ADVANCED

MEDIA

COMMUNICATION
& PRODUCTION

PETER MORRISSEY
SUE WARR

Heinemann Educational Publishers,
Halley Court, Jordan Hill, Oxford OX2 8EJ
a division of Reed Educational & Professional Publishing Ltd

OXFORD FLORENCE PRAGUE MADRID ATHENS
MELBOURNE AUCKLAND KUALA LUMPUR SINGAPORE TOKYO
IBADAN NAIROBI KAMPALA JOHANNESBURG GABORONE
PORTSMOUTH NH (USA) CHICAGO MEXICO CITY SAO PAULO

First published 1997
2001 2000 99 98
10 9 8 7 6 5 4 3 2 1

A catalogue record for this book is available from the British Library on
request

ISBN 0 435 452622

Typeset by TechType, Abingdon
Printed in Great Britain by The Bath Press

Contents

Acknowledgements

Numerous individuals and organisations have kindly contributed material and advice for this textbook. The help and support we have received has come from college staff and students, research and media organisations, our publishers and our families.

We would particularly like to thank the following:

Students Mark Pearson, Mike Sewell, Becket Jones, Hannah Ratcliffe, Iolanda Vittese, Tim Philp, Gary Battisson, Joe Bailey, Adrian Bird, Dean Callier, Eliot Kirkcaldy, Chris Collerson, Adam Hartopp, Hayley Dyer, Lisa Smart.

North Warwickshire and Hinckley College tutor librarian Sue O'Callaghan, and library assistant Jackie Malin.

We especially thank Adrian Huckfield, RTS and Central TV; Article 19; Steve Salmen, director, Griffindale Ltd, printers; Nick Carter (editor) and staff of the *Leicester Mercury*; Liam McCarthy (editor), John Florance (presenter), Helen Beevers (senior producer), at BBC Radio Leicester; Tony McKenzie, Radio City; CAA; the BBC; JICPAR; Film Education; Cross Counties Radio; Castlemead Radio; Catalunya Radio; the *Hinckley Times*; BFI; Gallup; BARB; RAJAR; CAVIAR; Market Research Society; RSL Media; BRAD; ABC; Campaign for Freedom of Information; All Party Media Group; NRS; NVLA; Outdoor Advertising Association; UNESCO; VFD; ITC; IBAR; BSC; MORI; Zenith North; UK Gold; Department of National Heritage; Prontaprint; Jenny Ludlam, manager, Diamond Cable 7; Barbara Jacobs; Ken Parker; Roger Wilkinson.

Thank you to the Heinemann team, Margaret Berriman and Jan Nikolic, for their support and guidance.

Finally a big thanks to our families: Tim, Jennifer and David Warr, and Annette, Sean and Drew Morrissey for their support and forbearance.

Sue Warr
Peter Morrissey
December 1996

Introduction

About this book

Welcome to *Advanced Media*. The eight main sections of this book relate to the eight **mandatory units** in the GNVQ award. Each unit is divided into chapters corresponding to the individual elements. We have set out to provide detailed background information, as well as case study examples, to guide students in developing an integrated understanding of the eight core units. The **evidence assignments** placed at the end of each chapter are tasks designed to enable students to show that they can meet particular requirements associated with the evidence indicators. We also provide **end-of-unit tests**, which give students practice in answering multiple-choice questions of the kind required to demonstrate a firm grasp of the underpinning knowledge for each unit.

Three compulsory **key skills** are also part of the GNVQ programme – Communication, Application of Number and Information Technology – and for an Advanced award they must be achieved at level 3. Key skills should be assessed within the vocational context, and many opportunities to acquire evidence occur throughout the activities and assignments in this book. **Tracking sheets** are provided to show which activities and assignments offer opportunities to achieve particular performance criteria in the key skills; however, students' work should always be checked carefully to ensure that suitable evidence has been produced.

Throughout the Advanced Media programme, issues concerning **health and safety** and **legal and ethical** considerations are a recurring theme. Therefore we provide appendices addressing these issues in detail, so that they can be referred to in conjunction with any area of study. Also provided are an appendix listing details of the major **media organisations**, and a select **bibliography**.

Outline of the course

For students to obtain full benefit from this demanding course, it is not recommended that the units are taught in a linear order from one to eight.

Students should have the opportunity to practise audio-visual and print and graphic skills throughout the course, to give them a chance to develop their work.

Many of the assignments to cover the evidence indicators for the Advanced GNVQ in Media can be interlinked according to the way the course is delivered over two years. Given below is a suggested course outline and details of work which would cover the evidence indicators.

There is no single correct way in which to deliver the units. This will vary from institution to institution, depending on such factors as:

- the number of students
- whether the year is divided into three terms or two semesters
- the availability of specialist teaching staff
- the availability of equipment and other facilities
- the timing of projects set up with outside agencies, such as newspaper producers or radio stations, or work placements
- other courses that students may be attending.

It is possible, however, to suggest a general order in which elements could be delivered in order for one unit to support another. There are certain areas that need to be tackled first, and some which work well with other topics. There is also a need to mix practical with theoretical subjects, and it is often possible to teach the theoretical *through* the practical.

Flexibility lies at the heart of successful delivery of this GNVQ. Information from within elements should be taught when needed to support other work, rather than waiting until that particular unit is listed on the timetable. It is not possible to say how long it will take to deliver each element, or how many hours should be spent on each one, as that will depend on the number of students, their abilities and their previous experience. The grouping of elements given below is therefore an indication of how the course can be delivered. The groupings can be overlapped.

The following elements, grouped loosely together, could be delivered in year 1 of the course (see the diagram on page ix):

Group 1

Unit 1 Element 1 (Analyse media texts) introduces the student to the vocabulary used in all areas of the media and to basic communication theory. The understanding of codes and conventions is fundamental to successful production work, and perhaps for the first time students will begin to look at media products not as consumers but as critics. They will start to evaluate and analyse in an objective manner.

Unit 2 Element 1 (Investigate research methods) is an important element to introduce early, as this will stress the importance of planning and research in media production.

Unit 4 Element 2 (Record audio material for programmes) is a practical element. As video production includes sound recording, it is suggested that audio is taught first. It is vital that students learn to handle equipment effectively, confidently and safely right from the start. They will not, however, be able to complete this element satisfactorily until much later on in the course when they have analysed professional audio products, researched and planned their own, and learnt how to write scripts.

Unit 1 Element 2 (Investigate representation in the media) is about more than stereotyping people. It explains how the media can represent events and ideas through the way in which texts are constructed.

Group 2

Unit 2 Element 2 (Plan and carry out research for print items) will enable the student not only to plan a print product but also to develop his or her writing and design skills. Good written work is essential for this course.

Unit 4 Element 3 (Edit audio programmes) continues the introduction of the student to various practical skills and equipment used in audio production. Students can be given an indication of the standard of their work at this stage, but the final evaluation of their products should not be made until the end of the course.

Unit 1 Element 3 (Analyse media genres) will reinforce and extend general knowledge about media products, how they have developed and their social context.

Unit 6 Element 4 (Carry out audience research for media products) enables students to carry out research themselves by constructing effective questionnaires and applying interview techniques. This will be useful also for the final element in each of the production units.

Group 3

Unit 1 Element 4 (Investigate narrative structures) is vital to support the production of appropriate AV scripts, and articles and stories for print publications.

Unit 2 Element 3 (Plan and carry out research for audio items) enables the student to plan and research audio material for a specific project.

Unit 6 Element 2 (Explore the relationship between media and audiences) looks more deeply at the relationship between media products and audiences. This will help students evaluate the effect of their own products on consumers.

Unit 5 Element 2 (Production – record moving images) introduces students to another area of practical skills and different types of equipment with which to familiarise themselves.

Group 4

Unit 5 Element 3 (Post-production – edit moving image products) continues the familiarisation of students with video equipment and practical skills, this time for editing. This is essential knowledge to impart to students before they start preparing treatments or writing scripts.

Unit 7 Element 1 (Analyse the role of marketing in the media) strengthens the idea for students that a media product has to be commercially viable and is produced to satisfy the needs of a customer or client rather than the producer, even if the producer is a student.

Unit 8 Element 1 (Investigate ownership and control in media industries) may be useful before students go out on work placements. They will now have a broad view of production and theory, and need to know the industrial context of media products.

Unit 3 Element 1 (Plan the production process for print products) starts the print production process, possibly using material already produced by the student.

In Year 2 of the course the major production units can be achieved. Students by now will have had sufficient time to practise individually all skills and techniques, and they can come together in teams to work on major projects. Elements could be grouped in the following way (see the diagram on page x):

Group 5

Unit 3 Element 2 (Originate and edit print material) sends the students out collecting material for their main print assignment.

Unit 3 Element 3 (Sub-edit and layout print products) needs to be run alongside, to simulate industrial working practices.

Unit 4 Element 1 (Plan the production process) plans out an audio programme, which can now be recorded and edited to achieve elements 4.2 and 4.3.

Unit 2 Element 4 (Plan and carry out research for moving image items) will revise the video work already done and take it a stage further to scriptwriting.

Group 6

Unit 5 Element 1 (Pre-production – planning the production process) plans out a moving image production, which can now be recorded and edited to achieve elements 5.2 and 5.3.

Unit 6 Element 1 (Investigate the use of audience research in the media) gives further emphasis to the importance of research, giving essential information on where data can be found.

Unit 7 Element 2 (Prepare marketing plans for media products) enables the students to use products they have already made for a marketing assignment.

Unit 8 Element 2 (Investigate regulation of media industries) – in explaining how media products and producers are controlled, this element will also give students another way in which to evaluate their work in comparison with a professional product.

Group 7

Unit 3 Element 4 (Review and evaluate print products) lets students use knowledge and skills from other units to review their own print product.

Unit 4 Element 4 (Review and evaluate audio productions) lets students use knowledge and skills from other units to review their own audio product.

Unit 5 Element 4 (Review and evaluate moving image products) lets students use knowledge and skills from other units to review their own moving image product.

Unit 8 Element 3 (Explore the development of the media industries) can utilise information from any work experience or industrial visits that the student has undertaken during the two years.

Group 8

Unit 8 Element 4 (Investigate employment in the UK media industries) will add to the knowledge students will already have gained through practical experience about the various personnel employed in the industries and the skills needed.

Unit 6 Element 3 (Analyse and interpret published data) will also be easier to do when students have investigated how audiences react to their own products. They will understand why the media needs accurate data and they will use their own experience and knowledge developed over the two years to interpret the data in a mature way.

Unit 7 Element 3 (Produce drafts and treatments for advertisements) and the following element can use all the practical skills achieved in other areas to produce materials for a marketing campaign.

Unit 7 Element 4 (Present drafts and treatments for advertisements) should be an opportunity for them to realise their full potential in presenting themselves and their work – an invaluable experience just prior to entering the competitive world outside.

We wish tutors and students every success in their work.

Peter Morrissey
Sue Warr
December 1996

YEAR 1

1.1 Analyse media texts

2.1 Investigate research methods

4.2 Record audio material for programmes

1.2 Investigate representation in the media

2.2 Plan and carry out research for print items

4.3 Edit audio programmes

1.3 Analyse media genres

6.4 Carry out audience research for media products

1.4 Investigate narrative structures

2.3 Plan and carry out research for audio items

6.2 Explore the relationship between media and audiences

5.2 Production – record moving images

5.3 Post-production – edit moving image products

7.1 Anlayse the role of marketing in the media

8.1 Investigate ownership and control in media industries

3.1 Plan the production process for print products

YEAR 2

3.2 Originate and edit print material

3.3 Sub-edit and layout print products

4.1 Plan the production process

2.4 Plan and carry out research for moving image items

5.1 Pre-production – planning the production process

6.1 Investigate the use of audience research in the media

7.2 Prepare marketing plans for media products

8.2 Investigate regulation of media industries

3.4 Review and evaluate print products

4.4 Review and evaluate audio products

5.4 Review and evaluate moving image products

8.3 Explore the development of the media industries

8.4 Investigate employment in the UK media industries

6.3 Analyse and interpret published data

7.3 Produce drafts and treatments for advertisements

7.4 Present drafts and treatments for advertisements

The media is a business and like all businesses it makes products. These products can be in the form of something tangible, or they could be a service. Media products can be literally anything produced by the various media industries for consumption by a target audience. Posters, magazines, TV commercials, comics and films are all examples of media products.

This unit allows you to examine how media products are constructed, that is, put together. It is, therefore, an important unit for both theoretical and practical purposes. First, you will be given the opportunity to analyse the various parts of a media product, such as its content and structure, its style, purpose and its potential effects on media audiences. Secondly, if you critically examine the case-study examples of products made by media industries, it will help you when you put together your own media products.

*In addition, the unit will explain the terminology used in the different media industries. We have already started to use various terms such as **product**, **consumption**, **target audience** and **construction**. These have an everyday meaning but take on a more specialised significance when applied to the study of the media.*

Chapter 1

Analyse media texts

In the opening section we introduced the idea of media products which are *consumed* by audiences. The process of consuming is often referred to as *reading*. Because of this, we refer to the product as a *text* that can be read.

Text is commonly understood to be the written word: a page from a novel, a letter, or the content of a report. In media terms, however, text is much more than this. Besides being newspapers, books, etc. it also includes sound, whether it is the spoken word, music or sound effects, and visual material, such as photographs and films. So a 'reader' of media 'text' can be a TV viewer or a radio listener as well as a magazine reader. Thus, a pop record is a media text; a newspaper is a media text, and so too is a single clipping from that newspaper. The advertisement in Figure 1.1 is also a text.

Elements of media texts that produce meaning

We now need to identify the various components of a text. In other words, what are its contents (elements) and how do they work to give meaning to the text?

Print texts

When we look at a print product, we – the consumers – derive meaning from the text, not only from the words themselves and the simplicity or

Figure 1.1 A holiday advertisement is also a text

complexity of the vocabulary, but from other elements. Another word for these elements is **signifiers**. These can include:

- photographs, including their composition
- diagrams
- line drawings
- colour
- typeface
- print size
- captions and other headings
- cropping, i.e. selecting part of an image
- the selection of items
- page layout
- sequencing of items.

Case study: *Marie Claire* magazine

Analysis The main image in Figure 1.2 is a close-up photograph of the face of an attractive young female model. The

photograph is posed and she is obviously made up. The top of her head has been **cropped**.

As part of the sequencing of items, the model's face is positioned centrally and is approximately in the upper two-thirds of the page. The date, price and edition are at the top whilst the free offer is near the bottom. There is also a bar code at the bottom.

The photograph of the original is in colour, as are the title and alternate sub-headings (some of which use bright orange). Typefaces are in upper and lower case, using both serif and sans serif (see Chapter 10 in Unit 3 for explanation of font types). The largest print size is the title, although there is variation in the size of other sub-headings, depending on their significance.

Many of the articles to be found in the magazine are listed, mostly on the left-hand side.

Discuss the purpose and effectiveness of these elements.

Activity

Look at the front covers of the two magazines shown in Figures 1.3 and 1.4.

Figure 1.2 A *Marie Claire* magazine cover

Marie Claire/Robert Harding Syndication

Figure 1.3 *Personal Computer World* cover

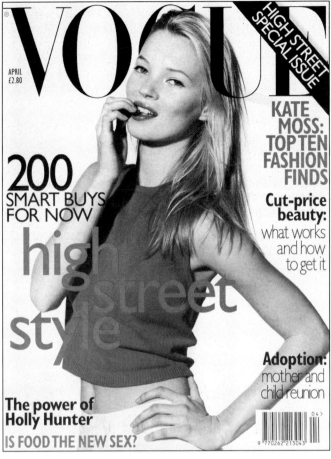

Figure 1.4 A *Vogue* cover

Miles Aldridge © Condé Nast PL – British Vogue

Identify the elements listed on page 2. List how they differ from each other.

Audio-visual texts

With an audio-visual product, the meaning is given not only through the scripted words read by actors or presenters but also through the following:

- visual images
- camera shots
- camera angles
- camera movement
- framing
- narrative structure (how the story is told)
- location
- props
- strength of colour
- lighting
- clothes and costume
- music
- titling.

To learn more about camera work refer to Chapters 8 and 18.

To identify all of these elements in a moving image text you would need to see a sequence of that text. However, even with a still image selected from the text it is possible to recognise some of these elements.

 Case study

Analysis The image in Figure 1.5 is of the hero holding a flag during battle.

Figure 1.5 Dramatic depiction of a hero

The *framing* centres the soldier, and also places him in the foreground. The low-angle *camera shot* gives him stature. The *lighting* makes him stand out against the background. Also in the frame are other soldiers, who are part of a rather indistinct backcloth which serves to highlight the central character in the frame.

The lighting and framing which crops the top of the standard gives a sense of action by providing an impression of movement. Prominence is given to the flag by framing it against a light-coloured sky.

The *location, props* (e.g. weapons) and *costumes* indicate that the scene is set in medieval times.

Discuss the purpose and effectiveness of these elements.

Activity

Look at these still images from the films *Sense and Sensibility* and *Rob Roy* in Figures 1.6 and 1.7. Identify as many of the elements listed on page 3 as you can and state how they differ from each other.

Figure 1.6 *Sense and Sensibility*

Relationship of elements in specific media texts

All of the elements of a text are important but a producer or editor also has to consider how they interact with each other and how they can change meaning. The sense that a film is a thriller may be given through the use of a close-up of vivid red blood or dramatic music or a look of tension on an actor's face. However, the deliberate over-use of these

Figure 1.7 *Rob Roy*

elements, in particular combinations, can result in one element under-cutting the other to produce a *parody*, or 'spoof' as it is commonly known.

Case study

Peter Sellers and Steve Martin are actors who have made an art form of parody in such spoof films as *The Pink Panther* and *Doctor Strangelove, Airport* and *Smoking Gun*.

A parody or spoof uses the forms of a particular genre (see Chapter 3) and exaggerates its elements to create comic effects. For example, in the Pink Panther films Peter Sellers exaggerates the French accent and the *stereotypical* detective clothing, thus creating caricatures. Why do you think we find such exaggerations funny?

Activity

This Activity allows you to demonstrate your understanding of how a particular meaning can be given to a media product. You are to make a presentation to the rest of your group which demonstrates how changing the music (or sound effects) can signify a different meaning to a film sequence.

First, choose an action sequence from a film, for example a chase or a fight scene, and select four different types of music to play with it. Watch the film without the music. What effect does this have on the meaning, i.e. what the audience thinks or feels?

Now run the action sequence through with a different selection of music each time, and note the different feelings and moods each induces.

Finally, run the sequence with its original soundtrack. What does this tell you about the film and its characters?

We have already mentioned that the use of clothing and colour can influence an audience's interpretation. A good example of this is their use in the classic Western to signify good or evil: the cowboy dressed in black is, in these old films, almost invariably the villain. The heroic Lone Ranger was always in white, whereas the killer cowboy in *Westworld* is clad in black. Meaning can, however, be signified even more subtly by, for example, the use of camera angles or lighting.

For example, a low-angle camera shot will make a character look important or dominant. If you then light their features from below you would produce quite a sinister effect. Try doing this yourself by holding a lighted torch below your chin and observing the result in front of a mirror.

Activity

Printed text, as we have mentioned, also contains signifiers. Demonstrate your understanding of this by looking at the following headline:

DANGER FROM FREE-RANGE CHICKENS

How would your expectations about the topic be changed by adding different accompanying **graphics**? (*Note*: A 'graphic' can be simple line drawing, as in a cartoon; a diagram, such as a chart or map; a painting or a photograph.)

Figure 1.8 Healthy chickens?

Figure 1.9 Road-hog chickens?

Role of anchorage in the production of meaning

Anchorage is the way in which a number of techniques are used to pin down or narrow the range of meaning of a text or part of a text. It applies to audio-visual products as well as print and graphics.

In a film the passing of time between two shots can be shown through a fade to black between the scenes. This can be reinforced by titling saying, 'Five years later...'. A **whip pan** is the term used when a camera moves so quickly that the picture is blurred. This effect was often used between scenes in 1960s adventure series, such as *Batman* or *The Man from Uncle,* to show events happening simultaneously in different places. The meaning can be reinforced by a caption giving the name of the place where the new action takes place.

Captions and headings

The use of **captions, headlines** and **subheadings** is particularly necessary in newspapers and magazines. They indicate the content or story within articles and still images, and can signify whether we are looking at fiction, non-fiction, tragedy, humour or perhaps even an advertisement.

Case study

Look at the photographs in Figure 1.10 and 1.11 below. What do you think is happening in them?

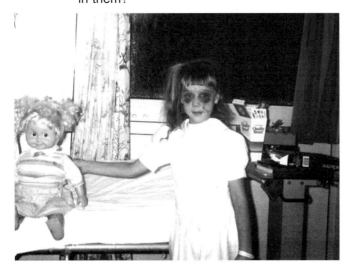

Figure 1.10

Figure 1.11

Without a caption the pictures could be about:

Figure 1.10: Shortage of hospital beds
Pop star's child on road to recovery
Miraculous recovery of 'hit-and-run' victim
New operation pioneered
An advertisement for health insurance

Figure 1.11: Summertime in the countryside
New housing estate planned
Farmers plan new crops
Walkers seek rights of way
An advertisement for country holidays.

Activity

Figure 1.12

Try selecting the actual caption for the picture in Figure 1.12.

Possible captions are:

- Happy days: the tragic couple on a previous skiing trip
- Whiteout: enthusiasts enjoy the exceptional conditions
- Snow White: the Prince with his new companion yesterday
- Cosy, comfortable and safe: make sure you have the right skiwear

The list above includes some actual captions. Look at some other newspaper or magazine pictures to get further ideas on how captions are written. They tend to be written in a brief but informative manner, with a few introductory words which are sometimes cryptic and perhaps in upper case or emboldened. This is then followed by the 'body' of the caption text.

Activity

Select a picture. This can be one which does not have a caption or perhaps a picture where you remove the caption. **Anchor** its meaning in four different ways by writing four captions that give entirely different viewpoints.

Captions can reinforce an obvious meaning of an image or they can contradict the image to create an entirely new meaning. Look at the example in Figure 1.13.

Figure 1.13 A government anti-drugs poster

Crown copyright, reproduced with permission of Controller of HMSO

Headlines

The positioning of two headlines, possibly placed alongside each other, i.e. juxtaposed, can also change meaning.

Figure 1.14 A sub-head can change the meaning of a main heading

The main purpose of headlines is to attract attention. They are often short. For example:

Scandal in High Places!

What does this actually tell a reader? That a member of the royal family or government has been caught stealing? That someone climbing Mount Everest is having an affair with another member of the expedition?

Headlines, therefore, often need sub-headings to narrow down their meaning. Look at the example in Figure 1.15.

HIS HIGHEST TRIP OF ALL
Timothy Leary dies aged 75

Figure 1.15 A sub-head can narrow down the meaning of a main headline

Now find your own example and explain the relationship between the headline and the sub-heading.

'Speech bubbles'

Cartoons and comic strips rely on visual images to tell a story. However, in order to clarify a situation or describe the action, words are used in a very stylised way, through speech bubbles and text placed next to the pictures or to represent and bring to life the action itself.

Figure 1.16 Cartoons and comic strips use speech bubbles and text alongside drawings

Typeface

The typeface or font used is also part of how meaning is anchored. For example the text in this book is sometimes emboldened or enlarged in order to indicate significance: perhaps an important word, a new topic or an Activity. There are many different typefaces available. Some have names which indicate that they are particularly suited to an area or genre, e.g. Computer or Gothic; others are more general but work better for some areas than others, e.g. children's books rather than a computer magazine.

Activity

Figure 1.17 shows a number of different fonts.

Death by Chocolate

Death by Chocolate

DEATH BY CHOCOLATE

DEATH BY CHOCOLATE

Death by Chocolate

Figure 1.17 Five different fonts

Which would be most appropriate for the following?

- titling for a 1930s detective programme
- a science fiction cartoon
- a subheading for a serious (hard) news article
- titling for a horror film
- a menu for a French restaurant.

Positioning

Anchorage need not only be done through words. Two images positioned or 'juxtaposed' in a certain way can strengthen their meaning or create a new meaning. The juxtapositioning of images to create a new meaning is known as **montage**.

In cartoons it is obvious that understanding is created by the **sequencing** of the line drawings, i.e. the order in which they appear. However, in magazine articles, the sequencing of pictures on a page is also important to create sense and to draw the eye along the article and maintain interest.

Figure 1.18 Magazine pages use the sequencing of pictures and text to draw the eye along

Analysing specific media texts by applying concepts

Before reading on, try the following task:

Activity

Select a magazine article on food. You have been asked to analyse it by looking at the pictures and language and assessing the effect they might have on readers. **Brainstorm** the ways in which you might approach this task. For example, you might count up the number of words that you don't understand, or you might read through the article once to see which parts can be remembered.

The ways in which we and the mass media industries communicate have been of interest to researchers for many years, and there are now a number of theories, all aiming to be as scientific as possible and to discover useful generalisations. A comprehensive list of them can be found in *A Dictionary of Communication and Media Studies* by James Watson and Anne Hill.

The success of all media industries is based on their skill at communicating the right message to the right people at the right time. It is therefore a good idea to have a basic understanding of communication theory in order to examine how these processes work.

Communication models

The communication models that have been developed apply both to straightforward one-to-one contact and to the use of electrical and mechanical means of transmitting messages.

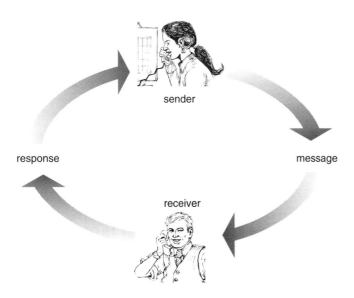

At its most basic level, communication consists of the following components:

- the sender of a message
- the means by which the message is sent
- the receiver of the message.

In a more developed form of communication, the line becomes a circle, with the sender checking that the message has been received correctly.

For students of the mass media the way in which the message is sent (and how it is received and interpreted) is of prime importance, whether it is on the Internet or through the local free newspaper.

Activity

Make a list of all the different means of mass communication. What are their strengths and weaknesses? Consider these in terms of reach, cost, suitability for different purposes, and so on.

In **Shannon and Weaver's** model of communication, developed in 1949 to explain how telephone and radio communication occurs, the additional issues of noise and redundancy are introduced.

Noise in the system can be literal noise owing to technical problems, but it could also be something occupying the receiver's mind or any other interference which causes distraction from the message.

Redundancy is when a message is repeated. This often occurs naturally in speech, where the same message, or part of it, is given again, perhaps in a different way. Redundancy can be used as a deliberate technique to help reinforce a message. Too much redundancy will, however, have a detrimental effect as it can cause the receiver to 'switch off'.

The advertising industry is well aware of both the value and the dangers of redundancy. This is why they do not deal in single advertisements but in advertising campaigns, where the advertising message is repeated and sometimes varied.

Essentially, the process of communication involves the five stages identified by **Harold Lasswell** in his analysis of mass media communication (1948):

- Who says something?
- What do they say?
- Through what channel, in what way do they say it?
- To whom do they say it?
- What effect does it have?

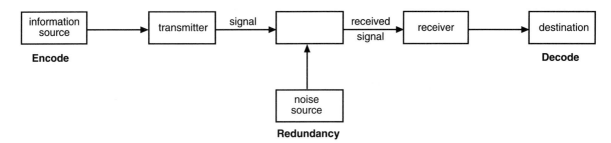

When a message is communicated, something called **mediation** takes place between the sender and the receiver. When the mass media communicate with us, the 'message' could be any newspaper story or any television or radio programme. All these messages are mediated, not only by the interpretation placed on them by media owners, editors or producers, but also by the nature of the medium (newspaper, TV, radio). This is because each medium has its own special characteristics.

Television news, for example, tends not to go into the same detail as newspaper news and will, in addition, have moving pictures to help tell the story. This may seem obvious, but when you bear in mind that out of all the events happening around the world just a few are chosen and these have to be summarised, you will then perhaps begin to wonder what has been left out, why it was left out and who made these decisions. Furthermore, in the case of television, you could ask yourself who shot the film, who selected and edited it, and on what basis these decisions were made. Because of these issues, academics who study the media often refer to the news as **selective** and **manufactured**.

By asking yourself these kinds of questions you will realise that mediation is in fact a process of interpretation. Take, for example, a news story which goes through the following stages:

1 In China a chemical disaster occurs. A Chinese journalist employed by the state newspaper records parts of the disaster.

2 This report is translated and sent to an international news agency.

3 A Western reporter reads it and investigates a little further, concentrating on the human interest angle.

4 The story is rejected for TV news.

5 However, it is sent to a European broadsheet newspaper editor where it is reshaped and shortened. Certain facts are omitted and others distorted to make the story more exciting, and the owner of the newspaper does not have the same political ideology as the Chinese government.

6 A photograph from another source is added. The importance of the article is diminished because of an outbreak of rioting in Britain. The story is relegated to a middle page of the newspaper.

7 On the day it is published, the newspaper has distribution problems.

8 You are told about the disaster by a friend during the tea break at the factory where you are doing part-time work.

Activity

In a group, discuss how each of these different stages can affect readers' understanding of the situation in China, depending on their age and cultural background.

Between the original event and its report, mediation has occurred. The final report would probably be quite different if various circumstances were altered, such as the choice of reporter, the length of the article, the time allowed for research, what is going on elsewhere, etc. The choice of vocabulary and supporting images will also radically affect the impression made on the reader. The choice of medium, such as local radio as opposed to the BBC World Service, will determine how many people hear the report or message.

Signification

There are now many different theories on the process of communication and, more importantly from our point of view, **mass communication**. These theories generally acknowledge the importance of **semantics**, in which the meaning of language is studied, and **semiotics**, which is the study of signs and their meaning.

Semeion is the Greek word for sign, and a lot of the theory surrounding how we interpret media texts is concerned with semiotics or semiology. Apart from the study of the meaning of signs it looks at how they are constructed and their role in creating meaning. Some of the earliest work on this subject was done by a Swiss linguist, **Ferdinand de Saussure** (1857–1913).

At the heart of semiotics is **signification**. De Saussure thought that language itself was a 'deposit of signs'. Just as we can see visual images, so can we hear acoustic images, i.e. the spoken word. Both types of images consist of two parts: firstly, their physical attributes such as colour, size, volume, length; secondly their concepts, that is, the ideas and emotions which they arouse. The first (more concrete) elements he called the **signifiers**. The second (more abstract) elements he called the **signified**. The relationship between these two is known as signification. We have already used the word 'signify'

in the previous pages. You can now see how it is used in its specialised, media sense.

Charles Pierce (1834–1914), an American philosopher, saw the relationship in the form of a triangle (see below).

Both men agreed that, for its interpretation, the meaning of the sign depends on its *context*. In other words, it depends on which culture or period in time it belongs to. So sign systems are not fixed. Instead, meaning is forever changing. This is why semiologists prefer the term **reader** to **receiver**, because it implies a greater degree of active involvement.

The French philosopher **Roland Barthes** (1915–80) extended the scope of the study of sign systems to music, dance, clothes and even eating. More research based on film and news images was done during the seventies, by people such as Christian Metz and Guy Gauthier.

Denotation and connotation

We read images just as we read words. As children, we learnt to read books by recognising individual letters which built up into words and sentences. We encountered written language in certain situations, such as on posters, in books or on signs. Sometimes written language was learnt through formal situations, such as in a classroom, but often it was assimilated through informal contact, such as reading road signs or advertisements. Unless we have attended art or design classes, our ability to read signs has been subconsciously learnt. The way in which it has developed depends on cultural and social factors.

There are two main concepts to consider with regard to images: **denotation** and **connotation**. These ideas are closely related to the concept of signification.

The process of denotation is very objective or 'scientific'. It involves noting down precisely the physical attributes of what is in a drawing or photograph. It does not matter who is looking at the picture, whether they are sixteen or sixty, male or female, African or Chinese, as long as they can see or are not colour blind, they will see the same thing. For example, look at the picture in Figure 1.19.

A *denotative analysis* of this picture might be:

This is a picture of a girl aged about 10 years old, standing in front of a grand piano. She has long brown hair pushed back with a hairband. She is wearing a jumper and jeans. She is holding a violin in one hand and a trophy in the other.

Denotation is, therefore, the literal interpretation of an image.

'TREE'
sign
(describes the object)

green forest
environment nature
countryside

interpretant
(signified)
i.e. mental concept

object

Figure 1.19 What does this picture show?

A *connotative analysis* could say:

This child has just won a prize in a music competition. She is quietly proud of her success. Her casual clothing is an indication of her relaxed attitude.

Connotations of colour

Colours in particular arouse different emotions in people. Generally, blue is considered a 'cold' colour, brown a 'warm' colour. Blue is associated with the cold sea, brown with the warm earth. Red is an exciting colour associated with heat, blood, danger, fire, sexuality.

Activity

As a group, brainstorm the connotations of the following colours: black, white, brown, green, blue, yellow, red and purple. You should bear in mind that connotative interpretations of colours can be determined by the cultural experiences of the viewer. In Britain for example, black is considered to be the colour of mourning, but in other countries white is worn at funerals.

Activity

Study the picture in Figure 1.20 and carry out denotative and connotative analyses.

Figure 1.20 Can you write an analysis of this picture?

Codes used in media texts

Signification is not produced by accident. Editors, producers, directors, advertisers and designers spend considerable time choosing material and considering how to combine the different elements to produce the effect they want. When certain signs, words or actions are used they can be referred to as **codes**.

Codes are a series of signs and **symbols** which mean certain things to certain people. Some may be meaningful only to a relatively small number of people, for example:

Morse code . . . – – – . . .

or:

13

Some have become almost universal, as for example the signs in Figure 1.21.

Figure 1.21 Some signs are universally recognised

Language itself is a type of code. We have to put our thoughts and ideas together in a way which, we hope, makes sense to people. We generally do this with words, although non-verbal cues, such as a handshake or a person's posture, can also be considered as codes. For example, we can usually tell if someone is friendly, threatening, sad, happy, etc. by the way they look.

Whether we intend to send a particular message or not, the information is *encoded* by the sender and *decoded* by the receiver. We all know, of course, how easy it is for the receiver to get the 'wrong end of the stick' when we send a message! This is why it is important to give feedback so that misunderstandings do not occur. In some organisations, particularly the Armed Forces and emergency services, it is standard procedure to build in feedback – perhaps by repeating back the message – as a check on understanding. In the same way, when you carry out the activities in this book they serve as a means of checking your understanding.

Types of codes

In the media, codes are divided into three main types:

■ technical
■ presentational
■ aesthetic.

Technical codes are considered to cover such factors as the type of microphone used, the choice of camera lens and filter, and the quality of paper for a magazine or newspaper.

Presentational codes can include such factors as the method of acting, gestures and expressions, the use of camera work and lighting, the style of drawing, the choice of typeface and the use of slogans.

Some codes are fixed, such as mathematical codes. Others can alter according to the period or situation in which they are used. 'Aesthetics' concerns such concepts as ideas of beauty, taste and style. **Aesthetic** codes especially are altered by their *cultural context*. This encompasses people's political views, educational standards, ethnic background, how they speak, dress and behave, and where they live.

Some codes may start off by being understood only by a relatively small number of people, but then become more widely known. 'Street' language is an example of this. So too is development in art. With a lot of new art, the encoding makes its interpretation accessible to a relatively small proportion of the population. However, over the years, with familiarity and popularisation, it can become accepted by many people as art and its meaning and purpose identified.

Another example of the encoding process is the use of a specialised vocabulary (sometimes known as 'jargon'), by such groups as the legal and medical professions. Doctors, for example, may state on medical records that someone has a fractured femur when they mean that the casualty has a broken upper leg. The media studies terms we are using are another example of encoding.

 Case study

Look at the two examples of art shown in Figures 1.22 and 1.23.

Figure 1.22 *Hannibal Crossing the Alps*, by J. M. W. Turner

Figure 1.23 Thangka of Padmasambhava

Figure 1.24 *Perpetual Motion* by Rene Magritte

The Turner painting was considered to be progressive, 'avant-garde' or extreme at the time it was painted. People complained that they could not understand it. It was considered different and disturbing. 'Now it could be used for the lid of a chocolate box', one art expert said. Do you agree?

The second example seems exotic and strange to a Westerner. It could be seen as exciting and even classed as 'modern'. But for the artist who created it, it represents traditional values going back hundreds of years, and the individual symbols have precise meanings to a Buddhist. Can you identify its codes?

Surrealism, as depicted in Figure 1.24, used to be considered a very progressive form of art, based on dream images aimed at shocking the viewer's codes and disturbing conventional ways of thinking. However, this sort of technique has become quite commonplace in current advertising. We have become so used to reading this type of media text that a significant number of us can successfully decode it.

Iconography

Cultural codes can also include iconography. An icon can be an image of a person or an object which comes to represent a particular meaning for a social group.

In the twentieth century the swastika become the symbol of the Nazi party,

signifying horror and oppression to millions of people. In earlier civilisations, however, similar symbols represented fertility and the spirit of good.

Images of Marilyn Monroe and the Virgin Mary are also used as icons, each idealizing a different type of womanhood.

Figure 1.25 Classic horror films have their own codes

Icons are supposed to represent the true likeness of somebody or something. In orthodox Christianity they are believed to be true images of Christ or other sacred figures, such as the Virgin Mary. However, the true likeness of a person or thing can also be represented by their *essence,* that is, their essential or defining features. Thus another idealised picture of womanhood is the iconic portrayal of Marilyn Monroe, the essence of which is parted red lips and waved blonde hair. Another example of an iconised object is Andy Warhol's painting of a Campbell's soup tin, which has become a symbol of the consumer society. It should be noted that, whereas a symbol is not necessarily an icon, an icon is necessarily a symbol.

Case study: A Hammer Horror film

Between the 1950s and 1970s some horror films were produced at the Hammer film studios which have since become classics and, arguably, a **genre** (see Chapter 3) in their own right. Of course, all classic gothic horror films have certain codes but Hammer Horror had, in addition, other characteristics.

Consider the following codes of this media product:

■ **technical**
   – approximately one-and-a-half hour feature film
   – stereo sound

   – colour
   – lighting

■ **presentational**
   – strong, even stylised use of expression
   – contrasting lighting
   – low-angle camera shots
   – shadows
   – creepy music
   – dark costumes, including cape, for the anti-hero
   – location in a castle or large rambling mansion

■ **aesthetic**
   – sense of foreboding, gloom, fear and horror
   – types of characters, e.g. dominant males versus subordinate females
   – sexual metaphors, e.g. Dracula's nocturnal visitations to young women in their bed chambers; the fatal kiss as seduction
   – good versus evil
   – puritan ethics versus corruption and debauchery
   – will power versus weakness.

In addition, the Vampire or Dracula, particularly when played by Christopher Lee, could be seen as embodying iconic status.

Look at the advertisement in Figure 1.26. Describe what technical, presentational and aesthetic codes it uses.

Figure 1.26 Describe the codes used in this advertisement

Codes and conventions

Conventions are established and accepted ways of performing certain activities. They are often synonymous with codes but not necessarily so. Consider the handshake example mentioned earlier. When we meet someone, particularly in formal circumstances, there is an established practice (convention) called shaking hands. This is also a code, the connotations of which signify friendliness, politeness, etc. However, if the convention of shaking hands was subverted by a deliberately short or limp handshake, this could then be a code for unfriendliness, impoliteness and so on. This encoding could also be strengthened by other accompanying codes, such as an icy smile.

A further example of codes and conventions working together would be the use of jingles on a radio station to signify a change of programme. In addition the jingle also serves as the station's 'identity' (see Chapter 13) and, as such, is a code. Generally speaking, the whole of the way a radio show is constructed would be classed as a convention because its constituent parts, such as jingles, presenters, introductions, information, as well as the music, would be packaged and presented according to certain established ways.

In literature, individual words in themselves have meaning but the way in which they are strung together – the grammar and syntax – also create other meanings. Small pieces of understanding are built into bigger structures.

With a film there are similar conventions. We sit down expecting some music and the title somewhere near the start. At the end we expect to see the credits accompanied by more music. In film, when all the different codes and conventions combine in a certain way, we can usually categorise the film as being an example of a particular genre. Therefore, we may well expect the story to unfold in a certain way and the characters to move and speak differently from us.

It is conventional for a film which we call 'realistic' to contain many unrealistic conventions. For example, we are not surprised when the camera switches rapidly from one scene to another and we accept zoom shots taken from the air where no human being would be naturally observing the action. Whole string orchestras accompany armies into battle or share the intimacy of a love scene. Our understanding is not upset by 'flashbacks' or seeing words appear on the screen telling us, for example, that the year is 1485 or that we are in Pennsylvania.

The world of the media is an artificial one. It offers us a false reality, full of devices (codes and conventions) which we accept as normal because we are accustomed to them.

Record a TV news programme. Describe the codes and conventions used. Consider the following points:

- What effect does the music and lighting give?
- What images do you see, and how are they arranged?
- What camera shots and angles are used and how do they affect what we feel?
- Why are the presenters often in pairs?
- What expressions or gestures do the newsreaders and journalists use?

- Where and how do the presenters sit?
- Comment on the looks, clothing, gender and age of the newsreaders.
- What locations are used?
- Whose point of view is given? Is it the journalist's, the producer's, the public's, the politician's, the owner's?

Analysing possible readings of media texts

The word 'reader' is preferred to that of viewer or listener regardless of the medium, i.e. radio or film, because it implies a greater degree of activity on the part of the audience or consumer. Both Stuart Hall in *The Determination of News Photographs* (1973) and Frank Parkin in *Class, Inequality and Political Order* (1972) recognise three ways to read a text. Later research by David Morley has stressed the importance of other factors in influencing the reader.

Preferred reading

The preferred (dominant) reading of a text is the one 'preferred', i.e. intended, by the transmitter of the text, who could be, for example, the writer, photographer, producer or designer. The editor will also help to create a preferred reading by techniques such as cropping, captioning, framing and juxtapositioning. In moving image production the same thing is done through camera angles, choice of music and so on. The interpretation will conform to traditional viewpoints and values present in contemporary society.

Negotiated reading

A negotiated (subordinate) reading is one in which the reader does not totally accept but questions the intentions of the producer and the social values generally. The reader may believe that subgroups or certain topics within society are not always treated fairly or without bias. Here the personal experience of the reader has influence. Someone who is young, black and female may not react in the same way to a media message as an elderly, white male.

Oppositional reading

In an oppositional (radical) reading, the reader recognises but rejects the dominant meaning of the text and gives it another meaning.

You can learn more about different possible readings in Chapter 4.

Case study

Look again at the heroin poster that we discussed on page 7.

Preferred reading: the intention of the government was to dissuade young people from using heroin.

Negotiated reading: a young person might agree with the intention of the poster but does not identify with the person in it; or the image does not match up with his or her own experience of drugtaking.

Oppositional reading: many young people may remain unaffected by the poster and admire the looks and attitude of the model.

Design a poster for young children with different possible readings in these categories.

Evidence assignment

Analyse two media texts: the front page of a broadsheet newspaper, or an article from a lifestyle magazine, and a television advert.

You may choose to analyse a printed publication or a moving image product which can be compared with a product you are planning to make in Unit 3 or Unit 5.

Give a brief synopsis of the chosen texts and their purpose. How do you think they could be interpreted in different ways? Identify where the words or images have been influenced by current trends in our society or culture, e.g. politics or fashion.

Identify the elements of each text. For the print item, count the number of words and describe the layout. Highlight significant words and describe their position within the text and their effect. Identify the typeface used and explain why different sizes were used. Discuss the use of photographs or other graphic illustrations. Consider their size, colour and position within the text. Explain how captions, slogans or headings relate to the images. How necessary are they? Explain the role of anchorage and the operation of codes.

For the television advert, identify the type of camera shots used and their effect. How is atmosphere created through the lighting, clothes, location and music? Again, explain the role of anchorage and the operation of codes in the advert.

Which elements are the most important in each case in getting the message across?

Conclude your report by writing notes on the types of element found in other media texts.

Investigate representation in the media

It is recommended that this section is read in conjunction with Chapter 22, which explores the relationship between media products and audiences.

Using words, images or sounds, the media can present us with a view of the real world or they can share with us an imaginary experience. The media present us with meaning, they give us their interpretation of events or situations, feelings, or ideas. They recreate emotions, ideas and events for an audience. What we see on our screens, listen to on the radio and see in print is not an accidental view but is instead *constructed.*

Thus the process by which the media carry to us their construction of reality is called *mediation,* as we noted in Chapter 1. The result of this process, that is, how the end product treats ideas and shows us people and events, is called *representation.* In other words, people and events are *re*presented to us.

Concept of representation within the media

Representation is about much more than how individuals or even social groups are treated in newspapers or on TV. It is about how audiences can be encouraged to identify with certain social and cultural attitudes and behaviour through the codes and conventions of a media product. There is always debate about how much a great work of art (whether music, painting or literature) is a product of its time or how much it is ahead of its time and influences future art. The same can be said about the media: how much do they reflect society and how much do they control or influence it?

Representation is also about what is not shown or is omitted from inclusion in media products. It can be about exclusion, censorship or neglect. Of course, as we noted in Chapter 1, a large degree of selectivity necessarily takes place as media producers cannot cover everything. They also have to take account of political, legal and ethical considerations, public opinion, media owners and consumer organisations. In addition they have to take into consideration consumer tastes and – in the case of commercial

producers – the advertisers who provide the bulk of the revenue.

Codes and conventions (see Chapter 1) are used to signal the status of the subject to the audience/consumer. The choice of format, for example, whether something is a poster or film, a five-minute radio interview or serialised TV documentary, is the first clue. The **treatment** (see Chapter 5) assigned to the product, that is, whether it is, for example, humorous, glossy, sophisticated, intellectual and so on can confirm our expectations. Camera angles, choice of typeface and style of music can all indicate to us what we should be feeling.

Activity

Compare the advertisement in Figure 2.1, from a nineteenth-century newspaper, with one of your choice from the 1990s that

Figure 2.1 An advertisement from a nineteenth-century newspaper

advertises a babycare product or a hair product. List the differences. The older one tells you about the qualities of the product. Is the later one selling you an image, a lifestyle? What is being represented in each?

Activity

Read the article in Figure 2.2, taken from a tabloid newspaper, concerning the drugs problem.

Agony of Ecstasy

By LYNDA LEE-POTTER

LEAH Betts grew up in a close-knit family but this morning she lies unconscious and close to death after taking an Ecstasy tablet on her 18th birthday. 'It could be your child', said yesterday's *Daily Mail* headline. We grieve for Leah's parents and feel terror that one terrible day we might be in the same position.

'What can we do?' we cry when it comes to bringing up our children – and we can only do our best. We must love and protect them without making them feel trapped and stultified. We have to provide protection without making them fearful and timid. We must have the wisdom to give them responsibilities but not let them grow up too quickly. We need the courage to say 'No' when other parents are saying 'Oh, all right then'.

We must accept that they will learn more by example than by force, and treat everybody in the family with civility and respect. We have to show our children that language is to be valued and that swearing is lazy and ill-mannered.

We should help them to enjoy pastimes that require neither money nor possessions. We mustn't make them feel guilty by being totally selfless. We need to realise that an over-inquisitive mother is as bad as an indifferent one.

We should be willing to apologise when we are in the wrong. We should never say coldly: 'You are in my house so you will do as I say.' We ought not to provide endless material possessions which dull their imagination. We need to help them to observe and to be visually aware. And above all, to teach them the continuing strength of joy, fun and laughter.

Figure 2.2 A *Daily Mail* article

Copyright © Associated Newspapers Ltd.

In a group, discuss whether the newspaper reflects attitudes in society or whether it hopes to influence people's attitudes. Whose viewpoint, beliefs, knowledge or emotions are being represented?

It is not only serious articles or programmes that offer us representations. Entertainment in the form of quiz shows, comedy programmes, comic strips, etc. all tell us something about human nature or life situations.

Activity

Consider a TV programme such as *Blind Date*. In a group, discuss what it might tell us about relationships and social behaviour at the end of the twentieth century. How typical is it of normal dating patterns?

The way that the media portray occupations and places can affect our behaviour and lifestyles. For example, regular news coverage of the Troubles in Northern Ireland has affected trade and tourism to Ireland. It has influenced not only how people view certain areas of the country but also how they view Irish people. Most English people do not have any direct experience of Northern Ireland and therefore their opinions are not based on firsthand knowledge but on impressions gained from brief and selective TV or newspaper items.

Activity

Look at the two images in Figures 2.3 and 2.4 below. What representation do they each give about the country? How much is our knowledge of each country based on media images such as these, and how much is based on hard facts about the economy, the population and so on?

Figure 2.3 An image of Africa

Figure 2.4 An image of Greece

Our choice of career can also be affected by what we see in films or on TV or read in magazines. TV dramas about the life of a vet, or of police officers, can emphasise the excitement and 'glamour' of the work and ignore the mountains of paperwork involved or the need for continuous studying to keep up-to-date with legal and technical changes.

Activity

Look at the picture of a female flight attendant (or air hostess, as they were traditionally called).

What image does it give about the status of the job, the duties involved and the type of person who is a flight attendant?

Would you feel differently about the job if it was known as an aeroplane waitress/waiter or a 'plane conductor'?

Is this how an air hostess is always portrayed in the media? Do you think that the reality of the work would be different?

Considerations relating to the representation of different issues

As noted above, issues that representation can cover include ideas, social groups and concerns, events, occupations and places. The media industries control *what* is represented and *how* the representation is carried out. Individual writers or artists are free to represent the world or their ideas in whichever way they want but if the material is to be published and distributed, then they must take into consideration the following:

■ legal responsibilities
■ ethical factors
■ social conditions and attitudes
■ the political climate.

Legal and ethical considerations

There are a number of laws, particularly those concerning equal opportunities, race relations and censorship, and ethical issues, such as bias and honesty, which media producers have to obey or take into consideration when they present their programmes or products.

Activity

Details of laws and ethical problems are dealt with fully in Chapter 30 and the Legal and Ethical appendix. Read these through and make notes of those which you think will affect representation.

Case study

In 1996 there was a media scandal in Germany because film footage for the *Stern* TV magazine programme, which supposedly showed real terrorists and members of illegal organisations such as the Ku-Klux-Klan, turned out to be fake. The film-maker used his friends as actors and filmed them pretending to plot bombing campaigns and training with guns. This is illegal as well as unethical and the film-maker ended up in prison. Why do you think the film-maker had been tempted to work in this way?

Activity

Answer the following questions:

1   What law would prevent an editor of a tabloid newspaper from publishing an editorial claiming that English people are mentally superior to the Welsh?
2   Is there any law which could prevent a TV company from making a comedy series about an Indian family?
3   Would it be illegal or unethical to write a series of articles which discussed only the problems of old people?
4   Is it illegal or unethical to make a documentary for a schools career programme in which girls are encouraged to become hairdressers and boys to be engineers?
5   Would it be illegal to state on the same programme that girls are unsuitable to be employed in the mining industry?
6   Which law might be contravened if a film showed Christ selling drugs to his followers?
7   What law would be contravened if someone criticised the Koran on a radio talk show?
8   A comedian tells sick jokes implying that disabled people are useless. Is this illegal?
9   A sports writer reports only on the Scottish team in a football match and uses glowing terms to describe their playing. There are no interviews with the opposing Russian team, whose playing is described as 'wimpish'. Is this unethical or illegal?
10 An advert shows images of a poor black person in a Third World country and the caption reads, 'If you don't want to end up like this then save with the Bigshire Building Society'. Is this unethical and, if so, why?
11 An advert describes England as the only safe place in the world. Is this illegal?

Social considerations

The media have a lot of status in our society. How they treat and understand various social groups is very important.

People can be classified by age, race, gender, occupation or ability. People in any of these categories can be depicted as 'salt of the earth' or 'a menace to society'. Different groups can sometimes be 'marginalised' or ignored, either because they are unattractive or because they are economically unimportant.

Western society in the last few decades has become more aware of the needs of minority groups in its midst; and disabled people, for instance, now receive more coverage in the media in both fictional and non-fictional products. But it is not only minority social groups that can claim to be unfairly treated. Women have often complained about their image on screen and in print and now men too are beginning to complain about manipulation by the media. At the beginning of the nineties they were portrayed as 'New Men', by the mid-nineties they had become 'Lads'.

Activity

Divide into three groups. One group will look at a local newspaper, another at a national broadsheet and the third group at a national tabloid.

First, count how many stories are about old people, unemployed people, religious groups, sportswomen, criminals, disabled people or a specific place. Secondly, count how many of these reports or articles have a positive approach to what they are dealing with and how many are negative.

Discuss your findings with the other groups and consider these points:

1   Was there any difference in coverage between the local newspaper, the broadsheet and the tabloid? Were some areas neglected? What reasons can you give for this? For example, was the time of year important or was it a particular event that drew a topic to public attention?
2   Were you surprised by the amount of positive or negative coverage?
3   Which groups of people made the front page and which were relegated to the middle or end pages?
4   Do you think that the coverage reflects the actual situation and significance of these groups in our society?

Case study

On the next page are two newspaper reports on the same issue. They differ quite dramatically. Study the reports, in Figures 2.5 and 2.6, and discuss the differences between the representation of political issues in tabloid and broadsheet newspapers.

Tories probe Serb links to funding

Patrick Wintour, Chief Political Correspondent

THE damaging secrecy surrounding the Conservative Party's funding re-emerged to blight John Major yesterday when the party chairman, Brian Mawhinney, was forced to order a full investigation into allegations that Serbian-born businessmen had given £100,000 to party funds.

The internal inquiry came as the CBI's incoming chairman, Sir Colin Marshall, urged British executives to stop using corporate cash to fund the Tories, and a survey for the *Guardian* showed financial support for the party from Britain's biggest companies had collapsed. It was also confirmed that accountants Touche Ross told the Tory party in July 1993 that £365,000 it had given by fugitive tycoon Asil Nadir had been stolen from his company.

Both opposition parties claimed it would be one of the most serious scandals of this parliament if Mr Mawhinney's investigation confirmed that Serbs with links to the Serbian war leader Radovan Karadzic had indeed given cash to the Tory party in the midst of the Balkan conflict.

The investigation was prompted by a *Sunday Times* story – hotly denied by one of the businessmen involved – claiming a donation from a British-based Serbian entrepreneur had been made of "less than £100,000" and was regarded as so sensitive that it was reported to security services, the Cabinet Office and Mr Major.

The second donation of £50,000 from a second businessman in late 1994 was – according to the *Sunday Times* – arranged by the known acquaintance of Karadzic, John Kennedy, a Tory candidate.

Jeremy Hanley, the party chairman at the time, conceded yesterday he had met the businessmen in a Mayfair club at the instigation of Mr Kennedy, but refused – as a matter of principle – to disclose whether any donation was made subsequently.

Mr Kennedy dismissed the *Sunday Times* story as fantastic nonsense whilst the businessman, who remained un-named yesterday, issued a statement through solicitors Carter-Ruck rejecting the newspaper's claims.

They said their client was a British citizen of Yugoslav birth with substantial assets who had lived in the UK for more than a decade. "Our client is outraged by any suggestions that he is linked in any way to Radovan Karadzic or the Bosnian Serbs. We are instructed that our client has never met, communicated with, or been associated with, Radovan Karadzic in any way whatsoever." It said the businessman had never been associated with anyone in the Bosnian Serb leadership, and never handled money or assets from them.

Mr Mawhinney said he would be speaking to Mr Kennedy about the allegations, as well as to party treasurers.

Mr Kennedy said he had not raised any money from outside the UK, nor had he "raised any amount, either in total or in part, of either £50,000 or £100,000".

Figure 2.5 A political article in a broadsheet newspaper

AND IT'S TROUBLE AS USUAL FOR MAJOR...

TORIES PROBE SERB £100,000 GIFT

TORY chief Brian Mawhinney last night ordered a probe into claims that the party was given £100,000 by a henchman of evil Serb leader Radovan Karadzic.

John Major has been warned about the payment made by a businessman with ties to Karadzic, who is wanted by the UN for ordering the slaughter of thousands of civilians in the Bosnian war.

by PASCOE WATSON

Yesterday the *Sunday Times* claimed the donation was made between 1992 and 1994 – when British troops were battling to keep the peace in Bosnia.

Last night Dr Mawhinney said: "These are serious allegations. I have asked the party's treasurers to look into it.

"If any rules are found to have been transgressed, the money will be returned."

The Tories were also rocked by reports that most of the £440,000 given to them by Polly Peck fraudster Asil Nadir was stolen.

A secret report showed that £365,000 from Nadir should have been paid back – but wasn't.

Figure 2.6 A political article in a tabloid newspaper

Activity

Divide into two groups, male and female. Each group is an investigative TV journalism team working for an international news agency.

There has been a fire at the largest school in Holland and many children have been badly injured. Brainstorm the areas you will investigate, the angle of the news report and who you will want to interview.

Afterwards, compare your list with the other team and then with the list of things you might have come up with. How different might the final programme be? Are there certain groups you might have omitted?

The list could possibly include:

- safety in public buildings
- teaching of safety rules to staff and students
- inability of emergency services, such as fire brigades and hospitals, to deal with disasters
- criminal negligence by builders and architects in designing this particular school
- possibility of arson, terrorism
- EU fire regulations
- comparison of Dutch fire disasters with British disasters

- bravery of rescue services
- underfunding of rescue services
- suffering of children
- bravery of individuals, including staff and children
- overcrowding in schools and overworked staff, leading to dangerous situations
- parents' concern over children's safety
- interviews with: parents, children, teachers, fire brigade, local politician, government education official, doctors, EU officials.

Theories of representation

There are two main theories covering representation in the media. The **pluralist** model argues that influence between the media and society flows two ways. In a commercially competitive society, for economic reasons, a media product has to attract customers by reflecting their viewpoints and giving them what they want. It can influence but not dictate. Also, many if not all of its producers – journalists, scriptwriters, photographers, directors and so on – belong to our society and have probably grown up in it and accepted its values.

Case study

The images in the advertisement shown in Figure 2.7 represent 'traditional' values. The aim is to give us a sense of belonging to a quintessential Britishness which can, in a commercial sense, make certain products into institutions with which we identify. Tiptree's is a good example of how advertising uses the **myth** of national identity so that we are then attracted to a product which seems to embody it. Analyse the messages in this advert.

The **hegemonic** model claims that ruling classes or bodies maintain power by exerting control over every aspect of cultural life and that includes the media. This theory has been applied to such diverse political ideologies as capitalism and communism. Both groups want to maintain the status quo, and one way to disguise their domination and manipulation and yet to exert them subtly is through the media. They use the media to distribute and reinforce their beliefs or doctrines. At the same time, they recognise that the media, especially popular media, can be a threat to them by directly challenging or slowly eroding their ideology. This use of the media is usually called **propaganda** and is dealt with more fully in Unit 6 and in Chapter 30.

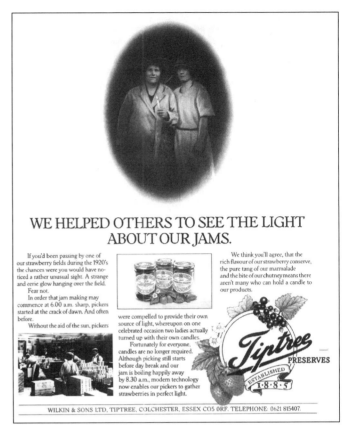

Figure 2.7 Some advertisements appeal to 'traditional' values

Political considerations

During the Second World War, in order to support the war effort, many women were encouraged to find jobs in the factories where for the first time they earned wages comparable with men. A problem for the government after the war was that the men returning from the Front needed to find jobs and so women were again discouraged from working. Among the methods used to encourage women to stay at home were the screen and magazines. Fictional tales showing that the good wife and mother's place was in the kitchen, and not in the masculine world of the office or factory, became very popular.

Unfair representation

Television is popularly thought of as neutral and trustworthy in its handling and portrayal of the news and current affairs. In contrast to newspapers, for example, broadcasters are not allowed to take sides or express an opinion in favour of one side or the other when covering an industrial dispute.

Some groups do, however, claim to be unfairly represented. This view is supported by the Glasgow University Media Group who have analysed thousands of hours of news broadcasts. In the 1984–5 miners' strike, for example, they claim that skilful news management by the National Coal Board (as it was then known) and the government misrepresented the miners and adversely affected both public opinion towards them and their own opinion of their fellow miners in other coalfields.

However, it is not just in this one industrial dispute that researchers claim this takes place. Rather, it is part of an ingrained process where the values of the controllers of our media and the values of the controllers of political and industrial power are shared.

Case study

As an example of how the Glasgow Media Group and other critics of TV news find fault with the way viewpoints are represented on the news, we have constructed a fictitious dispute which nonetheless contains the kinds of codes which, it is claimed, influence the audience.

This scenario concerns an industrial dispute between the management of a factory and the workforce. The TV news producer wants to represent 'both sides of the story' to the viewers. We have already discussed how assumptions can be made, often stereotypically, which are commonly shared ideologies, conveyed from producer to audience, by certain mutually accepted codes. Thus, the spokesperson for the workers may well be interviewed on the picket line. He or she may feel very cold, and perhaps look somewhat dishevelled. The spokesperson may not be particularly articulate and could have a strong regional accent. There could be noise, including shouting, going on in the background.

In contrast, the management spokesperson is likely to be interviewed in the calm and sophisticated environment of the TV studio. He or she will probably wear a suit and speak with a refined accent.

The connotations attached to trade unionists, especially those in low-status occupations who go on strike, are very likely to be the result of negative stereotyping. So, the signifiers carried by the workers' spokesperson

could signal to the audience that this is a scruffy, inarticulate troublemaker, if the audience have come to share in the commonly accepted codes and thus accept the dominant reading intended by the producer.

Any voice-over narrative could anchor this dominant reading even more. Selective framing, camera angles and shots, and editing could also contribute to the impression that the shop steward is the leader of a greedy and mindless rabble who are destroying the country's economy, putting jobs and lives at risk; while the management side is represented as calm, reasonable, 'legitimate' and 'civilised'.

Representation of royalty

An essential part of the political structure of our country is the position of the Royal family. It can be argued that the way the media have treated them, and how they themselves have used the media, can be shown as examples to support both pluralist and hegemonic theories of representation.

The hegemonic theory claims that the media can 'legitimise' the beliefs of the ruling classes and, indeed, both tabloid and broadsheet newspapers treat the Queen as 'special'.

There is very little questioning of the Queen's actual position. Political speeches questioning her right to rule are regarded with scorn by the majority of the press. The Queen is still seen as the symbol of the moral and cultural strength of Britain. Newspaper reports on her activities tend to be very bland, more concerned with how she looks than the work she undertakes.

The pluralist theory, however, argues that the regular media interest in the Royal family is fuelled by an insatiable public demand to know what is happening in the lives of the rich and famous. There is genuine popular support for the Queen (and also the Queen Mother) both as a person and in her role as monarch, and the press reflects that support. It has to be admitted that in the last decade the rest of the Royal family has been sharply criticised by the media and treated with little respect. Hegemonicists would argue that, whilst the government may want to support the Queen as a figurehead, they would be only too pleased to end the country's financial support of her relations.

It is undoubtedly true that media coverage of royalty has greatly changed. When Edward VIII abdicated because of his wish to marry the divorcee Wallis Simpson, the press were very discreet in mentioning

ROYAL TERROR TARGET ALERT

Queen's future plans open to all on Internet

Exclusive by Robert Jobson
Royal Correspondent

TERRORISTS anywhere in the world can discover the Queen's exact whereabouts months in advance on the Internet.

At the touch of a button, IRA activists can call up her diary on a computer screen.

Times, dates and venues of engagements for the Queen and nine other senior Royals appear within seconds.

The *Daily Express* accessed the information supplied by the Government's Office of Information in 30 seconds – there are no secret codes or passwords but we have chosen not to reveal how.

The sensitive information is available to millions who use the information superhighway. The IRA already spreads propaganda on it. So much detail is provided that a would-be assassin, crank or stalker would have months to plan an attack. Last night a senior establishment source close to the Prime Minister condemned the decision to release such sensitive information as "complete lunacy".

And leading Tory backbench MP Sir Ivan Lawrence called for the person responsible for the "appalling breach of security" to be sacked.

The list – issued "with the compliments of the Press Secretary to the Queen" – details the engagements of the Prince and Princess of Wales, the Princess Royal, Duke of Edinburgh, Prince Edward, Princess Margaret and Princess Alexandra.

Even visits scheduled for the Duke of York – a serving naval officer who the IRA claim is a "legitimate target" – are given.

The astonishing security lapse comes amid growing fears about the Queen's safety following the end of the IRA ceasefire.

Tight security surrounded Her Majesty as she celebrated her 70th birthday quietly at Sandringham yesterday after documents indicating that senior Royals are being targeted were found at the home of IRA Aldwych bus bomber Edward O'Brien in February.

Scotland Yard refused to discuss royal security. But whatever was uncovered at O'Brien's flat led to a drastic increase in protection and suggests that the IRA were planning their first royal attack since murdering Earl Mountbatten in 1979.

Ironically, the Queen yesterday moved the location of her birthday family dinner for security reasons after its original venue at a restaurant near Windsor was leaked.

The royal diary, which is updated every week on "the Net", provides engagements up to August 1996.

In stark contrast, the Prime Minister's movements are kept top secret. In America secret agents have uncovered 11 serious plots to kill President Clinton, on the net, showing the type of people who can get access to it.

Royal engagements are noted in the Court Circular published on the day of a visit. But issuing the information to such a wide audience so far in advance clearly puts the Royal Family at risk.

Sir Ivan said: "It really is appalling. It is time that those who are responsible for such a monumental breach of security woke up and if they are that stupid were sacked."

The senior establishment source added: "Whoever authorised this must be out of their tiny minds.

"It clearly gives the IRA or any other terrorist the upper hand and puts our Royal Family at risk."

the scandal and obeyed directions from the government to delay official announcements. Nowadays, royal scandals are openly and quickly reported in great detail by all sections of the press. In the same way, at one time TV camera shots maintained a respectful distance between royalty and the viewer. Now zoom lenses give us close-ups of a tearful Princess Diana.

Media ownership

The problem of who owns the media and how the owners may exert or try to exert control is the source of a wide-ranging and ongoing debate. It is of fundamental importance to our ideals of democracy, with its underlying assumptions of freedom and responsibility. One of the most constructive examinations of this issue is to be found in *Power without Responsibility* by James Curran and Jean Seaton, which is continually updated. In Britain there is legislation concerning the number of media products that can be owned by one person or corporation. (See Chapter 30 for details.) Rupert Murdoch's control of various newspapers and TV companies is a cause for concern. But there is also a worry that the media are largely controlled by people with similar ideological viewpoints.

Activity

Why are many individuals and organisations worried about the concentration of ownership of the media?

Can you identify which newspapers have right-wing sympathies and which lean to the left?

Case study

Look at the editorial column from *The Sun* shown in Figure 2.8.

What attitudes or viewpoints does this reinforce about:

■ politics?
■ homosexuality?

Activity

Record an edition of the BBC 9 o'clock evening news. Compare the items covering politics with the coverage of the same events in a broadsheet newspaper such as *The Guardian* and in a tabloid such as *The Daily Express*. Do you feel that the opinion and actions of the ruling party are supported or challenged?

If you have completed the exercises given above and discussed the work with students of your own age and with older people, you will have begun to realise that representation is a complex and contentious

---

THE SUN SAYS

Gentle John

WHAT this country needs is strong leadership.

Twice a week, John Smith leaps up in he Commons to ram home that message.

But what happens when the Labour leader gets the chance to show John Major how it should be done?

Smith proves to be about as firm as a wet lettuce.

Inept

He should have booted MP George Galloway out of the parliamentary party for his disgraceful sucking-up to Saddam Hussein.

Instead Galloway got a ticking off and was made to say sorry.

You'll have to do better than that, Mr Smith.

The inept Opposition's in danger of making the Government look good.

Empty vessels

WE'VE been conned by the gay lobby.

For years they've told us that one man in 10 is homosexual.

Governments pump millions into AIDs propaganda as gay actors mince into No 10.

Teachers tell children homosexuality is normal.

A campaign grows to make gay sex legal at 16.

But now the truth is out: A survey shows that barely one man in 90 is gay.

The loud-mouthed luvvies should belt up.

In memory

THE fans have turned Old Trafford into a shrine to Sir Matt Busby.

Manchester United should go one better.

Rename the ground Matt Busby Stadium.

Hans off!

LORD OWEN has an impossible task in Bosnia.

He is no nearer getting the Serbs, Croats and Muslims to talk peace.

But he's given it his best shot.

Sadly the political pygmies of the European parliament demand he should be sacked.

It shows how much that small-minded bunch dislike Britain.

If Owen was a German they'd be giving him a medal.

And finally ...

THIS really takes the biscuit.

Shops are calling gingerbread men "gingerbread persons".

They reckon it is politically correct.

What will they do about fairy cakes?

Figure 2.8 An editorial from *The Sun*

subject. You will be aware of what can be represented and how differently things can be represented. In the next section we will look more precisely at how this is done.

Analysing how issues are represented in media products

Now that different considerations relating to representation have been recognised, the next stage is to identify what is the intention of the author (and this can be a multiple authorship in which the owner of a company is also involved). Secondly, the intended audience and its nature must be recognised. Then the different techniques used in forming a representation can be identified. At this stage it may be helpful to re-read the section on the elements of a text as described on page 1 of Chapter 1.

When the BBC was originally formed in the 1920s, its philosophy, as stated by its first Director-General, John (later Lord) Reith, was to 'inform, educate and entertain' the public. Reith saw the BBC as acting in the national interest on behalf of the public. There was, however, an assumption that this government monopoly knew what was best for the public and it was their responsibility to provide it for them. This

IF KINNOCK WINS TODAY, WILL THE LAST PERSON TO LEAVE BRITAIN PLEASE TURN OUT THE LIGHTS

UP YOURS DELORS

FREDDIE STARR ATE MY HAMSTER

GOTCHA!

parental (even paternalist) attitude has changed over the years and a more sophisticated and critical audience now expects a far greater level of consultation over what is provided. At the same time, however, it is still argued that the media shape people's opinions and do not simply follow them. For example, most newspapers, particularly the popular tabloids, will claim to represent the views of the British public. Yet at the same time they will seek to shape their readers' views in an unashamedly explicit manner, as with the headlines shown below.

Some sections of the media, particularly TV and film, are aimed at an international market, whilst radio and local newspapers have a much more restricted target audience.

We can now begin to look at how representation of issues has changed in different periods and what effect this has had on individuals, groups and populations.

Social groups

Age

It is well documented that the 1950s saw the emergence of the teenager as a social phenomenon. Superficially it seemed as if the media and the music industry, in particular, were largely responsible for the rising importance of the tastes of this age group, their choice of music and fashion. However, there were more important economic factors such as increased leisure time, more money in their pockets and new inventions, such as the transistor radio, which contributed to their importance.

Young people today are represented in a number of ways, sometimes as being vulnerable, innocent and in need of protection or otherwise as wild, aggressive, unfeeling, ignorant and selfish.

Activity

Look at the images of young people in Figure 2.9 on the next page. What qualities do they each represent?

Figure 2.9 Different images of young people

Older people, too, have had mixed representation. On news programmes and in the newspapers, where there are plenty of images of older people, they can be seen as intelligent, wise, experienced and powerful.

It is interesting to note, however, that whilst it is acceptable to have a female news presenter, they tend to be younger and more obviously attractive than the male news presenters. Will the news ever be presented by a grey-haired woman with glasses?

By contrast, old people can also be portrayed as senile, living in the past, losing their memory, physically unattractive and usually deaf, with no sexual qualities, a burden on society and an easy target for violence. Even in the contemporary comedy series *One Foot in the Grave* the main character is grumpy, unattractive and anti-social, although still active.

The 1990s have seen a change in the situation because of the growing numbers of affluent pensioners. Comedy programmes such as *The Golden Girls,* about four elderly women, have shown that older people can share contemporary viewpoints and moral values, want to have fun, be sexy, travel, go out, and they are witty and intelligent. There have been films, too, in which the stars have been old, for example, *On Golden Pond* and *Cocoon.*

The media have responded to the rise of the pensioner, not only through the moving image but also through radio and in print. Advertisers are very keen to tap the savings of this age group by producing adverts that will appeal to and not insult the older reader and listener, and media producers therefore have to make a product that will support this type of advertising.

Activity

Listen to the radio station Classic FM. List the music played and the products which are advertised.

What signifies that this station targets older people? Listen to the adverts, the music and the style of presentation. Do you think that an older listener will be a typical British pensioner?

There has also been a rise in the publication of magazines for the over-sixties age group. Many of these are aimed at promoting health and financial issues.

Gender

Our sex is determined at conception, but it has been suggested that gender is something created through our upbringing and culture. Over the last few decades, there have been great efforts in the media and in education to give equal opportunities to both boys and girls, men and women. As is often the case, it is economic causes rather than natural justice which have changed the way in which men and women have been represented. One of the main areas of debate has been concerned with fiction.

Case study

'Jane and Peter' books for young children have been obvious targets. Jane was always given the traditional female role, 'helping Mummy in the kitchen', while Peter had a more active life, working with Daddy in the garden and being waited on by his mother and sister. In contrast, modern children's books allow girls and boys freedom from traditional gender roles. In an interesting reworking of traditional fairytales, there are stories of 'Prince Cinders' and 'Princess Smartypants', where the girls take on the more active roles.

Activity

Look at two different comic strips such as Alex from the *Daily Telegraph,* and Andy Capp from the *Daily Mirror.* How typical are they of contemporary men and women? Minnie the Minx and Dennis the Menace comic strips have been popular for generations. Their activities and attitudes towards education, culture and older people have not changed, but are they typical of today's children?

A change has been noticeable on the small and large screens. In early films, heroines were looking (whether they realised it or not!) for a man to rescue them so that they could live with him happily ever after, raise his children and give him a comfortable home. They were morally upright and tremendously pretty. Bad women could also be attractive but were independent, money grabbing, wore exciting clothing, were capable of physical violence and could look after themselves until defeated by a good man or woman (see Chapter 3).

These early films were a form of escapism which did not really reflect the experiences of most women at the time, who led very hard physical lives in domestic service or factories and in the home as well. Women were not the frail breed represented on screen.

In 1960s adventure films and serials, women came to be shown as intelligent, resourceful, independent and physically able to take care of themselves. However, their main role was still very often to support the dominant male and look attractive, for example, in James Bond films and *The Man from Uncle.* Again there are exceptions and the cult appeal of *The Avengers* may in part be due to the rather enigmatic Mrs Peel who fulfilled what could easily be termed a 'man's role' as the partner of Steed, except that her independence and resourcefulness also found expression in a single-minded sex appeal that left us in no doubt that she was her own woman.

There are now stronger roles for women on TV and in film. In *Prime Suspect* the main character is a mature, hard-working and hard-living woman who is successful in the traditionally male-dominated world

of the police. *The Bill* has a tough female boss in its portrayal of a woman police inspector. Women can also be portrayed as economically or physically powerful, as in the film *Disclosure* where a female boss sexually harasses her male subordinate.

Children's programmes such as *Blue Peter,* and even soaps such as *EastEnders* and *Neighbours,* have shown that both sexes can share the same qualities and not only want but are able to do the same things.

Activity

Split into two groups, male and female. Each group has to describe to an alien from outer space a typical woman and a typical man in their thirties. Make a list of attributes, including:

- physical details, such as hairstyle, colour of eyes, body shape
- mental qualities, such as kindness, toughness
- their most likely occupation
- leisure activities, such as football or knitting
- tastes in food and drink
- type of clothing, including colours associated with them
- good and bad habits
- what type of films they prefer.

Compare your list with that of the other team. Discuss whether the list was compiled from experience or images in films or on TV.

Look at the two adverts in Figure 2.10. How many of the qualities or activities that you listed are represented in these images?

Although TV and newspapers show some recognition of the equal importance of women's interests and needs, the greatest gap lies in magazines. Special-interest magazines are generally targeted at one particular sex. It is interesting to note that boys and men tend to buy magazines relating to one particular topic, such as computers, cars or gardening, whilst many women prefer to buy 'lifestyle' magazines that cover a number of subjects including cooking, fashion, short stories, problem pages, personal relationships and so on.

Activity

Look at a magazine aimed at a young female readership, such as *19.* List the main subjects covered in it. Discuss how representative it is of the lifestyle of young women.

Figure 2.10 Advertisements can subtly suggest appropriate roles for men and women

Finally it is interesting to note that, although they form over half the population, women are not employed in proportional numbers within the media industries. Read the article in Figure 2.11.

In 1993/94 *Skillset* commissioned and subsequently published a major study of working practices within the industry. They identified that, because of the structural and technological changes taking place within the industry, there had been a shift from permanent employment to freelance... The researchers estimated that, at the time of the survey, there were approximately 15,000 freelances in the industry, about 13,000 of whom were economically active. This represents approximately 60% of the workforce in TV, film and video. Most freelances are male (63%) but there is wide variation between the different skill groups. In the traditional technical areas (camera, sound and lighting) there are very few women. However, women predominate in wardrobe, make-up, production support and – just – amongst writers and researchers. Most freelances are white, with only 3% of respondents to the survey coming from ethnic minority backgrounds and most are young – 70% of women freelances are under 40 (47% men). This figure may indicate the likelihood of a more equal gender distribution as time goes on.

Figure 2.11 Information contained in a report by Skillset Careers Information Service

Race

The media have probably shown more deliberate bias and prejudice against people of different races or ethnic background than against any other group. Racism occurs when people consider others from a different culture or born in a different country are inferior to them.

For many years, in the film world, black people were used in minor roles, given the parts of servants or minor villains. It is ironic that the first movie to use sound starred Al Jolson, a white man portraying a black musician. This reflected the position of non-white people in American society. In Margaret Mitchell's book *Gone With the Wind,* the author depicts blacks as stupid and loyal, physically strong, and needing firm guidance from a white man to prevent them turning to crime. The book even indicates a certain sympathy for the Ku-Klux-Klan. When the film version was made, conscious consideration was given by the producer, perhaps for the first time in Hollywood history, to the representation of black people, although the end result was still very conservative. It is noteworthy that even in the 1990s, the voice for a subordinate or

servant in a cartoon is often given to a black person with a 'negro' accent.

In Britain in the 1960s, comedy programmes aimed to show that racist attitudes were stupid. In *Till Death do us Part,* the lead character Alf Garnett, played by Warren Mitchell, was an ignorant, loud-mouthed old man who referred to black people as 'coons'. However, later research showed that many people actually sympathised with his sentiments. Other comedy programmes made rather obvious points that black people were as intelligent as white, such as the well-spoken black student in *Rising Damp,* and *Love thy Neighbour,* which was about a racist white man living next door to a professional black family. Eventually black people, like women, were given supporting roles in TV adventure series, which showed that they too could be active, good looking, responsible and talk properly.

But even when minority groups were portrayed sympathetically, they were still shown as adjuncts to the white man, with amusing cultural differences built in to emphasise their essentially subordinate role.

In *The Lone Ranger,* a popular children's cowboy series of the 1950s and 1960s, the hero had Tonto as a loyal, trusty Indian friend. Tonto was very useful in awkward situations but couldn't string together two words grammatically, even after several years with the white man. He persisted to the bitter end in introducing himself as 'Me Tonto'!

It is the success of black people in music and the sports world that has really increased positive media coverage. Many black people are now role models for teenagers (whether black or white), such as Naomi

Figure 2.12 Trevor McDonald has become a 'star' as a newsreader

Campbell, the model, or John Fashinu, the footballer and TV presenter. No one now questions why Trevor McDonald should read the news.

Xenophobia (a hatred of foreigners) is often evident in the press. Sometimes this is because of political influences, as in reporting about immigration.

Standing firm on bogus refugees

So much for consistency. The Asylum and Immigration Bill – one of the few robust and necessary measures in a depressingly thin Queen's Speech – may be neutered from the start.

What has inspired John Major to contemplate turning the Bill over to a special, all-party Commons committee? Certainly not a sudden diminution in the problem. Forget the countless numbers of illegal immigrants. Last year there were more than 32,000 applicants for asylum. Fewer than 1,000 were found to be genuine. Britain remains a magnet for bogus 'refugees' intent only on an easier life.

Now it seems the Prime Minister is being blown off course by allegations that the Tories are just stoking up racial tensions for their own ends. Tony Blair lost no time before descending to the cheap jibe of racism. The entire race-relations industry is up in arms. In a particularly nasty personal attack, one of its representatives even sneered that Home Secretary Michael Howard might not be in

this country today had the Asylum Bill been in force when his Jewish father fled to Britain.

But this kind of tendentious rubbish should play no part in the debate. Bogus refugees undermine good race relations. They make it more difficult for genuine victims of persecution. They cost millions in benefit payments. The Tories need not apologise for trying to do something about them. John Major is right not to want the Asylum Bill to exacerbate racial prejudice. But there is no reason why it should, since it applies equally to white Poles and black Nigerians.

To set up a special committee would hand Labour a propaganda victory. It would lend credence to allegations that the Tories have been caught trying to play the race card – and arouse fears that the measure might be nobbled in the interests of political correctness.

The Prime Minister must brush off the snide attacks and stick to his guns. The Bill should go through Parliament by the normal means.

Sometimes it is more subtle, as in the use of photographs, and how they are cropped or the camera angle.

Racist attitudes still exist in the media industries, even though they are considered unethical and unprofessional. In February 1996 the *Daily Mirror* carried the story of how photographs of black Ford car workers in an advertisement were removed and replaced by white workers. The bad publicity forced Ford to launch an inquiry into why this was allowed

to happen. But the fact remains that racist attitudes are held by people who are influential and have proprietary access to the media, in this case in the advertising industry.

British patriotism is evident whenever there is conflict with European legislation, in the vocabulary used and the words given to describe French or German actions and opinions. They are often ridiculed. Consider again *The Sun's* 'Up Yours Delors' headline.

This feeling of superiority or sense of condescension is also evident in the methods sometimes used to describe conditions or situations in Third World countries, such as Asia, Latin America and Africa. Bias can occur because these countries appear on our screens or in the newspapers only when some disaster happens or war breaks out. Sometimes reports concentrate on the activities of foreign, particularly British, aid workers and neglect the efforts of local people. A documentary series on TV that commenced in February 1996 tried to represent a more positive side of Africa. It aimed to show that there is more to African life than a primitive tribal existence, poverty and famine. After all, it is a large continent consisting of numerous different countries with great cultural, economic and geographical diversity.

Occupation

Legislation has ensured that newspapers can no longer carry advertising for jobs asking only for men or only for women, unless the circumstances are exceptional. Part of the success of media products is their novelty, so we find examples of women and men doing unusual jobs or finding themselves in unusual or strange situations.

For example, on television in 'Casualty' there are male nurses with important roles. A recent serial on BBC TV, *Hetty Winthrop Investigates*, has a middle-aged, northern, working-class, female private investigator with a male teenager from a deprived background as an assistant.

There are many TV programmes that are centred around occupations. It is useful to examine how the jobs themselves are represented in such programmes. For example, we could consider the following:

- *All Creatures Great and Small* (vet)
- *Casualty* (hospital)
- *Shortland Street* (hospital)
- *London's Burning* (fire services)
- *Soldier, Soldier* (the Armed Forces)

33

- *The Bill* (police)
- *Dangerfield* (police/doctor).

These occupations have been chosen as the basis for series because they give scriptwriters the opportunity to introduce new characters on a regular basis. The type of work gives excellent dramatic possibilities as life-and-death situations can occur. Is it a coincidence that most of these jobs involve uniforms and the status of individual characters is easily identifiable?

All the above series claim to reflect and copy the activities of real firefighters, nurses, vets and so on. However, because of the 'star' status that the actors develop when the series becomes popular, does this glamorise the occupation? Also, the need to tell an interesting story each week can disguise the monotonous, routine work that is the reality of many of these jobs. Much of a firefighter's work is taken up with training, testing and maintenance, and safety visits to premises.

Activity

A new TV series is centred around the world of a college librarian. Briefly describe the activities that you think this job involves. How do you think the producer can make this idea exciting, glamorous and interesting? Think in terms of characters and situations. Go and talk to your college librarian!

The media give us expectations about jobs. Numerous jokes from comedians reinforce how boring and conservative are accountants and bank managers, insisting on the insincerity and deviousness of estate agents and sales people, or the moral self-righteousness of teachers and social workers.

Images are very powerful in indicating a person's job and status to us. The smart suit indicates power; the leather jacket a feeling of freedom and a job with more individuality, such as photographer.

Activity

Look at the adverts in Figures 2.13, 2.14 and 2.15. Discuss the lifestyles they represent.

Figure 2.13

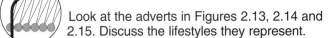

Figure 2.14

CHANEL photograph by Karl Lagerfeld

You needn't lose any sleep over money.

Hectic life being a student, isn't it?

So the last thing you want to worry about is how to make ends meet. Which is why our Student Package is specially designed to help you control your money more easily.

You'll have a Bankcard, cheque book and a free overdraft facility. (Just in case your grant doesn't cover everything.)

You can also keep completely up to date with your spending by getting full, up to the minute statements from our numerous cash machines.

Or, if that sounds like too much hassle, stay in and use our free PhoneBank service. Finally, if you fancy a break from the student bar, we'll throw in £20 worth of cinema vouchers when you open the account. Good night.

Student Package   **TSB** We want you to say **YES**

Figure 2.15

Disability

Until recently, disabled people have been dealt with very negatively in the media – if at all. Disability, whether physical or mental, was little understood by society in general. As late as 1977, a bestseller from Susan Howatch, *The Rich are Different*, could leave the reader with the impression that epilepsy is a hereditary disease causing physical and mental malformation in the children of epileptics.

For centuries, people with learning difficulties have been shunned and hidden away and people with physical disabilities have been displayed as freaks. The film *The Elephant Man* gives a powerful and tragic account of the Victorian man John Merrick, who was born with severe deformities and spent part of his life in a circus and the rest in institutions. The media at the time were certainly curious, but his life story is still of enduring interest to the modern media which periodically produce a documentary or article about him.

Physical disability was often considered to be linked with mental disorders. Deaf people often found that

people talked slowly as well as loudly to them, as if understanding as well as hearing was a problem. Disabled people were to be pitied and were seen to be largely helpless. They were also expected to be very grateful to society for any help they received.

In early films, it was acceptable for a character to be in a wheelchair, especially if he or she could manage to walk by the end of the film. A character with Down's syndrome was not considered suitable for viewing.

Ironside, the popular 1960s drama series, was based around a wheelchair-bound lawyer. Although he was played by an able-bodied actor, the representation was at least positive.

One of the earliest sympathetic portrayals of a person with learning difficulties was Benny in *Crossroads,* who was an accepted part of the soap's cast for many years. It has often been the case that disabled characters in films or on TV have been played by able-bodied actors such as Daniel Day-Lewis in *My Left Foot.* However, in *L.A. Law,* an American series of the 1980s, a regular member of the cast was an actor with Down's syndrome who played the part of a clerical assistant with the law firm. His role brought to the attention of the average viewer the problems and wishes of someone with learning difficulties, such as independence, sexual relationships and so on.

Gradually, society is recognising the needs of disabled people, and is starting to make their integration into general public life easier, with practical measures such as ramps and specialised transport. This has been weakly reflected by the media. As a group, they are seen on TV, heard on radio and their viewpoints and experienced related in the press. There are specialist magazines and programmes on TV and some news and current affairs programmes have sign language for the hearing-impaired. There have been dramas about all types of mental illness and the Oscar-winning film *Rainman* had Dustin Hoffman starring as a man with autism.

However, unlike other groups, such as women or old people, many disabled people are not economically or politically strong and advertisers are generally not interested in them. Indeed, it would be incorrect to put disabled people under one umbrella. The label covers so many types of disability that it becomes meaningless. What is the connection between someone who walks with a limp and someone who has advanced Alzheimer's disease? Their physical and mental needs, viewpoints and behaviour will be entirely different.

Activity

Analyse the representation of disabled people in your local newspaper. How many articles are about charity events raising money for disabled people? How many are about disabled children rather than adults? How many articles are there about the success of a disabled person? What type of disabilities are covered? What is the attitude of the writer towards the disabled person? What photographic images are there? Are there articles on the front page?

Ideas

The media can represent not just physical phenomena which we can see or hear, such as people and events, but also ideas, including political and religious ones.

The hegemonic theory can be useful to explain how the media treat religious ideas. It claims that the extensive coverage of the state religion serves to maintain the status quo. Britain is not a religious country. It tolerates many different types of religion and the state church itself is not particularly well attended. However, many people still choose the Church of England as the religion in which to be married and to be buried. They may not go to ordinary services but they accept its place as an important and traditional part of our culture. An alien reading a broadsheet newspaper or local newspaper could be forgiven for thinking that we are deeply interested in the Anglican religion. There is the broadcasting of religious services and the 'Thought for the Day' on radio, regular reports from Church Synods, deep interest in the lives of our spiritual leaders, lists of church services – even reviews of church services – in newspapers, lists of church appointments made by the Queen, long lists of weddings, funerals and so on. The vocabulary used in articles may be critical of individuals and practices, but there is an overall feeling that the Church is a respected institution, part of the fabric of society.

Religions outside the Anglican Church, other than Roman Catholicism, are not usually given the same status or amount of coverage.

Political ideas are also of deep concern to the media. Media owners or publishers may want to promote their own views. What makes the political bias of a newspaper apparent? The vocabulary itself is a big clue. Are the members of one political party referred to as Conservatives or Tories? What adjectives are used to describe the politicians or their parties?

Social issues

Crime

In many cases, how newspapers treat criminals depends not only on the crime but on the criminal's status in society. They are unlikely to demand a brutal prison regime for a middle-class financier who embezzles millions, although they will for the teenager from a deprived background, who has stolen much smaller amounts of money. Robin Hood, a medieval outlaw, and possibly a fictional character, has had many books and films made about him. Over the years, many other crimes have been made to appear glamorous and exciting, from highwaymen to gangsters.

Recently the media have been criticised for concentrating on the criminal rather than the victim. There was criticism over the film *Buster*, starring Phil Collins, because it trivialised the seriousness of the Great Train Robbery in which he took part.

Whether someone is a criminal, or what constitutes a crime, can also be seen as debatable. During the Afghan war in the 1980s the Afghans were depicted in the British press as freedom fighters, whereas to the Russians they were terrorists. However, whilst the British press might consider the Afghans to be worthy people, on home ground the IRA are definitely seen as terrorists. The IRA are considered by the British government to be an illegal and therefore criminal body. This led to a ban on the live transmission on TV of speeches by representatives of the IRA or Sinn Fein (their political wing). Until the ceasefire of 1994 any film footage had to be accompanied by an actor's voice-over so that the audience could not hear the actual voice of the person representing the illegal organisation.

The newspapers are generally seen as supporting the police, and journalists have to work closely with them to get information. This bias is subtly confirmed in photographs, which are generally taken from the viewpoint of the police rather than that of protesters or rioters. More recently there has been a new development as amateur camera people and photographers provide material for the media.

The media view of police work, as seen for example in *The Bill* and *Thieftakers*, may also be influenced by the amount of help given free of charge by the police to producers. A *Wired World* programme, in February 1996, revealed that the police were vetting scripts free of charge, something a consultant would charge thousands of pounds to do. They also gave free firearms training to some actors and supplied not only equipment, including cars and helicopters, but also officers to use as props and extras. Location fees for the use of police stations were half the normal price. The police must expect a sympathetic image in exchange for all this. Being in the position to vet scripts may also be useful in exerting pressure to change anything they do not like.

But real life does not always match up to the TV dramas. In the Rodney King case of 1992, American news programmes showed a black man being viciously beaten up by the Los Angeles police. The film footage had been taken using an amateur video recorder. A similar example took place in Wales when an amateur video recording captured a number of policemen beating up a suspect.

Case study

In the coverage of the Newbury bypass 'save the trees' campaign, environmentalists complained that journalists were keener to take photographs of protesters dressed like hippies and climbing trees than of middle-aged, middle-class female protesters. What does the photograph in Figure 2.16 suggest about the protesters?

Figure 2.16 Newbury bypass protesters

Activity

Look at the front pages of a tabloid newspaper over the space of a week. What crimes make front page news? How much disapproval is expressed at various crimes? Does it depend on the criminal? What words express disapproval of the crime and what words can glamorise the crime?

Crime, unemployment and homelessness are serious social issues that have received prominence though differing coverage over the past twenty-five years. In the 1960s, the *Cathy Come Home* drama documentary on homelessness had a seminal influence on British society and was the major spur for the founding of the charity 'Shelter'. But not all the media's handling of these issues is quite so sympathetic.

Health

Health is dealt with by the media from two aspects. There is the healthy, keep-fit image, beloved by advertisers who hope to sell us lots of products from pills to aerobic classes. Then there is the 'doom and gloom' approach which concentrates on telling us we are a dying race, sentenced to extinction through disease, beef eating and pollution.

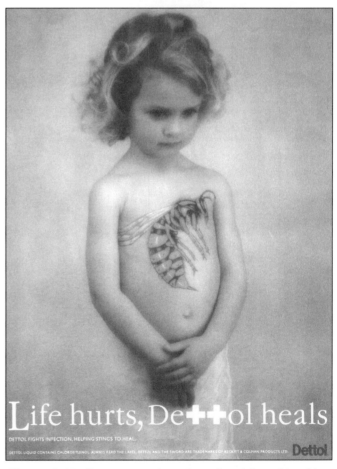

Figure 2.17 One approach to the advertising of health products

Courtesy of Reckitt & Colman.
With thanks to photographer Joyce Tennison

Figure 2.18 Some advertisements sell a healthy, keep-fit image

Activity

Look through a selection of women's magazines. How many articles and adverts promise a bright future and how many are scaremongering? How does this compare with health articles in a newspaper such as *The Guardian*?

(For a more detailed discussion of advertising please refer to Chapter 28.)

Events

It has been accepted that novels can mix fiction and non-fiction. Real events such as a war, or a disaster like the sinking of the *Titanic,* can form the background for a story including both historically real and imaginary characters. All the dialogue is usually made up but the producers strive to recreate the emotions and actions of the time.

Sometimes, however, events are distorted or changed, not to deceive the reader or film-goer, but to enhance a dramatic effect or simplify a situation. A novel or film has to conform to a certain length. Not everything can be shown or described within the space of a couple of hours in the case of a film. This is not generally considered to be unethical.

In Schiller's famous play, *Mary Queen of Scots,* the central dramatic action is based on a meeting between Mary and Queen Elizabeth I of England. In reality the two never met. In Sergei Eisenstein's film masterpiece, *Battleship Potemkin,* the reasons behind the failure of the 1905 revolution in Russia are symbolised in the massacre of civilians on a long flight of steps leading to the harbour in Odessa. In fact the massacre took place elsewhere and the length of the steps is extended by the use of repeated shots. The further away in time are events, the less critical we are of these distortions.

There also tends to be a bias in films and novels, as we see events unfold through the eyes of the main character, usually an heroic figure. So in *Reach for the Skies* we see the Second World War from the point of view of British pilot Douglas Bader (played by Kenneth More) who is shot down over German-occupied France and spends the rest of the war trying to escape. In *The One That Got Away* we anxiously follow the adventures of a German pilot shot down over England who makes several daring escape attempts before finally heroically succeeding. (As a matter of interest, both stories are based on fact.)

Activity

Make a list of action films. Alongside each entry, state who this film sympathises with, for instance Indians or cowboys, gangsters or police, and so on.

However, although we find it acceptable in films and novels for changes to be made, in newspapers and TV news programmes, we expect the truth!

In films such as *Superman* and *The Pelican Brief,* a main character and hero is a reporter, someone seeking to report the truth to the world against all odds. However, in reality, the truth can be distorted by the need to arouse the interest of readers or by constraints of time and money. We shall look at two examples.

Case study

A photojournalist working for the *Leicester Mercury* was asked to cover an Open Evening at the local college. Figure 2.19 shows a photo he took to show the type of activity that went on.

However, it is a constructed image; the photographer arranged this picture very carefully. When he arrived there was no one being talked to by the lecturer; in fact, very few people were around at the time. However, the table with the boards of student work behind and the equipment made a more interesting background. The

Figure 2.19 A college open evening

Mercury would be pleased to have their posters in shot. The college would also be pleased to promote this new course. So two girls interested in business courses were asked to pose by the side of one of the lecturers. The camera was moved to a central position and the students pretended that they were being shown how to make a film. Is the image successful? Is it truthful?

The arrangement of materials, whether text or pictures, is quite usual in journalism. This is particularly the case with regard to local newspapers, where most of the stories are unbelievably dull and only of interest to a minority of people. In the case above, it does not seem unethical. However, that is not always so.

A current issue is the way newspapers pay people for stories. Criminals are not supposed to benefit financially from their crimes, but it seems distasteful to the public that close relatives can. For example, Sonia Sutcliffe, wife of serial killer Peter Sutcliffe, has made money from selling her story to the newspapers. The tabloids reply to criticism by pointing out that they are only satisfying public demand for this type of story.

The amount of coverage given to any event will depend on the publication and especially on its readership. For example, a Royal wedding will be analysed in detail in all newspapers and magazines, but the emphasis will change. Women's magazines will go into great detail about the bride's dress and the romantic angle, a broadsheet may look at the need for security and the guest list.

Political bias will also affect the way in which some events are reported. Particularly when there is a war, or any event concerning a European angle, the news reporting may become more nationalistic. The Crimean War was possibly the first to give the public real information about how appalling the conditions on the frontline could be. Journalists covering the Vietnam war were instrumental in revealing the true state of affairs and turning American public opinion against the war. The vocabulary used is highly significant. Newspapers may try to avoid accusations of bias by giving as many viewpoints as possible, but the order in which these are given in the text is also important.

There are always problems in reporting from the frontline; for example, journalists may be deliberately fed wrong reports in order to mislead the enemy, or they may give information that is too detailed and so endanger troops. In the Gulf War, reports were closely monitored and all information was closely controlled, even though the large numbers of journalists present suggested that information was freely available.

Places

Exotic locations such as the Taj Mahal, the Sahara desert with camels or the Amazon jungle, can dominate our perception of a country. Too much coverage of the coastline of southern Spain, as shown in holiday programmes or in comedies, has made people forget about inland Spain and its culture.

Portrayals of other cultures are usually shown from a Western viewpoint. Even documentaries about other cultures, and their customs and rituals, which are supposedly sympathetically handled, can treat them as if they are in a theme park for the amusement of the civilised armchair tourists of Western suburbia. Consider the camera work on a TV documentary featuring natives or nomads in parts of the world remote from the West. It has a steady, slow, even hypnotic quality which is supposed to reflect the pace of life and the exotic strangeness of it all. But this is more to do with the perceptions of the producer than the reality for the people who actually live there. There is probably just as much going on in their lives in terms of social, romantic and economic interaction as there is in the average Westerner's. Yet a nomadic tribe will be portrayed as leading a simple life, with a documentary pace that encapsulates the myth of their essential stability, even if they are, in actuality, eking out a precarious existence. And, in these kinds of documentary, stability equals slowness. So the camera work is slow, and the voice-over narrative is soporific.

The portrayal of life in the West, even for the unemployed, is always much pacier. The camera action is faster and there is the sense that life is involved and complicated.

Apart from other countries, there are numerous stereotypical assumptions made about people from different regions of Britain. There is a popular image of Scousers, Cockneys, Brummies, Geordies, as well as the Irish and the Scots.

Activity

As far as England is concerned, there are ideas of 'Northerness' and 'Southerness' which contain within them many stereotypical connotations. As a group, brainstorm these and list the denotations from which they derive.

Activity

What media images do you associate with certain countries? Discuss the images of the countries shown in Figure 2.20.

Figure 2.20 The countries of Western Europe

Not only adverts but serious news reports like to link certain places and issues in our minds. News reports from Russia tend to have the reporter standing in front of St Basil's cathedral at the Kremlin. A report on American politics shows the White House.

Reporting about riots in Brixton gave a very negative image of the area. We can end up feeling unnecessarily fearful about such places. Whenever a bomb goes off in London, it affects the tourist trade, even though there may be little danger of a repeat. Statistically, there is much more chance of being killed on the roads than by a bomb.

Media access

The concept of access to the media is concerned with how easy it is for the public, whether individuals or groups, to influence the media product itself in terms of content and style.

There are a number of ways in which people can have access to the media, either as amateurs or professionals. These include the following:

- **Newspapers:**
  - letters to the editor
  - news items sent in by the public
  - features on local groups
  - quotes as part of news story
  - births, marriages and deaths columns.

- **Magazines:**
  - letters pages
  - short stories
  - features.

- **Radio:**
  - requests
  - phone–ins
  - 'vox pops'
  - interviews, for instance members of the public may be expert on a particular subject.

- **TV:**
  - amateur video documentaries
  - phone-ins (such as *Watchdog*)
  - entrants on quiz shows
  - audience participation chat shows, for example, *Central Weekend*
  - as experts
  - on magazine programmes
  - points of view programmes
  - public service or charity adverts.

- **The Internet:**
  - assessing and exchanging information by sending or downloading from one computer terminal to another.

Case study

Read the letter in Figure 2.21 sent to the TV programme *Points of View* with Anne Robinson. Does it successfully put across the writer's point of view?

Activity

- Write a letter to the local newspaper about a topical issue, preferably one that concerns local people in your area.
- Select a TV programme which either interests you or about which you feel strongly. Write your own letter to *Points of View* either to complain about the programme or to praise it.

Mark Pearson,
15 Cavendish Street,
Nuneaton,
Warwickshire

14 June 1995

Dear Anne,

I stumbled upon BBC 1's "The Invisible Wall" programme last week, while channel-hopping during the commercial break in "Coronation Street". Rarely have I found a documentary intriguing, shocking and enlightening enough to keep me away from Weatherfield; even rarer still have I felt compelled to write. I think it should be made compulsory for anyone who has ever doubted that discrimination is dead in this country, to watch at least one episode.

Of course it's impossible for any able-bodied person to fully understand the difficulties and discrimination the disabled population of the U.K. face on a daily basis but I think that "The Invisible Wall" went some way into showing the kind of unjustified bigotry perpetuated by, in this instance, nightclub staff, bar staff, and even charity committees.

There was a question asked in the show:

"When was the last time a woman was turned away from a nightclub, or a black man was refused entrance to a train?"

Obviously, it made me think, don't be silly, that wouldn't happen, there are sexism and racism laws that cover that sort of thing. The answer to the question was "Today, yesterday and the day before...., the people were disabled!"

Congratulations on a brilliant, well-made documentary, and thanks to the team for letting the public in on their lives.

A plea though, to "them upstairs", and you, please publicise this programme so that more people will watch, and realise these attitudes that still exist and are not legislated against.

Yours sincerely,

Mark Pearson

Figure 2.21 A letter sent to the BBC's *Points of View* programme

Sometimes pressure groups will send in material to programmes or they may even be consulted as experts by producers, as was noted earlier in the relationship between the police and producers of crime programmes. The people may be protesters in a local or national campaign, such as for making a road safer outside a school or to 'Save the Whale'. These pressure groups can range from MPs and environment groups, such as Greenpeace, to miners or parents of sick children.

Some pressure groups will be stronger than others because of numbers of membership or social status or economic wealth. (See Chapter 21 for more details of these pressure groups.)

Media conventions

There are certain conventions relating to the methods of access to the media by the public, as outlined above. These are:

- **How** – using video cameras, format of letters, phone-ins.
- **Where** – in the studio or on the street. Generally, interviews take place where the action is. So MPs will be interviewed with a backdrop of the Houses of Parliament, nurses outside a hospital, environmentalists in the woods! The amount of coverage given to news stories will depend too on location. There are more journalists and photographers living and working in London and the major cities, so it is inevitably easier to gain access to newspapers there.
- **When** – the public have very little say about if and when their work will be published or broadcast.

- **Why** – the motives for wanting access to the media are mixed. Some people want to publicise a cause or a point of view; some want Andy Warhol's '15 minutes of fame'; some may want to get money for an article or video.

Employment in the media

Another aspect to consider with regard to access is where the people come from who actually work in the media. What is their cultural and social background? What of their training, age and gender? How will this influence what and who they write about? How difficult is it for a young white graduate from a wealthy, well-educated middle-class background to report with understanding and without bias on topics such as unemployment, poverty and racial tension? Some groups tend to be over-represented, and some under-represented in media jobs.

Stereotypes in the media

Activity

Look at the pictures of the people shown in Figure 2.22 below. Imagine that you are a casting director for a comedy programme set in a block of expensive flats. The plot centres around the group of rich, successful people who own the flats and the people who look after them. Who would you cast for the following roles?

- an athlete
- a business person

Figure 2.22 Actors available for a comedy programme

- a cleaner
- a caretaker
- an opera singer
- a window cleaner
- a top chef
- a maid
- a film star

After you have chosen, look at the lists made by other people in your group. Did you think that the black person should be the athlete, the fat woman – the opera singer, the top chef – a man, the maid – a young female? How did you arrive at your decision? Did you choose the person you thought was typical of that job in real life or did you go for someone who was atypical, to make it funny?

Either way, you arrived at your decision through stereotyping.

It is an essential part of human existence to stereotype. We need to identify objects, people or feelings; we need to name them. We group together things that are similar to others and give them the same name. So, for example, some objects of a certain size and shape, with four legs, which we can sit upon, we call chairs. It makes communication much easier if we can say to someone, 'Fetch me a chair' rather than having to describe the object.

We use a similar form of shorthand to describe people. If we mention that someone is Chinese, we immediately begin to get some image in our minds of the physical characteristics of this person. However, when we use stereotypes we use words which very often imply physical and mental characteristics. If a woman is described as 'a blonde bombshell', more is understood than that she has fair hair; we also understand that she is young, attractive and lively.

Case study

The humour and romance of the film *Pretty Woman* relies on our recognising the different stereotypes that are represented within it. It is very like the Cinderella fairy tale. It opens with the successful business person, a man in a suit, young, attractive, with a magnificent house and a fast car. The action then switches to the heroine, who at this stage is a prostitute. We know this because she has blonde hair, lots of make-up, thigh-length black boots, short skirts and suspenders. A little later in the film, humour is created by breaking the stereotypes. He does not know how to drive the car whereas she is not only skilled at driving but knows how the car works. When the heroine shows that she is really a 'good' girl and worthy of the hero, she loses the blonde wig to show long wavy dark hair and she dresses in more conventional and less revealing clothing. She becomes financially and emotionally dependent on the man and spends her time shopping, bathing and getting dressed. Not only does she become less independent but she becomes more ignorant! The street-wise girl who could strut down the street in skimpy clothing and look after her friends becomes shy, and incapable of eating a meal in a restaurant without making social 'gaffes'. What do you think of this use of stereotypes?

Stereotyping by gender is still common. Look at adverts on TV or in magazines. The traditional role of the woman as carer, homemaker and someone intensely interested in her appearance is still there. If these stereotypes are reversed it is usually to create humour. Men are sometimes shown doing the washing or cooking but are usually shown doing it badly or stupidly.

Activity

Put together a storyboard for a short TV advert for pasta, in which the traditional gender roles are reversed.

Sometimes, in an attempt to break the stereotype and change roles, an equally unrepresentative image can be created. In the TV magazine show *The Girlie Show*, the female presenters are loud and aggressive and the material is controversial. The effect is shocking and the message is that they are trying to outdo the men.

Activity

Consider a TV programme with a predominantly male or female audience, such as *Top Gear* or *Delia Smith's Cookery*. How would you change it to attract more viewers from the opposite sex? Think about the presentation style, theme music, locations, content, and so on.

Racial stereotyping is still very common, particularly as the source of instantly recognisable humour in TV comedies. So Frenchmen are stereotyped as good lovers, Englishmen have a stiff upper lip, etc.

Activity

Make a list of the various attributes associated with other races, such as meanness, being 'laid back', stupid, male chauvinist, kind to children, fond of garlic, and so on.

Not all stereotypes are negative or bad. The stereotypes that portray Welsh people as good singers or Germans as methodical are positive. There may even be truth in these images. For instance, hard work is part of the official ethos of Japanese culture. When we meet people of different races we either consciously or subconsciously match them up to these images. Where stereotyping is wrong is when we assume that everyone should be like the stereotype and treat them accordingly.

So it has taken a long time to change the stereotype of a black person to one who can be good at more than sport and have more than a sense of rhythm! Unfortunately, sometimes it is in the political interest of a country's government to maintain these attitudes. Under the apartheid regime in the 1970s and 1980s, South African newspapers needed to reinforce the idea of blacks being a lesser race.

As has been noted earlier (page 28) we also stereotype people by age. Again, if the stereotype is broken, it is often for the purpose of humour. In the children's TV programme *Supergran,* the heroine is an extremely active pensioner, capable of intelligent thinking, riding a motorbike and fighting – a contrast to the traditional frail old lady in, for example, the story of Little Red Riding Hood.

Evidence assignment

Describe briefly what is meant by representation in the media, and make notes assessing the use of stereotypes. List how different media products can be accessed by the public, and give examples. This work can be stored in your production handbook. Identification of issues arising in your own productions should be noted and added as they occur.

You also need to produce two case studies, one relating to a print product and one relating to an audio-visual product.

As a group, make an exhibition of your individual case studies relating to representation in either magazines or newspapers. You should each find an illustration and an article relating to one of the issues of representation listed below. Write a brief accompanying explanation identifying the issue, and showing how it is represented.

For the audio-visual case study, the group could edit together excerpts from television advertisements with a voice-over explaining the issues involved. Each student should find an example and record it on tape. This should be submitted for editing with a brief script explaining the issue, and showing how it is represented.

The group exhibition and group video tape should cover all of the following:

- social groups
- ideas
- social issues
- events
- occupations
- places.

Chapter 3

Analyse media genres

Television and radio, film and video, newspapers and magazines are all media *forms,* with their own strengths and weaknesses. Each form has its own particular subgroups and these are known as *genres.* Genre basically means 'type'.

We talk about books and poems as being of certain types, such as historical and romantic novels, or ballads and sonnets. So when we talk of media genres we are talking about *types* of films, TV and radio programmes, and types of newspapers and magazines.

We have already looked at the various elements, codes and conventions used in media texts and at the representation of people, events and emotions. When all these different aspects are combined repeatedly in a certain pattern or format, for a particular purpose (to frighten or amuse us), they are said to become a genre.

Genres commonly used in media products

Most people can identify the genre of an audio-visual or print and graphics product through its **content characteristics**. For example, when we see a film set in a frontier town in America, with actors dressed as cowboys, riding horses and having gunfights, and with music played on a harmonica, we know we are watching the film genre called a **Hollywood Western**. But if some of the action seems unreal, the fights look like slapstick, the plot is silly, there are lots of witty speeches, and we laugh a lot, then we know we are watching a **comedy Western**.

Similarly, if a film is set in a city and uses soft focus shots to show the developing relationship between two people, with violins playing in the background, then this must be a **romance**. If every now and then the characters burst into song and dance routines, then the genre we are watching is a **musical**.

Other types of film which can be easily recognised include science fiction, action, horror, comedy, war, historical, children's, fantasy, thriller, detective, cartoon and so on.

We are all familiar with the main genres. They arouse certain expectations in us. For example, we expect to be frightened or we expect to laugh – we know which one to expect from a poster like the one in Figure 3.1! We are surrounded by different media genres as we grow up and have unconsciously developed the visual and aural skills that help us to recognise them without too much trouble. If you say to me that you like soaps or music magazines, then I know what you are watching or reading without having to have these products described in great detail.

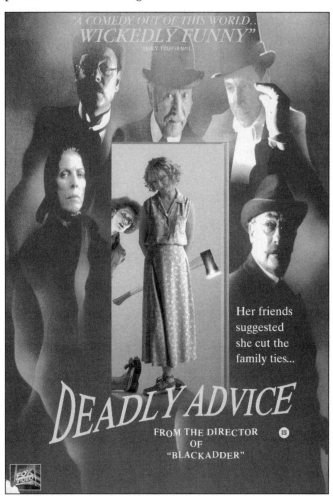

Figure 3.1 The genre of a film can easily be recognised in its advertising

Activity

As a group, look at the list of popular films given below and identify their genre. List the content characteristics that enable you to recognise each one as a particular genre. For example: *The Sound of Music* – this is a combination of romance and musical. It has song and dance routines and a love story.

- *Alien*
- *Sense and Sensibility*
- *Home Alone*
- *Braveheart*
- *Sleepless in Seattle*
- *Apollo 13*
- *Lion King*
- *Seven*
- *Superman*
- *Nightmare on Elm Street*
- *Hunt for Red October*
- *Goldeneye*
- *Apocalypse Now*
- *Tombstone*
- *Big*
- *Star Wars*

Television genres cover both fiction (drama, comedy, soaps and so on) and non-fiction (news, sport, quizzes, educational).

Activity

Read this description of a particular genre:

This type of programme has at least one 'reader' and very often two. These provide a link between us and the stories they are telling; sometimes they give the whole story, usually with the help of still or moving images; at other times they 'wrap' the story with an introduction and an ending, with the bulk of the story told by another person who could be where the story is happening and who may in turn be supported by interviews.

The start of the programme is signalled by a catchy, dramatic jingle, designed to get our attention and inform us of a change of mood. Lighting is dim and the presenters are in long shot which then pulls to medium shot as they at last become illuminated, seated behind a desk. They deliver the stories directly to you by talking straight to the camera.

What is this programme?

From all the clues you can probably guess that the description above is of television news. Of course, not all news programmes are like this. Some, like those on Breakfast TV, have a more informal style. It can, however, be regarded as 'typical'. The

characteristics described to you are about more than the content; they also describe technical, formal features.

Activity

Now make a list of the characteristics of a TV genre of your choice. Show it to a partner without telling him or her what genre it is, and see if they are able to recognise it.

Radio also has different genres, but here similar types of programme are often concentrated in one station. Thus, on BBC Radio One we expect to hear mainly music programmes, whilst on Five Live we can hear current affairs and sports programmes.

Activity

Look at the list of programmes on BBC Radio 4 shown in Figure 3.2. Which genres can you identify and why?

Sometimes, genres are combined to form a **hybrid genre**. Often, this can be a genre with the comedy genre mixed with it, such as the comedy western already mentioned, or a comedy thriller. A hybrid could also be, for example, a drama documentary. Although a hybrid will combine the characteristics of more than one genre, one genre will often dominate.

Activity

Brainstorm programmes which combine genres. Discuss the balance of characteristics in a hybrid genre, such as *Drop the Dead Donkey*, which combines comedy and current affairs, or *They Think It's All Over*, which combines comedy with sports knowledge.

So far you probably have not found these tasks very difficult. In the next section we shall be looking at not only content characteristics but the more technical, formal characteristics that make up an individual genre. We shall look at specific genres, their content and treatment.

Each different genre will be described and analysed in turn, considering all the performance criteria as outlined in the headings. It may help you if work in the related elements of Unit 2 is studied at the same time, as the basic skills such as writing or camera operation will support your understanding.

RADIO 4

6.00am News Briefing

6.10 Farming Today

6.25 Prayer for the Day
With the Rev Peter Jackson

6.30 Today
With Sue MacGregor and James Naughtie
7.25, 8.25 Sports News
7.45 Thought for the Day
8.40 Yesterday in Parliament

9.00 News

9.05 Call Nick Ross:
(0171) 580 4444
A topical discussion
LINES OPEN from 8.00 am

10.00–10.30 *FM only*
The Secret Life of Marineville
Stingray scriptwriter Alan Fennell provides a
guide to the fictional homes of Troy Tempest
and the World Aquanaut Security Patrol

10.00 Daily Service *LW only*

10.15 *LW only*
This Sceptr'd Isle
The history of Britain
188: *The Arrow War*

10.30 Woman's Hour
Marian McPartland, whose virtuoso
performances at the piano and personal
style of jazz have won her an international
reputation, talks to presenter Jenni Murray

11.30 All in the Mind
On call 24 hours a day, never tired or
irritable and always on form – Professor
Anthony Clare investigates the Cyberdoctor
and mental health

12.00 You and Yours
With Lesley Riddoch

12.25pm Quote … Unquote
Joining Nigel Rees to exchange quotations
and anecdotes this week are Kit Hesketh-
Harvey, Denis Norden, Sandi Toksvig and
Polly Toynbee, Reader William Franklyn

1.00 The World at One
With Nick Clark

1.40 The Archers

2.00 Thirty Minute Theatre
An untitled play by Sam McCartney
Sam .... GEORGE PARSONS
Helen .... TESSA WORSLEY

2.30 Comparing Notes with Brian Kay
Brian Kay talks to two of Britain's leading
cellists, Stephen Isserlis and Julian Lloyd
Webber, both of whom take particular
interest in expanding the repertoire of their
instrument

3.00 The Afternoon Shift
With Daire Brehan, Mark Tully remembers
the assassination of Indian Prime Minister
Rajiv Gandhi five years ago

4.00 News

4.05 Kaleidoscope
Paul Vaughan meets Russian baritone Dmitri
Hvorostosky and reviews a novel by Tim
Binding. And Christopher Logue reads from
his new collection of poems

4.45 Short Story: Down Under
By David Stenhouse. A family evening
around the Ouija board sent Aunt Julia to
Australia in search of her sister. Read by
Tom Smith

5.00 PM
With Chris Lowe and Charlie Lee-Potter

6.00 Six O'Clock News

6.30 Some Tame Gazelle
Elizabeth Proud's six-part
dramatisation of Barbara Pym's novel.
5: Harriet and Theor meet at the magic
lantern show, but nothing is as it seems, and
why is Mr Donne going away?

7.00 News

7.05 The Archers
Eddie comes to a standstill

7.20 File on 4
Major issues, changing attitudes and
important events at home and abroad.
Reporter Mark Whitaker

8.00 Science Now
Georgina Ferry presents highlights form this
year's Rhône Poulenc prizes for science
books

8.30 The Network
Art is communication and artists use
whatever is available to communicate their
message. So has art embraced the
information age?
Presented by Alun Lewis

9.00 In Touch
Peter White with news, views and
information for visually impaired people

9.30 Kaleidoscope
Paul Vaughan meets Russian baritone Dmitri
Hvorostovsky

10.00 The World Tonight
With Isabel Hilton

10.45 Book at Bedtime: Next of Kin
By Joanna Trollope
7: Dilys's confused emotions of sadness and
relief find an unlikely outlet in Zoe, drawn
back once more to Tideswell and to Robin

11.00 Mediumwave
The week's events in the media

11.30 *FM only*
Word of Mouth
The last programme in the series about
words and the way we speak. Street Talk.
Russell Davies checks out those wicked
jives from the street

11.30 *LW only*
Today in Parliament

12.00 News

12.30 am The Late Book: The Stone Diaries
By Carol Shields
7: *Work* 1955–1964

Figure 3.2 A Radio 4 schedule

Formal characteristics of genres

For **film** and **television**, the selected genres are:

- science fiction
- film noir
- documentary.

The **formal characteristics** that will be investigated here are stylistic ones (the use of sound, lighting, camera work and *mise-en-scène*), the use of icons and narrative structure. This last component will be dealt with more fully in Chapter 4.

Mise-en-scène is the way that the different shots of a production are assembled, how different scenes are put together and the arrangement of characters and props within the scenes. It is *mise-en-scène* that can give a film its particular meaning and significance, although there is also the **Auteurism** school of thought which gives primacy to the author (which usually means the director) in this respect.

The physical attributes and settings are examples of **iconography**. This term can be attributed to any *recurring* image which can be found in a production and as such is characteristic of it. Clothing (such as cowboy outfits in the Western example) and props (the desk in the news example) can also form part of the iconographic elements of a production. Even camera shots can be so characteristic of a particular genre that they are, in themselves, iconographic.

Iconography is part of the inter-related concepts of codes, **signification** and **connotation** that we discussed in Chapter 1. The related practical skills can be found in Chapter 8.

For **radio** the selected genres are:

- drama
- current affairs
- pop music.

The **formal characteristics** to be investigated are speech, music and sound effects, as these form the backbone of radio work. The spoken word on radio has changed, not only in what can be said but how it can be said. Local accents are now acceptable, as are women's voices.

Music can be used as the basis for a single programme or for an entire station, such as Classic FM or Radio 1. It is used to support a programme, it can be memorable in its own right or a mere background. Many programmes, such as comedy and drama, rely heavily on sound effects to bring alive in the listener's mind what they physically cannot see.

The associated practical skills are to be found in Chapter 7.

For **print** the selected genres are:

- tabloid newspapers
- broadsheet newspapers
- specialist magazines.

Here, the **formal characteristics** to be considered will be writing, typography, photography and graphics. The associated practical skills are to be found in Chapter 6.

Thematic concerns and functions will also be dealt with as each genre is discussed.

Analysing genres in terms of thematic concerns

Thematic concerns can be:

- *social* – how society affects and is affected by a media product.
- *metaphysical* – discussions, viewpoints on the nature of a media product, the reasons for its existence, its aesthetics, its 'meaning'.
- *ideological* – the purpose of a media product may be influenced by politics or cultural concerns.

Analysing genres in terms of functions

The **functions** of a media product will cover:

- *audience recognition* – how audiences understand and relate to texts and how the familiar format or formula of a programme or magazine help this recognition.
- *audience segmentation* – how certain types of people are attracted to and targeted by different media products and how this can affect distribution or scheduling.
- *entertainment* – most media products aim to entertain in the widest sense of the word, but they may have other purposes such as to inform, persuade or educate.
- *financial* – behind most media products is the need to make money. Of course there are also many products which are produced as a public service or for government purposes. However, the general aim is usually to maximise benefit to the organisation and, where the organisation is a

business such as a film company, then the general aim is to make a profit. In these cases the product is a commodity which needs to justify the level of investment that has been put into it. The products are then marketed with a particular audience in mind.

Some media companies specialise in one type of genre, others cover a whole range. There are advantages to specialisation. The audience becomes familiar with a particular type of product, for example, the Hammer Horror film. They recognise its characteristics and do not have to go through that initial 'learning curve' of getting to like the product. They already like it and are now on the lookout for more of the same. In business terminology, audiences develop a certain 'brand loyalty' and can be segmented and targeted. The film producers are then well placed to give the audience more of what they want. They have the sets built, the actors have been tried and tested, and so have the plots. Thus in business terms, the producers can achieve 'economies of scale' by gearing up for the production of a certain genre.

Economics control production, distribution and development. A new product which is commercially viable will generate further examples. We have seen this with numerous successful film products, such as *Batman, Police Academy, Star Wars* and many others, that have spawned sequels.

Analysing genres in terms of their development

The **development** of genres – and how and why media products evolve, change, become widely accepted and sometimes decline – cannot be easily separated from their characteristics, themes and functions. Sometimes it is technology, sometimes economic prosperity, that is the reason behind the development of a particular media product. Alternatively, it can be the changing needs of society or the educational and cultural backgrounds of certain groups of people that create a need for a certain type of media form or genre. Recent developments in the media industries are dealt with fully in Chapter 31.

Each genre is discussed in detail below, with case studies given and activities suggested. The GNVQ specifications suggest that only three in-depth reports, covering one example of genre from radio, one from TV and film and one from print and

graphics, are necessary. Students should read and attempt all of the range, however, as they can be asked questions on any of these genres in the unit tests.

Film and television

Science fiction

Formal characteristics

Science fiction films (or SF films, which is the abbreviation preferred by science fiction purists rather than 'Sci-Fi') are futuristic in content, with an emphasis on gadgetry and special effects. There is a prevailing theme of control, which can be by intelligent machines (Daleks in *Doctor Who*), machines used by other humans (HAL in *2001*), other life-forms (*Alien*) or by other humans (*1984*). Often, there is the mass manipulation of people who are subjugated by brain-washing, strange supernatural powers or overwhelming physical and technological force. Occasionally alien life forms are portrayed sympathetically, as in *Close Encounters of the Third Kind* or *Star Trek*.

Science fiction usually involves travel and exploration. It is about survival in strange and dangerous circumstances, and about people being stretched to their limits. A successful hero or heroine will be mentally and physically strong, and dedicated to searching for truth or justice.

Figure 3.3 Science fiction films emphasise exotic locations

The location can be set on the planet Earth of the future, on a space craft or other planets. In *Star Trek* and *Red Dwarf,* the space ships have characters of their own and play an important part in the stories. The space ship can be considered an icon, representing the human wish to travel and explore.

Costumes tend towards the fantastic, although there is a liking for uniforms. Many SF films are like early westerns or war films, in that good and bad forces are easily identifiable, not only through the behaviour of characters but through what they wear. Designers can let their imaginations run free, but it is interesting to note that although the costumes may look to the future, they also reflect contemporary fashion trends in terms of style or materials used, with shoulder pads or silver lurex, and so on.

Background music is generally electronically produced or computer-generated and stylistically unusual, in order to strengthen the impression of other-worldliness.

SF is also a brilliant opportunity for the creators of *special effects* to come into their own. *2001* was an early film which used state-of-the-art special effects and almost psychedelic visual sequences. Computers have since made many of these special effects

standard. In the film *Tron,* the hero is trapped inside a computer world, and live actors are mixed with graphic line drawings.

Lighting effects, and camera angles too, are other ways in which the forces of good and evil can be distinguished.

The narrative of most SF films is straightforward, often chronological, relying on visual and special effects to keep the action moving. Compared with other film genres, there is rarely great psychological insight into the characters. The situations themselves provide the motivation and interest.

Because SF films are set in the future, there is always an implication that the narrative structure is open – because the future is unpredictable. One particular danger may be averted, some antagonistic alien life-form defeated, but viewers are left feeling that the particular characters in the story have the potential to travel on to new adventures. Individual characters seldom age in the course of an SF film; time is telescoped in a certain way. In a historical or contemporary drama, we often see the actors physically age and their bodies change to show that time is passing. However, Buck Rogers in the *Twenty-First Century* series does not grow older as the series progresses. Time is static.

Figure 3.4 Lighting effects can make 'evil' characters look more terrifying

Thematic concerns, functions and development

There has always been a human fascination with anything strange, fantastical or grotesque. From antiquity our rituals, religions and superstitions have referred to hopes, beliefs and fears that 'we are not alone' and the possibility that 'there is something else out there'. The associations with the horror genre are numerous and overlapping, demonstrating again that there are limitations in attempts to classify the various elements of literary and audio-visual art forms.

SF has its modern antecedents in the novels of Jules Verne (*Twenty Thousand Leagues Under the Sea*) and H.G. Wells (*The Time Machine, War of the Worlds*). The works of writers such as Arthur C. Clarke, Isaac Asimov, Ray Bradbury and Ursula Le Guin have influenced or been the basis of classic SF.

From the outset, the moving image has seen the potential of this genre. If you visit the Museum of the Moving Image in London, one of the earliest films you will see is Georges Méliès's *Voyage to the Moon* (1902).

Figure 3.5 One of the early science fiction films was *Things To Come*

Other early examples include *Metropolis* (1926) and *Things To Come* (1936) (see Figure 3.5), based on an H.G. Wells story.

But it wasn't until the 1950s that science fiction really took off. Examples of this are *The Thing* (1951), *War of the Worlds* (1953), *Invaders from Mars* (1953) and *Invasion of the Bodysnatchers* (1956). In this post-war era, people were looking for new challenges and new enemies to fight. Audiences wanted to be entertained and SF provided excitement and novelty; it was good escapism from the relative drabness of everyday life.

Around this time, people were also beginning to have lots of new electronic gadgets in their homes, vacuum cleaners, fridges, food mixers and washing machines. Advertisements for these products gave them visions of a new world in which they would have more time for other activities. This liking for gadgets is reflected in early SF programmes such as *Space Family Robinson*.

Even a science fiction society wants servants of some description, and robots supply this need. There are still class distinctions and social hierarchies in space, as is evident in *Star Wars* and *Star Trek*. Authority and leadership are dominant themes, giving a sense of security in insecure worlds.

It is also fascinating how some inventions imagined by SF writers actually become possible years later. Novels about landings on the moon, satellites and robots were sheer fantasy for the public at the beginning of the century; but all these things are now part of our experience. Science fiction reflects contemporary technological advances and takes them a stage further.

Real space travel literally took off in the second half of this century, and this coincided with some of the most impressive SF films, such as *Planet of the Apes* (1968) and *2001: A Space Odyssey*.

Some films of the 1970s foretold grimmer visions of the future, with robots running amok in *Westworld* (1973), and *The Man Who Fell to Earth* (1976) with David Bowie as an alien visitor.

However, the general optimism of the 1970s was reflected in such films as *Star Wars* (1977) and *Close Encounters of the Third Kind* (1977). This last film showed alien life-forms as non-threatening, a theme which continued in *ET* (1982). People in society generally were becoming more tolerant of minority groups and different lifestyles. SF was becoming less preoccupied with action and more reflective about the human situation and moral dilemmas.

This benevolent view of aliens can also be seen in *Star Trek*, the classic American series presented by the BBC. It originated in the 1960s when the crew of the USS Enterprise were inspired to 'boldly go where no man had gone before'. The starship had a crew of 430 aboard her eight decks. It was never able to land and the crew were 'beamed' down to other planets.

Mr Spock, the first officer, was half human and half Vulcan, with pointed ears and green blood. Other principal officers included a Japanese man, a Russian, a Scotsman – and even women! The crew were ambassadors for peaceful co-existence and, although ready to defend themselves, would always try to seek non-violent solutions. All of these characters and features make moral statements.

Figure 3.6 The *Star Trek* crew were ambassadors for peaceful co-existence

Figure 3.7 *ET* showed alien life-forms as non-threatening – even cuddly!

It can be said that the SF genre reached its peak commercially in the late 1970s with the three films mentioned above. All of them were gigantic box-office hits. They were big-budget films and very expensive to produce, but they still managed to make large profits. Merchandising for *Star Wars* and *ET* was particularly profitable. Children collected model figures of the characters, creatures, machines and space ships from *Star Wars*. Even ET himself was turned into a sort of cuddly toy! Both have now been issued as videos. *Star Trek* too has retained its popularity, and as the original crew became too old, a new TV series, *Star Trek: The Next Generation,* was produced and is sold around the world. (Indeed, a third *Star Trek* series, *Deep Space Nine,* has been seen on television and a fourth, *Voyager,* has been produced.)

In other films and programmes, however, SF was combined with other genres. It was combined with horror in *Alien,* and in *Red Dwarf,* the British TV series, it is combined with comedy.

Another development was the appearance of the sequel. *Star Wars* eventually became the first part of a trilogy, and *Alien* and *Star Trek* have also been continued (as mentioned above). There have also been remakes of earlier films, such as *The Thing* (1982) and *Invasion of the Bodysnatchers* (1978). *Star Wars* has already been re-issued with a quadraphonic soundtrack.

But the science fiction genre has not only been popular in the cinema but also on TV, with programmes such as *Quatermass, Lost in Space, Doctor Who, The Hitchhiker's Guide to the Galaxy, Blake's Seven, The X-Files,* and so on. The *Star Trek* stories were transferred to the big screen from television.

Perhaps more than any other genre, SF attracts cult followings. 'Trekkies' form fan clubs all over the world and have their own magazines and meetings. *Red Dwarf* too has become a cult series, although this usually attracts mainly younger male viewers.

Science fiction is such a visually creative area that it will continue to appear on both large and small screens. The subject matter appeals to the human longing for immortality; we want to know that life goes on indefinitely into the future. Ultimately, SF can be considered an optimistic art form because it makes the assumption that humans can continue to exist in some form or other after our deaths.

Case study: *Dr Who*

Doctor Who, a *Timelord,* travels through time and space in his Tardis (Time and Relative Dimension in Space) – a converted police box. The series was produced by the BBC and began in 1963. The leading role was played originally by William Hartnell (see Figure 3.8), but over the years the part of the Doctor has been assumed by Patrick Troughton, Jon Pertwee, Tom Baker, Peter Davison, Colin Baker and Sylvester McCoy.

Figure 3.8 Dr Who was originally played by William Hartnell

The electronic title music by Ron Grainer was very atmospheric and it was a significant part of the opening in setting the mood of adventure and space.

Each series consisted of several episodes. Although one particular storyline would come to an end, viewers knew the Doctor would return. Each time the actor playing the Doctor was replaced, the new Doctor took on a totally different personality and appearance; that was part of the fantasy. The monsters too were changed regularly, gradually becoming more sophisticated. However, none were so frightening as the early Daleks, with their mechanistic shrieks of 'Exterminate, exterminate' as they trundled around the set.

This programme was originally scheduled for many years at teatime on Saturdays. It was something the family could view together: children were genuinely frightened by it and parents too were glued to the screen. It was good escapist entertainment.

Figure 3.9 A cover of *Dr Who* magazine

Early episodes now seem very dated. They were filmed in black and white and the first studio sets were very basic. As the years went by, the series became more sophisticated. It had to compete with the American *Star Trek* series. Although the plots continued to be centred around aliens trying to take over other worlds, they became a lot more sophisticated, with complex storylines involving deeper issues and using technical jargon. This reflected the growing sophistication of audiences and the acceptance of computer technology. However, the stories became too complex for younger viewers and the programme was eventually rescheduled to a weekday evening. But the basic formula remained the same. The Doctor, accompanied by at least one female assistant (changed every few series), would travel in time and space, encounter alien enemies and ultimately defeat them. One of the most popular characters was a robot dog called K9.

The Doctor has been 'merchandised'. There have been T-shirts, caps, mugs, lampshades, wallpaper, and a massive range of toys and plastic models. Books about the series have appeared, such as *Doctor Who: The Universal Databank* (Dr Who Books, 1992) which is the A to Z of everything about Dr Who. Virgin have brought out a range of novels, with new adventures continuing from where the series ended on TV.

After an absence of six years, the Doctor returned not as a TV series but as a film made for television in May 1996. It was shown first in America. In Britain it was released on video before appearing on television. The BBC had invested heavily, providing half of the £3.2m that the film cost. There was also the intention to use the film as a pilot. If ratings and video sales are good then a new TV series of 45 episodes will be produced.

The film was given a '15' rather than a 'PG' or 'U' certificate because there is a violent scene at the beginning involving gang warfare. Recent violent events in society, such as the Dunblane massacre, caused the censors to worry, so the film had to be shown in the evening from 8.10pm to 9.40pm. The new Doctor Who is Paul McGann, who may be signed on for another five years. He is an established drama actor who also appeals to women.

Activity

Take a recent SF film or TV series and discuss its narrative structure. How typical of the genre are the plot, the locations, the characters and the motivation for the action? How is time and space represented? Include details of when it was made and when it was released or scheduled.

What type of audience has it attracted and how popular is it? It might be helpful to make comparisons with *Dr Who* or *Star Wars*.

Film noir

Formal characteristics

The term **film noir** came to describe the style of Hollywood films from the early 1940s to late 1950s. They echoed the gloomy post-war mood of America.

Film noir is generally recognised as a genre that is chiefly concerned with thriller, gangster and detective films. These are, however, also genres in their own right. Moreover, film noir is also evident in other genres such as melodrama and even the Western. Because of this, it can also be seen not just as a genre, but as a 'movement' (see page 56) or even simply as a 'period'.

Whichever way this genre is labelled, there are certain stylistic characteristics which we can examine. The typical film noir explores the themes of corruption, betrayal and despair, with characters who seem dogged by fate.

The *femme fatale* is often a central character in these films, a prime motivation behind the narrative. The woman leading the tough hero astray is a symbol or icon for corruption, for instance Barbara Stanwyck in *Double Indemnity* (1944). These female protagonists are powerful women and this is mirrored by the harsh, shallow beauty created by the camera and lighting techniques. Their beauty takes on the hard and unattainable form of a statue (see Figure 3.10).

The setting of a film noir is generally the city or urban streets, shrouded in fog or drenched with rain. Strong contrasts between light and shadow, distorted perspectives and unusual camera angles help create atmosphere.

The use of lighting is probably the most significant feature of film noir. Characters and objects are framed by black shadows so that they appear isolated and overwhelmed by a sea of darkness (see Figure 3.11). Familiar objects take on new shapes and meaning and, rather like the objects in a bedroom when the light is off, they can appear strange and threatening. The key light (see Units 2 and 5) is used with little or none of the softening effect of the fill and back lights, producing a harder image with starkly contrasting light and dark. The three lights are changed about radically to obtain startling effects. Using night-time for night shooting, with the areas of action artificially illuminated, gave a greater contrast between light and dark. Previously night

Figure 3.10 Ava Gardner as the typical *femme fatale*

Figure 3.11 Alan Ladd and Veronica Lake in *The Blue Dahlia*: lighting is a significant feature

scenes were shot in the day using filters to limit the amount of light entering the camera. This gave a more natural, balanced look as did the conventional studio lighting system (three-quarter lighting). However, it was not a look compatible with film noir imagery.

The *mise-en-scène* has a fractured, uneven quality which jars and unsettles the senses. The composition of camera shots is unbalanced, with characters and objects in a discordant rather than compositionally harmonious relationship within the frame. Framing is tight and claustrophobic, making use of doors, windows, the tight circle of shadows already mentioned, and big close-up camera shots.

The camera work and lighting instils a sense of the characteristic moods of pessimism, foreboding, paranoia, claustrophobia and doom. In addition, by increasing a scene's **depth of field**, all the characters and objects, even when at varying distances from the camera, are in sharp focus, thus again obtaining the starkest contrasts between the trapped, closed world of the characters and the impenetrable nothingness around it.

The narrative in film noir often used an intricate flashback structure. There were also new levels of screen violence, with an emphasis on brutality.

Thematic concerns, functions and development

The term *film noir,* meaning 'dark and gloomy film' was first used by French critics. The term is derived from the *roman noir* (the dark novel) which described the English gothic fiction of the late eighteenth and early nineteenth centuries. Its cinematic antecedents can be found in the German Expressionist films of the inter-war years including the brooding *Nosferatu* (1922) and *Metropolis* (1926), the gritty detective fiction of Raymond Chandler (who also worked as a scriptwriter), and most directly in the fatalistic French dramas such as *Pepe le Moko* (Julien Duvivier), and Marcel Carne's *Quai des Brumes* (*Port of Shadows*) and *Le Jour se Lève* (*Daybreak*). It was French film-makers who produced the early examples of film noir, although they called it **poetic realism.**

Good examples of film noir include the following:

John Huston's *The Maltese Falcon* (1941)
Fritz Lang's *The Woman in the Window* (1944)
Dmytryk's *Farewell My Lovely* (1944)
Howard Hawks's *The Big Sleep* (1946)
Jacques Tourneur's *Build My Gallows High* (1947)

Figure 3.12 Humphrey Bogart and Mary Astor in *The Maltese Falcon*

Jules Dassin's *Night and the City* (1950)
Robert Aldrich's *Kiss Me Deadly* (1955)
Stephen Heath's *Touch of Evil* (1958)

America in the 1940s was still coming to terms with the aftermath of the war and economic depression. These films echo the disillusionment of the period and the potential breakdown of society and the family that many people feared. There was also resentment by unemployed men of the growing importance of women in the workplace, and male-dominated Hollywood liked to represent women as either homemakers or victims. The strong women in film noir are neither of these.

These films were aimed at an adult audience. Brutality and pessimism became stronger in the later films. Films focused on the twisted psychology and neuroses of the characters, such as the mother-fixated gangster Cody Jarrett, played by James Cagney in *White Heat,* or the thug-like sadist private eye in Robert Aldrich's *Kiss Me Deadly* (1955).

The mood of the American public changed, however, during the Eisenhower period and the cinema's experimentation with widescreen and colour process signalled the end of this type of film making.

There have since been more recent films which contain significant film noir characteristics, such as *Klute* (1972), *Chinatown* (1974), *Body Heat* (1981), and

After Dark my Sweet (1990). Directors such as Oliver Stone and Quentin Tarantino have adapted the genre with the new violent dark movies such as *Taxi Driver* (1976) and *Reservoir Dogs* (1992), and now *Seven* (1995) which are a development of this genre. They too are somewhat nihilist and are concerned with violence and crime. The role of women too (e.g. Jodie Foster as the young prostitute in *Taxi Driver*) is typical of the genre.

It is, in fact, even debatable whether the film noir is a genre. The Clint Eastwood Western *High Plains Drifter*, *Black Narcissus* (based in a Himalayan nunnery) and the disturbing *Witchfinder General* (set during the English Civil War) all contain noir characteristics. Indeed Janey Place uses the term 'movement' (with Peterson, *Some visual motifs of film noir*, 1974; *Women in film noir*, 1978). She argues that '... film noir is defined by a remarkable homogeneous visual style with which it cuts across genres'.

Case study: *Double Indemnity*

The influential American film *Double Indemnity* came out in 1944. It was directed for Paramount by Billy Wilder. It is remembered by film-goers for Barbara Stanwyck's portrayal of a *femme fatale*. She plays a bored housewife, Phyllis Dietrichson, who sexually ensnares an insurance salesman, Walter Neff. She persuades him to help her kill her husband. At first he refuses and walks out, but she tracks him down and eventually his passion for her makes him agree. Together they make

Figure 3.13 Barbara Stanwyck in *Double Indemnity*

Figure 3.14 Shadows frame Fred MacMurray and Barbara Stanwyck in a scene from *Double Indemnity*

an elaborate plan, which they carry out seemingly without a hitch. But just as the double indemnity insurance claim is about to go through, Neff's boss, Barton Keyes, becomes suspicious. He starts an investigation which puts the relationship of the two killers under a lot of strain and eventually turns them against each other, with tragic results.

Apart from the visual motifs of camera angle and framing and light and shadow, the narrative style adds to the sense of doom: the film begins with a badly wounded Neff staggering into Keyes's office to record a confession. The story then unfolds through flashbacks. Thus we already know that Neff is doomed, in the same way that we know a bull at the beginning of a bullfight is doomed. Yet an audience will still watch this to see in *what way* the tragedy will unfold.

Film noir characteristics to note whilst watching the film include:

- the leading female role: destructive, deceitful, seductive and manipulative
- the leading male role: someone who is strong but not innocent, disillusioned and ready to be led astray
- the use of voice-overs by the character Neff to relate the narrative
- the use of low-key lighting, particularly in the scene where Phyllis and Walter meet in his apartment
- shadow: for example the use of shadow to frame the protagonists is well illustrated in Figure 3.14
- the camera angles: for example the scene where Neff creeps up the back stairs to his apartment, is a good example of the use of lighting/shadow and

- camera angles to create eerie, disconcerting effects
- the iconic symbolism of the insurance business is connected with the paternalism of American authority
- the location: the significance of the rain.

Activity

Choose an example of film noir from the 1940s or 1950s. Write an analysis of its narrative structure, concentrating particularly on how the camera is used to record the action and the motivations. Comment on the use of close-ups, establishing shots and lighting.

Report on how you – the audience – felt about it in terms of entertainment. Compare it with a modern film with a pessimistic outlook, dealing with city violence or other problems.

Documentary

Formal characteristics

The purpose of the documentary is to *document,* that is, to report with evidence, something that has actually happened. It can show this by using **actuality footage**, or **reconstructions.** It can use a narrator's voice-over to anchor the meaning, or rely on the participants themselves, with perhaps the occasional interjection by an unseen narrator.

The term documentary shares the usual problem of definition with other genres. Strictly speaking, there are numerous examples of documented events which have been portrayed on film. These may bear some resemblance to the truth but are essentially fictitious, even when they claim to have a real event as their basis.

What distinguishes documentary is the portrayal of the 'recorded sounds and images of actuality' (John Corner, *Television Form and Public Address*, page 78, Edward Arnold, 1995). This would imply that the audio-visual equipment records what has actually happened, with the people who were actually involved.

But giving factual accounts of real-life occurrences does not always mean using actuality footage, and some types of documentaries are partly or completely staged. A wartime documentary, *Fires Were Started* (1943), depicts fire-fighting scenes from the Blitz which were completely staged – even to the extent of re-igniting bombed-out buildings. This sub-genre, where events are re-constructed, either using the

actual people involved or actors, is usually called **drama documentary**. *Crimewatch UK* on BBC TV is an example of this style.

Not all the devices used in fiction, such as whip pans or low-angle shots, are appropriate to develop character and storylines in documentaries. But even when the filming consists of actuality footage, people are directed and sets organised, so there is still a high level of **construction** taking place.

Documentaries do not necessarily contain analysis. They may be merely descriptive and may just leave it to the viewer to reach conclusions. This is certainly true of another kind of documentary, the **fly on the wall** or vérité type, such as 'The Living Soap', which seeks to make the depiction as plausible as possible by concealing the intervention between the documentary makers and their subject.

Documentaries may deal, for example, with political, historical, social, religious, artistic or cultural phenomena. They may or may not be classed as **current affairs**, depending on the topicality of the events they portray and how directly they are related to events in the news.

There are, then, tensions between two broad aspects of documentary style which we can term **documentary as art** and **documentary as reportage**. The former emphasises the aesthetic qualities which makes documentaries attractive and entertaining. A good documentary should be about the topic and not the style of presentation. However, the content alone, without any intervention from the producers, would seldom be enough to make the documentary coherent, let alone interesting. To give a product a sense of pace and structure, they draw on many of the characteristics of fiction in their use of, for example, camera angles, framing, lighting and editing. The questions of selectivity and, more importantly, the criteria used for selection, will then be the same as those raised in Chapter 1 where we discussed **signification** in terms of news broadcasts.

Thematic concerns, functions and development

The principles behind the documentary genre were being defined during the 1930s by John Grierson and his team at the GPO (General Post Office) Film Unit. (This became the Crown Film Unit during the Second World War.) Important examples of this work are *Industrial Britain, Housing Problems* (1935), *Coalface* (1935) and *Nightmail* (1936); these were produced for cinema audiences, as television had yet to be established. The idea was to use real-life situations to give the public a glimpse of other people's lives and show the country at work, thus establishing a sense of empathy and national identity. This theme continued during the war, with documentaries such as *Target for Tonight* (1941) and *Desert Victory* (1943). There are elements of persuasion in these documentaries, not only in the war-time films, which were used to boost morale and unite the war-time population, but also in the peace-time works which had as patrons either government or other vested interests.

Famous documentaries have included:

- The controversial *Death on the Rock,* about the shooting in Gilbraltar of three IRA members by the SAS.
- *Culloden,* made in 1963 and featuring the famous battle where the army of Charles Stuart ('Bonnie Prince Charlie') was destroyed by the forces of George II, as if it was taking place in front of TV cameras, with reporters giving a commentary of the battle and interviewing those involved.
- *Death of a Princess,* which looked at capital punishment in Saudi Arabia but more specifically examined the fate of a princess and the ideology that condemned her.

There are numerous others which could be added to the list. Some of these, for example, *The Cook Report,* feature regularly on television.

In TV and radio, scheduling of genres is an important part of the business of media. Once a target audience is identified, it is not only the product itself that is important but where it is positioned in the schedules – in terms of the time and day and what may be shown before and after. Audience research plays a crucial role here (see Chapter 24). Some documentary series, such as *Panorama,* are well known and can command a prime-time slot. Some documentaries are more like the tabloid newspapers in style and tend to be emotional or sensational, clearly attempting to direct the opinions of viewers. They can be considered as having strong entertainment value and are aimed at a popular audience. Others are more restrained, offering a balanced viewpoint and leaving the viewers to make up their own minds: they make more demands on viewers.

British documentaries are renowned for their use of investigative journalism which often is directly opposed to the views of the government and sometimes to the prevailing view in society.

Case study: *Here and Now*

This programme appeared in the *Here and Now* series on BBC1 television on Wednesday 15 May 1996 at 7.30pm. The following analysis looks at its construction.

Anchor introduces programme and main feature: a tale of incompetence concerning a spy plane project.

The feature starts with dramatic Gulf War footage showing 10 different camera shots. An equally dramatic voice-over states that it is *'1991 and our boys fight it out in the Gulf. They are waiting for a vital bit of kit'* then, after pausing for effect, adds ominously, *' – but it never arrives'.*

The scenes are accompanied by a rousing musical score which sounds like a cross between Wagner's *Ride of the Valkyries* and the 'News at 10' theme.

The scene cuts to a quick glimpse of the spy plane in flight, with the only sound the noise of the aircraft as it roars overhead. The connotation is that we are now in the present. We then cut back to more dramatic music, war footage and voice-over, which states that it is now *'1994 and our lads are in action in Bosnia'* (pause for effect) *' – but that crucial piece of equipment is still missing'.*

The footage this time consists of six shots, one of which is framed with a close-up of the union flag showing prominently on an armoured vehicle. We then see the plane again and at the same time catch a close-up of a wrist-watch as somebody looks through binoculars. Again, we are 'back' in the present, with the visual images giving us the impression that time is passing and we are still waiting.

Dramatic music, and footage consisting of seven shots showing action scenes returns, along with the urgent voice-over telling us that it is now *'1996 and the army are out on manoeuvres in the north of England. Do they have all the tools for the job now?'*

The last shot shows a tank halting abruptly. This visual is synchronised with the voice-over answering his own question: *'No!'.* The image and sound come to the same sharp halt.

The terms 'our boys' and 'our lads', the flag and the whole tone sets the mood of patriotic concern. The terms bond us with the troops, give us a sense of belonging and involvement. The war footage was given a mellow, soft-focus look, whilst the 'here and now' shots of the aircraft are shown as sharper and more vivid.

Next comes a close-up of the plane, which zooms out to show it is in fact a model. The voice-over has now become a person in the form of the reporter, Mark Easton. He then says to the camera: *'The bit of kit they are waiting for isn't actually that different to this model plane'*. The name 'Mark Easton' appears at the bottom of the screen.

'What the army ordered in the mid '80s was a remote control pilotless aircraft with a spy camera on board. The idea was to go behind enemy lines and beam back pictures so that artillery could target their guns. It was supposed to be ready in 1990 but ...'

As he talks, he looks at the camera i.e. he is looking at 'us'. He is in an informal, squatting position and uses his hands expressively. He appears relaxed and friendly towards us. He is telling us a story.

As he says 'but' he points to his wrist-watch. This links him with the anonymous watcher of the model aircraft seen earlier with close-up of binoculars. *'I'm afraid take-off has been rather delayed.'*

The 'rather' is an ironic understatement and is in keeping with the informal and gently mocking tone of the feature. The dramatic music, footage and tone of voice all give a sense of urgency, danger and concern. The concern is heightened by the patriotic references to our armed forces. The pace of the story is maintained by these techniques and the editing which allows the film to cut quickly from one situation and time period to another, but keep the sense of continuity. For example, the wrist-watch links the scenes, as well as giving us a sense of time passing.

There are then three shots of British soldiers standing around next to their armoured vehicle, drinking tea and giving the impression they are 'kicking their heels', while the commentator adds that: *'while the British army continued to wait for their spy drone the Americans have got one...'* (Shot of plane taking off.)

We then have a **talking head** (an expert brought in to comment) in close-up on the right side of the screen with the rest blanked out. Words printed underneath tell us it is Paul Beaver, defence analyst. This is replaced by another shot of a plane taking off and Mark Easton saying: *'... the French have got one.'*

Cut to another talking head this time Lt. Col. John Mesch of the Ministry of Defence, 1984–88, again on the right-hand side, while Mark Easton continues: *'... the Israelis have got lots.'*

Cut to talking head, Bruce George MP, House of Commons Defence Committee, framed on the left-hand side of the screen. We are then shown footage of precision bombing of Kuwait, accompanied by voice-over.

Next comes an **over-the-shoulder** shot. This means the interviewee has his back to the camera and the camera shoots over his shoulder to frame the interviewer (Mark Easton). The technique allows us to see the interview from the interviewee's point of view. At the same time, we can see Mark Easton nodding his head in encouragement. The idea is to continue to build a trusting relationship between Mark Easton and the viewers.

The interview continues and is interspersed with a photographic still, showing the interviewee in previous years as a serving officer. This, again, is another example of a 'linking' device, giving credibility and depth to the interviewee by showing the relevance of his past and linking it to the present. There is also aerial footage with reporter's comments and a clip from the interview is used as voice-over material.

After this interview and footage the format changes. The programme makers use cartoons to continue the story, sometimes animated to help explain, and with an accompanying musical score that is associated with early film. The effect is to depict the follies as almost comical bungling – a 'Mr Bean' in uniform!

The scene changes again to black and white footage of another spy aircraft called the Sprite. The voice-over and music give a science fiction feel at the beginning, thus adding a sense of mystery. But it then undercuts itself by the voice-over rather chirpily announcing that the Sprite was developed in a 'Berkshire workshop'. Compared to the portrayal of foreign agencies there is an almost affectionate celebration of the British 'amateur boffin' approach. When mixed with the portrayal of big business complacency and government bureaucracy, we get the distinct feeling that Britain has a positive attitude towards lost opportunities. This feeling is certainly not allayed when we are next informed that the drone is in fact in use with the Swedish authorities to whom we have sold it!

A shot of the Eiffel tower and the strains of the 'Marseillaise' **establish** that we are now in France. The voice-over informs us: *'over the channel the French have also bought a system.* Here and Now *were given exclusive access to the secret base somewhere in France.'*

We too can feel part of this exclusivity, which helps bolster the credentials of *Here and Now*. A French officer in smart dress uniform, standing by a spyplane, helpfully points out to Mark Easton that the system they have bought is actually British.

The scene moves to Ashford in Kent where a spokesperson for the company that sells the system to the French explains that it is a modified version of their main product, which is the design and manufacture of target aircraft for the British Armed Forces. As this is discussed we are shown footage of one of these target aircraft being tracked and then hit by a missile.

It is not strictly relevant to the documentary as it shows the aircraft being used for a completely different purpose, but it does make for exciting visuals to show something being blown up. Whilst this is being explained we are shown inserts and diagrams.

Following this, Sir Geoffrey Pattie, the Chairman of GEC-Marconi which has been developing the British project, is asked some pointed questions about why other countries already have a system which the British are far behind schedule with, yet the British have produced and sold systems to other countries. Again, there is an over-the-shoulder shot.

The film then cuts and is edited in order to give the impression that Paul Beaver is replying critically to Sir Geoffrey Pattie's attempts to justify GEC-Marconi's position. This is followed by cartoons giving a quirky snapshot of previous defence project flops, which all reinforce the preferred reading of the text.

Next, there follows a further pointed interview with Sir Geoffrey Pattie, in which he defends his company by saying that it builds projects to the army's specifications. However, the scene cuts to another clip of an interview, this time with Lt. Col. John Mesch. Mark Easton says to him: *'but the army didn't have a system'.*

'No' came the start of a reply, which is abruptly edited after that first word. We then cut back to Sir Geoffrey who is left saying: *'We are all wise after the event'.*

Victory to Mark Easton who can now go forward after establishing guilt and boldly refer to the project as the 'Phoenix fiasco'. This is followed by a summing up in a concerned voice, saying that it will be at least 1998 and *'Let's hope they get it right'.*

The feature ends with Bruce George MP saying: *'maybe they could put it right. If they can't put it right to the satisfaction of the government very quickly then they should do what the defence ministry suggested and scrap it.'*

The *Here and Now* logo then appears. The anchor informs us authoritatively that the project has cost £200 million and we still might not get it. GEC has rectified the problems and a final decision will be made 'in the summer'.

Activity

Analyse a documentary in terms of presenters, locations, and camera shots.

How was the programme structured? Were there flashbacks, dramatisations, etc? Was music used to reinforce actions or emotions? Was there any bias? Whose viewpoint prevails at the end? Who is the target audience for this programme? When was it scheduled?

Radio

Drama

Formal characteristics

It has been said that radio restored the ancient art of the story-teller in its drama programmes. Like the story-teller, the radio dramatist has to stimulate the imagination of the listeners to 'see' an experience, through the use of the spoken word and assisted by sound effects and music.

BBC Radio is renowned for its drama. It has been called the 'National Theatre of the Air', a phrase used in 1961 for an ambitious season of plays covering 400 years of English drama, from morality plays to Oscar Wilde. But the BBC does not restrict itself to the classics; it also puts on serious original works, and translations of foreign plays. Commercials, trailers, comedy shows and story-tellings such as *Book at Bedtime* all contain drama.

Radio drama relies on sound and sound alone. Tyrone Guthrie and Val Gielgud were pioneers who exploited the essential quality of radio. They recognised that when provided only with sound, every listener has to create his or her own mental picture. There is no lighting, costumes, props, make-up or scenery to evoke characters or actions. Music and sound effects are vital to set scenes and define emotions. However, one of the unique properties of radio is that even on a small production budget, exotic places can be evoked or mass crowds conjured up. It can be very convincing: as on the occasion of Orson Welles's adaptation of H.G. Wells's SF novel *The War of the Worlds*. The radio broadcast of this in 1938 caused large-scale panic in the USA, with its realistic descriptions of Martians invading Earth. It is estimated that a quarter of the six million listeners believed what they were hearing.

Different scripting techniques were needed for this medium that were not necessary in the theatre, where people could see the action. Some writers, such as Samuel Beckett and Harold Pinter, excelled at this. Later influential writers were Tom Stoppard, Bill Naughton and John Mortimer. We will now look at some of the problems they would have met.

Novels recreate fictional worlds and experiences through the words on the page; radio drama does the same through **dialogue** i.e. speech. There are restrictions, however, on the type of plays that can appear on radio. The general rule is to restrict major speaking parts to about four or five characters, and they must all have distinctive voices. On television whilst one person is speaking, we can see how other characters react. This is not possible on radio. Neither can radio characters stay silent for too long; they must maintain their presence within a scene by making some comment, however brief. Because of the limits of the medium itself, sound levels are compressed within certain bands: shouts cannot be too loud, nor whispers too soft. Sound, however, must be continuous!

How are these problems solved? Visual codes have to be replaced by auditory codes. The dialogue or narration has to contain all the information that the theatre-goer can see. The dialogue must tell us *what* is happening, to *whom* and the *where* and *how*.

For example, on stage you can see a woman enter the room crying; you remember from her appearance in an earlier scene that she is called Jane. On radio, one person needs to say to another, 'Oh, look, Jane's just walked in.' The other person then may say, 'What's the matter, why are you crying?'

Speech can quite easily indicate someone's personality and status to us through accent and the way in which they talk, which could, for example, be loudly, quietly, quickly or with a stutter. However, it is harder to convey someone's appearance in a natural manner. So a comedy which relies on the way someone is dressed and walks for the joke may not be suitable for the radio. However, the essence of drama should be personal conflict rather than re-enactment of events. Because radio is blind, a monologue recounting an individual's thoughts can be very effective, as thought itself is invisible. Shakespearean monologues (soliloquies) on stage can seem contrived. After all, why should anyone talk out loud to themselves for such long periods of time! On the radio, this seems much more natural.

So radio drama sometimes has to adapt stage drama. The significance of scenes such as chases or battles can be lost on radio, so the dramatic climax may have to be altered.

There are two types of **sound effects:**

■ *noises* – such as banging doors, gun shots
■ *acoustic treatments* – echoes, fades.

Both of these can be used to depict the environment and distances. For example: bird-song tells us we are in the country; the sound of people typing and telephone calls tells us we are in an office. But the codes can be more sophisticated than that. We can identify from the type of bird-song, whether it is light or dark: so larks and blackbirds indicate a sunny afternoon in a garden, whereas the hoot of an owl is more likely to indicate a graveyard in the middle of the night. However, just as a newspaper photograph needs a caption to anchor its meaning, so does a sound effect need dialogue for the same reason. We can hear the sounds of someone rowing a boat but we need speech to tell us whether the boat is on the sea or on a lake.

Fades can be used in two ways. As one character leaves the room or walks away, the voice fades. Fades are also used to indicate the end of a scene, similar to the fall of the curtain in the theatre.

Time can also be indicated through sound effects, such as the chime of a clock. The passing of the seasons or events can be indicated through carol singing, the *Wedding March,* the song *Happy Birthday,* and so on.

Music can be used in different ways as well:

■ It can introduce and end a programme.
■ Besides telling us that the programme is starting, some signature tunes set the mood, the style or the period. So a song by the Beatles will set a play in the 1960s, a Mozart symphony in the eighteenth century. A folk song can evoke a rural scene, guitar music a Spanish hacienda.
■ Music can be used to indicate the end of a scene, a change in location or time.

All these symbols can be considered **icons**, through the way in which they represent real life.

Actors generally like working in radio drama. They don't have to dress up or even learn their lines! They are judged solely by the quality of their voice rather than their appearance or age.

Thematic concerns, functions and development

Early radio drama was produced in a small studio, often with only one microphone. Soon more sophisticated results were achieved with the development of sound effects and mixing desks.

The first drama broadcast (February 1923) consisted of three scenes from three different Shakespeare plays. Later that year, the first complete play to go out was *Twelfth Night* and the first play specially written for radio was *Danger* by Richard Hughes in January 1924. It was set in the dark, in a coalmine; and began with the line: 'The lights have gone out'. Hughes hoped people would listen in the dark and share the experience of the characters.

The first novel to be adapted for radio was *Westward Ho!* by Charles Kingsley (April 1925). Then the first soap opera was *The English Family Robinson* in 1937. (*Note*: The first 'soaps' appeared in America when washing powder companies funded popular TV programmes about everyday life in which their products appeared.)

The first daily serial was *Dick Barton – Special Agent!* in 1946.

The BBC has always supported contemporary works and the first living dramatist to have a major season of his work performed was the Irish playwright Brian Friel, on Radio 3 and 4 in 1989. In the 1980s, however, there was a lot of criticism of radio drama, which, it was claimed, was too gloomy and preoccupied with marital splits and sexual infidelity.

The BBC Radio Drama Department has now grown into the largest commissioner and producer of plays in Britain, about 350 each year. Drama has a much smaller role to play in independent radio.

There are actually two distinct types of audiences for radio plays: those who sit at home and listen to it on the radio and those who watch and listen to it being made in the studio. Audiences are surrounded by the distractions of their own environments. A live audience in the theatre can affect the performance of the actors. Audiences who come to listen to radio plays are different. They have not paid for their seats and are as likely to be just as interested in how a performance is put together as in the performance itself.

Radio is for mass audiences, yet they usually listen in isolation. Like a book, radio is portable and intimate.

It is generally middle-aged and middle-class audiences who listen to BBC Radio 3 and 4. But fewer of the working-class audiences who listen to Radio 1 and 2 move on to 3 and 4 as they grow older. Radio 4 is, therefore, concerned with the need to attract younger listeners. Once people get to like a particular radio station they are less likely to change than if it was a TV channel. Historically, this may be partly due to the difficulties sometimes encountered in re-tuning. This bond may be somewhat weakened now that radios are more sophisticated. But in any case radio has always fostered a more personal relationship with the listener and, generally speaking, the bonds of loyalty are stronger.

Case study: *The Archers*

The Archers is the best-known soap on radio and certainly the longest running. It started because the Ministry of Agriculture needed to give advice to farmers. Similar motivations lay behind the soaps being sent to Russia to tell people about capitalism.

The radio soap *The Archers* appeared at a time shortly after the Second World War when the government wanted to encourage farmers to grow more food. In 1948, there was a meeting in Birmingham between the BBC and farming representatives. It was a farmer, an enthusiastic fan of Dick Barton, who suggested that it would be more interesting and subtle to spread the word through the medium of radio drama.

The first episode was broadcast on the Light programme on Monday 1 January, 1951. The *Radio Times* described it as, 'The daily events in the lives of country folk'. Its advisory team included representatives from the National Farmers' Union and the Ministry of Agriculture.

The programme centred round the home of Dan and Doris Archer at Brookfield Farm, Ambridge, in the fictional county of Borsetshire. The soap has mirrored

Figure 3.15 The Grundy family in *The Archers*

events in the farming world: the shift from shire horses to Range Rovers, foot-and-mouth disease, sheep worrying, milk quotas, BSE, unemployment and poverty in the countryside.

Yet millions of its listeners have nothing to do with farming. For many it provides nostalgia, a link with people's roots, a view of a slower, possibly safer world. There has been a shift in the programme's purpose from being an adviser on agricultural topics to relating a tale about country life.

During the Gulf War the BBC responded to requests from the troops for the serial to be carried on the British Forces Broadcasting Services. Sometimes famous people have appeared as themselves on the programme; for example, Princess Margaret playing herself in an episode in 1984. As President of the NSPCC she visited the Ambridge fashion show to raise funds and had 85 scripted words to say!

The Archers is broadcast twice every weekday and there is an omnibus edition on Sundays. Even if they don't listen to the programme, most people in Britain seem to be able to hum the signature tune to *The Archers.* It has become a national institution.

Activity

Record a drama on the radio. Discuss how the use of music enhances the style and setting of the play. List the various characters and identify specific speeches that tell you about the appearance of an individual or what actions are taking place. Make a list of the sound effects and explain their purpose.

Current affairs

Formal characteristics

The current affairs genre shares many of the features of news and documentary, but is concerned with topics of immediate i.e. 'current' interest.

Current affairs programmes are often in-depth features on news stories which they amplify and interpret. They involve greater depth of analysis and use experts or well-known personalities to contribute their views on a topical area. This can then take the form of a debate between the participants.

Current affairs programmes do use a documentary style but the topics discussed concern contemporary newsworthy issues which tend to affect us all. On the one hand, a documentary may be on some matter of

national importance, such as firearms, in which case it could also be classed as current affairs (particularly when tied in with current events such as the terrible shootings at Dunblane). On the other hand, a documentary may be an in-depth study of the history of firearms, in which case it would be a documentary rather than a current affairs programme. This would be of particular interest to enthusiasts and historians, although it may have a more general appeal because of the way it is presented and the type of audience listening in.

There are also current affairs elements in the radio **magazine** formats, which combine a popular mix of news analysis, features, comment and chat in varying degrees of seriousness.

Radio 4's *The World Tonight* and *The World This Weekend,* and Radio 5's *The Magazine,* are examples of current affairs programmes. In fact, over two-thirds of Radio 4's output are types of current affairs programmes.

The greatest competitors to radio stations are the newspapers. The BBC radio stations in particular compete with their news coverage and current affairs programmes. With a newspaper, you can see at a glance what stories are covered and in what depth. There are supplements on particular topics, such as business or sport, that you can pick up or ignore. Radio, being a format that exists in time, has a distinct problem. The listener does not know what is coming up. If a topic in which they have no interest is on air for longer than anticipated then they will switch off. They may never listen to that programme again. So it is important that a regular format for the programme is established, that its style is recognised and maintained. A newspaper reader expects the newspaper to have a consistent layout, but it is even more essential that a radio programme has a certain predictability.

Listeners have to be regularly reminded about what future items will include, so they will hear comments such as 'Later in the programme we shall be hearing from ...' or, 'Coming up shortly there will be a report from ...'.

Other news media can indicate the status of items through the order in which they are presented – through the serious or smiling expression on a TV presenter's face or the size of a headline in a newspaper. Generally, on radio, the importance of items is indicated by the order in which they are presented in the programme; so a serious topic which affects the entire nation will be dealt with first. However, 'heavy' subjects might well be interspersed with lighter ones so that the listeners can afford to relax their concentration. This gives variety and avoids monotony as well.

Language too, presents a problem. It has to be quickly comprehended and assimilated by a widely varying audience. If you, the reader, have not understood this last sentence, you can read it again, think about it, ask someone to explain it or look up words in the dictionary. Then you can return to the text. This cannot be done with radio. The pace of the programme must match the rate at which the listener can absorb information. So even complex subjects must be treated in a straightforward manner and simplified. More colloquial words, i.e. words used in everyday language, are used and there is more repetition and paraphrasing of information than would be appropriate in literary or written styles. Sentences are short. Significant words have to be stressed by the presenter.

The sound of a current affairs programme can be made more lively by a change of voices. Different qualities of tone, pace and volume will keep the listener's attention. Acoustics are important too. The studio can be given a warm sound or background noise can be included, such as the reactions of other participants in the debate.

As with other programmes, both on TV and radio, the opening theme music often indicates the genre, its content and style, whether the programme is sophisticated, serious, popular, etc. Themes for current affairs programmes need to be dramatic rather than sad, urgent rather than cheerful, with volume, pace, and a sense of authority. They tend to have sharp rhythms and a sense of timelessness. Some sound more like jingles, which can act like the fades in drama, to separate items. However, unlike the TV documentary, the current affairs programme does not use music to arouse an emotional reaction.

Thematic concerns, functions and development

Radio, or wireless as it was first known, was invented and developed as a means of communication to transmit messages over long distances. In Britain, the Post Office had the right to control broadcasts from 1904. It was worried about congestion of the airwaves but was also reluctant to let one wireless manufacturer have a monopoly. So, in 1922, the British Broadcasting Company Ltd was established as a consortium of manufacturers. Its first general manager, Lord Reith, established radio as a public

service with a strong moral and educational responsibility. By 1925, over three-quarters of the population were able to receive transmissions. From the beginning, news, information, speeches, lectures and weather reports were an essential part of the service.

Even at this early stage, the newspapers were aware of a challenge. The Newspaper Proprietors' Association influenced the government so that the BBC was banned from broadcasting news bulletins and commentaries on the news before 7pm. In 1927, the British Broadcasting Company was replaced by the British Broadcasting Corporation. By Act of Parliament it became a public institution, designed to be free of commercial pressures and political interference. Its aims for both radio and television were to inform, educate and entertain. Its obligations also included the need to report on Parliament, to broadcast government messages in emergencies, but to retain a political balance.

Radio's tradition for strong coverage of news and current affairs stems from the days of the Second World War, when the radio was the main source of information for most families. The nine o'clock news had huge audiences and in 1940 *Radio Newsreel* started. This was an early current affairs programme which gave more detail and commented on the news bulletins. About this time, the quality of broadcasts also improved, ironically because of new sound recording technology – often pioneered by the Germans.

During the War, the National Service was split into two: the Home Service, which continued in the same style, and the Forces Programme, which was much lighter and aimed at the working classes. This included dance band music and variety shows.

After the war, three networks were set up: the Home Service (which combined national and regional services); the Light Programme (largely dance and sport); and the Third Programme (concentrating on the arts and intellectual discussion). For the next decade, the radio ruled supreme.

However, radio listening figures had dropped dramatically by the 1960s because of the competition from television and because the three stations were no longer giving audiences what they wanted. Radio was saved by the new technology (described in greater detail below under 'Pop music') and also because of a radical shake-up in the reorganisation of the networks. Radio 1 was established to play contemporary pop music, Radio 2 took over older pop music, Radio 3 was to cover classical music and

Radio 4 concentrated on entertainment through the spoken word, but also specialised in news and current affairs programmes.

Today, the majority of commercial, independent radio stations are predominantly music based. The BBC local radio stations have given a local, community-based slant to their current affairs.

When radio news was first developed, the readers were very impersonal. It was only during the War that presenters' names were first mentioned so that listeners could recognise that this was an authentic British, rather than German, report. However, BBC radio news has retained a reputation for objectivity and impartiality. The current affairs programmes are less impersonal; they have more individual comment with differing styles and more of an editorial 'feel'.

The advantage that radio has over the newspapers is its immediacy. Because it is comparatively cheap it is quicker to get news on air and the personal style of delivery can make the listeners feel that information is being reported to them personally. There is also the convenience factor. The business person can be kept up-to-date whilst travelling in the car, whilst homeworkers can get on with whatever they are doing. Radio is portable! If people are doing something else whilst listening they are able to do an aural scan. They will concentrate on their work whilst topics which are not of particular interest to them are on the air, but will switch to give their full attention to subjects that do concern them.

The definition of broadcasting is the transmission of radio or TV programmes to the general public. However, the radio audience is scattered and the listener is more likely to be on his or her own, rather than in a large group as for film-going, or in a small family group as for watching television.

In the last decade, with greater competition, there has been a greater need to identify and attract audiences.

The BBC no longer has a monopoly, so it has been anxious to attract new listeners. Radio 4, for example, has traditionally had a loyal, well-educated following but this audience, as it dies out, needs to be replaced. Younger people have grown up with the visual images of TV news. A long, purely verbal commentary on events can be difficult for them to accept. So formats have had to adapt, for example, introducing phone-ins and changing the **mode-of-address.** How the presenters actually speak to us has changed. In the early days, when a radio set was known as a wireless, the poor quality of sound meant that presenters had to speak as if they were in a church pulpit in loud, slow voices.

	Adult (15+) Pop'n '000	Weekly Reach 000	Weekly Reach %	Average per head	Hours per listener	Total Hours '000
BBC NETWORK RADIO						
BBC Radio 1	46957	12283	26	2.4	9.2	113090
BBC Radio 2	46957	8987	19	2.3	12.2	109395
BBC Radio 3	46957	2380	5	0.2	3.5	8426
BBC Radio 4	46957	8517	18	1.9	10.3	88012
BBC Radio 5 Live	46957	4275	9	0.4	4.2	17803
NATIONAL REGIONAL						
BBC Radio Scotland	4147	867	21	1.4	6.7	5775
BBC Radio Ulster	1220	356	29	2.8	9.5	3367
BBC Radio Wales/Cymru	2335	541	23	2.9	12.5	6780
LOCAL						
BBC Local Radio	36858	7864	21	1.9	9.0	71152
BBC Radio Berkshire	612	56	9	0.4	4.5	253
BBC Radio Bristol	1162	284	24	2.1	8.6	2431
BBC CWR	472	37	8	0.4	5.3	197
BBC Radio Cambridge	550	116	21	1.9	9.1	1052
BBC Radio Cleveland	685	115	17	1.4	8.3	952
BBC Radio Cornwall	397	156	39	4.6	11.8	1832
BBC Radio Cumbria	373	124	33	3.2	9.7	1206
BBC Dorset FM	171	26	15	1.0	6.8	178
BBC Radio Derby	563	182	32	3.1	9.6	1741
BBC Radio Devon	872	218	25	2.8	11.1	2422
BBC Essex	1116	245	22	2.3	10.5	2566
BBC GLR	9829	384	4	0.2	3.9	1499
BBC GMR	2033	276	14	1.2	8.9	2463
BBC Radio Gloucestershire	348	67	19	1.5	7.6	506
BBC Hereford & Worcester	467	101	22	2.2	10.3	1034

Figure 3.16 Radio listening figures for BBC services in the second quarter of 1994

In many of its programmes the BBC now has a more personal feel. At one time all news presenters would have spoken in a formal, rather correct voice, using conventional grammar rather than colloquialisms. This was popularly known as 'speaking the King's English' or **received pronunciation**, or even BBC English. However, for two reasons society now accepts that news and current affairs programme presenters can speak with regional accents. First, because of the influence of the media themselves, people can become accustomed to hearing different accents on the television and radio as more programmes are produced in the regions. Secondly, many more people are better educated. It is not only students from Oxford or Cambridge with middle-class backgrounds who are successful in the professions or industry. These influential people may also speak with regional accents. A different accent can sound fresh and natural. However, as a general rule, the heavier the status of a current affairs programme, the more likely it is that the presenter will still speak with received pronunciation.

News and current affairs programmes continue to be at the heart of 'spoken word' programmes on the radio. Even in the early days, newspaper proprietors recognised the challenge that radio would bring to them and have responded in different ways, whether by trying to restrict radio or to 'buy in' to radio.

Case study: *The World This Weekend*

In order to illustrate the kind of content to be found on a current affairs programme, the following is a synopsis of *The World This Weekend*, a regular current affairs programme, which was broadcast on Radio 4 on Sunday 14 April 1996 from 1.00pm to 1.55pm.

The programme was introduced with a summary of the contents, and then related the 'hard' news stories. These included a major story about the bombardment of Southern Lebanon by Israel. After the hard news section there followed an interview with the Israeli ambassador in London.

Then came comment on the evangelist Billy Graham's latest campaigning tour in Britain, with points of view both from the presenter and members of the public. The topic was then widened out to discuss concerns about how Christianity is presented by, for example, the Billy Graham approach and by pop influences. This was delivered partly via an interview with Cliff Richard.

This was followed by discussion of the by-election defeat of the Conservatives in South-East Staffordshire three days before. This was still a current issue. The implications for the survival of the Conservative government, its chances in the next election, whether the general election would be brought forward and how Labour fared in crises whilst it was in power, were all discussed and analysed.

In this example we can identify some defining characteristics of current affairs programmes: the stories were in the form of two-way comment and analysis; the stories came out of news items which were examined in more breadth and depth; and several issues were examined.

Activity

Find two examples of current affairs programming: one for local radio and the other for national BBC radio. Provide a brief summary of their purpose. What are the differences and the similarities between the two programmes? List the different topics covered and how they were dealt with, for example through interviews or debate. Describe the introductory music and comment on the overall sound, the presenter's voice, background noise, etc.

Pop music

Formal characteristics

From the earliest days of radio, it has been recognised that music is especially suitable for this medium as it is an aural art form. It does not need visual images to aid understanding or add to its enjoyment.

What do we understand by the term popular music? When we talk of 'pop' we can mean all the different styles of contemporary popular music, including rock, heavy metal, rave, or we can mean light, commercial chart music from the last few decades. Nearly all pop does have its roots in other musical forms, such as swing, blues, gospel, rhythm and blues and rock 'n' roll and folk. We do, however, tend to distinguish it from classical, folk or jazz music, even though these might have as large a following and greater CD and record sales than heavy metal, for instance. Some people would argue that Classic FM (the first national commercial station) which plays light, well-known classical music, is also a popular music station. It is interesting to note that its presentation style is similar to that of existing rock and pop stations.

The essential part of a popular music programme is the music, i.e. records or, these days, CDs. For about the first three decades of radio, however, the music programmes played live rather than recorded music. The change to records occurred about the time when radio began to compete with television, but there were a number of reasons for this. First, the quality of records had improved and so had the decks they were played on. Besides, the mistakes in a live performance were a problem not found with recordings. It was also cheaper to use records and dispense with the big bands, orchestras and live performers that were attached to the radio stations. From the 1960s onwards, certain types of electronic music were impossible to perform live and even the most basic pop group needed their playing mixed and enhanced by sound engineers. Records offered far more variety than a few musicians crammed into a studio.

A special relationship has developed between radio and recorded popular music, with each industry contributing to the success of the other and both influencing and being influenced by the popular culture of the day. The recording industry supplies the music and is eager to *plug* new products. Any record played regularly will make the charts. Radio sells records: presenters recommend albums, run

4.00am Clive Warren

6.30 Chris Evans
The loudest crew, the Hair Bear Bunch, the UK's biggest traffic, the Closet Classics, lightning links and the best new music, plus *Newsbeat* with Tina Richie.

9.00 Simon Mayo
With the daily Golden Hour from **9.00**, the retrospective threesome in the **11.33** and the Dead or Alive? challenge on Freecall 0500 110100.

12.00 Lisa I'Anson
Maximum music over lunch, including **12.30–12.45** *Newsbeat.*

2.00pm Nicky Campbell
Including the Number Nine Game.

4.00 Mark Goodier
Entertainment for the afternoon drive, with the *Newsbeat* late report at **5.30–5.45**, the ongoing Batman *Knightfall* saga and three great radio records back-to-back in the nightly Drive-In at **6.00**

7.00 Evening Session
Steve Lamacq and Jo Whiley with Eska and Massive Attack in session.

9.00 Cling Film with Mark Kermode and Mary Anne Hobbs
Movies, videos, on-set reports and reviews, and a weekly cinematic guest chooses three favourite flicks, getting a one-way ticket to spend A Night in Casablanca.

10.00 Mark Radcliffe
Manchester's Studio 5 transmutates into the Palace of Glittering Delights with the aid of a boy called Lard.

12.00 Wendy Lloyd

Figure 3.17 A Radio 1 schedule

RADIO SOUTHSIDE FM

The early evening show – programme format
DJ: Jenny Warren
Slot: 7–8

1900	Programme introduction
1901	'Something changed' – Pulp
1904	'Creep' – Radiohead
1907	Commercial break and jingles (on cart)
1908	Promo for Manic Street Preachers
1909	Oasis: 'Don't look back in anger' 'Wonderwall' 'Slide away'
1918	Commercial Break and jingles
1919	Interview with lead singer about tonight's concert
1921	'Suicide and painless' – Manic Street Preachers
1924	Commercial Break and jingles
1925	'Jesus hairdo' – Charlatans
1928	Commercial Break and jingles
1929	Trailer for Matt's Early Morning Show
1930	News
1933	Sport
1935	Commercial Break and jingles
1937	'Too sussed' – These Animal Men
1940	'Kung Foo' – Ash
1943	'Give it away' – Red Hot Chilli Peppers
1946	Travel reports – air, road and rail
1950	'Sally Cinammon' – Stone Roses
1954	Commercial break and jingles
1956	'Common people' – Pulp
1959	Programme outro and jingle

Figure 3.18 Running order for a radio music programme

---

competitions where the winner goes to see a live band, the chart shows tell listeners what is currently available to buy. The records themselves act as samples. So, in a sense, even the BBC advertises!

Most of the popular music on air is easy to listen to and does not demand total concentration, so it is suitable to be listened to at work, in the factory or office, in the car or at home.

In the 1960s, to make an identity for themselves, radio stations adopted a pattern of programming known as **format radio.** This is where the output is specialised rather than mixed, so that there are several hours of continuous music interspersed with short bursts of talk, rather than, for example, a news documentary followed by a quiz, followed by a music concert and then a play. Figure 3.18 shows a typical format for a popular music programme.

There are numerous other items that can be put between songs, such as phone-ins, competitions, comedy sketches, interviews with stars or the public, requests, sports results, gossip, and so on.

Some stations have been criticised for having too much small talk or adverts and not enough music. To avoid this criticism, records are sometimes played back-to-back, i.e. one after another, and some stations will play three or more in a row.

These days the music can be chosen by computer rather than by the presenter. The computer will hold several banks of music, old and new, which are suitable for specific target audiences. A list is

Figure 3.19 DJ Chris Evans of Radio 1

produced, according to the time of day and who is thought to be listening, and to give a good mix of male/female singers, solo artists/groups or to group songs about a certain theme, such as romance or travel. Besides the music itself, the presenter is the person who gives a programme its style and identity. For most people, music without a human presence would be dull. The presenter is a companion with whom pleasure is shared. Popular presenters can attract thousands of listeners through their personalities, which was why the BBC was so keen to attract the lively, extrovert Chris Evans (see Figure 3.19) to host a breakfast show. Presenters may be chatty, they may be outrageous, but they should be memorable.

There are basically two types of presenters. The first talks mainly about the music, giving details of recordings and information about the bands, often in an objective, analytical manner. This is the approach that John Peel uses. These presenters are more likely to be fronting a programme playing new releases, experimental music or a specialist programme. Typically they will be on air later in the night.

The second type of presenter talks about other topics, such as films they have seen or what happened to them coming to work. They tend to play current hits from the Top Forty charts and may not even give the name of the record. A usual time for this sort of presenter would be in the morning or late afternoon. They have a more frivolous approach. Examples are Virgin's Russ 'n' Jono, whose show runs from 6 to 9am and who are very funny.

DJs have become stars in their own right, attracting publicity for themselves and their programmes. It is not an easy job, although the presenters make it sound simple. For example, the language used by DJs is informal. Although they are addressing a mass audience, they will use the words 'I' and 'you' to establish a close relationship with individual listeners. They will ask a question of the audience, 'Is it cold where you are today?' They know they are not going to get an answer! They will refer to individual listeners who have written or phoned in by their Christian names.

Jingles are an essential part of the popular-music programme; they are a type of slogan which gives the station or programme its identity. These will be recorded onto **carts** (cartridges) ready to slot into the schedule every so often. Jingles announce adverts; they announce the news. They aim to encourage loyalty. Most importantly, they announce the wavelength on which the station can be found. For example,

'This is the all-new Mercia FM, Coventry and Warwickshire's better music mix: 97 Mercia FM'.

Thematic concerns, functions and development

In the 1950s came rock 'n' roll. The BBC resisted playing this and instead hoped it was a passing phenomenon. But, of course, it did not go away although many listeners did – by tuning into Radio Luxembourg.

In 1948 Radio Luxembourg had been the first station to play pop music on a Sunday night. At the time it was a programme of the best-selling sheet music and was sponsored by Outdoor Girl lipstick. In 1952, with the creation of the first pop charts in *New Musical Express,* it became a programme of best-selling records. At its peak in 1959, Luxembourg was said to have attracted twelve million listeners with its continuous light music. There was little competition until the rise of the pirate stations in 1964 and Radio 1 in 1967, when it lost most of its audience.

The music itself was only one expression of a developing 'pop' culture in the 1950s and 1960s. The term 'teenager' was first coined in the 1950s to describe a new type of young people who, by their clothes, music, language and attitudes, differentiated themselves markedly from the pre-war generations. There have, of course, always been differences between the young and their parents – the generation gap – but this was far more pronounced because of other changes in society.

One major factor was the increased spending power of young people in the 1950s. Other factors included the development of the transistor, which made radios cheaper and more portable because they were smaller and the components more robust. Cheapness and portability made the radio far more attractive to young people, who could then listen to the new rock 'n' roll and 'pop' with friends wherever they were able to gather. They no longer had to depend on the large valve-operated wireless sets sitting in their parents' kitchen or living-room.

Other technical developments, such as stereo sound and VHF, also helped radio by improving its sound quality and reach. By 1964 there was such a demand for pop music that **pirate stations**, transmitting from ships off the coast, began to come on air, most notably Radio Caroline and Radio London. These differentiated their product sufficiently by broadcasting round-the-clock pop music; they had jingles and disc jockeys and soon became the main source of pop for listeners in Britain.

Although these pirate stations were illegal, the government and the BBC had to take notice of their phenomenal success. The audience for the pirate stations was claimed to be 24 million by 1966. There was, however, no appreciable decline in the Light Programme listening figures, so it was obvious that there was an untapped market for which the BBC had not catered. To be fair, the pirates did not have to take notice of agreements with the Musicians' Union and paid no royalties, whereas the BBC were severely restricted by this. The pirates were to be eventually forced off the air by the Marine Broadcasting (Offences) Act, passed in August 1967. Then in September the BBC launched its first all-pop station, Radio One, copying the format of the pirate stations' programmes and even employing some of their disc jockeys.

Tony Blackburn was the first of the 22 DJs recruited by the BBC to play a record on the new national pop station with 'Flowers in the Rain' at 7am on Saturday 30 September 1967. At first it was poorly funded and had to share airtime with Radio 2. Although popular, especially amongst teenagers, it was criticised for what has been described as 'pop-and-prattle'. But Radio 1 was for many years extremely popular, especially for its programmes which played the Top Twenty Hits from the charts, compiled for many years by Gallup. It also became well known for its roadshows, which since the mid-1970s have toured

the country, publicising their programmes and providing entertainment.

In the late 1980s Radio 1 was faced with a crisis: it was failing to attract new audiences, partly because of a fall in the teenage population, and partly because of increasing competition from independent radio. In 1988 Radio 1 was given an FM frequency and in May of that year went on air for 24 hours a day.

It then issued a policy document in May 1990. This stated Radio 1's objectives, to:

- retain its public service principles
- maintain a high level of listeners
- support new music
- increase the number of non-musical programmes
- have more presenters from a number of different backgrounds.

What is meant when it refers to **public service principles**? As far back as 1979, there have been *Action Specials,* giving information to teenagers on job training and educational opportunities. Similar campaigns have been on air about homelessness, drugs, debt, AIDS and so on. There are 24-hour telephone help-lines to offer listeners advice and support from various experts, including voluntary agencies and social workers.

In 1971 Independent Local Radio (ILR) was established, which allowed privately owned radio stations to be funded by advertising. Advertisers like music programmes. A sequence of records is short, compared to the longer spans needed by a current affairs programme or a play, so there can be frequent interruptions for commercials. The main function of such programmes is entertainment; listeners are more likely to be in a receptive, positive mood to hear about new, desirable products than if they are listening to a news programme about poverty in the Third World.

Since the 1970s the number of radio stations has increased dramatically and many of the new stations cater for different types of popular music. Some appeal to older listeners with their concentration on 'golden oldies' – the music of the sixties, seventies and eighties. The following is just a small selection of popular music stations:

Radio 1
Virgin FM
Atlantic 252
Heart FM
Kiss FM
Mercia FM and Mercia Classic Gold

Red Rose Gold and Red Rose Rock FM
Viking FM

Can you name any more?

New technology has also affected the popularity of some stations. In 1990 the BBC changed its four major networks to the FM signal, used by independent radio stations, which gives a better-quality sound. The latest developments include the development of digital radio and RDS (Radio Data System) in cars, which means that motorists do not have to retune to a station every so often as they travel out of reach of local transmitters.

The main problem for music stations lies not in the fact that people don't want to listen to radio any more, but that the market is becoming oversaturated and there is too much competition for smaller stations to survive.

Case study: *Radio City*

Radio City consists of two stations, City FM and Radio City Gold. Between them they aim to cater for the musical tastes of everyone throughout Merseyside, the North West and North Wales. We will look at the music mix of 96.7 City FM. Their own publicity (see Figure 3.20) indicates the target audience.

Radio City Gold 1548 AM adopts a similar approach (see Figure 3.21)

The way Radio City differentiates its music output to cater for different market segments is dealt with more fully in Chapters 25 and 26.

24-Hour Service, Every Day Of The Year

MONDAY TO FRIDAY

2–6AM JON JESSOP.. the City Nightcruiser, keeping the music going through the night, with regular news and trivia quizzes to keep the insomniacs alert.

6–9AM TONY SNELL... the breakfast show that's breaking all the records, pulling in over 100,000 listeners; with a brilliant mix of music, news and the infamous Snelly Scams... THE show to wake up to!

9–12NOON DAVE MASON... our morning man maintains The Best Music Mix and also specialises in star interviews. This show also features the daily action Desk and the Top Nine at Nine.

12.3PM NEAL ATKINSON... Mr Nice Guy Neal attracts an army of housewives and office workers as well as his young admirers for a show full of music, comedy, phone-ins and competitions.

3–6PM TONY MCKENZIE... drivetime presenter Tony hit the road from his native South in 1988... now he's a real North West favourite and it's music all the way, spiced with his dry wit and those essential drivetime news and traffic updates.

6–7PM TOP TEN OF THE DAY... the songs most requested by City FM listeners, compiled afresh every single day.

7–10PM RICK HOUGHTON... the voice of the North West's young people... presenting the very latest music, reviewing releases... keeping his audience in touch with what's on plus his regular Panic Attack and 4 Play features.

10PM–2AM BRIAN MOORE... the Late Night Show, featuring the legendary and original Peaceful Hours 60 minutes of ballads and listeners' dedications.

Figure 3.20 Publicity material for City FM

ROUND-THE-CLOCK PROGRAMMING

MONDAY TO FRIDAY

7–10AM JOHN O'HARA ... starting the day with a warm, welcome mix of music, comment, wit and all the important weather and traffic news.

10–1PM RICHARD DUNCAN... selecting the best music from the 50's through to the 80's for his dedicated followers... plus the popular 'Trading Post', individual horoscopes and birthday celebrations.

1–4PM ERICA HUGHES... posing the question. 'What was the year?' of the day's Classic Top Ten... and inviting the North West to join in the tricky 'Gold Rush'.

4–7PM TERRY LENNAINE... bringing you all the local, national and international news in the Radio City Gold reports, the very best drive-time listening... and asking listeners to choose their favourites on 'Jukebox'.

7–10PM DEBI JONES... our local celebrity and TV presenter answers listeners' questions on consumer concerns... and plays a great range of music too.

10–1AM PETE PRICE... the late night show that has proved a fantastic success. It's the most popular on any station, and has attracted national coverage in the press and on TV!

1–2AM BRIAN MOORE and

2–5AM JON JESSOP... playing right through the night, with shows shared with sister station 96.7 City FM.

AND AT THE WEEKEND

All-round entertainment

all around the clock... including

FRANKIE CONNOR on Friday nights... the best of country music with JOE BUTLER... the Radio City Gold fans' choice JUKEBOX for three hours on Saturday mornings... and TUTTI FRUTTI with ROY KELLY.

PLUS... SIR JIMMY SAVILE, the most legendary and loved of all DJ's presents 'Savile's Travels' every Sunday lunchtime... with two Top Tens from golden years gone by.

Figure 3.21 Radio City Gold's publicity material

Activity

With a partner, analyse a music programme from a local station and compare it with one from a national station which is on at the same time on the same day. Identify the target audience and discuss how this is affected by the scheduling. Compare the type of music played, the presenters' styles and the content of the two programmes.

Print media

Broadsheet and tabloid newspapers

Formal characteristics

A tabloid or broadsheet newspaper can be defined as a publication, usually produced daily, which contains information and stories about recent local, national or international events and issues of interest to the public. Western newspapers also contain a lot of advertising. Revenue from advertising is the main source of income for newspaper companies rather than the **cover price**, i.e. the price the person in the street pays for the newspaper.

The content of a newspaper is divided into three broad components: text, pictures and advertising. The text can be further categorised into:

- hard news
- features
- supplements
- sport, including details of fixtures, and horse-racing guides
- editorial, sometimes called the leader or comment
- comic strip
- cartoons
- horoscopes
- weather
- stock market figures
- crosswords, chess, bridge and other puzzles
- TV and radio schedules
- births, marriages and deaths
- obituaries
- book, film/theatre/concert reviews
- competitions
- free offers.

We can recognise from a distance which is a tabloid and which is a broadsheet newspaper by their size. The size of a broadsheet newspaper is 72 x 60 cm. The size of a tabloid is 38 x 40 centimetres. This makes it easy to handle and is the reason why a number of papers, for example the *Daily Express,* changed to this format. Even *The Guardian* uses a tabloid format for its second section (see below).

The size of a newspaper does tend to signify its intellectual content and style. Tabloids have very short articles with short words, colloquialisms and catchy phrases. They are either light-hearted with a cheeky wit, or self-righteously presume to speak for the vast majority of 'right-thinking' people. Broadsheets have a more restrained, considered approach, with more complicated words and phrases.

Tabloids are often divided between the **red banner** variety, for example, the *Daily Star,* and the **mid-range** types, such as the *Daily Express.*

Examples of a broadsheet newspaper are: *The Times, The Guardian, Independent, Daily Telegraph.*

Although newspapers do still carry out their original function of supplying the latest news, they have also had to adapt owing to the competition of television and radio, which the majority of people use as their primary source of news. Newspapers, therefore, particularly the tabloids, have moved into entertainment, while broadsheets put a lot of emphasis on features, particularly on news analysis.

Tabloids, particularly the **red banner** variety, have blatant mastheads (see Unit 3) and tend to use large headlines and **sans serif** typefaces, with relatively small amounts of easy-to-read text broken up by cross-heads and pictures. The text is similar to the spoken word and is often referred to as 'tabloidese'. This is a shorthand language which is often used to sensationalise a topic. For example, a story reporting job losses could well use the term 'axed' instead of 'sacked' or 'laid off'.

Broadsheets are more serious in their appearance and place far more emphasis on detailed content. The language is more elaborate, although it tends not to sensationalise events. Still, broadsheets wish to attract readers so they do place a lot of emphasis on good layout and photography. They are, however, more subtle in their appearance with layout and typeface, particularly for the masthead. They like to convey an image of sophistication, intellect, stature, respectability, reliability, tradition, integrity, and so on.

There are two types of advertising that newspapers can attract: classified and display. **Classified** ads are found in designated sections in a newspaper where articles and services are advertised under certain headings, such as cars, electrical goods, computers,

WANTED

WANTED: Diagnostic equipment for new model Range Rover Discovery, best prices paid – Tel 512738, fax Trade.
RANGE ROVER LHD 4-dr Diesel, air cond. £10,00-£20.000 waiting – Write to Mr Singh, 295 Rayleigh Road, EastWood
2.5 PETROL ENGINE, Suitable rebuild, with/without head, no casting damage. S. East Lond/N Kent area, or delivered, also ancillaries. Tel 834235 after 6pm
WANTED 1986–1989 LAND ROVER COUNTY station wagon 5-door turbo-diesel in good condition. Tel 953 0902, Fax: 905 1231.
HEADINGS FOR SIII TRUCK CAB wanted, must be genuine Land Rover, new or good secondhand. Tel 822516.
WANTED: SWB LAND ROVERS Light-weight Series 1, 2 and 3 and 90. Any condition considered, fair

prices paid Ring Robert 378078 office hours Monday–Saturday
SERIES III LWB v.g.c. 2.25 Diesel post-1968. No Q plates. F.s.h, will pay £2,500 dependent on spec and extras. tel 475624.
WANTED: TDi engines and gearboxes and radiator, also V8 3.9s and body panels for Range Rovers, L/R and Discoveries. Also alloy wheels and tyres. Late salvage always wanted (T). Tel: 810827.
WANTED: LAND ROVER 88" 109" AND STATION WAGONS pre-1971, must be good all-round vehicle. Will pay good cash prices for good vehicles. I will travel anywhere.
WANTED: 1986–1989 LAND ROVER COUNTY STATION WAGON 5-door Turbo Diesel in good condition. Tel: 953 0902.
WANTED: SWB LAND ROVERS. Lightweight Series 1, 2 and 3 and 90. Any condition considered, fair prices paid – ring Sarah, 314821 office hours.

Figure 3.22 Classified ads are a cheap and simple way to buy or sell

audio equipment, etc. Very often it will be private sales of used cars, bicycles, washing machines and so on placed by individuals. They are comparatively cheap and rely on just a line or two of text to sell the article. There is little involvement by the classified sales team in ad design. This is basically a 'no frills' approach, where the item sells itself through its description rather than through an advertising image.

Figure 3.23 Display ads generally contain artwork and logos

Display is basically a space in the newspaper, which can be in varying proportions up to the size of a page and even beyond. Display advertising space is normally bought by businesses and other organisations because of its cost, although there is nothing to stop a private individual from placing a display advert. Display ads can be placed in the classified sections of a paper but generally speaking the business customer will select a space in the **editorial** (news and comment) pages. The positioning of the advert will determine how much the customer will have to pay. A customer will receive advice and help with the design, placing and frequency of the display ad. They want to attract potential customers to look at the 'display' so it will generally have to contain attractive artwork, including a memorable logo.

Thematic concerns, functions and development

There has always been a need for methods to communicate information. In ancient Rome, written announcements of political and social events were posted up daily in the city. In medieval Britain the town crier told the citizens about local and sometimes national events. Later, when printing was developed, single pieces of paper called 'broadsides' told of the most important happenings in the country. In the seventeenth century, printed papers appeared on the Continent and in England, where the first daily newspaper *The Daily Courant* was published between 1702 and 1735. In 1771, Parliament gave journalists the right to report on its proceedings. *The Times* was founded in 1785 by John Walter and *The Observer* in 1791.

Circulation figures were in the low thousands for the early newspapers, but in the nineteenth century there was a dramatic rise. There were a number of reasons for this:

- technological advances, such as the rotary press
- improvements in communications and transport
- an increase in the population
- improved education – more people could read
- cheaper prices for newspapers.

The Times cost 7 pence to buy at the beginning of the nineteenth century. When *The Sun* was started by Benjamin Day in New York in 1833, he only charged one penny; it was a great success. In 1835, Gordon Bennett began the *New York Herald*. This was more like a modern newspaper in that it had a wider coverage and was more entertaining.

Meanwhile, in Britain, Lord Northcliffe introduced a national newspaper, the *Daily Mail,* in 1896. It had a low price to attract readers and raised most of its revenue through advertising. In 1903, he launched the first tabloid, the *Daily Mirror*. He was responsible for turning the newspaper industry into big business. At this time the major proprietors had both financial and editorial control. Lord Beaverbrook ran the *Daily Express* and the *Sunday Express* and Lord Camrose the *Daily Telegraph*. These were the Fleet Street press barons who wielded power until the 1960s. They reflected the power and opinions of the upper classes.

By the 1980s, most of the 13 national dailies and 10 of the Sunday newspapers published in London were owned by big industrial groups with diversified interests. The personal attitudes and opinions of the proprietors became less important than commercial pressures, and this resulted in aggressive marketing. The accountants gained greater power; they wanted to cut editorial costs and increase the amount of advertising in papers. This inevitably affected the content.

Accountants also wanted an efficient, streamlined industry. This was achieved through new technology, particularly computerisation. The number of overseas correspondents was cut, with international news stories provided by agencies. In fact, most of the news distributed internationally is provided by only four agencies: Reuters, the Associated Press, United Press International and Agence France Presse.

It is generally recognised that there is still political bias in newspapers. Most are interested in maintaining the status quo in the economy and society. The interests of the big multinational companies have replaced the interests of the press barons. The underlying ethos of most newspapers is to support the Conservative party.

The price of a newspaper varies from being free to about £1. If a newspaper drops its price then its competitors try to equal that in order to keep circulation figures high. What affects the profits most, however, is the cost of newsprint (i.e. paper), which has escalated enormously in recent years. Whereas over the past decade there has been a proliferation in the number of supplements a newspaper offers, some newspapers may now have to consider reducing the number of pages in order to remain financially viable.

Case study: *The Sun*

The Sun started life in 1912 as the *Daily Herald*, metamorphising into *The Sun* in 1969.

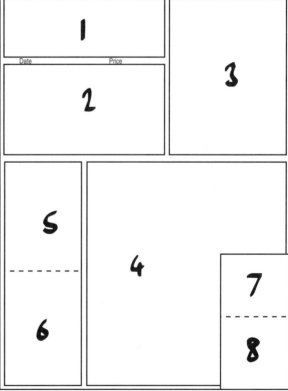

Figure 3.24 Front page of *The Sun*

The Sun is owned by Rupert Murdoch's News International which has 37 per cent of all national paper sales. The group also owns The Times, the book publisher Harper Collins and 40 per cent of the satellite company BSkyB. In addition, Murdoch has a lot of shares in media organisations in many other countries, including America, Australia and Asia.

Since 1994, the editor of The Sun has been Stuart Higgins. He took over from the extrovert Kelvin MacKenzie. MacKenzie ran The Sun for thirteen years. During that time he built up a reputation for being ruthless in his management style and crude in his ideas for the paper, many of which were thought to be in poor taste. Others, however, point to his hard work, dedication and ability to tap in to the national 'pulse'. He felt he knew what people wanted in a newspaper. He was probably right because, admire him or loathe him, he made The Sun's position as Britain's best-selling newspaper pretty well unassailable. The daily circulation for 1995 was 4,080,000.

Rupert Murdoch started a newspaper price war in 1993. The cost of The Sun dropped from 25p to 20p, forcing other newspapers to follow suit. In July 1996, it raised its price back to 25p because of the increase in the cost of newsprint. The price of The Sun is currently 27p.

We will now look at an analysis of the content and layout of a typical Sun front page: Monday 20 May 1996.

Box 1 contains the bold Sun masthead. As the cost of the newspaper has recently gone up, the price is now printed in very insignificant type.

Box 2 contains a coloured picture of Kermit the frog advertising a special offer – a free beefburger for every reader.

Box 3 contains details about a competition. This is about a scratchcard found in the newspaper which is linked with Coronation Street. There is a picture of a young attractive girl holding the card.

Box 4 contains the headline for a hard news story about a van driver stabbed to death by another motorist on the motorway. The article starts in Box 8 and uses the following emotive words and phrases:

'Road rage nut knifes man to death on M25' (headline)

'stabbed to death'

'he was left dying with his teenage sweetheart trying to stem blood from his wounds'

'massive hunt for the killer'

'shocking and tragic incident'

Box 5 contains the photo, and Box 6 contains the story about a football star's affair with an MP's daughter. A **strap** over the headline proclaims: 'EXCLUSIVE'. The headline itself says: 'England ace Robbie and the MP's girl'. The use of the player's Christian name suggests that he is a bit of a lad. The fact that the girl is the daughter of an MP adds the necessary bit of scandal.

Box 5 is a picture of the head and upper body of a smiling girl, leaning forward to reveal her cleavage. The caption states: 'Red-hot ... Amy romped with Liverpool striker'. Here the headline is reversed – the girl is named, Robbie is identified as a Liverpool striker. The word 'romp' suggests fun and naughtiness.

There is a much smaller photograph of the footballer. This has the caption: 'Robbie ... scored twice'. This has the double meaning of football (he scored two goals earlier that day) and sex (the girl had her friend with her).

This is the type of story that The Sun loves to have on its front page. It has all the right ingredients: a sports personality having sex with not just one but two attractive young girls. There is a suggestion that the Establishment is being made fun of, as the father of one of the girls is an MP.

Box 7 contains a photo of the 'horror scene' for the main road rage story.

Box 8 contains the text for the main story, which is continued on page 11.

Case study: The Guardian

The Guardian is a broadsheet national daily newspaper. The term 'broadsheet' refers to its dimensions, which in itself differentiates it from the tabloids. But the term also signifies that it is not just different in size but in the nature of its contents, which have little to do with the titillating entertainment offered, for example, by The Sun. Instead it is concerned with the serious business of in-depth news coverage and analysis. The Guardian would, however, argue that first, there is a lot more within its contents than 'just' news, and secondly, who said news coverage had to be boring?

The paper was founded in Manchester in 1821 in the aftermath of the Peterloo massacre. This took place when a peaceful rally demanding the right to vote was savagely attacked by mounted troops. The result was 11 people dead and hundreds injured. The spark of outrage moved one man, John Edward Taylor, to find a 'voice' that would speak out against injustice.

Out of this radical tradition the Manchester Guardian, as it was then called, was born, and it has maintained its independence to this day. Over the past hundred years it has stood out against British involvement in the Sudan and the Boer War, supported home rule for Ireland, and a Jewish state in Palestine, vigorously criticised Hitler's rise to power and opposed the Suez operation.

The Guardian is unique in that it is not owned by any individual or commercial organisation. Instead, the Scott Trust, named after C.P. Scott, the editor from 1872 to 1929 who left his fortune in trust to the paper, has meant that it has been able to maintain its editorial independence whilst withstanding takeover and closure. The Scott Trust was established to ensure the editorial independence of the newspaper, whose main purpose is not to maximise profits for investors (there aren't any) like other newspapers, but to continue to exist as a unique, independent voice. To help do this the paper has brought out a whole range of other products, including the excellent yearly *Media Guide*. It now also owns 15 per cent of GMTV. The Guardian Media Group also publishes *The Observer* and about 50 local papers and some magazines.

Although it started as a regional paper *The Guardian* quickly built up a national reputation. In order to establish this firmly it dropped the word 'Manchester' from its title in 1959, and in 1961 it moved its main operations to London, although it still also prints in Manchester.

In 1988 *The Guardian* was redesigned with new typeface and masthead. It now consists of two parts, the main newspaper and G2 – which is in tabloid format and

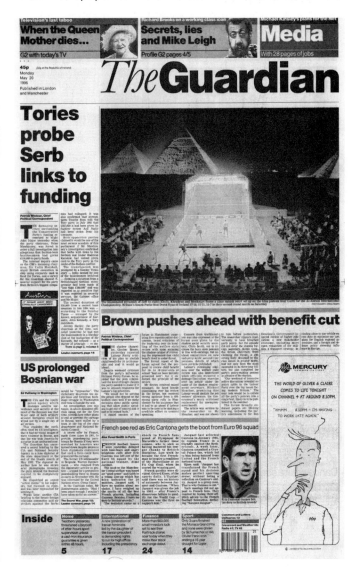

Figure 3.25 A *Guardian* front page

covers a specialist area each day. This market segmentation (see Unit 7) means that *The Guardian* can target its readers more specifically. For example, Monday's G2 is the *Media Guardian* with regular features on the media plus an average of 28 pages of jobs in media, sales and marketing. Its aim is to be the number one newspaper on Mondays for people interested in the media. G2 will also contain more general features on social or cultural themes.

G2 on Tuesdays is *Education Guardian*. Again there is detailed coverage of education issues and the same level of advertisements for jobs in this area. In addition, the paper produces learning resources, covering scientific, humanities or other educational topics which can be used in school or college projects.

We will now analyse the layout and content of *The Guardian's* front page for 20 May 1996, which can be considered a typical edition.

1   The top of the page consists of three 'boosts' in separate boxes, highlighting three items of content of the G2 section.

2   Below the boosts come the **masthead** with the price, date and where published.

3   Underneath this, and occupying 25 per cent of the page, is a typical *Guardian* photo story. *Guardian* front page photographs are often large and in colour and aim to appeal to the eye and the intellect. The story itself can be quite light-hearted but will still not seek to sensationalise or titillate. The photography aims to be interesting and thought-provoking without being over-sensational.

This picture shows a scene taken at night in the Egyptian desert. Within a circle of light is a glass box containing a full-sized squash court with a game in action inside. Outside of this spectacle is the semi-lit audience who frame the event, with a backdrop of the pyramids illuminated and with the lights of Cairo twinkling in the distance. The report of the Al-Ahram International Championship is contained solely within the **caption**.

4   The **banner** (main headline) announces 'Tories probe Serb links to funding'. It links allegations that money has been paid to the Conservatives by Serbs with previous scandals over the years, concerning the funding of the Conservative Party from dubious sources. This serious news item occupies approximately 15 per cent of the front page and then has a **turn line** to lead the reader to the continuation of the story on page two. Underneath the turn line is the line 'leader comment, p. 14' which indicates that, in terms of the public interest, the report is sufficiently serious to warrant the editor's comments.

Built into the story is a small cartoon which makes a 'serious joke' about the scandal, suggesting that the Serb money should have been 'ethnically laundered'.

5   Underneath the main story is another, related, article of approximately the same size revealing secret information about how the Americans deliberately prolonged the Bosnian war. This also has a turn line for readers to go to page 12 for more, and also a further leader comment on page 14.

6   The next story is a detailed account of the Shadow Chancellor's plans to abolish child benefit for 16–18 year olds.

Examples of the vocabulary used in this story which we would be unlikely to find in a tabloid are:

'closed session of the forum'
'endorsed the principle of the review'
'traditionalists'
'industry-wide second-tier pensions'
'inadvertently'
'stakeholder economy'
'regulation of the utilities'.

7   Underneath this is the story of the angry reaction of French football fans after Eric Cantona was left out of their national squad. The article contains a colour photo of the French hero.

8   This is an advert. The space it occupies is known as a **front page solus**.

9   Further 'boosts' under the heading 'Inside' inform the reader of articles to be found inside the paper.

Activity

What are the differences between the two papers in terms of layout and content? You should look at the type of story covered, the amount written and the vocabulary used.

Now carry out the following task: choose different examples of a tabloid and a broadsheet newspaper from those described in the case studies. Trace their history and any changes in ownership. Compare their contents and their choice of main news stories and how they treat similar topics. Compare layout. Discuss their target audience and what effect the difference in price between them might have. Make a comparison of the advertising carried in the two papers.

Magazines

Formal characteristics

What are the characteristics of a magazine?

Figure 3.26 Specialist magazines come in many different styles

- It should contain a number of different articles by different authors.
- It is produced periodically, usually weekly, fortnightly, monthly or quarterly.
- It can be bought over the counter or posted to subscribers.
- Its size is typically 21cm x 29.7cm (A4).
- It usually has a glossy, coloured cover.
- The main content of the front cover is artwork or a photograph of a person or item connected with the subject that the magazine covers.

Some magazines are general, covering lots of topics, whilst others are devoted to a particular subject. The content consists of text, pictures and advertisements. Text can include:

- a list of contents
- an editorial comment
- feature articles
- letters to the editor
- a problem page
- competitions
- special offers
- fictional stories
- advice columns.

The text style can range from the academic (*New Scientist*) to the less formal (*Leicestershire Now*).

A few years ago the inhabitants of Houghton-on-the Hill had a "scare". A proposal for an extensive development on nearby green-belt land, an area of rich meadows down on to which villagers looked directly, sounded alarm bells in the neighbourhood.

"Not in my back yard", I hear someone murmur. Yet since Houghton had just absorbed a fourfold increase in population within a comparatively short time, villagers felt that they had already "done their bit" in that direction. So, despite the popularity of sport in this "out and about" place, even the inclusion of a high-grade golf course in the proposals was not welcomed with any great enthusiasm. Visions of yet more roads and car parks loomed.

Figure 3.27 An excerpt from *Leicestershire Now*

TWICE in 20th century physics, the notion of unpredictability has shaken scientists' view of the Universe. The first time was the development of quantum mechanics, the theory that describes the behaviour of matter on an atomic scale. The second came with the classical phenomenon of chaos. In both areas unpredictable features changed scientists' understanding of matter in ways that were totally unforeseen.

How ironic then, that these two fields, which have something so fundamental in common, should end up as antagonists when combined. For by rights, chaos should not exist at all in quantum systems – the laws of quantum mechanics actually forbid it. Yet recent experiments seem to show the footprints of quantum chaos in remarkable swirling patterns of atomic disorder. These intriguing patterns could illuminate one of the darkest corners of modern physics: the twilight zone where the quantum and classical worlds meet.

Figure 3.28 An excerpt from *New Scientist*

Many of our gardens begin to deteriorate once August is nearing its end, or at least they would without bedding plants, so take a few minutes to look at the garden and plan how this can be avoided next year. Look at gaps in borders where there are dull shrubs, and think what would look good there.

READERS' TOP TIPS...

Each of this month's tips wins a pair of Standard Garden Shears. Your tips for better gardening are always welcome – send us a colour slide or print if you can!

Where to grow

As a group, they are accommodating plants which are not fussy about soil. Lime does not bother them, and most will tolerate heavy soils, especially the larger kinds, but it is best to add some grit if you have very heavy clay. Waterlogged gardens are not ideal for growing alliums, and they nearly all must have full sun.

How tall do they grow?

Because the leaves are at the base of the plants, alliums do not take up much room, but they can provide short-term extra height. The smaller sorts only reach 6in (15cm) but *Allium giganteum* can reach over 3ft (1m) with most of the taller species staying at about that height.

Instant impact

If you need to smarten up your borders quickly, there are plants in garden centres in flower now that will give them a late lift as we head into autumn:

■ Look out for the Yoder or 'cushion' chrysanthemums in full flower. These are hardy and don't normally need winter protection staying naturally dwarf in the garden.

■ Buy a pot or two of lilies (choose those in bud if you can) and plant in the bed, remembering that next year they will behave according to their natural cycle and flower earlier.

■ Fork over the soil and plant winter flowering pansies, or treat yourself to that shrub you have always wanted.

Figure 3.29 Examples of some of the typographical features you will see in magazines: drop letters, reverse-outs, cross-heads and bullets

The typeface will be chosen for both technical and artistic reasons. Some typefaces are more suited to certain types of paper and type sizes. The typeface will also carry a connotation regarding the image of the magazine.

Large drop letters, small boxes, or 'bullets', the use of 'reverse out' i.e. white on black, cross-heads and so on all visually enhance a magazine and give a certain image.

Pictures have always been an important part of a magazine's structure. Even before the invention of half-tone blocks, images were produced on the page using line drawings, engravings and woodcuts. Readers expect magazines to be illustrated with graphical material and for many, particularly the 'populars', it is the photographs that are the primary content. Even in the more serious journals, pictures are used to break up the text and make it more interesting for the reader. Pictures tend to be more of a feature in magazines than in newspapers and are usually better composed. The paper quality is generally better and the pictures tend to match this standard.

Thematic concerns, functions and development

The term 'magazine' was used for the first time in 1731 in the title *Gentleman's Magazine,* which described a periodical that drew its material from many sources. There were magazines before this, some of which were just single sheets with general knowledge, and discussions about history, philosophy and so on. In 1693 the *Ladies' Mercury* was founded. This contained many of the elements to be found in some women's magazines today. Its target audience were 'virgins, wives, and widows' and there was advice and comment on love, dress, adultery and pre-marital sex! The invention of half-tone blocks (see Chapter 9) made the reproduction of photographs possible. Magazines such as *Art Union* and *English Illustrated Post* (1884) were started.

Magazines had a general content in the eighteenth century and some, like the *Gentleman's Magazine,* were **digests** of material from other publications, although it did eventually start having original contributions. During the eighteenth and nineteenth centuries, magazines became more political in content, particularly as the law regarding sedition was somewhat relaxed. The *Edinburgh Review,* the *Quarterly Review* and *The Spectator* are all prominent examples of magazines that carried political and social comment.

The first mass-circulation women's magazine, *The Englishwomen's Domestic Magazine,* was established in 1852. Its contents included fashion, cookery and a problem page, along with dressmaking patterns and prize-winning competitions. Other magazines which are still popular today were *Good Housekeeping* and *Vogue,* both established in 1867.

Gradually magazines became increasingly specialised and many professional journals were started, such as *The Lancet, The Economist,* and *Nature.* These are still published today.

To be successful, magazines have always had to adapt to new readers and new technology (see Unit 7 for re-positioning of products). Advertising developed in the nineteenth century and so did sales, as leisure time, literacy, population and spending power all increased. Popular styles of journalism, suited to quick reads whilst travelling to and from work, were very much in demand. *Titbits* (1881) was the first magazine to sell a million copies with its human-interest stories, and prize competitions.

Life (USA 1936) and *Picture Post* (1938) came about as the result of further advances in photography, such as the development of the 35mm camera. More women's magazines came on the market, and these were followed in the 1950s by teenage magazines such as *Marilyn, Valentine* and *Boyfriend,* which contained picture-strip romantic stories. There were also gossip magazines like *Confidential* and *People Weekly.*

The *Which?* series of magazines started in 1957, providing consumers with independent reports, and

Figure 3.30 The *Radio Times* contains much more than just BBC listings

Radio Times/Nicky Johnston

then the early 1960s saw *The Sunday Times* start the era of newspaper colour supplements. These were devised to attract colour advertising. In the 1980s magazines became more international, with the French *Elle, Prima* and *Best* published in Anglicised versions.

The themes of specialist magazines are many and varied. Depending on the magazine, these themes often address the values and lifestyles (actual or aspired to) of its readership. There are now numerous specialist magazines catering for hobbies and interests as diverse as motorcycling, gardening, computing, photography, knitting, horse riding and DIY. In addition there are the limited-circulation titles which are bought by subscription only or, because of the advertising they contain, are used as giveaways to certain groups, such as *Girl about Town* which is targeted at 17–34-year-old women and handed out at stations or on the street.

Specialist magazines, like all genres, change over time. For example, the *Radio Times* has changed from listing just BBC radio schedules to including all public service and independent broadcasting, including terrestrial, satellite and cable television. It now also contains reviews, articles about the stars and problem pages.

Specialist magazines are produced to satisfy a niche market; whether they are for keen gardeners or photographers, for doctors or computer users, the aim for the publisher is to identify markets and to fill them. The marketplace has become increasingly segmented and so there is more and more emphasis placed on specialist publications. Magazines are continually closing and there is competition from other media, particularly television. However, publishers still launch new titles all the time, particularly in niche markets.

Desktop publishing has been instrumental in the proliferation of the magazine. It is now much cheaper to produce titles, and many more have appeared to cater for niche markets. The improvements in design and print technology, and their increased accessibility to non-specialist and home users, have meant that it has become much easier to produce professional print products and to target them precisely.

The Henley Centre, which does a lot of research into media consumption, has predicted that magazines will grow in importance and influence in the next century, despite the growth of electronic information services. People will use magazines to create an identity for themselves. They will identify with the target audiences that individual magazines address. Magazines will continue to cater for increased leisure activities and for growing sub-groups, such as the elderly, in society.

Case study: *Gardening Which?*

The magazine *Gardening Which?* is published by the Consumers' Association, who also produce *Which?* magazine. It is an independent monthly consumer magazine available only on subscription. This publisher is a subsidiary of the Association for Consumer Research, a registered charity which is a campaigning body for consumer rights. They state that *Gardening Which?* is committed to independent research and empowering consumers to garden more efficiently, safely, enjoyably and creatively. This independent research is funded by the sale of the magazines.

Figure 3.31 A front cover of *Gardening Which?* magazine

© Consumers' Association

The target audience for this magazine consists of men and women of middle age or over, who already have considerable experience in gardening. It is available only on subscription at a cost of £47 for ten issues per year. The main noticeable difference between this and other gardening magazines is that there are no adverts, so the main source of revenue for the magazine is the subscriptions. This type of magazine is designed to be collected together and stored, with an index, in a file at the end of the year.

The front cover is less thick and glossy than other magazines. Some gardening magazines give away free gifts, such as seeds or plant markers. Occasionally *Gardening Which?* does offer free seeds but they will also enclose a questionnaire, so that readers can report on how well the plants grew. This particular issue gave away a free wallchart on butterflies.

Figure 3.32 A front cover of *Garden Answers* magazine

As one would expect from a gardening magazine, there are lots of coloured photographs. These tend to be small, with several separate photographs covering a double-page spread. Tables are frequently used to give statistics on the success rate of plants or the capabilities of garden machinery.

Now compare this specialist magazine with the one below.

Case study: *Land Rover Owner International*

Land Rover Owner International is published by EMAP National Publications, which publishes 90 British magazines. There are 13 issues of the magazine per year and an annual subscription costs £36.40, although it can be bought from a newsagent for £2.80 per issue.

The 1996 figures from the Audit Bureau of Circulations show that 60,751 copies are sold each month, 52,000 in

Figure 3.33 A cover of *Land Rover Owner International*

The nature of this magazine is like that of a reference work. This is accentuated by the way the feature articles are listed and their page numbers given on the front cover. The use of photographs with no human figures is another clue to this more 'academic' approach. Compare the cover with that of *Garden Answers* (see Figure 3.32).

Inside *Gardening Which?* there are 184 pages packed with text and coloured images. It contains:

- features on how to grow or take care of plants
- details of gardening events around the country
- reviews of tests on garden machinery and plant trials
- problems page, for example: 'My spinach was ruined by brown spots last year'.

The feature articles are factual rather than emotive or anecdotal. They are concerned with objectively assessing the plant or gardening products in terms of efficiency and cost effectiveness.

the UK and the rest abroad. There are 10,000 purchased on subscription, so the majority are sold over the counter.

Car magazines are a bestseller in the world of periodicals. This particular magazine is aimed at a **niche** market. The typical reader of this magazine would be aged between 25 and 50, a male owner of a four-wheel drive vehicle, probably a Land Rover and almost certainly not new! He knows how to service his vehicle and drive it, preferably over rough terrain. This magazine is not aimed at the family who buy an expensive new Range Rover to drive around town to do the shopping. 'Land Rover man' is looking for excitement; he aspires to go on overseas expeditions; he likes to get his hands dirty; he likes the feeling of belonging to an elite club of specialists who talk his language and share his obsession.

What catches the eye on the glossy front cover is not the vehicle itself but the headings:

■ Land Rover (in bright yellow in the original)
■ the caption: 'No.1 4×4 magazine, original and best'
■ 'It's Torture! Surviving Europe's toughest off-road adventure' promises a glimpse into a more exciting world.

The vehicle pictured is covered in mud. This image has an open **narrative**: who has been driving it, where has it been, what is it winching up?

Having appealed to the spirit of adventure in its readers, the line at the bottom appeals to their interest in mechanics. The amazing free gift is a DIY guide for when you want to repair, overhaul or restore your vehicle!

This publication has 210 pages. There is an index. There are articles about drivers and their work in the countryside, vehicle conversions, etc. One typical feature is about the selection of motorists for the Camel Trophy rally. The pictures show young men covered in mud, physically exerting themselves as they prepare for the selection process. There is also a three-page photo-story about a Land Rover expedition. Many of the expeditions take place in exotic locations.

There are also competitions and offers, for example 'Driver of the Year' and an offer for some tools at a bargain price to readers. Then there are the regular features which include:

■ a comment from the editor leaning on his Land Rover
■ news of recent events such as rallies, talks, tests
■ readers' Rovers: pictures of readers with their cars
■ letters
■ a cartoon strip called 'Dipstick'
■ club news.

Unlike *Gardening Which?* there are lots of adverts to finance this magazine:

■ 30 full-page advertisements
■ 11 double-page advertisements
■ 9 pages with two advertisements
■ 2 pages with three or four adverts
■ 10 pages of classified adverts.

These adverts are predominantly 'old-fashioned', in that they list what is for sale and the price of each item and its capabilities. Here there are no evocative, emotional images to arouse interest. If a cylinder head is for sale, that is what the photograph shows; there are no scantily clad females here, draping themselves over a car bonnet! These ads do not offer a 'lifestyle'. The only advert not for car-parts or services is one for adventure clothing.

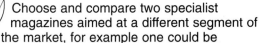

Activity

Choose and compare two specialist magazines aimed at a different segment of the market, for example one could be targeted at men and the other at women, or one at young people and the other at an older age group; alternatively one might be more up-market than the other. Find out who publishes them, their price and frequency of publication. Compare their content, layout and aesthetic qualities.

Evidence assignment

1 Find as many examples as you can of each of the genres listed in the worksheet on the next page. You can devise your own system of recording this information or you can use a copy of the worksheet, shown with some examples.

2 Choose one example of a genre from each of the media forms and produce a report describing its **characteristics.**

■ For film and television these are: sound, lighting, camera work, *mise-en-scène* and narrative structure.
■ For radio these are: speech, music and effects.
■ For print these are: writing, typography, photography and graphics.

In the report, you should describe how the genre has developed. You should identify the target audience, the purpose of the product and whether the popularity of this particular genre is growing or declining. Discuss whether the product reflects current social trends or political ideologies. Does it question human nature?

Media form	Genre	Name of product	Date or frequency of production	Producer/Owner	Where found
Film or television	Science fiction Film noir Documentary	Alien 3	1992	20th Century Fox	Video shops
Radio	Drama Current affairs Pop music	'Waiting around'	Sat 12 May 96 14.30-16.00	J. Edgar	Radio 4
Print	Tabloid Broadsheet Specialist magazines	Sun	Daily	News International	Newsagents, supermarkets, garages

Does it want the audience to reflect on the human condition and our own status?

This work may take the form of a written report produced by an individual student, or a video report produced by a team. If a video is produced, it should be accompanied by a production log identifying the work done by individuals.

Chapter 4

Investigate narrative structures

Investigating the content of media products

A *narrative* is defined in the *Oxford English Dictionary* as 'the spoken or written recital of connected events'. However, the narrative structure of any media text is more than the plot or story, delivered to an audience through the medium of sound, vision or print. It includes also the mechanisms or techniques used to deliver the story or plot. It is also concerned with how audiences *decode* or interpret the narrative.

All media products, even simple pictures, have a narrative, sometimes short, as in an advert, sometimes long, as in a film. They may be simple, as those used in a short story for children, or they may be complex, as those found in a pop video. Narrative structures belong to both fictional and non-fictional texts, to both comedy shows and TV news. Whether texts are print-based, including words and pictures, or time-based, such as radio, TV and film products, fictional or non-fictional, they may share the same type of narrative structure.

A novel is generally considered to be a narrative constructed by one person, the author. However, the narrative of most media products is a collective authorship because, as we shall see, the narrative consists of a number of parts or components. For example in a film, the scriptwriter, camera operator, costume maker, all contribute to the narrative. In fact the novel, too, has other people who can contribute to the narrative, such as the editor or the sleeve designer.

Narrative structures in media texts

Open and closed narrative structures

All media products must be either one or the other, i.e. open or closed. A story that has a definite ending, that seems complete, can be described as **closed**. A fairytale that ends with the words '... and they all lived happily ever after' has a closed structure. When the viewer, reader or listener is left to wonder what happens next, the product's narrative can be described as **open**. The TV adventure programme that ends with a voice saying, '... to be continued next week' has an open structure.

Case study

Figures 4.1 and 4.2 show two cartoon strips for children. Study their narrative structures. The first has a closed structure and the second an open structure. The closed structure will satisfy young readers, but the open one will make them want to buy the magazine again next week.

Figure 4.1 A *Spiderman* comic strip with an open structure

Figure 4.2 A cartoon strip from *The Beano* with a closed structure

© D.C. Thomson & Co. Ltd

THIS IS MY NEW SEXY BLACK DRESS. HOW DO I STOP IT GOING PREMATURELY GREY?

You're obviously no stranger to that washed out look. But it's a problem you don't need to have. Just call the Persil Careline and we'll tell you to always turn your dress inside out then wash it in Persil Colour. It's specially formulated to help prevent colours fading. In fact, the dress will probably grow old before the colour does.

We want you to get the best results from your wash. And for special fabrics you will need special care. So if you have any questions or comments, please call us FREE Monday to Friday 9am to 5pm on the Persil Careline. We're always here to help you.

The Persil Careline. All you have to do is ask.

If you need any washing advice, or have any comments or suggestions, simply phone the Persil Careline FREE Monday to Friday 9am to 5pm.

PERSIL CARELINE

RING 0 8 0 0 7 7 6 6 4 4
NORTHERN IRELAND - 0800 834484 · REPUBLIC OF IRELAND - 1 - 900 44555

Figure 4.3 Even advertisements tell a story

Activity

Design two cartoon strips, one with a closed and one with an open narrative.

A soap such as *EastEnders* or *Neighbours* is an obvious example of an open narrative. Some situation or event is left unresolved at the end of the programme so that viewers have to switch on for the next episode to find out what happens. The trailer for a film also always has an open structure. We are shown lots of action from the film itself, we gain an impression of what the story will be about, but we are not told the ending!

Even still images can contain a narrative. There is a saying that 'every picture tells a story'. Adverts such as the one in Figure 4.3 encourage us to think not only about what we see in the picture but also what happened before to create this situation and what is going to happen afterwards.

Sometimes, however, it is not quite so clear whether a narrative is open or closed. Are most horror films open or closed? At the end of a vampire film we are usually satisfied that evil has been defeated, but at the same time we know that Dracula will rise again. The first *Star Wars* film (1977) seemed complete in itself: Luke Skywalker triumphantly survived the forces of evil to be reunited with the Princess Leia and Han Solo, and audiences left the cinemas contented. But the story did not end there – two more films, *The Empire Strikes Back* and *Return of the Jedi*, completed the trilogy There is no sequel (as yet!) to *Silence of the Lambs*; this thriller ends satisfactorily with the release of the kidnapped girl. The mystery is solved but the escape of the psychopath Hannibal Lecter at the end leaves the audience with the feeling that new murders could occur.

A news report can sometimes appear complete, i.e. to have a closed structure. Perhaps after a series of stories about a civil war, a peace treaty is signed but then, a few days later, violence breaks out again. Look at the reports in Figures 4.4 and 4.5 for an example of the way news stories develop over time.

Consider the difference between a **series** and a **serial**. A series can use the same characters week after week, but each episode has a closed structure. On the other hand, a serial usually has a limited number of storylines which do not come to an end at the close of each episode.

Below are listed some closed and open narrative structures in fiction (imaginary events and people) and non-fiction (the portrayal of real events and people):

Open structure: fiction

These include:

- **on TV and radio**: any episode, except the last, of a serialised drama
- **on TV and radio**: any episode of a soap, except the very last!
- **in magazines**: any chapter, except the last, of a serialised book or story
- **in newspapers, comics and magazines**: cartoon strips whose story is to be continued; horoscopes
- **in films**: which leave the viewer feeling that the

Clinton aide feared dead in plan crash

Visit to US troops ends in disaster in a heavy storm near Dubrovnik

**Julian Broder in Zagreb
and Ian Katz in New York**

RON BROWN, the United States commerce secretary, a key pillar of President Clinton's administration, was missing presumed dead last night after his plan crashed in a heavy storm over the Balkans.

An unnamed US general was with Mr Brown on the flight from a US military base in Tuzla, northern Bosnia, to the coastal city of Dubrovnik.

Mr Brown, aged 45, had been visiting American troops with a delegation of government officials and US businessmen.

He grew up in Harlem, where his father ran a hotel, and became one of the more powerful figures in Washington. He was one of Washington's leading lobbyists, often drawing attention because of controversial clients, including former Haitian dictator Jean-Claude "Baby Doc" Duvalier.

Mr Brown, former chairman of the Democratic National Committee, was the first black to lead either major political party.

Reverend Jesse Jackson,

one of his closest friends, said last night: "Ron has been a faithful public servant and if the worst scenario materialises, he was in his full stride, travelling across the world connecting people."

Mr Brown's T43, a military version of the Boeing 737, vanished from Croatian radar screens a few minutes before 3pm in heavy rain and high winds.

There were some reports of wreckage being spotted in the Adriatic sea, but Dr Mladen Miovic, at Dubrovnik's main hospital said: "The latest reports we are getting is that the plane crashed in the hills north of the airport."

President Franjo Tudjman

of Croatia said the plan had crashed "10 miles southeast of Dubrovnik on the Hill of St John".

Local officials said Croatian rescue teams had found the bodies of three men and a woman near the wreckage.

Dr Miovic said the hospital had been put on alert to care for survivors, but none had arrived. US, Croatian and French planes and helicopters were searching the coastline and the sea near the airport at Cilipi, 10 miles south east of Dubrovnik.

Journalists waiting for the delegation at the airport were escorted back to town. "It was very windy, and there was a lot of rain", said

Adrijana Tomasic, from Dubrovnik Radio. "We were told the plane had not arrived but we have been given no more information."

It was raining heavily yesterday afternoon. All Croatian Airlines flights to Dubrovnik were re-routed to the Adriatic port of Split, 120 miles to the north.

Mr Brown had been due to meet local officials to discuss the potential for US investment in Dubrovnik's tourist industry, struggling to recover from the Croatian war of 1991, when the city's medieval port was damaged by Serb shelling.

'Super-salesman' from Harlem, page 12.

Figure 4.4 A report in *The Guardian* of 4 April 1996

situation could go on, or characters be used again
- **in film trailers:** these are never closed!
- **in adverts:** some of the TV ads are constructed like soaps, but even a single picture ad can tell a story.

Open structure: non-fiction

These can be:

- **on TV and radio:** news stories that are incomplete, for example, reports about a war or the first stages in a disaster; sports programmes covering events, such as the Olympics, that will not end for a few weeks; crime programmes that ask for information from viewers
- **in newspapers and magazines:** a series of articles about cookery or finance that will appear in several editions; chapters, except the last, of serialised memoirs or a diary.

Closed structure: fiction

These include:

- **on TV and radio:** the episodes in a series, this could be a crime detective story, an action series, a sit-com, etc. The final episode of any serialisation usually makes the whole programme closed
- **in newspapers and magazines:** short stories; single picture cartoons, especially political ones

- **in films:** those that are unlikely to get a sequel, such as a fairytale or a romance.

Closed structure: non-fiction

These might be:

- **on TV and radio:** some documentaries, particularly those about events in the past or individual people; a magazine programme; a variety show; a single sports programme, for example on the Grand National
- **in newspapers and magazines:** feature articles; some news stories, such as exam results; obituaries; instructional articles, like knitting patterns or recipes
- **in films:** those based on real events, such as the Battle of Britain, or on the life story of a person
- **in adverts:** the more factual ones which do not attempt to create a lifestyle.

Activity

Find examples for each of the above categories. Compare your answers with those of a colleague. Are there any that you disagree about? The most controversial will probably be films and documentaries. Can you add to the above list? Where would you put something like the weather report?

14 | INTERNATIONAL NEWS

Lack of black box hinders crash inquiry as bodies are recovered

US counts cost of fatal Bosnian trade mission

Julian Broder in Zagreb and Mark Tran in New York

IN HIGH winds and driving rain, the bodies of the United States commerce secretary, Ron Brown, and at least 32 of his entourage were brought off a rugged, mine-strewn Croatian hillside yesterday as investigators tried to discover exactly why their aircraft crashed moments before landing in Dubrovnik on Wednesday.

A temporary morgue was set up in Dubrovnik airport where Croatian and US pathologists were expected to identify the remains. President Bill Clinton telephoned Mr Brown's widow yesterday morning to inform her his body had been identified.

President Clinton ordered flags to be flown at half mast in Washington, and the New York Stock Exchange observed a moment of silence.

The victims included 13 American businessmen, 12 US government officials, an American journalist, and two Croatians – a photographer and an interpreter.

There was uncertainty whether 33 or 35 passengers and crew had been on the aircraft when it crashed.

It was still unclear yesterday why the T43 – the military version of the Boeing 737 – slammed into a hillside on Wednesday afternoon on its approach to the airport. The 23-year-old aircraft was not carrying a "black box" voice and flight data recording system.

Miomir Žuzul, the Croatian ambassador to Washington, said the plane first hit the mountain with its right wing, then its right engine, followed by the fuselage.

A local villager, Ivo Djuricic, the first person to see the wreckage, said he heard a scraping sound just before the crash.

Dubrovnik residents said Wednesday's storms were the worst for decades. Attention also focused on Dubrovnik's airport, whose instrument landing system was destroyed in fighting over four years ago.

Aviation sources at the airport and US Air Force officers denied that the lack of sophisticated landing equipment caused the crash.

"Many aircraft have landed at the airport here at Dubrovnik with no difficulty. If we thought it wasn't a safe approach we wouldn't allow our aircraft to use it," said Lieutenant-General Howell Estes, from the Pentagon.

It is possible the pilot tried to abort his landing at the last moment. Instead of turning west towards the runway, he appeared to have veered east into a 2,300-foot hillside. A US joint military and civil team was dispatched to Dubrovnik yesterday to investigate.

The high-profile Balkans trip led by Mr Brown was part of the multi-national effort involving the World Bank and the private sector to attract business and investment to Bosnia and Croatia. Mr Brown said his job was to help US companies capture a share of the $5.1 billion (£3.4 billion) in estimated aid that international financial institutions and governments are putting together to help the region.

The deaths of the senior executives on the plane have cut a swathe through a range of American companies, not just in construction, but also technology and banking. Many were the chairmen and chief execu-

tive officers.

A number of the executives, were infrastructure experts. Leonard Pieroni was chairman and CEO of Parsons, based in Pasadena, California, the USA's fourth largest construction company.

Another well-known engineering company that lost its top man was Foster Wheeler Energy from New Jersey: its chairman Robert Whittaker went down. Chairman John Scoville of the Chicago-based Harza Engineering was travelling with Mr Brown to discuss rebuilding dams and other water resources.

The telephone giant AT&T was represented by the Senior vice-president Walter Murphy, the company's top expert on global operations and telecommunications.

Chairman Claudo Elia of Air & Water Technologies was an expert in environmental cleanup and anti-pollution work. A top banker was on the plane, Paul Cushman, chairman of the Washington-based Riggs International Banking.

Obituary, page 17

Figure 4.5 *The Guardian*'s follow-up report of 5 April 1996

Single-strand and multi-strand narrative structures

In single-strand structures, there is one storyline or plot. For example, in a simple story, the reader, listener or viewer follows the actions of the hero or heroine. Other characters are usually minor, and what happens to them does not distract our attention from the central character. An example is shown in Figure 4.6.

In a multi-strand structure, there is more than one story unfolding and several contrasting characters are of equal importance. Either type of story may also have an open or closed structure.

Look at the newspaper report in Figure 4.7.

This is a single-strand narrative. However, the newspaper column in which it appears (see Figure 4.8) follows many different stories from around the country, so the product itself is multi-strand.

Activity

Find a magazine short story which has a closed, single-strand structure. Now list features that would make the product multi-strand and with open narratives.

The Robin family

A froggy day

The Woodlanders go exploring

For several days a soft grey mist had been hanging over the Woodlands, trying to get into the cosy houses. The older Woodlanders found it tiresome, but the young ones thought making their way in the mist was fun.

"Your know," said Roley Robin to Rosemary, his sister, and Richard, his cousin, "I think it's a bit like being an explorer." His friends, Sam Sparrow and Morris Mouse agreed, but Mr Rabbit, Miss Olivia Owl's gardener, hearing them, shook his head.

"The trouble with this sort of ol' mist," he said, "is that it's often followed by FROG – and we don't want that!"

The little Woodlanders were very puzzled.

FROG? Why didn't Mr Rabbit want their friends Flossie and Freddie?

Mr Rabbit realised what they were thinking and chuckled. "Bless my soul. I'm not talkin' about young Flossie or Freddie but FROG, when it's frosty and foggy at the same time."

And he was right. FROG did arrive and very horrid it was, too. Jack Daw, Blakeney Blackbird and Wilberforce Weasel hung lamps in the trees to guide those who had to go out. At the Woodlands School, Miss Olivia Owl sent her pupils home early, with Police Sergeant Serena Hare and PC Bullfinch to guide them. Even Roley Robin decided that being an explorer when it was FROGGY was not fun, and was really happy to get back to Tree Stump House in time for tea!

Figure 4.6 A magazine story with a single-strand structure

A TV or radio soap such as *Coronation Street* or *The Archers* is perhaps the most obvious example of a multi-strand product. Each episode tells part of the story about certain characters. In some episodes, a certain storyline is completed and others are left to carry on next week.

Case study: *Home and Away*

Choose a different soap and analyse the stories in the same way as in the Case Study on the next page.

Princess Di out of the picture

OXFORD: Royalist Sioux Dellow had to cut Princess Diana off a string of bunting for Prince Charles's visit to Oxford.

Miss Dellow (39), of Oxford, bought the bunting, featuring pictures of the Prince and Princess, to celebrate the Royal Wedding in 1981. To mark the Prince's visit she put up the bunting outside her house – after removing the pictures of Diana.

Figure 4.7 A single-strand news report

NEWS DIGEST

Princess Di out of the picture
OXFORD: Royalist Sioux Dellow had to cut Princess Diana off a string of bunting for Prince Charles's visit to Oxford. Miss Dellow (39), of Oxford, bought the bunting, featuring pictures of the Prince and Princess, to celebrate the Royal Wedding in 1981. To mark the Prince's visit she put up the bunting outside her house – after removing the pictures of Diana.

Man due in court
NORTHAMPTON: A man arrested after a siege at a cathedral was due to appear in court today.
The 39-year-old man was expected to appear before magistrates in Northampton charged with firearms offences, affray, making threats to kill and criminal damage following a siege at the town's cathedral at the weekend.

Union in dispute
PORTSMOUTH: A dispute by Immigration Officials at Portsmouth Docks is set to spread to other British ports and airports. It follows the suspensions of seven union members taking part in a protest over new shift rotas requiring 5am start times. The Immigration Officers' Union warned that the dispute would spread unless the members were reinstated immediately.

Hoaxer goes free
NORTH LONDON: A bomb-hoaxer who threatened to blow up Heathrow Airport had the case against him thrown out by magistrates. Neil Rennie (37), of Brae, Inverness, told a customer service agent at Heathrow Airport's Terminal One in February that he had a bomb. Magistrates in Uxbridge, north London, agreed there was not enough evidence to show Rennie had intended his joke to be taken seriously.

Boost for housing
NATIONWIDE: The Government is to award £30 million to housing projects which boost economic and employment opportunities around Britain. Housing Minister David Curry said 238 schemes in 181 housing authorities would benefit from the money from the Housing Partnership Fund over the next 12 months.

Figure 4.8 A multi-strand news column

Reproduced by permission of *Leicester Mercury*

Thursday March 28
Selina left the commune after Saul claimed he loved her. Ailsa refused to let Kelly stitch an open wound on Duncan's hand. (HIV danger.)

Friday March 29
Chloe saved Curtis from certain death. Ailsa came under fire from local residents, but found her actions defended by Kelly.

Monday April 1
Michael gave Jack and Sally a hard time about their romance. Shane and Angel decided to let Alex move into their spare room.

Tuesday April 2
Jack and Sally caused Michael problems. Marilyn and Sally won the quiz night. A ceremony was held in memory of Selina's child.

Wednesday April 3
Jack and Sally overheard Donald asking Marilyn to a concert. Irene called in the police after Saul took Selina hostage.

Thursday April 4
Alex rescued Selina from Saul's clutches. Jack and Sally struggled to find a place to be alone. Alex told Shannon he loved her.

189
Everything seems to be as you left it. The Karosseans have no interest in this area, and no desire to get any closer to the monsters than they have to! What will you do:

Leave your robot and go to the Administrative Building?	Turn to **85**
Leave your robot and go to the other building?	Turn to **171**
Stay in your robot and cross the electro-fence?	Turn to **129**
Leave the Dinosaur Preserve?	Turn to **150**

190
Test your Luck. If you are Lucky, you can get behind the case and remove the sword without either guard being the wiser. You hide it under your Cloak and leave the Capital Building (turn to **296**). If you are Unlucky, one of the guards notices the sword seemingly hanging in mid-air. Turn to **215** and fight.

191
If you had a robot, lose 1 STAMINA point as you are thrown from the wreckage. If you are still alive, you flee on foot as the Nothosaurus demolishes your robot. If you have not already explored the south of the city, you may do so (turn to **225**). Otherwise, you flee into the jungle (turn to **64**).

Figure 4.9 An example of investigative fiction, from *Robot Commando* by Steve Jackson and Ian Livingstone

Investigative structures

Some narrative structures can take a more random form. For example, reference books such as dictionaries or encyclopedias are never read through from beginning to end. The reader has a specific need, to find out information, and knows roughly where in the book it will be found. Other types of fiction can also be considered investigative. Children reading an adventure novel may come to the end of a page and be told to make a decision as to what the characters will do. Depending on their choice, they turn to a certain page or paragraph and continue with the story. Sometimes they will be moving forwards in the book and sometimes backwards. An example is shown in Figure 4.9.

Computer games also have an investigative structure which can be followed in a similar manner, depending on the dexterity and skills of the player. Interactive media or multi-media products are used in a similar way to the encyclopedia. The user chooses a particular subject to investigate and is led further into the programme by the use of hot spots and hidden pages. Other suggestions or options will be made to the user as progress continues.

Teletext on TV can be considered another form of investigative narrative. The viewer can turn to the index and, for example, choose to look at the day's weather report. When this page appears, the viewer is then invited to look at more detailed information, such as continental weather maps.

What about time-based texts such as film or video? A fly-on-the-wall documentary can be unpredictable in the way the narrative unfolds. In a series such as

Figure 4.10 A strip cartoon is only meaningful in chronological order!

The Living Soap, which followed the lives of a group of students, the weekly narrative was unpredictable because the events in the lives of real people are not predictable. The camera-work and editing can control how events are represented, but cannot control what is happening.

Linear and non-linear structures

A strip cartoon is a good example of a linear structure. To create sense, the pictures are sequenced in a particular order and we follow the action through chronologically.

 Activity

To make the cartoon in Figure 4.10 meaningful, in which order should the pictures appear?

A simple children's story starts at the beginning, progresses through the middle and finishes at the end. However, many narratives are likely to be non-linear. Instead of following this formula:

beginning – middle – end

they may be like this:

middle – beginning – end

or even:

end – beginning – middle – end

Take for example the traditional British detective novel. In a linear structure the story might unfold like this:

1 Several different characters meet over a period of years
2 Some event takes place, such as a fight or a burglary
3 The characters meet up again
4 There is a murder
5 The police are called in
6 A famous detective is called in
7 Suspects are interrogated and the detective detects
8 The detective explains to colleagues how the crime is committed
9 The murderer is confronted and arrested.

This structure is not usually used, because it does not allow for much in the way of dramatic surprise or tease our imagination.

The traditional Agatha Christie style of detective story is more likely to follow this pattern:

1 Several characters who know each other meet up again
2 The famous detective appears
3 A murder is committed
4 The police are called in
5 Suspects are interrogated and the detective detects
6 The past meetings of the characters are shown
7 The important event from the past, the burglary or fight, is shown
8 The murderer is exposed
9 The crime is explained.

Both linear and non-linear structures are used in non-fiction as well as fiction.

Case study

Look at the news report in Figure 4.11. It follows the pattern of end (the current situation), beginning (where did it all start?), middle (reasons for the problem, talks with experts, etc.) and future (predictions of what will happen). Write an analysis of this news report, explaining its use of a non-linear structure. Find other examples of newspaper or magazine articles with linear and non-linear structures.

The hockey doctors retire hurt

A DOCTORS' hockey team was forced to retire injured from a tournament after a pre-match meal turned into a brawl.

One of the doctors had his jaw smashed and another suffered a broken nose when they came under attack at the Kismet Tandoori in Paignton, Devon.

The trouble started after a group at another table challenged the team to toss a coin for the price of their meals.

Other diners fled in panic as glasses, plates of curry, chairs and fists began flying.

The doctors – all members of the Spirochaetes hockey team, based at Guy's Hospital in London – were unable to compete on the last day of the Torbay Easter Hockey Festival, which they have attended for 12 years.

Festival organiser Tony Forward said: 'I understand they were quietly having their meal and were then set upon. The whole team were pretty shocked.'

But he added: 'They aren't one of our strongest sides. I don't think they've won a game.'

Police were last night questioning three women and two men about the incident.

Figure 4.11 A newspaper report with a non-linear structure

Realist and anti-realist structures

What is 'real'? Reality is something that human beings as individuals experience through the senses. Everyday life is 'real' to us: we use our sight, hearing, touch, taste and smell to understand what is going on around us. That familiarity and understanding gives us a sense of reality, but because each human being is an individual, with different experiences and different mental and physical abilities, reality is not necessarily the same thing for two people. If I were to wake up in the morning and find myself in the desert, then I would feel the same sense of unreality as would the desert-living nomad who is suddenly transported to a supermarket. Both places are real, but one situation is outside the experience of either the nomad or me.

Drama, whether on screen or in a book, is considered realistic by many people. The closer it comes to representing the lives and activities of ordinary human beings, the more typical are the locations shown and the more contemporary is the setting.

Activity

Compare two programmes such as *The Bill* and *Star Trek*. Make a list of the real and unreal aspects of both programmes.

Realism with regard to media products can be confusing. There are two aspects to be considered: **form** and **content**.

Images and sound are central to our perception of reality. The more similar they are to things occurring in nature or life generally, the more they are recognised as real. So photography is often described as realistic ('the camera cannot lie') because generally it can duplicate exactly what is seen through the lens. It can show only something that has existed in 'real life'. This ability to resemble things in the real world is called 'iconic'.

Activity

Compare the four images in Figure 4.12 below; two are 'snapshot' photographs and two are paintings. Which do you find most realistic and why?

a

b

c

d

Figure 4.12 Which of these images are realistic?

We would usually consider a photograph to be a more realistic form than a written description, yet in the examples in Figures 4.13 and 4.14 below, which gives most information about the character?

A soap opera series is described as realistic because events happen in time similar to our own. There is no

Figure 4.14 Can a picture paint a thousand words?

Another door opened noiselessly, and Mr Verloc immobilizing his glance in that direction saw at first only black clothes. The bald top of a head, and a drooping dark grey whisker on each side of a pair of wrinkled hands. The person who had entered was holding a batch of papers before his eyes and walked up to the table with a rather mincing step, turning the papers over the while. Privy Councillor Wurmt, Chancelier d'Ambassade, was rather shortsighted. This meritorious official, laying the papers on the table, disclosed a face of pasty complexion and of melancholy ugliness surrounded by a lot of fine, long, dark grey hairs, barred heavily by thick and bushy eyebrows. He put on a black-framed pince-nez upon a blunt and shapeless nose, and seemed struck by Mr Verloc's appearance. Under the enormous eyebrows his weak eyes blinked pathetically through the glasses.

Figure 4.13 A new character is introduced in a novel (from *The Secret Agent* by Joseph Conrad)

awareness of an audience, no clapping or laughter, background music is used seldom and discreetly. Time and events happen at the same speed that they do in real life. However, although described as 'real', the form itself is actually very contrived. Western audiences with decades of cinematic and television experience accept the various codes and conventions as part of our reality. When a film such as *Robin Hood, Prince of Thieves,* uses aerial shots to show battle scenes, we do not think that this is far-fetched or unrealistic; we accept this convention as normal. We do not think the action is unreal simply because we could not see people like this in the Middle Ages.

In Soviet **film montage** of the 1920s and 1930s, ordinary objects were given symbolic meaning through rapid cutting and juxtapositioning of shots. For example, shots of a river would be interspersed with shots of printing presses and human crowds to show the power of the press in communication. A good example of this is *Oktober,* made in 1928 by Eisenstein.

As media audiences, we are less concerned with the reality of form than with the reality of content. We are not worried by the unnatural appearance of small figures on a screen in our living room. We are not worried if the story is interrupted by adverts or the news. However, we would immediately become sceptical if the main character in *Robin Hood* wore a wrist watch or spoke in contemporary slang.

There are two types of media products, both quite different in content but both of which we often call realistic:

1 Films, books, radio plays and so on which may be *fictional* but look natural. In reality the characters are actors, pretending to talk and behave according to the period in which they lived, for example, the film *Schindler's List*.

2 Programmes, magazines and photographic exhibitions which are non-fictional and use images and sounds from real life, such as the news or documentaries.

Activity

Look at the TV listings for today in a newspaper or magazine. How many of these programmes could you describe as realistic, and into which category – 1 or 2 (as described above) – do they fall?

To be realistic, therefore, media products must conform to accepted codes and conventions; they satisfy our expectations, they do not try to confuse us. However, some media texts can be described as anti-realist. They use images and sounds that disrupt meaning, rather than clarify it, or disturb our expectations. These techniques have tended to be used by producers outside of mainstream media production, by independent film directors, for example, rather than someone connected with Hollywood. Sometimes this is done for political or social reasons – many examples can be found in European film-making.

Case study

The German film *Aguirre Wrath of God*, produced by Werner Herzog in 1972, about the conquistadores, includes surreal scenes such as a Spanish galleon stuck in the tree tops of the Amazonian jungle. The film was concerned with the self-delusion as well as the barbarity of the Spanish invaders. The film starts realistically enough but becomes more like a dream or nightmare and metaphorically represents the descent of the invaders into chaos. The film was made on a very tight budget under difficult conditions in South America. What advantages, both artistic and otherwise, did the film-makers gain from setting aside realism?

The techniques of surrealism have also been used commercially to great effect. The classic example of this is the use of images by cigarette advertisers. They use images that puzzle and intrigue us because they wish us to absorb the brand name of the cigarette;

they are not concerned with describing its taste or burning quality.

Use of components within narrative structures

When talking about the narrative structure, we mean the elements or the 'ingredients' out of which it is built or constructed. From the information above, about the different types of structures, you will have already begun to recognise some of these components. They can be divided into two main categories: content (characters and storyline) and techniques (production and editing).

Narrative content

Much of the theory concerning how narrative structures organise material is based on film studies. Some of these in turn are based on the work of **Vladimir Propp**, a Russian critic of the 1920s, who analysed Russian fairytales. He observed that similar characters and similar events happened in many of the stories.

Characters

The same situation is to be found in our own experience. If you have ever been to a British pantomime, you know what to expect – whether it is *Cinderella* or *Jack-and-the-Beanstalk*. There will be a hero, his helper or friend, the Princess, the King, the villain, who may be a witch or an ogre, one or two minor villains and an object which will help the hero, such as the magic boots in *Puss-in-Boots* or a magic lantern as in *Aladdin*. Amateur theatre companies are able to use the same casts, year after year, because of this recurrence of the same characters.

Neither will you be surprised by the storyline. The pantomime will open, perhaps with happy villagers singing. Then the villain will enter, happiness is disturbed and the hero will be sent on his way to meet the challenge. He will have some help from a magic person in his quest, which will involve travelling. After a fight, the hero will win through to achieve wealth and a wife in the form of the princess. Happiness will be restored to the kingdom.

Case study

In modern films, such as the James Bond series, these characters can still be identified:

Propp's characters	=	*Characters in the films*
the hero	=	James Bond
the villain	=	Dr. No, or Blofeld
the donor, who provides the magic object	=	Q, who provides the fast cars and technological gadgets
the dispatcher, who sends the hero on his way	=	M, head of the British Secret Service
the helper	=	Felix Leiter or the 'Bond' girls
the princess	=	the 'main' girl
the king	=	the British government

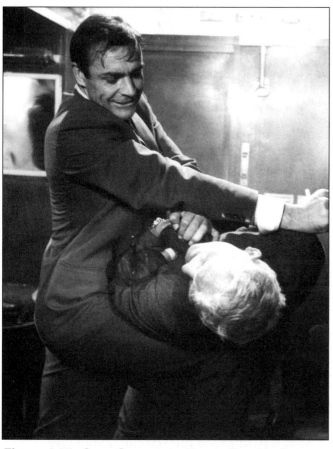

Figure 4.15 Sean Connery as James Bond in *From Russia With Love*

Choose a film, such as *Star Wars* or *Indiana Jones*, and analyse the characters in the style of Propp.

Besides these basic characters, there is one we have not considered yet – that of the **narrator.** Narrators can introduce us to characters or explain complicated events and situations to us, whether we are listeners, viewers or readers. Compare the excerpts from two classic novels shown in Figures 4.16 and 4.17.

As I rose and dressed, I thought over what had happened, and wondered if it were a dream. I could not be certain of the reality till I had seen Mr Rochester again, and heard him renew his words of love and promise.

While arranging my hair, I looked at my face in the glass, and felt it was no longer plain: there was hope in its aspect and life in its colour; and my eyes seemed as if they had beheld the fount of fruition, and borrowed beams from the lustrous ripple. I had often been unwilling to look at my master, because I feared he could not be pleased at my look: but I was sure I might lift my face to his now, and not cool his affection by its expression. I took a plain but clean and light summer dress from my drawer and put it on: it seemed no attire had ever so well become me, because none had I ever worn in so blissful a mood.

I was not surprised, when I ran down into the hall, to see that a brilliant June morning had succeeded to the tempest of the night; and to feel, through the open glass door, the breathing of a fresh and fragrant breeze. Nature must be gladsome when I was so happy. A beggar-woman and her little boy – pale, ragged objects both – were coming up the walk, and I ran down and gave them all the money I happened to have in my purse – some three or four shillings; good or bad, they must partake of my jubilee. The rooks cawed, and blither birds sang; but nothing was so merry or so musical as my own rejoicing heart.

Figure 4.16 From *Jane Eyre* by Charlotte Brontë

SIR WALTER had taken a very good house in Camden-place, a lofty, dignified situation, such as becomes a man of consequence; and both he and Elizabeth were settled there, much to their satisfaction.

Anne entered it with a sinking heart, anticipating an imprisonment of many months, and anxiously saying to herself, 'Oh! when shall I leave you again?' A degree of unexpected cordiality, however, in the welcome she received, did her good. Her father and sister were glad to see her, for the sake of showing her the house and furniture, and met her with kindness. Her making a fourth, when they sat down to dinner, was noticed as an advantage.

Mrs Clay was very pleasant, and very smiling; but her courtesies and smiles were more a matter of course. Anne had always felt that she would pretend what was proper on her arrival; but the complaisance of the others was unlooked for. They were evidently in excellent spirits, and she was soon to listen to the causes. They had no inclination to listen to her. After laying out for some compliments of being deeply regretted in their old neighbourhood, which Anne could not pay, they had only a few faint enquiries to make, before the talk must be all their own.

Figure 4.17 From *Persuasion* by Jane Austen

The first excerpt is written in the first person singular; the reader sees what happens through the eyes of Jane. This creates a great feeling of involvement. Its limitations are that we can experience only what the heroine experiences – it is a very subjective viewpoint. On the other hand, the excerpt from *Persuasion*, written in the third person, can tell us more about the characters and situations in the book than the individual characters themselves know. An altogether more objective viewpoint can be given, not limited by the attitudes of the main protagonist.

Activity

Adapt the children's short story on page 89 into two brief plays for radio. The first script will use a narrator, the second will use only the voices of the characters and sound effects. Afterwards, read aloud the two plays to other people. The audience should assess which play is the most understandable and which the most effective. Which play was the easiest to write? (See Chapter 7.)

CRICKET, LOVELY CRICKET

Richardson and Atherton are chips off an older block

It is a sorry world we live in. Everest is filthy, and cricketers are coarser. The crisp confidence of white flannels has succumbed to enforced inelegance. Test matches threaten to go the way of the dodo, pushed to extinction by the meretricious allure of the game's abbreviated form. Small boys swear when they play in parks: imitation is the worst form of flattery. What once were vices are now manners; cricket, that exquisite dowager of games, is in danger of damnation.

Two men now have the job of shaking the dust from creeds forgotten. Michael Atherton, a dour Lancastrian unspoilt by Cambridge, and Richie Richardson, a phlegmatic Antiguan with the most cultured cover drive, promise to kiss cricket's frog back to its old princely state. England's endearing cricketers, after a harrowing season of unseemly battle with Australians, will face a chivalrous team of exuberant West Indians in a series of some considerable importance.

Significantly, there are new men at the helm. Vivian Richards, Richardson's predecessor, was a brooding genius who saw cricket as more than a game. He sulked and scowled, obsessed with ethnicity and a bloated

sense of mission. And Graham Gooch, careworn and unshaven, lacked what Robert Burns called "a spark o' nature's fire". The two teams are now led by captains of higher style and step, and this will enrich the cricket played.

The West Indies under Richardson, and bound by the rule that permits no more than one bouncer per over, are the "gentleman" of international cricket. Combative and unyielding on the field of play, they rely for victory on the eloquence of cricketing skills rather than on sharpness of tongue, or length of moustache. Of the major cricketing sides, they share this proclivity for values from the age of sepia tint only with England and India. Australia and Pakistan today do not – a cleft that defies all facile explanations.

The series with the West Indies will be a muscular context between upright men, and should restore the fading nobility of cricket. Richardson, the gangling Ambrose, Lara – the first great Trinidadian cricketer since Sonny Ramadhin – and Haynes, will adorn the game as much as Robin Smith, Salisbury, Hick and skipper Atherton. England will probably lose, but they will have sustained a "defeat without a war".

Figure 4.18 A *Times* editorial

Times Newspapers Limited, London, 1994

Figure 4.19 A *Sun* editorial

In newspapers, editorials can use the form 'we', thereby creating an even greater intimacy with the reader. People whose viewpoints they disagree with are called 'they'. Compare the examples in Figures 4.18 and 4.19.

Films, too, such as *The Rocky Horror Picture Show, The Go-Between* and *Citizen Kane,* have retained the use of a narrator – either through the use of a voice-over or through the introduction of a special character who acts the part of the narrator.

'Characters' occur not only in fictional but also in non-fictional texts. In a wrestling match, for example, there are often heroes and villains, such as 'good' Big Daddy versus 'bad' Hulk Hogan. Even in a sport such as tennis, players have been allocated roles as heroes (Bjorn Borg in the 1970s) and villains (John McEnroe). The narrator takes the form of a presenter, who not only tells us about the technical action but gives us insights into the motivations and personalities of the players. Viewers can observe the physical struggles on court, but the presenter can create more tension and excitement by giving his or her own opinions and revealing inside knowledge.

News presenters, commentators, hosts on game shows and experts brought in to explain events can all take the part of narrators. The narrators or presenters not only increase our knowledge and help our understanding, but also control the unfolding of the narrative by what they say, how much they say and the way in which they give or do not give information.

Activity

Choose a non-fictional programme from the television. This may be a sports programme, a documentary or an entertainment programme such as *Gladiators*. What 'characters' can you identify?

Motivations

When considering characters, we rely significantly on **stereotypes**. (Refer back to Chapter 2.) If certain types of people are put together in certain situations, then this will result in friction which can create action, i.e. narrative. These different characters (often stereotypes) provide **motivations** or reasons for the narrative. The narrative of all comedy, and cartoons in particular, relies on the skilful interaction of characters and situations to create a humorous effect.

Case study: *Red Dwarf*

The successful SF series *Red Dwarf* gets its comic effect from the interaction of the stylised characters. Although the main characters are played by an all-male cast, they make up the nucleus of the average family: father, mother, son and daughter.

Rimmer is the father figure; he is a pompous, ineffectual character with authoritarian tendencies.

Kryton is the stereotypical mother, a gentle caring person whose main concern is to cook, clean and look after the others. He will sacrifice himself for the welfare of the others.

Cat has the stereotyped attributes of a teenage girl – extremely vain, he adores fashionable clothes and although expressing interest in the opposite sex is most interested in himself.

Lister is a young rebel representing the younger generation, who mocks the tastes and ambitions of Rimmer. He is the character whom many viewers, male or female, will identify with. He is a 'real lad' – careless of his appearance, with a controlled wildness, liking to get drunk, carefree yet ultimately caring.

The comedy may be set in the future, but the humour is based on situations within the experience of viewers.

Choose a sit-com such as *Absolutely Fabulous* or *Men Behaving Badly*. Describe the characters and identify the stereotypes they are based on.

Often, after seeing a film or reading a newspaper report, people ask themselves why something happened. They need to be satisfied about the motivation behind the action. Sometimes a narrative is built around a **cause–effect** chain. Certain events take place and build up to create a *climax*. Films are sometimes constructed with one event or situation seemingly leading inevitably to another, giving a sense of movement and occasionally of doom.

Organisation of material

Now we have considered characters, we can look at how the storyline, plot or material is organised in terms of **time**. This has already been discussed briefly when we were considering open and closed, linear and non-linear structures.

Many conventions govern the **opening** and **closure** of media texts. The openings are significant. The reader (in the wide, media sense of the word) has to be attracted, expectations have to be raised, and interest must be maintained ready for the main part of the text. The content may be novel, shocking or unexpected, but conventions of form can help reassure the reader that it is possible to cope with the demands. For example, the opening part of horror films, such as *The Curse of Frankenstein* or *Seven,* may be deeply disturbing but the conventions of titling and music, even the BBFC certificate beforehand, can reassure readers that they are not in personal danger.

Written texts use headlines and sub-headings to signal that the text is about to begin. The opening of a newspaper story is also constructed to be of great significance to the reader. All the essential details –

97

Fire heroine honoured

A NINE-YEAR-OLD girl hailed a heroine after saving her mother's life in a horrific blaze is to receive a letter of commendation from fire bosses.

Sophie Steer, from Warren Street, Leicester, doused mum Carole in water after she accidentally set herself on fire.

She then ran to a payphone in another street and called the emergency services in such a calm manner operators suspected a hoax.

Community fire safety officer Bill Wells said today: "She did a wonderful job. The call she put in to the ambulance service was amazing. I have spoken to people there who said it was so good and clear and that the girl was so composed they thought it might not be genuine.

"Sophie did exactly the right thing and her mother was very lucky to have her around or else she would probably have died in the fire."

Sophie, who goes to Fosse Primary School, will receive a special letter from the county's chief fire officer, Norman Dickerson acknowledging her efforts.

Mrs Steer (47) is still recovering at Leicster Royal Infirmary from 20 per cent burns.

Fire bosses have yet to determine the cause of the blaze. One theory is that Mrs Steer's dress caught fire as she lit an ornamental candle.

Figure 4.20 Openings are very important in newspaper stories

Reproduced by permission of *Leicester Mercury*

the who, what, where, when and how – are contained in the first paragraph or two. This has to attract readers and assure them that this is a story that will interest them and contains people and events about which they want to know more. Study the example in Figure 4.20.

The feature article in a specialist magazine differs in its opening. The reader has an interest in the topic –

When an actress friend of mine had a baby she was given a detailed horoscope for the child. The predictions were unanimous; 'great theatrical talent', 'certain for a career on the stage'. Her mother was delighted. Her father, a civil engineer and something to do with Wandsworth sewers, was less impressed. He eyed the chart again. 'Are you sure it says nothing about a career in waste disposal?'

The fact is, no parent can reliably predict whether they are more likely to attend their child's Nobel Peace Prize ceremony in Stockholm or a Parole Board Review in Holloway. I went through a naughty stage as a child, which might be to do with the change of name I adopted when I was 8. My father was Foreign correspondent for a Danish television company and we – my mother, older brother, younger sister and I – moved to America, where I was instantly transformed by Sandra to Sandi. Sandra was a good girl but Sandi was a lot more fun and consequently much less controllable. I parted company with several schools under what can only be described as a 'cloud'.

Figure 4.21 The opening of a magazine feature article

that is why he or she bought the magazine in the first place – so the feature writer can be more **enigmatic** in the opening. *Good Housekeeping* is a magazine aimed at families and, particularly, housewives with children. Figure 4.21 is the opening of an article by the actress Sandi Toksvig, about her childhood. (For more details on feature and news writing see Chapter 10.)

After the opening, the text, in whatever form it takes (whether fiction or non-fiction, written or moving image), reaches a **climax**. Usually this is near the end but sometimes there can be more than one climax. In the Hitchcock film *Psycho,* the horrific murder of the girl in the shower takes place one third of the way into the film. It is certainly a climax, even though the murderer is not revealed until the end of the film. Hitchcock manages to retain the tension even though nothing quite so shocking as this occurs afterwards.

With moving images, the climax is often highlighted by camera work and editing. This can be seen through the increased number of shots and angles or, on the other hand, through the use of slow motion or freeze framing. Music will often become more prominent or can suddenly cease. In a soap or a serial, the climax comes at the end of the episode; we anticipate it partly because we are aware that the programme ends soon and it is a convention to end with a climax, but also through the use of camera work and music.

In printed text, such as cartoons and stories, vocabulary and illustrations disclose the climax: vocabulary becomes more vivid, illustrations become larger. The climax of a newspaper could be considered to be the main picture on the front page.

The general public are experts at recognising the **closure** of a text. This is signalled to us by certain conventions and not merely by the plot. How something ends depends on its purpose and what action the authors expect us to take, if any. Even if the text has an open ending, we, the readers, are aware that the text has come to an end for the time being. In the case of a soap, the final camera shot is usually frozen before the appearance of the credits. On a radio programme the presenter or DJ will 'sign off' with a set phrase. The comics, the Two Ronnies, always used to end their comedy show with the words: 'So it's goodbye from me ... and it's goodbye from him'. In a variety show, the applause of the audience tells us that the end is near. Likewise, in cartoon strips, the words *To be continued* tell us that the text has finished for now – but that there is more to come.

Figure 4.22 The 'closure' of an advert is the part that tells us what to do next

In the advert in Figure 4.22, the closure is the telephone number and address. It means that we know what to do next – buy the product at this outlet or ring up for further information.

Activity

Describe the opening and closure of a news programme on TV. How does it differ from a fiction-based programme? What kinds of reassurance are viewers offered?

In order to create dynamism or movement within a narrative, two different types of codes can be identified: the **action code** and the **enigma code**.

An **action code** is a type of shorthand for describing how events are progressing. In a film or on TV, a shot of a plane taking off lets us know that the heroine has travelled to another country. The hero buckles on his sword and we realise that the battle is soon to take place. We do not need to see the heroine buying her air ticket or checking in her luggage. We do not need to see the hero put on all his armour and call for his horse. We know what action is taking place.

Activity

List other sequences of camera shots that symbolise action in a similar way. Are viewers conscious that they are being offered codes, rather than being shown specific action?

An **enigma** code controls narrative in a different way, through releasing only certain amounts of information at certain times. This code arouses interest and attention by giving information that puzzles us. The traditional 'who-dunnit' could be considered a giant form of enigma code! The initial murder intrigues us, but only gradually are the full facts given to us, and the final solution is revealed in the last section.

Newspaper headlines commonly use enigma codes. They abbreviate information and present it in an attention-grabbing manner so that we need to read the article in order to find out what it means. Look at the headlines in Figure 4.23.

Beefy scare puts England in a stew

Feb 29

Marry me– 500 times!

Chainsaw massacre? Not in Wisconsin

Figure 4.23 Enigmatic newspaper headlines

The article under 'Chainsaw massacre' is not about serial murders but about cutting down trees. 'Marry me 500 times' is about a marriage proposal backed up by a petition. And 'Beefy scare' does not refer to the BSE health risk from infected cows but accompanies a report on cricket and the prospect of Ian Botham becoming a cricket test selector!

Stages within the narrative

In addition to his analysis of the characterisation, Propp also analysed the organisation of the action within fairytales. He recognised six stages in the course of the narrative:

- preparation – the scene is set
- complication – a problem occurs, some evil takes place
- transference – the hero receives help and leaves on a quest
- struggle – there is a fight
- return – the hero attains his objective, fulfils the quest
- recognition – villains are punished and the hero receives his reward.

Activity

How well does Propp's analysis (six stages of action) apply to a modern film you have seen, such as *Batman* or *Die Hard*? Does the formula apply as well to a romantic film?

The main criticism of this plan is that is only suitable for simple texts and those which follow a chronological order. Another theorist, **Tzvetan Todorov**, developed a looser analytical structure with three main stages:

1 There is equilibrium, an established state of affairs.
2 There is disequilibrium, i.e. disruption, an event happens which disturbs the order
   - there is a recognition of disruption, an awareness of the problem
   - efforts are made to solve the problem or trouble.
3 There is a return to equilibrium, although this may not be the same as at the start.

Case study: *Jumanji* (1996)

Three main stages can be identified in this film, according to Todorov's analysis:

1 We meet an ordinary boy living an average life in small-town America.

2 He finds a board game buried in a building site. When he starts to play it terrifying adventures happen.

3 The bad magic is defeated and the boy survives to grow up and create a new life.

How adequately does this describe the movement of the narrative in *Jumanji*? Write a brief synopsis for a new science fiction film which would follow this three-stage structure.

This more flexible approach can be used to describe both fictional and non-fictional texts. A news programme such as the *News at Ten* follows this pattern:

1 Equilibrium is established by the familiar opening credits, music, studio and presenters.
2 The actual news reports bring disruption into our homes.
3 The return to the studio, the final 'soft' news item and closing credits and music return us to equilibrium, though the situation is not identical, because we are changed by what we have learnt.

Narrative techniques

We shall now look at the technical side of narrative, and how production and post-production methods can affect it.

These techniques are particularly noticeable in the handling of time. A live televised football match follows 'real time' and the radio coverage of a live pop concert also covers real time. But although gardening magazines cover the seasons and soaps, too, try to mirror 'real' time so that Christmas is celebrated by actors and viewers/listeners alike, few other media products attempt to do this. Even the live football match if shown again may be altered to fit a shorter time slot. Any film or documentary about the Second World War will not take six years to watch! So time is often manipulated by the producer or editor.

Representation of time

The main techniques to show the passing of time are given below:

1 **Compression** – we see on screen the seasons rapidly changing; the calendar may be flicked

over to show the passing of days, there may be a fade-out to black between scenes. All these things can indicate to us that time has passed.

2 **Ellipsis** – (see action code above) a long series of events is cut down to a few significant shots.

3 **Freeze frame** – a still image appears on screen and a narrator or voice-over tells us that a few years have passed.

4 **Slow motion** – time can also be stretched and emphasis given to a scene through slow motion.

5 **Flashbacks and flash-forwards** – the film-maker can make us travel in time, either to the past or to the future.

6 **Repeats** – in music videos, some shots are repeatedly shown to create coherence – they come around again and again just like a musical chorus. Repeats of the action are also usual in a sports programme; parts of the Grand National are run several times so that we can experience the most exciting bits again and the same race is shown from the point of view of a different camera.

7 **Parallel actions** – as viewers, listeners or readers, we are able to know and experience what is going on in different places at different times. We are not just flies on the wall in one room but in several rooms!

Activity

List films or programmes which manipulate time and identify which techniques they use from the list above. How successful are these techniques?

The use of sound, particularly music, can affect how we feel about time. It can give coherence to a sequence with many different, fast-changing shots. It can reinforce images but, it can also contradict them.

Space

In printed texts the equivalent of time is **space**. The feeling of movement is created in the layout. One of the rules of advertising governs the use of space, particularly white space. Text wrongly positioned can look as if it is dropping off the page. The space left around a headline can indicate its importance.

Activity

Look at the magazine extract in Figure 4.24. It is crowded with textual information. Where is there most white space? How is it being used to attract your attention?

Jolly good news!

A less-than perfect figure is the lot of many women. Is there anything you can do to make yours better? Or should you accept that you are meant to be imperfect. Here we have sensible guidelines for those who prefer a trimmer profile and support for those who don't.

What do supermodels have that other women don't? Actually, it's more a question of what they don't have. Watch them shimmy down the catwalk, skimpily attired in the latest unwearable Paris wisp. Boobs may be in this year, hips may be in, but one little item is always out – the tummy. My tummy, like the cost of living, is always with me. Unless I suck my tummy in, it bulges comfortably under the belt of my jeans, undulates under the waistband of my skirts and ruins the line of my best dress. It's not fair. When I lost some weight recently, my bosoms vanished, my buttocks deflated, but my tummy did not budge one inch.

Having a baby hasn't helped, of course. I remember my fury at my six-week hospital check, when a young male doctor told me gravely, "Your scar has healed beautifully, and you'll be able to wear a bikini this summer." Was there something wrong with his eyes? Did he really imagine that a woman like me would swan around in a thong?

The truth is, pregnant or not, my tummy has never held it in for more than 30 seconds at a time – on the beach I have always been a one-piece black Speedo woman, and I still look forward to the day when those concealing, knee-length Edwardian bathing costumes come back into fashion.

Let us be honest – I have a tummy because I am a woman. Yes, when God made Eve, her perfection included an endearingly curved belly. It is as much a part of our natural make-up as ovaries. So why do we all hate our tummies so much? Why do all fashion designers fail to cater for the one attribute women share?

Even the most gazelle-like female icons have tummies. A friend of mine recently met the Princess of Wales and instantly spread the glad tidings: "She's as skinny as a rake – and she's got a little sticking-out tummy!" Several years ago, article about those fabulous models Marie Helvin and Jerry Hall made a startling revelation. They had flat tummies only when they sucked them in! In other words, despite their glorious beauty, they were exactly like the rest of us in the navel department. Even supermodels have them.

Now it can be told. We can do sit-ups and muscle-clenchings, we can puff and blow and endure painful contortions in a leotard, but unless we have what cosmetic surgeons revoltingly call an "apronectomy" – our dear old tums are here to stay. Perhaps, instead of trying to wish them away, we should learn to love them. So wear a skin-tight frock and flaunt that tummy with pride – I will if you will.

Figure 4.24 On a magazine page, the layout of text must make interesting use of space

In film-making, **space** is important in the way the characters are shown from different camera positions; the viewer sometimes has the bird's eye view (for example, in battle scenes or where there are vast crowds).

Alternative narrative structures

The word **alternative** has often been applied to the press and small, non-mainstream film producers. It implies an independence of viewpoint and the ability to cater for minority groups. 'Alternative' producers show a commitment to innovation and experimentation. They are radical, they break the rules. Their work is not the 'norm'.

An alternative narrative structure is one that is 'different' in either content or form. It may ignore or alter the usual codes and conventions, or it may treat the various components in unusual or unexpected ways.

101

Pop videos are still considered alternative by some older people, although they are generally accepted as the norm in popular culture. They do not follow a narrative that could be analysed according to Todorov and, at first, their use of fast edits and special effects, such as strobe and unusual camera angles, did make them different. However, their meaning is now understood by mass audiences. Some TV adverts, particularly those for lagers or beers aimed at a younger market in their twenties and thirties, commonly use an alternative narrative. Guinness adverts led the way in this area with their adverts starring Rutger Hauer.

The surreal form of some advertisements such as those for cigarettes have already been noted. They provide an enigma code that may never be solved!

Narrative structures do not have to be new to be alternative, however. James Joyce's novel *Ulysses* was written in the early 1900s. It is what has been called a 'stream of consciousness' novel. The entire novel takes place over the period of one day and the thoughts of the writer are not written down in an orderly, constructed fashion but poured out as they occur in his brain. Compare the two passages in Figures 4.25 and 4.26, which both depict someone thinking. The first is taken from Thomas Hardy's *Jude the Obscure* and the second is from *Ulysses*. Which is conventional and which is alternative? Also consider which is more 'real'.

> When he had had something to eat he walked out into the dull winter light over the town bridge, and turned the corner towards the Close. The day was foggy, and standing under the walls of the most graceful architectural pile in England he paused and looked up. The lofty building was visible as far as the roof-ridge; above, the dwindling spire rose more and more remotely, till its apex was quite lost in the mist drifting across it.
>
> The lamps now began to be lighted, and turning to the west front he walked round. He took it as a good omen that numerous blocks of stone were lying about, which signified that the cathedral was undergoing restoration or repair to a considerable extent. It seemed to him, full of the superstitions of his beliefs, that this was an exercise of forethought on the part of a ruling Power, that he might find plenty to do in the art he practised while waiting for a call to a higher labours.
>
> Then a wave of warmth came over him as he thought how near he stood to the bright-eyed vivacious girl with the broad forehead and pile of dark hair above it; the girl with the kindling glance, daringly soft at times – something like that of the girls he had seen in engravings from paintings of the Spanish School. She was here – actually in this Close – in one of the houses confronting this very west façade.

Figure 4.25 From *Jude the Obscure* by Thomas Hardy

> Open your eyes now. I will. One moment. Has all vanished since? If I open and am for ever in the black adiaphane. *Basta!* I will see if I can see.
>
> See now. There all the time without you: and ever shall be, world without end.
>
> They came down the steps from Leahy's terrace prudently, *Frauenzimmer*: and down the shelving shore flabbily their splayed feet sinking in the silted sand. Like me, like Algy, coming down to our mighty mother. Number one swung lourdily her midwife's bag, the other's gamp poked in the beach. From the liberties, out for the day. Mrs Florence MacCabe, relict of the late Patk MacCabe, deeply lamented, of Bride Street. One of her sisterhood lugged me squealing into life. Creation from nothing. What has she in the bag? A misbirth with a trailing navelcord, hushed in ruddy wool. The cords of all link back, strandentwining cable of all flesh. That is why mystic monks. Will you be as goods? Gaze in your omphalos. Hello. Kinch here. Put me on to Edenville. Aleph, alpha: nought, nought, one.

Figure 4.26 From *Ulysses* by James Joyce

Activity

Which of the following is an alternative use of a media convention?

1. Using a whip pan to show the passing of time.
2. Using black and white to show a flashback.
3. Using white print on a black background for the front page of a newspaper.
4. Using soft focus for a romantic scene.
5. Dispensing with a presenter for the news and using only a voice-over.
6. Having music to accompany weather reports.
7. Using stills in films.
8. Having background music to accompany sport on TV.
9. Putting local news before national or international news.
10. Using flashbacks on TV in documentaries.
11. Using footage of real people in action films.
12. Using different angle shots for the Queen's Christmas Speech.
13. Using a robot to present programmes.
14. Writing a magazine story in which readers choose the ending.
15. Producing a TV commercial with no music.

In addition to this, the word 'alternative' can be applied to media forms. The adult comic *Viz* is an example of this. It took the format of a product associated which children and turned it into an adult product. Although considered alternative, it did become a mainstream media product in terms of popularity.

The term could also be applied to the narrative structure used by a new media form, such as the developing multi-media or computer-based technology like the Internet. Their alternativeness is based on their 'drop-in' nature, their accessibility and interactive nature.

Relationship between narrative structures and audiences

The term 'audience' can be considered similar if not identical to the term 'reader' in this context. It can mean a reader of a magazine or newspaper, a listener to radio or a viewer of TV, films and videos.

This book is about the **mass** media, but audiences consist of individuals consuming products on their own at home at different times, such as magazine readers, as well as large groups of people watching films in cinemas together at the same time. There is obviously a difference between studying individual responses and those of the masses. There is also a great deal of difference caused by the amount of attention audiences give to a product in terms of primary, secondary and tertiary viewing. (For further details see Chapter 22.)

At the end of Chapter 1, the possible readings of media texts were briefly discussed – how there could be preferred, negotiated or oppositional readings. The meaning of any media text is never 'fixed'; it depends on its audience, i.e. the social, educational and cultural experiences of the media audience or readers and on their age and mental capabilities. Individuals will bring their own prejudices, attitudes, opinions and experiences with them when they 'read' a text.

For example, one group of film-goers may consider a film such as *Pulp Fiction* to be entertainment, another group may consider it to be a comment on contemporary violence in society, and a third group may consider it to be so violent that it should be banned.

Unfamiliarity with certain texts can affect how we respond to them. The preferred, intended meaning of an alternative advert, such as a cigarette advert, is that the attention of potential adult consumers is caught and they will remember the brand name when buying cigarettes. However, other people will admire the artwork rather than the product and may want to buy the poster. The intended reading of the Levi jeans advertising campaign was that the jeans were desirable, but even more people went out and bought the music ('I Heard it Through the Grapevine' and 'Stand By Me') that accompanied the visual images in the advert.

Some of the most well-known research in this area has been done by David Morley, on television audiences between 1975 and 1979 at Birmingham University. The project focused on the analysis of one particular example of a genre, the TV magazine/current affairs programme *Nationwide*. The project explored, first, narrative structures, and secondly how the programme was interpreted by individuals from different backgrounds. Morley wanted to prove that watching television is 'an active process of decoding and interpretation, not simply a passive process of "reception" or "consumption" of messages.'

One experiment investigated the use of preferred, negotiated and oppositional readings. Videotapes of two *Nationwide* programmes were shown to groups of different people, who were then interviewed to establish their interpretations. The first programme was shown to people from different educational backgrounds in the Midlands and London areas. The second programme about the Budget was shown to a different variety of groups. See the diagram in Figure 4.27.

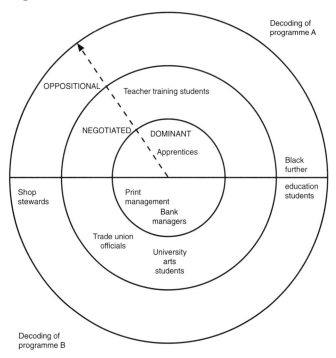

Figure 4.27 The 'decoding' of programmes, from David Morley's *Television, Audiences and Cultural Studies*, Routledge (1992)

There's no place like

Home...

What about

insurance?

If you haven't made a home insurance claim in the last three years, why subsidise the bad risks? Provided your home has four bedrooms or fewer and contents worth no more than £30,000, call us FREE now. You could save £40, £70, £90 or even more on your home insurance

quoting reference below. Lines open 8am–8pm Mon–Fri, 9am–5pm Sat.

CALL FREE 0800 1000800

TRIED & TRUE
Motor and Home Insurance

Figure 4.28 Some adverts aim to attract the clients of rival companies

One response (**dominant reading**) from a white working-class apprentice was: 'It creates the impression that Tom Coyne [a presenter] sort of is your local mate from up the road that's in there on your behalf ... the presenters have got to be the most authoritative, because you see most of them ... you mistrust the person they're interviewing, straightaway, don't you? I mean, you don't know them, you're suspicious, you know they're out for themselves. The interviewer isn't, he's only presenting the programme.'

Another response (**negotiated reading**) from a white, middle-class, university arts student was: 'It's meant to give the impression that we're all in this together. We're a great big happy family as a nation, and we're doing all these things together ... the programme tries to give you the impression that Michael Barratt [presenter] is a very nice guy.'

A response (**oppositional reading**) from a shop steward, white, working class was: 'I don't think you can take *Nationwide* in isolation ... I mean ... add *The Sun,* the *Mirror* and the *Daily Express* to it, it's all the same whole heap of crap ... and they're all saying to

the unions, "you're running the country ..."'

Texts can also be considered to **position** audiences by structuring the content so that audiences respond in a predictable way. If a text addresses the audience in a certain way and encourages them to see things from a certain viewpoint, then **subject positioning** or **interpellation** can be said to have taken place. Market researchers and advertisers are eager to position markets and not merely accept pre-existing groups of clients, so they will create targeting strategies. (See Chapter 25.)

The advert in Figure 4.28 aims at enticing homeowners away from their usual insurance company.

From adverts to soaps and documentaries, media texts want us to identify with certain feelings or roles. The advert for medicines in Figure 4.29 wants us to identify with the mother and implies that she will fulfil her maternal and wifely responsibilities by

Figure 4.29 Some adverts aim to make us identify with 'ideal' roles or feelings

going to the pharmacy to purchase goods for the welfare of her family.

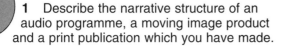

Activity

Choose an advert and a short hard news story about a social issue, such as unemployment, and ask everyone in the group, including the teacher, to write down briefly what they think the intention of these texts is, and if they agree with them. Analyse the results in terms of preferred, negotiated and oppositional readings. Then compare these results in terms of the age, gender and general background of the group.

Evidence assignment

1 Describe the narrative structure of an audio programme, a moving image product and a print publication which you have made.

You can show how you used different components by including your scripts or running order, storyboard and newspaper articles or magazine features. Explain why you chose this structure. What alternative structures could you have used?

The meanings which the audience or readers have taken from your product can be researched as part of Unit 6 Element 4 (Chapter 24).

Alternatively, you can analyse the narrative structure of the three media texts which you chose to investigate in depth for Unit 1 Element 3 (Chapter 3). This work can be included in the written report or video report for that unit. Describe the use of components in the narrative structures. Discuss the meanings of the text and how different audiences may interpret the texts differently.

2 Collect some examples of different types of media products that have 'alternative' narrative structures, and explain why they may be described as alternative.

Investigating the Content of Media Products: Unit Test

1 A magazine is a media text. Which aspect of the cover is an important element which suggests meaning to potential readers?
a the name of the photographer
b the font used for the title
c where it is printed
d the type of ink used

2 In a film, which of these is an aesthetic rather than a technical code?
a the style of the costumes
b the use of establishing shots
c the stage directions
d the use of boom microphones

3 What clothes would you expect the presenter of a breakfast magazine programme for young people to wear?
a a suit
b fashionable casual clothes
c a shirt and tie
d a denim shirt and jeans

4 Which of the following visuals is a political icon?
a a map
b a crucifix
c a swastika
d an election poster

5 Which of these signifies that a cartoon character is thinking?

6 What anchors the meaning of a photograph in a newspaper?
a a subheading
b a slogan
c a headline
d a caption

7 Which of the following is a convention in BBC radio but not in BBC television?
a a studio audience for comedy
b jingles and idents within a programme
c regular commercial breaks
d news bulletins

8 Which types of camera shot will make a subject look insignificant?
a a tracking shot
b a high-angle shot
c a low-angle shot
d a panning shot

9 Which of these captions for a photo of a young girl crying by herself would be a denotative statement?
a It's sad to be alone at Christmas
b A child's heart breaks
c Why is this child unhappy?
d A child cries on her own

10 A connotative statement accompanying a picture of a tree would be:
a The mighty oak of England
b A thirty-foot-high oak
c This tree was planted in '93
d This oak is covered in leaves

11 Which of these is generally considered a cold colour?
a brown   **b** blue
c orange   **d** purple

Here are some descriptions of moving image productions. Use them to answer question 12–14 below.

a an often violent story set in the past, in a city with tense, isolated characters who have a bleak future
b an imaginative story which relies on many special effects about two people with unusual travelling companions
c a discussion of contemporary issues by invited guests in front of a live studio audience
d a true story about space travel which is introduced in a studio and whose events are reconstructed on location

12 Which of these is **most** typical of the documentary genre?

13 Which of these is **most** typical of the film noir genre?

14 Which of these is **most** typical of the science fiction genre?

15 What is the purpose of a documentary on the drug trade in the Third World?
a to entertain the audience
b to persuade viewers to change their lifestyle
c to inform the audience about the topic
d to encourage viewers to lobby politicians

16 A magazine targets readership amongst the Asian population. What is this known as?
a audience recognition
b profile marketing
c market segmentation
d magazine specialisation

17 Which of the following best describes why film noir became popular in the 1950s?
a it appealed to a wide audience
b it reflected American society's disillusionment
c most cinemas couldn't show colour films
d male cinema-goers liked dominant women

18 In night scenes of a film noir, what is the lighting technique called which creates the extreme contrasts between light and dark areas of a shot?
a night for night
b back lighting
c day for night
d key lighting

19 Which of the following is a reason why there are now so many specialist magazines on the newsagents' shelves compared with twenty years ago?
a they are cheap to buy
b distribution methods are better
c newsprint is cheaper now
d people have more leisure time to pursue specialist interests

20 Which social issues do many science fiction series, and especially *Star Trek,* try to highlight in a positive way?
a homelessness
b racism
c poverty
d crime

21 Why could the themes in a science fiction film such as *2001: A Space Odyssey* be said to include metaphysical considerations?
a it explores space
b it questions the meaning of existence
c one of the main characters is a robot
d it relies on science and technology

22 When real events are reconstructed using actors, what can this be called?
a faction
b actuality footage
c vérité
d drama documentary

23 Which of these items for television always has an open, multi-strand narrative?
a an advert
b a documentary
c a murder story
d the evening news

24 If a story ends with the words '... to be continued', what sort of narrative structure is suggested?
a open
b closed
c realist
d investigative

25 Which of the following items in a newspaper uses a linear structure?
a the news in brief
b the problem page
c the horoscope
d the editorial

26 An advert puzzles the reader at first glance. What technique is being used?
a cause–effect   b teaser
c enigma   d equilibrium

27 Sometimes a film uses a narrator to describe the action. Which of these television programmes **always** uses a similar technique?
a a chat show
b televised sports
c a situation comedy
d a soap

28 How, in a film, is time compressed?
a by the use of flashbacks
b by omitting some stages in an event
c by parallel actions
d by the use of flash forwards

29 What is meant by representation of an event in the media?
    a whether the people involved are stereotyped or not
    b the techniques and information the media selects to show us what has happened
    c that information is accurate and the event is shown as it happened
    d that all ideas, groups and issues are covered equally

30 Which of the following programmes often relies on the use of stereotypes?
    a the news
    b a sit-com
    c sport
    d a thriller

This unit is concerned with how professionals plan material for media products and how students should approach similar projects. It covers the origination, development and refinement of ideas and the research and scheduling necessary for a successful product. Units 3, 4 and 5 contain the basic production skills and it will be useful for the student to have covered these in order to be aware of the capabilities and potential of various pieces of equipment before they start planning.

Any media project can be divided into three broad stages:

- *pre-production*
- *production*
- *post-production.*

Although this unit is primarily concerned with pre-production, effective planning still requires you to have a good idea of how the product will end up and the production processes which are to be used.

Chapter 5

Investigate research methods

This element looks at the generic skills associated with research, which can be applied to all three product areas. It looks at the way in which information is located, collected, analysed and presented. The research for any product will be wide-reaching. Take, for example, a quiz for commercial radio: not only will the questions and answers need to be found, but the target audience must be defined, sponsors located, certain types of contestants selected and a studio booked and presenters chosen.

Pre-production planning

Whether you are producing a thirty-second advert, a major film epic or a series of documentaries for radio, you will spend more time on pre-production planning than in actually making it. A classic example is the blockbuster film *Gone With The Wind*. The rights to this best-selling book were bought in 1936, but it was well over two years before filming started because of problems with finance, scripting and casting. At the other end of the scale, an advert for Guinness, lasting about 30 seconds, also took over a year to prepare; in this case because of the amount of research needed rather than because of financial difficulties. The actual filming took two months.

The final media product which we hear, watch or read is the culmination of thousands of hours of production time by a team of people. The final product is the metaphorical tip of the iceberg. The vast majority of hours allocated to production will have been spent on research and planning. This is done not only to secure high quality but ultimately

to save time and money. Some people will be exclusively employed in the pre-production stages for research and planning. With very few exceptions, all jobs within the media industries will be involved at some stage with planning, especially the planning of time, and many will also involve some research, from the lighting engineer to the director. The research will cover not only the content of the product itself and how ideas can be assessed, but also how it is going to be produced, the problems which may arise and how they can be solved.

The importance of thorough planning cannot be over-emphasised. If a project is not planned properly, the result will be very costly in terms of time, money and your reputation! Good planning helps you to identify what you are trying to achieve and how you are going to set about achieving it. You will then be able to identify the resources you need and how to make the best use of them. This planning framework will allow you to develop a product that is on time, within a budget and to the agreed specifications wanted by the client.

Sources of information relevant to researching content

When researching media products (or any other project), there are two main sources of information for the researcher:

- primary
- secondary.

Primary research takes place when the researcher personally accesses the source of information, i.e. talks to a living person or visits a particular location. **Secondary research** takes place when a researcher uses existing information sources, such as books or films.

There are specific organisations and archives set up to help professionals with their research in the various media industries, such as Reuters or the National Sound Archive. Students will be unable to access some of these, mainly for financial reasons. However, there are also useful handbooks and reference works which a library should be able to get for you. An excellent book is David Spark's *A Journalist's Guide to Sources*, Focal Press, 1996.

Information can be in the **public** domain, that is, freely available to members of the public. Alternatively, it might be **proprietary** knowledge, i.e. owned by an individual or an organisation, and therefore not so accessible. There is an old saying that 'information is power' and while this has always been true, there is now so much information available that it has become a gigantic industry in itself with many agencies specialising in handling and controlling information of different types. Information is seen as a commodity to be bought and sold. You will, therefore, need to identify your information requirements and assess how much it will cost in terms of time, inconvenience and perhaps money to obtain them.

When we talk of the *content* of media products, we mean the ideas which make up the product. These may be fiction (based on fantasy or unreal people or events) or non-fiction (based on true facts, people or events). (See Chapter 4, page 92 for further discussion of realism and anti-realism.)

Finding new ideas

Many students find the most difficult part of production planning to be the generation of suitable ideas. The media are always looking for novelty – no other industries use up ideas so quickly – but where do these come from? The simple answer is that they come from people. Sometimes these people are already established and have made their reputations, such as famous authors. But ideas can come from someone who is not yet known – like yourself.

How are ideas generated? Many films, for example, are based on books, plays, TV dramas or even cartoons. They may also be based on events or social issues.

Activity

Where were the ideas for the following films found?

Mary Poppins
The Sinking of the Titanic
The Flintstones
Superman
The Madness of King George
Gandhi
Little Women
Dances with Wolves
The Fugitive
Equus
Schindler's List
Much Ado About Nothing
Batman

There are two main reasons for an idea being developed further:

- the product will be a money-spinner
- there is public demand for the product.

Making money is an obvious motivating factor – but what does the public want?

- there may be a strong interest in some current social or political issue
- people need to be informed about certain situations or events
- there is a demand for a forum to voice opinions on a topic
- there is a hobby which has had little coverage from the media
- people need some means of sharing emotions, such as laughter or outrage
- there are issues and situations in society which could be turned into a comedy
- everyone enjoys some sort of escapism from life's realities.

Activity

Make an ideas list based on the following:

- What hobbies or activities interest you?
- What areas of knowledge do you know most about?
- Conversely, what would you like to know about?
- What sort of people fascinate you?
- What events in the news have caught your attention?

- What sort of films, radio and TV programmes, newspapers and magazines would you most like to have produced yourself?
- Has anything happened to you recently that has amused, shocked, horrified, surprised or annoyed you?

All of the things you have listed could become the basis of a magazine article or a TV serial.

However, a production idea is not only about the content of ideas but also about their **presentation** or **treatment**. For example, there are lots of sports programmes dealing with football, so another football programme would not sound like a new idea. However, if a new programme was started which discussed footballing issues using cartoon characters in a daily ten-minute TV slot, then it does become something new.

In terms of generating ideas, **primary sources** can also be said to include short stories, poems, films and press releases; in fact, it could be anything that stimulates ideas, anything that you come across that gives you the first idea for a product.

Investigative methods for carrying out content research

Primary research can take place in a number of ways:

- personal interview
- telephone interview
- through personal correspondence
- by observation
- by taking photographs
- by making video recordings
- by making audio recordings
- by surveys and questionnaires.

It is very important to choose a cross-section of these methods. The researcher can guide the research to meet specific objectives; for example, asking 'leading' questions in an interview or structuring a survey to get certain responses.

Secondary research also takes place in a number of ways, but it is one step removed from the researcher, who cannot influence the shape it takes. It is very useful for checking original research. It includes all the material you expect to find in a modern library:

- books
- newspaper articles

- magazine articles
- documents, such as reports
- maps and diagrams
- videotapes
- audiotapes
- electronic retrieval devices such as CD-ROM, the Internet and multi-media reference works.

Activity
Look at the ideas list you made above. Choose four different ideas and identify the primary or secondary sources of information.

Communication skills

You will need to develop interview techniques and your interpersonal communication skills. You will need to be able to make appointments.

Activity
Identify someone whom you wish to interview in order to gather information for your production.

Write a brief letter outlining who you are and what your production is about. Give an indication of the kind of information you are looking for and ask if you could have an interview. If the information you are looking for is brief and quite straightforward, it may be that you could obtain it all by letter, without having to meet personally.

Write out the same information in the form of a check list, with questions, for a telephone enquiry asking for an appointment. It may be that you could conduct the complete interview over the telephone, even if it means ringing again at a pre-arranged time.

It could be that you have never met a particular individual before. In this case, it is a good idea to identify the factors that influence communication. Physical appearance, personality and body language all contribute to how people react to you.

Activity
List as many individual factors as possible, such as hairstyle or accent, that might alienate an interviewee or set them at ease.

Importance of team work

Now you have some ideas that interest you, but you will have to work at them to make them interesting for other people. Even at this stage, it is important that individuals get together in a team to discuss their work.

In a business situation, the idea may not be your own. You could be working for an agency that is commissioned to produce, for example, a promotional video for a company. It is vital to ensure that the user/customer is involved in the drawing up of the specifications for the product, and at regular intervals thereafter, as a means of reviewing and checking that the work remains 'on spec'. You will not get paid for producing what you *thought* the customer wanted. Also, it could be that the customer does not know exactly what is wanted or what will work. This is why you need to build in regular reviews, called 'milestones', so that you can check on progress and decide on modifications.

Regular meetings should take place with the production team and, if there is a client, then the client should be involved, or at least briefed after the meeting. To ensure that a record is kept and words are put into action, minutes of each meeting should be taken and produced in time for the next meeting. In order to aid efficiency, meetings should also have an agenda. The case study below gives an example.

Case study

A student group are involved in a production simulation and have called themselves Picturehouse Productions. Their brief is to

> **There will be a meeting of Picturehouse Productions in the student common room at 10.00 on 10.09.96.**
>
> # Agenda
>
> Present (those in attendance at the meeting)
> Apologies (from anyone absent)
> Minutes (of previous meeting)
> Matters arising (from minutes of previous meeting)
> Suggestions for titles/credits
> Video packaging
> AOB (Any other business)
> Date of next meeting

Figure 5.1 Meeting notice and agenda for a student production

add moving images to a selected piece of music which is no more than five minutes long. Their meeting notice and agenda is shown in Figure 5.1.

What are the advantages for the students of taking minutes?

Activity

Using the format above, devise an agenda and then hold a meeting on what research needs to be done for your chosen ideas.

Key approaches to researching audiences

You could take any of your ideas to a producer. How will they then be evaluated? Why are some ideas accepted and other rejected?

You could be lucky and a producer or client might immediately consider yours a brilliant idea. It is more likely, however, that a producer will expect you to have done all the research listed below in order to convince him or her that the idea is worth developing.

One of the first points to consider is the appropriateness of the idea for the target audience. It is crucial to identify your audience and the purpose of the product, so that you can ensure fitness for purpose. You must be quite clear in defining who the product is intended for in terms of age, gender, social class and interests. It is not sufficient to state that this cartoon is intended for young people. How young? Pre-school, age 10–12, older teenagers? The interests of a particular age group will also vary according to their affluence or if they live in a rural or urban community.

Methods of research

There are a number of ways to approach audience research and these are dealt with in more detail in Chapter 21. Methods of research cover:

- **quantitative** research, which collects and compares statistics
- **qualitative** research, which collects attitudes and opinions and makes generalisations from them
- **demographic** and **socio-economic** research, which looks at how people of different age, class, sex, financial background and so on, react

- **psychographic** research, including lifestyle groupings.

This last category is of particular interest at the ideas stage. It is a technique well used in the advertising industry, because it cuts across socio-economic and demographic boundaries. **Psychographic** methods look at how individuals see themselves and what they want to be like. You may be sixteen and female, or you may be sixty and male, but both of you may want the same lifestyle. You might want to be free and travel the world or you might want to do something to help the environment. This means that you are susceptible to similar influences and may buy the same products.

Lifestyle grouping

Through interviewing sample groups, the lifestyle grouping research method builds up profiles of the type of people who share or want to share a lifestyle.

The advertising agency Young and Rubicam divided the population into four main groups:

- *Mainstreamers*
  These people want security, to play it safe. They tend to conform, they do not want to stand out from the crowd or be controversial, they like to buy brand names. They will be attracted by pensions adverts. They shop at high-street stores such as Marks and Spencer.
- *Aspirers*
  These are interested in material success and the trappings that go with it. They are outward-looking types, they like novelty and gimmicks. In the 1980s they would have been called Yuppies. They like status symbols such as the Porsche and Rolex watches. Designer labels are important for them.
- *Succeeders*
  These are people who have already achieved some status in their lives, either through birth or through their work. Their main driving force is their wish to control. They are less ostentatious than the aspirers. They do not flaunt their money. They have classic tastes, for example preferring the Rolls-Royce to the flash sports car. They identify with products which command respect and not just material envy.
- *Reformers*
  This is the most educated group, who are interested in public and social concerns – not just concern for themselves and their immediate families. They wouldn't necessarily buy branded goods, or things just because they were cheap.

However, they might actively seek out something environmentally friendly. They would be the group most likely to respond to Benetton advertising with its stress on social issues. People from the education and caring sectors are well represented in this group.

Activity

What category would you put yourself and your colleagues into? Develop a profile of yourself and compare it with those of your friends.

Of course, no-one resides completely in one category. Most of us are a mixture of two or more of these groupings. We may also be in different categories for different products.

Activity

Look at the articles and adverts in a cross-section of magazines, such as specialist ones and Sunday supplements. Which of the four groups listed above do you think they are aimed at and why?

Demographics

However, it is still usual and useful to divide audiences up by **demographic** criteria.

Activity

Look at the statistics in Figure 5.2 on the next page, showing which age groups and genders like certain programmes.

Are there any surprises here? Do we make assumptions about the type of programmes people like to watch?

You must decide whether there is a gap in the market for a particular audience. You will need to carry out market research to establish this. If there are already suitable products that fill this gap then no matter how good or original your idea is, the chances are it will not be pursued.

Monday 01.01.96 (percentage of population viewing)

Start	Title	Min	Adults %	Men %	Women %	Housewives %	Children %
17:40	Early evening news	015	10	9	11	13	3
17:55	Weather	002	11	9	12	13	4
18:01	Home and Away	023	11	8	14	13	13
19:01	Catchphrase	026	20	15	24	25	13
19:29	Coronation Street	028	33	26	40	41	23
20:01	The Bill	028	26	22	29	30	19
20:33	Strange but True	025	22	20	25	25	17
21:02	Peak Practice	057	19	15	23	24	8
22:02	News at Ten	028	10	8	11	12	2

Figure 5.2 BARB statistics on viewing habits

Activity

Can you identify any gaps in the TV schedules for your age group?

Justification

Funding for any project will also depend on the purpose of your project. There are three main justifications for a media product. These are:

■ **information** – what facts are you trying to tell somebody? What knowledge will they acquire by watching or listening to your production?

■ **entertainment** – will they watch or listen as a form of escapism from their ordinary lives? Or to relax after work, fill in their leisure hours in a pleasant manner or to give them the thrill of different experiences, from romance to horror?

■ **persuasion** – will the product result in action on the part of the viewer or listener? Will it induce physical or mental change in the way they live or behave? For example, will they change their voting habits after watching a party political broadcast or buy the latest designer trainers after seeing the advert?

When the BBC was formed, its brief was to inform, educate and entertain. The chances are that just about any programme you choose to watch will fit into one or more of these categories. Other channels too follow a similar formula.

Activity

Look at a sample of one day's TV schedules. For example, the extract below:

1.00 ITN News (Teletext) and weather

1.30 Racing round Britain and Ireland. Colin Forbes' insight into the 1993 Teesside Round Britain and Ireland Yacht Race

2.00 The Motor Show. Will Hoy samples the delights of stock car racing

2.30 Cartoon Time

2.50 The A-team: Judgement Day. In this feature-length episode of the action series, the Vietnam veterans travel to Europe aboard a cruise ship.

4.35 London at War: The Making of Modern London. Nina Hibbin, who had the unenviable task of inspecting the overcrowded street shelters in 1940, tells of the complete lack of facilities for those seeking shelter from Hitler's bombs.

5.10 The London programme: NHS Bed Shortages with Trevor Philips

In between each programme there will also be adverts and trailers.

1 Which programmes are primarily concerned with giving information?
2 Which programmes may be considered balanced between information and entertainment?
3 Do any of these programmes aim to make us change our spending habits or our lifestyles?

Activity

Look at your own ideas listed above. What is the main purpose behind them? What other reasons may be involved?

Most media products will contain elements of all three 'justifications' but usually one reason will dominate, depending on the intention of the producer and the attitude of the viewer/listener. For example, some gardening programmes are produced primarily to give information to existing gardeners about new methods of planting or the availability of different plants. Another programme may be made to persuade young people to take up gardening. Both these programmes may be entertaining in order to keep their audience, but the underlying reason behind them is different.

Activity

Find current examples on TV of programmes which superficially cover the same topic but where the purpose is different, for example, holiday/travel programmes.

Form and content of ideas

Sometimes producers are approached by clients or sponsors who already have a basic idea or concept: they know what the purpose and the target audience are to be. What they want is an idea for the presentation of their concept.

How this purpose will be best communicated will affect the content in terms of choosing non-fiction (when the characters and events are real) or fiction (with imaginary characters and events) for the narrative or storyline.

Some products can mix the two:

- a film based on real historical events but with dialogue made up yesterday
- an advert about a real product, such as gravy, which is used by a 'pretend' family.

A decision must be made about which medium or format will be the most successful for the purpose. These will include:

- **Audio**: tape is cheap to produce and can be used either as part of a radio show or be produced to be sold as cassettes. Nearly every home has a cassette player and it is a popular format for people to play in their cars. It is a familiar format, for example, for stories for children, language courses, music.

- **Video**: the popularity of the video as a format has increased enormously over the last decade, as video players have become accepted in the home, college and workplace. They are particularly popular with young people because of their demand for music videos and films on video. Despite their high price – not only for the producer but also for the purchaser – their quality and availability will always make this a format to consider.

- **Audio/still image**: the tape-slide production is still used in schools and colleges and in industry to give presentations. It is cheaper and easier to make than video. The final production can be quite sophisticated, depending on the equipment used. For a large audience it can be better than video because it can be shown on a large screen. It is also cheap and comparatively easy to update or alter in length.

- **Computer graphics and animation**: these are becoming cheaper, easier to produce and more sophisticated all the time. They are invaluable in presenting boring or complicated information in an attractive and comprehensible way. Animation has in recent years been used not only for children but for adults, in a variety of products from adverts to opera. The new capabilities of computers are making sophisticated animation easier to produce.

- **Newspapers**: these are cheap to access and cheap to buy and provide up-to-the-minute information. They contain lots of short items, both pictures and text. They can reach a large target audience in the case of national broadsheets and tabloids or a localised audience, as in the case of regional and free newspapers.

- **Magazines**: these are aimed at specific audiences. They come out less regularly and are more expensive. However they excel at in-depth articles of a specialised nature and the quality of their paper means that people keep them for longer than newspapers.

(For further detail on the characteristics of different genres, refer to Chapter 3.)

Case study

A doctor wishes to be able to explain a difficult heart operation to patients in a clear, concise and sympathetic manner. A media consultant sketches out the following specification:

115

Purpose: to give information about the operation and to persuade people that the operation is not something to worry about but will benefit them.

Target audience: adults, mostly over the age of 40, who are not only unwell but are probably feeling vulnerable.

Preferred format: video using computer graphics. Most health clinics these days will have access to a TV and video player and the patient can also have the option of borrowing the video. It will also appeal to a wider section of the population than a magazine article, which patients might take away and then either not read or misunderstand. They are more likely to express concern or ask questions after watching a video.

Content: the fictional scenario involves a worried male patient visiting his consultant, who will explain briefly the problems which make the operation necessary and the main steps in surgery. The video will end with a former invalid explaining how well he felt afterwards. The operation is explained using animation rather than scenes from real operations, as these might be too disturbing and not sufficiently clear. Computer graphics will be better able to illustrate the complex procedures.

Treatment: bright colours and lively modern music will generate a cheerful optimistic atmosphere. The presentation will be shared between a male and female consultant. The video should last approximately ten minutes.

How well does this specification fulfil its purpose?

Activity

Write a mini-specification for each of the following clients, which will include the purpose, the target audience, the format, the content (fiction or non-fiction) and technical details such as length or colour. Explain how you reached your decision.

1 The manager of a small sports shop who would like an advert to promote its opening in the locality.
2 A manufacturer of a new type of bubblegum.
3 A history teacher needing an information pack on the Battle of Bosworth, 1485.
4 The manager of a rock band wishing to promote their latest record.
5 A manufacturer wanting to show new employees the various departments and personnel in the factory.

Remember that there will be a number of ways of approaching each assignment; there is not one correct answer.

Content considerations related to the development of media ideas

There are many legal and ethical issues to be considered at the planning stage. If these are ignored, there could be serious problems which might either hold up or even stop production and the quality of the product and its eventual success will be affected.

Details of the following can be found in the Legal and Ethical Appendix at the back of the book:

- **Legal** considerations
  - defamation
  - copyright
  - race relations
  - equal opportunities
  - sex discrimination

- **Ethical** considerations
  - confidentiality
  - privacy
  - offensive material
  - representation (see also Chapter 2).

Sources of information relevant to production research

Location

As part of your planning for the generation of print and audio-visual material, you will have to identify a suitable location. For example, in the case of film or radio, you have to decide whether you will shoot in a studio, on location, or both; how easy it is to get to a location and what the conditions are like.

A location may look ideal for your needs on a particular day, but you need to do some research into possible changes in conditions. For example, there may be more people or traffic about than you anticipated, or even roadworks or a demonstration, carnival, etc. If recording for radio, then you may be looking for a particular quality of sound only available at certain times. Weather conditions also need to be considered, especially if shooting or recording in an exposed position. Time of day will possibly affect production, so the natural light and shadow will need to be checked for the camera crew. You also need to find the best vantage points for cameras and tape recorders and decide whether they are in a safe and secure position, which will not interfere with other activities in the area, and that the equipment will not be interfered with. You should also make sure that you will be able to get the full range of shots or sounds that your script requires.

It may be that access to a particular location is restricted, at least at certain times. You will need to find this out before going to all the trouble and expense of travelling over with the rest of your team and with all the equipment you need. For many students, locations will need to be within walking distance of the college.

Above all, make sure that the rest of the team know where the location is and what time they should be there! Contact numbers are also essential, so that if anything goes wrong, people are not waiting around for hours.

Transport

The problems of transport should not be under-estimated. Cars, vans and lorries and their drivers, will need to be booked well in advance. If the location is in too isolated a place, then you may have to reconsider because of the expense. It can be useful to use a studio which can be accessed easily by public transport, for example, if making a quiz programme with the public as contestants.

For reporters, where you interview people is of considerable importance. It may be more comfortable to interview them in a restaurant, but this may take up too much time. Sometimes the only opportunity may be on the steps of a courtroom. The reporter has to investigate each individual circumstance and decide where will be the best place and how they will get there.

Most importantly, location and transport can affect continuity so you need to keep this constantly in mind. The continuity person is responsible for ensuring that errors do not occur, such as an aeroplane appearing in the sky during a period drama or a scene which is supposed to be continuous in which the actor is standing in sunshine one minute and then in cloudy conditions.

Talent

'Talent' refers to the people who will appear in a programme. Actors, actresses and performing animals will need to be auditioned and booked through an agency.

Decisions have to be made about whether you need any 'non-professional' people to be in certain parts of your production. Extras, such as experts e.g. politicians or scientists, or representatives of social groups, such as the homeless or environmentalists, or participants, such as sportspeople or gameshow contestants, are also referred to in TV, film and radio as talent. They too have to be researched, from their addresses to their personal backgrounds, and especially as to their availability on a certain date.

Journalists for newspaper and magazines also have to undertake similar research about the people they want to interview.

Friday 19 September

SET UP AND READY TO RECORD:	0900
LOCATION:	Burbage Village, Nr. Hinckley
CONTACT:	Mr & Mrs Evans The Post Office Tel: 01455 681 Mr & Mrs Peters (Ye Olde Pub) Tel: 01455 623
DIRECTIONS:	Take the A5 out of Nuneaton (Watling Street). Just after passing through Burbage there is a sign for Hinckley on the right-hand side of the road. Take this road, Burbage is about 5 miles further on. Do not take the first sign for Burbage before Hinckley – this is a very congested road.
PARKING:	Technical vehicles by telephone kiosk on left-hand side of road outside the post office. The coaches and private vehicles in the pub car park.
ARTISTES:	Time req. on loc. Alice.....................................0830 Jan..0830 Shaun..................................0830 Drew.....................................0830 Ben.......................................0830
SUPPORTING ARTISTES:	Old road-digger ....0830 Young road-digger ....0830 3 girls....................................0830 Postman ....0830 4 school children................0830

Figure 5.3 Location details

Props

Apart from equipment, you may need to consider whether you will need any 'props' such as furnishings, ornaments, scenery, etc. These will have to be arranged well in advance. It can take considerable time in the case of period drama to collect together furniture appropriate to the period. Equally difficult problems can arise for photographers working for a glossy food magazine. The food has to be ordered and prepared to a very specific timescale.

Figure 5.4 shows a props list for an outside broadcast.

Property Requirement

Project No. 49K		Copies to:	
Production: THE POST OFFICE EPS.4/5	Reh Room	Producer	2
		Designer	2
Producer: Pete Allen Ext.2017	Filming Date 11-18 August	Buyer	2
		Asst Handling	1
Designer: Harry Drum Ext.2018	Location see below	P/C Buyer	1
		Stores Sup.	2
Prop buyer: Alice Ext.2019	Studio Dates	Scene Sup.	2
AFM: Jan Berry Ext.2020	Setting Date	Date Issued	
Sheet No. 4		Date Received	

O.B.ACTION PROP LIST-VEHICLES & ANIMALS

BURBAGE COMMON 12-AUGUST -On Loc.at 0830hrs.
                        (req. all day)
44. Bill's Landrover (continuity for Ep1)

POST OFFICE, BURBAGE 12 AUGUST-On Loc.at 0830hrs.
                    (req. until 1300hrs)
44.1 Labrador dog tied up to lamp post

VILLAGE CHURCH-13 AUGUST-On Loc. at 0900hrs.
                     (finish-TBA)
45.3 parked cars (black, blue and red sports)

N.B.Please inform Production of the cost of the cars before ordering, as it maybe necessary to cut numbers.

Figure 5.4 A props list

Sometimes graphic designers have to be involved in changing the props to suit the action (see Figure 5.5).

Music

Music is an integral part of any audio-visual production, especially the opening titles and end credits. It can affect the entire treatment and needs to be considered from the beginning. The main choice will be between using original music, written specifically for the production, or copyright music

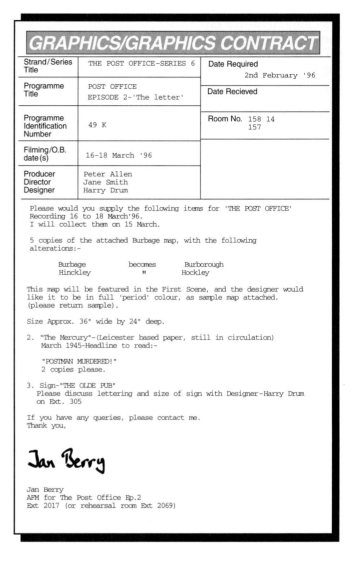

Figure 5.5 List of changes to props

written for another purpose. In the case of the former, a suitable composer or music group will need to be found and booked and a recording session organised. In the case of copyright music, legal clearance will be needed. (See the Legal and Ethical appendix for more details on this subject.)

Sound or special effects

You should also think of any sound effects or special effects. Obtaining the correct ambience and wildtracks can often take considerable time to prepare and rehearse and need to be built in from the start. You may save time and money by using pre-existing sound effects, such as bird-song on disc or explosions and other effects found on samplers. Special effects such as pyrotechnics, for example ships on fire, must also be ordered well in advance. A BBC producer will contact the London Visual Effects Department as soon as possible.

Permissions

Permission must be given by the owner before you can use private property for photography, filming or sound recording. Professional media producers expect to be charged, sometimes thousands of pounds, for working in someone else's house or on their land. After use, they must return the property to its original condition unless requested otherwise by the owner.

Journalists face similar problems. It may be necessary to liaise with certain people, for example, security guards, custodians, police, gatekeepers and so on, in order to gain access and it is better to anticipate queries about what you are doing. These arrangements should be made sensitively, and in good time. Nobody likes to be taken for granted and it is courteous to ask permission or to let people know what you are up to in their immediate area. Sometimes, for example, if actors are using imitation firearms in a public place, it is necessary to inform the police.

Students should get into the habit of obtaining written permission for wherever they film outside college. This is not only good public relations, but may cover them legally too in case of accidents. It is particularly important when students are using pubs or graveyards, for example, that they contact the publican or vicar, respectively, to gain permission. Security guards in arcades and supermarket managers can be unwilling to allow filming, photography or interviewing to take place on their premises if not approached in advance.

Permission will also be needed if copyright material, either music or words, is to be used. (See Legal and Ethical appendix.)

Risk assessment

Risk assessment covers health and safety matters, including general hazards such as personal safety, fire, electricity and emergency procedures. It is essential that regulations are followed or production may be delayed or even halted; an individual or a company sued for negligence could lose thousands of pounds.

Activity

Design a form which you can use as a checklist for all the factors to consider when you carry out a pre-production location visit.

Evidence assignment

Compile a production handbook. This could be in the form of a loose-leaf file or it could be a database stored on a computer with regular printouts. The chosen format should permit you to add or change information with ease and be simple to access. The handbook should contain the following information:

- list of the content of products which needs to be researched
- names, addresses and telephone numbers of contacts, e.g. interviewees, individuals within the public services, librarians, team members
- completed booking forms for equipment and studios
- details of locations that could be used
- permissions needed for locations
- details of props needed
- lists of transport needed, including timetables
- details of risk assessment for particular situations and locations
- a bibliography of sources of information for content of productions
- a list of suitable music for audio-visual productions
- notes on copyright restrictions
- details of permissions to use copyright material
- notes on research methods to be used
- notes about research relating to the target audience for different products
- notes on key legal and ethical considerations
- notes on issues of representation

This handbook will be an important part of your portfolio. It will have further material added to it as you progress through your course.

Chapter 6

Plan and carry out research for print items

This element gives you the opportunity to originate ideas and to research and develop them as far as the copy stage. The ideas should be for individual small pieces of work, such as news stories, features and comic strips, rather than for entire products. The work can then be used in Unit 3 to compile a complete print publication.

You should practise writing in different styles and at different lengths for a cross-section of publications, from children's comics to broadcast newspapers. At all stages you should consider not just text but graphic illustrations, diagrams, drawings, photographs, etc.

Origination and evaluation of ideas for print items

In Chapter 5 you will have generated some ideas already. Perhaps some of these will be suitable for a newspaper, magazine, brochure, poster or comic? However, let us also look at where professionals get their ideas.

Newspapers

Where does the content for newspapers come from? Most of the pages are filled with items that appear regularly, such as the editorial, the horoscope, the cartoon, the weather report, the TV schedules, display adverts, classified adverts, obituaries, entertainment listings, letters, and so on. The content of these may change, but there is a formula there in terms of length, vocabulary and style which the journalists follow.

Activity

Find an example of a horoscope, cartoon strip, obituary and editorial in a tabloid or local newspaper. Analyse the construction of each, considering length or size and type of words used. Choose two and write or design your own. Change the content, using different names and events, but closely follow the structure used in the newspaper.

The remaining space in a newspaper is filled with features and news articles. These do not appear out of thin air. Journalists do not stumble every day upon a major story worth reporting, especially if they work for a small town's local newspaper. They have to *create* the news. They get their ideas not only from personal observations and face-to-face interviews, but from the following sources:

- the emergency services
- the general public
- interesting photographs
- reports from councils (including public notices) and other official bodies, such as Parliament
- press releases from businesses and other organisations
- international news sources
- national news sources (if they are local)
- local news sources (if they are national)
- TV, radio and other newspapers
- job vacancies, obituaries, etc.
- contacts.

When this material is collected and put on their desks, it can look very boring. It is the job of the journalist to make it attractive and exciting for the reader. So do not worry if your original idea may seem bland or uninteresting, it is how that idea is treated which is important.

Case study

Each morning the *Leicester Mercury* has an editorial meeting to decide on the content of the newspaper and the various editions for the day. Here is the first part of the **minutes** of one such meeting.

Working as a team, decide which of the stories referred to in Figure 6.1 you would give priority to – in order to provide an interesting and balanced selection of news for the reader. Then make a list of possible ideas that you could contribute to your local newspaper or to a college news-sheet. Try to find at least one from each of the sources listed above.

THE EDITORIAL NEWSDESK

7.45 am   The news editor and sub-editors report to editor

The newspaper already has some sections prepared – consisting of advertising copy, features and stories from the overnight list. A proportion of the paper, including parts of the front page, are left blank for 'live' stories. Pages 1, 7 and 9 are usually 'live'. In the next hour or so these blank spaces must be filled. In the editorial meeting the following topics are briefly discussed and decisions are made rapidly on what to select for the blank spaces.

News editor's report

- Rothley four-year-old believed to be first child in Europe to have life-threatening diseased spleen removed by keyhole surgery. Another first for Leicester Royal Infirmary [PIC]
- Nurses at risk through bus service cancellation, claim. [PIC]
- Jealous rivals blamed for wrecking prize-winning Broughton Astley gardener's show exhibits. [PIC]
- Seven-year-old Birstall girl, who was an inspiration to everyone, has died of cancer. [No pic]
- City Council ad in *Mercury* inviting 30,000 County Council employees to learn truth about local government re-organisation appears to break gentlemen's agreement. (To be updated with reaction after first edition).
- State of the art technology brought into play to catch The Bank pub armed robber – a videofit. [PIC]
- City Leisure services debate Guildhall video system and Tudor Road pub move. (Previews done on both so decisions needed.)
- Leics. police launch child safety initiative.
- City Council response to road humps.
- Vandalised allotments – victim blames 'rivals'. Ed. asks to 'pull cuts' to check whether any legal implications (i.e. could be only one serious rival, implied suspicion). [Dep. Ed. decided to chop all ref. to 'jealous rivals'.]
- Tuna war
- Pools winner harassed by 'Sun'.
- Queen Mum.
- Councillors set to give go-ahead to £250,000 spy camera scheme in Leicester – 19 sites in city centre.
- Old soldiers selling off their cherished medals because they're broke. [PIC]

- Glenfield Parish Council wants to capture vandals on film and prosecute the parents.
- Police, magistrates, councils and clubs to sort out the bully bouncers who racially, sexually and violently harass customers.
- 'Kids from hell' terrorising Mowmacre council tenants ... and City Council meeting as Saffron Lane old folk to keep diaries of crime.
- 85 people want to be education director.
- Parish bobbies idea proposed by Government's law and order think tank. (Cross ref. to centre.)
- Rail supporters' meeting.
- £5,500 raid on Humberstone Heights Golf Club.
- 8 Leicestershire millionaires.
- CAMRA results.

District reports:
Market Harborough traders' non-payment of rent
Loughborough man stuck in Sarajevo
Melton pedestrianised area problem
Coalville/Ashby Leisure Centre alterations
Hinckley local government reorganisation.

National reports:
Shot policeman (made TV news the night before)
Rail strike
Snatched baby
Interest rates
Dollywood
Kelvin McKenzie resignation
Atheist vicar
Asthma and road pollution.

Sports reports:
Current fixtures
City haggling over purchase of a new player.

Pictures
Reunion of family with brother not seen for 37 years
Shetland ponies.

The news editor will be responsible for allocating tasks to reporters, photographers, copywriters, and others. He will write some of the important front page live copy himself.

Figure 6.1 Editorial meeting of the *Leicester Mercury*

Magazines

Magazines also hold regular conferences, either weekly or monthly depending on the type of publication, in which they will plan the contents. Editors will decide what features to commission. It is rare for the majority of publications to use **unsolicited** work. These are articles which unknown writers send in the hope that they will be published. Established freelances seldom submit work 'on spec', but put forward ideas for features they would like to write or photograph.

Editors may want something which is:

- **topical** e.g. about a current film
- **fresh** e.g. a medical breakthrough
- **seasonal** e.g. Christmas recipes
- **a follow-up** e.g. the life of a soccer star a year after scoring the goal that won the World Cup
- **promotional** e.g. sponsorship of a fashion show.

All of these apply to photographic as well as written assignments. As with newspapers, magazine editors will be looking for a mix of lightweight and more serious subjects.

Activity

Look at a music magazine or other hobby magazine of your choice. Write down some ideas for the next issue that would be topical, fresh, seasonal, promotional and a follow-up.

Some magazines use a **'think tank'** to **brainstorm** ideas, where a group of people get together to discuss possible features. Sometimes one person will pick up a half-hearted idea from another and see its potential.

Most of the ideas you have thought about so far have been for **non-fiction** material. **Fiction** is provided in magazines through their short stories. These too will reflect the nature and style of the magazine and the interests of its particular readers. You would not usually expect to find a sci-fi story in *Woman's Own* or a serialisation of a Catherine Cookson novel in *Loaded*.

Activity

In small groups, brainstorm ideas for a new comic strip for children. Identify fresh characters, situations and behaviour that

would make this cartoon original. Do rough sketches of the main character. Everyone should be given the opportunity to make a contribution.

Anyone should be able to originate a cartoon character without amazing drawing skills if they follow the basic steps given on pages 144–9.

By now you should have identified several possible ideas for newspapers, magazines and comics. If you want to add to this list any other interesting ideas for posters or leaflets, then you may do so.

Evaluating ideas

How do you decide which ideas are worth developing? Some of the reasons have already been discussed in Chapter 5 and in the text above. The three main criteria for evaluation are: fitness for purpose, resource requirements and aesthetics.

Fitness for purpose

This covers suitability for the target audience: is it appropriate for their age, mentality, interests? It includes whether it entertains, persuades or informs readers. Will it form a cohesive part of a larger publication in terms of subject matter?

It must also meet the physical needs of the publication. Is it the sort of idea that can be expanded or cut down to a specified number of words? For instance, the *Leicester Mercury* recommends the following number of words for certain types of story:

- a lead story   – approximately 200/300 words
- a square story – approximately 80 words
- a small story   – approximately 60 words
- NIBS (News in   – approximately 50 words
  Brief stories)

Resource requirements

Resources can be categorised as follows: human, financial, materials, time.

Human resources: personnel should be identified in advance. Will you need a photographer as well as a reporter or can one person do both jobs? If an event in the evening needs covering, will there be a member of staff available? Many local newspapers cannot afford to pay a staff photographer over-time to go out and photograph many evening or weekend events, such as school fetes or annual dinners. Instead they rely on freelances to provide coverage. The essential personnel are the photojournalist, the editor and the printer. (For a list of jobs in the printing industry see Chapter 9.)

Financial resources: even for a small feature article, expenses will be incurred in both generating and producing the material. The journalist will make phone calls and have travelling expenses. The photographer will have to buy film. If a glossy up-market brochure is planned then production costs will be much higher than for a black and white leaflet. (For examples of costings see Chapter 9.)

Materials: paper, pencil, a computer and a film for the camera are the most important materials that the journalist needs. At a later stage expensive newsprint and inks will be needed. For producing print products generally you will need to have access to the following: a drawing board and T-square (but you can get by with a large flat surface and a long, transparent ruler), compass, pencils (preferably H series for the compass because they are hard, and HB or B series for freehand), a protractor, two set squares (one 30 and 60 degree angle, the other 45 and 90 degrees), an eraser, pencil sharpener, scissors, masking tape and sticky tape, and a craft knife.

For posters you will, of course, need paper. These range in size from A0 to A6.

Time: for newspapers, one of the biggest constraints is time. Material must be prepared to meet the **deadline**. A newspaper cannot go into circulation with empty spaces. Editors have to be realistic in assessing how quickly information can be collected and written up and photocalls arranged.

Aesthetics

This refers to the artistic and creative side of the idea, rather than commercial considerations. Is the idea worth pursuing for its own merits?

Some newspaper and magazine articles are classic pieces of writing and some photographs have a

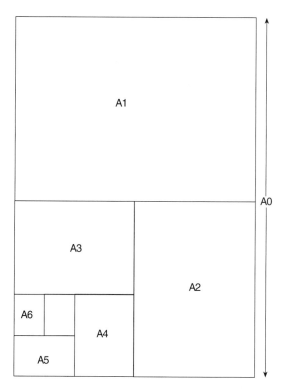

Figure 6.2 Paper sizes

Figure 6.3 Photographs from the *Hinckley Times* by Jim Tomlinson. News photos can have a beauty of their own

123

beauty or meaning of their own, which transcends the publication they were written for. It is not unusual, for example, to have exhibitions of photographs taken by journalists in the course of their work.

Activity

Evaluate the ideas you have collected so far. How realistic are they? Assess them under the headings of fitness for purpose, resource requirements and aesthetics. Which ones do you feel are now worth progressing?

Key features of print items

The key features to consider are the **target audience** and the **concept** behind the idea – its purpose, design, style, content and layout. The ideas have so far embodied assumptions about the type of person who will want to read or look at the print items. The audience will have been suggested already in terms of age, gender, class and interests; but now research will need to be done to ensure that the correct audience has been defined.

The underlying **purpose** for many publications is the need to make money – for the writers, the photographers, the printers and the publishers, and retailers such as bookshops or newsagents.

Certain genres traditionally appeal to certain target audiences, for example comics appeal to young children, novels with some line drawings appeal to teenagers. However, if adapted, different genres can also appeal to different target groups, so comics can also appeal to adults, such as adult fantasy comics.

The target audience and the purpose will influence not only content but style and layout, or the choice of fiction or non-fiction. People can just as easily be persuaded or informed through an imaginary story as through a serious article, which may not grab their attention or their interest.

Case studies

Look at the print and graphic items on pages 124–6 produced by GNVQ students.

Mike Sewell needed to produce a CV. He is interested in a career as a photographer and decided to present his CV in a different format from the one generally used for a CV (see Figure 6.5 on the next page).

His **target audience** are employers and university/college admissions tutors. He wanted a high-quality product that would show off his technical abilities, but also one whose aesthetic qualities would show that Mike has the ideas to succeed in a media industry. He wants to **inform** people about his qualifications and work experience and **persuade** them that he is a suitable candidate. The style of a 'Wanted Poster' gives novelty.

Figure 6.4 A poster warning against drug abuse

The **target audience** for the drugs poster by Becket Jones (see Figure 6.4) is teenagers. The purpose is to attract attention through the set of images that are associated with both horror and heavy rock music. There is very little text. Its message is simple and clear: its intention is to shock and **persuade** young people that drug taking is to be avoided.

Joe Bailey had to design an advert for McDonald's. The target **audience** included both children and parents. The cartoon characters he suggested would attract the children and the text would inform parents of the advantages of having a party at

MEDIA MOGUL

Produced by Michael Sewell at Griffindale Limited Printers, Lutterworth • January 1996

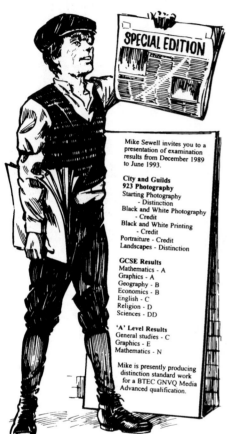

Mike Sewell invites you to a presentation of examination results from December 1989 to June 1993.

City and Guilds
923 Photography
Starting Photography
 - Distinction
Black and White Photography
 - Credit
Black and White Printing
 - Credit
Portraiture - Credit
Landscapes - Distinction

GCSE Results
Mathematics - A
Graphics - A
Geography - B
Economics - B
English - C
Religion - D
Sciences - DD

'A' Level Results
General studies - C
Graphics - E
Mathematics - N

Mike is presently producing distinction standard work for a BTEC GNVQ Media Advanced qualification.

SEWELL EXPOSED!

Within the last few hours it has been announced that Leicestershire student, Mike Sewell, needs a career in Press Photography.

Mike Sewell, 20, has only a few weeks left in a secure media course before he is thrust onto the job streets to fend for himself. Mike is currently studying for a BTEC GNVQ Advanced at the Hinckley College, and a leaked report states his intentions to pursue a photographic career.

The artistic confession came just after his work placement at the local newspaper, Hinckley Times. He spent two weeks with a team headed by Chief Photographer, Jim Tomlinson to experience the life of a Photo Journalist.

In those weeks Mike tackled many assignments ranging from the opening of a playground for special needs children to Member of Parliament David Tredinnick visiting a South Leicestershire school.

Communication became a key factor in the job. Talking to and organising children, sports stars, High School achievers, and teachers was a task equal to Sewell's talents. In addition to the photography he was able to further his printing knowledge by producing colour photographs of the jobs he covered and orders that the public had made at the front office.

Colour contact sheets, cataloguing prints, and making the coffee were also high demand activities which Sewell undertook.

His photographic knowledge grew from studying a City and Guilds course at night school with his DIY fanatical dad. Having completed the final module Sewell realised that he loved the art and scratched down a career plan.

During 'A' Level studies his photographic urge was locked up, only let out to photograph students for the college yearbook and to take pictures for his assignments. Everything was going to plan, when disaster struck. Damaging 'A' Level results left Mike at a loss meaning a Degree at Wolverhampton was impossible.

The career plan was revised and after a year out working in retail he was back on track with his present media course.

Recent news from a Hinckley College source reveals that Mike is working with colleagues to produce a four-page supplement for the Leicester Mercury provincial newspaper, to be published in March this year. The pull-out will promote Hinckley College and try to attract students to the area.

As well as providing support to the advertising team, Sewell's main role will be to head the photographic department.. Our source, which cannot be named for legal reasons, believes his experience, knowledge and enthusiasm will help the newspaper team to produce a high quality publication.

We at the Media Mogul also hope that Mike Sewell realises his dream of becoming a Photo-Journalist.

Mike in action with the Hinckley Times

Part-Timer

For the last Four years, along with my education, I have been working part-time at my local Safeway Superstore in Hinckley.

Some may say that stacking shelves in a supermarket is a boring job but the people I work with make it bearable, often a laugh. I've seen staff come and go and I must be one of the only employees to have been there from opening in march 1992. I think of Safeway as a big family and that's probably why we all work well together as a team.

In organising social events and team building exercises we get to know each other better and therefore work together better. Our recent technological developments such as our Self-Scan system and other new ideas have kept my interest in working there. I have no intention of pursuing a career in supermarket retail but as a part-timer feel proud to be working in a professional business.

My retail experience comes from assissing sales. Starting out on the grocery department I was promoted to handling wines and spirits to end up in my present position on the produce team. While working with liquor I had the responsibility of holding the keys to the wine store and occasionally now have the keys to the main delivery door and other secure units.

The Safeway experience will continue to keep me occupied until I find my way into press photography.

Spare-Timer

In between studying the media and working part-time at my local supermarket I enjoy several sporting activities.

The summer months see me cycling through winding countryside lanes and spending time on the golf course. Come winter I follow the ups and downs of Leicester City Football Club. Better still I'm indoors playing badminton or ten-pin bowling.

Figure 6.5 A CV with a difference

Figure 6.6 An advert for a local McDonald's

McDonald's and persuade them to ask for further advice (see Figure 6.6).

The target audience for Figure 6.7 are teenagers and young adults. The purpose of this adventure cartoon strip is entertainment.

Activity

Take a magazine such as *Smash Hits*. Identify the purpose of each article. Is it to persuade you to buy something? Which articles inform you about what groups are doing? Do any educate you, for example about the music business? Which items are entertaining or amusing?

Research will also support the choice of content and its appeal and effect on readers. However wonderful the idea is, its accessibility must also be assessed. Access to a product implies not only physical access (where can I buy this magazine?) but mental access (do I understand this writer?).

Figure 6.7 An entertaining cartoon strip

Investigative methods and research for print items

The range of investigative methods has already been described in Chapter 5. Questionnaires and interviews can provide valuable information but when should you use them? A prime consideration for the researcher will be the time available for the investigation. Statistics from official research bodies are generally reliable (see Chapter 21), and information from other secondary sources, such as books and magazines can be quick and cheap to access; but primary sources have their own unique benefits.

Personal interviews

What are the advantages of personal interviews for writing articles or adverts, or fiction such as comic strips or novels?

Answers to this question include the following.

- The material is fresh and comes direct from a living source.
- Information is up-to-date, even up-to-the-minute.
- It adds human interest to a subject, through personal anecdotes.
- It is the only way to get quotes which add life to an article.
- It is 'unique' in that you will be able to bring your own experiences and personality to the interview.
- You can modify the interview to suit the approach that you feel is most appropriate for the article. A change of approach can be made during the interview itself, depending on how you judge the situation.
- It's cheap – there are no copyright fees to pay unless you are writing for the papers and are paying to get an 'exclusive'.
- Most people prefer to talk to another human being rather than write things down or even use the telephone. A face-to-face interview gives you the opportunity to develop a rapport with the interviewee.
- It makes an article sound authentic.
- Readers want to know how the people actually involved in an event felt.
- Comments and opinions, other than from the author, give another viewpoint or dimension to a topic.
- You can get intimate details that may be unobtainable elsewhere.
- You can obtain small personal details, such as what the person likes to eat for breakfast.
- A good interviewer can pick up on non-verbal communication, such as whether someone is ill at ease and possibly lying, or whether he or she is being modest or reticent and there is more information to find out.
- You can ask people what they think about a product.
- You can ask people what they think about certain types of adverts.
- Interviewees can give you ideas you may not have thought of.
- You can get ideas from talking to people from your target audience.
- You can find out about people's everyday lives, or their jobs, i.e. what society is like now.
- You can take photographs during or after the meeting.
- There may be no published written data on this subject or event!

Telephone interviews

What are the advantages of interviewing over the telephone?

- You can obtain quotes.
- It saves time, you may be able to obtain all the information then and there.
- It saves transport costs in getting to a face-to-face interview.
- You may be so many miles apart from the interviewee that a meeting is impossible.
- You can use it as a preliminary interview to prepare someone for the face-to-face interview.

Personal observation

What are the advantages of personal observation?

- Readers expect the reporter of a football match, the reviewer of a pop concert or the critic of a play to have actually seen these events.
- Extra detail can be added, such as the expression and gestures of someone found not guilty after a trial, or the colour and style of a wedding dress.
- You don't have to rely on other people's views or information; they might not have noted something that you think is significant.

Images

What are the advantages of taking photographs?

- They are a good record of what research was done and how it was done.
- They give a face to a name, they pin-point a location.
- They can job your memory, when you actually come to write an article about a person or place, about what it was like at the time.
- They can tell a story for you – you may be able to dispense with words.
- They can support and give emphasis to written, factual information; for instance, a story about an old person being mugged is horrific, but a photograph is even more moving.
- They are essential for feature articles.

Audio or video recordings

What are the advantages of making audio or video recordings?

- You can give your full attention to the interviewee if you are not writing notes.

127

- You have a complete record of what is said, so quotes can be accurate.
- A small cassette recorder is unobtrusive, but the video camera will provide visual images.

Questionnaires

Why should you use questionnaires?

- They collect the opinions and attitudes of lots of people.
- They are fairly cheap to run and analyse.
- They can give you information about your target audience, their likes and dislikes, when planning your book or comic strip.
- They are good for assessing reactions and getting feedback.
- Results of questionnaires can be used in books or newspaper articles to support your viewpoint.

(For detailed information on how to design a questionnaire, see Chapter 24, page 405.)

How do you decide which method to use? In practice you will probably mix a number of these approaches.

Case study

The well-known author Sue Townsend officially opened the new library at Hinckley College in 1996. The media students wrote the article shown in Figure 6.8 about the event.

Can you identify what sources of information could have been used?

Here is a brainstorm of the research that was suggested by the students.

Personal interviews:
with the author, Sue Townsend, to get information, anecdotes and quotes.

Possible questions include:

- how she writes, with word processor or by hand
- her inspiration for writing
- how she got involved in writing
- her opinion of the TV version of *Adrian Mole*
- what else has she been, besides a writer
- future projects
- whether she prefers writing novels or plays
- her background; children, age, marital status, etc.
- does she live locally?
- has she visited the town before?
- did she go to a college?
- the books she reads.

Writer opens new college library

Sue Townsend recently visited Hinckley to open Hinckley College's new Library and Learning Resources centre. She was honoured to do so, as she acknowledges the importance of libraries as essential and integral to the learning development of individuals.

Former College Principal Mr Ifor Jones began proceedings with an introduction to the £330,000 centre.

The audience were entertained by a humorous and honest speech by the writer, who talked about her success story which came in the form of a spotty teenage boy with the name Adrian Mole. She also talked about her plays, such as 'The Queen and I'.

Inspired

Sue's early influences came from the popular Just William series of books, and she was inspired to write after witnessing a murder as a child. She has also worked within the Social Services as a youth worker, from which she has gained a valuable insight into the minds of teenagers and their secret lives.

Sue's literary talents were discovered by accident, when an actor friend of hers needed some material with which to audition for a play. Sue offered her book for material. When she learnt of the positive response from the people present at the audition, she decided to send off her hand-written copy of the work.

The writer, who is married with three children, said: "Librarians have made me and taken me from a dreary life." After the speech the author proudly cut the ribbon which was tied over the library entrance and the official opening was final. The new library holds a variety of individual study rooms and a GNVQ/NVQ seminar room. It has the latest in information technology, a series of Pentium computers and CD ROM facilities, a multi-media facility, access to the Internet, and World Wide Web.

Figure 6.8 Media students' article about a library opening

with the librarian, Sue O'Callaghan, to get information about the event, the library and quotes.

Possible questions about the event include:

- details of the ceremony itself
- what does the event involve?
- will it be formal or informal?
- who else is she meeting?
- what is their relationship to the author or the college?
- the name of the main organiser of this event.

Other information must include:

- description of the old library
- advantages of the new library
- opinions of staff and students.

with the students at college to get quotes about the old library and the author.

Questions to include:

- have they read the books or seen her play?
- ask for permission to photograph in the library
- where does the librarian suggest journalists and photographer stand?

Telephone calls:

to her agent, for background details on the author and to ask if the students can interview her personally

to her publisher, for permission to quote from books

to the principal, of the college, asking for a quote.

Personal observation:
of the site

- visit the library to look for photo opportunities
- where can the reporters stand?

of the official event

- what did she wear?
- what did she look like?
- what happened?
- for how long did she speak?
- what did she say?
- who else was there?

Photography:

- photograph of her with students
- photographs of the library
- photographs of the moment the ribbon is cut.

Audio/video recordings:

- of the official ceremony and the speeches.

Secondary research:

- read the books
- read the plays
- read critical reviews of her work.

As you can see, not all the information collected was used. The editor decided that the story should run on the front page as **hard news**, rather than as a **feature**. As a result, the article had to be edited to fit the front page requirements.

Primary research: interviewing

There are three basic types of **interviewee**:

- experts
- celebrities
- the general public.

All of these should be considered when doing any sort of research. But whoever you are interviewing, there are some basic skills you should learn. A recommended book is *Interviewing for Journalists* by Joan Clayton (Piatkus, 1994).

Activity

The secret of good communication is to be a good listener. This is important in an interview situation so that you can develop a rapport to show that you are interested and value the interaction.

Many people are not good listeners. Find out whether you are by answering the following questions:

- Do you look at people while they are talking to you?
- Do you break into a conversation whenever there is a pause?
- Do you keep your mind on the topic of conversation?
- Do you always insist on having the last word?
- Do you manage the physical environment so that you and the interviewee are comfortable and can hear what is being said?
- Do you give non-verbal clues, such as nodding and facial expressions, to indicate that you are giving them your attention?
- Are you sensitive to a speaker's need for privacy?
- Are you sensitive to the tone of a speaker's voice and 'body language'?
- Do you consider the other person's point of view, even though you may disagree with it?
- Can you ignore what someone looks like and concentrate on what he or she is saying?

Some people, such as celebrities and experts, may be experienced in handling requests for information. Interviews with experts are necessary to check the accuracy of material already gained or to find out new facts.

Case study

Crime writer P. D. James sought advice from a member of the mortuary staff working for a local authority for one of her murder mystery novels, *Original Sin.* She wanted to learn about post-mortem techniques. Specifically, she needed to know if a micro-cassette, hidden in someone's mouth and then removed after their murder, would leave a mark. She also wanted to check whether the roof of the mouth is examined in a routine post-mortem and, if so, would any bruising be noticeable? Why did the author feel that this forensic background information had to be thoroughly researched?

Secondary research

Professionals also use a number of secondary sources to gain material for print and graphics products.

International, national and regional news agencies find news stories and take photographs and sell them to newspapers and broadcasters. They provide up-to-the-minute news reports and images. Some can also provide features.

The leading international news agencies are:

- **Reuters**
  This is the most famous electronic supplier of news and information, including images, to the print and broadcasting media throughout the world. The Reuter World Report gives 24-hour global coverage from political to sports news. The organisation was founded in 1851 and now has 123 news bureaux in approximately 80 countries, employing more than 1,200 journalists, photographers and camera operators. It also has interests in television news.

- **Agence France Presse**
  This is a large international French agency, providing a news and picture service to the UK and disseminating British material to the foreign media.

- **Associated Press**
  This is a huge American agency, owned by US media companies, which supplies news and pictures to the UK and disseminates British material to American media outlets.

The main UK agencies are:

- **The Press Association**
  This is owned by the regional newspaper publishers and was for many years the main agency.

- **UK News**
  This is now a major challenger, established in 1993 by Northcliffe Newspapers and Westminster Press, and is based in Leicester.

Some agencies provide specialist services:

- **Extel Financial**
  This agency supplies financial and business news around the world.

- **Parliamentary & EEC News Service**
  Reports on political developments in Britain and the European Union are provided by this agency.

There are many regional news agencies. A few examples are given below:

- **Croydon News Agency**
  Specialises in reporting law courts.

- **Fleet Street News Agency**
  Covers London and the Home Counties.

- **Frontline News and Sports Agency**
  Covers Scarborough and the Yorkshire coast.

Illustrations can also be found from secondary sources. For example, the National Picture Agencies and Libraries specialise in still photographs. The trade association BAPLA (the British Association of Picture Libraries and Agencies) publishes an annual directory of its members. Some important sources are listed below:

- **Action Images**
  Specialises in sports photos.

- **BBC Photograph Library**
  Contains more than 2 million programme stills.

- **British Library Reproductions**
  Reproduces images and pictures from its collection.

- **Capital Pictures**
  This specialises in portrait photography, especially of people in showbusiness.

- **Greater London Record Office**
  Besides written material, this contains over half a million photos of London, especially useful for official and historical photographs. Other record offices throughout Britain are equally useful sources of information.

- **Hulton-Deutsch Collection**
  At one time owned by the BBC, this is one of the largest photo collections in the world, holding over 15 million images covering most subjects and periods.

- **Popperfoto**
  Another very large collection, with over 12 million images, it collects not only historical pictures but also photos from the leading news agencies.

There are numerous other picture libraries, some general, some specialising in specific topics or areas, events or people. *The Picture Researcher's Handbook* by Hilary and Mary Evans (Chapman and Hall), is the standard reference book of picture sources.

When budgeting for a print product you should bear in mind that a charge may very well be made for these types of specialised service.

Activity

Look at your chosen ideas and identify which areas will need research. List the information you will need to find out, including the names of people to be interviewed.

Potential content considerations

The legal and ethical considerations of an idea will need to be researched, so it is a good idea to refer to the Legal and Ethical Appendix at this stage. Newspapers are ever conscious of the need to protect themselves against accusations of libel, invasion of privacy or the use of insensitive language that can cause offence.

A national tabloid was forced to pay out substantial damages to singer/songwriter Elton John after it failed to substantiate serious allegations concerning his sex life.

On the other hand, some publications appear to accept the risk of court action and publish controversial material, either because they believe it is true or because it sells.

Activity

Find other cases in recent years where newspapers have been sued, either successfully or unsuccessfully. The easiest way to do this is to carry out a CD-ROM search. What do you think prompted the decision to publish the offending material? Was it justified in your opinion?

Look at your own ideas for print items. Could any of them be considered unethical? Take two of them. How can you ensure that they are unbiased? Explain how, in some of your other ideas, you are considering issues of representation.

Select material for development

Selection of material depends on numerous factors, including the nature and purpose of the product, the target audience, and the limitations of resources such as time, personnel and money.

Case study

Look at the notes in Figure 6.9 of the decisions taken during one morning at the *Leicester Mercury*, and the editorial meeting they held. They show which leads were to be followed up and developed for the front page, and explain why. Difficulty in obtaining some information, and the arrival of dramatic news of a mountaineering accident, altered the front page considerably. For example, the intention to have a photograph of a pub serving the beer awarded a prize by CAMRA was ultimately thwarted because the photographer was unable to contact the landlord in order to obtain permission for a picture.

The editor, Nick Carter, has taken into consideration the key features: he shows continuous awareness of the target audience of the *Mercury* and the purpose of the newspaper. Priority is given to local news. He and the sub-editors ensure that the style is consistent and the layout visually attractive and helpful to the reader. There has to be a balance between novelty and familiarity.

The two main categories to consider with any print and graphics material are:

- **text**
  body copy, captions, headlines and sub-headings

- **visuals**
  photographs, graphics, cartoons.

By **copy** we mean written material, from the few words in a press release to the 200,000 words in a novel. You can learn skills that will help you write good copy – they are described in the following pages.

Produce material for print items

From your work in this chapter, you should now have a firm idea of what material you are going to develop.

Read the notes below on writing. You will also find the section on proofreading (Chapter 11) of value here.

1 Choose the appropriate vocabulary

Always keep in mind your target audience. Whether they are children or politicians, do not try to impress them with long words! Clarity is the aim of good writers, and short words can be just as effective as

8.00 am   *Decisions made on front page, where to include other stories and what further action needs to be taken.*

1   Check pictures on Braunstone. Has this story been run before?
2   Find a pub that serves the winning beer for photo.
3   Locate millionaires and their photos.
4   Saffron Lane can lead on page three.
5   Bouncers in clubs should be in relatively unimportant position as most readers don't come into contact with them. More people will have experience of and interest in parish bobbies so that story should have a more important position.
6   The old soldiers' story would be suitable for front page news except there is no photo as they were too proud to admit to having sold their medals.

9.30 am   *First deadline. All copy to have reached the news editor.*

9.50 am   *The news editor decides to switch lead story to that of child with spleen operation but photo is needed.*

9.51 am   *Child's mother is telephoned at hospital but she decides he is too groggy this morning to be photographed. Better this afternoon or in an hour's time. So news editor decides to stick with family reunion lead.*

10.00 am   *News comes in of a Market Harborough couple killed in a mountaineering accident on Jungfrau. This can become the lead story for the Market Harborough edition as the deadline for its copy is 10.30 am and it is late in the running order of County editions to be printed. Library is asked to locate map of Jungfrau.*

10.05 am   *Editorial meeting to discuss overnight list. This is to prepare news for the following day's paper.*

Discussions are led by the assistant news editor, whose job it is to compile the overnight list. He has approximately 12 strong stories and 6 potential leads. His sources are:

1   *Phone calls*
2   *His post in-tray*
3   *National stories with local interest.*

Also discussed are regular features, page layout and use of colour. The photographer has a major input.

Topics submitted by the assistant news editor at this meeting:

Carnival page
The best village shop at Thrussington
Trade unions for clergy
Safety routes for school children – has this been done already?
YTS trainee has joined police – picture needed
Holidays abroad & weather. (*Hot or wet weather has a considerable effect on newspaper sales as people's buying habits change.*)
Burglaries, gun offences, armed officers
Raw sewage in Groby.

Features:

Loros – an article on coping with death. Copy of about 600 words and photo needed, black and white.
What's in store – 600 words required and three pictures.

Sport:

Signings
Matches
Sports other than football
Colour photos of superstars in action.

Figure 6.9   Selecting material for the *Leicester Mercury*

long ones. Newspaper language has now become simpler and closer to the spoken word. Colour can be given to a dull text by the careful use of adjectives and adverbs: if you find yourself using the same words again and again, use a thesaurus to find new ones. A thesaurus is a book rather like a dictionary that gives you a range of alternative words with a similar meaning.

There are also words that you should avoid when writing reports because they have racist or sexist overtones. For legal reasons, the **generic** term for a product should be used, rather than its trade name.

The following is a sample of words to watch out for:

vacuum cleaner	*rather than*	Hoover
ball-point pen		Biro
public address system		Tannoy
vacuum flask		Thermos
photocopy		Xerox
business people		businessmen
disabled people		cripples
manufactured		man-made
police officers		policemen
flight attendant		air hostess
firefighters		firewomen

Activity

Make a list of similar words that might cause offence or are trade names. Think of a suitable alternative for each.

Jargon is the use of specialised words, such as medical terms – for example, *fractured femur* instead of *broken leg*. Jargon should be avoided wherever possible, unless you are writing for a specialist audience. The use of highly technical or 'in' words can be very off-putting in general writing – and fashionable terms tend to date quickly.

Different types of newspapers use specific language to give a certain sort of style. 'Tabloidese' language as used in *The Sun* or the *Daily Mirror* is easily recognisable. The tabloids use very short, melodramatic words. They are often highly descriptive words which imply a physical action, and they tend to exaggerate, e.g.:

axe	*rather than*	cancel
threat		possibility
slam		criticise
fury		annoyance
row		controversy
vow		pledge
quit		resign

Sometimes the tabloids will link two words to create a vivid image and add colour. In tabloidese, for example, people do not just have sex, they have *sex romps*. The connotations are that the sex is silly and naughty, which is (presumably) what people find

Figure 6.10 A 'death plunge'

titillating. Again, a fatal fall will probably be reported in a tabloid as a *death plunge*.

Activity

1 Go through any tabloid and make a list of the tabloidese you encounter.

2 Compare any editorial from a tabloid with one from a broadsheet newspaper.

3 Take a front page news story from a tabloid and rewrite it using the longer words associated with broadsheets. You will find a dictionary or thesaurus helpful.

2 Always check the spelling of your work

Use a dictionary as well as the spellcheck facility on a word processor. Remember, a computer will not pick up all misspelt words if their spelling is correct when the word is used in a different context, e.g.:

There bicycles were left here.

It is a common mistake amongst students to use there instead of *their*.

Try looking up the word *alot* in a dictionary – it is another common mistake. You will find that there is no such word. The correct spelling is *a lot*. But the spellcheck on your word processor may suggest *allot*, which would make nonsense of your writing.

You should also take into account that there are often differences in spelling between British English and American English. Many word-processing packages such as WordPerfect and Microsoft Word favour American spelling because they were developed in the USA.

3 Always check the punctuation of your work

The most frequent punctuation mistake is in the use of the apostrophe, e.g.:

Its a fine day.

The car looked good but *it's* engine was worn out.

These are both wrong. Remember, *it's* is an abbreviation of *it is*.

4 Check your syntax

Syntax is the construction of sentences. When students first start writing for newspapers, they tend to write sentences that are too long. Simple short sentences are best, but vary their length to give your writing an interesting rhythm.

Avoid the overuse of clichés, similes and metaphors, e.g.:

> horror attack
> desperate attempt
> blazing inferno
> honeymoon period

You will find all of these hackneyed terms in newspapers, but it is refreshing to see more individual language being used. For further detail on grammar read *Fowler's Modern English Usage* (Oxford).

 Activity

How many clichés and overused metaphors or similes can you find in one copy of a tabloid newspaper? What is their effect?

5 Planning, drafting, revising

Your first task in writing is to give some thought to the structure of your piece and its content. Refer back to the section above on investigative methods and research. Will you need to interview people? When will this be done? How long will it take you to write the piece? What photographs need to be taken, or what illustrations drawn? You need to decide at this stage whether the item is to be formal or informal, as this will affect the content. Do you need lots of statistics, or do you need lots of people's opinions?

Are you going to use direct speech or reported speech? The effect can be quite different: direct speech gives authenticity and immediacy to a report. Take this example from an interview for a magazine feature:

> I asked why he had said this. He looked straight at me. 'I don't know why', he replied, the faintest suggestion of a smile on his lips.

Compare this with the example below.

> I asked why he had said this. He looked straight at me and with the faintest suggestion of a smile told me that he didn't know why he had said it.

More drama is conveyed by the use of direct speech, and it has far more immediacy. In this particular example, reported speech has deadened the impact of the moment rather than allowing the reader to savour it.

Direct speech can be tedious, however, if there is a lot of material to quote. In this case, reported speech can avoid the tedium by summarising what was said. This practice can, however, cause distortions. Take this interview with a manager at a hospital. A reporter is attempting to interview her about an incident at work:

> 'Whose job is it to do this?'
> 'I don't really know, as it's not my department.'
> 'Don't you think you should know?'
> 'My main concern is with my own department.'

When summarised, the story could be given a rather unsympathetic interpretation:

> When asked who was responsible, the manager replied that it was none of her concern.

Alternatively, a sympathetic reporter could have made the manager sound more helpful than she really was.

When you have gathered the necessary information, you can write out a rough draft of your work. The best techniques for structuring your writing are described below. Your first draft will probably be revised several times before the final copy is submitted to the editor.

6 Check the accuracy of your facts

At the revision stage it is vital to check your information with another source, either primary or secondary. Also, as you can see from the examples above, if you are quoting someone, it is important that you use his or her exact words.

7 Structuring the text

Writing a news report for a newspaper is a different task from writing a feature article for a magazine. The 'shape' of a news report is often represented diagrammatically as an inverted triangle (see Figure 6.11). The idea is to get the key facts, i.e. the who, what and when, into the report as early as possible. This is followed by the non-vital, but still important, details of where, why and how. If the story is edited down to just the 'head', then it can still be used in the News In Brief section of a newspaper.

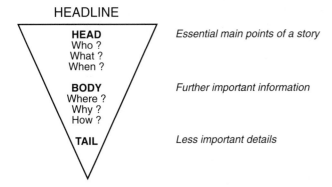

Figure 6.11 The shape of a news report

The report is constructed so that the important information goes in first, and less important details go towards the end. This means that if need be, the report can be edited by chopping off the 'tail' without harming the body of the text by editing out important information. If the story is constructed properly according to these guidelines, then the body of the report, or part of it, could also be edited out without losing key material.

These guidelines are not set in stone, however; you should note that sometimes, for example, the *where* fits more naturally into the 'head' of the report. The best practice is to use the guidelines but also to be flexible and use common sense when constructing a report.

'Hard' news stories are written with language that concentrates on reporting the facts not only as concisely but as fully as possible. The style here is less concerned with the aesthetics of creating atmosphere and drama or conveying emotions.

A 'hard news' report seeks to put the essential points across in the first paragraph, which often consists of just one sentence.

Case study

HEAD

WHO	A **postman and an off-duty firefighter**
WHAT	**saved the lives of two young children**
WHEN	**yesterday** when their Derby home became engulfed in flames.

BODY

WHERE *WHY*	Gemma Nicholls, 7, and her 3-year-old brother Darren were playing **upstairs at their home in Desford Street** when a **chip pan caught fire** in the kitchen.
	Off-duty fireman Sam Horris was decorating the outside of his home when he heard the children's mother Dawn Nicholls screaming for help.
HOW	Together **with postman Pat Walker they were able to use Mr Horris's ladder to climb in through a bedroom window** where they found the children huddled together clutching their teddy bears.
	They carried them down the ladder to neighbours, who had called the emergency services.

TAIL

Two firecrews and an ambulance attended the fire, which started shortly after 5 pm, and gave the children oxygen.

The children were taken to Derby Royal Infirmary, where they were treated for smoke inhalation, but were later discharged.

Their grandfather, Mr Albert Nicholls of London Road, Swadlingcote, said he was grateful for the rescuers' actions.

'If it wasn't for them my grandchildren wouldn't be alive,' he said.

Activity

Write a short news report of 100 words following the Head, Body and Tail formula. Now answer the following:

1 If you chop off the 'tail' does it still make a good story?

2 If you chop off the 'body' and 'tail', does it still make sense?

Feature articles

Feature articles are generally on a larger scale, and can afford to give space to a 'tantalising' opening that sets the scene and draws the reader into a story. A piece of creative writing, such as a feature article, can be represented by a triangle with its apex at the top. The apex indicates that it is not essential, factual information that necessarily comes first. In fact, it is more usual to create atmosphere first, and then, perhaps, create tension by a sudden unveiling of the drama of the story.

Feature articles allow you the space to examine the background of a story and establish personalities, features of communities, etc. The article below looks at the house fire story again, but this time from the point of view of a feature writer.

Getting started on writing articles

Sources of inspiration for articles include books, especially encyclopedias, books of quotations, yearbooks, and books of dates. Telephone directories can throw up some interesting names. Newspapers and magazines will also give you plenty of source material; get into the habit of cutting out articles and photos that catch your interest or that look useful, and keep them in a cuttings file.

Two or more disparate ideas can often be merged to create a third theme. For example, you may have seen a report or TV programme expressing concern about adolescents' diets. If you had been commissioned to write an article with adolescents as the target audience, how could you make it popular and interesting? One way would be to research some well-known sports personalities and talk to them about their diet. This would be tackling the task from a 'human interest angle', which is generally more interesting to readers than a plain report.

If you do have the subject for an article in mind, write it down in the middle of a blank sheet of paper. Then use a process called 'free association' (rather like a brainstorming session) to write down associated ideas about the subject. Each new idea can, in turn, branch into further ideas. Let's look at an example; say you have been commissioned to

IT HAD been a lovely sunny afternoon, and Sam Horris was using the good weather and free time to get some much-needed paint on to the windowsills of his comfortable, three-bedroomed semi in the quiet residential area of Desford Street.

He was enjoying the time off from his job as driver of Blue Watch's 12-ton Dennis tender – for Sam's normal occupation is as a firefighter. But today was destined to be anything but normal for Sam, even on his afternoon off.

It was just after 5 pm when Sam first heard the shouts coming from along the road. Looking down, he saw his neighbour Mrs Nicholls waving and shouting frantically. Then in the next split second, he saw the reason for her screams. Smoke was billowing out of the door and windows of her home and, although he was at least 100 yards away, he thought he could make out the ominous sound of crackling as the fire took hold.

'I didn't stop to think', said Sam. 'When we get a call at work we just go on automatic pilot, and get on with it, and this was just the same.'

Sam grabbed his 20-foot, two-piece ladder and began running and dragging it down the road towards the flames. But even he with his 15-stone, 6'2" frame was grateful when help arrived in the form of postman Pat Walker and Mrs Nicholls herself. The three of them managed to get the ladder into position against a bedroom window, and Sam was soon at the top and smashing his way inside.

'The room was full of smoke, but I spotted the kids almost immediately. I'll never forget the look on their faces when I appeared. I think I gave them more of a fright than the fire! Anyway, I grabbed the smallest one and passed him to Pat who was at the top of the ladder and hanging through into the bedroom. It was getting very hot so we had to move quickly. I then stretched out and took the older child by the hand. She was beginning to choke quite a bit, but all the same she was very brave.'

Sam carried her down the ladder to where Mrs Nicholls and her neighbours were waiting desperately.

Shortly afterwards, Sam's colleagues from Blue Watch were on hand and they soon brought the fire under control. The children made a full recovery and the family is now staying with relatives.

Mr Horris didn't feel he had done anything special on his afternoon off, but to friends and neighbours in Desford Street he is a hero. All Sam wants to do now is to get back to work. 'I need a rest,' he said.

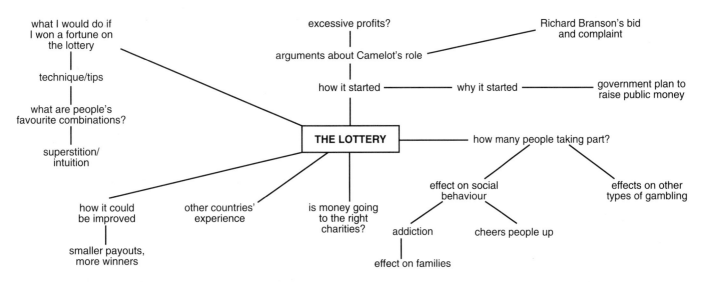

Figure 6.12 'Free association' ideas about the National Lottery

write an article on the National Lottery. You could begin to develop your ideas as shown in Figure 6.12.

Carry out your research, reading, observing, interviewing, and so on about the topic in such a way that you develop a 'feel' for it. Be committed, and convey that commitment to the reader. If the writing feels like a chore, then it will be dulled by your lack of enthusiasm.

The introduction

Americans call the 'intro' of an article or story the 'lead'. This is a good term as it captures the main purpose of the introduction, which is to lead the reader into the story. You need to make the reader sit up and take notice, and there are numerous techniques to help you do this. Try these:

Tell an anecdote, e.g.	Last week, I went to Jeremy's wedding and ...
Make a revelation, e.g.	Jeremy has a secret. His five wives don't know about each other.
Ask a question, e.g.	Would you know how to keep on top of five wives? Jeremy does.
Give a quotation, e.g.	'Jeremy was the most charming man I had ever met – and the slimiest!'

These could all serve as the lead into a popular article on bigamy or the state of marriage today. The point is,

you have to take a fresh approach so that an editor feels it will capture his or her readers' imagination.

Activity

Using one of your ideas, write two possible openings for a feature article using some of the suggestions above.

The middle

Once you have got the article under way, it is essential to maintain interest by keeping up the pace and sticking to the main point of the article.

Be specific, and add details so as to paint a vivid picture and gain authenticity. Try to describe actions closely so as to convey mood, feelings, attitudes, etc. For example, a certain travel story involved relating an encounter with a customs official, including the words: '... *with a look of disdain he sifted through the contents of my laundry bag.*' This could be altered to: '... *he picked through the contents of my laundry bag, holding the edge of each item between finger and thumb then letting them drop back into the bag before wiping his hands up and down the sides of his trousers.*'

This description conveys a sense of the customs official's disdain through the use of certain key words and phrases. The situation is communicated through the action, rather than by adding adverbs such as *disdainfully, gingerly, slowly,* etc.

137

Activity

1   Identify the key words and phrases in the example above that convey the customs official's feelings.
2   Try describing one of the scenes listed below with the same amount of detail.

  a Closing the curtains
  b A punch
  c Getting off a crowded underground train (or bus).

Remember, too many generalisations make subjects intangible and uninteresting. Bring your writing to life wherever you can.

Endings

Endings can also be problematic. You should seek to use much the same strategy as your openings and end strongly, rather than trailing off.

One common ending technique is the 'twist' where something unexpected or quirky is stated at the end. It is a good idea to leave the reader with something thought-provoking.

For example, an article was written with the tourist industry in Burma as its main subject. However, the article also mentions the Burmese government's policy of using forced (often child) labour to develop the country's infrastructure to facilitate tourism. It ends like this:

> The railway is a remarkable engineering achievement. It has opened up a beautiful country for the first time to western eyes. But like so much of the world's treasures, it is built on the shoddy, dismal foundations of cruelty and injustice.

What started as a point made in the body of the article has now become the main point with which the article is concluded.

With a different ending, this point could have been diminished:

> Although the local peasants have carried out 'national service' on the railway, there is no doubt that the influx of tourism can only bring benefit to their communities.

8 Decide on the balance between text and visual images

In children's stories and tabloid newspapers, lots of pictures, preferably in colour, are needed, although colour printing is expensive. Black and white photographs can give a feeling of sophistication or nostalgia, however.

When you take photographs for a feature or report, take lots! Try unusual angles and close-ups, as well as distance shots.

Use diagrams, including maps, graphs and pie charts, to explain complex situations or to present figures.

Case study

Student Hayley Dyer wrote a feature for a Sunday supplement on offensive material in popular young people's magazines. One of her first areas of research was readership. She collated the results of her questionnaire and presented them as a pie chart (see Figure 6.13). This is an effective method of presentation as it can be understood at a glance and also makes an attractive visual for the article itself.

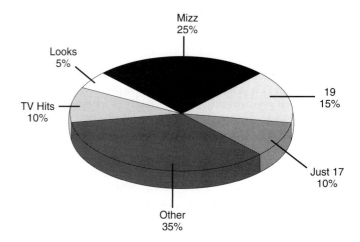

Figure 6.13 Readership of popular magazines

Activity

Sketch the illustrations or list the photographs you will need to accompany your articles or stories.

9 Retain your motivation, enthusiasm and creativity

It is all too easy to become tired of a project and to lose your initial enthusiasm. There is a lot of work involved even in a short news report. Set yourself short-term targets or milestones so that you can measure your progress. Most of all, accept that articles do need re-writing, often many times. Do not try to avoid revising your work! It is a most important part of your task.

10 Develop your own style

Style is a personal way of using words or language. You can analyse someone else's style and model your own writing on it, using the types of words and sentences that seem effective in communicating information about events, emotions and people. Good writers tend to be good readers. However, eventually you have to find your own style. Everyone's style is as individual as their handwriting – indeed, as individual as their personality.

11 Presentation of body copy

All your material should be word processed. Industrial standards require that each **folio**, i.e. page, of the text is:

- double-spaced
- written on one side of the paper only
- identified by the author's name, date and catchline (that is, a word taken from the story that is used to identify it to the typesetter. For example, the fifth page of an article on graduates searching for jobs could have the catchline 'Careers 5').

If you have to add an insert, say between pages five and six, then the catchline should read: 'Careers 5 (5A follows)', or 'Careers 5A (6 follows)'.

Ordinarily, each page should end with 'more follows', and the final page should have 'ends' written at the bottom. The number of words should also be given.

Headlines and captions

The job of headlines, sub-headings and captions is to draw attention to stories and (in the case of captions) pictures on the newspaper page. They have to give a succinct and interest-arousing impression of what the story or picture is about. But it is not just the words themselves that tempt people to read a story. The shape of a page is very important in ensuring that it looks attractive. Therefore, the design and arrangement of the headings and captions, as well as the allure of the words, help to highlight a particular story so that it catches the reader's eye.

Headlines, sub-headings and captions often use a pun or 'play on words' to make an impact. Nevertheless, the headline should always be clear and unambiguous, and it should describe what the story is about.

Captions are different from headlines in that they should not simply seek to describe a photograph to a reader, no matter how informatively and eloquently. They should expand on the photograph by alluding to the story it accompanies. In other words, the caption should form a link between the visual and the text. For examples of how captions work you should refer to Chapter 1.

Activity

Write a caption for the photograph in Figure 6.14.

Figure 6.14 Try writing a caption for this photo

Its accompanying text is included in the Case Study on page 155. You need to refer to it now in order 'contextualise' the caption.

Headlines do not generally have punctuation, except to replace the word 'and'. For example, the phrase *Men and women*, if used in a headline, would read *Men, women*.

Headlines usually miss out words such as 'and', 'is', 'have', etc. so that the result is a very condensed language with a predominately active rather than passive style. For example:

ISRAEL POUNDS LEBANON

is more powerful and immediate than:

LEBANON IS POUNDED BY ISRAEL

The headline is often accompanied by a **strapline**, which is an auxiliary heading in smaller type, usually placed above the headline. In the example above, the headline could be accompanied with the strapline:

Chaos as thousands flee tank and artillery onslaught

Activity

Try re-writing these into acceptable headlines:

DOG IS BITTEN BY MAN

GIRL IS MET BY BOY

A WOMAN IS HURT WHEN FIGHTING OFF THUGS TRYING TO SNATCH HER HANDBAG

For 'hard' news, headlines should be clear and unambiguous. If, however, there is more of a feature-style approach, the headline can afford to be more tantalising.

Photography

It is easy enough to take a photograph, particularly if you have a modern instamatic camera of the 'point and shoot' variety and you want to take a 'holiday snap'. However, it is not so easy taking an *effective* photograph, that is, a photograph that achieves its purpose and communicates your visual message. To do this you need to have a grasp of two concepts:

- how the camera works.
- how to compose a picture.

Although it is certainly possible to take decent photographs with a cheap instamatic camera, we will specifically discuss the **SLR (single lens reflex) camera**, as this allows you to make manual adjustments which will help you to learn how to take good photographs. It is regarded as a 'serious' camera by professionals. Let's see how it works.

In a homemade pin-hole camera, light enters the box through a hole and the image is focused by a lens on to light-sensitive paper. The SLR camera works on the same principle. The advantage of the SLR over an instamatic or direct viewfinder camera is that its mechanism makes the image in the viewfinder the same as that seen by the lens. Focusing on an image can be much more accurate, and lenses and filters can be changed.

The main parts of the SLR camera are shown in Figure 6.15.

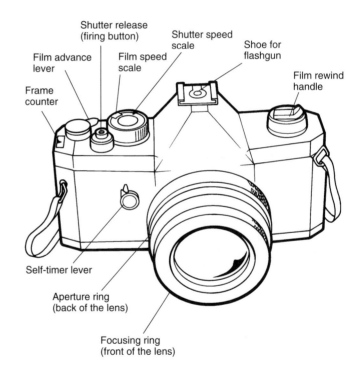

Figure 6.15 Main parts of a single lens reflex camera

Activity

With the help of Figure 6.15, locate the various parts on an SLR camera.

You should get used to the camera so that you can handle it confidently. Open up the back by pulling up the rewind spindle.

Examine the film speed scale. What are the most commonly used film speeds? Whenever you use film, ensure that the film speed scale is set to the speed of the film. Get used to loading, winding on and unloading film, preferably by using cheap out-of-date stock; practise adjusting the aperture ring and the focusing ring.

Types of film

It is important to use the appropriate type of film and know how to load it correctly. There are two types of films:

- positive – for colour slides
- negative – for colour prints or black and white prints.

Positive films have names ending in -chrome, e.g. Kodachrome. **Negative** films have names ending in -color, e.g. Agfacolor.

Prints are convenient but many professionals use slides. They are more economical because you do not have to produce prints from negatives. Also, they are appropriate for talks and presentations because they can be projected on to large screens. In addition, they produce better detail and colour at lower shutter speeds.

The more sensitive the film, the higher the **ASA/ISO rating**. ASA stands for American Standards Association. ISO stands for International Standardisation Organisation. ASA 200 and ISO 400 are both a numerical indication of film speed. Film speed is referred to as fast or slow.

Fast film is for taking photographs in low light conditions. With this type of film you can use fast shutter speeds – this cuts down the risk of blurring because of camera shake. However, you can see the grain of this type of film, which makes it look less sharp.

With **slow** film you need more light, and the more you can get the faster the shutter speed you can use. There is generally no grain apparent in the photograph, so it appears sharp.

The shutter speed determines how much light falls on your film. The scale is in fractions of a second. If, for example, you set the speed to 1/250, this means the shutter will be open for 1/250th of a second.

Techniques

Turning the **focusing** ring brings the subject into focus. Move through this until the subject starts to blur, then turn the ring back until the subject is in sharp focus again.

The **aperture** ring is the one closest to the camera body. It also determines how much light falls on to your film. To see how it does this, first make sure there is no film in your camera and then unscrew the lens from the camera body. There are numbers on the aperture ring which are called 'stops' or 'f' numbers. Look through the lens and at the same time change the 'f' numbers. You will find that the size of the aperture changes. The aperture is at its largest at the lowest 'f' number, probably f2 or f1.8, and at its smallest at f16 or f22. Each time you change the aperture you halve or double the amount of light you allow through the aperture and on to the film. If the film gets too much light it will be **over-exposed**. If it does not get enough light it will be **under-exposed**.

You need to be aware of the effects of sunlight when planning your composition. Sunlight is constantly changing throughout the day in terms of its direction, its strength and quality, its colour, and the effect it is having at any one time on objects or the landscape.

For example, direct sunlight can be harsh, especially on people's faces. It also creates shadows on their faces. You can soften the effect by moving the subject into open shade, or you can use a reflector – which can simply be a sheet of white cardboard held below the face (and, obviously, out of shot) – or you can wait for clouds!

Composition

A basic camera can achieve excellent results providing you use the controls as described and take the trouble to **compose** the picture.

There are several considerations concerning composition. A photograph is a form of visual communication so you should first of all have an idea of what you are trying to communicate.

You should start with a good idea of why you are taking the picture, what kind of image you are trying to achieve and how you are going to organise yourself, the equipment and the subject in order to achieve it.

A simple framing device can help you to plan a composition. You can make it yourself. It consists of

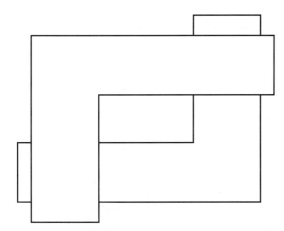

Figure 6.16 A framing device

two cardboard right angles which you place together as shown in Figure 6.16. You can then increase or decrease the size of the frame. Just as importantly, you can change its shape to make it more or less square or rectangular.

Always have a point of interest in the photograph. Do not put the centre of interest exactly in the middle, nor allow a 'line', whether it is the horizon or a washing line, to cut the picture in half. You should instead apply the 'rule of thirds', whereby the picture is divided into thirds rather than halves. It looks less contrived to have the subject sitting off-centre rather than right in the middle.

Figure 6.17 The horizon cuts the picture in half and makes it a very static composition

Figure 6.18 The girl at the front is the main subject. Her positioning in the left-hand third adds movement and interest to the photo

Use natural lines such as a road or fence to lead the eye into the picture.

With people, do not cut them off at their natural joints, such as where the neck joins the shoulders, or at the waist, elbows, or knees – this gives a rather strange impression and can make people look silly!

Figure 6.19 Natural lines lead the eye into the photo

Use any available framing devices such as doorways, trees, etc. to 'frame' a composition. Figure 6.20 shows a good example.

Get as close to the subject as possible, and be aware of background. It is easy to miss unwanted and distracting objects in the background, as in Figure 6.21.

Figure 6.20 Frame your subject if you can

Figure 6.22 The author complete with swans

Figure 6.21 Be aware of distracting background objects

Also ensure that subjects do not end up with trees, lamp-posts etc. 'growing' out of their heads! See Figure 6.22 for an example of an unusual headdress …

An essential concept is **depth of field**. All photographs show a certain amount of distance both in front of and behind the main subject which is also in focus. You can increase or decrease this area (the 'field') by altering the aperture. This increases or decreases the 'depth' of the 'field'. The rule is that the smaller the aperture, the greater the depth of field. Therefore, if you want to put the background of your picture out of focus you would shorten the depth of field by increasing the size of the aperture (see Figure 6.23).

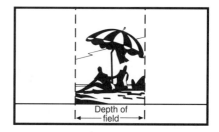

A large aperature gives a narrow depth of field

A small aperture gives a greater depth of field

Figure 6.23 Changing the aperture alters the depth of field

Pressing the shutter

When taking the picture bear the following in mind:

- use a tripod or rest where possible, especially if you are using shutter speeds of less than 1/30 of a second
- keep both feet firmly on the ground
- keep your elbows tucked in
- breathe out and, at the point before you draw breath again, gently press the shutter release.

When you take photographs to support your work, fill in a log like the one in Figure 6.24 so that you have a clear record of the conditions under which you took the photos. This should help you improve your technique!

GNVQ in Media Communication and Production

35mm PHOTOGRAPHY

Name ....

Type of camera ....

Make of camera ....

Make of film ....

Type of film ....

Where processed ....

Date ....

Shot no. ....

Date ....

Subject ....

Distance from subject ....

Lighting conditions ....

f stop ....

Shutter speed ....

Comments ....

....

....

Figure 6.24 A photographic log sheet

Cartoons

A cartoon is a drawing that creates characters and humorous situations through exaggerating the features and characteristics of faces and bodies. This is the world of fantasy where realism is suspended. It is also the world of stereotypes, where boys wear blue and girls wear pink!

An excellent book on the subject is Christopher Hart's *Everything you ever wanted to know about cartooning but were afraid to draw* (Watson-Gupthill Publications, 1994). This gives detailed instructions on how to draw cartoons from the earliest stages through to advanced techniques.

The most important skill to learn is how to draw a head and how to keep this face recognisable when it changes its position.

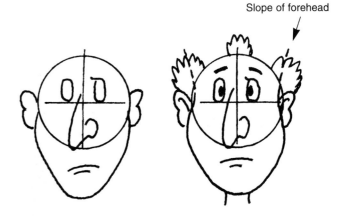

Slope of forehead

Figure 6.25 A basic face

Begin by dividing the head into two parts:

- a circle on which to place the eyes and nose
- a jaw which will contain the mouth.

As the head rotates, the features retain the same proportion and position within the circle (see Figure 6.26).

The horizontal line on which the eyes are placed can be raised or lowered. Babies or young-looking characters have a low horizontal line so that they can be drawn with big foreheads and eyes (see Figure 6.27).

The basic circle shape of the head can be changed to an oval or even a cylinder for different effects. Figure 6.28 shows an example of using a cylinder shape.

Figure 6.26   Rotating the head

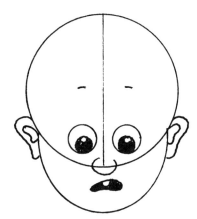

Figure 6.27   A baby's face

Figure 6.28   A cylinder-shaped head

Facial expressions are created by the eyes (as in Figure 6.29) and/or the mouth (as in Figure 6.30).

Bodies, too, come in easily recognisable shapes such as the ones shown in Figure 6.31. What does each shape suggest to you? Leg spacing can also be important – the heavier the body, the wider apart the legs are drawn.

Traditionally, cartoon characters have hands with only three fingers and a thumb! Figure 6.32 shows a typical example.

Figure 6.29   The eyes can create vivid expressions

145

Figure 6.30 Different expressions indicated by the mouth

Figure 6.32 The traditional cartoon hand has only three fingers

Figure 6.31 Body shapes and leg spacing

Figure 6.33 The action line and motion line

Movement is created in cartoons by the use of action and motion lines. The action line runs through the spine and shows which way the body is leaning. The motion line indicates the way in which an action like a throw or a punch is proceeding, and is not necessarily the same (see Figure 6.33).

Cartoon people are timeless. Fred Flintstone is essentially a twentieth-century man except that he wears animal skins and lives in a cave! It is not his body or facial characteristics that make him a Stone Age man, but his fur clothing, the fact that he lives in a cave, and his pet dinosaur.

In the cartoon world, location, customs and props must always be stereotypical of the chosen period, nationality and character. So a Spanish man is often dressed as a matador, and a queen must wear a crown and a long dress, as in Figure 6.34.

Backgrounds are suggested, rather than shown in detail. If someone is sitting reading in the lounge, it is not necessary to draw in all the furniture. Perhaps only an easy chair, the book and a standard lamp will be enough (see Figure 6.35).

Figure 6.34 Stereotypes abound in the world of cartoons

147

Figure 6.35 A few props can suggest an entire background

Certain objects in the drawing can be symbolic. For example, a crescent moon tells the reader it is night. The sun with broken lines around it, as in Figure 6.36, indicates searing heat.

Figure 6.36 The sun can be a symbol suggesting searing heat

Figure 6.37 A short word can be used to suggest action

Figure 6.38 A speech bubble lets us know what a character is saying

There are also many conventions surrounding the use of words in cartoons. Actions can be strengthened by short, onomatopoeic words such as SPLAT! and VROOM!, or cries such as AAUGH! and WHAAA! Speech bubbles can let us know what a character is saying. Text below or above the drawing can explain an action more precisely.

Other symbols have traditional meanings. Thought clouds, halos, stars or hearts floating over characters' heads also indicate their moods or what has happened to them, as in Figure 6.39.

Figure 6.39 Symbols indicate characters' moods or what has happened to them

Realism can be suspended in the cartoon world. Eyes can jump out of heads, animals can be flattened by a car and then rise again.

Activity

Draw a one-panel cartoon with a punch line (sometimes called a **spot gag**), or a short cartoon strip, or design an advert using a cartoon character. You may choose a political or social subject or a fantasy such as a sci-fi adventure to work around.

You will need to practise all the techniques described above many times before you can create an effective, individual character. For this Activity you may prefer to work in a team consisting of:

- a writer who produces the jokes and suggests the layout
- a cartoonist who draws the characters, props and backgrounds
- an inker who inks and letters the final drawing.

If you decide to use colour rather than a black and white line drawing, keep to colours that are symbolic of certain emotions or status, e.g. red for anger or purple for royalty.

Graphic design

A graphic designer is involved in discussions about a project from the very start. For example, the book jacket or cover of a magazine is one of the first items to be produced, long before the content, so that it can be used in market research and promotion.

The designers will be responsible for the overall look. They not only suggest pictures, their size and colour,

Figure 6.40 Copy often needs to be divided into blocks according to its importance

but also recommend how text should be laid out, what typeface will be appropriate and its size. They will need to know about the target audience, the product itself and what sort of 'look' the client prefers, such as traditional or futuristic, bright or subdued.

We are now living in the age of computer graphics, but there are still many practical skills that the graphic designer has to learn. These are the various stages that designers go through:

1 They first need to see the **copy**, i.e. the text. They will begin to select different types of lettering. They will decide how the blocks of text will be arranged.

2 Then designers will prepare **thumbnails**, i.e. tiny sketches to try out different ways in which the information can be arranged.

Figure 6.41 Thumbnails are drawn in proportion to the full-size job

3 A selection of the best thumbnails will be re-drawn to full size and possibly in colour. These are called **roughs**. At this stage the text and headings

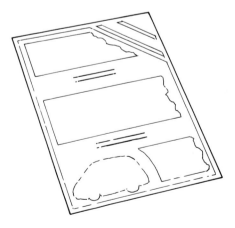

Figure 6.42 Roughs are used to refine ideas

149

may use 'dummy' or sample wording rather than 'live' or real copy.

4 The client will be shown a **visual**. This will be in colour and will be very close to what the final piece of work will look like. For best effect, these should be mounted on black card.

Figure 6.43 A visual gives a good idea of the finished work to a client

5 **Artwork** is the finished work that is ready for printing. Sometimes it is referred to as **mechanicals** or **camera-ready artwork**.

Figure 6.44 Artwork is finished work ready for printing

Lettering

A major part of graphic designers' work is deciding on the type of lettering, its size and how it is spaced. They will consider the spacing between individual letters, words and lines.

Calligraphy is the art of beautiful writing. When it is done by hand, the different effects are created by the changing angle of a broad nib (see Figure 6.45).

Figure 6.45 Calligraphy uses the different angles of a broad nib to produce its effects

Today, similar effects to those produced by hand-written calligraphy can be created by using the different typefaces available on a computer. There are two basic types of typefaces:

- **text** or **book** faces – used for blocks of text
- **display** faces – used for headings and titles.

Any lettering consists of a number of elements which can be combined to give contrasting effects, such as formal or informal, modern or old-fashioned. Figures 6.46 to 6.50 illustrate the use of differing size, style, weight, colour and case in lettering.

MEDIA LIFE
MEDIA LIFE

Figure 6.46 Size

MEDIA LIFE
MEDIA LIFE

Figure 6.47 Style

MEDIA LIFE
MEDIA LIFE

Figure 6.48 Weight

MEDIA LIFE
MEDIA LIFE

Figure 6.49 Colour

Media Life
MEDIA LIFE

Figure 6.50 Case

The same principles also apply to numbering. Some styles look traditional, others look modern. The two main styles of numbers are illustrated in Figure 6.51. Old-style numbers have the **3**, **4**, **5**, **7** and **9** dropping below the baseline, and the **6** and **8** extending above the topline of the other figures. Modern numbers all line up at the top and bottom, and tend to look better with modern type styles.

1 2 3 4 5 6 7 8 9 0

1 2 3 4 5 6 7 8 9 0

Figure 6.51 Old style (top) and modern (or ranging) numbers

For further information on typefaces see Chapter 11.

Not all lettering is produced by computer. You can use stencils, rub-down lettering, or spray painting using an airbrush. Spray painting is especially useful for creating 'fading' effects. Follow the steps shown below.

1 Trace letters on to the surface you want to use.

Figure 6.52 Letters traced onto the surface to be used

2 Stick special art masking tape over the letters and cut around their outline. Alternatively, you could cut a stencil instead.

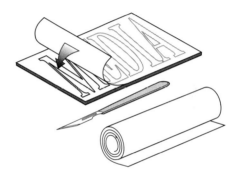

Figure 6.53 Masking film overlaying the letters

3 Spray the lightest colour first, either with aerosol spray paints or modelmaker's airbrushes. **Be sure to do this in a well-ventilated room.**

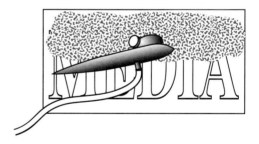

Figure 6.54 Spraying over the surface

4 Let the paint dry.

5 Apply other colours and allow them to dry. A darker colour will look most effective across the bottom.

151

6 When you are satisfied with the effect and the paint is dry, remove the masking tape.

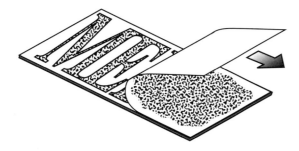

Figure 6.55 Removing the masking film to reveal the finished product

Producing a paste-up

In order to produce artwork, the graphic designer has to get together all the various components such as lettering, copy, photographs and drawings, etc. and do a **paste-up.** The following procedure should be followed.

1 Camera-ready artwork is always prepared flat on a line board. First, draw a **grid** in pale blue pencil. Photographic blue pencil will not show when a negative is made from the artwork. This grid gives a framework to work around. Books like this one are based on a simple grid, such as the one in

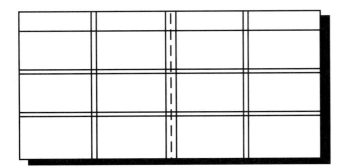

Figure 6.56 A grid for a two-column book

Figure 6.56. Newspapers with eight or nine columns to a page are more complicated. Use a ruler and set square to draw the lines around the edges of the page. Draw in the other columns and guide lines.

2 Take a photocopy of all the different components and cut them up.

3 In a **rough paste-up**, text and picture proofs are assembled together on layout sheets or tracing paper with the grid mapped out on it, to check that everything fits. Accuracy is vital, so dimensions must be checked and re-checked.

4 Trim the originals to within 3 mm of their edge. Keep your equipment very clean or you will leave marks on your originals.

5 Position the larger, straightforward pieces first, then drop in illustrations, and finally the smaller details.

6 Glue the back of each piece. Rubber solution, adhesive sprays or warm wax may be used. The board should be cleaned with lighter fuel to remove excess glue and dirt.

7 Position each piece on to the grid, following the rough paste-up, checking that each is straight with a ruler and set square.

8 Always protect your artwork with overlays. A transparent sheet covers the work first, and this can have instructions on it for the printer. Over that goes an outer cover to give greater protection.

Using computers

All graphic designers need to have a certain skill in drawing. It is still quicker to sketch by hand than to draw with a computer. However, computers can be a great aid, and several software programs such as Coreldraw have been developed as a design tool.

One area where computers are useful is for **scanning** in images for alteration. The shape, size and colour of pictures can be changed.

Industrial designers have found computers to be an invaluable aid for technical drawing, and the three-dimensional effects available can make a product look more realistic.

The latest collaboration between artists and computer researchers has been the development of **virtual reality**. By wearing special glasses with movement sensors, you can 'enter' your computer drawing, giving you the effect of walking or flying along a computer-generated landscape. This technique has already been used effectively to simulate flight conditions for trainee pilots.

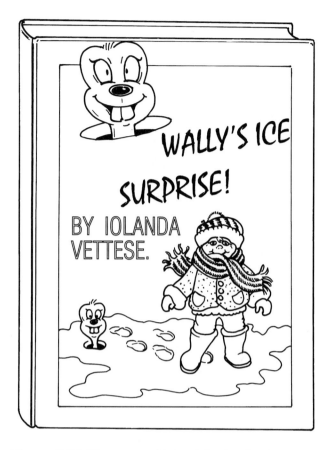

Activity

Design a poster for a film. Write an evaluation of your work, including both a discussion of the production method and the reasons for your choice of components for this particular design.

Two books recommended for further reading on graphic design are the *Usborne Book of Graphic Design,* 1987, published by Usborne, and *Practical Graphic Design Techniques,* 1991, edited by Lydia Darbyshire, published by Tiger Books International.

Justifying completed print items

Writing text and working with visuals are skills that need to be practised regularly before you can produce items quickly and to the required standard.

To justify or evaluate your work, you will have to consider the following questions:

1 Does it meet the needs of the target audience?

One of the best ways to assess this is by asking a sample from your target group to read the piece of work and give their opinions. You can learn a lot by asking people what they liked and disliked in a piece of work, and which parts they found most useful and/or interesting.

Case study

Student Iolanda Vettese wrote a short story for children for one of her GNVQ assignments. Part of her research involved visiting a local crèche to find out what type of stories and characters the children liked. After writing and producing her storybook, she attended another session at the crèche to read it to the youngsters. She noted down their comments to use in her evaluation. Figure 6.57 shows the cover Iolanda used for her short story.

Figure 6.57 The cover of Iolanda's storybook

2 Does it fulfil the original purpose?

No matter how clever, amusing or witty a text is, it must meet the needs of the client. It will be rejected if the intention was to give detailed information and it fails to do so. Alternatively, an advert will not be successful if it describes all the desirable features of a product in detail but fails to catch the eye of readers.

Case study

The two adverts in Figure 6.58 are quite different but are both suitable because their purpose is different. The first gives a lot of written details because its target readers are trying to locate a particular holiday at a certain price. They do not want fancy pictures; the purpose of the advert is to give information. The second advert has more pictures with less text, because the advertiser is trying to

153

Figure 6.58 Two holiday adverts aiming at different purposes

convey an impression of the attractions of the destination on offer. The underlying purpose is persuasion.

3 Were the necessary people or other resources available?

It is frustrating when writing is delayed because interviewees have failed to turn up or the photographer is late. When you were doing initial research, you may have found that a larger team was needed to do surveys effectively. You might also decide that you need someone in your team with particular skills. For example, if you are writing for a children's comic, you might decide in your evaluation that input from a graphic artist is essential. Were other resources, such as artist's materials, adequate for your tasks?

4 Has the cost remained within the agreed budget?

All professionals keep receipts of personal expenses incurred as they work, including charges for such items as faxes, postage, travel fares, film, processing costs, photocopying, etc.

5 Was there sufficient material to complete the task?

In other words, were you able to collect enough background information from either primary or secondary sources to enable you to write something fresh on the subject you had chosen? Perhaps you did not prepare the right questions for an interview, so you came away with too little material or the wrong material.

6 Did you run out of time?

If you cannot meet deadlines, then you will not be suited to working in the print and graphics industries. A newspaper article that is completed too late for the print run is useless. Newspapers do not want copy that is a day out of date, however well researched and well written it may be. The same is true for magazines and even book publishers – they always want their publications to be up to date and out in the shops before those of their competitors.

7 Is the writing of a high enough quality?

It sounds obvious, but people very often do not read what they have written – they skim over the words. They know what they mean, and what they intend to write, but that is not always the same as what appears on the page. So try reading your work out loud. Amongst other things, this tells you if your sentences are too long! Be critical. Do the sentences flow? Does the piece 'feel' the right length? Would the reader lose interest long before the end, or does it terminate too abruptly? It is hard for a writer to be objective, so get used to other people reading your work and to accepting criticism!

Case study

Student Hannah Ratcliffe wrote an article for her local newspaper about the college gym. As you can see from Figures 6.59 to 6.61, the production process went through several stages. First, as part of her research she had to interview the manager of the gym (see Figure 6.59).

She then wrote up her story and submitted the copy (see Figure 6.60).

At the offices of the newspaper her article went through the editing process, and it finally reached the public in the form shown in Figure 6.61.

As you can see, the article has been re-written in a different style. Secondly, the story was originally planned as an article in its own right with its own headline. Instead its format was altered by placing it within the context of a larger article.

```
COLLEGE GYM INTERVIEW
PAUL KNIGHT

What is your involvement with the
college gym?

Basically I run it, programme it and
instruct. I also lay down rules for
its use.

How did you get involved with the
college gym?

I spoke to Clive Robinson, who is a
friend of mine. I explained that I
was unemployed and Clive offered me
this job.

What experience do you have?

I am a fully trained fitness
instructor and before working here I
was working at the Leisure Centre.

Why did the college feel they needed
a gym?

Health-related courses needed a gym,
and nowadays people are more fitness
conscious. A lot of students had been
asking for lunch-time facilities.

Who is the gym open to?

Staff and students.

When is the gym open?

Monday to Friday, 12-2 pm.

How did you promote the gym?

Posters, leaflets, a newsletter, and
by word of mouth.

How popular has the gym been?

Last term there were about thirty
regular visitors to the gym each
week, and this term we expect more
widespread interest.

How much does it cost to use the gym?

It costs 50p for a session.
```

Figure 6.59 Hannah's notes of her interview

NEW COLLEGE GYM

Hinckley College recently added a fitness studio to its list of new developments. The college is going from strength to strength in terms of expansion, and predicts that these new developments will be a great asset to the college.

The gym is managed by Paul Knight, who is a trained fitness instructor with extensive experience in fitness and management. Since his involvement with the college gym he has been responsible for its programming, promotions and instructing customers in a fitness programme suitable for them.

Paul commented: 'The college needed a gym for health-related courses, and because nowadays people are more fitness conscious.' He went on to say, 'The gym has been very popular among students and staff, and we expect a more widespread interest in the future.'

The gym is open to anyone involved with the college, from Monday to Friday between the hours of 12 noon and 2 pm.

The cost of a session in the gym is only fifty pence.

- ends -

Figure 6.60 The copy Hannah submitted to her local newspaper

Gym

As well as a new library, Hinckley College has recently added a new fitness studio to its list of new developments. The gym is managed by Paul Knight, who is a trained fitness instructor with extensive experience in fitness and management. He has been responsible for their promotions and the instructing of customers in a fitness programme suitable for them.

Paul commented: 'The gym has been very popular among students and staff, and we expect a more widespread interest in the future.'

The college is going from strength to strength in terms of expansion, and predicts that these new developments will be a great asset.

Figure 6.61 Hannah's article in print

Activity

Justify the copy you have written using the seven criteria listed above. List the things that you consider were successful about your work, and make a separate list of things you could improve next time.

Comparing your work with published items

It is a valuable exercise to compare your own work with that of professional, established authors and journalists. There are three areas in particular which are worth studying: style, format and representation.

Style

Different styles suit different print publications. What type of style do you have? What type of words do you like to use? How long are your sentences? Do you prefer to write formally or informally? Are you able to adapt your style to suit different purposes?

Activity

Find some writing by: a) a newspaper or magazine journalist and b) an author of text-books or novels, which you think matches your style in some respects. What can you learn by studying their writing? Are there any aspects of their style that you do *not* admire?

Format

Sometimes it becomes apparent after you have started to write that a short story would be better as a novel, or that a news report would cover its topic better if it were recast as a feature article. Matching content to an appropriate format is vital – how well have you done?

Activity

Find a magazine article, hard news report or short story which covers the same subject as one of yours. How similar is it in style and treatment to your own? How does it compare in length and sequencing of the material? What angle does the other writer concentrate on? What can you learn from it about the use of different formats?

Representation

Have you been fair and unbiased in the way you have written about people, places and events in your work? Have you given a balanced viewpoint? In the case of news stories, did you interview different people to get both sides of the story? Tabloid and broadsheet newspapers usually do have certain political and cultural leanings, as we discussed in Chapter 2.

Activity

Compare a newspaper report you have written with one on the same subject in either a national or a local newspaper, aimed at the same target audience. How do they differ? Consider the words used to describe the events or people who are being represented. Do either you or the professional writer show a bias towards any particular group of people, or towards any particular attitude or opinion? Is the overall impression given by your article the same as the one given by the professional writer? If not, can it still be said that both are fair and accurate?

Evidence assignment

Produce three print items, one of which should be image based.

Here are some examples of work you could do:

- a hard news story
- an article on a hobby
- a short story for children
- a horoscope
- an advertisement
- a cartoon strip
- a photograph with captions.

The work should be presented with a specification identifying the target audience, style and purpose of the items. List other ideas you considered, and describe how you assessed them. Why did you progress with your chosen three rather than with the others?

You should evaluate your work by comparing it with a similar work from a professional publication.

In your production handbook, you should include the following evidence:

- a record of your research and why you chose certain methods
- identification of legal, ethical and representational issues.

Plan and carry out research for audio items

Planning and carrying out research for audio items should be more than a theoretical exercise. You will need to know the skills and equipment involved in production so that you can plan effectively and realistically.

At this stage, you should be practising making part of a programme rather than the entire programme. For example, adverts, jingles, interviews and weather reports are ideal short items to attempt.

At every stage, you should be concerned not only with the content but also the *quality* of sound that is produced. You will all have listened to the radio or cassette tapes or CDs, but in many cases this will have been a secondary function, a background to another activity such as homework, socialising or exercise. You will now have to give primary attention to the sound and learn different criteria in order to be objectively critical.

You need to develop an understanding of a range of audio equipment, from a basic domestic cassette recorder to digital editing equipment. If you fill in a log sheet, such as the one shown in Figure 7.3 on the next page, when you make sound recordings you will begin to identify what type of microphone is most suitable in different circumstances, what quality tape is satisfactory, which recorder is most convenient to use, and so on.

As you progress through the activities, it may sometimes be more appropriate for you to record ideas and discussions on tape rather than write them down.

Background information

Theory of sound

It is essential for you to be aware of basic sound theory before you start this module.

Sound is the vibration of particles of air. If you hit a drum or pluck a guitar the skin or string will move, i.e. **vibrate**. This movement will make the air next to it move in a similar pattern. These vibrations, known as sound waves, will travel and eventually fade away.

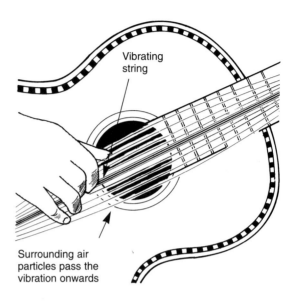

Vibrating string

Surrounding air particles pass the vibration onwards

Figure 7.1 Vibration – how sound travels

Our outer ears are designed to 'catch' these vibrations and direct them towards the ear drum. The auditory nerve then changes the vibration into electrochemical impulses that are interpreted by the brain. As humans have two ears, they hear sound in stereo.

These bones pass the vibrations along from one to the next

Vibrations pass through bones and fluid to the auditory nerve which sends a signal to the brain

The shape of the outer ear helps to collect sounds

The sound waves make the ear drum vibrate

Figure 7.2 How we hear sounds

Sound recording

Student name:..

Date:...

Content of recording:..

Recorder	Mic	Tape	Evaluation

Figure 7.3 Sound recording assessment sheet

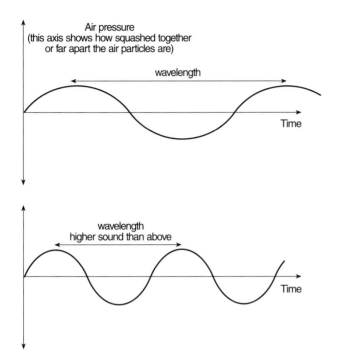

Figure 7.4 Sound waves

When vibrations are random, the sound is called **noise**; when the vibrations are organised and arranged into patterns, this can be called **speech** or **music**.

Figure 7.4 shows an illustration of a sound wave. The distance between the two peaks is called the **wavelength**. The shorter the wave length the higher the sound. The number of times a sound vibrates per second is called its **frequency** and this is measured in **Hertz**.

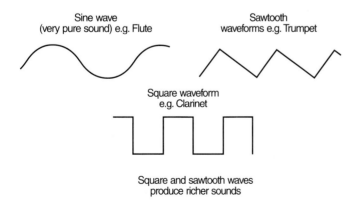

Figure 7.5 Different-shaped sound waves

Different sounds have different shaped waves, as can be seen from Figure 7.5.

The basic shape of the wave will remain the same regardless of how loudly an instrument is played or whether it is playing high rather than low notes.

The loudness or **volume** of sound is measured in **decibels (dB)**. If you listen for long periods to sounds, whether music or machinery, which is over 105 dB, then you can damage your hearing. If the rating of a dB is increased by ten, the intensity of sound will increase tenfold.

dB	Sound
20	quiet country lane
60	normal conversation
80	alarm clock
90	underground train
110	jet aircraft
130	threshold of pain
160	ear drum ruptures

Recording and storing sound

Here are some ways to store sound:

- on vinyl
- on tape (cassette or open reel)
- on CD
- on hard disk
- on video tape

Activity

Discuss the advantages and disadvantages of each of these formats. Consider cost for producers and consumers, ease of use, quality of sound and durability.

In the recording industry, music or speech is first recorded on to tape even if it is going to end up on record or disc.

This is the basic recording process:

- a microphone picks up sound vibrations and converts them into an electric current of varying strength or **voltage**
- these electrical signals are fed into a tape recorder, and the recording head converts them into magnetic forces of varying strength
- magnetic patterns are laid on to the surface of the tape where they are stored

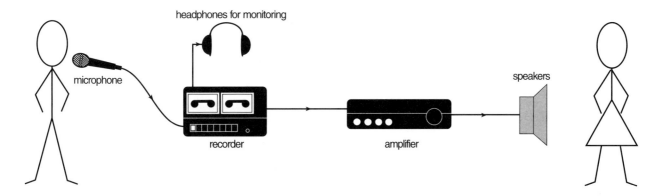

Figure 7.6 How the basic recording process works

- the electrical signals can be converted back into sound using an amplifier and speakers.

The description above is for **analogue** recording. In **digital** recording the voltage from the microphone is measured by a digital tape recorder and stored on special tape as **binary numbers** (0s and 1s) which represent on/off signals **(digitisation)**. Sound can now also be stored by digitisation on to the hard disk of a computer. Digital recording and editing is becoming the norm in the audio industry (see Chapter 31).

Digital recording is more accurate than analogue: the voltage from the microphone is measured up to 50,000 times per second. This ability to detect tiny variations in a voltage results in sound quality.

Recordings, whether from a radio station or a music studio, are put on to a **master tape**. They can be stored like this or converted into cassette tapes, vinyl records or CDs.

In order to make a record, the magnetic patterns on the tape are converted back into voltages. These are used to control a needle, which carves a groove on a circular sheet of aluminium covered with plastic. From this, metal moulds or stampers are made which are used to produce multiple copies in vinyl.

When you play a record, the grooves vibrate a stylus. Its movements are converted back into voltages which are amplified and sent to the loudspeakers.

CDs, however, store music in digital form. The disc is made of aluminium coated with a transparent, protective vinyl layer containing millions of tiny pits. Inside the CD player, a laser beam scans the disc surface. It can sense the pits and converts this information into binary numbers before converting them back into voltages which are amplified and

sent to the loudspeakers. CDs are more robust than vinyl in that there is no contact between the laser beam and the disc.

For more detail about the different items of equipment used in sound recording, and their capabilities, read Chapters 14 and 15 on recording and editing audio material.

Originate and evaluate ideas for audio items

Activity

Radio can sometimes be considered the 'poor relation' of the media world in comparison with television or newspapers. Before progressing further, list six advantages that radio has over these formats. Consider both practical and aesthetic reasons; for example, cost of production, ability to stimulate the individual's imagination, etc.

In Chapter 5, you may have come up with some ideas for radio programmes. However, not all recording is done for radio. You may decide to record some original live music, which is also a useful exercise. Of course, this can then be incorporated into a radio programme, either as an item in its own right or as part of a jingle, advert or theme music for a drama.

It may be helpful at this stage to read Chapter 3 again, looking closely at the section on the different radio genres and their codes and conventions. Even at these early stages in originating and evaluating ideas, you will have to consider the purpose and style of the final product.

161

Types of radio programme

There are basically two types of radio programme: **speech based** (including fiction and non-fiction) and **music based**.

Speech-based radio

Non-fiction includes news, current affairs, quizzes, educational and magazine programmes. Most of these follow the same format, week after week. The length of individual programmes remains constant, e.g. 'Gardener's Question Time' will always last half an hour. Only under exceptional circumstances will the length of the news alter. Obviously, there is a change in content, such as the contestants and questions in a quiz, guests on a chat show, records on a music programme, but introductions, length, presenters and style remain the same.

Activity

Working in groups of three or four, record an example of an advert and a travel news report from the radio. Analyse their construction, considering length, the use of music, sound effects, the vocabulary used and the style of presentation. Now write and record your own. Choose a different product to advertise and some current or imaginary travel news for your area, but closely follow the structure used in the professional radio examples.

This activity can use the following basic equipment: cassette recorder; omni-directional microphone (see Chapter 14 on microphones); a keyboard with a choice of demo tunes (or make up your own) and possibly sound effects to fade in and out.

Source material for these non-fiction programmes will be found from personal observation and face-to-face interviews but also from the following sources:

- the emergency services
- the general public, e.g. phone-ins
- reports from councils (including public notices) and other official bodies, such as Parliament
- press releases from business and other organisations
- national news sources
- local news sources
- TV, newspapers, magazines and other radio stations around the world
- encyclopedias and other reference works.

Fiction items on the radio include plays, comedy, readings of books, poetry and so on. A new programme may be based on:

- **classical works**, a series of plays or excerpts from plays, or poetry linked to a theme, such as war, or to a period, such as the seventeenth century.
- **adaptations** of classic works, where a different approach is given, for example the setting is changed from Italy in the 1500s to America in the 1920s. Or a story is changed from an objective, straightforward account of events to a narrator telling what has happened in a series of flashbacks to a friend.
- **new commissions**, which can be based on anything from personal experiences or emotions to something that happened way back in the Stone Age or may happen in the thirtieth century. (There will be more information on how to construct a play on page 171, in the section on writing for drama.)

Radio Four is well known for its different drama productions. These are scheduled to meet the needs of the various different type of listener who will switch on at that particular time of day or night.

Besides the daily dose of 'The Archers' (from 13.40 to 13.55, repeated from 19.05 to 19.20 the previous evening) there are regular slots for drama throughout the week. Here are some examples:

- *Saturday 18 May 1996*
  14.30–16.00: Saturday Playhouse: 'Football Play for Girls' by Stephen Butchard and Pat Anderson.

  19.50–21.20: Saturday Night Theatre: 'Lady's Maid', an adaptation of Margaret Forster's novel, dramatised by Ed Thomason.

- *Monday 20 May 1996*
  19.45–21.15: The Monday Play: 'The Taxman' by Paul Brennan, a black comedy about luck, love and the lottery.

- *Tuesday 21 May 1996*
  14.00–14.30: Thirty Minute Theatre: 'Baby on Board' by Alison Joseph. Gillian has just been promoted and is now the most senior woman in the company.

  18.30–19.00: 'Some Tame Gazelle' a serialised dramatisation of Barbara Pym's novel by Elisabeth Proud.

- *Wednesday 22 May 1996*
  12.25–13.00: 'Are you from the *Bugle*?', a sit-com about life in a local newspaper office by John Gradwell.

- *Thursday 23 May 1996*
  14.00–15.00: 'One Day I'll Fly Away' by Helen Kluger.

Some of these plays are based on classic novels, some on contemporary life. Different genres are represented such as soap, sit-com and thriller. There are different narrative structures: some are serialised, some are a series and others are complete in themselves. The Monday Play and Thirty Minute Theatre are usually by contemporary writers, including new writers. The theme can be about anything, from the trauma of war to an hour in the life of a shelf stacker in a supermarket. The treatment, however, can be more experimental. The Saturday Playhouse is traditionally for family listening and uses the more popular genres such as who-dunnits and thrillers. It is one of the longer slots – 90 minutes – as is the Monday Play. This tends to be more thought-provoking and challenging to understand.

Activity

Listen to plays and readings of novels and poetry on the radio, and choose one to analyse. Give a brief synopsis of the content and who you think this play was aimed at. Now choose a novel, short story or series of poems you have read and suggest what new approach could be given to them and what sort of person they might appeal to.

Music-based radio

These programmes have three main sources of material:

- **recorded music** – every radio station has a library of sound recordings, preferably on CD or even on hard disk.
- **live music** – this could include recordings of concerts, recitals or gigs, or even a studio performance.
- **talk** about music and musicians. Ideas ranging from gossip to critical reviews can come from interviews and personal observation, but also from books, newspapers and magazines.

Activity

Suggest a 'theme' for a music programme: it could be songs by a particular performer or group, or music from a particular year. Write down a possible playlist and the names of people whom you would like to interview.

Recording companies and radio stations will want their audio product, whether it is a CD or a music magazine programme, to be something that is:

- **topical** e.g. it follows a new musical trend
- **fresh** e.g. an up-and-coming pop star
- **seasonal** e.g. Cliff Richard's Christmas record
- **a follow-up** e.g. the second album from a group
- **promotional** e.g. a competition to win tickets for a concert.

Activity

Listen to either a current affairs or a music programme on the radio and list its contents. Write down some ideas for the next edition that would be topical, fresh, seasonal, promotional and/or a follow-up.

Now you should have listed a few ideas which could be developed into an audio product. If you have any additional ideas that you think would be original, then add them to the list.

Evaluating ideas

How do you decide which ideas are worth developing? Some of the reasons have already been discussed above and in Chapter 5. The three main criteria for evaluation are: fitness for purpose, resource requirements and aesthetics.

Fitness for purpose

This covers suitability for the target audience. Is it appropriate for their age, interests and where they live? It includes whether it entertains, persuades or informs listeners. Does it fit in with the style and ethos of the radio station or record company?

Is the individual item the appropriate length? Can an advert or jingle be cut in length to fit a particular spot without losing its sense? For example, most adverts are seldom above 30 seconds long, an on-the-hour news spot on a music programme is usually three minutes.

Resource requirements

Resources can be categorised as follows: human, financial, materials, time.

Human resources: in contrast with filming, only a small team is necessary for collecting information for audio. The radio journalist usually works alone. He or she will conduct the interview and record it. This, however, takes practice and, with student work, it is recommended that a minimum of two should work together. Thus, one person can do the interview whilst another is responsible for the equipment, monitoring the recording levels and the quality of the sound. (See Chapter 13 for further details on this.)

There is also the question of personal safety, and permission should always be gained for off-site activities.

Depending on the programme, other essential personnel are actors, the guests, contestants, presenters, sound engineers, programme editors, controllers, and others. (For a complete list of jobs in the radio industry see Chapter 13.)

Financial resources: the cost of producing the average hour-long radio programme may be cheaper than producing its equivalent on television or an edition of a newspaper or magazine, but it is just as essential to have a budget and stick to it. Some programmes will be cheaper to make than others in terms of materials, such as transport or recorded music, and staff, such as technicians or actors.

One expense that music-based programmes have to pay is royalties for the use of pre-recorded music. So, by law, a radio station has to compile a playlist of each record played (See Figure 7.7.)

Activity

Make a list of the expenses you might incur for a:

- talk show based on a public phone-in
- record review programme
- local current affairs programme.

Case study

On the next page is the budget sheet from a small studio for making a radio advert for a local businessperson (1993). The studio is run by one person who is both musician and sound engineer.

The words and melody for the jingle were supplied by the customer.

The work was carried out over a three-day period.

Castle Radio **PLAY LIST**				
Haverford Hospital				

Presenter's Name .... Date ....

Show's Name .... Time ....

All presenters must fill in a play list in CLEARLY READABLE BLOCK CAPITALS. Please now include the catalogue number of the record if the CR record library copy is used. If the record is played because of a request then please tick the request box. On the back of this document please list any taped interviews and guests etc . . .

	Name of artist	Title of recording	Cat No.	Req.
1				
2				
3				
4				
5				
6				
7				
8				
9				
10				
11				
12				
13				
14				
15				
16				
17				
18				
19				
20				

Figure 7.7 A radio station playlist form

Work activity	Cost in £
Composition	500.00
Singer for lead vocals	30.00
Voice-overs	20.00
Recording (2 hours)	300.00
Editing and mastering	700.00
Other expenses (phone calls, tape etc.)	50.00
Total cost	**1,600.00**

1 Why should an individual need to keep details of bills or a budget?

2 If you were making a recording from a home studio, what other costs might you add?

Materials: have you got the most appropriate equipment for the job? Have you got enough tape for the amount of recording you want to do? Can you use a power supply or do you need batteries?

At the very least you will need a microphone, a tape recorder and a set of headphones. You may need on-site resources, i.e. a studio, or transport to get to off-site locations.

Time: deadlines are as important in radio as in any other media industry. Programmes have to go on air at specific times, personnel and studios must be booked and appointments made with interviewees have to be kept. Studio time and staff wages need to be kept to a minimum.

The more careful the planning and research stages, the more likely it is that the project will meet its **deadline**.

You need to be realistic in assessing how long it is going to take to organise your research, interview people or visit a library. For example, when will the necessary equipment be free? One of the first things to be done is to book this equipment. The booking forms in themselves will then form part of your production log so you should ensure that these are filled out accurately and in detail.

Aesthetics

This is about the actual physical sound of an audio item, and also how creative and original it is.

Here the style and presentation of the work must be assessed, particularly in relation to the target

Sound recording equipment booking form

Student name ....

Date ....

Time...

For what purposes do you need the equipment/studio?

Equipment needed:

If recording outside college, have you obtained permission from a lecturer? Yes/No

Studio needed:

Has equipment been returned?

Has studio been locked where appropriate?

Has all equipment, including microphones, been switched off?

Have there been any problems with the equipment?

Figure 7.8 Sound recording equipment booking form

audience. Something that is aesthetically pleasing or satisfying to a middle-aged professional person may be boring for the teenager who looks for novelty and excitement. However, the aesthetic quality will be spoiled for both types of person if, for example, the sound of the recording is flawed, if speech is overwhelmed by background music, or if there is tape hiss on the recording.

Case study

Ken Parker is 53 and has lived all his life in an industrial town in the Midlands which has a small hospital radio station run by volunteers. Most of the patients are over fifty years old.

Three years ago Kenny was asked to present his own radio show to run from 20.30 to 22.00 on Wednesday evenings. He had to come up with an idea which would make his programme different from those running in the other slots. Other presenters were playing music from the seventies onwards, but Kenny is a big Tommy Steele and Rick Nelson fan with a large personal collection of records from the 'rock 'n' roll' years, so he decided to use this type of music for the programme. Patients are asked for requests and feedback and this is also obtained from the nurses on the ward.

Ken has called his show 'Handful of Songs', after one of Tommy Steele's hits. An important part of the programme is the 'Guess the Year Quiz' which covers the years from 1955 to 1980. Listeners hear the music, news headlines and film titles from the chosen year and are invited to guess the date. The most popular years have proved to be 1959 and 1963!

Ken is also a big fan of local sport, especially football, and each week gives an eyewitness account of one of the local games which are not covered on other radio stations.

Interesting snippets from the local newspaper are also read out, along with 'What's On' locally, the chemist's rota and the weather. National news is fed in from satellite on the hour. Besides the station and news jingles, Ken has to fit in health promotion carts (cartridges) on such topics as 'Quitting smoking'.

Introducing this session of easy listening music, Ken sounds like a friendly neighbour with a bit of chat and gossip – he likes to tell listeners about any interesting graffiti he has seen this week, as well as the naughty bits from the tabloids!

1 What makes Ken's idea suitable for the target audience?

2 How feasible is the idea in terms of resources?

3 Why is a radio format suitable for hospital?

4 What is the main purpose of the programme in terms of information, entertainment and persuasion?

5 How important is Ken's personality and background in making his idea successful?

Activity

Evaluate the ideas you have collected so far. How realistic are they? Assess them under the headings of fitness for purpose, resource requirements and aesthetics. Which ones do you feel are now worth progressing?

Key features of audio items

The key features to consider are the **target audience** and the **idea** itself. What is its purpose, design, style, content and structure?

Target audience

Research needs to be done to confirm that assumptions made about the **target audience** are correct in terms of age, gender, social class, and interests.

For example, we might assume that an item reporting about a football game is aimed at males over the age of ten. However, if the subject is presented in a certain way then women too may be attracted. Very few women have had the opportunity to play football at school and may fail to understand fully the skill involved. If the tactics of the game were explained in

Figure 7.9 The target audience for a programme on football may include women!

a non-condescending manner during the football report, a new audience could be attracted. A variety of research could be done to define this audience, for example on women's attitudes to the game, whether they watch it on television, whether they listen to the radio on Saturdays, what sort of sports presenters they like, etc.

The accessibility of the programme for the target audience needs to be checked. There are two aspects to consider: timing and content.

Will the target audience be able to listen at a certain time? The most brilliant feature for young teenagers on new trends in pop music will be wasted if it is included in a daytime magazine programme on Radio 4 at a time when they will be at school!

Will the target audience understand the content? Accessibility of a product also implies that the style and presentation, the type of vocabulary used, the type of background music or jingles, matches the tastes and experience of the listeners. The brilliant feature for young teenagers on new trends in music should use the language of the streets rather than that of a university professor with a degree in sociology/music.

All genres – if adapted – can appeal to a variety of target audiences. Children can enjoy a quiz as much as an adult, provided the level of question is correct. The structure might need to be changed in terms of length, the presentation may need to be more lighthearted, for example.

Activity

How might you change an adult current affairs programme, such as 'The Magazine' on Radio 5, to appeal to seven-year-olds? Discuss content, presentation style and structure.

Ideas

As with any media product, the main purposes of audio items are to inform, to educate, to persuade and to entertain.

Activity

Look through the radio schedules for the day for both a music- and a talk-based station. Can you identify the purpose of the different programmes? Are they to persuade you to buy something, such as a record? Can you find programmes which are intended to educate the listener rather than give information? Are any programmes purely for entertainment?

The **structure** of the audio item is also highly important, not only in terms of its length but in the order in which material is presented within the item. There are codes and conventions surrounding this, not only for music-based programmes but also for speech-based programmes such as current affairs. Listeners have expectations about the length of a jingle, or when the news bulletin should be heard and how the presenter will tell what is coming up in the programme. Our recognition of the genre of a programme is based on the use of these codes and conventions.

The structure is dealt with in more detail in the section on scriptwriting, page 171.

Technical requirements

At this stage you should make yourself familiar with the basic technical and resource requirements for sound recordings so that you can judge whether your ideas are feasible. For details on the equipment and practical skills needed, turn to Chapter 14.

In the studio the basic equipment includes:

- microphones
- records, compact discs, cassettes, cartridges and the equipment to play these
- telephone lines.

A **mixing desk** combines all of the above. The result can be recorded on to an open reel-to-reel tape recorder or sent to a transmitter to be broadcast.

The technical aspect to be considered for an **outside broadcast** (OB) involves the way in which information is to be sent back to the studio:

- through a **broadcast link**. This is a common method; a radio car sends the material over the air using a frequency that is unavailable on domestic radio receivers. Other electrical equipment in the vicinity can, however, cause interference.
- by **landline**; a cable owned by a telecommunications company. This is expensive and has to be booked in advance. Material sent over a landline can go straight on air.
- by **telephone links**. The mobile phone has replaced the rush by journalists to get to a telephone box. Telephone output is generally of low quality, but if used as an audio item it can

give a sense of immediacy and atmosphere to a broadcast.

- a **courier** to transport tape back to the studio is possibly the least satisfactory way. The live feeling of an outside broadcast is lost in the delay.

Investigative methods and research for audio items

Earlier, in Chapter 5, we looked at a range of investigative research methods, including both questionnaires and interviews. The choice of method depends on time and budget and the type of information needed. Statistics from official research bodies can be useful in researching target audiences (see Chapter 21, pages 358–9). However, the programme researcher will also use a number of secondary sources, including books, magazines and reports as well as primary sources for finding content material and checking its accuracy.

Figure 7.10 Investigative methods can be varied

What are the advantages of personal interviews, telephone interviews, personal observation, taking photographs and making audio and video recordings for the research of either fictional or non-fictional programmes?

Read the reasons given in Chapter 6 (page 127) and also the section on interviewing. Most of these reasons for research and the skills involved apply equally for audio as for print and graphic items, with the addition of the following comments.

Personal interviews

Some radio genres are built around the personal interview, such as the hospital radio request show. Hospital DJs tour the wards regularly to chat to patients, and find out the type of person who may be listening as well as what they want to hear.

If a personal interview is recorded, the recording can be incorporated into a programme where a fresh voice can add a lot of interest.

Interviews over the telephone

These can either be used for initial research or broadcast live over the air.

Phone-ins are a cheap and successful part of radio programmes. Fresh voices can help keep the listeners' attention. As well as appealing to people working at home, a growing number of motorists – who form a large part of the daytime radio audience – have mobile phones and enjoy accessing the radio network in this way. It emphasises the intimacy and the immediacy of radio as a medium. The Internet is also being increasingly used to gain people's opinions.

There are two different types of phone-in:

an open-line: anybody can ring in to discuss a general topic suggested by the presenter.

an advice-line: an expert, such as a doctor, lawyer or gardener, will answer specific questions asked by listeners.

Personal observation

Roadshows can be an important part of the publicity machine for a radio station. This is one of the rare occasions when presenters, producers and the listeners can see each other!

Images

Photographs are obviously of less use in radio than for newspapers and magazines, but they do form a visual record of people who have been interviewees, guests or contestants and can be useful for publicity.

Audio recordings

This method of collecting information is obviously far more important for audio items than it is for print and graphics publications. After editing, these recordings will be the 'lifeblood' of news, current affairs, documentary and magazine programmes.

Vox pops are a popular convention of radio, where the opinions of people in the street are collected. The expression 'vox pop' is an abbreviation of the Latin *vox populi* which means 'the voice of the people'. These opinions may be about local or national events, trends such as fashion or food, and can be about something trivial or serious. It is a particularly successful technique for radio, because the change of voices gives variety and pace to news items. A single question is asked and answered by a number of people.

A **Q and A** (**Question and Answer**) interview is usually live, for example between the presenter in the studio and the reporter at the scene of a crime or accident. These interviews are called **two-ways** by the BBC.

(For more information on radio interviews see page 175.)

Activity

Choose a topic suitable for a series of vox pop interviews. It could be on people's favourite television soap or whether they think violence in their local town is increasing. Go to a public area of your college or school and record the opinions of six people. Try to choose people of different ages, sex, ethnic background and occupation.

You will need a microphone and portable cassette player for this.

Case study

A small town is soon to get its own radio licence. The local media students were asked to do a five-minute feature on this,

to be included in a music show for young people. Here is a brainstorm by the students of possible research. Would you add anything to the list?

- **Personal interviews**:
  with people bidding for the licence
  Possible questions include:

  - what sort of service do you hope to provide?
  - how will you be different from the competitors?
  - what financial backing do you have?
  - what experience have you had in the radio industry?
  - what sort of music will you play?
  - where will the station be based?
  - what is your chance of success in gaining the licence?
  - are you going to go on air for a trial run?

  with students at college
  Possible questions include:
  - what stations do you listen to at the moment?
  - do you think our town needs a radio station?

- **Telephone calls**:

  to established radio stations to ascertain their views on a potential competitor.

  to the local newspaper to ask if they support the new venture.

  to the leader of the Council to find out if they welcome this new facility for the town.

  to local business people to ask if they will pay for advertising on the new radio station.

- **Photography**:
  It may be useful to have a visual record of the people bidding for the licence and of potential sites for the new radio station.

- **Audio recordings**:
  Both personal interviews and telephone calls might provide sufficiently good quotes, comments or opinions to be used in the programme itself.

- **Secondary research**:
  - read the regulations about how to apply for a radio licence
  - make a list of other stations that might be affected by the new station
  - search through newspapers on CD-ROM to find out about similar bids for other areas for a radio licence.

Not all the information collected could be used in five minutes. When talking to the people bidding for the licence, the interviewer would need to show that he or she had taken the trouble to find out about the process; but detailed financial and legal information would be inappropriate for the target audience.

Secondary research

Professionals also use a number of **secondary sources** to gain material for audio products. All the sources available to researchers for print and graphics professionals will be available to people working in radio, such as satellite news. However, there are a number of additional sources that are especially useful:

- The BBC Written Archives Centre near Reading holds all the radio scripts, programme information and other written material about the BBC.
- The BBC also has a separate Sound Library containing 500,000 sound recordings.
- The National Sound Archive is part of the British Library. This is the national collection of recorded sound and covers music, spoken work, and sound effects both of nature and of machinery.

Some publications are written especially to help radio presenters and DJs. The magazine *Broadcaster's Bulletin* is aimed at people working in hospital radio. It provides information for quizzes and gives details of companies who will sponsor a competition with their product as the prize.

Note: Record libraries are also useful for getting ideas about the type of music to be used in a programme, whether it is a music programme or to use as theme music or background music for a play. Music librarians will be pleased to suggest different pieces of music that suggest a certain mood or period in history.

 Activity

Find examples of pre-recorded music that would be suitable as theme music for the following radio programmes:

- a children's quiz
- a gardening programme
- a comedy series set in France
- a drama about two doomed lovers in contemporary Britain
- an educational programme about Elizabethan music.

Potential content considerations

The legal and ethical considerations for any audio item will need to be researched. They are explained in detail in the Legal and Ethical Appendix. Radio producers have to protect themselves against accusations of libel, invasion of privacy, blasphemy and copyright infringement.

A radio programme is considered to be published material so if you defame a person (i.e. say something bad about someone that is not true) on air, you are sued for **libel** not **slander**.

Music copyright involves both mechanical rights (the right to record a piece of music) and performing rights (which includes the right to broadcast music). Radio stations must record the number of times each record is played so that the composers and musicians can collect royalties.

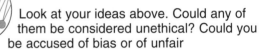 Activity

Look at your ideas above. Could any of them be considered unethical? Could you be accused of bias or of unfair representation? What legal aspects do you have to take into account?

Select materials for development

The material you have selected to develop should cover a range of items. It is recommended that you choose to write and record:

- a news report
- a short drama.

These additional items should also be attempted, however, as they can be incorporated into larger products for Unit 4:

- studio interviews
- vox pops
- adverts
- weather reports
- presentation of some music.

Your notes should include something on each of the following areas:

- You should be clear about the *purpose* of each item and have identified a specific *target audience*.
- You should be aware of any *legal or ethical implications*.

- You should have identified *people* to work with you.
- You should have made a list of *deadlines* for each audio item and booked equipment and studio time.
- You should be aware of all the *research* needed to collect material.

Activity

At this stage you should also be working on the various practical skills necessary for all of the above. Experiment with different sound effects, choose different music for intros and outros. Always remember to keep a log of the resulting quality of your work and any problems that arise.

Make samples of the above items – they will help you make a decision on which materials to select. Do not worry at this stage if your work does not sound very original; it is good to copy professional recordings closely. Imitate the structure of items from the radio; imitate the presenters' styles. This is an important part of the learning process.

Produce proposals and scripts for audio items

Proposals

Any idea for a radio programme, whether it is for a quiz or a current affairs programme, needs to be accepted by an editor or producer of a station. The proposal is the blueprint which describes content (the synopsis) and style, and justifies the suggestion in terms of audience and resources. It is important that the proposal is accepted before too much work is done. However brilliant your programme, if there is another one already in the pipeline that is rather similar, your idea is going to be rejected. In the case of plays, writers often send in proposals plus a sample of scripting to give a feel of the overall production. New dramatists, however, should send in a complete script.

The success of radio depends on the strength of the presenters or actors – on the people who do the talking. Sometimes this is fully scripted, as in a play, or partly scripted, as in a current affairs programme. There are two areas we shall look at: radio drama and news.

HAVING AN ARGUMENT

A play for radio by Sam Smedley

Sam Smedley
14 Burton Road
Hockley
0145 32212 **Time:** 30 mins

CHARACTERS

Henry Ashby	(early sixties)
Tracey Ashby	(mid forties)
daughter Becky	(aged 17)
twins Richard and Alec	(aged 12)

The play is set in the home of a vet and his family in Wales during the 1950s.

Theme: the play takes a lighthearted look at the problems facing parents as their children get older and leave home, and the ways individuals adjust to this.

Plot: Becky wants to leave home to go to Art School in London. The boys, too, want to go away with their friends on holiday. The wife feels deserted and resentful but has to come to terms with what is left in her life when the family goes. The argument is over a missing application form to go to college.

Resolution: Becky stays at home, mother goes to college and father goes on safari with the twins.

The music is an orchestral version of Elvis Presley's *Heartbreak Hotel*.

Figure 7.11 A proposal for a radio play

Writing radio plays

Writing a successful radio play is difficult. You have to make the listener 'see' or experience the feelings that you want them to see or feel, without the help of visual images. This has to be done through the skilful use of **dialogue**, i.e. speech, assisted by sound effects and music.

First you need a **plot** or **theme**. Keep this simple. When you start writing, think of some *event, issue* or *feelings* within your own experience. For example:

- *event:* every morning a student gets up, meets a friend and goes to college
- *issue:* drugs in society
- *feelings:* a wish for adventure.

This is not yet a plot; it is a starting point. What is needed is disruption! (It may help at this point to re-read the section on narrative structure in Chapter 4.) You could make the story unfold as in the fairytale structure analysed by Propp:

- *preparation:* a student gets up to meet a friend as usual to go to college
- *complication:* the student sees the friend being kidnapped
- *transference:* the local shopkeeper knows who the gang are but warns the student not to go to the police as there is a corrupt officer
- *struggle:* the student finds out that the friend has been kidnapped because she had been dealing in drugs but wants to leave the gang
- *return:* the corrupt police officer is exposed but the friend dies
- *recognition:* the student is thanked by the local community and goes back to college.

This could be rather a dull story, but what will make it interesting is its **treatment**: the actual words used, the strength of the characterisations. Now you have the basic idea, you can add to the story, even change the genre from thriller to black comedy. You need something that will make this idea unusual. The play could be set in the future or in a different country. The gang could all be female.

There are many ways to add colour. The order of events can be changed. The example above could begin with the funeral of the friend.

When the storyline is written out in more detail, it will be called a **synopsis**.

Activity

Write a synopsis for a play following the formula given above.

The writer must be clear in his or her mind about the different characters. Monologue (where there is only one person talking) has been successfully used in radio drama, but you will find it easier at first to use four or five characters. The contrast between them and the way they interact will help define the action and emotions in the play.

Activity

Give a written sketch of the physical appearance, age, gender, behaviour, interests and occupation of each of your characters. Think about how they will speak – slowly, or with a refined accent, for example. Try not to rely on stereotypes unless this is a comedy.

What the dramatist has to do is arouse the interest or the curiosity of the listeners and make them use their imagination. This is perhaps the most difficult thing to do for the writer who is just beginning. In attempting to describe what is happening or who the characters are, the beginner may write speeches that are unnatural and obvious, and leave little to the imagination. For example:

SANDRA:	Oh, there's Paul getting out of his car. Hello, Paul.
PAUL:	Hello, Sandra. You don't seem to be in a good mood today.
SANDRA:	No, I'm not. The cat's died.

This could be written differently (SFX stands for sound effects):

SFX	Sound of car driving up, man whistling, door slams.
PAUL:	Hi, Sandra!
SANDRA:	*(quietly)* Oh ... Hi.
PAUL:	The traffic's bad this morning. Did you have trouble getting in?
SANDRA:	*(abstractedly)* ... hmmmm.
PAUL:	*(getting cross)* What's the matter? Cat got your tongue this morning?
SANDRA:	*(bitterly)* Actually, it's dead!
PAUL:	What is?
SANDRA:	The cat, you horrible man.

This second piece of scripting is far better at revealing the situation and giving insight into the characters and their relationship than the rather 'dead' first example. The sound effect of a car can adequately replace the sentence, 'There's Paul getting out of his car.' The whistling tells us that he's in a good mood far better than words do.

Another important point to remember, in order to make dialogue sound convincing, is that although an individual character may have a distinct personality trait, such as grumpiness or shyness, he or she will respond with different words and expressions when in confrontation or conversation with different characters.

For example: Gladys is a middle-aged woman, who hates unpunctuality. Here is how she might respond to another character who is late:

■ she talks to her daughter:
GLADYS: *(angrily)* You're late. Where have you been? I've been worried sick about you.

■ she talks to an ageing parent:
GLADYS: *(concerned)* Oh, I'm so glad you've arrived. Everything okay?

■ she talks to the plumber who has come to fix the washing machine:
GLADYS: *(complaining)* Oh, you're here at last. The shop said you'd be here half an hour ago. I can't spend all day hanging around for you, I've got to get to work.

■ she talks to her boss at work:
GLADYS: *(crisply)* Good morning, Mrs Wright. How was the traffic this morning? I've got everything ready for the meeting.

Writing for Radio by Colin Haydn Evans (W.H. Allen, 1991), gives useful hints on how to write radio drama.

Presentation of the script

Your work should follow the standard **layout**:

■ a **title page**, including the writer's name and address and the length of the play
■ the **character list** with a brief description of each character, followed by the location of the play and any suggested music
■ the body of the **script** itself.

Scripting for a fictional production

The script should be:

■ typed or word processed using **double spacing**
■ scenes should be **numbered**
■ speeches should be **numbered**, as this makes rehearsal easy
■ **characters' names** should be in **upper-case** lettering

WAXWORK

by *Peter Lovesey*

Adapted by *Geoffrey M. Matthews*

Directed by *Vanessa Whitburn*

Figure 7.12 Title page for a play broadcast on Radio 4

Sgt Cribb	BRIAN COX
PC Thackeray	JOHN CATER
Miriam Cromer	SARAH BERGER
Insp Jowett	ROGER HUME
James Berry	DON HENDERSON
Howard Cromer	GORDON REID
Simon Allingham	KIM DURHAM
Insp Waterlow	ROGER ROWLAND
Lottie Piper/First wardress	CLAIRE FAULCONBRIDGE
Mrs Berry/Dorothea Davenant	GILLIAN GOODMAN
Tussaud/Judge	EDWIN RICHFIELD
Prison Governor/Hundelby	ANTHONY BENSON
Second wardress	CYNTHIA CHERRY

Figure 7.13 Final cast list for the radio play *Waxwork*

- the dialogue is **indented** to the right of the character's name
- **directions**, such as how the actors should speak (for example, angrily, close to mic or pause) or sound effects should be **underlined** and in **brackets**. Production techniques such as 'Fade' should be in upper-case and underlined.
- all **scenes** begin or end with the following directions:
  Fade up – followed by the word *Interior* or *Exterior*, so that the producer knows whether to create acoustics to represent an indoor or an outdoor scene.
  Fade down – always indicates that a scene has ended.
  Cross fade – this is used to create a bridge between two scenes. The final speech in a scene will be marked *Fading* and will merge into the opening of the next.

Scene: 4 *(FADE UP exterior; football field. The sound of boots kicking a ball. A murmur of the crowd in the background. Some occasional cheers. Fred and Bill on the pitch.)*

1. FRED: *(shouts)* Pass me the ball. Now!

2. BILL: *(panting)* I'm getting too old for this. My back's aching and my feet hurt.

3. FRED: *(cutting in)* Stop moaning, pass the ball.

    SFX: *(sound of ball kicked hard. Cheers from crowd)*

4. FRED: *(excitedly)* It's a goal! It's a goal!

5. BILL: *(fading)* Yes, but my feet still hurt and my back aches . . . What I want is a nice cup of tea . . .

Scene: 5 *(CROSS FADE to sound of people talking in a pub. Chink of glasses. Laughter)*

6. ALICE: *(cheerfully)* Eh, you did well this afternoon Bill.

Figure 7.14 Part of a script for radio

Writing radio news

Radio news is tightly organised in terms of the order of the material and how it is presented. For local radio, local news may well take precedence over national or international stories. A balance must also be struck between light and heavy news items.

The serious nature of many news programmes or items is indicated in their jingles, which can include a brief, dramatic musical introduction, the sound of a clock chiming, or the pips of morse code.

Special terms are given to individual parts of the script:

- **copy** – usually three short paragraphs making up a story. This is read by the newsreader.
- **voicepiece** – sometimes called a **voicer** or **voice report**. This is a short report on a self-contained story told by a reporter and not by the news-reader. The BBC will use voicepieces of up to 50 seconds, whereas independent radio prefers them to be a maximum of 30 seconds.
- **cue** – an introduction of one or two sentences for a voicepiece, clip or interview read by the newsreader. The name of the correspondent will be given, 'and now over to Bill McArthur in Prague' or 'over to our political correspondent Maggie White'.
- **SOC (Standard Out Cue)** – the words often used to end a voicepiece, for example, Jane Smith Western College Radio News, Exeter.
- **interviews** – these are an important part of longer news broadcasts, although an individual interview is usually under a minute and a half.
- **clip** – this is a short section, approximately half a minute long, taken from a full-length interview.
- **wrap** – this is when a clip or interview is surrounded by a voicepiece. A **double** or **triple wrap** includes two or more audio clips. The term wrap is used in independent radio; the BBC will call this a **package**.
- **FX** or **SFX** – this stands for sound effects, a term normally associated with drama. But the sense of location and atmosphere can be established for the news listener by the appropriate addition of **wildtrack**, **ambient** (background) sound either recorded at the time or later.

Case study

Study the following analysis of a news programme. What patterns can you find in it?

Radio 4 News: 1800 hrs, 20 November 1994.

1800: The sound of the Westminster Chimes

Newsreader announces the programme:
It's 6 o'clock. The News from the BBC with Alison Roper.

CROSS FADE – Big Ben striking fades out after second heading.

The newsreader gives a synopsis of the main stories:

Bosnia
Criminal Justice Act

School League Tables
Rugby League result from Australia

Body of news programme:

1 *Cue*   Bosnia
Voicepiece (correspondent in Sarajevo)

2 *Cue*   Criminal Justice Act
Voicepiece (reporter)
SFX (protesters chanting)
Clip (protesters)
Voicepiece = Wrap

3 *Copy*   Anti-hunt demonstration

4 *Cue*   Education League Tables
Voicepiece (political correspondent)
Clip (Shadow Education Secretary)
Voicepiece
Clip (Education Secretary
Voicepiece
Clip (NUT General Secretary)
Voicepiece = Triple wrap

5 *Cue*   Hospital deaths
Voicepiece (reporter)
Clip
Voicepiece = Wrap

6 *Copy*   Prison story

7 *Cue*   Fighting in Gaza
Voicepiece (correspondent in Jerusalem)

8 *Copy*   President Mubarak

9 *Cue*   Angola
Voicepiece (correspondent in Lusaka)

10 *Cue*   Sport – rugby, football, tennis
Voicepiece (sports reporter)

11 *Copy*   Plane crash

12 *Copy*   National Lottery

13 Headlines are repeated
Outro: 'BBC Radio News'

Activity

Analyse a news broadcast from an independent local radio station and compare the structure and content with the one given above.

Interviews

Interviews should **not** be scripted, otherwise they will not sound spontaneous. However, interviewees should be prepared for likely questions so that they have something to say. Sometimes, however, experienced interviewers will put someone, especially politicians, 'on the spot'. It can be entertaining or exciting if their reactions are silly or angry.

You may not find it very easy at first to relax in front of the microphone, either as interviewer or interviewee. The following hints may be useful.

- Know exactly what the interview is about and what the main points are likely to be.
- Talk as you would normally, don't try to use big words or be formal as you might if you were writing down the replies.
- Notes might be helpful if they refer to statistics, dates or names that might otherwise slip your memory.
- You might be more comfortable doing the interview at home rather than in a studio. You might prefer somewhere with privacy rather than in a busy office (or classroom!) where people may be watching. Of course, this will depend on the acoustics to a large extent.
- Try to sit fairly still and not create extraneous noises by moving your feet around or playing with a pen.
- Everybody involved in the interview wants it to go well. Very seldom will they try to trip you up! Concentrate on the person you are talking to and what they are saying. Try to forget the microphone.
- Take a few deep breaths before you start.
- Remember – if it all goes wrong, then unless an interview is going out live, it can be re-recorded and/or edited!

Types of interview

In his book, *Broadcast Journalism* (Focal Press, 1988), Andrew Boyd lists the different types of interview. These include the following:

- **hard news interview** – this is short and asks very precise questions such as, 'At what time was the car crash?' or, 'At what speed was the car travelling?'
- **informational interview** – this can provide background detail by asking questions like, 'What sort of weather conditions lead to crop failure?' or, 'How safe are heart operations today?'

175

- **investigative interview** – this tries to find the reasons behind an event or the motive behind someone's actions. For example, 'Why did this particular building collapse during the earthquake?' or, 'Who was responsible for ensuring the tigers were locked in at night?'
- **adversarial interview** – although this can be carried out politely, this is a far more aggressive form of questioning. It challenges the interviewee, who might be asked, 'Do you agree that security should have been tightened for an event like this?' or, 'What measures will be taken to ensure that this will not happen again?'
- **interpretative interview** – this is particularly suited to the 'expert' interviewee, it asks for objective comments on what has happened and on potential new developments. It can invite speculation. For example, 'Is new legislation now needed to cope with immigration?' or, 'What will happen now to the ruling party after their defeat?'
- **personal interview** – this usually takes place with someone who is either a celebrity or is prominent in a particular field, such as politics or flower arranging. It may try to find out about the person's work or it may try to find out about his or her personality. 'What inspired you to paint that picture?' or, 'What is it that you like about breeding worms?'
- **emotional interview** – this aims to expose someone's feelings with questions such as, 'How did you feel when you saw her again?' or, 'When did you first realise you were in danger?'
- **entertainment interview** – this concentrates on the lighter or more trivial aspects of even serious events or situations. A soldier might be asked, 'What radio programme did you like to listen to when you were out in the Gulf?' or, 'How did you keep your spirits up when you were lost in the jungle?'

Activity

A controversial new play has opened in London.

Make a list of who you would interview and the type of interview you would like to conduct. Write down a few leading questions for each possible interviewee. Working as a team, record the interviews.

Once material has been collected, interviews done and the structure of the programme decided, the scripts for the newsreaders and reporters can be written.

There are two easy rules to remember:

1 **Keep it simple:**
   - use short words
   - use short sentences
   - avoid jargon
   - use concrete rather than abstract terms
2 **Keep it lively:**
   - use the present tense
   - be natural.

Activity

Below are some examples of abstract/concrete words. A concrete word conjures up more of an image in people's minds, which is especially useful for radio.

Abstract	Concrete
residence	house
converse	talk
antagonise	annoy
zenith	high point
strategy	plan
sustained serious injuries	badly hurt

Now provide alternatives to the following:

   fatality
   enhance
   executives
   induce
   communicative
   vacation
   substantial

If you have trouble in finding alternatives to words use a **thesaurus**, this is a type of dictionary specifically designed to provide lists of words which mean approximately the same.

Even on the Radio 4 News the vocabulary is plain; it is the tone of voice that sets the serious, authoritative style. All radio news shows restraint because of the wide target audience who listen in for the news; there is no certainty that children are not listening. The dramatic, hyperbolic style of the tabloids is avoided. Vivid descriptions of accidents or murders are not given, and gruesome details are avoided. Violent and sexual crimes are not reported using exciting language; for example, 'his brains were blown out' would be replaced by 'he was shot in the head at close range'.

Very often, radio news is scripted from press releases. Press releases are sent into newspapers, radio and TV stations by organisations, whether they are businesses, charities, clubs, societies, etc.

The journalists then re-write the press release as a news item or feature. The style in which it is written will depend on whether it is for the spoken or written word.

Case study

Look at the example of a police press release given in Figure 7.15. It has been written to pass on factual information to the media so that they can help publicise the crime. It does not, however, try to sound interesting or, dare we say it, entertaining. Try reading it to a colleague. Do you normally talk like this? Probably not! If you bear in mind that the radio should speak to you in a straightforward and fairly informal manner, you will realise that this written style is not appropriate for the spoken word. Therefore you need to re-write it so it sounds more natural and less technical.

Figure 7.16 shows an example of how it could be re-written. Let's look at the differences.

A Hampton security guard is in hospital with serious head injuries following an early morning raid on a city hosiery factory.

43-year-old Mr David Rosbotham of Barwell was bound and locked into a cupboard by attackers who made off with 200 thousand pounds' worth of cash and clothes from N.J. Smith and Sons of London Road.

He was found by a cleaner after a 5-hour ordeal.

Police are looking for a six foot three white man in his mid twenties and a scar on the left hand side of his face.

Two other men involved wore masks and one has a tattoo on his fist.

Figure 7.16 A rewrite of the police press release

The first point to note is that the important facts are all put into the opening sentence. Also because it is being broadcast by a Hampton-based radio station, the word Hampton is placed at the very beginning to make the story sound relevant to listeners. Secondly, the tense has been changed, where possible, from the past to the present. For example, 'was' becomes 'is'. This makes the topic feel current and up-to-the minute. It can even make it sound as if events are still unfolding.

Times are not given as, for example, 00.30. Instead they are either put as words (.e.g 'half past twelve') or, as in this case, they are written as approximate times of day ('early morning'). Similarly, the sum of money stolen is written in words.

The formal-sounding words 'premises' and 'entered' are replaced by 'raid', while the stilted 'blunt instrument' is not mentioned but is instead implied by 'in hospital with serious head injuries'.

Hamptonshire Constabulary
press release

At 00.30 hours this morning, the premises of N.J. Smith and Sons, 18 London Road, Hampton were entered. A security guard was attacked with a blunt instrument. He now has serious head injuries and is in hospital. The hosiery factory was ransacked and cash and clothes worth £200,000 were stolen. The security guard, Mr David Steven Rosbotham (43) of 20 Meadowfield, Blackwell was tied up and locked in a cleaners' cupboard on the first floor of the premises. He was found by a cleaner, Mrs Sarah Banks, at 5.30 a.m. Police are still looking for the weapon. They have now issued a description of the intruders as follows:-

1) White man 6'3" 20-25, scar on left side of face.
2) Male, 5'10" wearing mask over face and blue boiler suit.
3) White man, wearing balaclava over face. He wore a gold wristwatch and a tattoo on his fist.

Figure 7.15 An example of a police press release

The security guard's age is given because it adds to the 'human interest' element, i.e. it gives people some kind of a mental picture of a human being, and not just some functionary known as 'security guard'. Stating the area he lives in adds to this picture, but the full address is not given, both for security reasons and because it just isn't necessary. Radio should give an impression and not be cluttered up with inordinate detail. This is why details about the premises, the guard, the cleaner, exact times and some of the suspects' descriptions (where they were unhelpful) have been omitted.

Would you add anything to or delete anything from this report?

Not all press releases are interesting. Sometimes the content sounds dull and it is very often written in a dry, stilted manner. However, it is the journalist's job to make them interesting and find news where it is not immediately apparent. Here we have what could be classed as a rather boring subject which has been freshened up a little.

Activity

Compare the two articles in Figures 7.17 and 7.18 and identify the changes in style and vocabulary in the re-write of the press release.

Safety campaigners are claiming victory against cowboy gas fitters whose shoddy work puts lives at risk.

Sheila Black, spokeswoman for the Gas Consumers Council, said 'Cowboy and DIY installers have caused gas explosions and death by carbon monoxide poisoning. Sadly these tragedies often involve death or injury to others while the cowboy gets off scot-free. A price has to be paid, sometimes in human life.'

The new guidelines will help improve safety by making employers responsible for the work of individual installers.

Figure 7.17 A rewrite of the press release

Gas watchdog welcomes new standards for gas installers

The Gas Consumers Council welcomes a major safety advance for gas consumers that begins on Wednesday (   ) when a new Code of Practice for Gas Installers under the Health and Safety at Work Etc. Act 1974 comes into operation.

For some years the Council has campaigned against dangers arising from amateur or 'cowboy' installers and the Council's Chairman, Sheila Black today (   ) expressed the Council's approval of the new requirement of employer companies that they must ensure that their individual installers are competent. GCC also welcomes what it has long sought, the introduction of improved training, to ensure safe installation, servicing, maintenance, removal and repair of gas systems.

Miss Black said 'Cowboy and D.I.Y. installers have caused gas explosions and death by carbon monoxide poisoning by all burnt fuels. Sadly these tragedies often involve death or injury to others while the cowboy gets off scot free. Both cowboys and do-it-yourselfers tend to think they are doing customers favours with low prices and speedy work. They are totally irresponsible. A price has to be paid, sometimes in human life.'

Failure to observe the Code may be taken into account by a Court in criminal proceedings as proof of a contravention.

END

Note to Editors: 'Approved Code of Practice – Standards of training in safe gas installations' is published by the Health and Safety Commission (HMSO £4.50).

Figure 7.18 A gas safety press release

Justifying completed audio scripts

To justify or evaluate your work, you will have to consider the following questions:

1 Does it meet the needs of the target audience?

What is the purpose and does the item fulfil that purpose?

2 Have you considered the context in which the item is to appear?

Is the **content** interesting? Does it use the right level of vocabulary for the target audience? Does the **structure** help keep the listener's attention? Are individual items the conventional length? Could the ordinary listener recognise the **genre** of the audio item or would they be confused as to whether they were listening to fiction or non-fiction, whether the item is to be taken seriously or not?

 Activity

Read parts of your scripts to someone from the target group for whom you have written. Then ask them the following questions:

a What type of programmes do you think these could be part of?
b Can you describe the plot or list the main points made in the items?
c Did you understand everything that was said?
d What did you enjoy about these scripts?

3 In your scripts, are people and events fairly represented?

If you have stereotyped characters in drama, can this be justified, for example, because this is a comedy?

4 Has the work been delayed because people or equipment have been unavailable for collecting material or co-writing scripts?

It is unlikely that you will have gone over any financial budget in writing a play or interviewing people, but you may well have had difficulties in keeping to the agreed timescale, especially for research. Did you manage to collect enough material?

Figure 7.19 on the next page shows an example of professional scripting. Both content and layout are typical of the industry and the style and vocabulary use the expected conventions for the genre.

Activity

Compare your scripts with professional ones of the same genre. How do they compare in layout and content? What are the issues of representation, and how are they treated? Do they demand the same number of people to make the recording? Will you have the same time, budget or equipment available to you?

Evidence assignment

You should produce two scripts. One could be for a short play or a scene from a play. The other should be for the scripted part of a short section of a programme such as:

- a documentary
- a quiz
- a magazine programme
- a music-based programme.

The scripts should be supported by:

- a detailed proposal for both items
- a list of other ideas you had and how you evaluated them
- a comparison of the script with a similar professional script.

You should include the following as part of the production handbook which you began compiling for Unit 2 Element 1 (Chapter 5):

- the choice of research methods
- a brief record of what research was carried out.

		(FADE UP INTERIOR ACOUSTIC (SLIGHTLY ECHOEY)
HOWARD	1	Miriam … Dearest … Reconsider … I beg you …
MIRIAM	2	My mind is made up, Howard …
WATERLOW	3	A confession, Mrs Cromer! The consequences … ?
MIRIAM	4	Are fully accepted, Inspector … Now if you will be kind enough to write at my dictation …
		(RUSTLE OF PAPER, SCRIBBLING)
		I Miriam Jane Cromer voluntarily confess that on March 12 1888 I did wilfully and in cold blood murder one …
		FADE
		(FADE UP ON PASSING HORSE-DRAWN TRAFFIC. STREET CRIES 'Violets … pretty violets … Flowers for your lady' … DISTANT BARREL ORGAN WELL UNDER)
NEWSBOY	5	Kew Green poisoning … Murderer confesses … Read all about it … Kew Green poisoning …
		(FADE UNDER ANNOUNCEMENTS)
ANNOUNCER	6	Saturday Night Theatre … We present …

		(FADE UP ON DISTANT TOLL OF BELL SLOW AND DELIBERATE. HOLD UNDER FOLLOWING: AND FADE (INTERIOR ACOUSTIC)
JUDGE	1	Miriam Jane Cromer … That the deceased Josiah Percival behaved shamefully, even criminally towards you I concede … But there were other remedies open to you than murder … And even though you've chosen to confess … the Law allows only one sentence I may pass upon you …
		(SLIGHT MURMUR OF VOICES)
		Miriam Jane Cromer … this Court doth ordain that you be taken to the place from whence you came … And from thence to a place of execution … And that there you be hanged by the neck until dead … And that afterwards your body …
		FADE
		(FADE UP ON CRACKLE OF FIRE (INTERIOR ACOUSTIC) DISTANT CHURCH BELLS. HOLD UNDER)
BERRY	2	Lord let me know mine end and the number of my days; that I may be certified how long I have to live … The word of the Lord, woman …

Figure 7.19 The script for a play broadcast on BBC Radio 4: *Waxwork* by Peter Lovesey, adapted by Geoffrey M. Matthews (reproduced by permission)

Chapter 8

Plan and carry out research for moving image items

This chapter is concerned with how professionals produce material for moving image productions and how students should approach similar projects. It covers the origination, development and refinement of ideas and the research, scripting and scheduling necessary for a successful product. Moving image includes films, videos, TV programmes, commercials and animation.

Background information

In the first few decades of this century, moving image meant film. Now it can mean videos and television programmes as well. Television productions are broadcast to large audiences by either over-air or cable transmission. They can be **live** or **taped**, i.e. edited. These productions need to be of a high quality. Video productions can conform to the most advanced professional broadcast standard or they can be made to a low budget for distribution to small audiences. Video productions can be broadcast too, particularly music videos.

There are three basic stages to consider:

1 **pre-production** – this will be the longest stage. It includes planning the schedules, organising the budget, writing the script, hiring actors and crews, etc. This chapter is largely concerned with this aspect of production, but in order to work effectively, you will need to know about the skills used for the next two stages.

2 **production** – recording the action, either on location or in a studio.

3 **post-production** – this is concerned with the editing process. This consists of playing back selected shots and rearranging them, possibly in a different order, on to a master tape. Shots can be cut or have different effects added. Titling will also be added at this stage and music and sound effects dubbed. These techniques will be explained fully in Chapter 19. Then the product is ready for distribution or transmission.

On television there are basically two different types of programmes:

- **studio** programmes, where a location is created in a controlled studio environment through the use of sets
- **outside broadcasts (OBs)** where all the necessary equipment for filming is taken to an outside location away from the studio. This location may be in the open air or in a room inside a building.

Planning and carrying out research for moving image items will involve a lot of practical work. You will need to know how to use equipment such as cameras, lighting and editing suites. You will need to understand their capabilities and the different effects they can produce. It is worthwhile at this point to re-read the section in Chapter 3 on the codes and conventions used in various TV and film genres. How to achieve these in practical terms will be outlined in both this chapter and Chapter 17.

As the soundtrack is such an important part of a moving image production it is advisable to have done the practical work outlined in Chapter 14.

It is recommended that you design and produce several small products at this stage: a short advert, part of a music video or a section of a documentary or film. At the same time, however, you should consider the conventions and content, audience and style of the entire product in which these items will be included.

Originate and evaluate ideas for moving image items

There is an enormous range of different types of moving image productions – from the small five-minute cartoon to the epic movie. Some are designed to entertain, some to inform and some to persuade. They all have a purpose, and their design, their genre, the codes and conventions used, their style, should aim to make them fit for that purpose.

In Chapter 5 you may have come up with some ideas for media products. As already noted, some productions are inspired by literature, some by the experiences of real people or events, and some by other media products. They may be based on reality or on fantasy.

Activity

Generate some ideas for moving image items by answering the following questions:

- Is there a series on TV at the moment which you think could be made into a successful blockbuster film?
- Can you think of any films that would make a good TV series?
- Name a book which could be made into an action series for TV.
- Is there someone famous you would like to make a documentary about?
- Is there a new fashion or a new trend in music you would like to find out more about?
- What guests would you like to have on a chat show?
- What characters from a children's TV series or book would you like to make into a cartoon film?
- Has there been a true-life romance in the newspapers recently which you could make into a studio drama?
- Has there been a documentary about any group of people which could be made into a soap?
- Has anything funny happened to you recently that could be the basis of a comedy drama?

It is important not only to come up with ideas but to make sure that they are different from existing products.

Activity

Work on this activity first on your own and then in a group. Write down some fresh ideas for the following mixture of fiction and non-fiction products:

- TV sit-com
- TV soap
- sports programme for local cable TV
- children's news programme for Saturday morning
- film based on life in contemporary Britain
- advert for a new brand of soup
- animated graphics for a computer game for girls
- informative cartoon
- TV quiz

Discuss with your colleagues how similar your own ideas are to theirs.

Evaluating ideas

You need to be careful that, in order to make your idea original, you don't use gimmicks simply for the sake of novelty. You have to decide whether, for example, special effects, jingles, elaborate graphics and so on are really necessary or even desirable, or whether something more straightforward would be more appropriate. It is this **fitness for purpose** that you should continually bear in mind. It is easy to get carried away and start building in extra effects just because they are there. Equipment has become more sophisticated and, at the same time, more accessible and easier to use. However, these factors by themselves will not ensure the quality of your product. It can, in fact, just mean that it is now easier to make bad products! (See also Chapter 7, page 163, on this subject.)

Resource requirements

A major factor in deciding the feasibility of any idea will be the resources needed. These can be categorised as follows: human, financial, materials and time.

Human resources: are there people in your production team with the necessary skills to produce this work and will they be available at the right time? Feature films, radio programmes, cartoons, adverts and TV programmes all require many personnel for the three stages of production. Planning will include the producer, scriptwriter, location manager and so on. Production will involve camera operators, directors, actors, make-up artists and many more. Later on editors, technical operators, engineers and others will be needed.

Activity

Look at the credits at the end of a TV drama programme or film.

How many personnel are listed? With which stage of production are they most concerned?

Even for a small-scale student project for radio or video you may need the following:

- producer
- researcher
- secretary
- designer
- set and props manager
- wardrobe and make-up assistant
- floor manager
- camera operator
- lighting engineer

- sound engineer
- editor
- musical director (including the hundred-piece orchestra!)
- general assistants.

You may be able to combine some roles, but good organisation and control of your team will be essential. A producer with the characteristics of a managing director can often be the deciding factor in getting a production made!

A full list of the jobs involved in film and television is given and each is explained in Chapter 17.

Financial resources: without money no project gets off the ground. Even students have to budget for a production – however small. This is necessary, for example, for: the cost of cassette or video tapes, the cost of postage for letters asking for permission to film, or the cost of transport to interview someone on the other side of town.

At the other end of the scale from a student budget is the financial plan for a TV or radio programme, which will be much larger and include many more items.

Finance for some films comes from the film studios, but independent film-makers have to persuade banks, investment companies and wealthy individuals to part with their money. They will have to prove to these people that the film will make a profit after all the expenditure, either through the box-office, video sales, merchandising or other spin-offs. A general rule is that a film needs to make two-and-a-half times its production costs in order to make a profit.

A film budget is divided into 'above the line' and 'below the line' costs. The former covers the known wages of directors, performers and technicians. The latter covers the costs incurred after filming has begun.

Independent TV and radio producers also need financial backing. They will have to prove that the programme will attract a certain number of viewers/listeners if it is to appeal to an advertising sponsor.

Case study

This is the budget sheet for the British romantic film *The Racegoer* (1994):

46 days of location
19 days studio
21 days post-production

DESCRIPTION	Cost in £
Above-the-line costs:	
Story and other rights	411,189
Writing	145,375
Producer and staff	564,987
Director and staff	1,234,008
Talent	1,654,846
Tax & fringe	51,350
Total above-the-line	**4,061,755**
Below-the-line costs:	
Production staff	199,245
Camera	178,434
Art dept.	211,323
Set construction	523,805
Special effects	31,231
Set operations	81,122
Electrical	163,334
Set dressing	301,098
Props	35,176
Animals	93,808
Special photography	45,700
Feature – extra talent	235,156
Wardrobe	201,142
Make-up and hairdressing	66,450
Sound (production)	44,341
Locations	324,571
Transportation	238,454
Film-production	112,731
Tests	7,700
Facilities	124,145
Second unit	34,000
Special unit	31,000
Below-the-line fringe	114,343
Total production	**3,398,309**
Editing	233,450
Music	435,788
Sound (post-production)	167,786
Film and stock shots	122,233
Titles and opticals	45,340
Post-production fringe	15,070
Total post-production	**1,019,667**
Insurance	96,500
Publicity	35,756
General expenses	778,565
Other fringe	780
Completion bond fee	348,225
Contingency	565,566
Total other expenses	**1,825,392**
GRAND TOTAL	**10,305,123**

1 What are the most expensive parts of this budget?
2 Which costs are most likely to change, depending on the film genre?

Generally speaking, studio work is less expensive than work out on location. An episode of a sit-com or soap will be less expensive to make than one episode from a serialised period drama using expensive sets and costumes. Wages are a major part of most productions, whether a drama or documentary is being made. Game shows are one of the cheapest forms of television programme because they use the same set week after week, they usually have only one presenter, the competitors appear for nothing and prizes are donated. British television is noted for the high quality of its drama but this is matched by the high cost of production. Independent television companies now seek sponsorship to help meet these costs, and they depend on good sales of the programme abroad.

Activity

Which of the projects below do you think will be the most expensive and why? What major expenses will have to be taken into consideration?

- episode from an established soap
- war film involving unknown actors
- TV period drama using well-known stars
- music video for a major star
- training video for a small company
- TV advert for foreign holidays
- episode of a studio situation comedy
- chat show on late-night weekday television
- TV advert for a well-known brand of designer jeans
- Disney film cartoon using the voices of famous actors

You may be able to think of some wonderful ideas for your AV production, but you will have to work with the resources available to you. Try to be realistic about what is feasible. It is no good planning to shoot your video in an exotic location, with lots of extravagant extras, if it is all going to be impossibly expensive and time-consuming. Making a moving image product is a business activity as well as a creative one, and like any business activity you have to identify your resource needs and try to justify them.

Material resources: these include props, costumes, make-up, catering facilities, production equipment including cameras, editing suites, film, means of transport for the team, actors, equipment, etc.

This is possibly even more of a consideration for the student than it is for the professional! Schools and colleges have a limited number of cameras, recorders, mikes and editing suites. There may also be constraints in terms of quality and capabilities. Locations might need to be within walking distance of the school or college.

Time: for many productions, such as a political campaign or a Christmas show for TV, a deadline is crucial. A news report of a local disaster might be improved if there was more time to write the script, but the listener wants to hear about the event now – not a day later. Actors, studios and equipment may be available only for a certain length of time. Any production which goes outside the time limit will also go outside the budget. Students should work to deadlines as if they were professionals. Time-scales should always have extra time built in, to account for any disasters that occur – from the computer network going down to the absence of fellow students because of sickness or some other problem.

Case study

Anthony James is a young artist with an idea for a children's TV programme based around a puppet called Grubble.

Anthony started his career as a graphic artist working for Nintendo on their computer games. When he left the company he began working from home, making large-scale fantasy creatures from recycled materials which he then exhibited in museums and schools. He also ran workshops for young people on how to make the monsters. His work has been shown on *Blue Peter* and is now under copyright. Recently he has changed the main part of his exhibition to show life-sized models of dinosaurs. Because of the appeal of his work to children, Anthony began writing a story about one of his smaller creations which he thinks will be visually interesting.

1. How much has Anthony's previous work influenced his idea?
2. What experience has Anthony had with the target audience?
3. Why is Anthony's chosen format TV rather than radio or a comic strip?
4. What is the purpose of the idea in terms of information, persuasion and entertainment?
5. How expensive will it be to develop Anthony's ideas in terms of human and material resources?

Aesthetics

A decision you should make at the start of production is whether this is to be **live** or **edited**. This is not simply a practical decision, it also involves aesthetic considerations concerning the style and presentation of the work. In a live production the audience experiences a lot more excitement, the programme feels fresh and there is a feeling of participation. In an edited production a major advantage is that the boring bits can be deleted.

A live production will need more than one camera to make the action interesting, so that shots can be mixed from a number of different directions or angles. This is known as **multi-camera production**. However, if you plan to edit your tape, then a single camera may be sufficient.

In live multi-camera productions, two or more cameras shoot the action and their shots are selected or **intercut** using a **vision mixer** or **production switcher**. This requires a larger team than the single-camera edited version, as you will need at least two camera operators and somebody to be the vision mixer.

Key features and material for moving image items

As with all media products, the central consideration is the **target audience**. This affects not only the content but the finished product, and where and when it will be scheduled or distributed. Moving image is such an expensive product that research in this area is very intensive. In the case of commercial television, it has to be proved that not only will a substantial audience enjoy or appreciate the product, but that this is the right sort of audience to buy the products of advertisers or of a sponsor.

If you read the section on BARB (Broadcasters Audience Research Board), CAA (Cinema Advertising Association) and CAVIAR (Cinema and Video Industry Audience Research) in Chapter 21, pages 357–60, you will gain some idea of the detail which is required to support the activities of the various industries associated with the moving image. The figures collected indicate what sort of films people of a certain age and sex enjoy, or when, for example, most professional people or shoppers are watching the television.

Purpose and structure

Whatever ideas you have for moving image products, you must be very clear about their **purpose**. Films and videos aim to make money for their producers; they need to entertain in order to attract audiences. They may do this by making us laugh or cry, or be thrilled or terrified. Some films, such as *Forrest Gump* or *Schindler's List,* can at the same time inform, educate and persuade, as they make audiences aware of social issues, historical events or the actions of an individual.

Activity

Choose a current social issue, such as homelessness or a health issue. Write a brief synopsis for a film based around people from different or opposing sides falling in love, for example a refugee and an immigration officer, or a patient and a nurse. How could you make this idea original?

The **narrative structure** of a film can also clarify its purpose. (See Chapter 4.) The use of a narrator or voice-over to describe certain parts of the action, as in a film noir such as *Double Indemnity,* can give a sense of seriousness and authority to what is taking place. This is partly because documentaries use a similar technique: we, the audience, are having something explained to us by an 'expert', someone who knows what has happened.

Activity

Choose an historical event with a central character as the basis for an action thriller. Write a brief synopsis in which the action is described through flashbacks. What effect will this technique have on the audience?

If you glance through the TV schedules, it is generally easy to identify the purpose or purposes of different programmes. They tend to be associated with certain **genres**. Thrillers, police dramas, quizzes and situation comedies are primarily there to entertain. Documentaries, news and weather reports, travel programmes, etc. are informative. Adverts and party political programmes are there to persuade viewers. Many programmes have more than one purpose. A soap, such as *Brookside,* may be entertaining but it can also inform us about social issues, such as homosexuality or child abuse.

A competition, such as *Masterchef,* can educate us in how to cook complicated dishes, but at the same time it provides entertainment for many people who may prefer simpler food.

Activity

Pick one subject, for instance dinosaurs or flowers. Explain how you would adapt your subject to be the basis for the following programmes:

1 a soap for older viewers
2 a sit-com for children
3 a documentary for adults
4 an education programme for teenagers
5 an advert for a specific target group.

We have so far looked mainly at fiction items but the content of non-fiction programmes needs to be closely defined also, as does their structure and style. It is not enough to state that a network has so many hours of cookery or so much coverage of politics. The **treatment** is all-important. BBC TV put on a lot more sport in the summer of 1996, and has paid millions of pounds in order to cover the Olympics and retain *Match of the Day* until the next decade. But it is still criticised because the content of these programmes will contain too much pre-competition hype and recorded action highlights, rather than live games followed by analysis. It is claimed that BSkyB has more adventurous camera work and better explanations of the action.

Case study

Below are some suggestions by GNVQ students for images to accompany a music record.

Three students, Dean Callier, Adrian Bird and Chris Collerson decided to produce the visual images to accompany the single of rock group Soundgarden. The music, called *Jesus Christ Pose*, is a fast up-beat song with agonising guitar sounds.

First they analysed the song in terms of its structure (see Figure 8.1).

They wrote down the words to help clarify the structure and emotional content of the single. Then they brainstormed what the song suggested to them, as shown in Figure 8.2.

```
            Song analysis

Analysis of Jesus Christ Pose by
Soundgarden

Times
(min/secs)
0-30            Instrumental/use of
                instruments to
                Create atmosphere
31-58           Guitar fill
59-1:26         Main guitar riff enters
1:27-1:54       1st verse
1:55-2:10       Pre-chorus
2:11-2:21       Chorus
2:22-2:38       Break/instruments
2:39-3:03       2nd verse
3:04-3:35       Different pre-chorus
3:36-3:49       Chorus
3:50-4:08       Interlude
4:09-4:33       Vocals come in over top
4:34-4:47       Different pre-chorus mixed
                with chorus over top
4:48-5:49       Outro, feedback etc.

Drums basically the same all the way
through apart from on pre-chorus and
interlude.
```

Figure 8.1 Students' analysis of a song

They each suggested various visual ideas. These included:

- fast clips of statues in crucifix positions
- the statue of a woman with raised arms in the local park
- clips of someone playing a guitar

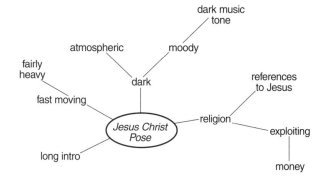

Figure 8.2 Results of the brainstorming session

- scenes representing the four seasons
- money being thrown
- shots of the group standing in a crucifix pose
- black and white and negative images rather than colour.

A more detailed explanation of how moving image products are structured is given on page 192. See also Chapter 4 on narrative structure.

Technical requirements

At this stage you should be practising camera and editing skills which will make you familiar with the equipment needed to produce a video or TV programme. For more information, study Chapters 18 and 19.

For **recording**, the basic equipment includes:

- cameras
- tripods or dollies
- power adapters or batteries
- cables
- lighting
- microphones
- headphones.

For **editing**, the basic equipment includes:

- two or three machine editing equipment
- titling facilities
- vision mixer
- special effects.

Students will probably have access only to analogue machines, but should be aware of the implications and capabilities of digital editing.

When all these key features have been identified and written down they will form a **proposal** which can be given to a client.

 Case study

Figure 8.3 on the following page shows a proposal for a programme for Cable 7 TV by Andrew Wright, who wishes to make a programme on local ghosts.

In a group, discuss the following questions relating to the proposal.

1 What other reasons could Andrew have given for wanting to make this programme?
2 Do you get an impression of the style of the programme from what he has written?
3 How will the choice of a target audience as general as this affect the material used?
4 What biased viewpoint could this programme give?
5 Instead of one long programme, do you think this idea could be developed into a series of shorter programmes?
6 What other information do you think could have been incorporated into the design of the proposal sheet?

 Activity

Write out a proposal, following a similar format to the one shown in Figure 8.3, for two of your own ideas.

Investigative methods and research for moving image items

It is important early on to identify the research needed to develop an idea. Do not, for example, think that it is acceptable to shoot lots of film without bothering to plan properly, because you think you will be able to edit it all at the post-production stage. If necessary, this can be done in an emergency situation, where, for example, dramatic events are unfolding in front of you and there is no time to plan. However, generally speaking, it makes good business and artistic sense to plan carefully so that time and money and other valuable resources, such as editing suites, are not used excessively as a way of getting out of poor planning.

General research

Even before the product specification is finalised, or a deal is drawn up with a client, many hours of research will already have been done. This will have centred on the following areas:

- Researching the **product**
  This can mean a close reading of the book on which a film is based, finding out about the particular qualities of a product for which you are making an advert. If you are requested to make a radio documentary about a famous person it may necessitate a visit to the library to find out what has been written about this individual. To sell your idea you must become an expert on it!

- Researching **similar** products
  What other competition is there in the market? How novel is your 'original' idea? Are similar

Cable 7 programme proposal

1. Why do you want to produce a programme?

Please tell us your reasons for wishing to produce a programme, what you hope to achieve and why community TV is the best medium for you:

A desire to contribute to a project of local interest and inform via the most popular medium - TV.

2. What is your programme about?

Describe the general content of your programme and how it will look: studio shoots/interviews/video inserts/remote shoots. Please be as specific as you can, particularly if you are thinking of doing a series. Use a separate sheet if necessary:

Folklore, legends and ghostly goings-on within the "Castle Park" area of Lanchester. Interviews, cases related, sites visited. An external location documentary taking in historical details and possible cause for legend, ghost story etc. and several participants relating their experiences first hand.

3. Who do you want to watch your programme?

Please state the age and interest of your target audience.

From 8 to 80! Anyone with a passion for hair-raising tales of a spooky nature!

4. Do you want your audience to respond to your programme? If so, how?

Indicate phone-in/competition/visits/mail etc.

Yes! As an investigator of paranormal activity, one is always on the lookout for "active cases" i.e. have any viewers been subjected to supernatural disturbance? If someone has a ghostly problem we will investigate and arrange for termination.

5. How much time are you prepared to commit?

Making programmes takes a great deal of time and commitment – your time! How much are you willing to spend on your programme?

12 hours, as arranged

6. How long will your programme be?

Less than   5 mins. _____   10 mins. _____   20 mins. _____   30 mins. ✔_____

               60 mins._____   Any other length *45 mins if new developments arise*

7. What facilities will you require?

Please indicate if you need film crew/equipment only/studio/edit facilities:

Film crew, edit

8. When, if at all, will your programme be out of date?

Should be valid for the foreseeable future

Figure 8.3 A proposal

products performing well or are they going out of fashion?

- Researching the **target audience**
  You will have to prove to any financial backer that there is an audience out there for your idea. This may be done through official audience statistics or local questionnaires or interviews.

- Researching the **resources** needed
  This will be essential in order to produce a financial plan.

- Researching the availability of **personnel**
  This involves a lot of letters and telephone calls, and the ability to negotiate.

- **Ownership**
  The first thing a prospective film producer must do is to buy the rights of the book, for example, on which the film is based. It will then become known as the *property*.

- Finding a **financial backer**
  This will involve a lot of letters, telephone calls and visits to banks, accountants, etc. It also means that all possible expenditure has been researched.

- **Legal issues**
  It is important to be clear at this stage that the idea will not contravene any laws such as libel, race relations or equal opportunities measures, etc. If any music is to be used, whether original or belonging to someone else, then there will be issues of copyright, mechanical and/or performing rights to be taken into consideration.

- **Location recce**
  A preliminary survey on possible sites for filming, whether in a studio or on location, will be useful at an early stage, not only for budgeting but to indicate the scale of the production.

The recce is sometimes called the **remote survey**. When you film in a studio, you know what to expect – anywhere else and there is a lot of checking to be done! Not all location work is outside; if you are filming inside any building other than a studio, that too is called being on location.

Figure 8.4 is an example of a checklist for a recce. There may be other details that you will need to add for your own work.

Activity

The horror film *Curse of the Killer Sheep* is about animal vampires and set in the last century. The crew is working to a very tight budget and time is limited, so all locations need to be as close together as possible.

The main studio for filming is in the area where you live. You have been asked to find locations as close to each other as possible for the following scenes:

- an old terraced house
- a stately home
- a graveyard
- an old library
- a church with a spire
- an old school
- a large field with sheep.

Locate all of the above and make a detailed remote survey of one of the locations.

If you have already completed Chapters 6 and 7 (and read parts of Unit 6), you should be familiar with the range of investigative research methods, including both questionnaires and interviews. For fiction as well as non-fiction it is essential to research your audience and your material in order to check for accuracy, and for aesthetic and legal reasons.

Primary research

The primary sources referred to before will be useful here, i.e. personal interviews (perhaps on location), telephone interviews, personal observation, taking photographs and making audio and video recordings. However, taking photographs and video recordings will be of greater significance than for an audio production as the final product may include these visual images if it is a news programme or documentary. Photographs of locations can also help script writers plan camera shots or construct a storyboard, and will also help set designers with their work.

Case study

For the Soundgarden music video, the team did a recce of the location and Adrian Bird took photographs of the site and of the team.

THE REMOTE SURVEY

Project ... Film: Curse of the Killer Sheep

Name of producer ... David Polinski

Name of person conducting survey ... Jennifer White

Date of survey ... 10 Sep 1996

Date when production is intended ... Oct 1996

Attach a sketch of location (indicate possible good positions for cameras) and a route map to location

Permissions needed: The farmer who owns the field is G. Slope of Merrydale Farm. Tel. 01865 445443. He has given a verbal agreement for filming to take place. Local police to be informed, as fake firearms will be used

Traffic problems: Heavy traffic around 08.45 because of schools and the local factory. Noise from aircraft taking off from the small, local airport at 08.05, 11.10, 14.00, 18.15 during the week. More flights at the weekend. Large car boot sale and market every Saturday in adjacent field.

Local conditions: Generally a windy spot. May cause problems with sound. No rain expected but frosts are predicted over the next few weeks. Additional lighting may be needed. No mains electricity available.

Intrusions: Horses and sheep on site. Farmer has agreed to move horses. Electricity pylon on hills behind the scene needs to be kept out of shot.

Continuity: There may be problems as lots of leaves were on the trees in the last outdoor sequence shot.

Set dressing: Nineteenth-century farmer's wagon needed.

Welfare: Crew and actors can use outside toilet at the farm. Refreshments available at Post Office in village.

Possible dates for production: Any day in October except the first weekend when there are sheepdog trials.

Figure 8.4 A remote survey form

Figure 8.5 Illustration used on Adrian's video

Later, these stills were used in the video and on the cover of the video case. They also had to go to the Council offices to ask for permission to film in the park. They checked whether equipment and personnel were available on certain days. What other primary research should they do?

Secondary research

Besides the usual books, articles, CD-ROM, videotapes and audiotapes, there are other collections that professionals find invaluable for source material. However, some can be expensive to access and are therefore unavailable to the student. Besides the news and picture agencies mentioned in Chapter 6 (page 130), the following are also useful. Some cover all topics, some specialise in certain areas:

- **BBC Worldwide Television Library Sales**
  This is Britain's largest library of film and videotape, including all recorded BBC programmes.

- **ITV Libraries**
  All these companies keep material which they have produced.

- **British Film Institute**
  Besides film footage, the library contains a data-base about film and TV, stills and posters. It was founded in 1935 and now contains over a quarter of a million items of film.

- **British Movietone News**
  This library stores the newsreels of Movietone which operated from 1929 to 1979.

- **British Pathe News**
  This covers world events from 1895 to 1970, which were recorded by Pathe News to show in cinemas between films.

- **Imperial War Museum Film and Video Archive**
  This holds all official war film shot since 1914.

- **Greenpeace Communications Video Library**
  This has the footage from the various Greenpeace campaigns.

- **RSPB Film Library**
  Naturally this contains lots of footage of birds, but also covers other natural history areas.

Activity

Brainstorm the areas of research you would need to cover in order to evaluate the viability of the ideas for a moving image product that you have suggested so far.

You will need to estimate the human and financial resources necessary to do this research. Most of all, you will need to look at how much time you have to complete the research.

Choose four ideas that you think will provide enough material after research to make different moving image products. Try to cover both fiction and non-fiction products, some studio-based and others on location. Remember, it will be sufficient to complete only part of each product; so if the intended war film involves mass destruction of tanks and aircraft, and a cast of thousands, you can get away with filming the love scene between two of the characters! However, you will need to have researched costume, locations, how people spoke and behaved, and so on.

Potential content considerations

The legal and ethical considerations for moving image products are explained in detail in the Legal and Ethical Appendix. The TV and film industries are tightly regulated, and you will find it useful to read the section on the official regulatory bodies in Chapter 30.

Representation has been discussed in Chapter 2. We know that film and television can reflect society and different cultures, but it can influence them too. For example, TV dramas can show women in powerful positions in industry or government – which is not (yet!) the case in reality. Ideas and attitudes can also be presented to audiences which will persuade them to change their viewpoints; this is especially true of political or economic issues.

Activity

Take two of your ideas and discuss within the group how a minority group could be represented to:

- *reflect* current attitudes in society
- *change* attitudes towards them within society.

Select material for development

You will now have researched a number of ideas. The amount of material which you have collected and its quality will indicate to you which ideas you should pursue. You should, however, choose at least one fiction and one non-fiction product, one studio-based and one on location. Possible items could include:

- a sports report
- an episode from a drama
- a documentary
- the news
- an advert
- a quiz
- an instructional video on a hobby.

Activity

At this stage, check that you have made some notes about each of the following:

- You should be aware of the *purpose* of your products and have a clear idea of the type of viewer they are intended for (i.e. *target audience*).
- You should have noted any *legal* and *ethical* implications.
- You should have made a list of *people* who are available to work with you and any special skills they might have.
- You should have begun negotiating *deadlines* with the client (probably your teacher).
- You should have completed any necessary *research.*

Produce treatments and scripts for moving image items

Treatments

The notes you have made will form the basis of a **treatment**. This states in abbreviated form the pictures and sound that will make up the programme. As work progresses, certain parts may change, new material may be added or the sequence of shots may change, but the treatment will give a clear indication of the scope of the work and the intentions of the producer. Some programmes, such as *Masterchef,* follow the same formula each week and this is what the treatment would describe.

Figure 8.6 is a treatment for *Get Moving,* a potential new series of short, 20-minute programmes on sport for young people aged between 10 and 15. It is intended for transmission on a Saturday morning, and the presenter will be someone who has starred in

	Picture	Sound
1	titling	lively music
2	professional tennis match	commentary: these are professional players. How did they reach the top?
3	presenter with tennis star	star tells of early years as a player
4	library film: player winning Wimbledon for the first time	star continues to talk
5	star practising basic shots	what he/she likes about tennis and the hard work needed
6	interview with tennis coach	explains training possibilities for youngsters
7	young tennis player with star	voice-over from presenter explaining the shots
8	lots of young tennis players	vox pop: why they are prepared to spend a lot of time practising and their ambitions
9	library film of star winning Wimbledon recently	theme music
10	young tennis player playing a winning point	theme music and commentary – could this be you?

Figure 8.6 A treatment for a sports programme for young people

a teenage soap. The sports celebrities chosen will be young, lively and colourful, and the locations will be varied. The first programme is on tennis.

Each sequence may involve a number of shots from different angles and distances. However, the formula above could be used week after week for a number of different sports from football to surfing.

Activity

Write a similar treatment for an advert for a chocolate bar.

Treatments include a fair amount of detail. They should indicate the angle or purpose behind the production. They can be used as a basis for the budget and the schedule. An experienced producer will be able to assess quite quickly how long a particular sequence of scenes will take to shoot; to that will be added the length of time it takes to travel, set up cameras, rehearse actors or brief interviewees.

The duration of each sequence can be estimated, e.g.			
Sequence	1		10 secs
	2		30 secs
	3	2 mins	20 secs
	4	1 min	
	5	4 mins	
	6	3 mins	
	7	6 mins	
	8	1 min	30 secs
	9		30 secs
	10	1 min	
Total		**20 mins**	

It will take approximately one shooting day to complete filming. The interviews with the tennis stars and the coach will take about an hour each, and filming the master class with a young person will take two or three hours. Additional footage of students playing and being interviewed may take another hour to organise and shoot. To this should be added the time it takes for a crew to travel to the location.

This assumes that all the tennis players will be available on the same day. Remember, the sequences do not have to be shot in the order in which they appear in the treatment, but can suit the convenience of the crew and the people appearing in the shots. If rain seems likely then all exterior shots should be taken as soon as possible.

Activity

Estimate the duration for shooting the chocolate advert for which you did a treatment above.

Scripts

Once a treatment has been prepared and agreed with a producer, a **storyboard** and a script can be written. A storyboard gives an overall impression of how the product will look. It is particularly useful for showing a client how an advertisement will look. In films, people doing dangerous stunts expect to see a storyboard showing how the sequence will be filmed.

It does not matter if you are not good at drawing when you make a storyboard. Stick people will suffice as long as the proportions are correct.

Activity

Draw a storyboard similar to the one in Figure 8.7 on the next page. Choose five different shots to show how to make a mug of coffee. Compare your choice of shots with those of your colleagues.

An author will submit a script giving *dialogue* and indicating *action*. The director will then make a visual interpretation of the author's script by adding camera shots, camera movements, editing directions and sound requirements. Scripts for TV use a standard layout.

For a live show, scenes or units will be shot in the scripted order, i.e. the **running order**. When taping a production which can be edited later, scenes are shot in the order that is most convenient for the crew and cast. This is known as the **shooting order**.

Camera shots

Before you start making a storyboard or writing a script you will need to practise some of the standard shots. This will help you to understand the different effects they produce so that you are able to describe the ones you need in the correct way. There are special abbreviations for different shots, as shown in Figure 8.8.

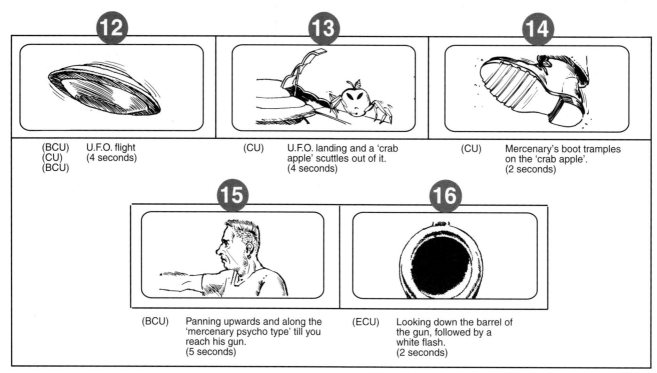

Figure 8.7 Storyboard images for a studio video

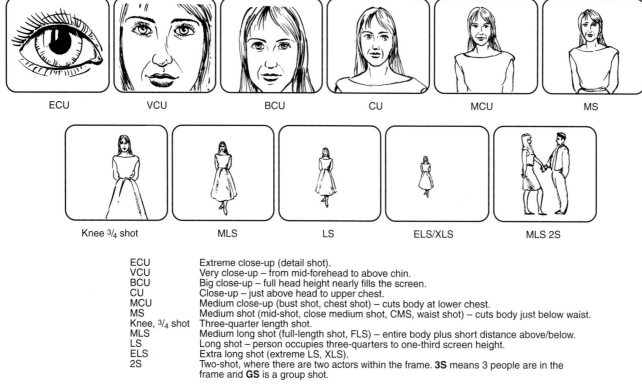

ECU	Extreme close-up (detail shot).
VCU	Very close-up – from mid-forehead to above chin.
BCU	Big close-up – full head height nearly fills the screen.
CU	Close-up – just above head to upper chest.
MCU	Medium close-up (bust shot, chest shot) – cuts body at lower chest.
MS	Medium shot (mid-shot, close medium shot, CMS, waist shot) – cuts body just below waist.
Knee, 3/4 shot	Three-quarter length shot.
MLS	Medium long shot (full-length shot, FLS) – entire body plus short distance above/below.
LS	Long shot – person occupies three-quarters to one-third screen height.
ELS	Extra long shot (extreme LS, XLS).
2S	Two-shot, where there are two actors within the frame. **3S** means 3 people are in the frame and **GS** is a group shot.

Figure 8.8 Camera shots

194

Other useful abbreviations include:

- **L/A** – low angle
  Low angle shots, with the camera pointing up at a person, make someone look intimidating or superior.

- **H/A** – high angle
  This type of shot can give the opposite effect and makes the person look insignificant.

- **POV** – point of view shot
  The viewer sees the action through the eyes of one of the actors. So in a fight, the camera might show what the victim sees (the victim's viewpoint) and we see the aggressor approaching or throwing punches towards the camera. The viewer sympathises with the victim and experiences his or her feeling of terror. This is a far more powerful shot than one showing the two people fighting.

- **Top shot**
  This gives a bird's eye view of the action or place.

- **WS** – wide shot

- **Insert shots** – close ups of significant detail, such as a clenched fist, a ring on a finger, the flashing light on an ambulance. At the editing stage, these shots are called **overlays**.

- **Pieces to camera**
  Sometimes known as **stand-ups** or **stand-uppers**, these are shots where a reporter stands in front of the scene that is being reported on.

  When filming, it is useful to take some standard shots:

- **GV (General view)** or **establishing shots**
  These should be taken for every building or location where shooting takes place. They are very often required at the editing stage!

- **Introductory shots**
  There should always be a shot of the interviewee doing something other than talking to the interviewer. For example, politicians are often shown walking away from the House of Commons talking to a colleague before being questioned by a reporter.

- **Wallpaper shots**
  These are general shots of people, places or activities that form a background for a commentary or narration.

- **Cutaway shots**
  A glimpse of something which is not part of the main action is called a cutaway shot. In a variety show, for example, there will be a brief shot of the audience. Whilst reporting from a race meeting, the scene may cut from the horses in the paddock to show a couple strolling hand in hand in the sunshine. Cutaways put the main action into context.

- **Overlap shots**
  These are two or more different shots that, when put together, will show a continuous action. Camera One films a small boy falling through a hole, for example, while Camera Two shoots his fall from the floor of the basement. These shots could be filmed with one camera, but the action would then have to be performed twice.

Not all shots are static. Some are moving shots, as described in Figure 8.10 on the next page.

Camera scripts

The BBC uses a standard format, which all production assistants are expected to use when writing a camera script. Instructions are written in a type of shorthand. Abbreviations are used, as there is little time for the camera operators to read detailed descriptions of what they are supposed to do.

Information about visual images (see Figure 8.9) is given on the left-hand side of the page.

Dialogue and information about sound and directions to actors (see Figure 8.11) are given on the right-hand side of the page.

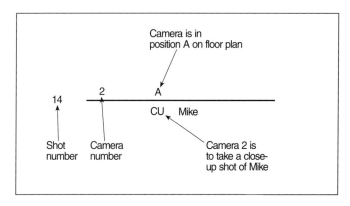

Figure 8.9 Information about visual images in a camera script

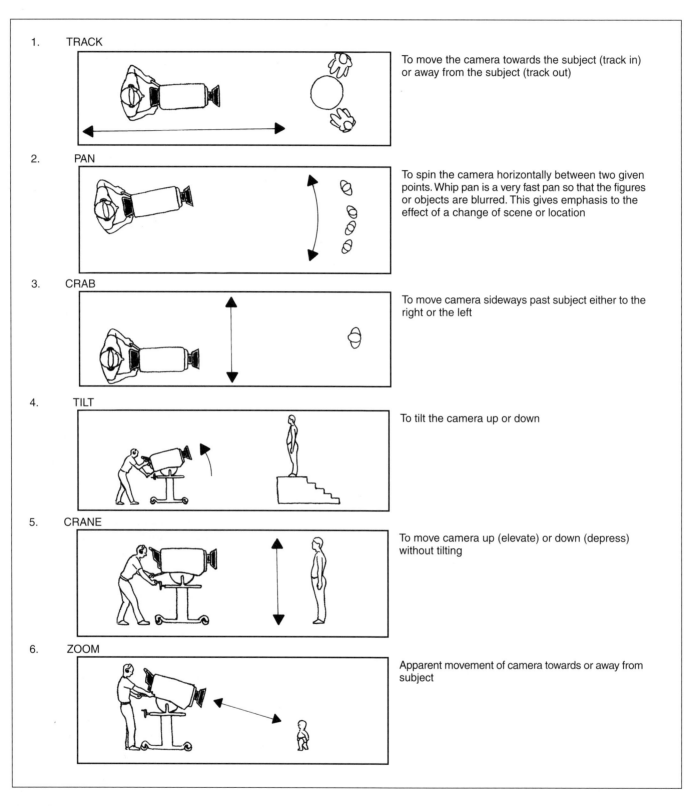

1. TRACK — To move the camera towards the subject (track in) or away from the subject (track out)

2. PAN — To spin the camera horizontally between two given points. Whip pan is a very fast pan so that the figures or objects are blurred. This gives emphasis to the effect of a change of scene or location

3. CRAB — To move camera sideways past subject either to the right or the left

4. TILT — To tilt the camera up or down

5. CRANE — To move camera up (elevate) or down (depress) without tilting

6. ZOOM — Apparent movement of camera towards or away from subject

Figure 8.10 Movement shots

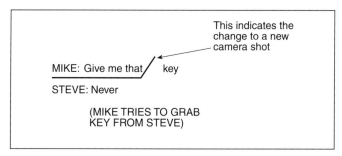

Figure 8.11 Dialogue and directions in a camera script

Activity

Describe what is happening in a studio using the camera script shown in Figure 8.12.

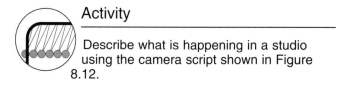

Figure 8.12 A camera script

Sometimes, camera movements and editing techniques are indicated such as PAN, ZOOM, MIX, FADE etc.

Other instructions might be:

■ **S/I** – superimpose

Figure 8.13 tells us that shot six is a long shot of a castle taken by camera 1 from position A. Superimposed on this will be the date – 1918.

Sometimes during run-throughs it may be decided that additional shots are needed. New shots are given the number of the previous shot followed by a letter, such as shot 43A.

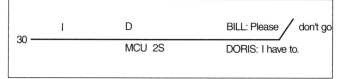

Figure 8.13 Camera script for shot six

■ **VT** – videotape sequence

Figure 8.14 shows a sequence already filmed and stored on videotape. Its sequence number on the videotape is 5, its title is LOCKED ROOM. It will last for 20 seconds and the production assistant will count it out for the crew. Earlier there will be a reminder in the script that there is soon to be a VTI.

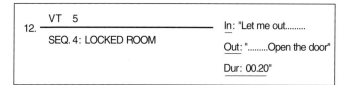

Figure 8.14 Script for a sequence stored on videotape

Other instructions you may see are:

■ **S/BY VT 5** – stand by for videotape sequence 5
■ **4 TO D** – means move camera 4 to position D
■ **MUSIC** – this indicates that music is to be used
■ **PL 14** – identifies the disc number
■ **TK 5** – identifies the track
■ **SOT** – sound on tape.

Activity

Figure 8.15, on the next page, shows a camera script.

Can you tell what is happening in this script?

From such a script **camera cards** are prepared. These list and describe all the shots for each camera and indicate the position of the camera on the floor plan. There is plenty of space on the right of the card for the camera operator to make notes of any changes made during a rehearsal called a **camera walk through**.

Activity

Look at the page of script in Figure 8.15. Write out a camera card for camera 2.

News scripts

Fictional products, such as films, soaps and drama, are fully scripted to show dialogue and action. Other programmes are not. There is far less time to prepare

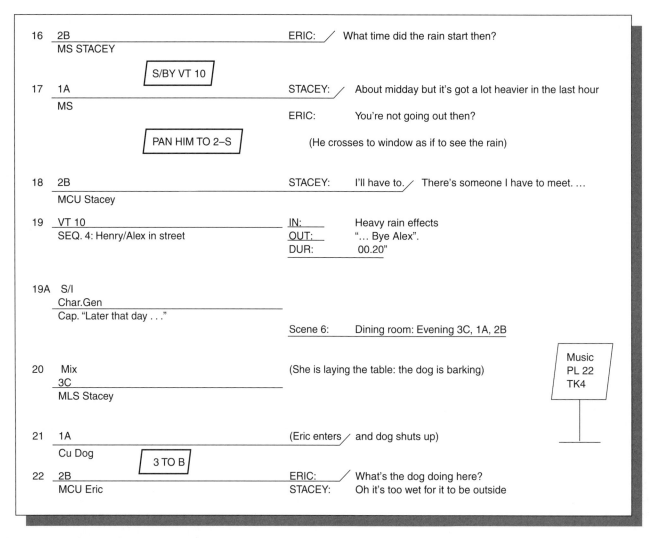

Figure 8.15 A sample camera script

a detailed camera script for programmes such as news, current affairs or magazine programmes, which contain items that arrive at the last moment, or interviews. Where additional footage is added, a sheet is inserted in the script giving:

■ the title of the item
■ the introductory words to be spoken by the newsreader or presenter in full
■ the opening and closing words of the insert on videotape
■ the duration or the insert
■ an outcue to be spoken by the newsreader or presenter.

Alternative outcues should be given with varying lengths, so that the programme does not overrun its transmission time.

When writing a script for a documentary or the news, some footage will have been shot already. Sometimes the script dictates what pictures need to be taken; sometimes the script is built around the images. A two-minute news report will probably have less than two hundred words. The newsreader or reporter's script should never describe what the viewer can see, but should clarify or explain the images.

Activity

Read aloud at a steady pace for two minutes. How many words have you read out?

Shot selection and script writing often need to be done together. First of all, a **dopesheet** or **shot list** is produced of all the footage taken. In the example below, the shots are intended to be part of a news report on a mining accident:

SHOT TIME	SUBJECT	TIME IN SECS.	CUMULATIVE
GV	Colliery	4	4
MS	Rescue workers	3	7
CU	Mining official	6	13
MLS	Crowd waiting by mine	4	17
CU	Wife of trapped miner	3	20
GS	Friends of trapped miner	3	23
LS	Ambulances arriving	3	26
MS	Miner brought up from pit	6	32
LS	Ambulance leaving	3	35

Activity

The sequence of shots shown above lasts a mere 35 seconds. A reporter would actually be able to say very few words in this time. Write a short script to accompany these pictures which will explain the situation and provide extra detail for the viewer. Read the script aloud while a friend times you precisely. You will probably need to amend the script several times in order to make it fit.

The newsreader will arouse the interest of the viewer in the story with an opening sentence introducing the topic, called a **cue**, **lead** or **link**. In the example, the cue might say 'as you can see from the pictures, there was a happy end to the disaster at Hockley Colliery today.' This cue may finish before the footage appears or may overlap on to the first establishing shot.

Long shots are usually used for the **establishing shot** or **opener**. As a rule, close-ups are bridged by medium shots. Panning and zooming shots are difficult to cut, so are taken sparingly by camera operators. **Sound-bites**, sometimes called **grabs**, are interviews used in reports and are usually much shorter than those used on radio.

Cutaway shots, 'noddy' shots, two shots of reporters and interviewees are known as **reverses**.

The script is written out as described above for fiction. There are a few extra conventions to note for news scripts:

Tell stories are when the newsreader only is **in vision** (I/V). For example:

JENNY I/V:	Tennis now – at Wimbledon today, a British player has succeeded in getting through to the semi-final.

Reports can use photographic stills and graphics. These are called **captions** by the BBC. For example:

SEAN I/V:	A helicopter is now on its way to pick up people stranded on the remote island of Eigg.
CAPTION: (Map)	They found themselves on the island after their yacht was swept off course during a storm.

Interviews

For interviews, the reporter or chat show host will have a list of guests, brief notes about their careers and so on, and a list of key questions. These will not be followed rigidly and may be abandoned if the interview takes off along an unexpected but interesting path. The important thing is to make the interview flow.

There are basically two types of questions that people can be asked: closed and open.

Closed questions have a 'yes' or 'no' or a couple of words as an answer. For example: How old are you? Do you like Britain? How many records have you made?

Open questions will demand a longer response. So: Why do you like fast food restaurants? What made you decide to become a brain surgeon? Why do you think the riot took place yesterday?

Key words in a news programme sum up the important points of the news. Key questions should be open ended, but they too must get to the heart of the topic that is being discussed. The interviewer should be prepared to follow them up with other questions which will develop that avenue of investigation further.

Activity

You are hosting a magazine programme. Your guest, Alice James, is a female jockey who has just won the Grand National. Script an introduction and then make a list of half a dozen key questions to ask her. For example, is she the first woman to achieve this success?

199

The individual items within such a programme are listed in the order in which they will appear. The names of people appearing in each sequence, the duration of each item and the sound and vision sources are given. This is known as a **running order**.

Interviews should not be scripted, because this destroys a natural atmosphere. However, questions should be prepared in advance. The advantage of television is that the audience can see the reactions of the interviewees, their body language, nervous gestures, etc. There are a few practical points that should be remembered. Don't let the interviewee wear dark glasses (people's eyes reveal a lot about their personality and feelings) or smoke (if material is edited, the rapidly changing length of a cigarette can look bizarre). Make-up, powder at least, will be necessary to stop speakers from looking as if they are sweating.

There should always be a run-through with the interviewee to check technical points such as voice levels, lighting and camera positions. Interviewees will also need to be set at ease. Unlike in the radio station, there will be a crew around, lots of lighting and equipment, and maybe a studio audience. Unless the interview is live, there may be the need to re-do the first couple of questions to give guests the opportunity to relax.

With only one camera, the interviewee should be placed in front of the camera with the interviewer next to the camera. By using a wide-angle shot, the interview can start with the back of the interviewer's head to one side and the face of the guest in the centre of the frame. The camera can then zoom in on the guest. This is known as an **over-the-shoulder two-shot**.

As a general rule, the camera lens should be level with the eyes of the person in the shot.

With two cameras, the interviewer and the guest can both sit in front of a camera, but at right angles to each other.

There are two types of cutaway shots used in interviews. A **noddy** or **listening shot** is when the interviewer can be seen to be listening; there may be a slight nod of the head. **Cutaway questions** are where the interviewer repeats questions to camera after the actual interview, possibly tidying them up if the original unscripted questions sounded rambling.

Activity

Video a short studio interview, to last five minutes. This could be, for example, about a film that a student has just seen or an event he or she has attended. It could be about something more controversial, such as the legalisation of cannabis. The interview can use either one or two cameras, but follow the advice given above. Take care that you have checked that there is no untidy background within camera shot, and that foreground objects such as books on a table are not visually distracting. You may be able to vision mix the interview as it progresses if you have two cameras, but think about using noddies and cutaway questions to add during editing.

Activity

Write a page of script for a fictional production, such as an advert, and a non-fiction production, such as the news, based on treatments you have prepared above.

Justifying completed scripts for moving image items

To justify or evaluate your work, you will have to consider the following questions:

1 Does it meet the needs of the target audience?

Have you clearly identified the purpose of your intended production and is this reflected in your script? Can you honestly say that you yourself are interested in the content? If not, why not?

2 Have you considered the context in which the item is to appear?

If you have written for television, in what type of programme do you think your item will fit? Where would it appear in the schedules? Is your style and presentation appropriate for your target audience? Does the text support the images or vice versa? Have you chosen the right images and words to illustrate your ideas? The level of vocabulary should match that of the target audience. Can your work be easily identifiable as fiction or non-fiction through your use of codes and conventions?

Activity

Read your script and show your storyboard to someone from your target audience. Then ask the following questions:

- What sort of programme do you think this is like?
- Could you follow what was happening?
- Can you describe the plot or the main events in the script?
- What did you like most about the script?

3 Are people and events fairly represented in your scripts?

If you have written a drama script, have you used any stereotypes? If so, can you justify their use?

In a news or current affairs programme, have you given a balanced viewpoint of issues or ideas? Have you allowed both sides of a story to be told?

4 Has the work been delayed because people or equipment have been unavailable for collecting material or co-writing scripts?

Did you find the time to do a thorough remote survey? Was enough time allowed for interviewing people? Did some types of research take a lot longer than you thought? If you have to pay for your own film or transport costs, did you run over budget?

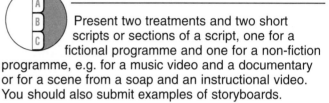

Case study

Figure 8.16 on the following pages shows a script which has been broadcast on Cable 7. Compare your script with it. How do they compare in layout and content? Identify any issues of representation and compare how they are treated. Will they need the same number of people to make the production, or require similar facilities? Will you have the same time, budget and equipment available to you?

Evidence assignment

Present two treatments and two short scripts or sections of a script, one for a fictional programme and one for a non-fiction programme, e.g. for a music video and a documentary or for a scene from a soap and an instructional video. You should also submit examples of storyboards.

Evaluate your script by comparing it with a professional script for a similar product.

Notes on research and identifying legal, ethical and representational issues should be kept in your production handbook.

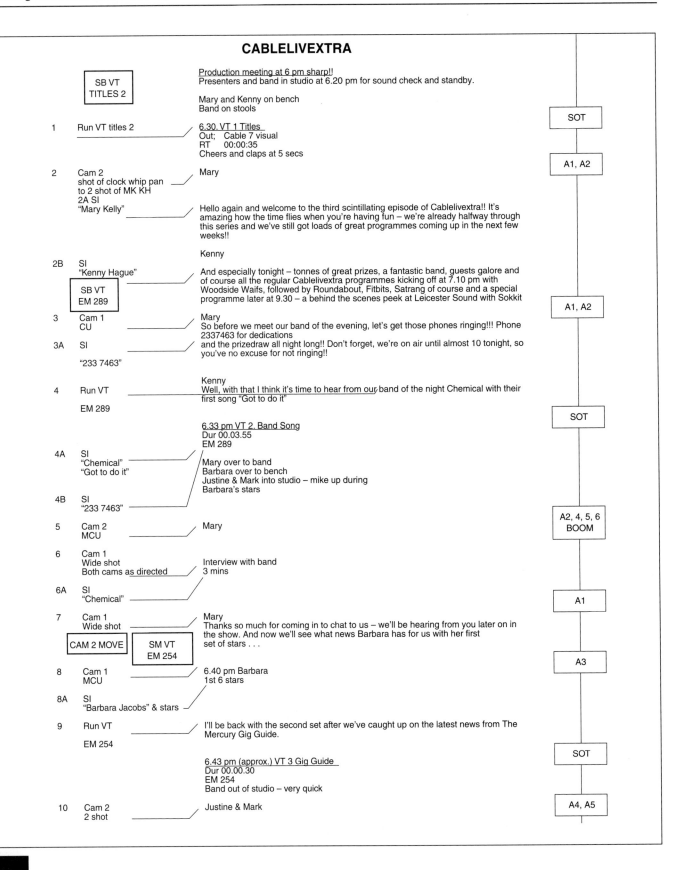

CABLELIVEXTRA

SB VT
TITLES 2

Production meeting at 6 pm sharp!!
Presenters and band in studio at 6.20 pm for sound check and standby.

Mary and Kenny on bench
Band on stools

SOT

1　Run VT titles 2

6.30. VT 1 Titles
Out;　Cable 7 visual
RT　00:00:35
Cheers and claps at 5 secs

A1, A2

2　Cam 2
shot of clock whip pan
to 2 shot of MK KH
2A SI
"Mary Kelly"

Mary

Hello again and welcome to the third scintillating episode of Cablelivextra!! It's amazing how the time flies when you're having fun – we're already halfway through this series and we've still got loads of great programmes coming up in the next few weeks!!

2B　SI
"Kenny Hague"

SB VT
EM 289

Kenny

And especially tonight – tonnes of great prizes, a fantastic band, guests galore and of course all the regular Cablelivextra programmes kicking off at 7.10 pm with Woodside Waifs, followed by Roundabout, Fitbits, Satrang of course and a special programme later at 9.30 – a behind the scenes peek at Leicester Sound with Sokkit

A1, A2

3　Cam 1
CU
3A　SI

"233 7463"

Mary
So before we meet our band of the evening, let's get those phones ringing!!! Phone 2337463 for dedications
and the prizedraw all night long!! Don't forget, we're on air until almost 10 tonight, so you've no excuse for not ringing!!

4　Run VT

EM 289

Kenny
Well, with that I think it's time to hear from our band of the night Chemical with their first song "Got to do it"

SOT

6.33 pm VT 2. Band Song
Dur 00.03.55
EM 289

4A　SI
"Chemical"
"Got to do it"

Mary over to band
Barbara over to bench
Justine & Mark into studio – mike up during
Barbara's stars

4B　SI
"233 7463"

5　Cam 2
MCU

Mary

A2, 4, 5, 6
BOOM

6　Cam 1
Wide shot
Both cams as directed

Interview with band
3 mins

6A　SI
"Chemical"

A1

7　Cam 1
Wide shot

CAM 2 MOVE　　SM VT
EM 254

Mary
Thanks so much for coming in to chat to us – we'll be hearing from you later on in the show. And now we'll see what news Barbara has for us with her first set of stars . . .

A3

8　Cam 1
MCU
8A　SI
"Barbara Jacobs" & stars

6.40 pm Barbara
1st 6 stars

9　Run VT

EM 254

I'll be back with the second set after we've caught up on the latest news from The Mercury Gig Guide.

SOT

6.43 pm (approx.) VT 3 Gig Guide
Dur 00.00.30
EM 254
Band out of studio – very quick

A4, A5

10　Cam 2
2 shot

Justine & Mark

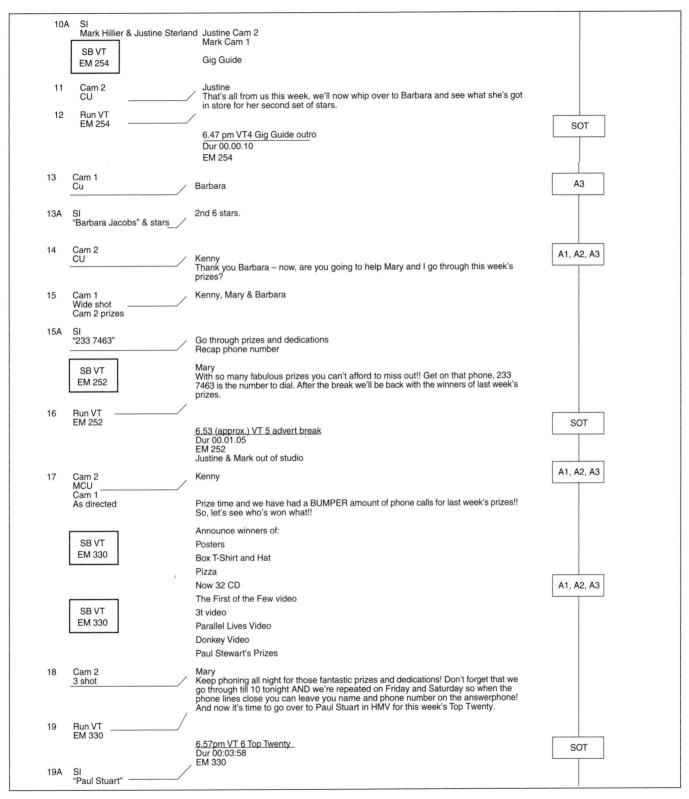

Figure 8.16 A script from Cable 7 for a non-fiction programme

Planning and Research for Media Production: Unit Test

Here are some research methods. Use them to answer questions 1 and 2.
- **a** distributing questionnaires
- **b** finding archive material
- **c** conducting interviews
- **d** searching on a CD-ROM

1 Which method would you use to obtain opinions about a new monument in the town for an article in a local newspaper?

2 Which method would you use to research the sound of a World War I fighter plane for a radio drama?

3 A new magazine claims that its target audience are 'aspirers and succeeders'. How has it defined its readers?
- **a** by demographic groups
- **b** by quantatitive analysis
- **c** by socio-economic division
- **d** by lifestyle groupings

4 BARB classifies TV audiences by occupation. If someone is in junior management or is a supervisor or a salesperson, how would they be described?
- **a** grade B
- **b** grade C1
- **c** grade C2
- **d** grade D

5 Look at these statistics

	Adult (15+) Pop'n '000	Weekly reach '000	Weekly reach %	Average hours per head	Average hours per listener
Local Radio					
BBC Radio Berkshire	612	56	9	0.4	4.5
BBC Radio Bristol	1162	284	24	2.1	8.6
BBC CWR	472	37	8	0.4	5.3
BBC Radio Cambridgeshire	550	116	21	1.9	9.1
BBC Radio Cleveland	685	115	17	1.4	8.3
BBC Radio Cornwall	397	156	39	4.6	11.8
BBC Radio Cumbria	373	124	33	3.2	9.7

How would you describe the analysis?
- **a** demographic
- **b** economic
- **c** psychographic
- **d** qualitative

6 What will the location recce tell a television producer?
- **a** what talent will be needed
- **b** how far the programme can be transmitted
- **c** what extra lighting will be required
- **d** how long production will take

7 From whom does a journalist need to get permission, before visiting a school to interview children for an article on school meals?
- **a** the headteacher
- **b** parents of children
- **c** the police
- **d** the catering staff

8 A photographer takes a picture of an MP kissing her secretary in the garden of her home. Why does the editor of a broadsheet think twice before publishing the photo?
- **a** it is offensive material
- **b** it is libellous
- **c** it breaks confidentiality
- **d** it is an invasion of privacy

9 Which of the following would offend against sex discrimination legislation?
- **a** if market researchers were mostly female
- **b** if male researchers were paid more than female researchers
- **c** if a research company advertised for only female interviewees
- **d** if only questionnaires filled in by women were analysed

10 A researcher passes on information spoken 'off the record', and this is published. What ethical issue is involved?
- **a** confidentiality
- **b** privacy
- **c** defamation
- **d** libel

11 A feature writer for a magazine is researching in a library. Which of the following would be a breach of copyright?
a to photocopy the words of a song
b to photocopy 4 pages from a book
c to photocopy a poem by a living poet
d to photocopy an Ordnance Survey map

12 A reporter is collecting material for a documentary about crime on the streets. Why should the police, the criminal **and** the victims be interviewed?
a to avoid charges of defamation
b because of equal opportunities legislation
c to represent the issue fairly
d to check that the material won't be offensive to anyone

13 Which is essential information to put into a flier advertising the opening of a new video shop?
a address and date of opening
b the name of the owner
c a picture of the shop
d details of films for loan

14 Which of these would be needed during an outside broadcast to make a link with the studio for a live radio programme?
a a satellite link
b a courier
c radio microphones
d a radio car

15 Which type of local radio programme could use vox pops?
a a magazine programme
b a phone-in
c a news bulletin
d a drama

16 Which of these is needed for a live television studio discussion?
a an off-line editing suite
b land lines
c a vision mixer
d chromakey

17 What is the purpose of a foreign soap opera such as *Neighbours?*
a to inform the audience about a different country
b to make social issues entertaining
c to persuade people to change their lifestyle
d to educate people about how to solve their problems

18 A local newspaper editor wants to have regular feature articles that will attract teenagers. What should the articles be about?
a a guide to good schools and qualifications
b financial advice and job prospects
c take-away restaurants and how to eat cheaply
d a local entertainment guide and chart music reviews

19 A leaflet about dental health is to be distributed in schools. Why does it include Disney cartoon characters?
a cartoon characters are cheap to copy
b cartoon characters are always colourful
c the characters will be small to fit on the leaflet
d children will be attracted and more likely to read the text

20 Which of the following types of television programmes, each lasting half an hour, will be cheapest to make?
a the news
b a quiz show
c a wildlife documentary
d period drama

21 In a science fiction film, why does the producer choose, as background music, an orchestral piece by a famous classical composer?
a it reinforces the serious mood of the story
b it will be out of copyright
c it will appeal to old and young people
d it is unusual for film music to be classical

22 Which will contain the highest number of colour photographs?
a a tabloid
b a broadsheet
c a glossy magazine
d a comic

23 What type of radio programme will include a live question and answer session or two-way interview?
a a quiz show
b a phone-in
c a drama
d a news programme

24 Whilst being filmed, a sit-com may have a live studio audience. Which of the following also needs a live audience?
a a documentary
b the news

c   a sporting event
d   a comedy film

25   Decide whether each of these statements is true or false.
i   positive films give colour prints
ii   if a film gets too much light, it will be over-exposed

a   i   is true and   ii   is true
b   i   is true and   ii   is false
c   i   is false and   ii   is true
d   i   is false and   ii   is false

26   What is the term used for photographs, drawings or illustrations for inclusion in a magazine when they are in a state to be sent to the printers?
a   proofs
b   camera ready artwork
c   roughs
d   inserts

27   Which of the following must a proposal for a radio drama contain?
a   a synopsis of the plot
b   names of actors

c   a list of sound effects
d   names of the production team

28   Which of the following will be scripted in a current affairs programme on radio?
a   vox pops
b   key questions
c   studio interviews
d   links

29   Which of the following must a treatment for a new magazine programme describe?
a   how the set will be made
b   what type of film will be used
c   the style of the presenter
d   who composed the music and when

30   Which of the following will be included in a script for a television soap?
a   the type of camera
b   the framing of shots
c   the names of the actors
d   the number of rehearsals

In Chapter 6 we looked at how you could plan and produce individual print items and the skills associated with these activities. In this unit we will, where appropriate, combine these separate items into a coherent, integrated publication. The development of ideas and the necessary research for large-scale products, such as magazines or books, will be discussed and the various print processes, as well as general design and layout, will be explained. Production management plays a key role, and decisions on how to budget and schedule are just as important for students as for professionals. Not only individual creativity but strong teamwork will be essential during the production stages.

At all times you must keep your target audience firmly in mind.

Plan the production process for print products

The production process begins when an idea is accepted, and ends with the publication of the product. The process covers the agreement of proposals, scheduling, collecting material and decisions on layout and the actual printing. It also considers how to overcome any problems, whether legal, ethical or concerned with safety.

Proposals for print products

Before any decisions can be made, it is first necessary to justify and agree the idea or **proposal**. Within the industry, the agreement will be with a client – which can be an individual person or a multinational company financing the project. With students, the agreement will be with a member of staff or possibly another client.

The proposed items should be justified in terms of their **fitness for purpose** and the available resources. There are many different types of print and graphics publications – newspapers, newsletters, magazines, comics, pamphlets, brochures, paperbacks, hardbacks, etc.

Choice of format

Decisions will need to be made about whether the **medium**, i.e. book, comic, magazine and so on, is appropriate for conveying the suggested material to a certain audience. A cheap paperback may be ideal for a teenager, but useless for a toddler. A doting parent or grandparent will prefer to pay extra for a product that is colourful and indestructible. This is also an example of a situation where the purchaser may not necessarily be the consumer!

The publisher of a government report will not be so concerned with aesthetics as the publisher of 'coffee table' books, the large glossy hardbacks with wonderful photography and minimal text on popular subjects such as food, travel or the countryside.

Activity

Discuss in a group which format (i.e. hardback book, paperback, pamphlet, brochure, glossy magazine, cheaper magazine, comic, tabloid-sized newspaper, broadsheet newspaper) would be most suitable for the clients or authors listed below. Suggest a target audience for each product. There is more than one right answer for any of these but you should be able to explain the reasons for your choice (such as the use of photos or lots of colour) by comparisons with similar print and graphics products you have seen. The clients/authors are:

- an environmental group wanting to raise issues about pollution
- the diary of an ex-president
- a zoologist's account of a year in the jungle
- a guide on how to play football
- a series of poems
- the scandalous biography of a living film star
- knitting projects.

How would your decisions be affected if the target audience is changed?

The choice of format will also be influenced by how readers acquire the publication and where they use it. They might buy it from a newsagents, bookshop or supermarket; they may be sent it through the mail or get it pushed through their letterbox; it may be something handed out at a sales presentation or given away in shops with a product. Publications that have to attract readers to buy them, and which have lots of competitors, need to be more eye-catching to customers than specialist material such as a textbook or a professional journal sent through the post.

Some publications, such as tabloids or catalogues, are designed for the person who likes to scan, with plenty of photographs to catch the eye. The adult novel can dispense with eye-catching headings or pictures, however, because it is aimed at someone who wants to spend a continuous length of time recreating a story in their own imagination. Light holiday reading aimed at the traveller is produced in paperback format so that it is easy to carry and pack. A foreign phrasebook needs to be small to fit in a pocket. Saturday and Sunday newspapers can be larger and heavier than during the week, as people will have more time to read them at weekends.

Your vocabulary and style depends on who you are 'speaking' to. Some publications will use quite academic language, such as a scientific or medical journal, or a literary magazine such as the *London Review of Books*. But, as a rule of thumb, you should keep it simple. Most people do not read long, complicated-looking discussions, so you need to be straightforward.

A print and graphics product is made up of a series of activities which work together to produce the final product. In the case of a newspaper or magazine, income is generated by the classified and display advertising departments and the sales department. In the case of a book, income can be generated not just by sales to the public but by selling the rights so that a film or play can be made or a serialisation done in a newspaper.

Financial resources

Financial considerations will influence the size of a publication and its quality in terms of paper, the amount of colour used or, perhaps, the quality and number of illustrations required.

Colour does make your product significantly more expensive, but there are low-budget ways of achieving a colour effect. For example, you can use coloured paper. There are hundreds of different shades available and they are only slightly more expensive than standard.

One of the first considerations in any professional project is the budget, i.e. how much money will be available. Some will be allocated for creative people, such as writers, photographers and artists, some for production staff, such as copyeditors or printers. There may also be copyright fees or advances to pay.

Material resources

The material and technological resources needed to produce a large daily newspaper, for example, are on a vast scale. For instance, paper in the form of newsprint is a key consideration. A newspaper uses many tonnes per week and the price of newsprint is a serious financial consideration for any print media organisation. Printer's inks can also be a major expense.

Newsprint

The *Midshires Chronicle* uses three different types of newsprint.

Supplier number one – the major supplier – provides more than 12,000 tonnes of paper per year. This is good-quality newsprint, made up of 65 per cent virgin fibre (i.e. fresh from trees!) and 35 per cent recycled newsprint. The wood comes from 'managed' forests in Wales. For every tree cut down, another is planted.

Supplier number two is a Norwegian firm which sells them 10,000 tonnes per year. This is high-quality paper made from 100 per cent virgin material with long fibres, which make it more durable and smooth. This is the most expensive.

Supplier number three provides them with 4000 tonnes of paper each year. This is 100 per cent recycled newsprint, and is the cheapest.

Activity

Look at your ideas for print products. Which of the above types of paper would you use and why?

Case study

The *Midshires Chronicle*, a large regional newspaper, uses the following material resources each week:

540 tonnes of newspaper @ £4.96 per tonne
60 tonnes of black ink @ £0.80 per kilo
3.6 tonnes of coloured inks (cyan, magenta and yellow) @ £2.95 per kilo.

Classified Advertising staff

At the *Mercury* they handle around 10,000 calls a week. The staff are organised in teams: some deal with calls from the public and others spend time phoning businesses to canvass them to place ads.

Display Advertising staff

The staff in this department deal either with a sector of Leicestershire and the customers in that area or they are responsible for a particular section of the newspaper, such as the Property Guide.

Page Planning staff

Once an advertisement is booked by the advertising staff, it needs to be planned for a particular page in the newspaper. Two days before the newspaper is produced, the page planners produce a dummy copy of the paper with ads marked in place which is then given to editorial.

Editor

In control of the content of the paper, the editor is totally responsible for everything that is published and will be the person taken to court if anything illegal is published.

Sub-Editor

Works with the editor to make decisions on content and then is responsible for planning the pages, making decisions on the size of the stories and where they should be placed on the page. Also checks stories written by reporters for spelling, grammatical errors and to see if they have covered all aspects of the story. Finally, once the space has been allocated and the story checked a sub-editor also writes the headlines.

News Editor

The *Mercury* also has a news editor who runs the news desk. This person is responsible for coordinating the news content of the paper. Together with the editor he or she helps to decide which news should be covered and allocates stories to reporters.

Reporters

General news reporters are the *Leicester Mercury's* news gatherers. They are often allocated an area of Leicester to cover and have to get to know all the influential people in that area: religious leaders, politicians, school heads and community group leaders. They spend a lot of their time on the phone investigating stories. Some reporters specialise in certain areas such as politics, education or business.

Features Journalists

A feature may not highlight an event or something which has just happened, but will instead perhaps comment on a trend or focus on a particular person, group or activity. A feature will have great interest value to readers and may take a lot of research. Journalists tend to start out as basic reporters then specialise in particular areas and the features desk is one of these options.

Apple Mac Operator

The Apple Desk team use the instructions from the sub editors to guide them in constructing the pages of news and pictures using the latest Apple Mac computers and a versatile desk-top publishing package to do so.

Pre-Press Team

The pre-press team interpret the plans made by the Advertisement Executives and the customers. They design advertisements of the right size, shape and content and a proof copy is often sent to a customer to ensure they are happy with the design.

The team who scan in the pictures and photographs are also part of this team as is the Page Management Unit. The task here is to bring the advertisements together with the editorial content of the paper then pair the pages as they will appear ready for printing.

Technicians

Once a pair of pages have been completed they are printed out in the form of a photographic negative. This is then used to create a printing plate by placing it on a sheet of aluminium coated with a material sensitive to the light. A strong light is shone through the negative, hitting the plate and developing the image of the pages. This plate is then sent on to the press team. The technicians in this area often work under great pressure and must ensure the correct plates are processed in the correct order, for the time they are needed.

Press Team

The people in this section work in teams who are all responsible for their particular area of the press. They have to clean and maintain the presses in between print runs which is a difficult job because the presses are occupied almost 24 hours a day.

Publishing Dept.

This department ensures that as the newspapers come off the presses they are counted into bundles of the right number for each newsagent, labelled and despatched to awaiting vans.

Newspaper Sales Dept.

This department is concerned with making sure that the company sells as many copies of the paper as possible. This involves everything from liaison with the editor at the outset over the choice of front page news to making sure the delivery vans take the correct routes and deliver the newspapers on time. A team of sales people also work with newsagents to promote the *Leicester Mercury*, and are responsible for canvassing new customers by phone, doorstep calling and through promotional shop parties and in-store events.

Publicity Dept.

The publicity department work to promote the newspaper in many different ways. They add to its value by negotiating special offers and money-off coupons, competitions and in-paper games. They organise holiday offers for readers and reproduce promotional items, branded with the *Leicester Mercury's* name, as well as advertising campaigns which involve posters, bus shelters, buses, TV, radio, cinema, and in-paper advertisements.

Finance Dept.

The finance department must underpin every area of the company's activity. Advertisements sold need invoices despatching to bring in the promised revenue. Newsagents need billing for the newspapers they purchase. Bills for services and commodities need to be paid and the staff need wages!

Training Officer

The staff often need the input of some training to help them on their way. The training officers, supported by the Assistant Managing Director, work with every area. They evaluate systems of management and give input at all levels to ensure everyone is able to give their best.

Figure 9.1 Staff needed to produce a *Leicester Mercury*

The *Chronicle* has, on average, 72 pages; 50 of these newspapers will use up 10 kilos of newsprint.

The newsprint costs them £4.96 a tonne because they are part of a larger newspaper group which buys in bulk at the beginning of the year. (This is known as **economy of scale** where the price becomes cheaper because such a large quantity of a commodity is bought.) On the open market the price per tonne is £5.60.

Besides their own eleven editions, the *Midshires Chronicle* also contract prints for other newspapers. These include a national Sunday newspaper, three sporting papers and 35 other titles. The presses will run throughout the night. The total number of newspapers printed each week is three million. 60,000 copies can be run off per hour. Even large print runs are completed at great speed – the **web** is 60 metres long but a page can travel along it in 2.1 seconds.

Work out the following calculations:

- How much newsprint is used each year?
- How much ink is used each year?
- What is the total cost of materials over a year?
- How many newspapers are printed on average in the course of twenty-four hours?

You have decided to print a Sunday newspaper. You plan a print run of 150,000 copies for six months. Based on the figures given above, how much will it cost you in terms of materials? How long will it take the presses to complete the run?

Human resources

Some products, particularly daily national newspapers, need a large team to produce regular publications.

The team for the production of a book will be smaller than that for newspapers and will use more freelance staff. Which of the jobs listed in Figure 9.1 would appeal to you?

The first thing always to keep in mind is an overall product. Then individual items (**proposals**) can be evaluated according to the specifications laid down, both for the individual items and for the overall product.

Case study

To demonstrate what we mean by a proposal, we will examine the example shown below in Figure 9.2. The North Warwickshire & Hinckley College/*Leicester Mercury* Project proposed the following:

medium: a four-page insert into a tabloid-sized newspaper.

purpose: to provide media students with realistic and 'hands on' learning opportunities within the newspaper industry.

- to promote the college and particularly its media courses by producing a publication that prospective students and parents will find informative and entertaining, and provide attractive and entertaining articles about the college and surrounding area.
- to produce a product that will be considered an attractive advertising medium for businesses and other organisations.

target audience: prospective students and their parents; advertisers.

content: human-interest stories about individuals associated with the college; articles about new college faculties, new developments, etc.

aesthetics: mid-range tabloid style, in keeping with the style and editorial policy of the parent product (the *Leicester Mercury*); plenty of photographs, especially those showing human interest. Some colour, but see budget; articles to be quite light and lively.

resource requirements:

human: 19 students in a number of teams and roles: editor, assistant editor, reporters, feature writers, photographers, advertisement design and page make-up, newspaper promotion and sales.

financial: £2000 needed for a 120,000 copy (circulation of *Leicester Mercury*) print run to be inserted into all editions. The price quoted is for black and white only although some colour may be available for adverts. Sales team to sell at least sufficient advertising space to break even. College to purchase £1000 of space and to underwrite the other £1000.

materials: Leicester Mercury Resource Centre with access to computerised page make-up equipment (Apple Macintosh computers, Quark Xpress software, scanner, A3 photocopier), all newsprint, inks and web offset litho printing system.

time: overall time allocation is 12 weeks. It will take this long because the main objective is to educate (i.e. for students to learn the processes involved). Details are as per the schedule in the project case study below.

All decisions made should be recorded. The basic format for doing this is through the use of agendas (the list of topics for consideration) and the minutes of meetings held by production teams. This will ensure that decisions regarding role allocation and specific tasks agreed by individuals, are all recorded. At the next

Figure 9.2 The front and back pages of a four-page student supplement

meeting activities can be progress-chased by reading the minutes of the previous meeting and looking at matters arising from those minutes. If a member of the team had agreed to contact, for example, a photographer at the *Mercury*, then it is in the 'matters arising' that the team member can report back. If he or she has not done so then this fact, and any explanation, is recorded in the minutes. This then serves as part of the evidence to demonstrate the process of planning and production that was gone through.

Schedule and secure resources for the production process

Schedules

The schedule is an extremely important part of any media production as time means money. Newspapers in particular have to keep to very tight schedules as the customer expectation is that they will be on the news stand or delivered at a certain time of day.

Case study

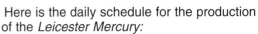

Here is the daily schedule for the production of the *Leicester Mercury:*

■ At 07.45 every morning there is a meeting of the editor, news editor, sub-editors, sports editor and picture editor to plan the newspaper that will appear on the streets four hours later.

The newspaper already has some sections written and page layout planned (see page 212). Dummy pages show the spaces allocated to advertising copy. The illustration in Figure 9.3 shows an example of the page layout from the newspaper section designed by the students. They allocated certain spaces for adverts. What was left could be filled by editorial.

Figure 9.4 shows an example of how page 13 was designed for the *Leicester Mercury*.

As you can see, advertising boxes are always allocated before the editorial sections are entered. Adverts already have their spaces allocated and this makes

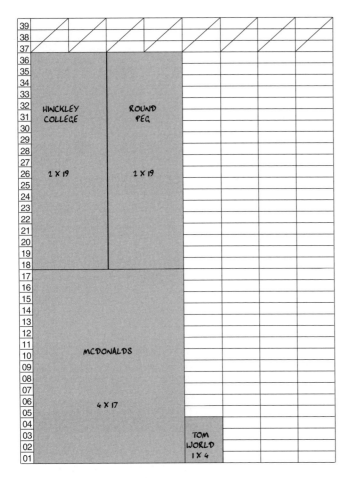

Figure 9.3 Dummy page for the back page of the student supplement

page planning easier. In addition, a newspaper like the *Mercury* depends on advertising as its major source of revenue. The advertisers, therefore, have some scope – particularly on the inner pages – for negotiation about position. There are, however, limits to this. Aesthetic considerations and house style could rule against adverts being placed wherever an advertiser wanted them.

The page is divided into eight columns and is marked off in centimetres. Advertising is sold in column centimetres. Apart from the advertising copy and spaces, the newspaper already has some features and stories written from the overnight list. This leaves a proportion of the paper, usually pages one, seven and nine for 'live' stories, i.e. stories which have recently broken and are perhaps still unfolding.

In the next hour or so these 'live' pages will be filled with the stories that are selected from a list provided by the

news editor of stories which have recently broken. This list is reproduced in Chapter 6, along with lists for district and national news, the sports news and the photographs that were available.

It is the news editor who is responsible for allocating tasks to the reporters and photographers.

- by 08.00 decisions have been made regarding what should go on the front page, where to include other stories and what future action needs to be taken.
- 10.05 – editorial meeting to discuss overnight list. The assistant news editor may have approximately 12 strong stories and six potential leads. His sources are phone calls from contacts, his incoming post and national stories with local interest.

Regular features are also discussed. Apart from considering the individual stories, the meeting also takes into account the overall product by looking at where the stories will be placed in relation to each

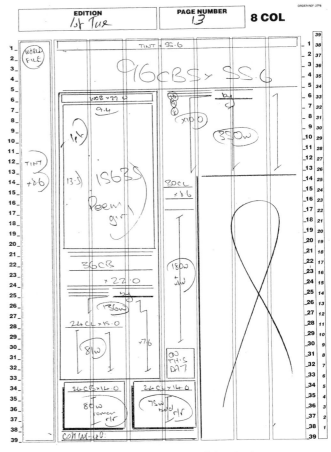

Figure 9.4 Dummy for page 13 of the *Leicester Mercury*

other in terms of the page layout and the use of colour.

- 10.00 – the front page is printed and checked.
- 10.20 – the first edition is printed and will be on the street by 11.00.
- 10.30 – the county editions are printed and will be available by 14.30.
- 12.30 – the city edition is printed and is on the streets by 14.00.
- 15.30 – the night-time edition is printed and will be on sale in the evening at the bus station and train station.

The first point to establish when developing the schedule is the print day or time of day when the product will be produced and distributed to its target audience. This will indicate how much time you have and allow you to plan the most effective use of the time available. There will be different **deadlines** for team members, depending on their job. The writer of a cookery book will have a different deadline for submitting copy to the editor from the illustrator or the photographer. When organising a schedule it is vital to be aware of all the resources that will be needed to generate materials and complete the production process. To do this effectively involves an understanding of printing methods, which will be explained later.

Another major point affecting the schedule, whether for a professional product or a student project, is the availability of personnel or staff and their capabilities.

Risk assessment, i.e. health and safety, should also be taken into account with scheduling. One of the major causes of accidents, both in production industries and in everyday life, is hurry or pressure of work where people have not allowed enough time for activities. This could affect the reporter racing to the next appointment in the car or the printer who has worked too long on the presses. Both could be stressed or distracted by thinking of all the work that needs to be done and the result could be a car crash, or the loss of a finger while using a machine!

In student projects there is a tendency to underestimate three areas of scheduling, i.e. the length of time it takes to:

- learn and *practise* new skills
- do research
- organise equipment and people.

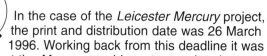

Case study

In the case of the *Leicester Mercury* project, the print and distribution date was 26 March 1996. Working back from this deadline it was decided that the *Mercury* would want artwork to be ready two working days before the print run, so the final deadline for setting the pages was 22 March. This was in order to give the page designers the time to shape the page finally. The deadline for copy was 20 March.

This information gave the production team a time-scale to which they could work. They also needed to know when technical resources, such as the page design facilities, were available. The newspaper pages were set on Apple Macintosh computers using Quark Xpress. Copy produced at college was word-processed using Word for Windows or Wordperfect 5.1. and transferred over on disk. Compatibility with the newspaper's software was checked to ensure there would be no difficulties in this area.

Material resources had to be identified and ordered or booked in advance. Computer disks had to be purchased. Some master disks were also required so that work could be copied across for downloading at the newspaper offices. In addition access was needed to computers, scanners, 35mm cameras and telephones. These had to be organised very early on in the project. A telephone directory, *Yellow Pages*, and other research material, such as *Thompson's Business Directory* and *Compass*, had to be located before the advertising team could start work. The students also had to book equipment such as portable tape recorders for interviews.

Financial resources: the paper cost £2000 to produce. The students therefore had to earn at least that amount in advertising in order to break even. The cost was underwritten by the college. This meant that the college guaranteed to cover costs if the students were unable to meet their target. The college, however, recognised this as a good publicity opportunity and felt that £2000 was a cost-effective way of advertising to the 317,000 people who read the paper each day.

In order to finance the supplement, the advertising team had to do the same as the *Leicester Mercury's* staff and sell advertising. They had to make £2000 to be successful. In the event they exceeded their target and generated revenue totalling £3500.

The process of identifying and developing the **human resources** started at the personnel selection stage. Project members were given a list of the different jobs available (see Figure 9.5).

```
EDITORIAL STAFF:
Editor x1
Deputy editor x1
General news reporters x2
Features journalists x2
Photographers x2

ADVERTISING STAFF:
Advertising manager x1
Deputy manager x1
Advertising executives x3

GRAPHICS AND PAGE DESIGN TEAM
Graphic artist and ad designer x1
Page design and layout specialists x2

NEWSPAPER SALES TEAM
Newspaper sales manager x1
Newspaper sales and promotions executives x2
```

Figure 9.5 Job roles for the student supplement

Students went through a selection process involving some of the techniques used by the advertising staff at the *Leicester Mercury*. This started with individuals researching and then applying for a particular job, using the standard application form and a covering letter.

Following this they took part in group interview sessions and role-play exercises to demonstrate initiative, confidence, flair and imagination. Another exercise was a spelling test. Despite the use of spell checks on computers (which do not pick up all errors), it is still considered essential that staff can take down information accurately.

Look at the list of words that the students had to check. Which would you correct and how?

ABREVIATE	OCCASIONALY
ADVERTISMENT	PLANING
ACCOMODATION	REFERED
ACQUAINTANCE	PRECEADING
BEGINING	SEPERATE
CORESPONDENCE	TRANSFERRED
DISAPOINTING	SURPRISEING
ESPECIALY	CERTANLY
IMMEDIATELY	SUCESS

Training was a crucial part of this project so that the right human resources were available. No member of the student advertising or newspaper teams had adequate experience of this very competitive area, although some had been involved with sales and customer relations through work experience at school or part-time jobs. Learning new skills had to be built into the schedule.

The editorial team was short of experience in writing articles to a professional standard. Writing news stories is very different from writing essays and academic reports.

The graphic design team (for designing ads) and the page make-up team needed to develop skills in using the Apple Mac computers and the Quark Xpress software. They were unfamiliar with this system, having previously worked only with PCs.

Photographers also needed advice on the kind of pictures that are attractive to readers. (See Chapter 6 for details.)

In order to promote and sell the product effectively, the sales team needed to be involved in discussions with the production team at regular intervals, to give advice on such things as the number of papers to be produced. (For more information on their work turn to the section on investigating and carrying out media marketing.)

Production methods: the schedule must take into account the production method selected. Some take longer than others depending on the sophistication of the product and size of print run. For example, the schedule for this book allowed one month for the printers to produce 5000 bound copies from film produced by the typesetter. The type of production method will also affect the order in which materials, for example visuals or text, have to be supplied for printing.

Different production methods and techniques

When planning the schedule for the production of a print product you will have to make decisions concerning the best methods of producing the material. You should, therefore, be aware of the various methods of production and their advantages and disadvantages.

Screen printing

This is a simple and effective method of printing products that do not require a lot of small body text and intricate detail. It is suitable for signs, posters, banners and tee shirts. It has the advantage of being

Figure 9.6 Silk screen printing

Figure 9.7 Letterpress printing

able to print on to many types of surface, such as metal, plastic, glass and cloth as well as paper. It is best for comparatively small print runs as it is rather slow, even though automatic screen print machines can produce up to three thousand impressions per hour.

Basically the print machine consists of a stencil with a fine mesh screen. The screen used to be made of silk, hence the term 'silk screen' by which it is still known today. The stencil is either cut by hand or produced photographically. It is then mounted in a frame and ink is spread over the stencil by a rubber blade called a squeegee. This forces the ink through the screen and on to the surface to be printed.

Photocopying

This uses the xerographic principle, which involves scanning the original with a bright light and tracing the image on to a drum in the form of an electrostatic charge. Very fine carbon is attracted to the charged image areas and also becomes charged itself. This electrostatically charged black image is then rolled against paper and transferred on to it.

Photocopying is becoming more sophisticated and can be cost-effective for short runs if colour and quality are not of paramount importance. Many machines can enlarge and reduce images, and collate and fold copies.

Photocopies tend to show photographic images as either areas of black or areas of white, with no gradations of tone between them (see 'half-tones' on the next page). This is usually a disadvantage but can be used deliberately to create a special effect.

Letterpress

In **letterpress printing**, ink is carried on surfaces raised in 'relief', and then transferred on to the paper by direct contact.

Changing single letters and lines is quick and cheap with this method but, overall, setting is slow and heavy work. The process has now largely given way to offset lithography.

Offset litho

With offset lithography, the image is not printed directly on to the paper. Instead it is transferred on to a rubber surface called a blanket cylinder, and then on to paper. The paper can be in continuous

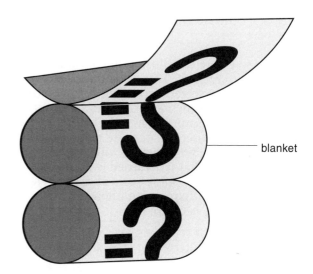

Figure 9.8 Offset lithography

form, known as a 'web' or in separate sheets. The *Leicester Mercury* uses the web offset litho method which produces 60,000 copies per hour.

Camera-ready artwork is made by putting together all the material (artwork) to be printed (origination). Printing plates are made by photographing it.

There are other techniques that are used in print products to give particular effects.

Half-tones

When we look at a person or object we see the image as made up of variations of a colour or colours. When a picture is printed this effect is largely lost, because the printing process gives an image a starker and more contrasted appearance.

Figure 9.9 A photograph printed in a book creates the illusion of continuous tones by screening

In order to create the illusion of continuous tone, images are 'screened'. This entails photographing them through a screen consisting of a pattern of dots. These are known as tints. The space between the dots will determine how light or dark the shade will look. The closer the dots are placed together, the darker that part of the picture will look and vice versa. An image that is screened is known as a half-tone. The idea is for some parts of the screen to have more dots than others, so an impression of continuous tone is created.

By using different types of tints, a designer or printer can create some interesting effects.

Outline and layout of products

Outline

The outline of a publication takes into account more than the physical design grid into which text and pictures are fitted, the number of pages or width of columns. It also considers the overall content, the **concept** behind the publication, its aims and the **angle** behind individual items or stories. What gives different newspapers their individuality is the emphasis given to entertainment (e.g. *The Sun*) or serious information (e.g. *The Guardian*). Tabloids and broadsheets may both be reporting on a similar story as noted in Chapter 6, but the position of the story, within the newspaper and the number of words vary enormously. The angle varies too: tabloids tend to emphasise the human interest in stories, whilst broadsheets may concentrate on giving a more objective, unemotive look at the same events. The political leanings of a newspaper may also influence how something is reported as well as where it appears in a newspaper.

The overall look of the page too is taken into consideration; for example, whether an item should be on a single page or a double page **spread**.

 Activity

Look at the list of topics listed below:

- Famous Hollywood star visits Britain to open new film studios
- Britain's beaches win an international award for beauty
- Public schoolboy is expelled for smoking cannabis
- Colleges and schools are reprimanded for wasting paper
- British girl becomes most highly paid model in the world
- A rare butterfly is in danger of extinction
- There is an outbreak of smallpox in Birmingham
- A six-year-old violinist plays at the Albert Hall
- A British space craft lands on the moon.

These topics are discussed at the editorial meetings of the following:

- tabloid newspaper
- broadsheet newspaper
- weekly women's magazine aimed at people with families

- glossy women's magazine aimed at young career women
- magazine concerned with environmental issues
- magazine published by the teaching union
- lifestyle magazine aimed at young men
- publisher of non-fiction books.

What importance would these publications place on the above? Would the topics merit a brief mention, a large feature article, or be ignored altogether? What angle would be taken by different publications? Don't forget that, by changing the angle, what might seem at first glance to be unlikely material can become a strong story. The item about beaches may seem irrelevant for the male magazine, but if the angle taken stresses the adventurous watersports on these beaches, then this could become an article with a strong appeal to the target audience.

Layout

Different print genres use different layouts for a number of reasons:

- to make them easier to read
- to attract the reader's attention
- to provide space for advertising
- for aesthetic reasons.

We would not expect a novel to use the same layout as a magazine or newspaper. Graphics, too, are positioned differently in books than they are in magazines. You can recognise at a glance a print genre from its layout and the relationship between the text and pictures.

Activity

Find your own examples of the following and make notes on the different layouts used for each:

- children's story
- adult paperback novel
- newspaper
- magazine
- comic.

Newspapers follow a regular format. This is not only so that readers know where to find the TV listings or the sports reports, but also so that both the advertising and editorial teams can quickly assess where adverts can be placed and at what price, or what live stories or features are needed. This enables them to put the newspaper together very speedily,

as we saw in the case study about the *Leicester Mercury* above.

Grids

If you are producing a student newspaper it is important to make sure it looks as much like a real paper as possible, designed to attract and hold the reader's attention. A lot of skill goes into the layout of a newspaper; it will determine how much copy you need.

Pages are generally designed around a **grid** which indicates how many columns there are and where visuals such as photographs, line drawings, and adverts should be placed. These grids are used as an aid to design and they can be changed if necessary. In desk-top publishing packages, the grids appear as vertical and horizontal lines that show up on the computer but not on the material when it is printed. The plan, blueprint or make-up sheet is also known as the **dummy**.

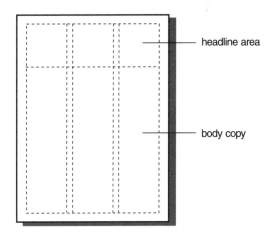

Figure 9.10 A page grid

Grids give a sense of proportion; they can help determine where **headings** and **body copy** should go (see Figure 9.10).

Except in some books, copy is normally arranged in **columns**. Column width dictates the line length; the shorter this is, the easier the text is to read because readers scan groups of words rather than individual words and it is easy for the eye to jump to the next sentence down. The width of a column is influenced by the size of type used. It is quite acceptable to use columns of different widths on the same page.

The more text you have the more columns you should use. Newspapers such as the broadsheets, with long columns of text, usually use eight columns. This means that the width of each column is narrow – five or six words – which makes it easier to follow the text without losing your place.

Text is often **fully justified** (spaced out to fit the column width) rather than **jagged right**. Generally speaking, **left justified** text (flush left) as in this column of type, is easier to read because the eye can pick out the individual ends of lines. However, when the lines are as short as those in eight-column newspapers it is not so important. What may be important, however, is the amount of text that can be placed on a page, and fully justified text uses the space more economically.

> Text is often **fully justified** (spaced out to fit the column width) rather than **jagged right**. Generally speaking, **left justified** text (flush left) is easier to read because the eye can pick out the individual ends of lines. However, when the lines are as short as those in eight-column newspapers it is not so important. What may be important, however, is the amount of text that can be placed on a page, and fully justified text uses the space more economically.

Text justified right

> Text is often **fully justified** (spaced out to fit the column width) rather than **jagged right**. Generally speaking, **left justified** text (flush left) is easier to read because the eye can pick out the individual ends of lines. However, when the lines are as short as those in eight-column newspapers it is not so important. What may be important, however, is the amount of text that can be placed on a page, and fully justified text uses the space more economically.

Text centred

You can help the reader to follow the columns through making their separation more pronounced by drawing (thin) vertical lines between them. As mentioned above, not all columns on a page have to be of the same width, particularly for magazines or 'arty' publications.

Grids show where the **borders** are. There are two types of border, **tangible**, where an actual line surrounds the text and graphics, and **assumed**, where the text itself creates an imaginary line in the reader's mind.

The use of **white space** in design is very important. The space created by **margins** can signify the

Figure 9.11 Wide or narrow margins give pages a different look

seriousness or difficulty of a publication. The space between columns or facing pages is known as a **gutter**.

In newspapers and magazines **rules** can draw attention and separate text to make reading easy; they can be horizontal or vertical, thick or thin. **Boxes** too can divide text. In magazines, short articles within articles are called **sidebars**. Boxes are useful for giving extra information, such as names and addresses of retailers, handy hints relating to an article, details of publishers, etc. The different parts of a newspaper's front page are discussed on pages 73–76.

Graphic design

A good layout is based on the following elements of graphic design.

Proportion – it is important that the different elements relate to each other in terms of size and emphasis. It is not just the text and images that are important, but their relationship to each other – how they are juxtaposed – that can enhance or diminish the overall appearance of your product. Not only the content but its relation to the background page – the white space – affects appearance. From a design point of view the white space is just as important as the items on the page. You need to bear in mind the effect of white space and make use of it. When used correctly, it adds balance and contrast.

If the white space is too large it can make the text appear insignificant, especially if that text is too small or light. Alternatively, if the text is too large or

TOO CROWDED

Over the past few years there have been a considerable number of changes in education. The introduction of Local Management and Grant Maintained status have radically altered how schools are funded, how they view themselves and how they are viewed by the public.

At one time it was possible for a school to simply settle down and try to provide the best education it could knowing that its catchment area of pupils was relatively safe and its funding assured.

The recent proposals to allow all state schools to select up to 15 per cent of their intake by interviewing parents and children to assess their suitability may or may not be successful, but over the past few years there has been a steady movement towards a two-tier system in British education. The number of schools with a genuine 'mix' of students in terms of ability has

dropped from just under 50 per cent to about 27 per cent now. There are now many comprehensive schools who have attracted a much higher percentage of top ability students and have effectively become grammar schools. This also ensures that there are a number of schools with a much higher percentage of low ability students who are finding it hard to maintain a good balance.

Over the past few years there have been a considerable number of changes in education. The introduction of Local Management and Grant Maintained status have radically altered how schools are funded, how they view themselves and how they are viewed by the public.

At one time it was possible for a school to simply settle down and try to provide the best education it could knowing that its catchment area of pupils

---

This is rather

insignificant

Over the past few years there have been a considerable number of changes in education. The introduction of Local Management and Grant Maintained status have radically altered how schools are funded, how they view themselves and how they are viewed by the public.

At one time it was possible for a school to simply settle down and try to provide the best education it could knowing that its catchment area of pupils was relatively safe and its funding assured.

The recent proposals to allow all state schools to select up to 15 per cent of their intake by interviewing parents and children to assess their suitability may or may not be successful, but over the past few years there has been a steady movement towards a two-tier system in British education. The number of schools with a genuine 'mix' of students in terms of ability has

dropped from just under 50 per cent to about 27 per cent now. There are now many comprehensive schools who have attracted a much higher percentage of top ability students and have effectively become grammar schools. This also ensures that there are a number of schools with a much higher percentage of low ability students who are finding it hard to maintain a good balance.

Over the past few years there have been a considerable number of changes in education. The introduction of Local Management and Grant Maintained status have radically altered how schools are funded, how they view themselves and how they are viewed by the public.

At one time it was possible for a school to simply settle down and try to provide the best education it could knowing that its catchment area of pupils

This rule is too heavy

This one is too light

Figure 9.12 Correct proportions are an important part of typographical design

bold in relation to the white space, then it will have a cramped, claustrophobic look.

You can also use a second shade or colour in selected parts of the publication, such as boxes and borders, in order to give emphasis to it. But do not over-use it or it will detract from the contrast.

White space can be the 'leading' (i.e. gaps) between lines of type or the space surrounding a headline or between columns. The amount of white space depends on the product. A poster may use large areas of white space, whereas there will be relatively small amounts on a newspaper. An advert on a newspaper or magazine editorial page will usually have relatively more white space than the editorial, as this will allow it to stand out.

Organisation – it should be clear to the reader how the information is arranged. This can be done in a number of ways. The most obvious is through the use of page **numbers** and an index, which can be placed at the front or back of a publication. An additional method for non-fiction to organise material is through the use of **bullets**, **asterisks** and **numbers**. Bullets make each point of equal value, whereas numbers tend to give a priority to the order.

Turnlines tell readers that the articles continue on another page.

Direction – a successful graphic layout of a page using headings, graphics and text will lead the eye in the order that the writer intends.

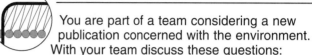

Activity

You are part of a team considering a new publication concerned with the environment. With your team discuss these questions:

How many pages? This will depend on the cost so some research is needed.

What size pages? A4 is easier but tabloid size gives a more authentic feel, especially if newsprint is used.

What font size? This will be partly determined by the size of the page and the number of columns proposed.

How many columns? Columns help to break up what otherwise would be long lines of text. Newspapers tend to have eight, but magazines vary quite a lot and may have only two. Again, it partly depends on the font and page size.

Will you seek advertising? Except for books (and even they will list other publications by the author or other books in a series) a large proportion of a publication will be taken up with advertising.

Will you use photographs and graphic material? The answer should be yes, whether you carry advertising or not.

Design the layout of the front page and one of the inside pages. Indicate the content in terms of adverts and topics.

Identify material for print items

After completing the work in Chapter 6 you and your team should have an idea of the type of publication you wish to write for and produce. So now you need to reassess the suitability of any ideas you may have had.

What kind of content will you have? Obviously this will depend on the type of publication, but you should have your target audience firmly in mind. As you prepare and write the content you should be continually asking yourself, 'Who will be interested in it?' and 'How can I make it interesting for them?' In addition, in your enthusiasm for appealing to an identified target audience, don't neglect to take into account the legal and ethical issues dealt with in the appendix at the back of the book.

Case study

Students on the *Leicester Mercury* project decided to go for **human interest** stories. This type of article, as the name implies, concentrates on people and personalities, and builds the story around them. This is a popular form of reporting and is often seen in the tabloids. Readers are generally more interested in people than in events. The idea is to use a person as the central point of an article and build in other details around this.

Production teams decided that they did not want to put too much emphasis on explicit articles about a particular course. Some individual items which had been produced using this approach were either altered or not used. We will now look at individual examples from the finished product. Because the end-result was a 'product within a product' it had to fit into the newspaper's style and policy objectives. The students therefore needed to know what kind of product the *Mercury* is. To do this they had to find out its purpose, target audience and content.

Research was carried out into the nature of the *Leicester Mercury* product. This was achieved by analysing examples of the product itself and by inviting the Newspapers in Education Manager, Annemarie Shillito, to deliver a workshop on the paper's marketing strategy. This involved looking at how the paper **segments** the market into different target audiences and how the product's appearance and content are **differentiated** in order to reach that target audience. Full details of this marketing strategy are given in Chapter 26.

Once they had an idea of the host product, the production team could start planning around it. Although the four-page insert could have its own style and image, it still had to be aware of the overall policy parameters within which it had to operate. These are in addition to the many legal, ethical and representational issues, which are dealt with in the Legal and Ethical appendix. The stories, therefore, had to be accepted by the client, who in this case was the *Leicester Mercury's* assistant editor Tim Cowen, whilst the advertising copy was vetted by the assistant display advertising manager, Barbara Hastings.

The purpose of the product was to publicise both the college generally and the media course in particular. Its purpose was certainly to inform and entertain, but its core concern was to persuade. That is, its aim was to persuade young people that North Warwickshire & Hinckley College has an attractive learning and social environment in which to study.

Activity

Choose a magazine, newspaper or fanzine similar to the one you are considering producing. Make a list of the contents and compare them with the material you have outlined. Don't just consider major features and hard news stories but also weather reports, horoscopes, editorials, cartoons or backgrounders by specialist writers, and the type of advertisements it might carry.

Identify potential content considerations

You can find the legal and ethical considerations described at the back of the book in the appendix. The laws and issues that you should be aware of include:

The Defamation Act
The Obscene Publications Act
The Official Secrets Act
D-Notices – no legal force
The Copyright Design and Patent Act
The Race Relations Act
The Sex Discrimination Act
The Equal Opportunities Act
Sedition
Contempt of court
Breach of confidence

Ethical considerations cover not only the content, such as issues of representation, but also the professional conduct of staff within the publishing industry, particularly journalists and editors. See the NUJ Code of Conduct on the next page. Look back at Chapters 2 and 6 for further details of representation and related issues.

Activity

Choose one of the stories or features you think your publication will cover. Make a list of ways in which it could potentially break the law or be unethical. Then identify how you would get around the problems. Remember, the media are concerned with re-presenting people, issues and events. Therefore there are *always* issues of representation. In addition, with anything that is printed there is a risk that someone may be defamed, or confidentiality may be broken.

NUJ Code of Conduct

1. A journalist has a duty to maintain the highest professional and ethical standards.
2. A journalist shall at all times defend the principle of the freedom of the Press and other media in relation to the collection of information and the expression of comment and criticism. He/she shall strive to eliminate distortion, news suppression and censorship.
3. A journalist shall strive to ensure that the information he/she disseminates is fair and accurate, avoid the expression of comment and conjecture as established fact and falsification by distortion, selection or misrepresentation.
4. A journalist shall rectify promptly any harmful inaccuracies, ensure that correction and apologies receive due prominence and afford the right of reply to persons criticised when the issue is of sufficient importance.
5. A journalist shall obtain information, photographs and illustrations only by straightforward means. The use of other means can be justified only by over-riding considerations of the public interest. The journalist is entitled to exercise a personal conscientious objection to the use of such means.
6. Subject to justification by over-riding considerations of public interest, a journalist shall do nothing which entails intrusion into private grief and distress.
7. A journalist shall protect confidential sources of information.
8. A journalist shall not accept bribes nor shall he/she allow other inducements to influence the performances of his/her professional duties.
9. A journalist shall not lend himself/herself to the distortion or suppression of the truth because of advertising or other considerations.
10. A journalist shall not originate material which encourages discrimination on grounds of race, colour, creed, gender or sexual orientation.
11. A journalist shall not take private advantage of information gained in the course of his/her duties, before the information is public knowledge.

Evidence assignment

Write a proposal for each of two print products, e.g. a children's book and a newspaper. The proposal should include details about:

- medium
- purpose
- target audience
- content
- aesthetics
- resource requirements
- technical requirements.

Produce outlines for both products, with notes on potential layout. Write a schedule for the production of one of the products, including resource requirements, production methods and deadlines.

In your production handbook make a note of any potential legal, ethical or representational issues.

Evidence of research done to support the proposal may be used for Unit 6 Element 4 (Chapter 24).

Producing print products

Chapter 10

Originate and edit print material

In order to get an idea of how the work of different areas comes together for a complete publication, we can look at the typical flow of work through a large national newspaper (see Figure 10.1 below). If it was a smaller, local paper then many of the staff would have more than one role.

At this stage you will be collecting information, taking notes and recording interviews. This material will need to be rewritten, possibly several times. It will help to discuss your work with other people and ask for their opinion on what you are writing.

You will be responsible for checking the accuracy of your work and proofreading the copy. Even when you are working individually as a journalist or a photographer, you have to keep in mind the fact that you are now working as part of a larger team.

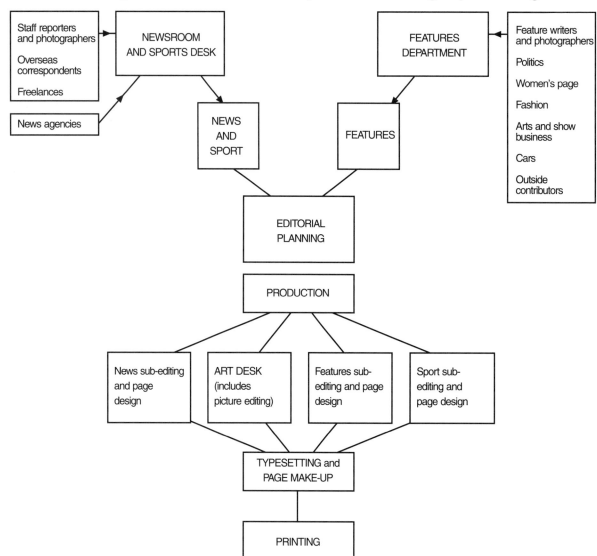

Figure 10.1 The flow of work through a national newspaper

222

Carry out the necessary research for material

The skills and sources of information needed here have already been discussed in Chapter 6. Newspapers and magazines obtain their stories from a wide variety of sources. The general public can contribute articles to the press, particularly the local papers, but usually they pass on information to a reporter or feature writer who then moulds the information into an article.

Journalists and newspapers build up contacts with all kinds of organisations and private individuals. The police, ambulance and fire service give out regular press releases and statements to the press. Newspapers also contact them routinely, perhaps every hour, to see if there is anything happening. Other contacts could be politicians and government and council officials, business organisations – the larger of which have their own PR (Public Relations) units, and educational establishments. Even criminals, or sources close to them, can be a point of contact for news gathering.

Sometimes a journalist will specialise in writing about a particular subject area, such as politics, sport or a gossip column. Others have more general responsibilities and will wait for the editor to direct them to a particular story.

Once the initial contact has been made, the commonest way of obtaining the information for a story is the interview. This can be used for finding out facts or people's opinions and attitudes. Press releases are also a useful source of information. They involve studying a written statement, which often has to be followed up with an interview.

But interviewing is not the first stage of the process. The first stage consists of information gathering, i.e. research. You will need to carry out research, first to identify the appropriate people to interview and, secondly, to gather some information about the topic you will be enquiring about.

For example, you may be writing an article about vandalism in your area. If the article is a hard news story then you will need to apply the 'who, what, where, why, when and how' formula detailed in Chapter 6 (see page 135) to find out what property has been damaged and to whom it belongs. The advantage of this formula is that you will always ask 'open-ended' questions – that is, questions which require more than a 'yes' or 'no' answer. For example, if you ask people who live in the area

where there has been vandalism, 'Do you like living in this area?', they may well reply with only a 'yes' or 'no' answer. However, if you ask them, 'What is it about the area that you like or dislike?' you should get a more extended response.

You could also decide to put the crime in context by giving some extra information at the end of your report about a number of related incidents within your newspaper's circulation area. This would require further research.

If you were carrying out research for a feature article on the same topic, you would apply the same formula but do more in-depth research. You would find out the number of incidents of vandalism in the area, and research the national and regional statistics so comparisons could be made. Individual residents, police, vandals, young people, old people, community workers, church leaders, neighbourhood associations, teachers, sociologists, psychologists and so on could all be interviewed, depending on how large a study you wished to make. To bring the article to life you would also need to research specific examples of vandalism and use quotes from victims, photographs of the damage done, etc.

You will need to be aware of the particular safety risks associated with the equipment and activities involved in the design and editing process. Refer to the appendix on Health and Safety for detailed discussion of this.

Generate material for print items in accordance with the agreed outline

In Chapter 6 we looked at ways of producing different types of articles for different types of publication or audience. We can now look at a particular type of publication and the approach it takes to generating material.

Case study

The publication is part of a project run by an organisation known as the Christmas Cracker Trust. The aim of this trust is to support young people who want to alleviate suffering in other parts of the world. In order to do this, the trust organises numerous initiatives, including one that has been running since 1989 called *The Cracker*.

The Cracker is a newspaper which is produced by various different groups of young people around the

223

country. Every year since 1989, school, college and youth groups have all participated in producing a newspaper in the run-up to Christmas. The purpose of the paper is two-fold. First, it increases awareness and raises money for those less fortunate than ourselves. It does this through the sale of the newspaper itself and by publicising fund-raising events that can run alongside the newspaper production and form part of an overall project package. Secondly, it gives young people the opportunity to develop the design and business skills necessary to produce a newspaper.

To start with, we can look at the advice given for generating the material (see Figure 10.2 below).

Getting the words right

WHAT'S THE ANGLE?
Any story or feature you might be asked to write could have several different angles that you could explore. Is there a key fact that is particularly attention grabbing?

Make the introduction work
If you don't grab the readers in the first paragraph, you might not grab them at all.

Telling them first that your school/church is having a carol service next Thursday and mentioning 3 paragraphs later that chart-topper Eternal have agreed to appear, is known as 'burying the lead'. 'Chart-toppers Eternal will bring soulful excellence to a special [your town] carol service next Wednesday [13 December]' has more appeal.

… And then explain
Always ask yourself the 'W' questions.
• Who are Eternal?
• Why are they famous?
• Where will they be appearing?
• What is the point of the carol service?
• What else will be happening?
• When will it start?
Never assume too much about what your reader knows. If you quote a vicar talking about Christmas, put him in context. Which church does he lead? What part of the town is it in?

PACE
When you've written your article, go back and check the length of your sentences. Try to aim for 12–15-word sentences. This makes your paper much more readable.

Going back over the material and shortening it can also help you avoid waffle.

Style
We recommend that you aim for a style similar to a national newspaper.
You won't be writing about the same subjects, but using them as a 'style' guide will help you.

The mix
Another style point relates to the different elements of your feature or article. You need a balance between:
• The facts – What is actually happening?
• The quotes – What do the people in the feature think about what's happening?
• The analysis – What does it all mean?
• The conclusion – What can the reader do? (if appropriate).

Research
If you're writing a feature, doing the diary section, reviewing a record or whatever, check out how others do it.

Read a similar feature in a magazine or newspaper and borrow and adopt their ideas. There's nothing new under the sun – we can all learn from other skilled and creative people.

THE BUILDING BLOCKS
You're writing short sentences, without obscure words, and your introductions are good. What else will make your copy sing?

Headlines
Aim for 3- or 4-word headlines that tell a story, or have a pun, or convey an idea.
These are as vital as your introductions. Work hard at them.

Subheads
For slightly longer features you may want to introduce a small sub-headline: 'Local churches are causing uproar by banning Santa in favour of St Nicholas. "We're leaving", claim hundreds of outraged parents.'
This gives the reader another chance to 'sample' the story and arouses further curiosity.

Crossheads
If the article is 700–1000 words long you will want to break up the text with crossheads. These are 2–5-word mini-headlines.

St Nick – a real saint!
Shopkeepers fear Santa recession

This helps break up the article visually. Big blocks of continuous text will put off the casual reader.

Quotes and fact boxes
You can't beat a juicy quote to draw in the reader.
'Today's Santa Claus myth is an excuse for wasting money on ourselves. The real St Nicholas gave to the poor.'

A fact box allows you to give information in short bullet-point style, e.g:
• The real St Nicholas
• St Nicholas lived x hundred years ago.
• Today's Santa Claus myth is a corruption of his story. Santa Claus means St Nicholas in Dutch.
• 80% of Christmas presents are unwanted and unused. St Nicholas gave his gifts to starving children.

Pictures
Every picture tells a story in itself. The picture caption is vital. A well-written caption draws the casual reader into the main story, or it can stand as a photo-story in its own right.

The details, the details
Don't forget the details. Check the following:
• Who are you – are you getting a credit for the feature or section?
• Has the photographer been given a credit?
• If the readers need to respond in any way, do they have details of time, venue, phone number, etc?

Figure 10.2 Advice on generating print material

Cracker project workers have the task of generating the material (i.e. stories) according to the agreed outline. This outline is a combination of their editorial policy and decisions on the types of content and their treatment (see Figure 10.3 below).

As you can see, there are numerous considerations relating to this editorial policy, many of which concern the issues discussed in the legal and ethical section of this book. Some, however, are issues which you may feel are 'not a problem'.

Activity

You may or may not agree with the content of the editorial policy in Figure 10.3. Discuss the points individually and state your own position. It will help if you bear the following points in mind:

- The Christmas Cracker Trust is a charity that aims to combat poverty and the injustices that accompany it. These injustices include
  - the exploitation of a country's resources, including its people, by international companies and governments.
  - not paying a fair price for a country's products (this comes under something called 'terms of trade').
  - the sale of arms to these countries.
- The Christmas Cracker Trust's Christian beliefs are founded in a moral code which finds certain activities and practices immoral.

---

1. **General coverage**
   While your paper will want to reflect the interests of all ages in your community, it should be youth orientated and pacey.

2. **Dodgy stuff**
   Your paper will be read by a very diverse set of people. Things to avoid include horoscopes, sexually explicit humour, gossip, and reviews of controversial films or books.

3. **Church groups**
   You shouldn't exclude a Christian emphasis from your stories – your daily newspaper doesn't – but find creative ways to express it. Remember that your audience may not share your beliefs and it is important to be sensitive and balanced in your approach.

4. **Legal notes**
   Be careful what you say!
   Our policy is not only to obey the law but to be wholesome in all we say and do. Therefore, you should avoid partisan comments or remarks about local schools, churches, staff, ministers, community leaders, political parties and other bodies or groups with whom you may not agree.

5. **Ethical advertising**
   Be clear in your own mind about what kind of advertising you would be reluctant to accept. This could include alcohol, tobacco and adult entertainment. You will need to create your own 'black list'. In any event, the disclaimer provided by Cracker HQ must be used in *every* edition of your paper.

   Every newspaper has legal constraints on it. There are two areas in particular with legal implications to watch:

I. **'Contempt of court':**
   This relates to references to Court proceedings in any court (High Court, Crown Court, Magistrate's Court, Coroner's Court). You are normally safe to refer to cases after the verdict and sentence, but as a rule it is best to try to avoid any legal comment or reporting if you can.

II. **'Defamation':**
   This is much more likely to lead to problems, and needs watching for carefully. Here is a very simple guide:

   The law of defamation embraces libel and slander. There is no definition of defamation, but one suggestion is that 'defamation shall consist of the publication to a third party of a matter which, in all the circumstances, would be likely to affect a person adversely in the estimation of reasonable people generally'.

   Guideline: 'If I were him/her, would I like that said of me?'

   What might constitute a libellous statement?
   - One that holds someone up to hatred, ridicule or contempt;
   - One that causes someone to be shunned or avoided;
   - One that lowers someone in the estimation of right-thinking people;
   - One that disparages someone in his/her office, trade or profession.

   Beware of:
   - Libel or innuendo
   - Nameless libel
   - Unintentional libel
   - Libelling someone just because everyone else is!

   Note As a general rule, if you must mention anything political or interview a political figure (MP, councillor, etc.) please remember that your coverage should reflect a principle of 'balance', which means that all major parties should have a fair hearing and share of the interview/coverage.

   One useful fact: a visit from the mayor or chairman of the local council is politics-free, as they are non-political during their year of office.

6. **Hoaxes or practical jokes**
   These are fine on April 1st. In all other cases they're prohibited!

7. **Keeping a record**
   For our own legal records Cracker HQ needs to receive a copy of everything you publish under 'The Cracker' name. Don't forget to keep back some archive copies for you and your team!

Figure 10.3 Material must be generated in line with editorial policy

---

Content

1. **The 'must-have' basics**
   Logo
   All the Cracker papers must carry the same (masthead) title logo on the front page. This will be supplied as part of the artwork disk.

   Address/Charity details/Distribution information
   Somewhere near the front you should have your local address, details of our charity status and a sentence or two about the project. We will supply this and you can insert your address details.

   Disclaimer
   Once again, this wording will be supplied. It will simply reflect that acceptance of advertising does not imply endorsement, and give the central office address for any feedback about aspects of the project. This is necessary for legal and ethical reasons.

2. **The 'must-have' project information**
   You should plan to have the following in every issue:
   a) *How to give:*
      Details of how people can give via:
      • Post – they may be moved by what they read
      • Your shop and events – where are they and when
      • Your paper sales – where can they buy further copies
      Once you've designed this, you can repeat it in every issue.

   b) *Events*
   Events are absolutely vital to the success of the project. Events are a brilliant, regular source of lively copy and pictures, so the more the merrier!

   Give details of forthcoming events. Don't just put times and venues but give details. Show pictures of people doing trial runs of their fund-raising activities. Nothing succeeds like success. So promote the event one week and report back the next. Tell your readers how much has been raised so far, how events have gone, who came and how people are reacting. Use lots of pictures, get interviews, get a real events 'buzz' going!

   c) *Project stories/Campaigning*
   One of the aims of 'The Cracker' is to promote justice in the world, highlighting the issue of 'blindness' in particular in the 1996 project. Cracker HQ will provide national articles on the issue, give contacts for further action, and generally give you topical ammunition to fire from your pages. There will also be stories on some of the people and projects that will benefit from Cracker, all of which will be key ingredients in prompting people to give and support your efforts.

   Be creative, too – do you know anyone who has been to Bangladesh, etc? What did they see?

3. **'Further ideas' section**
   Here's some ideas to develop further:
   • Fair trade shop window
   • Really useful guide
     Provide a regular update on what's happening in your town.
   • Christmas profile in your locality
   • Reviews
     Review or preview family entertainment, such as blockbuster films, pantomimes, major concerts, TV listings; or even music or food!
   • Sport
   • Recipes for Christmas
   • Christmas traditions around the world
   • Local news, stories and profiles
   • Competitions
     Lots of possibilities here, such as caption competitions and so on.
   • Schools
   • Human interest
   • Developing world issues

Figure 10.4 Content considerations

Keeping these values in mind, can you understand (even if you disagree) why the Cracker Trust built these points into their policy?

There is also the approach to the content to consider. Figure 10.4 shows the guidelines for the outline treatment.

We have already discussed photography in Chapter 6, but the Cracker Trust's advice on taking photographs (Figure 10.5) will help to emphasise the important points.

Get in the picture

PHOTOGRAPHY AND ILLUSTRATION
It's a cliché of course, but a picture is worth a thousand words. Here's some tips for the budding David Baileys in your midst:

Technical stuff
Several books have been written on this. If you're the editor, try to ensure that your potential photographer is not a complete novice. If you're the potential photographer, don't bluff about your abilities or knowledge – you don't have to be brilliant, but you should know your film speed from your 200mm lens specification.

Who's in the picture?
Make sure the people/actions dominate the picture. Even if they don't on the print, you may be able to crop them to ensure they do.
   A picture of lots of people needs to be bigger than normal, or it just looks like a sea of fairly hard-to-distinguish faces.

Compose, compose, compose
Not music, but your picture. If you cover an event, get an action picture rather than a 'proud finisher holding cheque' type of shot.
   People's attention will usually be arrested by something different or unusual. Try different angles or unposed pictures where the real emotion of the moment shines through.

The background
Many a good shot is ruined by a dodgy backdrop. Try to make good backdrops part of the picture.
   As much as possible, go for a light background to give contrast to your picture.

Figure 10.5 Tips on photography

When selecting photographs to include in your product you should ask yourself whether they add something to the story. The old saying 'a picture paints a thousand words' is true enough as long as it is the right picture. You therefore need to ask yourself whether it makes much difference to the story and whether it is sufficiently eye-catching to make a reader sit up and take notice.

Needless to say, the photograph should be in focus and correctly exposed (see Chapter 6). Don't use the picture just because it is the only one you've got; it could end up detracting from the story, and the whole publication.

You have now looked at a particular print project and the constraints associated with it. It should illustrate to you what it means to write within design and production guidelines, for a defined **purpose** which takes into account both **editorial policy** and the **target audience**.

At all stages of the process, **safe working practices** must be observed. So health and safety guidelines should be followed at all times, when using computers, for example, or when using any other design and editing tools.

Generating advertising copy

We have now discussed generating material for editorial content. You should not forget, however, that a large proportion of a newspaper, perhaps 50 per cent and often more, is taken up with advertising. You may also want to generate revenue through advertising and you need to go about it the right way in order to make a good impression.

For information on how to sell your advertising space you should refer to Chapter 27.

Through interviewing prospective advisers you will increase the opportunities of generating advertising material. If the initial interview works, then the next stage will be a further interview to find out exactly what the client wants. It is too easy for us to make assumptions about what we think people want. This is often a false assumption. However, the problem is that customers often don't really *know* what they want. You therefore have to develop skills in eliciting information from a client or member of the public.

These communication skills will decide whether or not you will be able to gather the material to generate copy, whether it is for editorial or advertising. In the newspaper industry, the possession of good communication skills is of paramount importance. At the *Leicester Mercury,* advertising sales teams participate in role-play exercises every morning to sharpen them up before they start making contact with prospective clients.

Remember, you simply cannot allow yourself to get off to a slow and sloppy start when it comes to conducting interviews. You need information from people in order to produce your product. Rightly or wrongly, people form impressions of someone very

quickly. Therefore the first minutes, even seconds, are vital. You do not get a second chance to make a first impression!

Another important thing to remember is to keep your editor informed about what you are doing, not only so that progress can be monitored but also as a matter of personal safety, so that someone is aware of where you are at all times.

Then, as the pages start coming together, the editor will be able to assess whether more material is needed and supervise the printing schedule.

Check information is accurately recorded and references and quotes accurately attributed

It is vitally important to carry out your research as thoroughly as possible in the time allowed. Even if you are rushing to meet a deadline there is no excuse for the misspelling of names and other personal details, or mixing up dates, ages, etc. Be particularly careful when it comes to photographs, as it is easy to get names and pictures confused. As a matter of good practice you should double-check these kinds of details by asking people to spell, for example, their names, repeating a spelling back to them, or showing them how you have written it.

The basic rule is to check everything that is checkable. The sub-editor is not always in a position to know, for example, whether an eye-witness account is accurate. However, experience should tell you that no two accounts are exactly the same and the more dramatic or stressful an incident, the more likelihood there is of a significant discrepancy. The answer in this particular scenario is to ask the reporter whether there were any other witnesses so you can make a comparison.

Another 'minefield' is concerned with quotes from those interviewed, or the use of famous quotes to illustrate a point, particularly in an editorial (leader comment) piece. We have already outlined in Chapter 6 how the editing of quotes can result in a misquote, which can lead to resentment and the loss of a useful source of information – or even litigation.

As far as literary quotes go, check them in a book of quotations. Quotes that should add to the authority of an article will, if misquoted, lead to loss of confidence in that article. After all, what else might be wrong? Grammar, syntax and conventions can be checked in Fowler's *Modern English Usage.*

Other facts, such as titles, addresses and the activities of certain famous people, can be checked in specialist reference works such as *Who's Who*. There is also the *BBC Year Book, Oxford Companion to Literature* (and another for music), and specialist *Who's Who*, in radio and TV, music, and the theatre. There is also the *Civil Service List, The Directory of Directors, Foreign Office List, International Who's Who, The Stock Exchange Year Book* and *Who's Who in America*. Other books which will help you to check facts about people are *Burke's Peerage,* (for instance, is someone a Lord or a Duke or whatever?), while books such as *Crockford's Clerical Directory, Catholic Directory* or *Jewish Year Book* will help you to work out how you should refer to members of the clergy. For the armed services there are also the separate Air Force, Army and Navy Lists, along with *Jane's World Aircraft* and *Jane's Fighting Ships.*

Sub-editors and typesetters can also make mistakes, perhaps by misreading a single character or digit. But this could, for example, put 10 years on somebody's age! Therefore, rewrites should always be checked against the original.

Above all, when you are gathering material for a story you need to take an interest in the surroundings in which you find yourself, and show awareness, sensitivity and empathy for the situation and the people involved. Taking an interest helps you to concentrate, and therefore listen better.

It is essential that you present yourself as an amiable and trustworthy person who is worth talking to about something perhaps very important or even personal.

You may have to conduct your interview over the telephone. In this case, checks on accuracy are even more important. You should also be even more aware of how you come across, and try to make a good impression.

Listening and taking notes is a skill that takes practice. If you are serious about becoming a journalist, you will need to learn shorthand. At the very least, develop your own 'shorthand' so that you don't laboriously write down in longhand everything a person says. Dictaphones or other portable tape recorders are also very useful. However, it may be that the interviewee will be intimidated by the sight of a recording device so you may not be able to use it. Try to put the person at their ease by making the recording equipment as inconspicuous as possible. It is no good cajoling someone into 'putting up with' a tape recorder. If they feel uncomfortable you won't get very good results anyway. You should always ask permission to tape someone, or even to take notes. If you create a relaxed atmosphere, people will soon forget there is any recording going on.

For more information on interviewing techniques try reading *Interviewing for Journalists* by Joan Clayton (Piatkus, 1994). It is full of advice and tips and is in an easy-to-follow style and format.

For more information on preparing stories see Chapter 6, pages 135–8.

Identify and resolve content considerations

These considerations are dealt with in the Legal and Ethical appendix and elsewhere.

Proofread written text

Proofreading is the process of checking for typographical and grammatical errors. Text should also be proofread for accuracy of material, sense and style, and the correct spelling of proper names. You should note that, while a proofreader will be able to spot spelling mistakes, it may take the author of a piece to spot a factual inaccuracy.

The first proofreading takes place when the **galley proof** is produced. The galley proof is a single continuous column of text, used before setting the text into columns and pages. The second stage (for books) is **page proofs**, which include spaces for illustrations or artist's roughs for these. With modern typesetting, the galley stage may be omitted and page proofs are the first proofs to check.

There is a British standard for proof-readers' symbols. The most commonly used ones are reproduced in Figure 10.6.

You should get into the habit of using these as they are a clear, quick way of communicating mistakes to the typesetter or printer. You need a pen with a very fine point to make the marks in precisely the right place.

Text mark	Margin mark	Correction to be made
copy	✓	leave unchanged
╪	delete	delete
and	delete	delete
foun̰d	delete	delete and close up space
in͡to	⌒	delete space between words
⋏	the /	insert word where indicated
⋏	⊙/	insert punctuation mark
⋋	⋎	insert superior character
self⋌discipline	⊢⊣	insert hyphen
understbod	and /	substitute characters
make	d /	substitute character
Note	⎵⎵⎵	change to italic type
home	≡	change to capital letter
Home	≢	change capital letter to lower-case letter
∼	∼	transpose characters or words
gre e n	Y	insert space between characters
gre/en	T	reduce space between characters
green door	Y	insert space between words
green↑door	T	reduce space between words
≍		insert space between lines or paragraphs
		reduce space between lines or paragraphs
		run on (no new paragraph)
The		indent
⊢The		cancel indent

Figure 10.6 Proof correction marks

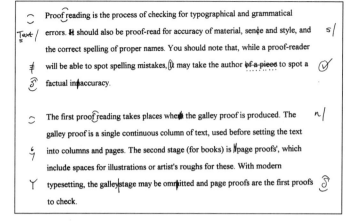

Figure 10.7 A piece of corrected text

Most people do not read their work through properly.

They think that once it has been written down once they shouldn't have to tough it again. Wrong! In Media this is just the first stage. You will have to get usedto writing and re-writing until you get it right, and this usually has to be don under pressure of deadlines.

It is, however, very easy to miss mistakes when you proofread your own work. We know what we mean and therefore we tend to read for general meaning, which causes us to miss mistakes. A good way of minimising the danger of missing mistakes it to read the work aloud. It will soon become apparent if something doesn't make sense.

Evidence assignment

Research and collect material for your chosen print publication. Keep a record of notes taken during interviews, and copies of rough sketches or original photographs taken for your work.

Write up your article or story. Keep examples of drafts and rewrites. You should proofread your own work, and also that of others.

Submit your copy, including written text and visuals to the sub-editor.

Details of research, names of interviewees, etc. and notes on content considerations should be kept in your production handbook.

Activity

Study the following text carefully and then proofread it using the correct symbols. There are errors of punctuation, spelling, and grammar. The layout also needs to be improved.

The job of proof reading is carried out by a vareity of people, depending on the types of print product. with newspapers, the first person to proofread is the person who wrote the article, so, always proof read your work, even more importantly, you should get someone else to proofread it.

229

Chapter 11

Sub-edit and layout print products

Once copy has been produced it is passed to a copy-taster; this is usually the news editor but it can be any experienced journalist who knows the publication and its audience. The copy-taster decides whether the story is newsworthy and checks that there are no obvious mistakes. If it is approved for inclusion in the newspaper it goes to the sub-editor, whose job it is to check the contents, shape it to the page, and write the headline for it.

Select, organise and edit material for inclusion in the print product

In addition to checking copy for mistakes in spelling, grammar, typographical errors ('typos' or 'literals'), inconsistencies, presentation style, structure and length, the sub-editor will also have to decide whether an article is appropriate for inclusion into a publication. This will depend, for example, on how topical the content is. A story has to have 'currency'. That is, it needs to be on a subject which is in people's minds and in which they are interested.

Some topics, such as capital punishment, arming the police or legalising drugs, are nearly always 'topical' and the debate about them re-surfaces again and again, often triggered by a hard news story. A terrorist attack or a particularly brutal murder, particularly of a child, will re-activate the debate.

Let's look at a typical 'chain reaction' of topical articles which could be set in motion by, for example, a heinous crime such as a murder. There would be articles and 'leader comment' for and against the death penalty, and also the human interest stories of those who have been affected by it or similar ordeals. There might also be articles making statistical comparisons between societies that do or do not carry out capital punishment, or that show rises in violent crime in particular areas, or claims that there was just as much violence fifty years ago. There would also be articles about the fear of crime, or psychological probes into the 'sickness in society' the breakdown in moral standards, claims that violent attitudes are caused by watching certain films, or by pornography, lack of parental control, lack of school discipline or lack of jobs.

All these give ample scope for a sub-editor to 'freshen up' a running story by giving it a new **angle**, of which the above are examples. These stories can either be given to a journalist to write or re-write or, if time is short, the sub-editor will make the change of angle. Subs will also re-write if a story is dull or badly written, or needs modifying because they judge it to be too outrageous for the readership, or even legally questionable. Some reporters are good at getting stories, but not so good at writing them up. They therefore rely on the sub to give the story its final polish.

Related to this is the question of the readership: the story could be very well written but if it is not aimed at the target audience then it could be rejected. If, for example, you are writing for a local newspaper, there is no point in writing about national or international issues, except where they can be related to a local context. Making use of news from other areas is a useful approach that is often used by local newspapers.

The secret is to get the angle right so that you are making it relevant to your readership. If legislation concerning beef cattle is made in Brussels, you can write about the effects on local farmers. You could even do a survey or vox pop on how it has affected local people's diets or their livelihoods.

A sub-editor must also be concerned with balance. Too many crime stories on the same page may be seen as rather disturbing, perhaps giving the impression that there is a lot more crime than there really is. In the Fred and Rosemary West case, many newspapers found the details so horrific that they were actually downplayed rather than sensationalised.

The editor of the *Gloucester Echo* decided that she would print the stories in a factual, low-key style, without any of the language style or design techniques that are used to embellish a story and grab the reader's attention. Her argument was that there was already so much publicity, and the crimes so awful, that it was causing an imbalance in the news. She was worried that 'the news' had become 'the West murders' and local people were beginning to avoid it because it was so depressing and unrelenting. Any more bold headlines would only accentuate this effect. No matter how awful the facts were, there was more to life than this.

A story may also be rejected if it is outside the newspaper's circulation area, or if it is not really of public interest. Editing not only involves checking the spelling, grammar and inconsistencies. It is also concerned with readability, the presentation of information, suitability of style and accuracy. In addition, there are legal and ethical considerations to take into account, which are dealt with in the Legal and Ethical appendix.

Apart from all this, individual items have to be considered in relation to other items. If, for example, another, more important story came in, then other stories might have to be scaled down (perhaps affecting the structure of the whole), or even lost altogether.

Design pages and sub-edit in accordance with layout, to produce finished print product

When you design a new product, typographical considerations, such as the design for both **headline text** and **body text**, are part of the planning process as dealt with in Chapter 9. Subsequently, these matters are part of the page design function and are usually part of the sub-editor's brief, although there will be matters of house style and editorial policy to consider. The editor, for example, would certainly be involved in how the front page looks.

The impact of desk-top publishing

There has been something of a revolution in the production of print products in the past 10 years. This has had a profound impact on how newspapers and magazines are produced and the working practices associated with their production. Technology, and particularly the development of the 'micro' or 'home' computer, has been the main reason for change. You can read more about these changes and their effects in Chapter 32.

The term 'micro' was used originally to differentiate the computer for the small business, or home user, from the mini and mainframe computers used in industry. Computers have, however, become smaller yet more powerful so the distinction between them is now increasingly blurred.

The desk-top (and the lap-top) computer is now a familiar sight whether it is sitting on a desk at work, college or in the home. They are becoming as common in household item as the video recorder. In 1996, over 28 per cent of adults owned a home computer.

The software has also become more and more sophisticated. Wordprocessing has moved on from being an elaborate method of typewriting to packages such as Word for Windows, which have so many facilities that they are basic DTP systems in themselves.

What is desk-top publishing?

DTP is the production of a print product by bringing together and manipulating, on one computer screen, the various components – text, pictures, graphs, tables, and artwork such as lines, borders, 'bullets', etc. – which go to make up that product. Traditionally these activities were termed 'cut and paste', because this is how they were done. Although this is no longer literally true, DTP does emulate the 'cut and paste' process.

The software available for DTP includes Quark XPress for the AppleMac and Aldus Pagemaker for the PC. These are two of the most widely used DTP packages for professional publishing. There are, however, other products available which offer a high standard of performance, output and ease of use; two of these are Microsoft Publisher, and Serif's PagePlus.

DTP software, especially when designed to operate in the 'Windows' environment, can be used to produce different parts of your publication on different 'stand alone' software. For example, wordprocessing applications such as Wordperfect or Word for Windows can produce the text, drawing packages such as Corel Draw can produce illustrations, and you may want to import some figures from a spreadsheet such as Excel. On the other hand, you could use an integrated package such as PagePlus. This incorporates all the characteristic features of DTP (and more).

All good DTP packages will allow you to import text and graphics and it is quite common to produce your *content* on other applications and use the DTP application for the *design* of these contents. Alternatively, you can, as we have already said, use the DTP package for both content and design, by making use of its built-in features. Depending on its **fitness for purpose** it may well be acceptable to produce the whole product using the built-in facilities of the DTP package. Its purpose will also help you to decide on the quality acceptable for a production.

Use of DTP

If you have a **scanner** as part of your DTP equipment, you can use it to integrate photographs, drawings and images into the document you are creating. Their quality of resolution is measured in dpi (dots per inch). A scanner can also be used to scan in text. Some are able to carry out OCR (optical character recognition), which means the text that is scanned in can be manipulated as individual characters, rather than a chunk of text being treated as a single object. Another 'image-grabbing' facility is the use on a video camera or a video recorder linked to a computer with a video card installed. This allows images on the camera or VCR to be scanned in to your document or saved as a separate file on disk.

With all the sophisticated features offered by DTP it is easy to think that all you have to do is switch the computer on and start experimenting on screen. Eventually, it is hoped, something presentable will come out of it.

This approach is just as time-consuming as when pages were designed manually. In fact it can be worse. There are so many features, including vast arrays of fonts and artwork including **clip art**, that users are tempted into including as many as possible, regardless of what it does to the appearance and readability of the publication. Clip art is drawings that have already been produced and stored for users. These illustrations do not demand individual effort, except in retrieving and positioning them. Although clip art and other off-the-shelf features do have their uses they can also introduce a degree of mediocrity, when all readers see is the same tired images put into documents without any real creative thought behind them.

This leads us to the first and most important rule of DTP: stay off the computer until you have researched, planned and sketched out your design on paper. As part of your research, you will have to explore the DTP package to find out what it is capable of. But there is no point in planning all sorts of elaborate designs if you cannot put them into practice on the computer, or if they are too costly, in terms of time or money, to be feasible. Other than that, you should keep away from the machine until you have a good idea what you are going to do with it.

Design planning

When planning your design, ask yourself the following questions:

- **Who is the publication for?**
  Define the target audience. Besides gender, age, social grouping and so on, decide if they are, for example, casual readers of a general product, or a specific group for a specialist product.

- **What is the main type of message?**
  Will it be information, news, entertainment or something else?

- **Where will it be seen or made available?**
  On kiosks, stalls, etc. or delivered to homes, displayed on a notice board or billboard, left on tables? You can make the product appropriate to its surroundings – for example, it can look like a beer mat.

- **What kind of response should it generate?**
  Perhaps humour, outrage, general interest...

You can then try to develop a style that matches the response you are aiming for, such as serious, traditional, light-hearted, dependable, 'arty', informal, etc.

You will, therefore, need to investigate the components, starting with typography, that make up the particular style of a publication. Read the descriptions of these different features and techniques below, and also examine a range of print publications. You should be starting to look critically at print products and deciding what it is about their look that you like or dislike.

Typography

Typography is the collective name for the art of designing, selecting and producing typefaces. It is an important part of design. There are thousands of different typefaces and each can have its own variations within that style. A single size and style of a particular typeface is called a font (or fount).

The major difference in type style is whether the typeface is **serif**, which has a decorative flourish, or **sans serif** which is plainer.

Typography rules OK

Serif

Typography rules OK

San serif

Figure 11.1 Serif and sans serif typefaces

Another difference in type style is whether a typeface is Roman (upright) or *italic* (slanting). Originally, this would have been classed as two separate typefaces. These days a single typeface can have Roman and italic versions. **Bold** can also be used to make a word or phrase stand out.

A further element of type style is **upper case**, often referred to as Caps (capitals) and **lower case**.

Letters in the alphabet have three components when they are printed. The part of the letter that fits on the line is the body. The height of this body is determined by the height of the lower case x in the particular typeface being used. It is therefore referred to as the **x height**. If a letter has a stem that rises above the x height, this is known as an **ascender**. If it has a tail that goes below, it is called a **descender**.

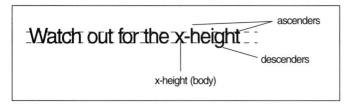

Figure 11.2 Components of printed letters

Another factor to take into account with type style is letter spacing and line spacing. There are no definite rules concerning spacing but it needs to take legibility and aesthetic style into consideration. If the letters or lines are too close together or too far apart, text is difficult to read. With line spacing the **leading** (pronounced 'ledding') must take account of the ascenders and descenders.

When letters set side by side are brought together, particularly to the point of overlap, it is known as **kerning**. Letters can be kerned (condensed) or extended as a means of varying the apparent weight. **Weight** refers to how light or bold the type is. By varying the width, the appearance of letter weights can also be altered. This gives a single typeface even more variations from which to choose.

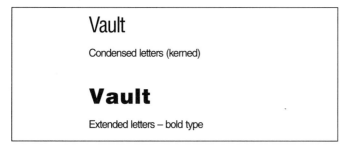

Figure 11.3 Condensed and extended letters

Sizes of typefaces are measured in various ways, including **points**, of which there are twelve in a **pica** (the equivalent to 1/6 inch). Metric equivalents are being used more and more, but the point system seems to be surviving for the present.

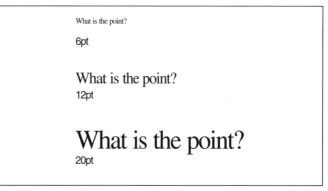

Figure 11.4 Point sizes

Print jobs usually employ print sizes within the range 5pt to 120pt. The size used in this book is 10pt.

Typefaces can also be divided into 'display' and 'text'. Display faces are used to attract attention and are therefore used for titles and headings. Some typefaces are designed specifically for display purposes and would be unsuitable for body text.

Text typefaces are designed to be legible even when printed quite small.

The width of letters and lines is also measured in picas, and in **ems** and **ens**. These refer to the widest letter in the alphabet, the *m*, and half its width, the *n*.

There are other stylistic ways of enhancing text, including:

> **T**HERE are other stylistic ways of enhancing text, as we can see here.
>
> **T**HESE can include drop letters (as above) and raised (as here).

Figure 11.5 Drop and raised caps

- **Drop** and raised (stand up drop) letters to draw attention to the text. The first letter drops or is raised several lines below or above the body text. The first word is also generally printed in caps.

The first paragraph or lead intro is often in bold and in a larger point size.

- **Reverse out**
  Reversing lettering by printing white on black attracts the eye and is a good method of highlighting a piece of text. It is frequently used in magazines. However, as with all highlighting, you should be careful not to over-use this effect as too much can detract from the message and give the page a cluttered look. The appearance is sometimes referred to as WOB (white on black).

REVERSED OUT

Figure 11.6 Reverse lettering

- **Masthead**
  The **masthead** (sometimes referred to as the **flag**, **titlepiece** or **title-line**) is the title of your publication, produced in a distinctive style that should remain the same in all issues and promotional material. It is, in effect, a 'textual logo' and forms part of the overall image of the publication. It is part of that publication's visual identity and people should be able to pick it out from similar publications at a glance. Its design embodies the values and image that the publication wishes to portray to the readership. However, it should never detract from the headlines, and the **banner** (main headline) at least, is normally bigger. The masthead is nevertheless crucial to the product's image and you should be prepared to work hard at getting it right.

Other major 'visual text' elements of page design are **headlines**, **sub-headings** and **captions**. These have been discussed in Chapters 3 and 6. It is, however, worth reiterating that they are part of the page design function and are therefore part of the sub-editor's duties. As we have mentioned before, the sub-editor has to make the page come together in an informative and visually interesting way. He or she will have to make decisions regarding, for example, the size of the headlines.

Cross heads and **side heads** break up long columns of text and are also used as 'tasters' to attract the reader's eye into the text. Sometimes the cross heads are replaced by quotes of two or three lines (sometimes called teasers) which also act as breakers.

(The word 'teaser' is an American term. It can also refer to contents lists and guides, etc.) Refer back to Chapter 9, page 217, for other details of layouts.

Although we are here dealing primarily with text, headings, reverse-outs, etc. are part of the visual elements of the product design. The idea is to produce a harmonious product which is pleasing to the eye and is easy for readers to find their way around.

In Chapter 6 (page 135) we illustrated how the stories should be written so that the sub can make edits as easily as possible. The sub will also ensure there are no **widows** (short lines left at the top of a column of text) or **orphans** (a single word left at the bottom in similar isolation).

Illustrations

Tear-out (**rag-out**) is a photograph or article from a previous edition, or other print source, which is given a deliberately ragged look as if it had been torn from a copy of an old paper or magazine. Our visual skills tell us that it is a flashback from the past.

Cropping is a form of editing. It involves selecting a certain section of a picture and excluding unwanted parts. This gets rid of distracting, unnecessary detail, and highlights the selected part of the image. Practically all newspaper and magazine photographs are cropped.

Figure 11.7 An overlay indicates the area to be used in a cropped photo

Scaling or sizing is the proportional reduction or enlargement of a picture. It is carried out by drawing a diagonal line from one corner of the back of the picture to the other. A horizontal line of the required measurement is drawn until it meets the diagonal, then an ascending line to the top of the picture.

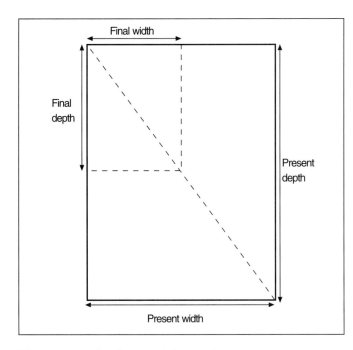

Figure 11.8 Scaling or sizing a picture

Cut-outs allow the text to flow around the content of a photograph rather than being excluded by its frame. This brings text and image together by allowing them to flow into each other, giving a more intimate feel to the picture.

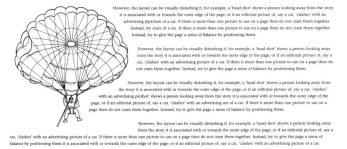

Figure 11.9 A cut-out

Re-touching can be carried out to get rid of genuinely surplus detail in a picture but it should not be used to misrepresent a person or event. If it does, this can be classed as a libel in the same way that text can be libellous. For more details see the Legal and Ethical appendix.

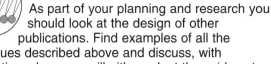

Activity

As part of your planning and research you should look at the design of other publications. Find examples of all the techniques described above and discuss, with justifications, how you will either adapt these ideas to your own design or choose something else.

Positioning

Pictures are part of the design element as well as the content. You therefore have to consider how you are going to position the pictures on the page – in relation to the text and in relation to each other.

A well-positioned picture attracts the eye, so that the person reads the caption and, in turn, is stimulated to read the body text. (Headings, of course, also play this role.)

However, the layout can be visually disturbing if, for example, a 'head shot' shows a person looking away from the story it is associated with or towards the outer edge of the page; or if an editorial picture of, say, a car, 'clashes' with an advertising picture of a car. If there is more than one picture to use on a page then do not cram them together. Instead, try to give the page a sense of balance by positioning them.

Pre-press

A the **pre-press** stage complete pages can be composed on computer, with text and visuals input from keyboard and scanner. Pages are then paired with their positive sides and sent to film output devices which produce the double page as a photographic negative.

The final stage is to turn these negatives into printing plates. This is done by placing them on top of pre-sensitised aluminium plates. Ultra-violet light is then directed through the negative on to the plate, producing an image of the two pages. This image is developed by using a processing unit and the plates are then fitted on to the press cylinders.

When producing an item in a newspaper style it is far more convincing to produce on authentic newsprint, rather than printing out on to photocopying paper. You should contact your local newspapers and organisations such as NIE (Newspapers in Education) and investigate the possibility of some collaborative ventures.

If you don't have access to professional printing facilities, you can still produce good work by outputting to a laser printer. Depending on the type of publication you are aiming for you could use coloured paper, or you may have access to a colour copier. You may have a scanner or perhaps you need to 'cut and paste' your images first.

If you are able to generate income from advertising, perhaps you will be able to send the product to a printer like Prontaprint. It is worth getting a quotation if you have money available for printing and finishing.

Proofread finished group product

We have seen that individual items go through a series of checks, starting with the writer of the item, then, in the case of newspapers, to the copy-taster and on to the sub-editor.

The sub is responsible not only for checking the individual items, but also for how the articles fit in relation to each other, and the overall look of the page or publication.

At the printing stage, sample copies are pulled from a trial run and these printer's proofs are checked for mistakes, particularly those concerning the quality of the print.

Books are proofread by a proof-reader. This person not only reads for 'literals', that is, spelling, grammar and typographical errors, but also for clarity, sense and consistency. For example, a passage of a book or manual might refer the reader to another passage in that book. However, that particular reference could have been taken out at some earlier stage. Of course, the author or copy-editor should have removed the reference but it is all too easy to lose track and it is left to the proof-reader to spot it and put it right.

Other mistakes might be concerned with ambiguities, sometimes arising from using the wrong word. For example, 'ambiguous' and 'ambivalent' are sometimes confused, as is 'affect' and 'effect'. See Chapter 10 for more on proofreading and proof-readers' marks.

Review production schedule and note any deviations

After the product has been printed you can start a review of the production process. This will allow you to identify where the plans were not followed. You can then carry out a review to find out why there were deviations and whether they were justified.

There are all sorts of reasons why you may have to change plans. These can include technical problems, human error and working relationships turning sour. Some problems may be foreseeable, but others may be quite unexpected. However, with any large project you are bound to encounter some difficulties and time should have been allowed for this somewhere in the schedule. Who can predict which adverts might not turn up on time, or which journalists miss deadlines?

Case study

On a student project the late arrival of advertising copy from either the advertisers themselves, or the advertising agencies they used, caused a delay in setting the pages. When the ads finally arrived there were technical difficulties in scanning them in, with very little time left to manage these problems. The result was that last-minute changes, such as altering some of the artwork, were made in order to get the images into full page make-up. Although this did not make a significant difference overall, it did detract somewhat from the final quality of the product. Some adverts were slightly different and one advertiser at least was less than pleased when a logo was slightly altered. How could these problems have been avoided?

Apart from instances of communication breakdown, there is also the related matter of human relations. In large projects, individual activities form only part of a much bigger picture. However, these various activities are inter-related so that one activity depends on another. For example, journalists have to research stories and make contacts. They also, in many cases, need to liaise with a photographer; sales staff have to chase up advertisers and perhaps liaise with the journalists so they can write a feature on an organisation; editorial copy needs to arrive in time for it to be copy-tasted and progressed to page make-up stage. Expensive and heavily used resources must be booked well in advance for page make-up, scanning in, etc. Copy must, therefore, be ready on time for this stage.

With so much inter-dependency, it only takes one person to neglect doing the job properly and the whole project time-scale starts to slip. When you have a deadline for a newspaper, you just cannot allow this to happen. It is imperative, therefore, that the production team operates as an effective unit and keeps the objective – the production of the print product, by a certain time, at a certain cost, for a certain target audience – firmly in mind at all times.

This means that team-building exercises should ideally take place prior to starting a project of this scale. In addition, the editor should be someone in whom the rest of the group has trust and confidence.

Activity

As a group, identify the changes to a production schedule. Why did they take place and could they have been avoided?

Evidence assignment

Submit for printing an edited copy of your print product.

This should be accompanied by:

- a draft page layout
- a layout with material in place
- evidence of sub-edited material
- evidence of the proofreading process
- notes explaining why certain material or items were accepted and others rejected
- a list of deviations from the production schedule.

237

Review and evaluate print products

Once the print product is produced it should be evaluated: in terms of the planning and production process, the persons involved in these processes, and the audience response. The research on audience response can then be used as evidence for Chapter 24 and the work on distribution for Unit 7.

A new product should always be market tested, but even established products such as the *Leicester Mercury* require continuous performance monitoring.

Distribute print product to target audience

The end product may be informative and attractive, but it must reach its target audience at the right time in order to fulfil its purpose. Effective distribution is a vital part of the **marketing mix**, and the different methods are discussed in Unit 7. If distribution methods are ineffective there will be a poor return on the investments made, whether these are in time, money, materials or human resources.

Customers may need inducements, such as free gifts or reduced subscriptions, to buy publications. Retailers too may need some special offer or exclusive deal to encourage them to stock the product. The ending of the Net Book Agreement has meant that books can be sold at whatever price a retailer wishes, so competition has increased. Classic novels, which are no longer protected by copyright, have been brought out in cheap paperback editions for as little as a pound. Supermarkets, for instance, have begun to stock popular books and are taking a significant share of the market.

Case study

In the case of the North Warwickshire & Hinckley College/*Leicester Mercury* project, introduced in Chapter 9 (see page 210), the student sales team had to promote and sell the product, i.e. the *Leicester Mercury*. They bought a total of two hundred of the newspapers at the wholesale price of 18 pence each and sold them at the retail price of 27 pence.

Tuesday 26 March

Special Feature produced by

Hinckley College students

FREE

SNACKS
WITH EVERY

𝕷𝖊𝖎𝖈𝖊𝖘𝖙𝖊𝖗 𝕸𝖊𝖗𝖈𝖚𝖗𝖞

PURCHASED

Available from:
Canteen, Information Centre & Business Block

Figure 12.1 An advertising poster for the *Leicester Mercury* project. See Chapter 28, page 483 for an analysis of audience reaction to it

The sales team had to research and identify likely vending sites across the college. In order to encourage people to buy a newspaper the sales team planned a promotions campaign. They researched and contacted several regional businesses in order to obtain sponsorship in the form of promotional merchandise i.e. free snacks. They were successful with KP Foods, who donated savoury snacks, Trebor Bassett, who gave Jelly

```
Consumer Snacks Dept
Walkers Snacks Ltd

11 March 1996


Dear Sir/Madam
            Re: Promotional Stock Donation
I am a student at Hinckley College of Further
Education, currently studying for an advanced
GNVQ in Media: Communication & Production.

As part of this course I am currently working in
a team, in conjunction with the Leicester
Mercury's Newspapers in Education department, to
produce a four-page supplement which will appear
in all editions of the Leicester Mercury on one
day, in the week beginning 25 March.

As part of the project, I and a few others are
working as a sales and promotion team, and we
have been asked to promote sales of the paper
within the college.

Hinckley College are buying 200 copies to sell on
the campus. We feel that the most advantageous
way of promoting the paper would be to give away
a free gift with the paper. This is where you may
be able to help us and we may be able to help
you.

We would be grateful if you would consider
supplying us with approximately 200 units of a
product you seek to promote. Your product would
be promoted around the college and surrounding
area and your help would, of course, be
acknowledged within the publication itself, which
will be seen by over 317,000 people across
Leicestershire.

Thank you for your time. I look forward to
hearing from you.


Yours faithfully



Tim Philp

Sales & Promotions Manager

(Leicester Mercury - Newspaper in Education
Project)
```

Figure 12.2 A student's letter seeking sponsorship

Babies, and Walkers Snack Foods, who contributed crisps.

The *Leicester Mercury* provided the packaging in the form of carrier bags decorated with their logo. Therefore the **product** became more than just the newspaper – it consisted of three assorted savouries and sweets along with a copy of the *Leicester Mercury*. Because the promotional goods were donated to the project they could all be bundled together and given 'free' for the price of the newspaper. In return, the donating companies benefited from the publicity.

Activity

Working in your production team, choose a professional publication which is similar to yours and brainstorm all the places where it may be distributed and *how* it may be distributed: for example, to supermarkets, pubs and homes, through the post or by home delivery. Suggest other marketing activities that may appeal first to retailers and, secondly, to the customer.

Test audience response to print product

A sample audience can be gathered together and given examples of the product. You can carry out qualitative research by asking the sample group to give opinions through the use of discussion groups. A reasonable size for this sample would be approximately eight, but they would have to be carefully selected to make sure that they belong to the target audience. You will find parts of Chapter 23 useful for planning discussion groups.

Activity

Make use of the headings and discussion points listed below on pages 240 and 241 and use them to compile a questionnaire for use in obtaining audience responses.

Circulation figures for newspapers and magazines are continually monitored and the results are published in the NRS (National Readership Surveys) (see Unit 6, page 356). Audience satisfaction with newspapers and magazines can be assessed by the numbers of readers who renew their subscriptions.

Trends in book sales are also closely monitored. For example, Heinemann, the publisher of this book, asks teachers and lecturers to comment on educational books, and their views are carefully considered.

You can find out more about research techniques, such as interviewing, questionnaires and sampling, in Chapters 21 to 24.

Activity

Go to your local bookshop and ask for the list of the top ten sellers. Then go to your local library and find out who are the ten most popular authors of books loaned to the public.

Compare the two lists and identify similarities and differences. For example, do people prefer to buy, rather than to borrow, certain types of books?

Evaluate the success and quality of the product

The evaluation of your product should examine both the audience response to the content and appearance of the publication, and your own assessment. Again, this should be in terms of content and appearance, and should also be concerned with editorial objectives and how they may have affected the end result.

For example, did the editorial objectives limit or constrain any of the articles, or the style of the whole publication, in any way? Editorial control is necessary to ensure that the publication stays within guidelines imposed by legal and ethical constraints (discussed in the Legal and Ethical appendix), and conforms to the objectives in terms of its style and ethos (beliefs and values). Publications tend to embody certain values or attitudes, and an effective editorial policy will ensure that this comes through in the look as well as the content of the product.

You should also examine the effect of the production and editing process on the readability, style and presentation of individual articles and on the overall appearance of the product.

Finally, you should evaluate your product in comparison with an existing, professionally produced publication. For this it would be advisable to use the sample evaluation form shown here.

Evaluating Print Products

Name of your product ....

Name of professional/commercial product ....

Appearance
Comment on the following areas, where it is applicable to your particular type of publication. To make the exercise meaningful, you should ensure that you are comparing yours with a similar product. For each item you should state the quantity (e.g. how many columns) where appropriate, and the quality (i.e. which is the more effective and why).

Text	*Your product*	*Commercial product*
columns		
boxes		
lines		
white space		
bleed		
reverse out		
drop caps		
masthead		
headlines		
straplines		
runs ons		
captions		
cross heads		
turn lines		

Fonts
weight
leading
spacing
kerning

Visuals
text alignment
(left, centre, right)
margins
gutters
bleed
use of colour

Type of paper
ink/print

Activity

Using the checklist headings as prompts, comment generally on the overall appearance of both publications.

Content

In order to compare the content of your publication with a similar commercially/professionally produced product, it will be necessary to examine such features as article concepts, editing, style of writing, etc. You should, therefore, make comments on all content issues. To help you do this you should be asking yourself the questions which follow each point.

- **Language style and vocabulary**
  What kind of language was used? What was the style of the language and the type of words used? Were they long, complicated words, short and simple, using direct or indirect speech, formal, colloquial, slang?

- **Subject matter and its angle/treatment**
  Were the articles interesting and informative? Did they show topicality or relevance in terms of the product's target audience and its perceived fitness for purpose?

- **Legal and ethical issues**
  Did the content defame anybody or cause unnecessary offence? How were different social groups (e.g. old, young, male, female, black, white, able-bodied, disabled) represented? Was it fair or was there negative stereotyping? (See the Legal and Ethical appendix for more details.)

- **Choice of visuals**
  Was the content of the visuals interesting? Why did you choose, for example, a sketch or drawing (technically speaking, a drawing is to scale), rather than a photograph?

Audience response

The results of your focus groups, interviews, questionnaires and other means of obtaining feedback from an audience or potential audience, should be collated and evaluated.

All responses, whether qualitative or quantitative, should be put into a coherent format, such as clearly labelled graphs, tables and so on, and into a report which clearly picks out common points and trends, and any deviations.

Activity

Present your audience response findings to your group, in a manner that demonstrates you have carried out a substantive audience response survey and are able to interpret those responses and understand their implications.

Assess the effectiveness of the planning and production process

A review of the planning and production stages should be carried out. This should include assessments of how much research went into the different production techniques, how much they cost in terms of time, materials, money, etc. and whether these were, in fact, the most appropriate methods for the scale of the project. Some methods may well give a very finished and sophisticated appearance but may also be over-elaborate and expensive in terms of the resources required.

You should ask whether the product is fit for the purpose intended. This measure of fitness for purpose includes:

- was it targeted at the right audience?
- were the research, production and distribution methods appropriate to the nature of the product?
- were they commercially viable in terms of the costs which ensued and the price charged?
- was there product satisfaction – does it fulfil the brief?

Activity

In your group, discuss what was successful in the planning of the production and in the production process itself. What would you keep and what would you change if you carried out the same project again?

Evaluate individual and team roles in the production process

It is now time to look at the effectiveness of your contribution and that of the whole team.

241

The importance of feedback

When carrying out any form of evaluation it is most important that you do so in a *positive* and *objective* manner. By this, we mean that self-evaluation and group evaluation will involve the giving and receiving of **feedback**. All products and processes are subject to continual monitoring and reappraisal. This also applies to the work of the staff. There is always room for improvement. No self-respecting organisation allows itself to sit back and think that everything that is done and everyone who works there are beyond criticism.

Criticism can and should be healthy and constructive. If it does not take place it doesn't mean that there is nothing that can be improved – it could well be that people are afraid to speak up. A situation can arise in group cultures where members become too anxious to keep everyone happy because the group itself becomes more important than its tasks. It is, therefore, important that your tutor facilitates a group culture where feedback is 'de-personalised' and debate is honest and open.

Group working

When carrying out production activities you will mostly be working in groups. Working groups are a collection of individuals who have come together to carry out a particular project. It is quite natural for a certain amount of doubt and uncertainty to exist within a group in the early stages. Group members have to feel comfortable about the tasks and about each other before they can perform most effectively.

Try to recognise group forming as a natural process. In working situations you very often do not work with people because they are your friends. You may, of course, become friends but people are usually put together to carry out a task because it requires more than one person and may also require different skills and attributes. Groups have to develop cohesion and a sense of purpose and this may take time. (Obviously, this is also the case in a working situation where you do not choose your colleagues – they may become friends but also they may not!)

Positive attitudes

Having established the need for feedback, the next issue is to ensure that the feedback is beneficial rather than harmful both to the individual and to the organisation. It is therefore important that this feedback is positive and *constructive,* so allowing the individual and the group to learn where improvements could be achieved, without being made to feel foolish or embarrassed.

The most important point to remember is to focus on the task rather than on personalities. It is easy to stray from the point, and to end up making personal remarks.

Understanding that other members of the group are in a similar position to you will help you to empathise with them. Members of a production team can experience a whole range of negative emotions, such as feeling left out and ignored, feeling devalued (for example, by being given what they consider to be only the menial jobs), feeling 'put upon', i.e. given difficult tasks or given too much work, or feeling that others are not doing as much.

These points should help you to comment on the overall effectiveness of the project team. For example, with hindsight, were individuals matched to the most appropriate roles? What was communication like within the group – e.g. were all team members kept informed of plans, changes, etc.? What was the working atmosphere like? Was it busy, with the attitude generally purposeful, or were there any significant levels of apathy, complacency or lack of direction that pervaded the group or part of it?

When discussing these points with your team try to keep an even and open tone rather than getting angry, moody or sarcastic. Let other people have their say without interrupting them, and do not always try to have the last word!

Body language

You should not under-estimate the importance of the impression you give to others when you are giving and receiving feedback. We communicate not only with words. Non-verbal signals (body language) can be more powerful than the words you speak.

First of all you should get into a position where you can see and maintain eye contact with fellow group members. It is best not to adopt a 'defensive' posture, by sitting with your arms wrapped round you. Instead try to be 'open', with your hands in front, and arms and legs uncrossed. Keep a calm expression and try to adopt a relaxed but attentive and concerned attitude. Do not slouch, drawl or behave flippantly. It is important to show that you are listening and valuing what others are saying to you – even if you do not necessarily agree with it.

Of course, just because you are trying to be mature and constructive does not mean that everyone else is. But neither does this mean that you should retaliate in like fashion if they behave inappropriately. Instead, you should assert yourself by standing up for your rights, without violating the rights of others.

You can and should accept constructive criticism where it may be justified. Accepting that there may be truth in what another person is saying clears the air and should stop you becoming defensive. However, you should resist receiving or giving criticism that makes sweeping accusations or judgements on personality. Remember, this is a learning process and people have a right to make genuine mistakes, providing they are prepared to listen and learn from them.

(See also Chapter 16, page 279 and Chapter 20, page 338 on evaluation of roles.)

Activity

Try working your way through the self-evaluation checklist opposite. Use the checklist points as prompts in making extended comments.

Producing Print Products

Self-evaluation checklist

Your name ....

Name of your product...

Evaluate your performance in each of the following areas, using the scale given here:

5 = excellent, 4 = good, 3 = average, 2 = below average, 1 = poor

- [ ] attendance
- [ ] time-keeping
- [ ] reliability in completing tasks
- [ ] meeting deadlines
- [ ] self-motivation
- [ ] appearance (appropriate for the occasion, e.g. meeting advertisers)
- [ ] professional behaviour in dealing with clients, the public, etc.
- [ ] ability to work in a team
- [ ] ability to motivate others
- [ ] relationship with peers
- [ ] relationship with staff
- [ ] coping with pressure
- [ ] use of initiative
- [ ] liaison with team
- [ ] use of equipment

Comments

Activity

Now use the following form to carry out an evaluation of the whole group's performance. Again, you should use the 1 to 5 scale.

Producing Print Products

Group evaluation checklist

Your name...

Name of your product ....

Evaluate the group's performance, using the points listed to help you write out your comments.

☐ team spirit and attitude

☐ attendance, time-keeping and reliability

☐ organisation

☐ effectiveness

☐ relationship with staff

Comments

Finally...

If you are serious about studying or working in the media you will have to get used to giving and receiving a high level of critical scrutiny. Reflecting on and analysing their work is something that doesn't come easily to most people.

As mentioned earlier in the section on proof-reading, the vast majority of people do not check their work and do not examine it critically. It is, therefore, very easy to say that everything in your piece of work is satisfactory and nothing needs changing. This is very convenient because it means that you don't have to put any effort into revising or re-doing it. In fact, it is almost certainly wrong! There is very little in the world that would not benefit from some kind of improvement!

All work that is produced for public consumption requires continual checking and modification. You may have formed an impression from the media world that the work is effortless and an endless round of fun. The reality is that it can be hard and often tedious to keep working at something until it meets the standards identified in the product's specification. But the reward, if you get it right, is a product you can be proud of.

Evidence assignment

Write a report evaluating your print product in terms of:

■ the content of the article and its angle
■ its presentation, style and readability
■ the layout
■ how professional it is
■ the editorial objectives
■ comparison with other products
■ audience response.

The report should also assess the effectiveness of the planning and production processes, documenting the distribution process and evaluating your performance within the team.

Details of the methods used for audience testing can be kept in your production handbook. This work may also be used as evidence for Unit 6 Element 4 (Chapter 24).

Producing Print Products: Unit Test

1 You have an idea for a magazine article. What should be described in the proposal to the editor?
   a the photographs to be used
   b a suitable typeface for the text
   c whether the article is to be serious or amusing
   d the possible layout of the article

2 Which type of illustration would be most suitable in a page designed for toddlers in a mother and baby magazine?
   a watercolours
   b line drawings
   c cartoons
   d photographs

3 Why might a publisher decide to bring out an encyclopaedia in paperback rather than hardback?

   a it is lighter for people to take on holiday
   b it is cheaper for students to buy
   c it will be more durable
   d bookshops prefer to stock paperbacks

4 From which source will a journalist obtain regular information about road accidents?
   a the general public
   b the editorial team
   c radio news
   d the emergency services

5 A film star has committed a crime. Which of these is a primary source of information?
   a a telephone interview with the star
   b a press agency report
   c television news showing the arrest
   d a film in which the star appears

6 Which of the following is **most** likely to be given a double page spread in the centre of a tabloid newspaper?
   a the Duchess of Kent opens a flower show
   b a child genius goes to Oxford University
   c a politician has an affair with a film star
   d exciting new recipes for summer meals

7 What is needed to design the layout of newspaper and magazines for each edition?
   a the specification

   b a proposal
   c a schedule
   d a grid

8 Which of these will be the first to be placed on a newspaper page?
   a the hard news stories
   b feature articles
   c advertisements
   d headlines

9 In newspaper production, which of the following cannot be altered within four hours of the paper being on the streets?
   a the time of the print run
   b the number of photographs to be used
   c the positioning of copy on the page
   d the content of the hard news stories

10 Which of the following pieces of text has been fully justified?
   a   Media: Communication & Production GNVQ is designed to provide opportunities for students to understand and analyse the professional practice found in media industries, and to develop the knowledge, conceptual frameworks and practical skills which underpin them
   b   Media: Communication & Production GNVQ is designed to provide opportunities for students to understand and analyse the professional practice found in media industries, and to develop the knowledge, conceptual frameworks and practical skills which underpin them
   c   Media: Communication & Production GNVQ is designed to provide opportunities for students to understand and analyse the professional practice found in media industries, and to develop the knowledge, conceptual frameworks and practical skills which underpin them
   d   Media: Communication & Production GNVQ is designed to provide opportunities for students to understand and analyse the professional practice found in media industries, and to develop the knowledge, conceptual frameworks and practical skills which underpin them

11 What is the space between facing pages known as?
   a a border
   b a margin
   c a gutter
   d a box

12 Which of the following fonts would be suitable for the newsletter of a society for science fiction fans?
 a Space Travellers
 b Space Travellers
 c Space Travellers
 d Space Travellers

13 Which of these will use the largest number of columns?
 a a magazine
 b a newspaper
 c a textbook
 d a comic

14 What is the duty of a sub-editor?
 a to write headlines
 b to choose the masthead
 c to write the editorial
 d to position the adverts

15 What is the responsibility of the editor?
 a to crop and scale photographs
 b to choose the lead story
 c to write the larger features
 d to supervise the print run

16 The house style of a publication should be consistent. What does this mean for a newspaper?
 a all articles have the same number of words, e.g. a hard news story will have 200 words
 b illustrations are all the same size, e.g. 4 cm by 5 cm
 c certain words are always spelt the same way, e.g. mic not mike
 d only one font can be used throughout, e.g. Times Roman

17 The picture editor wants to use only a part of a photograph and indicates this by a box. What is this technique called?
 a cropping
 b sequencing
 c cut-out
 d scaling

18 A photograph needs a few words to explain what it is about. This is known as:
 a a title-line
 b a sub-heading
 c a caption
 d a quote

Questions 19-24 relate to the following piece of text from *The Mayor of Casterbridge* by Thomas Hardy. Read it carefully and answer the following questions.

Behind the bench was a little promenade under the wall were[1] people some times[2] walked instead of on the gravel. The bench seemed to be touched by something; she looked round, and a face was bending over her, the face of the young woman she had seen yesterday.
Elizabeth-jane[3] looked confounded for a moment, knowing she had been overhead, though there was pleasure in her confusion. Yes, I heard you,[4] said the lady, in a vivacious voice, answering her look. 'What can have happened'[5]

19 What word should be used at (1)?
 a were
 b we're
 c wear
 d where

20 Which proof reading sign should be used to show that sometimes, at (2), should be one word?

21 Which of these is correct at (3)?
 a Elizabeth-jane
 b Elisabeth-jane
 c elizabeth-jane
 d Elizabeth-Jane

22 At (4), what punctuation is needed?
 a Yes; I heard you
 b 'Yes I heard you'
 c 'Yes, I heard you,'
 d 'Yes'. I heard you

23 At (5), how should the last sentence end?
 a happened!'
 b happened?'
 c happened.'
 d happened'?

24 After it has been typeset, the text needs to be edited because the last word, 'happened', is an orphan. What does this mean?
 a it is all on its own on the next page
 b there should not be a new paragraph after it
 c it needs to be made smaller to fit the page
 d it is the wrong word and needs replacing

25 You have to enter the print room when a print run is underway. What safety precaution should you take?
    a wear goggles
    b wear flat shoes
    c don't try to talk
    d wear ear defenders

26 Why might a magazine publisher invite a selected group of readers to discuss the latest edition?
    a to ask them which other magazines they read
    b to find out which sections they enjoy and why
    c to investigate the lifestyle of readers
    d to find out how many times they have bought the magazine

27 How can a newspaper editor compare the success of her publication with that of rivals?
    a through questionnaires to readers
    b by interviewing a sample of newsagents
    c by reading other publications
    d by consulting official statistics on sales

28 Which of these is the **best** indicator of the success of a book?
    a a revised edition has been printed
    b it has had good reviews in broadsheet newspapers
    c it has made a large profit
    d there are no similar books on the market

29 Which of these should you check to assess the **quality** of your product?
    a whether you kept within the budget
    b the readability of the text
    c how many people read the publication
    d whether it was produced on time

30 You chose screen printing rather than offset lithography to produce a poster for a college gig. What evidence will you give to your team to show that this was the right method to choose?
    a that it was much cheaper
    b that it was better for large runs
    c that it was most suitable for A2 sizes
    d that it produced better-quality graphics

This unit will allow you to put the planning skills you learnt in Chapter 9 into practice. Individual audio items such as a mini-play, advertisement, news broadcast, etc. *can now be brought together by a production team and made into a complete programme, of which those individual items could form a part.*

Plan the production process

As in Chapter 7, you will need to become familiar with the equipment that is described here and in Chapter 14. As a rule of thumb, the individual members of a team should each be responsible for approximately five minutes of an audio broadcast. A production team of four would therefore be expected to produce a 20-minute programme. For example, your production team could make a 'magazine' programme with current affairs items, interviews, news, weather and traffic reports. On the other hand you may want to consider a music station format with DJ introductions and comments, promos (for example, promotions of bands' tour dates and venues, or films), celebrity interviews, news, weather and traffic reports. Any music selections should last no more than 20 seconds each and consist essentially of the presenter's introduction, a fade up to a few seconds of the music and then a fade out or the ending.

Agree the programme brief and carry out any necessary research

Programme research

Let us first look at a particular radio programme and the radio station which broadcasts it. This should help to illustrate all the factors such as the resources (budget, time, personnel, equipment, materials), the research, fitness for purpose and target audience, and the legal and ethical issues which have to be taken into account when planning and making a programme.

Case study – Radio Leicester and the *Talkback* programme

BBC Radio Leicester is a speech-based public service station serving the county of Leicestershire. It came on air in 1967, making it the first station in the BBC's local area network.

In those days individual BBC local radio stations had a lot of freedom to choose their own formats and many of them were not that different from the music-based independent local radio stations such as Radio City. However, deregulation has made broadcasting far more competitive and BBC local radio has differentiated its product by concentrating on speech-based programmes. Conversely, ILR has conceded that talk radio is something which the BBC does best and they therefore concentrate on music. The financial implications of speech-based radio are also a factor. It is significantly cheaper to put on a record than to have someone (a journalist or presenter) putting resources into researching and discussing a topic, often with studio guests, and perhaps OB (Outside Broadcast) facilities etc.

BBC local radio therefore has the challenge of delivering a cost-effective product in the face of competition from ILR which has fewer overheads and a product ('music') which is assumed to be the 'natural' choice of the 15–45 age group. The answer, as far as Radio Leicester is concerned, is not to regard the local ILR station as in competition with it, but rather to think of the one as complementing the other. At the same time, Radio Leicester has to work at attracting the younger members of the community, whilst not losing their established listeners.

We will now look at the station's programming schedule and see whether it reflects the diversity of a multi-cultural city like Leicester and the mixture of small textile and market towns, farming and old coal-mining communities that form the county of Leicestershire.

PROGRAMMING SCHEDULE

- 0600–0900 *Good Morning Leicester* is a programme that deals with both local and national events from a Leicestershire perspective. It is strong on information services, such as traffic and travel news, and also has a 'diary' service of what's going on in the area.
- 0900–1200 *Talkback* is a live programme of topical debate and discussion. Although the public can access from 0845 until midday, the 0900–1000 slot is dedicated to phone-ins. Thereafter it is studio guests, roundtable discussions and outside broadcasts (OB). We will examine this particular programme in some depth below.
- 1200–1400 The midday programme offers accessibility to the audience for help and advice on a wide range of consumer issues. There are in-depth interviews with local people and it also accommodates the lunchtime news. The programme incudes a variety of light features such as 'Flash-back', 'All Abroad' and a general knowledge quiz.
- 1400–1700 The mid-afternoon programme covers all sorts of local events and topical issues, using OB to give that 'on location' immediacy to an event. Because of the time-scale, the programme has quite a wide age range. For example, in the late afternoon there are younger listeners who have come home from school and college. The programme tries to address this audience with features of family interest. Between 4 and 5 pm the programme acknowledges 'drive time' (rush hour) by providing increased travel bulletins.
- 1700–1900 *Leicestershire Tonight* reflects the day's main local, national and international news. It carries a large amount of live material on topical issues and provides a complete service of local information, which includes traffic and travel news

TALKBACK

We can now look at one programme in detail. As already indicated, *Talkback* is a phone-in programme devoted to news and topical features. It can be serious or light according to the topics discussed.

The programme goes on air at 0900. The first hour is a dedicated phone-in session and the lines are open from 0845, helped by **trails** put out during *Good Morning Leicester*. Trails are short pieces aimed at promoting something later on in a future programme or later in the same programme. Radio Leicester is always trailing ahead as a key element in the policy of continually inviting the public to look ahead with the station so they can be tempted, by attractive-sounding snippets, to stay tuned to Radio Leicester.

By 0800 *Talkback's* producer, Helen Beevers, is checking through the **running order**. This is a list of the topics for the day and how they will be covered.

The running order was prepared the afternoon before but it will be only a partial list of the activities. The producer wants to make the programme as 'up-to-the-minute' as possible so the search for a good story is never-ending, and is pursued right up until the end of the programme.

News is breaking all the time and Helen, along with presenter John Florance and researcher Claire Somerby, is involved with trawling through the newspapers and checking Ceefax and other on-line news coming through from news agencies. These include 'Rip and Read', the BBC's local radio news service which comes through and is displayed on VDU. It is Helen's job to access the newsworthiness of items and find the ones with a Leicestershire angle. John is interested in anything topical and relevant which could make interesting talk points.

News comes from numerous information sources. It can be from the emergency services, the general public, news agencies or even other news reports, whether in the press, on television or other radio stations. The point is to adapt the stories in order to make them interesting and relevant to the target audience. Very often it is a national story, but the newsroom or programme team will look for the local angle that will make it more relevant to local people. Topics chosen for today include school governors, local water quality, National Bike Week, and two huge local beech trees which are to be felled this morning after being struck by disease.

Meanwhile, preparations are well under way for *Talkback* to go on air. John Florance visits the *Good Morning Leicester* programme and trails his own show by saying who and what will be on and inviting phone-in contributions.

Already calls have started to come in. Each is logged and given a telephone line. The caller can then be rung back by the press of a button when it is his or her turn. At about the same time, the calls are typed into a computerised facility called **Visual Talkback**. The details of the caller and the topic are typed on to VDU and appear simultaneously on a similar screen in front of John in the studio. He then has some indication of what the call is about and can prepare himself mentally for it!

The presenter (and sometimes the producer) also has to write the cues. In this context, a **cue** is an introduction to one of the features in the running order. More specifically, the term is used to describe an introduction to a story read by a presenter before handing over to a reporter at the scene. For example, the 1045 slot involved a link up with reporter Jane Hesketh in the radio car at the spot where the beech trees were to be felled. Helen wrote the cue for John to introduce Jane and her report.

After the 0900 news and AA Roadwatch John starts to deal with the phone-in contributions. As John is talking to a caller, the next on the list is rung back and held in the queue until John brings him or her in. The programme is live and John, Helen and Claire must continually keep up the pace, getting the calls through, trailing for more of them and using other potential stories for later on in the programme.

John has to concentrate all the time in these situations because not only is he listening and responding to the present caller, he is also quickly reading about the next calls that are queuing in the system. The topics can change very rapidly and John has to use a lot of mental agility to keep on top of the different topics that people want to talk about.

Helen meanwhile has been informed that the first studio guests are in reception and brings them down to the studio. They sit in the production area, are helped to feel at ease and briefed about the procedure.

John is dealing with his last call and then cues the news, which is read from a different studio. In the meantime, the guests are shown into the studio by Helen where they are greeted by John.

Following the news and AA Roadwatch, John comes back on air, introducing his guests and leading a 'roundtable' discussion on school governors.

As the roundtable discussion is finishing, Helen brings down the next studio guest. She then accompanies the previous guests from the studio and has a quick word before they leave. The new guest is settling in while John plays some pre-recorded trails. By pre-recording these before he went on air he is able to take a breather whilst also giving Helen time to bring guests in and out.

Just then Jane in the radio car calls to report her arrival on location for the story about the beech trees. A quick equipment test gives the station the sound of chain saws coming through from location. John then cues Jane, who gives an on-the-spot report and interviews experts.

News in studio 4

After Jane gives her **outro**, news is cued, followed by a slot called the CSV action desk (about Community

service Volunteers), which outlines the voluntary activities taking place or needed in the community. Meanwhile, in response to trails given out since the day before, calls are being taken for the later features and guests.

At last John winds up the interview with his final guest and cues Peter Maas, a *Washington Post* journalist who has just written a book about his experiences during the Yugoslavian conflict. The interviewee is in London but the station is using ISDN (Integrated Service Digital Network) which gives studio quality sound, as if the guest is present in the studio. ISDN replaces telephone lines and can carry all sorts of data: voice, computer transmissions, music and video.

As John wraps up his discussion he trails for tomorrow's *Talkback* before giving an outro and cueing the midday news.

Claire's *Talkback* role has now ended for the day but Helen must keep on organising tomorrow's programme. She has some arrangements already in place, such as a 'round-table' discussion with representatives of four major housing estates in Leicester. Other features for tomorrow will include 'Are young people letting themselves down at interview?' and 'Are references any good?'

Now look at some examples of intros and links from a show aimed at a younger market (see box below).

- *INTRO*
  Good evening to you on this wet and cold Friday, the 11th of February, David Harris with you through till nine o'clock on BBC Radio Leicester's *Friday FM*.

- *TRAIL (PROMO)*
  Have we got an action-packed show for you tonight, with **your** chance to win record tokens, Radio Leicester goodie bags, and we have two pairs of tickets to see *Air America*.

Also, how about saying hello to someone? The dedication line will be open soon, and, as usual, we'll have the gigs guide – all on Friday FM 104.9 and 95.1 FM Stereo.

Now for your chance to win those record tokens, Radio Leicester goodie bags or two pairs of tickets for *Air America* in Radio Leicester's Cinema Competition.

Are you ready?

Which of these films hasn't had a remake?

a *The Fly*
b *Bonnie and Clyde*
c *A Star is Born*

Which of these films had the biggest audience?

a *For Your Eyes Only*
b *Jaws*
c *Raiders of the Lost Ark*

Which country produces the most films each year?

a USA
b India
c Australia

Answers on a postcard please to David Harris, Cinema Competition, Friday FM, BBC Radio Leicester.

■ Time for the *weather*...

■ *OUTRO*
Thanks for listening. If you would like to drop me a line about the competition or gig guide then write to .... Bye for now and I'll be back in seven days' time for the next **Friday FM on BBC Radio Leicester**.

Ideas

Other ideas for a show can include:

■ looking at the same date as today's in past years, for example one year, five years or ten years ago today.
■ devising a 'guess the year quiz' where clues from the records played, films made in that year and significant events are all given out throughout a show. The idea is for listeners to phone in before a certain time (perhaps five minutes before the end of the show) when the answer will be given out.

Planning a programme brief

Now that you have examined a programme in detail, and looked at some other styles and ideas, you can start planning your own programme. You should already have two scripts prepared from your planning work in Chapter 7. These scripts will consist of a piece of fiction material such as a radio play, and a non-fiction item, for example, DJ's dialogue, the news, a documentary, interview or quiz. You should then build these scripts into the rest of the production process, which we will now look at.

First, the programme brief or proposal has to be drawn up. You will already have investigated the ideas for the brief. These now need to be agreed with the rest of the production team. You will also have to agree on the recording format (cassette, reel-to-reel or DAT tape, or hard disk). See pages 256–8 on technical requirements to help make your decisions.

You may wish to go for a station with a mix of talk and music programmes, such as Catalunya Radio, based in Barcelona.

Study the Catalunya Radio schedule on page 252 closely. As you can see there is a lot of variety, both in Catalunya Radio's schedule and within the individual programmes. The policy here is to try to appeal to as much of the community as possible, in some cases within the individual programmes, and certainly within the day's schedule. You can learn more about this 'mix of products' in Unit 7.

Activity

Make a list of different types of programme content you can think of. There is, for example, a variety of pop and rock music, some of which is light chart music and others which you could term 'alternative' or 'indie'. There are also classical and blues, as well as numerous non-musical items.

Choose three programme types that you would be interested in developing further and give your reasons. You may, for example, be interested in researching and producing a children's programme, or one that is dedicated to sport.

Different formats

You will need to carry out some research into different programme formats. You should, therefore, listen to various radio broadcasts to get an idea of the different types and styles of programme. For example, if you want to produce a programme with sport and current affairs then Radio Five ('Five Live') would be a useful station to listen to at various *different* times of the day. To do this effectively you will need to obtain a copy of their schedule.

Make a recording of an example of the type of programme you are interested in. Analyse the programme in terms of its style and content. To do this you should re-create its running order or schedule. For an example of this see the running order for the music programme in Chapter 3 (page 67) or the schedule for the Radio Leicester *Talkback* programme. Identify the characteristics in terms of length, sound/music, vocabulary, tone and pace. Decide what characteristics of this programme (or programmes) you wish your group programme to embody, and where you would like to modify it or substitute your own ideas.

251

Time	Programme	Presenter	Schedule
06.06	SOL SOSTINGUT	Carmina Malagarriga	A 'wake up' programme for the weekend, based on a combination of classical music, weather and news.
08.06	ROTLLANA OBERTA	Dolors Busquets/Josep Ventura	All about 'sardanes' (the popular Catalan folk dance).
09.00	DE BOCA A BOCA	Llorenç Torrado	The cuisine and gastronomy programme. Listeners' recipes and knowledge are welcome in this programme, hosted by a well-known gastronome and food critic.
10.00	EL SUPLEMENT	Xavier Solà	The weekend magazine with quiz games, interviews, music and light entertainment.
13.06	L'ÀUDIO CLIP		
13.10	CATACRAC	Jordi Tenas	All about the pop and rock music made in the Catalan language. News and music.
14.00	L'INFORMATIU MIGDIA	Jordi Corbalan	Noon newscast.
14.30	L'ESPORT AL PUNT	Pere Flores	Sports news.
15.06	CALIDOSCOPI	Àngela Llaona, Mariona Anglès, Narcís Vives i Xavier Àvila	Addressed to children of 10–13. The listeners can take part in the actual making of the programme through an electronic mailbox on the Internet.
16.06	TARDA TARDÀ	Jordi Tardà	Long-format music show with information about international pop and rock music. Concerts, auditions, exclusive interviews and premieres of not-yet-released new songs.
19.06	DIA A DIA, ROCK A ROCK	Jordi Tardà	A complete and detailed history of rock and roll. With the details of political and social events taking place at every given moment. Broadcast of rare vintage materials.
20.00	L'INFORMATIUS DEL VESPRE	Jordi Corbalan	Evening news.
20.30	FORÇA ESPORTS	Pere Flores	Sports news.
21.06	TRANSMISSIONS ESPORTIVES		Live coverage of football matches and other events.
22.06	T'AGRADA EL BLUES?	Quico Pi de la Serra	Blues music presented by one of Catalonia's most popular musicians and song writers. Selected blues pieces from Pi de la Serra's private collection.
23.06	LA FINESTRA INDISCRETA	Àlex Gorina	The cinema programme, hosted by a prestigious critic. With reviews for the new releases, interviews, festival reports, etc.
01.06	TRES QUARTS DE MIG	Jordi Vendrell	The presenter and guests philosophise about a particular fact of life from contrasted points of view.
02.06	EL SOTERRANI	Xavier Escuder, David Talleda i Ignasi Julià	Music show featuring broadcasts, news and interviews on independent, unlisted rock music.
04.06	T'AGRADA EL BLUES?	Quico Pi de la Serra	Rerun of the programme.
05.06	DIA A DIA, ROCK A ROCK	Jordi Tardà	Rerun of the programme.

Your research should include background material about the various topics you are covering. Interesting little snippets of information about a band, a film, a sports personality, etc. are always handy to have and can give you the opportunity to project your personality. Admittedly, this is not always possible on format radio where all the output sounds much the same. Even if you do not use it all, a radio presenter needs to have enough material to tide him or her over in the event of an unexpected hitch.

Agreeing and producing the brief

Once you have carried out your own individual analysis and made your choice for a particular type of programme, you will have to justify it to the rest of the production team. The team will then have to come to a decision on the choice of programme that is to go forward into production.

At the same time that you have been researching and agreeing the brief, you should have also been carrying out research on the time, materials, financial resources and equipment required to produce your product. Obviously, it is pointless agreeing a particular type of programme if its resource requirements are outside your range. Ideas regarding your resource requirements should be gleaned from the information on equipment here and in Chapter 14.

Once the production team has reached agreement, you will need to obtain the go-ahead from your 'client'. This may be your tutor or somebody else who is commissioning a production, within the constraints imposed by specifications regarding resources, fitness for purpose and target audience.

To do this you should produce a brief (sometimes referred to as *proposal, specification* or *treatment*) such as the one from which this extract was taken. This gives an idea of the kind of programme you have in mind:

We have decided that our show will be a lively and bubbly morning show, similar to Chris Evans's, with a 'chit-chatty' air to it. We have also picked music which is from the '80s to the present day. We have decided to include such things as news/weather, a request line and a promotion for a party. As well as these we have traffic and travel, and some adverts.

To be able to create the right mood for the show the DJ (which is me) has to have the right voice to wake people up in the morning. I listen to the radio a lot to hear the way other DJs sound.

Equipment
Keyboards: Yamaha PSR 150 – for jingles, adverts
                 Yamaha PSR 300

$2 \times$ uni-directional microphones and stands

Panasonic CD/tape player – music

Fostex four-channel multitrack recorder – for mixing the different ingredients of items e.g. jingles

Coomber cassette recorder – to master from the 4-track

Tascam two-track open-reel tape recorder – for editing

Develop and mark up scripts for production

Examples of various forms of 'script' have been produced in Chapter 7 and on page 254 below and page 271 in Chapter 14. These are 'marked up' according to certain industry conventions in radio and sound production that you should follow. This allows everybody involved in the production to anticipate what is to happen next and to understand the 'marks' on the script.

Selector			
Number	Title	Artist	Intro/Run/End
00:00	News/Sport/Weather		4.00
A023	Try Me Out	Corona	D-90's-Chart
	Stuck on U	PJ & Duncan	P-90's-Chart
	Humpin' Around	Bobby Brown	D-90's-Chart
	Some Might Say	Oasis	R/H-90's-Chart
18:37	Adbreak		
	Always on my Mind	Pet Shop Boys	P-80's-
	Things that Make ...	C&C Music Fact	D-90's-
	Should I Stay ...	The Clash	I-80's-
32:14	Adbreak		
	I Need Your Lovin'	Baby D	R/J-90's-
	This Time	Donna Summer	P-80's-
	Think of You	Whigfield	D-90's-Chart
	Love in an Elevator	Aerosmith	R/H-80's
45:42	Adbreak		
	The Only Way is Up	Yazz	D-80's-
	Gonna Make You ...	Inner Circle	P-90's-
55:26	Adbreak to news		

Figure 13.1 A playlist generated by Selector

TIME	LINK	BREAK/JINGLE	DISC
00	NEWS	NEWS	NEWS
04	WEATHER	WEATHER BED	CORONA
	NO LINK HERE	PRESENTER'S CHOICE/ZAP	PJ & DUNCAN
	NO LINK HERE	NO JINGLE	BOBBY BROWN
	PRESENTER'S CHOICE	PRESENTER'S CHOICE	OASIS
18:37	AD BREAK	AD BREAK	AD BREAK
	NO LINK HERE	JINGLE	PET SHOP BOYS
	TRAFFIC & TRAVEL	TRAVEL BED	C&C MUSIC
	COMPETITION	PRESENTER'S CHOICE	THE CLASH
32:14	AD BREAK	AD BREAK	AD BREAK
	NO LINK HERE	JINGLE	BABY D
	COMP. CALLER	SHORT ZAP	DONNA SUMMER
	NO LINK HERE	PRESENTER'S CHOICE	WHIGFIELD
	NO LINK HERE	JINGLE	AEROSMITH
45:42	AD BREAK	AD BREAK	AD BREAK
	WHAT'S ON &/OR HELLOS	PRESENTER'S CHOICE	YAZZ
	BACK ANNOUNCE	NO JINGLE	INNER CIRCLE
55:26	AD BREAK	AD BREAK	AD BREAK
	NEWS LINK & BED	NEWS JINGLE	
00	NEWS	NEWS	NEWS

Figure 13.2 Plan of a music programme

The script for the radio play has 'marks' incorporated in it, and you can also see that there are numerous conventions attached to how the news bulletins are constructed.

Another example of a script is of a playlist for a music show that is generated by a computer programme called 'Selector'. The programme controller will key in certain parameters, such as the type of show, time, target audience, etc. and the computer will produce a playlist such as the example in Figure 13.1. For more details of this, see Unit 7.

We can also look at an example of how a music radio programme is compiled. Look at Figure 13.2 above. It details how the DJ has planned out the show for an hour.

The time, given in minutes and seconds past the hour is in the left-hand column. Next come the **links**. These include anything speech-based between the music. So, for example, the news would be a 'link', as would a 'promo' (otherwise known as a **trail**, e.g. 'what's coming up next'). **Jingles** or other

FADE UP Now for further radio chat. Our roving reporter DENNIS BUTTWORTHY took to the streets of Hilltown today to find out what you think about COMMUNITY RADIO coming to YOUR town.

(*vox pops*)

THANKS FOR THAT DENNIS and if you have any more comments you wish to add just give us your call on.... double 2 double 2 double 2 your LOCAL MUSIC MIX on RADIO LOADED.

FADE UP Music

CROSS FADE Coming soon to Radio Loaded, LIVE in concert Mr PAUL CALF. Hear his sensitive side....

CLIP 'It's not how they are on the outside.'

Hear him talk unashamedly about sex...

CLIP 'I'll say sex.'

Hear his sadness as he talks about how he's planning to win back the love he's lost...

CLIP 'I will change!'

That's Paul Calf, alias Steve Coogan, LIVE next SATURDAY EVENING, 10 o'clock. Now LISTEN in.

FADE

special effects are usually on cartridge (see Chapter 14), so they can be fired instantaneously by the DJ.

As a further example we can take a look at how a student's script for introducing a 'vox pop' and a 'promo' (trail) was marked up (see previous page).

The directions in CAPS are there to indicate where the presenter must emphasise a particular part of the script. In local radio this will include building in and emphasising the city, town or locality to make it sound relevant and interesting to local people.

There are also intros and outros where a topic or presenter signs on or off. In addition there is the **SOC (Standard Out Cue)**, which occurs when reporters identify themselves, their location and their station at the end of a report. For example: 'This is Annette Lee, Victoria Park, for Leicester Sound.'

The **cue** will introduce the topic, as we have seen with the news, vox-pop and promo examples. The cross fade, as described in Chapter 7 (page 174), involves two sounds – one being faded up and the other faded down. On a music station this often involves a **bed** and a **voice-over**. The bed means a music bed, usually of the instrumental opening or closing of a record. The voice-over is the presenter's voice laid over that bed.

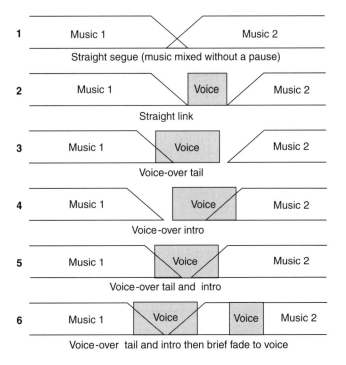

Figure 13.3 Types of cross fade – music and voice-overs

The illustrations in Figure 13.3 give various examples of how this can be done.

Activity

Choose a piece of music which is a suitable bed onto which you can lay a voice-over. Practise and record this, using the following example as a guideline:

- Choose a twin-tape player/recorder or CD player/tape recorder with a microphone socket
- Insert tape or CD for playback and tape for recording
- Connect microphone
- Press record button and play back the tape/CD
- Say voice-over
- Stop and play back recording.

It takes practice to pace your delivery in order to fit in what you want to say, without clipping the start of the vocals or the main body of the music.

Identify and secure resources for production

Budgets

Radio stations and their individual programmes are subject to certain financial constraints. Commercial radio obtains the vast majority of its income from advertising and sponsorship, whereas the public service broadcasting offered by the BBC raises its money from the licence fee charged to television owners. Neither sector has the luxury of unlimited amounts of money. Instead they are given a budget. An example of the budget for Radio Leicester, and its *Talkback* programme, is listed below.

From this you can see that the costs can be quite involved. Even a speech-based station like Radio Leicester pays £75,000 in rights clearances for music copyright!

A further example of budget implications can be seen in Chapter 7, where the cost of producing a commercial is shown.

Resources

Apart from the budget, you will need to consider equipment, materials, studio time and pre-recorded sources. Equipment and materials are dealt with below, on pages 257–63.

255

Radio Leicester Budget for 1996/7

The total budget for Radio Leicester is £1.96 million, of which £1.54 million is spent on the FM service, which provides the mainstream programming, and the Asian service (operating on the AM frequency). 54 per cent is spent on staff. There are 37 full-time staff and the hours worked by the approximately 60 freelance personnel take this to an equivalent of 52 full-time staff. Each person produces an average of 177 hours of output every year. This works out as 9204, although the plan for 1996/7 is for 9169 hours of output, of which 5194 will be broadcast on the FM service and 3975 on AM.

There are 219,000 listeners to the station. The cost per hour of providing the FM service is £217.

The overheads (costs) are as follows:

Staff wages and freelance fees	£1,065,332
Staff training	£35,000
Playing music. A fee has to be paid to the Performing Rights Society (PRS) for most music played (see Legal & Ethical appendix)	£75,000
Property charges (rent and rates)	£100,000

Talkback's **costs (i.e. share of the budget) are as follows:**

The programme's duration	– 3 hrs per day
It is on five days a week	– 15 hrs per week
Hours per year (after taking into account certain days when it isn't broadcast)	– 715 hrs per year

Staff costs per year:	– £93,000

- presenter
- producer
- news reporter
- RPA

Apart from the presenter and producer, nobody else works exclusively for the *Talkback* programme. For example, the RPA carries out other duties in the afternoon. These costs therefore have to be calculated as proportions of their equivalent full-time functions.

Overheads:	£37,000

These are as listed for the overall station budget, and include:
Studios and other facilities, for example OB (radio car or van)
Rent and rates
Central BBC costs include:

- lawyers who provide the legal framework for operating a public broadcasting service – they give legal advice on the content of broadcast material
- libraries which provide a wealth of research material
- news information services.

These overheads are part of the budget allocated to *Talkback*. They are a proportion of the overall station overheads.

Total *Talkback* budget per year – £130,000

By dividing the total number of hours (715) by the total programme budget (£130,000) we find that the cost per hour of producing the programme is approximately £182.

Figure 13.4 An example of a radio station budget

Pre-recorded sources for sound effects and jingles or signature tunes are known as **grams**, because they were originally stored on gramophone records, although they are now nearly always stored on one of the tape formats, CDs or computer. These are a valuable resource which either have to be produced in-house or bought in, with implications for copyright issues and costs. You can find out about copyright legislation and how it applies to music or sound effects in the Legal and Ethical appendix.

Studio time also has to be booked, or at least its cost taken into account. Like all resources it is not 'free' and should not be taken for granted. In practice, the cost would be worked out from the business rent and rates, telephone, heating and lighting costs charged to the studio owner (whether it is a radio station or a recording studio for bands), the cost of personnel and the cost of hiring/buying, maintaining and replacing equipment. Thus the cost of the studio for the *Talkback* programme is calculated as a percentage of the overall station costs, plus its specific additional requirements. In a commercial or professional environment there is generally a heavy demand on studio and equipment time. You should take this into account when planning your own productions. Equipment and studio time should be pre-booked and properly logged, using a form such as the one in Figure 13.5. This can be used to help assess your planning.

Identify technical requirements for production

Tape is still the main means of recording, although computer disk is becoming increasingly common. Computers can also act as sequencers. These are devices which allow you to put together different sounds, manipulate them and put them into various sequences. The Atari has MIDI connectors built in. MIDI stands for Musical Instrument Digital Interface and it is used for connecting digitised sounds from sources such as keyboards, synthesisers and samplers. Recordings are also stored on vinyl (although this is becoming obsolete), mini-disc and CD, which until recently had just the ROM (Read Only Memory) capability but is now evolving into CDi (interactive), which means we now have another recording medium.

Equipment booking form

Student name...

Date...

Time ....

For what purpose do you need the equipment/room?

....

Equipment needed:

....

....

....

....

Room needed:

....

Has equipment been returned? If so, on what date? ....

Has room been locked where appropriate?...................................

Has all equipment, including microphones, been switched off?.......

Have there been any problems with the equipment? ....

....

....

....

Figure 13.5 Equipment and studio time should be booked and logged carefully

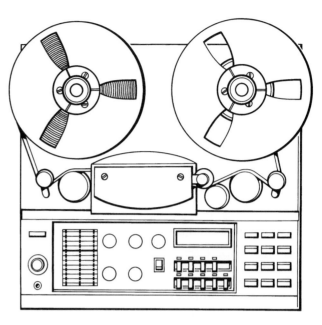

Figure 13.6 A reel-to-reel tape deck

that it uses up tape more quickly, so although you should ideally aim for the highest quality, you should ensure that you have enough tape to record it all! A speed of 7.5 ips produces a satisfactory result, and one reel will last 15 minutes at this speed.

DAT quality is excellent, as its recording process is based on the same principle as the CD (compact disc) but with the added advantage of being able to record onto it. CDi (interactive) is now becoming

Tape formats

Tape comes in various formats. **Reel-to-reel (open-reel)** tape is still used extensively in radio stations and recording studios, although DAT (Digital Audio Tape) and computer hard disk recordings are becoming increasingly common. Advantages of reel-to-reel tape include the high sound quality and its ease of editing, which will be discussed in Chapter 15.

For robustness and flexibility, the Uher reel-to-reel tape recorder is still hard to beat – and it is portable, although the Sony Walkman Professional is very compact and offers good quality for a cassette format.

The speed which the machine records at is either 7.5 or 15 ips (inches per second). The faster the tape speed, the better the quality. However, this means

Figure 13.7 A Uher reel-to-reel portable recorder

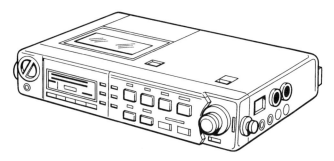

Figure 13.8 A portable DAT recorder

more common, so this will become a recording as well as a playback medium in the future.

Cassette tapes don't generally have the same quality but they are convenient. They are the commonest form of storage for a master copy of a recording produced by non-professionals. It is in this format that you are most likely to store your evidence for assessment purposes. It is probable that recordings will be made on reel-to-reel or DAT, and a copy of the master will be stored on cassette.

Another interesting medium is **video tape**. It may appear strange for audio products, but making use of a video tape's sound track gives good results. Many VCRs are designed to act as audio recorders and have 'mic' and 'line' inputs. The tape will also record for longer. It can give up to eight hours continuous recording if you use an E240 tape on LP (long play). This would not generally be a suitable length and speed, however. First, the tape would be relatively thin and therefore more susceptible to damage, especially if continually re-used. Secondly, as we have already indicated, the slower the tape speed as it passes the recording head the poorer the resultant sound quality. If the purpose, however, is to have a recording of output as a legal requirement of radio stations (see Legal and Ethical appendix), then it is very convenient. This medium is chosen by Radio Leicester to fulfil legal obligations.

Features

All professional (portable or studio) tape recorders, whether reel-to-reel, cassette or DAT, have the means of monitoring and controlling sound levels, input sockets for mikes and headphones and a battery check meter. Whilst all recorders have the means to monitor and playback through headphones, the Uher also has an integral amplifier and loudspeaker. The DAT and Walkman can be listened to only through headphones or by placing the tapes in DAT

and cassette machines linked to amplifier and speakers.

Sound insulation

Many of the principles and features associated with portable equipment also apply to studio-based equipment. However, although it is desirable, it is not strictly necessary to have a purpose-built studio. Plenty of good work can be produced using portable mixers, amps, speakers, keyboards, etc.

It will be important, however, to take **acoustics**, particularly sound insulation, into account. The larger the room, and the harder the surfaces, the more natural echo (*reverb*) you will get. This may be exactly what you want for a particular recording, but not for others. The solution is to create a neutral environment where the sound is 'dead'. You can then make adjustments to create the sound you want.

This process is referred to as 'sound insulation' rather than sound proofing, since sound proofing is very difficult to achieve and very expensive. You can, however, achieve acceptable results without excessive outlay.

A partition can be made by tacking fibreboard onto a wooden frame. This frame can be built onto an existing wall or, preferably, be free-standing with a gap between the existing wall and the new partition.

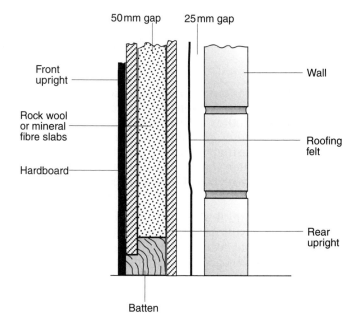

Figure 13.9 Sound insulation

This gap can be filled with rockwool or mineral slabs for greater insulation.

Even better results can be achieved if you can build a front and rear frame onto battens. Cover the front with perforated hardboard (to diffuse the sound) and fill the inside with rockwool or mineral slabs. Then position it next to the existing wall but with a 25mm gap, and a sheet of roofing felt hanging down inside.

Alternatively, you could use lots of old heavy carpet, which may not look very attractive but will help to absorb the sound!

Safety

Fibreboard and mineral wool create a lot of dust particles which are unpleasant and not particularly good for you if inhaled. Wear goggles and a face mask before working with this kind of material.

Mixing desk

The heart of any studio operation is the mixing desk, sometimes referred to as the console or simply 'the desk'.

The mixer allows you to balance and mix two or more sound sources. In a studio, you can have mixing desks with numerous channels and inputs such as microphones, CD and tape recorders, samplers and effects units and musical instruments.

A **sampler** 'samples' short sections of sound (a few seconds) which can then be played back at different pitches or within another recording.

Effects units can enhance or distort sound so, for example, you can make a voice faster or slower or give it an 'echo' (delay) effect or 'reverb' (reverberation).

'Effects' means deliberately changing a sound for creative reasons, and adding reverb gives a richer and fuller sound to voices or instruments.

Sound studios are designed to create a **dead zone** for sound, so that you can create precisely the quality you want for a particular recording.

A studio, particularly if it is used for music recording, will also contain a **compressor** which can control the sound range of various inputs. For example, some instruments and voices are louder or more uneven than others. The **noise gate** is the necessary counterpart to the compressor. The compression process reduces the ratio between the signal and noise so that the noise is more apparent. The noise gate cuts out the background noise when an instrument is not playing. The noise gate and the compressor can be used creatively for effects.

The mixing desk consists of controls for adjusting the different inputs. Each sound, keyboard, voice, etc. can be changed. Each column corresponds to one input channel.

The basic controls are:

- **Input selector** can be set for 'mic' or 'line'. It is important to choose the correct one, as mikes

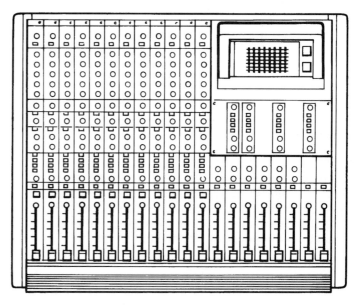

Figure 13.10 A mixing desk and 8-track recorder

259

have a lower output level.

- **Pad** is used to cut down any really high input signal before it distorts.
- The **trim** (gain, input) allows you to adjust the signal levels coming in. Mike signals are relatively weak, so their input channel may need its trim turned up.
- **Solo** or **PFL (Pre-Fade Listen)** allows you to listen to that particular channel alone. This is useful for listening to a sound on its own, before introducing it into the mix.
- **Mute** silences a particular channel.
- **EQ** (equalisation) allows you to adjust the high, middle and low frequencies.
- **Pan** allows the sound to be 'positioned' as you want it between the left and right speakers. On multitrackers, it assigns a channel to a track (see below).

Multi-track recorders

There are also multi-track tape recorders, portable mixers, and cassette-based multi-track recorders (multitrackers) which combine the mixing and recording functions.

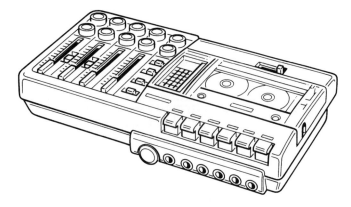

Figure 13.11 A multitracker

Essentially, a multi-track recorder allows different sounds to be laid individually on separate tracks. They can be laid down simultaneously or one at a time. This allows the tracks to be mixed, either on a separate mixing desk or on the built-in mixing facility.

When using these cassette-based machines you must be sure to use a high-quality tape such as TDK-SA or a similar Type II equivalent. Cassette tapes are really designed to record and play in stereo (two tracks) on

both 'sides'. Of course, the recording is not really on the other side, because there is only one side coated with the recording substance. The tracks are all on the same side, but two run in the opposite direction. To hear them you have to turn the cassette around so that the other two tracks are heard, playing in the same direction as the first side.

The multitracker, however, makes use of all four tracks because it has a tape recording/playback head that covers the full width of the tape. If you are laying the tracks one at a time you can lay the first track and then play it back while laying the second, then lay the third while listening to the first two, and the same with the fourth. You could also 'bounce' the first three tracks onto the fourth track by routing them to track four, mixing them and then, when you are happy with it, recording the result onto the fourth track. You could then erase the first three tracks and use them again.

It is vital for quality recording to get the sound levels right before you start. If the recording level is too high then the sound will distort, whereas if the level is too low there will be a lot of background hiss when you turn up the output in order to hear it. As a rule of thumb, the needle should peak just below the red, but don't worry if there is the occasional flicker over into the red.

Case study: Using a multi-track recorder to produce a jingle

The jingle can be very simple and does not require any musical ability. The equipment used here is typical of the basic portable assembly that can be taken away and used in a quiet corner. It is a simple arrangement which allows you to become familiar with the principles, without being overwhelmed by a mass of complicated-looking equipment in a sound studio.

Let us assume for this purpose that the jingle is to be the station 'ID' for a station called Jungle Radio. It will consist of:

- the beat of 'jungle' drums
- a simple tune – you can pick it out yourself, or select a 'demo'
- some 'jungle noise' sound effects
- a voice-over.

Equipment needed:

- keyboards and power adaptor
- portable 4-track cassette recorder, e.g. Fostex 18H and power adaptor

- cassette tape recorder, i.e. a 2-track (stereo)
- a unidirectional microphone, with a jack-to-jack lead, two phono leads and headphones.

The procedure is as follows:

Plug in the keyboard and 4-track using the power adaptors. Connect the keyboard to the 4-track using the jack-to-jack lead. Connect the 4-track to the 2-track with the phono leads. Insert the mike into the 'mic input' socket on the 4-track.

Make sure that the tape is wound back to the beginning. If it is new you should wind it through and then rewind. Let it run for a couple of seconds, then stop. Press RTZ (return to zero) so that the counter numbers read zero.

Play the drum beat and set the levels until you are getting a good signal on the display. When you are happy with the signal you can record the drum beat by sending the signal from the keyboard into an input channel and onto track 1. Turn the 'pan' knob on channel 1 to the left, and select this channel by pushing the 'rec sel' (record select) switch to position '1'. Ensure the fader is set at around 7. Close down the other faders to prevent 'leakage' (the recording going onto other tracks).

You do not have to match up the channels and tracks. Any channel can be sent to any track. You should note, however, that with the Fostex 4-track you have to use the channel 1 and 2 inputs for the microphone, although if you didn't need a mike you could use these inputs for something else. For this study, because we do need a mike we will assume that the keyboard is connected to channel 2.

Play back the tape. It will come through on the speakers of the ordinary tape recorder, or else you can listen through the headphones. Set up the recording of the next track, which will be the melody (tune). You should note that for a jingle this should be just a few notes (perhaps four or six). This may not seem very much, but try listening to some radio jingles – they are generally very simple structures.

The tune is played by the keyboard, so there is no need to change the connection. While it is playing you should listen to the drum beat already recorded. Again, ensure that only the channel 2 fader is open and that you have panned to the right and moved to 'rec sel 2'.

Follow the same procedure for tracks 3 and 4, always ensuring that you close down unused faders and that the pan and rec sel are in their correct positions. Track 3 will be the sound effects that you usually

find on keyboards. Track 4 will record voices chanting a little catch-phrase such as:

It's the Tree House Show on J-u-n-g-l-e R-a-d-i-o!

or something equally memorable!

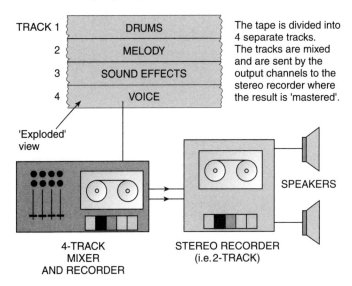

The tape is divided into 4 separate tracks. The tracks are mixed and are sent by the output channels to the stereo recorder where the result is 'mastered'.

Figure 13.12 Mixing the tracks for Jungle Radio jingle

Now that you have all four tracks laid down you can proceed to the mixdown stage. Play the recording and see whether it sounds like a harmonious whole or a collection of disparate sounds, all fighting for supremacy. If it is the latter, then you have to start making adjustments to the EQ of each track until they are suitably integrated (mixed). Once you are happy you can send it all to be mastered onto the stereo cassette.

This is a simple example of the use of multi-tracking. Although only four tracks were used and there were no 'effects', it demonstrates that quite sophisticated recordings can be made with this level of technology, providing the planning is carefully done.

Remember, you should always carry out a test on any piece of equipment before using it, and particularly before taking it out on location.

Microphones

The main types of recording mikes are:

- **Ribbon**, which is expensive but good quality. It is best used in the studio because it is rather delicate.

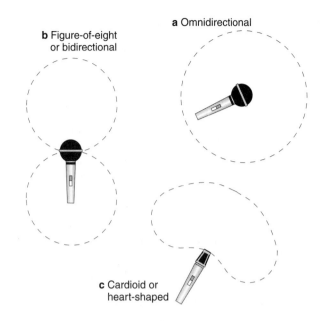

a Omnidirectional

b Figure-of-eight or bidirectional

c Cardioid or heart-shaped

Figure 13.13 Microphone pick-up patterns

- **Moving coil (dynamic)**, which is robust and reasonably priced, with good sound quality.
- **Capacitor (condenser)**, of which **electret** is a type. This is more expensive and has very good quality, although it is not quite so tough. It also requires batteries or some form of electrical charge to vibrate the element.

Dynamic and electret seem to be the most popular mikes for educational use.

Microphones defined by shape of pick-up area are divided into two types: the unidirectional, which picks up sound in the direction that the mike is pointing, and the omnidirectional, which picks up sound from every direction (Figure 13.3a).

Unidirectional mikes are useful for homing in on a particular sound source. There are different types, including the cardioid, which is unidirectional with a heart-shaped pick-up pattern (Figure 13.13c); the figure-of-eight, which picks up from front and rear but not the sides (Figure 13.13b); and the hypercardioid (or cottage loaf or heart shape), which is a combination of the cardioid and figure-of-eight pick up.

There are also gun (rifle) mikes, which have a very narrow pick-up area and are therefore highly directional, and lapel (tie-clip) mikes, which are discreet and generally quite good. The problem is that they can pick up the rustle of clothes if the person starts moving about during recording.

Connections

There are numerous types of connectors for linking different pieces of equipment.

a The mono jack plug

b The stereo jack plug

c The phono plug

d The female XLR (Cannon) plug

e The male XLR (Cannon) plug

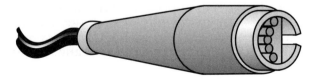

f The DIN plug

Figure 13.14 Connectors

Jacks can be divided into mono and stereo. You can identify them according to whether the plug has a single ring or two rings. Mono jacks are used for plugging leads into mixers, 4-track cassette recorders, amplifiers and synthesisers. Stereo jacks are usually found on headphone leads, which should be plugged into stereo sockets (normally marked 'phones') on amplifiers and tape recorders. Leads with a jack at each end are referred to as jack-to-jack leads.

Phono plugs are used to connect leads (phono leads) to cassette and open-reel tape recorders, CD players and amplifiers, as well as some four-track cassette recorders.

Female and male **XLR** (commonly called Cannon) plugs are used on microphones. The female is attached to the microphone while the male is inserted into the sockets on the mixing desk.

DIN plugs are used on some amplifiers and tape recorders. The initials stand for Deutsche Industrie Normen, which is the European standard for plugs and sockets.

There are also various adaptors which allow compatibility between different types of connection. For example, there are adaptors which convert from jack to phono, standard jack to mini jack, and vice versa.

Identify personnel and allocate production roles

There is a vast array of different job roles in sound and radio. A large number of these are in administration, finance and sales/marketing. Of course, without income and organisation there would be no product, and these roles are discussed in Units 7 and 8. This section will concentrate on those directly concerned with production.

Presenters

In radio, those involved with programming are the **presenters** and **journalists**. To most of us, the voice of radio *is* the presenter, whose output is the culmination of the collective efforts of everyone in the station. One of the attractions of radio is the personalities that shape individual programmes and make them unique. For example, Radio 1's Chris Evans, Terry Wogan on Radio 2, Classic FM's Henry Kelly, Five Live's Diana Modell and Sue Lawley on Radio 4, all give a programme its particular personal

style which attracts a loyal following. But this loyalty cannot be taken for granted, and many presenters are freelancers employed on contracts, perhaps for just one year, rather than staff employees, to give the stations flexibility.

One such presenter is John Florance, who presents BBC Radio Leicester's *Talkback* programme and also extends his freelance activities to arts and cultural features for other stations, including Radio 2 and Radio 4.

JOHN FLORANCE

BBC RADIO LEICESTER
EPIC HOUSE
CHARLES STREET
LEICESTER LE1 3SH
TEL: (0116) 251 6688

104.9 FM

Presenters are 'personalities', and the skills they need are, in fact, certain human qualities such as an ability to communicate effectively and to develop a rapport with people. Obviously, they need a good broadcasting voice to which people can listen for a long time without it irritating them. Presenters also need to develop a technical familiarity with their working environment, which consists of a mixing desk, microphones, and various types of recording and playback equipment.

John Florance feels that a presenter has to be quick-witted and able to absorb a lot of information quickly. This is particularly true on an interactive, speech-based programme such as *Talkback*, where there are numerous guests and members of the public who can respond to any comment that the presenter or guests make, or speak on any subject they like (within reason!). It's no wonder that another vital quality which John identifies is a sense of humour. All presenters need to project their personality and link in with their audience, particularly on a local service. They should know a locality and its people and have a good knowledge of local affairs, and current affairs generally, because what is going on in the wider world can often be given local relevance (as we saw when we took a look at *Talkback*). To do this they have to be interested in people and what is going on around them, and they shouldn't be too shy about asking questions.

Disc jockeys (DJs or 'Jocks') are presenters of popular music programmes. Again, the style is very individual and can be determined by the individual DJ or by the programme and the particular station 'sound'. All stations strive to differentiate themselves by developing their own particular sound, and music stations often refer in their publicity to their unique 'music mix'.

Activity

Listen to different presenters for different types of radio programme. Decide which one you are interested in, and make a list of the particular characteristics. Bear in mind that it is better to develop your own style rather than just imitating someone else's. Nevertheless, you should examine other styles and model yours on those aspects that appeal to you.

The production team

Producers, such as Helen Beevers, whom we profiled planning and running *Talkback*, are basically the coordinators and controllers of individual programmes. They need to have good organising ability, a rapport with other staff, particularly the presenter, and good journalistic skills, including a thorough grounding in broadcasting law (see Unit 8 and the Legal and Ethical appendix).

The producer is responsible for organising and carrying out, with varying levels of support, many different functions – planning, research and scheduling, liaising/negotiating with, for example, the news room, or over budgetary matters. Producers ensure that the programme comes together in an organised and creative manner. They maintain operational control over the programme throughout its duration.

Researchers provide invaluable support to the programme producers. Their role can be either to provide the specialist research for a particular programme, series of programmes or features, or to act as production assistants performing administrative duties, as well as carrying out general research, including contacting potential contributors, etc.

Contributors on radio can come from all walks of life. They can be unpaid members of the public, who are interviewed because they have an interesting hobby or lifestyle or are perhaps involved in a community campaign; or they could be the representatives of an organisation such as the water company or a political party, or a government officer. On the other hand, they could also be the cast of a radio drama or quiz.

Journalists need to have many of the qualities of the presenter and producer, in that they need to be curious, systematic and thorough in their research, accurate in their reporting, able to communicate with people and win their trust, and have a good grasp of the law relating to broadcast journalism. They also need to be determined, thorough and sharp enough not to miss a potential story that may at first not be apparent. News stories often contain other, potential news stories within them.

The following is an example often used to illustrate the need to have a 'nose' for a story. A reporter sent to cover the funeral of a famous person didn't get the story because the funeral did not go ahead – the officiating priest was involved in an accident on his way to conduct the service. Obviously, the point is that there was still a story and potentially a more interesting one, if only the reporter had been more imaginative.

Activity

Apply the information on the duties, responsibilities and qualities of a journalist to finding, compiling and reading news items. You should prepare enough items for a one-minute broadcast.

You will need to familiarise yourself with the content of 'Writing radio news', which can be found in Chapter 7, page 174, in order to do this. You should time each item and write down its duration on the sheet. Each news item should be typed, using double spaces between lines and one item per page. Remember that all numbers, etc. should be rounded off and should be read in an informal style. For example, 0740 hours is 'twenty to eight in the morning', it is not 'seven forty am' or 'seven-forty hours'.

The news also has to be put into a reading order. The order of precedence will depend on your target audience. As an example, let us assume that your radio station is local and covers the Barnsley area. Look at the following list of stories.

- Bomb alert in central London – area cordoned off
- New York hotel blaze – seven dead
- Barnsley armed post office robbery

Because it is a local station, the running order would probably be: (1) Barnsley robbery, (2) London bomb alert and (3) New York fire. This is despite the fact that the bomb alert has serious terrorist implications for the capital city, and the New York fire has cost lives.

Using this example as a guideline, put your news items into a running order, with justifications.

Radio stations and their individual studios consist of a mass of electrical components and their connections. The **studio engineer**'s role is to ensure that all of these function correctly and the station stays on air.

In sound recording studios the term 'engineer' refers to the role of operating the desk and other equipment, to *engineer* the mix. The person who does this is usually referred to as the **recording engineer**. In small studios (often with only one or two persons), the engineer is also the producer. The producer is in charge of all that goes on in the studio. In the larger studios there will be a separate producer.

Large studios will also have the benefit of assistant engineers who will keep a log of 'takes', test the mikes, stop/start recorders and generally carry out the day-to-day functions of a routine nature.

A **maintenance engineer** will perform the highly skilled job of carrying out alignments and calibrations and generally ensuring that the equipment is in good working order.

Carry out a reconnaissance of recording locations

The reconnaissance or 'recce' should be carried out prior to undertaking location work. You need to familiarise yourself with the area, and the conditions, whether temporary or permanent, that you will encounter. You will have to be sure, for example, that there isn't a busy aircraft flightpath, or road works, or marching bands at the place when you want to record the peaceful sounds of nature. For checking on permanent features, an OS (ordinance survey) map is used. The check list for the recce (or remote survey) is the same as for video purposes (but without continuity and set dressing) and is detailed in Chapter 8 (see page 190).

Activity

You have been asked to carry out a recce for a choral performance in a cathedral, church or hall. Using the video 'recce' form for guidance (see page 190), create an audio recording 'recce' form.

You should bear in mind that it will still be essential to have a sketch of the inside of the building, so that the producer will know where to position the mikes and mixing desk (if you have one). You will also need to work out the volume of the building to assess its acoustic properties.

Organise the production schedule

Production schedules are that part of the pre-production work which puts activities into a sequence of dates and times, details production crew and cast 'calls' (the agreed time when people will meet), script units (the length of time of a designated portion of a script and the start and finish recording time for it), and the times required for a studio or 'set' (this could be a room or area you have booked). In order to plan a production effectively, you need to map the activities within a time-scale and in the order in which they should occur. This will include:

- Dates and times for when activities such as planning meetings, remote surveys and other planning and research activities such as appointments, recording, 'live' interviews or broadcasts are going to take place.
- Places that will be used, whether studio-based or on location. They need to be identified and booked for certain dates and times.
- The logistics (for example, how long it will take you to get to a certain location).
- The personnel needed and their roles. Are they available at certain times?
- Equipment needs.
- Bookings, whether of equipment, rooms, specialist support (such as technicians, guides), or of transport and accommodation.
- Risk assessment – this is planned and carried out at specified stages of the production in order to maintain an on-going assessment of risks to both personnel and equipment. Any potential changes of situation can be monitored and the new situation will be re-evaluated in the light of those changes.

Activity

Using the Video Production Schedule as a guide, design an Audio Production Schedule form which you can use for planning your schedules.

Evidence assignment

As a team, submit two scripts for a fictional radio programme and a non-fictional radio programme. These could develop further the scripts written for Unit 2 Element 3 (Chapter 7), and place them in a larger context.

The scripts should be accompanied by:

- the programme brief
- notes on research such as recces (for your production handbook)
- a list of technical resources
- a production schedule
- a list identifying production roles within the team
- an evaluation of your own contribution within the team
- minutes of meetings.

Chapter 14

Record audio material for programmes

Now that you have learnt something about the equipment and recording techniques available for audio materials, you can put this knowledge into practice by making a programme.

Appropriate equipment for the recording

If you refer back to the *Talkback* case study in Chapter 13 (page 248) you will realise that a large amount of equipment was needed to produce the programme. A student production would not need (or, probably, have access to) all the equipment used by a production team such as the one working on *Talkback*. However, certain items – such as microphones – are essential for recording audio material.

Microphones vary a great deal in terms of their characteristics, as we saw in Chapter 13. Depending on what the purpose is – whether studio or location, interior or exterior – you will have to decide on the appropriate choice of microphones for the different activities that make up the show.

In the *Talkback* studio there was one mike for each person. These were unidirectional because they needed to pick up the voice of one person only, without the risk of distracting sounds coming from other people 'off mike'. For one-to-one studio interviews you should use a unidirectional mike, but if you wanted to record a discussion then a PZM or other omnidirectional mike would be best.

For the OB (outside broadcast) the producer wanted the sound of the chain saws buzzing away in the background, and so an omnidirectional mike was used. A similar decision would have to be made if, for example, you wanted to record some vox pop interviews in a busy street. You may feel that you would want to use a unidirectional mike because it would concentrate on the people's voices. It is more lively, however, if you capture the street sounds to give atmosphere to your piece. But again, if a straightforward interview has to be 'grabbed' in a noisy environment, you should choose a unidirectional mike.

Operate equipment according to industry working practices and record material according to programme brief

Studio recording

When recording in the studio you should use a mike stand. Handling the microphone creates a surprising amount of noise. Try to use a free-standing mike stand, or an angle-poise arm, rather than one that sits on a table. People can cause vibrations by knocking the table or putting items down next to the mike.

We have discussed news bulletins in Chapters 7 and 13. We can now look at good practice when reading news broadcasts and speaking into the microphone in general.

When reading the news or any other script you should bear in mind the following:

- **Read it through beforehand**. Learn to pronounce any difficult words and build in some natural breaks.
- **Pace of delivery**. This is typically 180 wpm (words per minute) but can be anything from 140 wpm for the BBC World Service, which is broadcasting to people for whom English is not their first language, to 240 wpm for a fast-talking music station.
- **Pause**. Make sure you build in pauses so that you don't become breathless. Learn to breathe from the diaphragm and avoid making gasping noises which will certainly be picked up with embarrassing clarity.
- **Projection**. Radio is an intimate medium, so you do not have to sound as if you are addressing a political rally. However, unlike television, people cannot see you so there is no illusion of eye contact. Also, you probably have less of their attention as people are quite often doing something else when they are listening to the radio. The rule of thumb is to imagine you are talking to someone who is doing some tidying up at the other end of an average-sized room. Learn

to make your voice carry without shouting, by using your diaphragm rather than your throat.

■ **Emphasis** (stress). Identify the key words and put them in caps or underline them. Be aware, however, that changing the emphasis can change the meaning. Take the example, 'Shut that door'. Any of the three words could be stressed:

SHUT that door – means shut it, don't leave it open
shut THAT door – means a particular door, not the other one
shut that DOOR – means shut the door, not the window.

■ **Pitch** (modulation). This is the 'up and down' quality of a voice which, along with emphasis,

gives it rhythm and makes a voice sound interesting. Lack of these qualities make it sound robotic.

Location recording

If you are recording on location there are certain procedures which you should follow as a matter of good practice. First, check all equipment you are going to use. There is nothing more maddening (or embarrassing) than taking out a piece of equipment and finding the battery is flat, or that it doesn't appear to be working. Appearances can be deceptive. Equipment may seem to be faulty when, in fact, it is the user's lack of familiarity with it which is the problem. The solution is simple. Put more time into learning how the equipment works. The more you use a particular type of equipment, the more naturally you will think a problem through. For example, people can often assume a piece of recording equipment is defective when in fact the 'record protect' tag on the tape is missing.

In the case of a Uher recorder, or any other open-reel for that matter, you need to check that the tape is laced up correctly. There is only one correct way it can go (see Figure 14.2).

The rule to remember is always to carry out a test on any piece of equipment before using it, and particularly before taking it out on location. A book should be available in which to report and record any faults. This is good practice because it tells other people that there is a problem before they find out the hard way. It also stops you from getting the blame! Try to give as much indication as possible of what the problem is or where the fault might lie.

Sound Recording

Student name:...

Date:............................

Content of recording:...

Recorder	Mic	Tape	Evaluation

Figure 14.1 Use a checklist to keep track of your recordings and your developing skills

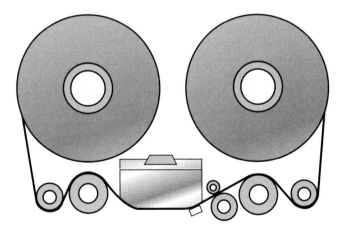

Figure 14.2 Tape transport route

Noise hazards

When you are out on location you should check the environment for any noise hazards. Road or building works, heavy traffic, low-flying aircraft, factory or office machinery and telephones are all examples of potential noise hazards. You should always choose your location with care. If you are carrying out an interview, try to avoid large rooms, or at least don't stand in the middle of them, as they give reverb to the recording. Reverb is also produced in rooms with hard, bare surfaces, such as tiles and stone, and this should be avoided (unless this is the effect you seek, of course).

Microphone leads can pick up interference from fluorescent lights and any electrical equipment or appliances, such as television. Hold the mike about 9 to 12 inches away from you. When speaking into the mike on location, wrap any excess cable around your hand to prevent it from swinging about and causing noise.

When using the mike be wary of 'popping'. This term is used to describe the noise sometimes made when the speaker forces air very rapidly onto the mike diaphragm, causing a popping sound. It usually happens when you pronounce the letter 'p' and 'b'. You can reduce the risks by talking or singing *across* the mike rather than *into* it. Another remedy is to use a **pop shield**. You can make a cheap one by stretching a pair of tights over a wire coat hanger, and use this as a shield to talk through.

'Popping' and the sound of the wind blowing through the mike can ruin any recording. You know when popping is taking place, but even a light breeze can cause a surprising amount of interference. Preferably you should use a **wind shield**. These can be made of foam but the more expensive ones are shaggy, sock-like objects made from sheep or goats' wool. At the very least, turn your back to the wind and use your body as a shield as much as possible.

If the environment is noisy, you may have to bring the mike closer to your mouth. A 'lip' mike has a facility for allowing presenters to press their lips against them, to exclude background noise.

Interviews

Before carrying out an interview, or other recording, you should record at least ten seconds of wildtrack, or background sound. This could well be useful for adding atmosphere to a piece, or as a lead-in to the interview or commentary.

You should also ask the interviewee to carry out a sound test by stating his or her name and address. Monitor the levels, play back and adjust if necessary. If you do notice the VU meter needle at too high or low a level, try moving the mike closer or further away, rather than adjusting the controls on the recorder. Also, if the interviewee moves about make sure that the mike goes with him or her at the same distance.

Once the interview is complete you should play back at least a few seconds of it to ensure that it has been recorded properly.

Vox pops (from *vox populi*, meaning 'voice of the people') are a type of interview carried out with a number of people to seek opinions on a topic. The question is usually short, and so should be the response. Because quite a number of people, perhaps six to ten, are all asked the same question, it makes rather tedious radio for the listeners to hear the same lines over and over again. Therefore the best technique is to ask the question with the pause button on the recorder down and then release it when the person starts to answer. If this is a little tricky, you can always ask the question while the tape is recording and then edit it out afterwards. There may well be some responses you also want to get rid of!

This type of interview tends to work best with fairly light topics, or at least one where people have a ready opinion. Questions about the royal family seem to work well.

Here is an example of how it works. A radio station notes that the royal family is getting a lot of unwelcome attention in the newspapers and decides to ask people in the street about it. The CUE, that is, the introduction to the piece, is given by the presenter and will be something like this:

> CUE: As you know, the royals have been getting a fair bit of stick in the press recently. We *know* there's a lot of interest out there so we thought we'd better get down and find out what *you* think about how the press is treating the royal family.

The question by the reporter is simply, 'What do you think about how the press is treating the royal family?' Although the audience won't actually hear that.

The responses will vary, and you should choose a mixture of young, old, male and female in order to get a cross-section of opinion, and also a varied selection of voices. Radio is, after all, about having a 'good sound'. At the editing stage you can cut out all the 'ums and ers' and swear words, etc. You can read about editing in Chapter 15.

Vox-pop is an interesting way of giving the listeners a direct involvement with the radio station. Being interviewed may not, however, be such an appealing proposition for some people you approach in the street, so if they don't want to give an opinion, don't force the issue.

Phone-ins

The phone-in is another popular form of radio which allows listeners access to a particular programme and a forum for their comments. Sometimes people may be given a free rein to ring in about absolutely anything (within the constraints imposed by legal and ethical considerations – as discussed in the appendix). This, as we have seen, is how the first hour of *Talkback* is allocated. On the other hand, phone-ins can be on particular topics, as for the last two hours of *Talkback*. Some dedicated phone-in slots can be on subjects such as health or the law and they will usually have an expert (such as a doctor or lawyer) to answer queries.

You have to rely on the presenter to make general phone-ins interesting, because you certainly can't rely on the public. Many people are interesting and articulate, but some are not. Unfortunately, it's people in the latter category who often tend to phone in! What makes the phone-in successful is how it is handled by the presenter and monitored by the producer and staff. The *Talkback* case study at the beginning of Chapter 13 is an example of a successful phone-in. An experienced presenter like John Florance can use a phone-in as a cue to define the subject and articulate it more eloquently. He can also give his own comments and judge how much he should intervene or add. This can lead to a proliferation of ideas and subject matter, and sometimes it can really snowball and be very interesting and thought-provoking. It doesn't just 'happen', however, and John often has to play devil's advocate keeping a balance between creating controversy and causing offence. (Another good example is BBC Radio 4's *Call Nick Ross* programme, which takes a topical – and often controversial – subject each week.)

There are times, however, when enough people just won't ring in – no matter what you say! As a presenter, you then need to use your personality and conversational skills. This is when the benefits of

knowing the community and what is going on in the world really pay off. John Florance recalls the time when, after failing to provoke much reaction from the listeners by raising various social, political and family issues, he happened to mention the words 'ice-cream'. After this he was inundated with calls from people bemoaning the fact that 'ice-cream isn't what it used to be' or else claiming it is only good from one particular source!

Procedure

Calls are usually taken 'off air' by the producer or production assistant, who takes down details about the caller and feeds them through to the presenter, as we saw with *Talkback*. In this way the presenter can be given some prior warning of what the calls are about, and the calls can be 'screened' to ensure that they are not just cranky or foolish. In some stations there is a 'delay' (or 'dump') button. This means there is a 7 to 10 second delay between what is said and what actually goes out on air, giving the producer time to delete anything that could cause legal or ethical problems.

Documentaries

Radio documentaries are features that, in a similar way to their print and TV counterparts, allow a subject to be covered in more depth. The feature could involve looking at issues behind a news story, or it could be on something of general interest. The documentary could, for example, be a follow-up to a train crash looking at rail safety, or on a local or famous railway station.

Figure 14.3 shows how it could start.

Identify and resolve issues relating to content considerations

These considerations are dealt with fully in the appendix concerning legal and ethical issues. Content considerations concern legal issues such as defamation, copyright and discrimination and ethical issues such as confidentiality (which can also be a legal issue), privacy, accuracy of sources, avoiding sensationalism and exploitation. Issues of representation concern gender and race, social issues and groupings (e.g. minority groups), and age.

CUE It is now six months since the tragedy of Drewington, when sixteen passengers lost their lives in the country's worst rail disaster in recent years. The report into the disaster has now been made public. But how many of its recommendations will be implemented? Ministers and rail officials are insisting that there will be no cover up, but already there are accusations that the government is dragging its feet on the issue of passenger safety. Tonight Annette Lee brings you the first of our special reports on the state of the country's rail network.

FX: Sounds of trains, STATIONS and so on.

REPORTER: Linend station, at six o'clock in the morning. The Linend to Gophar express is about to pull out. The log sheet states that all safety checks have been properly carried out. But, according to some of the workforce, the work does not conform to the rail industry's or the government's own minimum safety guidelines. We spoke to one maintenance worker who didn't want to be identified. His voice has been disguised.

AUDIO: The management may well claim that there's no safety risks but there's some of these trains that haven't been properly serviced for months. Basically, there's not enough of us, not any more anyway. So many have got laid off and if anyone's off sick or on holiday, well, there's no one to cover and the job just doesn't get done.

Figure 14.3 Start of a radio documentary

Follow safe working practices at all times

This area is dealt with fully in the Health and Safety appendix. Apart from personal health and safety, safe working practices are also concerned with your responsibilities to colleagues and the wider public. In addition they involve preventing damage to equipment and to recordings.

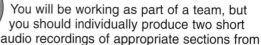

Evidence assignment

You will be working as part of a team, but you should individually produce two short audio recordings of appropriate sections from the scripts prepared in Unit 4 Element 1 (Chapter 13), selecting the appropriate equipment. You should submit these for evaluation in cassette format, properly labelled and protected.

One audio recording may be an insert for a speech-based programme or music programme such as an advert, an interview or travel news. The other should be a short play or a scene from a play.

The log of the work should be included in the production handbook produced for Unit 2 Element 1 (Chapter 5). It should include the following information:

■ identification of health and safety issues concerning the production team and the public
■ details of how risk of damage to equipment and recordings was limited
■ actions taken to solve any problems
■ identification and solution of legal issues
■ identification and solution of ethical and representational issues.

Chapter 15

Edit audio programmes

Unless you are broadcasting live, as in the *Talkback* example, you will need to go through an editing process with your recordings to produce a finished programme.

Log sourced recordings

You will need to play back all your recordings and make a careful note of all the content and the timings for each of them, using either a watch or the counter on the playback machine.

Tape counters can, however, be misleading because they tend to vary from machine to machine. This can cause inconvenience if you carry out the logging activity by using one machine and later try to put your 'paper edit' into practice by using another machine. There is every chance that the log record will not correspond to the counter on the machine you are now using.

One solution to this problem is to use the same machine all the time, but this is not always possible in a learning or professional environment where there is a lot of activity going on and share resources are in much demand. Using a watch is a better policy, but it really needs to have a stop-watch facility in order to be sufficiently accurate. You can then time your recording without worrying about variations between counters. The logging process should make a careful note of all the content, including how usable all the recorded footage might be.

Relevance and recording quality

When recordings are being played back for logging it is essential to check their **relevance** to the:

- script
- programme purpose
- narrative context.

For example, with regard to the narrative context, the process of logging might indicate where in a narrative sequence (which might be fictional or non-fictional) a recording would work best.

The **recording quality** is also an important criterion when logging recordings. Issues to consider here include the following:

- acceptable recording levels
- ratio of background noise (whether ambient or mechanical) to intended sound signal
- microphone technique
- presence of handling noise, i.e. the rumbling sound picked up through hand movement on the mike or lead
- 'popping' (loud 'p's and 'b's causing sound break-up)
- sibilance (distortion caused through excessive hissing of 's' sounds).

It is worth remembering for future reference that repositioning the microphone (or even changing it) can help to avoid or at least minimise the problems of popping or sibilance. These issues of recording quality are considered in more detail below.

Select material for editing into finished programmes

Editing material involves not only getting rid of the pauses and stutterings. It also involves making creative decisions on where a piece of audio is best placed. Just because a particular piece is in a particular place in a recording does not mean it cannot be moved and inserted somewhere else.

You will also have to decide whether the recording quality is acceptable. Generally speaking if there is background 'noise' (i.e. any unwanted signal in the system) then the recording will have to be done again.

Noise can be caused by feedback. This happens when the microphones are too close to the speaker output and the output volume has not been turned down. You can get feedback if the recording levels are too high, i.e. consistently moving into the red area of a VU meter.

Conversely, you can obtain an unwelcome background noise called 'hiss' which is the result of recording levels being too low and picking up 'atmospherics' (electrical activity in the atmosphere). Hiss can also be found on tape, particularly cassette tape, without a sound reduction facility. Therefore most systems have something called Dolby B or C (named after its inventor Ray Dolby who produced it for cinema sound projection). Dolby B is usually suitable, but for multi-tracking it doesn't really cope. The Fostex multi-track machine, for example, uses Dolby C. There is another system, called dbx, which is used by Tascam and Yamaha.

Other forms of noise, such as popping and that caused by handling and vibrations, have been dealt with earlier.

You may decide that you need to instil a little atmosphere into your programme and this is where **wildtrack** (see Chapter 14) can be useful. In Chapter 14 we saw that some train and railway station sound effects were needed, and it is in situations like this that you can add some of that pre-recorded wildtrack sound.

One of the most creative acts of editing is to give 'pace' to a recording. This takes careful editing to remove all or part of a natural pause, or to juxtapose two or more voices. A good example of this technique is when it is used in vox-pop interviews, such as the one we discussed in Chapter 14. As we pointed out, all the stutterings, mistakes, crude or crass remarks, even the repetitive questioning and any other chat from the interviewer, can be taken out to make it a really tight, fast-moving sound.

Alternatively, you could slow down a piece and give it atmosphere, perhaps even status, by adding silences and/or other sound effects (SFX or FX) such as a clock ticking or chiming. There are many different sound effects that can be added, as well as various types of music, depending on the mood you are trying to induce in your audience.

When editing, you have to be aware of the need for continuity. In an interview situation, for example, you could end up with mismatched questions and answers. You also need to pay particular attention to background sounds as these can easily become disjointed through editing. So it can be useful to edit the natural pauses, but be careful not to edit these out completely or the recorded voice will sound like a Dalek! Conversely, be careful not to splice two breath pauses together.

You can see that this is an extremely important stage of production. It is vital that you allocate and book sufficient time and resources to carry out the editing process thoroughly.

Produce an edit script following the conventions of audio production

There are various methods of recording editing decisions. They should all, however, contain certain standard characteristics, i.e. **conventions**, which are common to all styles. These are: the **layout**, which should be in columns with counter numbers (or times) in the left-hand column to indicate **durations**; and the **running order** of the contents, with any **technical instructions** indicated.

The edit sheet in the case study below shows how you can log a piece of audio, whether fiction or non-fiction, prior to editing. You should have a copy of the actual script (where applicable) for reference.

Case study

This example is based on the script produced for the documentary on rail safety discussed in Chapter 14 (page 271). The edit decision list shows the order in which the material was originally recorded, with the reporter's words, followed by the maintenance worker's comments, and the presenter's introduction and finally the wildtrack.

Counter number	Recorded words/FX	Edit decision
005	Linend station ...	
010	The Linend to Stopov ... sorry	DELETE: The Linend to Stopov ... sorry
	The Linend to Gophar ... pull out	
019		
033	... disguised	
038	um ... the bloody management	DELETE: um DELETE: bloody
048	er ... basically	DELETE: er
058	... get done	
063	it is now six months	MOVE 063–097 TO START OF TAPE
097	... network	
102	train/station wildtrack	FADE IN 102–105 WILDTRACK AND 107–108 AT 003 AND CROSS-FADE WITH REPORTER
108		

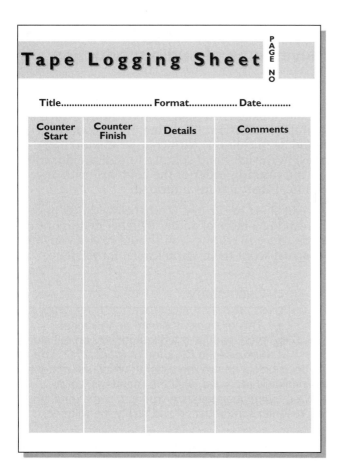

Figure 15.1 An example of a tape logging sheet

Activity

Making use of the tape logging sheet reproduced in Figure 15.1 (or using your own design), carry out the logging tasks for your own work as described above.

Ensure you have sufficient resources booked, in terms of time and equipment, to do justice to the recordings. Make your bookings in the book provided and keep a record for evaluation purposes (i.e. to prove that you have carried out your planning correctly).

Edit selected material into finished programmes

You should by now have made your selections for the final product and the decisions you have made and logged can be put into practice. This involves the final selection, sequencing and mixing of material (possibly from a number of tapes recorded in different situations) and either dub editing or splice editing.

Splice editing

Reel-to-reel editing is called cutting and **splicing**. It involves cutting the tape, removing the unwanted section, and then joining (splicing) the two ends of tape back together again. Splice editing is still widely used in radio news production and can be a very accurate method of editing speech, for example for interviews. To do this you need the following equipment and materials:

- a non-magnetic single-sided razor blade
- an editing block
- a yellow or white chinagraph pencil
- $\frac{1}{4}$ inch splicing tape
- red and green or yellow leader tapes.

To demonstrate how cutting and splicing works, let us assume that there is a sneeze which you want to remove from your recording. You will have already logged this, so go to the time or counter number where it is located. Most reel-to-reels have an 'edit mode' which allows the tape to be in contact with the heads, but with the reels in freespool.

After engaging the edit lever, you can cue up the tape by rocking the spools backwards and forwards gently. The tape will sound extremely slow and, with a little practice, you will be able to locate the beginning of your edit exactly.

Once you have done this, take the chinagraph pencil and make a mark where the tape is on the play head (see Figure 15.2).

Wind the tape on until you come to the time or counter number that indicates the end of the edit.

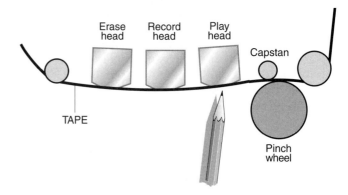

Figure 15.2 Cutting and splicing audio tape (1)

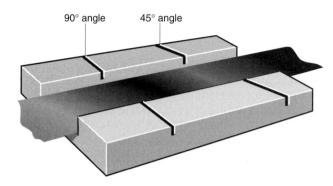

Figure 15.3 Cutting and splicing audio tape (2)

Cue up and mark the tape, using exactly the same procedure as before. With the machine still in edit mode, slacken off the spools until the piece to be edited is lying loose.

Pick it up and lay it into the channel running through the centre of the splicing block where it will fit quite snugly (see Figure 15.3).

There is a 45 degree slot cut into the block. Insert the blade here and cut. By cutting at this angle you ensure that the edit is seamless, whereas a vertical cut would give a little 'pop' as it goes past the playback head.

Now do the same for the other end of the edit.

Take out the edited piece and keep it safe. It's a nightmare if you destroy it or throw it into a bin with hundreds of other cuttings – then discover that you need it after all!

Next, push the two ends together so that they abut without overlapping; the smoother the join, the better the recording, so don't leave any gaps. Cut off

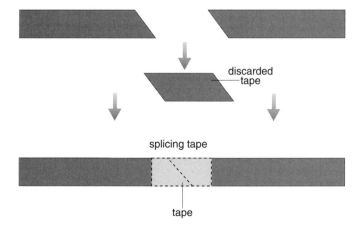

Figure 15.4 Tape editing

a small piece of the splicing tape and join the two ends together (see Figure 15.4).

Be careful when handling the razor blade and store it away carefully after use.

Take up the slack and replay the tape to check your work.

Apart from reel-to-reel editing you can also edit your digital recordings on computer by carrying out much the same process on screen.

With DAT recordings you can edit them using the same process as that used for video recording. You need a source and an edit machine. Then identify and mark the 'in' and 'out' points and initiate the edit.

Another method that you can use with cassette tape is known as **crash editing**, and is the same principle as used for crash video editing. It simply means finding the start and end of an edit and starting and stopping at these points. It is rather rough and ready, and therefore unsuitable for intricate work.

Dub editing

Dub editing is the name given to the same process of editing when it involves the straightforward copying of material from one tape to another in the correct sequence.

You should note that even when recordings are made initially on cassette they are often transferred to open-reel because of the precision editing it offers. This can also be done with DAT if there are not two DAT machines available for editing.

Prepare tapes for playback

Leader tapes and labelling

The tape should be clearly marked for identification purposes by cutting the recording tape before the start of your recording and inserting green (or sometimes yellow) 'leader' tape between the two ends, then splicing each of the two joins together with the splicing tape. Next use the same procedure to insert red leader at the end of your recording.

These brightly coloured 'leaders' let you see where your recording is, even when the reels are in motion. This is better than calculating it with a counter or watch. You will be able to cue the tape up to the exact start of your recording and know where it will end.

The disadvantage of leader tape is that you cannot record over it. If you want to reuse the tape you will have to remove the leader tape, otherwise there will be 'drop out', i.e. blank spaces, on your subsequent recording.

The tape should be clearly identified with neatly written or typed labels. This not only makes it look more professional, it also helps people to read the label.

Cue sheet

You will also need a 'cue sheet' which contains all the information about the recordings on the tape. It should have the name and contents of each recording, their start and finish times, or counter numbers (with a note of which machine you used), with the duration of each section or recording.

Cassette tape or 'cart'

Your final product will probably end up being copied onto a cassette tape. This also should be clearly and neatly labelled with a cue sheet attached. Alternatively, if you had a cartridge machine, you could copy it across onto cartridge, which is a plastic box containing a tape set up in an endless loop, commonly referred to as a 'cart'. A cue pulse is placed on the tape when the record button is depressed in the cart machine. When the start button is pressed, the cart immediately 'fires' (i.e. plays instantaneously). When finished it will use the cue pulse automatically to cue itself back to the precise start of the recording again.

Carts are extremely useful and all radio stations will have various jingles, advertisements, and news items on cart for instant playback without the worry of having to cue up tape.

Carts cannot be recorded over but instead need to be **wiped**, using a machine called a bulk eraser. This consists of a powerful electromagnet which wipes clear the magnetic patterns on the tape. It is important that you do this, otherwise the previous recording will still be audible.

Activity

Prepare your tape for playback using the methods described above. Prepare a cue sheet to accompany the tape.

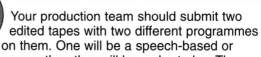

Evidence assignment

Your production team should submit two edited tapes with two different programmes on them. One will be a speech-based or news programme, the other will be a short play. The tapes should be labelled and cued.

Accompanying the tapes should be:

- a log sheet with notes on recording quality
- an edit script showing any alterations to the running order
- an evaluation of the relevance of the material.

You should also put in your portfolio personal evidence of carrying out mixing, dub editing and splicing.

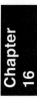

Chapter 16

Review and evaluate audio productions

Now that your audio product has been produced, you should review and evaluate it in terms of its planning and production as well as its final quality – technical quality and content – and the audience response. This will also involve an assessment of individual and group contributions during the production process.

Present finished products to an audience

When you planned the programme, you identified a target audience for your product. You now need to organise a **sample** of people from this target audience in order to obtain feedback from them.

The most obvious way to do this is to gather a sample audience together in one place to listen to your programme. Feedback can then be obtained by completing a questionnaire, group discussion and interviews, or by combinations of these.

Alternatively you may feel that people need to spend some time reviewing the product. It might also be difficult to gather all the sample audience together. You could, therefore, decide to give out copies of the programme with questionnaires, to be completed and returned. You will have to judge how much you can rely on individuals to return their responses on time! The questionnaires will also need to be constructed carefully, in order to cover all the responses required, if interviews are not also carried out.

Analyse audience feedback on products

You should refer to Chapter 24 to find out how to organise audience feedback, whether this is from a discussion group, interview or questionnaire.

Whichever way you decide to obtain your feedback, the audience will need to be analysed and their responses evaluated. You should try to find people for the sample who are not too close to you (such as friends and family), as their responses may be biased!

 Activity

Devise a plan for the gathering and analysis of the responses of a targeted audience. The plan should include:

Method selected for gathering and analysing audience responses.
Justification of the choice (questionnaire, interview, discussion group) or combination of choices.

Selection of sample.
When choosing your sample of the target audience you should take into account the time of day and location you have chosen. You need to consider the time and place where you may find a representative sample.

Resources for gathering information.
The design of the questionnaire, list of interview questions and the key points to help focus the discussion should all be concerned with obtaining responses to the following issues:

- **Relevance** – was the programme subject or topics relevant to the audience?
- **Topicality** – did the programme material have 'currency' i.e. did it deal with issues that are happening now and use material that the audience could identify with?

  Relevance and topicality are related and overlapping, but nevertheless they can be distinguished. For example, the subject may be relevant in that it is about, for example, youth culture but it would lack credibility if it did not contain topical (up-to-date) references to the latest fashions, attitudes, etc.

- **Entertainment** – did it have entertainment value and more importantly, was it supposed to? The term needs to be clarified because it is associated with enjoyment. The programme may have aimed to inform or to educate, so entertainment in the sense of being amused may not be an appropriate term. We can hear a radio report, for example, on an awful atrocity somewhere such as Rwanda or Bosnia. We listen primarily to be informed and to learn something. The impact of this could be shock, anger, pity, horror or a whole range of emotions, but we would hardly call it entertainment.
- **Technical quality** – how did the audience respond to the sound quality? Was it recorded properly so it

could be played back without having to adjust the volume, without hiss or distortion? Was the sound full and well balanced, was it thin and reedy?

- **Originality** – how original was the material or the treatment of it? Even if the programme is relevant and topical, the treatment can still be tired and it may be worth thinking about novel ways of presenting a topic. Perhaps a different location and a different style of presentation could make a topic more interesting. However, be wary of gimmicks which do not really add anything to a programme and get in the way of its message.

You can also ask other questions, such as the ones below, which aim to get to grips with what people feel about the programme, i.e. its **perceived impact**.

- Did the programme measure up to the expectations of the audience?
- Did it sound like other programmes in that genre (e.g. a magazine programme or a chart show) to them?
- What images did the words/music bring to the minds of your listeners?
- What information did they gain?
- What emotions did they experience?
- Did they feel it was the right length?

Finally, as part of your plan you should define the means of quantifying, collating and drawing conclusions from the feedback received. Will you, for example, be able to give a numerical value to the comments so that they can be quantified? This can then go forward as 'audience feedback' when evaluating the quality of the finished product (see below).

Evaluate quality of finished product

You should carry out an evaluation of these three areas of your production:

- technical quality
- content
- audience feedback.

Refer to your diary or log entries, and to the minutes of team meetings, when making your responses. They will help to remind you of various problems and decisions, such as those noted in these extracts from a student evaluation:

> *The script was changed each lesson until we were completely satisfied with it. Our radio show was edited each lesson and changed quite significantly as our knowledge of editing increased. We came across difficulties such as the fact that the keyboards we used did not sound right when recorded on tape.*

> *Another problem occurred when we tried to insert the songs. There was usually a distinctive 'clonk' at the beginning of the song and at the end. This did not sound at all professional. As well as this, the volume levels of songs were all different and so were the speaking levels. At one point it could be too quiet, and then it went too loud.*

Technical quality

Consider and comment on the following aspects of your audio production:

- **Sound levels**
  Were the recordings at levels which produced a clear sound, untainted by hiss or feedback?

- **Mixing**
  Was the mixing carried out smoothly so that the final sound was integrated? This may have been a 'live' sound with fades, cross fades, etc. It may, however, have been a mix laid down and compiled on a multi-track recorder and mixer. In either case, you should comment on whether it sounds like one complete sound, with its different components in harmony, or whether it is disjointed, with some parts drowning out the others.

- **Editing**
  How accurate was the editing? How seamless were the edited portions of the tape? Were there any noticeable jumps as the edited tapes passed the heads on the tape machine?

■ **Microphone technique**
Were there any recording problems which can be related to the way the mike was used? For example, was there feedback caused by the mikes being too close to speakers with output volume too high? Was there any evidence of popping, rattling, vibrations, or wind noise picked up by an unprotected mike? Were you able to control your breathing, or were intakes of breath recorded onto the tape?

Content

You should go through the content of the programme and comment on each of the content issues (see below). For each issue you should make comparisons with the original proposal, noting and explaining any changes. You should also indicate whether the codes and conventions relating to audio recording, and radio broadcasting, were adhered to. These codes will include the correct marking up of scripts (where they were used), the use of jingles and station signatures, the use of **links** between music, and **anchors** to introduce topics and provide continuity.

	Your programme	Original proposal	Comments
Choice of jingle/ station identity			
Script mark-up (where appropriate)			
Pace of delivery			
Tone of presenter's voice			
Language style e.g. formal, informal			
Vocabulary			
Choice of topics			
Fitness for purpose			
Overall sound			

Audience feedback

Once you have analysed the audience responses you will be able to decide whether the product was a success in terms of its fitness for purpose.

Activity

Using the audience analysis above on page 277 as a guide, decide whether you have successfully matched the product to its target audience.

Assess own and team's role in the production process

You should carry out an evaluation of your own contributions, and the work of the team as a whole. You need to be able to reflect on the issues, such as the various roles allocated, with a view to considering how the production process could be improved if a subsequent product was commissioned.

Activity

Use the forms provided in Chapter 12 in order to evaluate your own performance and that of the team. The self-evaluation checklist is on page 243 and the group evaluation checklist can be found on page 244.

Justify completed audio product and compare with existing broadcast material

In order to fulfil this requirement you should go through the content of your programme, comparing it with another – professional – programme, using the checklist on this page.

Again, you should refer to your diary or log entries and to the minutes of team meetings when making your responses.

In addition to completing the checklist you should comment generally on this central question:

■ Was the choice of topics and their treatment – using available resources – suitable for their perceived purpose and for the target audience?

Case study

As an example, let us consider a radio play which seeks to explore the reasons for the conflict that exists between two communities. Its **purpose** is to *inform* people of some historical facts, but also to try to get them to appreciate the many complex issues that are involved (*educate* them). The play's content should, therefore, reflect this.

Let us assume that the play's **target audience** has been defined as educated, well informed, with a sense of history, concerned about society, etc. If the treatment of the main characters and dialogue presented the arguments in a superficial or unsubtle way (*representation* would be an issue here), perhaps with Rambo-like melodrama but little analysis, then clearly the **fitness of the material for its purpose** would have to be seriously questioned.

Similarly, the content of a music programme would have to be questioned if it was supposed to be modelled on a 'gold' station line-up, but had a presenter's style that was more in keeping with a chart show featuring current hit singles.

In terms of **justifying the resources**, if the purpose of an advertisement, for example, was to give some diary dates for local community activities, this would hardly justify the cost of employing a national celebrity for the voice-over.

When carrying out your evaluation you should be asking the following questions:

- Were the resources employed appropriate for the agreed production?
- Were the individual items suitable for the target audience?
- Were they successful in meeting the 'fitness for purpose' criteria?
- Did they come together to produce a coherent overall product with a consistent identity?

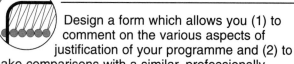

Activity

Design a form which allows you (1) to comment on the various aspects of justification of your programme and (2) to make comparisons with a similar, professionally produced product.

Evidence assignment

Play your audio recordings to an audience. Record feedback from the audience and analyse the findings.

Write a report evaluating your audio products in terms of:

- how much it kept to the original proposal
- whether the content used accepted codes and conventions
- its relevance for the target audience
- topicality, entertainment value and originality
- technical quality, including microphone technique, sound levels, accuracy of editing, etc.
- audience response.

The report should also assess the effectiveness of the planning and production processes, and will evaluate your own performance within the team.

Details of the methods used for audience testing can be kept in your production handbook. This may also be used as evidence for Unit 6 Element 4 (Chapter 24).

Producing Audio Products: Unit Test

1 What will set the style of a music programme in order to appeal to a specific audience?
a the station ident
b the commercials
c the DJ's personality
d the number of music tracks played

2 Which part of a music programme is designed to retain the attention of the listeners and prevent them changing stations?
a the national news
b the jingle
c the names of the records
d a competition

3 Which type of programming needs the largest production team and the most equipment?
a a studio discussion
b a chart show
c a phone-in
d a live outside broadcast

4 On what sort of radio programme would you expect to hear the presenter say 'Jane in Glasgow wants to give a big thank you to all her friends at work'?
a a magazine programme on Radio 4
b a music programme on Radio 2
c the news on Radio 5
d a request programme on Radio 3

5 Which of the following costs will be included in the production budget for a particular programme?
a rent and rates
b studio time
c licence fees
d marketing

6 What would a researcher working on the production of a period drama be responsible for finding out?
a the background of the actors
b how to make sound effects
c where to position the mikes
d who owns the music copyright

7 You have gone on location to interview a vicar in his or her church for a religious programme. What is the **most** important thing you will need to check?
a the quality of the acoustics
b that there is an electricity supply
c that there is sufficient parking
d what the vicar is intending to say

8 What will a writer need to know first, before he or she starts scripting a new quiz show?
a the age of potential listeners
b where the programme will be made
c the names of the contestants
d when the studio has been booked

9 If a drama script is 'marked up', this means that:
a it has been put on to the computer
b it includes directions as to how different sound sources should be mixed
c the actors have rehearsed and made alterations
d the running order has been attached

10 Decide which of these statements is true or false.
i the slower the tape speed, the better the quality
ii a UHER is an analogue recording machine

Which of the answers below is correct?

a i is true and   ii is true
b i is true and   ii is false
c i is false and   ii is true
d i is false and   ii is false

11 Which of the following tells you what is coming up next on a programme?
a a jingle
b a cue
c an outro
d a trail

12 What is a Standard Out Cue or Back Anno?
a the presenter signing off the programme
b the signal that a music track is ending
c the reporter identifying who and where he or she is
d the script mark to show an actor is to exit

13 Which of the following could be described as a segue?
 a one track of music following another without a break
 b a voice talking over a music track
 c a cue followed by an interview
 d theme music preceding a play

14 You are recording a dramatisation of *Tess of the D'Urbevilles*. Where would you record the scene set in a field to get the right acoustics?
 a in a large room
 b in a dead room
 c in a field
 d in a live room

15 What will give a richer quality to a sound?
 a a reverb unit
 b a compressor
 c a sampler
 d a noise gate

16 A pressure zone microphone is omni-directional. What does this mean?
 a it picks up from only one direction
 b it picks up sound from every direction
 c it can be used in all circumstances
 d it is best when used outside

17 Which control enables you to adjust the amount of signal coming in from a microphone?
 a the EQ
 b the pan
 c the fader
 d the trim

18 Which of these would you expect to find in the production **schedule** for a drama programme?
 a the edit decision list
 b listener figures from RAJAR
 c crew and cast calls sheet
 d the marked up script

19 Why do some presenters speak more slowly than others on radio?
 a the script is too short for the length of time allocated
 b the producer has asked for a relaxed style
 c listeners are more likely to remember what is said
 d it helps people who are hard of hearing

20 You are asked to interview a politician outside the Houses of Parliament. Why do you ask her to answer a few questions before recording?
 a to check the sound levels are correct
 b to check that she can use a lapel mike properly
 c to check that she will not say anything inappropriate
 d to check that she is speaking clearly enough

21 What can a radio station do to prevent a swear word being heard on air during a phone-in?
 a nothing, ask the presenter to apologise
 b use the delay button and edit it out
 c screen the callers, asking what they will say
 d warn callers about using bad language

22 When will a recording for a current affairs programme need to be redone?
 a when the items have been recorded in the wrong order
 b when an interviewee has stumbled and stuttered
 c when an interview goes on for too long
 d when there is too much feedback

23 What problem does the Dolby system correct?
 a popping
 b compression
 c poor tape quality
 d tape hiss

24 Some programmes make use of wildtrack. What is this?
 a sound effects which give atmosphere
 b animal and bird sound
 c exciting background music
 d outside broadcast inserts

25 Who is responsible for organising the budget for an individual programme?
 a the traffic controller
 b the personnel manager
 c the producer
 d the station accountant

26 Which colour of leader tape should you use to indicate the start of an item?
 a green
 b red
 c yellow
 d white

27 Which of the following can damage a cassette tape?
    a splicing in the wrong place
    b playing it at the wrong speed
    c leaving it on top of a speaker
    d removing the tab on the side

Here are some suggested ways in which a radio producer could evaluate the success of a programme. Use them to answer questions 28–30.

    a consult the official statistics from RAJAR
    b interview shoppers in the local streets
    c send out questionnaires to selected listeners
    d hold group discussions with the production team

28 Which would be most useful to find out whether the technical quality was good?

29 Which would be used to find out why women don't tend to listen to the show?

30 Which would be the best way to find out how many women listen to the show?

283

Chapter 17

Chapter 8 was an introducion to the pre-production stage for making a film, TV programme or video. You should now be aware of the various camera shots and movements and how to prepare and understand the use of storyboards and camera scripts. This unit will help you take your ideas and produce them. There will be explanations of different filming and editing techniques,

and the type of equipment used. There will also be a look at how professional productions are put together in a TV studio.

You will need to have a specific role within a team for larger productions, but you should also build up a personal portfolio of work showing evidence of your own camera work and editing.

Pre-production – planning the production process

Careful planning at the pre-production stage not only saves time and money but results in a high-quality product, whether you are a student or a professional.

The individual items you have considered in Chapter 8 could perhaps now be made part of a larger production. For instance, if you have researched and written a script for a mini-documentary, then it could be included in a current affairs programme. Maybe you have attempted a scene from a film or a soap; these can also now be taken a stage further.

Television production involves two types of planning:

- *contingency planning* – here the content of the programme is unknown or may need alterations, as in news and sport. So the outline of the programme is planned based on predictions of what is *likely* to happen: for example, these types of microphones will probably be all right for this interview, these cameras will be placed around the football ground like this to pick up the action.
- *content planning* – here the material is known well in advance, as in studio drama, so everything can be very precisely planned.

Activity

Decide which type of planning will be required for your ideas for moving image productions.

Agree the programme brief

The word 'programme' should be interpreted in its widest context to cover all the various types of

moving image production, not just those seen on the television.

There will not be sufficient time or resources to put into practice all of the ideas of everybody in the team. So you will need to negotiate within your team about which idea will be the best to progress. This is an important part of pre-production to get right. By this stage you and others may feel very committed to your own ideas and don't want other people trampling on them or dismissing them out of hand. It is difficult to admit that your own ideas may have flair but be impractical or, on the other hand, be rather dull. Each proposal submitted to the group should be discussed carefully; all team members should take time to read or listen to prepared treatments and have the opportunity to give their opinions about each suggestion. Try to make objective comments and not emotional statements. If someone hears such comments about their programme as 'Oh that's really boring' or 'That's just stupid', it is not only unhelpful but crushing; that person is unlikely to become an enthusiastic worker on your programme if it is chosen. Always give specific reasons such as, 'This item is too long to keep people's attention' or, 'If this soap was set in the college library it might be more practical'.

Remember also that the target audience may not be you. So whilst you may think that people dressed up as rabbits look silly, as presenters of a quiz show for young children they may be ideal.

Your decisions about the programme brief should then be discussed and agreed with your tutor, who may be acting in the role of client.

Developing the brief

In professional TV, the producer writes the proposal around a new concept or idea and submits it to the management or board of directors of a commercial or public service TV station or cable system. If the producer has been approached by a client to make a film or video, for example, then not only the target audience but also the wishes of the client have to be ascertained. Can the following questions be answered?

- What is the client's purpose in making the film – to make money or change the world?
- What is the film or video about? What viewpoint, bias or angle does the client want to give to it?
- How much does the audience already know about the subject or topic of the film or video?
- Who will have the final say as to whether the project goes ahead?

In the film and TV industry the programme brief will form the basis for more binding legal contracts, so this initial stage is very important. The programme brief itself should start with the proposal, which will include:

- format
- content
- purpose
- target audience
- medium.

This will then be developed to include:

- treatment
- budget
- production schedule.

Later on there might be added:

- pre-production script
- set design
- pilot on videotape.

When this has been agreed, shooting scripts can be prepared and production work started.

Some of the above you will have already considered if you intend using material from Chapter 8, but now more detail will be necessary.

Format

What is meant by **format?**

Format and genre are very similar. Particularly in television, many forms of presentation have developed into stereotypes. The format will divide the programme into segments. So, in an entertainment programme, an outline will be given indicating how many minutes of speech, how much dance, how much music and how much comedy.

The breakdown may also have to include how many breaks for commercials.

A common television programme format is the talk show. It is popular because it uses a very small production team, a very basic studio facility with usually only one set and not much in the way of talent, yet it can offer a lot of variety in the range of topics that can be covered and the guests chosen to appear. The quiz show offers the same advantages. News, current affairs programmes and documentaries also tend to follow an established format. (Refer to Chapter 3 for further discussion of the format of TV documentaries.)

Different aspects of the brief

These are questions your brief should answer:

- Is the production fiction or non-fiction?
- Will the production be live or recorded?
- Are you using a studio?
- Will this be an outside broadcast?
- Will there be an audience?
- Will this be a single-camera or a multi-camera production?
- Are any special sound or lighting effects needed?
- Are any extra inserts needed, such as library tape or special sequences using slow motion?
- Will all the production be in colour, or will any black and white sequences be included?
- Is background music to be used?
- If you are using reporters or presenters, will they be seen on screen?
- Will you need to design any special studio sets?
- Will any scenes be dramatised?
- Are any costumes needed?
- How much of the production will need to be scripted?
- Instead of people, do you intend to use puppets, cartoons or models?
- Will any graphics be needed, such as diagrams, drawings or photographic stills?
- Will captions be included at any point?

The programme brief will have defined the **target audience** but you will need to identify what is known as **production values**, i.e. those elements which will attract and hook the attention and interest of that particular audience. This might be the music used (e.g. classical music to attract a mature sophisticated audience) or sequences using fast cutting of images (to attract teenagers).

Particularly when choosing a fictional production, it will be necessary to consider the following point.

Although your work should not be graded for the quality of the acting in it, the final product will look less professional if the acting or presenters appear very amateurish. It will also take longer to film if you use people who have never spoken without a script before and who feel embarrassed when talking in front of a camera. If you can find people with theatrical experience, this will make life much easier. It may be worthwhile finding out if there are any local theatre groups who might help you with a project.

Activity

Write two programme briefs for:

- a documentary or talk show
- a soap or a drama series.

Present the programme brief to a client.

Keep minutes of the meetings you have with the rest of your team and make a note of any comments made by the client.

Carry out any necessary research

As with any media product, research will need to be done before the programme brief can be put together, and afterwards for both the content of the programme and the production. The 'where, what and how' of researching has been discussed in Chapters 5 and 8.

Content research

Here are some examples of content research:

- finding background information on carnations and roses for a gardening programme
- researching details about costumes worn in the eighteenth century for a period drama
- interviewing sailors for a new soap based on the Royal Navy
- finding maps and geographical accounts of the interior of Africa for a film about a Victorian explorer
- telephoning the agents of stars due to appear on a magazine programme for biographical details
- finding out what sort of prizes would be suitable for a teenage sports competition.

Production research

Here are some examples of questions asked in production research:

- when is a certain director available?
- what studios will be free in July?
- which facility house will be cheapest to produce the titling?
- how long will it take to produce a five-minute animated cartoon sequence for a children's programme?
- how much will it cost to hire a stately home for a week to film in?
- how long will it take to get a camera crew to Scotland to report on the Highland Games?

Activity

Brainstorm the research needs for the content and the production of these TV programmes:

- a drama about a murder which took place on a train in France in the 1920s
- a quiz for children about cookery.

Research will provide the essential information for many areas of work, and is important in helping you to produce effective scripts, to identify technical, human and financial resources and to organise a schedule.

Develop production/shooting scripts from the programme brief

There are two approaches to organising the camera work for a script. Either you observe the action (as in a drama rehearsal or sport) and choose a good viewpoint, or you decide what will be effective shots and arrange the action around them (as in a studio magazine show).

The type of scripts used will also vary according to the personnel using them. The script for the actors will certainly include the dialogue, how to speak and where to stand and move. As a general rule, one page of script is equal to one minute of completed video. The television director will have all the camera shots, positions and movements marked on the script. Camera operators will not have all the dialogue. Sometimes, as for advertisements and drama productions, sketches and storyboards will appear with the scripts. They show the significance of certain shots, i.e. **key shots**.

Storyboards can also be helpful in films and drama when scenes are shot out of order. Rough drawings show changes of scene for every major sequence and make it easier to check if all the necessary footage has been taken.

You should refer back to Chapter 8, pages 193–8 to remind yourself how to lay out a production script, storyboards and camera cards. Here are two examples of scripts from commercial TV. One is for a quiz show, the other for a crime programme.

Case study: *Tellystack*

Tellystack is a new quiz show produced at Carlton studios by Steve Pinay of Zenith North for UK Gold.

Steve was asked by UK Gold to come up with 'something different' and on that basis he formulated his ideas. Because budgets are confidential we do not know

---

	PLAY IN VTR	**1. OPENING TITLES** RT: .30″
1.	5 W/S TELEVISION	**2. PAUL'S INTRO (V/O?)** STACK IS OPEN & CLOSES AFTER ENTRANCE.
	TELLYSTACK LOGO ON EACH SCREEN	PAUL ENTERS THROUGH STACK TO APPLAUSE.
2.	2 CENTRE SET MS PAUL	**PAUL** Hello and welcome to the game in which real life takes a back seat to the wonderful world of television. Yes, it's time to meet three of the nation's finest couch potatoes as they prepare to do battle with each other and the mighty 26 screen Tellystack.
	(CAM 4 NEXT) (ON CAM 2)	**PAUL** Are they the kind of people who can tell their Rosamund Street from their Albert Square, or will they fall apart in Crinkley Bottom?
3.	4 W/S FROM RT TO CONTESTANTS ON TURN	Why don't we find out?
	(CAM 2 REPO)	**3. INTRO CONTESTANTS & CHAT** MUSIC STING PAUL MOVES TO CAMERA RIGHT OF CAMERA RIGHT CONTESTANT.
4.	2 MS PAUL U/S OF CONTESTANTS	**PAUL** Now, let me see if I've got this right. You're X from X, you're X from X, and you must therefore be X from X. So let's start with you X – tell us something about your good self!
5.	CAMS AS DIRECTED 1 – S/BY ALT 3S OR O/S PAUL 2 – MS PAUL 3 – 3S CONTESTANTS 4 – MS CONTESTANT 5 – W/S TELLYSTACK	

	(CAM 2 NEXT) (ON AS DIRECTED)	
		THREE CONTESTANT CHATS WITH PAUL WORKING ON CAMERA RIGHT TO LEFT AND IN WHICH EACH MUST END WITH A STATEMENT ABOUT THEIR FAVOURITE TELEVISION SHOW OF ALL TIME.
6.	2 MS PAUL CAM R OF CONTESTANTS	**PAUL** Well, there you are. Three favourite programmes and not a single mention of Crime Monthly, Big City or The Big Breakfast – The Paul Ross Year. Still, I shall hide my disappointment and hasten swiftly along to rouse the slumbering stack into action. Time to summon up a testy telly gem for your delectation.
7.	5 W/S TELLYSTACK	PAUL TURNS TELLYSTACK
	PLAY IN VTR CLIP	VTR CLIP OF TV HERO
	VTR PLAYED TO ALL 18 SCREENS AS ONE PICTURE	[CAMERAS REPOS DURING VTR CLIP – RT: .20″]
	MIX TO FULL FRAME OF VTR CLEAN	
	(CAM 1 NEXT) (ON VTR INSERT)	**4. GUEST INTRO VTR CLIP** RT: .20″ ARCHIVE CLIP INTRODUCES TV HERO. PAUL TO HIS PODIUM POSITION. **5. TV HERO ENTRANCE & CHAT** PAUL
8.	1 MS PAUL	Yes, it's today's TV Hero – Melvyn Hayes.
9.	5 WS TELLYSTACK	SCREENS PART & GUEST ENTERS,

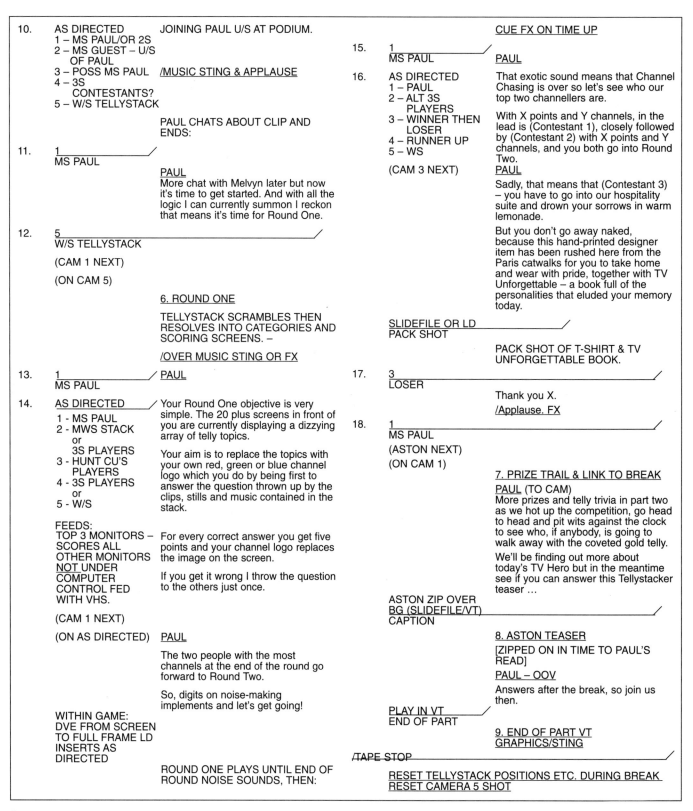

10. AS DIRECTED
1 – MS PAUL/OR 2S
2 – MS GUEST – U/S
   OF PAUL
3 – POSS MS PAUL
4 – 3S
   CONTESTANTS?
5 – W/S TELLYSTACK

JOINING PAUL U/S AT PODIUM.

/MUSIC STING & APPLAUSE

PAUL CHATS ABOUT CLIP AND ENDS:

11. 1
MS PAUL

PAUL
More chat with Melvyn later but now it's time to get started. And with all the logic I can currently summon I reckon that means it's time for Round One.

12. 5
W/S TELLYSTACK

(CAM 1 NEXT)

(ON CAM 5)

6. ROUND ONE

TELLYSTACK SCRAMBLES THEN RESOLVES INTO CATEGORIES AND SCORING SCREENS. –

/OVER MUSIC STING OR FX

13. 1   PAUL
MS PAUL

14. AS DIRECTED   / Your Round One objective is very simple. The 20 plus screens in front of you are currently displaying a dizzying array of telly topics.
1 - MS PAUL
2 - MWS STACK
   or
   3S PLAYERS
3 - HUNT CU'S
   PLAYERS
4 - 3S PLAYERS
   or
5 - W/S

Your aim is to replace the topics with your own red, green or blue channel logo which you do by being first to answer the question thrown up by the clips, stills and music contained in the stack.

FEEDS:
TOP 3 MONITORS –
SCORES ALL
OTHER MONITORS
NOT UNDER
COMPUTER
CONTROL FED
WITH VHS.

For every correct answer you get five points and your channel logo replaces the image on the screen.

If you get it wrong I throw the question to the others just once.

(CAM 1 NEXT)

(ON AS DIRECTED) PAUL

The two people with the most channels at the end of the round go forward to Round Two.

So, digits on noise-making implements and let's get going!

WITHIN GAME:
DVE FROM SCREEN
TO FULL FRAME LD
INSERTS AS
DIRECTED

ROUND ONE PLAYS UNTIL END OF ROUND NOISE SOUNDS, THEN:

CUE FX ON TIME UP

15. 1
MS PAUL   PAUL

16. AS DIRECTED
1 – PAUL
2 – ALT 3S
   PLAYERS
3 – WINNER THEN
   LOSER
4 – RUNNER UP
5 – WS

(CAM 3 NEXT)

That exotic sound means that Channel Chasing is over so let's see who our top two channellers are.

With X points and Y channels, in the lead is (Contestant 1), closely followed by (Contestant 2) with X points and Y channels, and you both go into Round Two.

PAUL

Sadly, that means that (Contestant 3) – you have to go into our hospitality suite and drown your sorrows in warm lemonade.

But you don't go away naked, because this hand-printed designer item has been rushed here from the Paris catwalks for you to take home and wear with pride, together with TV Unforgettable – a book full of the personalities that eluded your memory today.

SLIDEFILE OR LD
PACK SHOT

PACK SHOT OF T-SHIRT & TV UNFORGETTABLE BOOK.

17. 3
LOSER

Thank you X.
/Applause. FX

18. 1
MS PAUL
(ASTON NEXT)

(ON CAM 1)

7. PRIZE TRAIL & LINK TO BREAK
PAUL (TO CAM)
More prizes and telly trivia in part two as we hot up the competition, go head to head and pit wits against the clock to see who, if anybody, is going to walk away with the coveted gold telly.

We'll be finding out more about today's TV Hero but in the meantime see if you can answer this Tellystacker teaser …

ASTON ZIP OVER
BG (SLIDEFILE/VT)
CAPTION

8. ASTON TEASER
[ZIPPED ON IN TIME TO PAUL'S READ]

PAUL – OOV
Answers after the break, so join us then.

PLAY IN VT
END OF PART

9. END OF PART VT
GRAPHICS/STING

/TAPE STOP

RESET TELLYSTACK POSITIONS ETC. DURING BREAK
RESET CAMERA 5 SHOT

Figure 17.1 A script for *Tellystack*

what he had to spend, but the upper limit on the budget influenced his choice of ideas towards popular, light entertainment.

The idea was to produce a fast-moving quiz on TV programmes and personalities, full of quickfire questions and answers, a fast-talking presenter and with a different celebrity guest (the 'TV Hero') for each show. It has similarities with *Telly Addicts* but has individuals, not family teams, and a pace similar to the *Crystal Maze*.

The set includes a sofa for chatting to the contestants, chairs and buzzers, and a 'stack of tellies', consisting of sixteen televisions each with a different category or topic on its screen. When one of the three contestants chooses a category the camera zooms in and reveals what is inside the box in terms of archive clips and stills. These are researched and compiled beforehand and transferred from tape onto laser disk. This is controlled by a computer which plays the clips, stores the questions and answers and reveals the blanked-out words that are sometimes part of a printed question's clues. The computer also controls the titles and other graphics. The contestant then has to identify personalities or programmes.

Each show will have a guest celebrity known as the 'TV Hero', whose role it is to bring some variety to the action. The appearance of the TV Hero is preceded by some archive clips of past shows and productions in which the celebrity has appeared.

The script in Figure 17.1 is for the pilot programme of *Tellystack*. Read through the script and answer the questions that follow.

1 What style does the script suggest for the presenter, Paul Ross? Sophisticated, serious, light-hearted, cynical? Pick out examples of vocabulary or phrases that support this style.
2 How important is the set design, i.e. the 'Tellystack', in writing the script?
3 How many cameras are used?
4 Make a list of what the wide shots will show.
5 Make a list of what the close-up shots will show.
6 What sound effects are used?
7 How many times are there VTR inserts?
8 What parts of the script would need to be changed each week?
9 Can you think of other quiz shows which have similar prizes?
10 What role does the star guest play in the programme?

Activity

Adapt the script in Figure 17.1 working from shot number 2 to shot 9, so that you and your team can produce it later on in this unit.

If you have a vision mixer it is possible to rework this script for two cameras, so that you can video part of it for yourselves.

Choose any lively music to introduce the guests. You will need one person to be the presenter, one person to be the TV Hero, and you could limit the number of guests to two. Instead of the 'Tellystack' the presenter could pretend to pick a card from a box at random.

Case study: *Nightstalker*

This is a weekly popular crime series based on real-life crimes, presented by John Stalker, an ex-policeman, and Mary Nightingale.

This type of programme may well include library or archive material.

Read and compare the two scripts in Figures 17.2 and 17.3 and answer the questions which follow.

1 How many stories are covered in each programme?
2 Which do you think is the main story and where does it appear in the programmes?
3 Does the order in which the presenters speak change from one week to the next?
4 Does the way they introduce the topics and sign off change?
5 What style does the script suggest for John and Mary? Friendly, pacey, formal, optimistic?
6 What comes over as being the main purpose: to inform, entertain or influence people? What is the overall mood of the programmes?
7 Who do you think is the target audience for this programme and why? Consider the vocabulary, the type of stories chosen and the angle they take.
8 How many inserts on videotape (Beta) does each programme have?

Activity

Write a script following this formula for a news programme about your school or college. Add to your script suitable camera shots and camera movements.

The titles and credits for a programme and any graphics which appear in it, such as drawings, maps, graphs and diagrams, would be prepared in the early stages. The opening titles particularly can contribute enormously to the success of a programme: they are what the viewer will see first and will either attract or repel them. The choice of music could also be sorted out at this stage. Titling and graphics can range from writing or drawing on a board and videoing that, to using computer-generated material.

Activity

Make a list of the programmes whose opening sequences you enjoy. What is it that attracts you – the music, the images, the title itself?

Now consider in particular the titling. What fonts are used? Is upper or lower case used? How do they appear on the screen? Are they scrolled upwards or sideways?

Now suggest two new titles for the quiz programme and the crime programme discussed above. Do a rough sketch of how they would appear on the screen, or you may find it just as quick to use a computer package to produce the title.

Choose what colour the lettering and the background will be. Perhaps the words will be superimposed onto a scene from the production. A black or coloured ending to the lettering may help to make it more legible.

Decide which part of the picture the words will appear

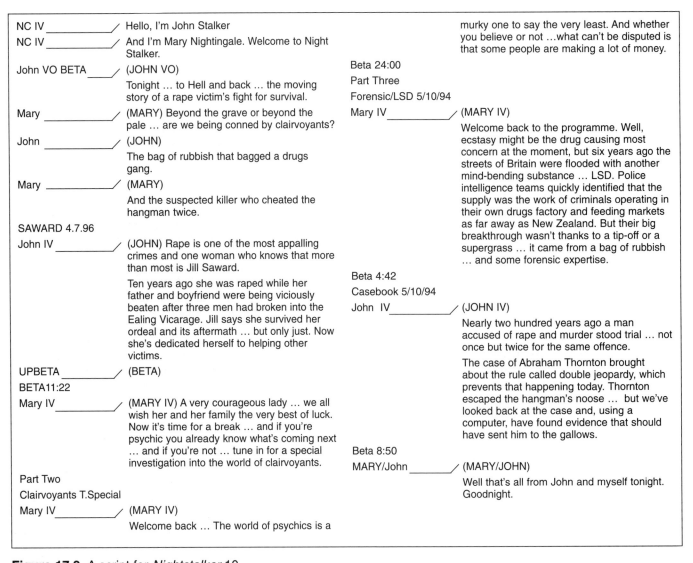

NC IV _____ /	Hello, I'm John Stalker
NC IV _____ /	And I'm Mary Nightingale. Welcome to Night Stalker.
John VO BETA _____ /	(JOHN VO)
	Tonight ... to Hell and back ... the moving story of a rape victim's fight for survival.
Mary _____ /	(MARY) Beyond the grave or beyond the pale ... are we being conned by clairvoyants?
John _____ /	(JOHN)
	The bag of rubbish that bagged a drugs gang.
Mary _____ /	(MARY)
	And the suspected killer who cheated the hangman twice.

SAWARD 4.7.96

John IV _____ /	(JOHN) Rape is one of the most appalling crimes and one woman who knows that more than most is Jill Saward.
	Ten years ago she was raped while her father and boyfriend were being viciously beaten after three men had broken into the Ealing Vicarage. Jill says she survived her ordeal and its aftermath ... but only just. Now she's dedicated herself to helping other victims.
UPBETA _____ /	(BETA)

BETA 11:22

Mary IV _____ /	(MARY IV) A very courageous lady ... we all wish her and her family the very best of luck. Now it's time for a break ... and if you're psychic you already know what's coming next ... and if you're not ... tune in for a special investigation into the world of clairvoyants.

Part Two

Clairvoyants T.Special

Mary IV _____ /	(MARY IV)
	Welcome back ... The world of psychics is a

murky one to say the very least. And whether you believe or not ...what can't be disputed is that some people are making a lot of money.

Beta 24:00

Part Three

Forensic/LSD 5/10/94

Mary IV _____ /	(MARY IV)
	Welcome back to the programme. Well, ecstasy might be the drug causing most concern at the moment, but six years ago the streets of Britain were flooded with another mind-bending substance ... LSD. Police intelligence teams quickly identified that the supply was the work of criminals operating in their own drugs factory and feeding markets as far away as New Zealand. But their big breakthrough wasn't thanks to a tip-off or a supergrass ... it came from a bag of rubbish ... and some forensic expertise.

Beta 4:42

Casebook 5/10/94

John IV _____ /	(JOHN IV)
	Nearly two hundred years ago a man accused of rape and murder stood trial ... not once but twice for the same offence.
	The case of Abraham Thornton brought about the rule called double jeopardy, which prevents that happening today. Thornton escaped the hangman's noose ... but we've looked back at the case and, using a computer, have found evidence that should have sent him to the gallows.

Beta 8:50

MARY/John _____ /	(MARY/JOHN)
	Well that's all from John and myself tonight. Goodnight.

Figure 17.2 A script for *Nightstalker* 10

in, i.e. top third, bottom third or centre frame. Will they appear to the right, left or in the middle of the screen?

Sometimes you will need captions. In a non-fiction production this might be the name of a reporter or, in a gardening programme, the name of a flower. In a fiction production a caption could tell the audience the location and date of the action, such as Bosworth Field, 1485. Captions should be kept short and left on screen long enough for a slow reader to take in the information.

Film and TV companies generally have a policy as to who should be on the credit list at the end. Again, try to keep this to a minimum.

Graphics and animation

Graphics, particularly animation, can really help explain a complex situation in an easy way. You can add movement to a photographic still or diagram by zooming in to a close-up of a particular spot. If you do use photos, try to use ones with a matt rather than a glossy finish.

You should be able to put stills and drawings onto videotape by using an ordinary studio camera, but professional studios use a rig called a **rostrum camera** which gives maximum control of camera movements over small areas. This camera is supported on a moveable bracket facing downwards onto a lit, flat bench. Its control is finely calibrated for panning, tracking, zooming and focusing onto the mounted artwork, stills, animations and models. The result is known as a **rostrum shot**.

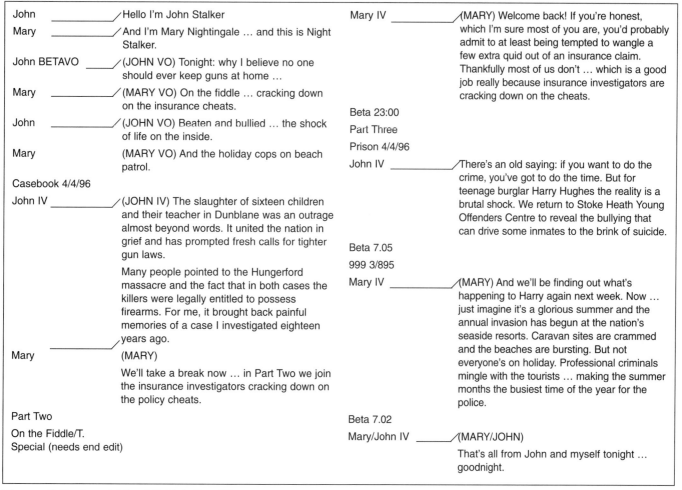

John	Hello I'm John Stalker
Mary	And I'm Mary Nightingale … and this is Night Stalker.
John BETAVO	(JOHN VO) Tonight: why I believe no one should ever keep guns at home …
Mary	(MARY VO) On the fiddle … cracking down on the insurance cheats.
John	(JOHN VO) Beaten and bullied … the shock of life on the inside.
Mary	(MARY VO) And the holiday cops on beach patrol.
Casebook 4/4/96	
John IV	(JOHN IV) The slaughter of sixteen children and their teacher in Dunblane was an outrage almost beyond words. It united the nation in grief and has prompted fresh calls for tighter gun laws.
	Many people pointed to the Hungerford massacre and the fact that in both cases the killers were legally entitled to possess firearms. For me, it brought back painful memories of a case I investigated eighteen years ago.
Mary	(MARY)
	We'll take a break now … in Part Two we join the insurance investigators cracking down on the policy cheats.
Part Two	
On the Fiddle/T. Special (needs end edit)	

Mary IV	(MARY) Welcome back! If you're honest, which I'm sure most of you are, you'd probably admit to at least being tempted to wangle a few extra quid out of an insurance claim. Thankfully most of us don't … which is a good job really because insurance investigators are cracking down on the cheats.
Beta 23:00	
Part Three	
Prison 4/4/96	
John IV	There's an old saying: if you want to do the crime, you've got to do the time. But for teenage burglar Harry Hughes the reality is a brutal shock. We return to Stoke Heath Young Offenders Centre to reveal the bullying that can drive some inmates to the brink of suicide.
Beta 7.05	
999 3/895	
Mary IV	(MARY) And we'll be finding out what's happening to Harry again next week. Now … just imagine it's a glorious summer and the annual invasion has begun at the nation's seaside resorts. Caravan sites are crammed and the beaches are bursting. But not everyone's on holiday. Professional criminals mingle with the tourists … making the summer months the busiest time of the year for the police.
Beta 7.02	
Mary/John IV	(MARY/JOHN)
	That's all from John and myself tonight … goodnight.

Figure 17.3 A script for *Nightstalker* 12

Nightstalker is a Carlton Production for ITV. © Carlton UK Television Limited MCMXCVI

Figure 17.4 Cutout animation

Cartoons such as those produced by Disney are complex, time-consuming and expensive to make. However, simple animation is possible and can be very effective.

The best sort of camera to use is one that can take a single frame at a time, such as the old Super 8mm cine-cameras. When the frames are played back rapidly in succession an illusion of movement is created.

There are a number of techniques you can experiment with, as described below.

separately a head and neck, arms and legs. Cut them out and flatten the neck, legs and arms to the body, using paper fasteners so that they can move about fairly freely. The cardboard person can then be laid on the background of your choice. The rostrum camera, or an ordinary camera set upside down on a tripod, videos the first position. Then the head or legs and arms can be moved slightly and a shot is taken of this new position. Gradually a series of different positions is filmed which, when played back, gives the impression of movement (see Figure 17.4).

Cutout animation

This is one of the simplest techniques. On some lightweight card, first draw a body, then draw

Cel animation

If you were successful at drawing cartoons, as explained in Chapter 6, then you might like to

Figure 17.5 Cel animation

Figure 17.6 A sequence for an animated drawing

extend your skill and create a series of drawings that could make up an animated cartoon. A cel is a thin, clear acetate sheet on which a character or an object is painted. A background is placed behind the cel. The part of the character or object on the acetate which moves is then redrawn and videoed again. The background can stay the same (see Figure 17.5).

Sand cel animation

In sand cel animation, sand, which can be coloured, is laid on backlit glass. The sand can then be changed into a different position and another shot taken and so on.

3D animation

For three-dimensional animation an object or model made of plasticine or pipe cleaners is placed in front of a free-standing camera. It is then moved step by step, and each position is filmed using a stop-frame camera.

Animated drawings

Another simple but effective method is to draw the basic outline of an object, such as a tree or face, and gradually add more detail to it, filming each stage. This gives an impression of something appearing from nowhere or growing (see Figure 17.6).

Computer-generated animation

There are now software packages run on PCs which can be used for two- and even three-dimensional animation. The graphics can be manipulated on screen and then 'dumped' onto video.

Resources needed for production

The personnel needed for production, the time to be allocated and the technical requirements, such as studio space or editing facilities, will be discussed below. What we will look at here are the financial resources needed, i.e. the budget.

Budgets

The financial planning for both television and film production has to take a vast number of factors into account. Two blockbuster movies released in the summer of 1996, *Twister* and *Independence Day*, both cost about £50 million to make. The way in which a film budget can be broken down was explained in Chapter 8. Here we will look in more detail at the cost of television production.

Television production

The cost of a television programme obviously varies a great deal depending on the type of programme it is. A period costume drama, such as *Pride and Prejudice*, will cost a great deal more to make than a quiz show such as *Blockbusters*.

If a producer is making a one-hour drama, he or she can expect to budget for somewhere in the region of £500,000 to £600,000 per hour. On the other hand, a half-hour sitcom (situation comedy) or quiz show could cost between £10,000 and £60,000. You can see immediately that a schedule full of light entertainment of this kind is far cheaper than making drama or documentaries.

However, good television is about obtaining a balance between the different types of programme. The success of lavish productions based on classic novels, such as *Middlemarch, Martin Chuzzlewit, Little Dorrit, Silas Marner* and *Pride and Prejudice,* illustrates that it would be short-sighted to take the cheapest alternative and broadcast an endless diet of studio-based quiz shows. At the same time, productions that cost vast sums have to be carefully considered, first with a judgement on their viability and secondly in their relationship to the other programmes.

In television this relationship between different programmes manifests itself in what is termed programming or scheduling. As audiences, we are becoming more and more specialised and differentiated in the media products we consume. Just as there are now a vast array of specialist or hobby magazines, so too there is an increasing number of television channels. These cater for specific tastes such as in film or in music; they might specialise in sport or wildlife documentaries or what is termed 'adult entertainment'. There are still, however, the 'mainstream' channels BBC1 and ITV, whose mission is to cater for mass audiences.

The television companies have to ensure that a mainstream channel reflects audience diversity. There are numerous different audiences. This is demonstrated by the amount of research needed to monitor them, which you can read about in Unit 6. Market research and the marketing mix (discussed in Unit 7) further highlight this and also illustrate the commercial nature of production activities.

However, even between the same types of television programme the cost of production can vary enormously. Let us look again at the examples of costs given earlier and consider why they might differ so much.

When a programme is commissioned, the producer or production manager of that programme has to organise, all the resources, human, material and financial necessary to produce the broadcast.

Figure 17.7 shows an example of a blank budget sheet; it lists all the resources needed for an imaginary light entertainment show.

A. Programme

Date: 24th May 1996
Budget prepared by: A.N. Accountant
7 x 30 min programmes

		Series budget £	Per EP £
3011	Artiste fees		
3012	Walk-ons		
3013	Production & rehearsal days		
3014	Artiste overtime		
3015	Artiste expenses		
3016	Artiste NI		
3019	Artiste accommodation		
3031	Locations		
3071	Music		
3091	Script fees		
3092	Package fees		
3094	Writers' expenses		
3132	Photographs		
3133	Photographers		
3174	Direct hire of staff		
3231	Picture & sound stock		
3321	Scenery		
3325	Scenery storage		
3341	Props		
3361	Costume		
3381	Make-up		
3401	Graphics		
3423	Lighting		
3425	Telephones		
3427	Supp tech equipment		
3428	Power		
3440	Catering		
3441	Hospitality		
3442	Vehicle hire		
3443	Location catering		
3445	Taxis		
3446	Stationery & printing		
3492	Mileage allowance		
3495	Meal allowances		
3496	Overnight allowances		
3502	Rail fares		
3504	Hotel accommodation		
3506	Misc. expenses		
3610	Rehearsal rooms		
3612	Producers/directors		
3615	Stage manager		
3616	Casting director		
	Total direct cost		
3644	Television house labour		
3645	Television house equip		
	Total indirect cost		
	Total production cost		

Assumptions

Studio day:	Audience only for evening show
	Prod sec to arrange audiences
Location day:	1 day location inserts/titles
	No location caterers
	Read-through & record same day
Artistes:	2 x guest artistes per episode
	Assuming deal with main artistes – no fee increases
	Artistes to travel by rail
	Main artistes to travel by car
Freelance crew:	
	All assumed to be schedule D
	Lighting director (local)
	Floor manager (local)
	Asst. floor manager (local)
	Costume designer (London based)
	Stage manager (London based - sch E)
Other:	

Figure 17.7 A budget sheet for a light entertainment show

You might think this looks detailed, but each of these headings can be broken down further, as shown in Figure 17.8 (see the next page).

As you can see, practically everything is included in a budget. Budgets are commercially sensitive. In other words, they include a lot of confidential information about a production, including, for example, the fee being paid to an actor. So much of a budget is open to negotiation that this kind of information is not generally made available. Other interested parties, such as the agent for another actor or actress, could use the information as a basis for negotiating a favourable deal for a client.

Activity

Freeze frame a scene from a contemporary TV drama. Make an estimate of everything you can see in the frame which you think has to be paid for.

Let us suppose that it involves a character standing in a street outside a house. What are the costs involved? Obviously the actor or actress needs to be paid, as do the camera crew who filmed the scene. But there are a vast number of other costs to take into account. Props and costumes have to be bought or hired. Where did the lighting come from, is it all shot using natural light? Probably not. Therefore the lighting rig and crew have to be budgeted for. Is it raining? If it is, then this is not due to a stroke of either good or bad luck but depends on whether rain was supposed to be part of the set or not. These events are not left to chance but are instead 'constructed' by the production team, and anything that is constructed costs money.

The whole scene is constructed, as are the characters that are in it: their make-up or haircuts, the ashtray in which they put out their cigarettes or the house they are standing in front of. They generally have one factor in common: they are all representations of a real or imaginary world that has been artificially constructed, with a storyline, characterisation and props. All of it has to be paid for.

Treatments

What makes some dramas, or sitcoms or quiz shows, cost more than others? The answer is that it depends on what kind of product is envisaged. Will it be a big commercial blockbuster, with lots of spectacular scene and effects, or will it be a more low-key affair for a minority audience? This information will be contained in the **treatment**.

Film producer Patrick Cassavetti explains how the process works in an interview printed in Film Education's *Movie Mogul* pack. (The pack is available free from this film industry-sponsored organisation at 41–42 Berners Street, London W1P 3AA and is highly recommended.

'Is it a project that might prove to be very commercial, appeal to a very wide audience, attract a well-known star and is therefore likely to cost in excess of $20 million? If so, it should probably be made in conjunction with an American Hollywood studio, because only they can really afford budgets of this scale. Or is it a smaller, more delicate idea that might only really work in England or possible Europe? In which case you might be thinking in terms of a smaller, more modest budget in the range of one to two million pounds, funded locally by British Screen or Channel Four. Having weighed up the project in terms of what you think you can raise for it, you then consider the type and cost of your actors and director.'

Whether it is for film or TV, the cost of casting will have major implications for the budget. Do you want a big-name celebrity, or can it work with lesser-known talent? Well-known screen personalities help to sell a new film or programme to the public. If the public like a certain actor or presenter then this person's name will help to recommend the programme to them and increase the chances of a successful launch. (You can read more about these marketing activities in Unit 7.)

The treatment will also detail the kinds of places where the filming will be carried out and the various ingredients of a scene. Is the scene to be filmed in the studio, and if so what sets are required? Does the scene require only a table and two chairs or does it need to look like the inside of a palace? Will the location shooting involve hiring properties and obtaining 'permissions' from private individuals, companies, police, local authorities, etc.?

Patrick Cassavetti gives an example of what can be involved:

'I did a low-budget TV series about bomb disposal during the Blitz. It was set in south London so I had to go and find streets that could be done up to look like wartime London ... Not only do you have to find the locations and set them up, you have to negotiate the use of them, sometimes move people out and put them in alternative accommodation. You are also responsible for about 60 people turning up in trucks, getting them into the location, liaising with the police and then getting them out again.'

295

3011 **Artiste fees**
Budget
Main artistes
Guest artistes
Warm up _____

3012 **Walk-ons & extras**
Budget
Walk-on 1's
Walk-on 2 upgrades _____

3013 **Production & rehearsal days**
Budget

Standby   Attdnce   Travel
Inclusive Contract

Main artistes
Guests
Total numbers
Rate
Total cost _____

3014 **Artiste overtime**
Budget
Studio record days
Assume 09.00–22.00 hrs
  13 hrs less 1.5 hrs break and 7 hr
  day = 4.5 hrs overtime
Artistes
Walk-on 1's
Walk-on 2's _____

3015 **Artiste expenses**
Budget
Exp per ep:
Rail & taxi   Eve meal   OOP   Total
                              Per EP
£   £   £   £
Studio
Main
Guests x 2 per EP
Warm-up
Total expenses per studio EP x 7 trips
Hair cuts _____

3016 **Artistes' National Insurance**
Budget
Artiste fees
Walk-ons
Prod & reh days
Artiste overtime
Artiste NI @ 10.2% _____

3019 **Artiste accommodation**
Budget

EPs	Nights	Forte Crest	Cost
		Incl B/F	
Main			
Guests x 2			_____

3031 **Locations**
Budget
Total budget _____

3071 **Music**
Budget
Total budget
To include composition, md, musicians,
  mrs session, etc. _____

3381 **Make-up materials**
Budget
Make-up purchases _____

3401 **Graphics materials**
Budget
Total budget for materials & external
  graphics _____

3423 **Lighting**
Budget
Studio   Gels, gobos, etc
            Tech stores
Location   Generator
            Other equipment_____

3425 **Telephones**
Budget
Office calls   Prep/clear
Buyer – mobile   Hire & calls
Designer – mobile   Hire & calls
Location manager
Costume designer
Misc crew claims _____

3427 **Supplementary technical equipment**
Budget
Tech stores, etc.
Location _____

3428 **Power**
Budget
Studio power _____

3440 **Catering**
Budget
Office tea & coffee
Read-through/rehearsals
Props _____

3441 **Hospitality**
Budget

Entertaining writers
Entertaining artistes
Record night drinks
Last night buffet _____

3442 **Vehicles**
Budget
Fuel for minibus,
  facility vehicles _____

3443 **Location catering**
Budget
None required _____

3445 **Taxis**
Budget
Taxis
Chauffeur car _____

3446 **Stationery/duplicating**
Budget
Audience tickets
Stationery
Duplicating _____

3502 **Rail fares**
Budget
Executive producer
Director
Stage manager
Read-through
Tech run
Producer/Prog. Manager _____

3504 **Hotel accommodation**
Budget
Exec. producer Nottm based
Costume designer
Director
Producer/Prog. manager _____

3506 **Misc expenses**
Budget
Parking – London
Couriers
Prodn. Misc. _____

3610 **Rehearsal rooms**
Budget

3612 **Producers/Directors**
Budget
Exec. producer prep
                studio
Director   prep
            studio _____

Figure 17.8 A breakdown of budget items

The more a location is used the cheaper the overall costs will be. If a project has numerous different locations then this will increase the costs. The production crew will be continually setting up and **striking** (breaking down the equipment, rigs, etc. after shooting). One-off 'permissions' will have to be negotiated and risk assessments made.

Conversely, if a project can make use of the same 'locations' then the costs will be less. A good example of this is the game show. This will usually have the same set, the same presenter and work to a certain formula. The more predictable and repetitive a production, the cheaper it will be.

The purpose of the budget, therefore, is to estimate realistically all possible costs of a proposed production, from pre-production through to post-production. It will cover personnel, equipment, time and materials. It should also recognise any hidden costs. Projected costs can be researched from a number of sources such as the rate cards of facility houses, acting agencies and travel companies. Story rights, copyright clearances and performing rights fees may also need to be paid. Opposite, in Figure 17.9, is an example of a rate card from a professional company which also shows how much professional tapes cost.

Activity

For your own moving image production, you will need to put together a budget sheet – and remember, very little in life is free! You should have more on your costing sheet than the price of a few videotapes. Even if you have been able to borrow props free of charge, or the college van has given you a lift to a location, you should cost these out as if you were a professional who would have to pay for them. If you are filming in the college hall, ask the administration staff how much it would cost per hour for an outside body to hire the premises.

You could use the information in Figure 17.9 to work out how much it would cost to use a professional camera crew and editing facilities.

Case study

Figure 17.10 shows some publicity material written by a student, Carl Vivian, who teamed up with others to set up a production company in order to produce videos after leaving college with a BTEC qualification and going to university. It gives production rates.

VALIANT VIDEO CO.
Current rates effective from May 1996

EFP/PSC units
2-person Betacam SP crew	£720.00 per day
3-person Betacam SP crew	£820.00 per day

Post-production
Main edit suite	£175.00 per hour	£1,380.00 per day

The suite comprises 1", Betacam SP, BVU/SP and Lo-Band VTR's. Digital mastering is available on D2, D3 or Digital Betacam.

Computer Graphics
Graphics system with designer £85.00 per hour	£640.00 per day
A/V slide production from tape	£35.00 per slide

Off-line
AVID non-linear edit with editor	£400.00 per day
AVID non-linear edit without editor	£275.00 per day
Digitising	£35.00 per hour
Dedicated Betacam machine	£50.00 per day
VHS and lo-band edit suites	£120.00 per day

Additional facilities
Studio suitable for pack shots, slide transfer and graphics, including basic lighting, camera, VTR and operator	£120.00 per hour
Burnt in time code (any format)	£60.00 per hour

Tapes: 3M professional high-grade stock
Duration

Quantity	5 mins	10 mins	15 mins	20 mins	30 mins	60 mins
1	8.50	9.45	11.50	12.00	13.50	20.00
2	8.10	9.05	11.00	11.50	13.00	19.50
3	6.00	7.00	7.85	8.50	10.00	15.00
5	4.30	4.90	5.40	5.75	6.80	10.15
10	3.20	3.50	4.00	4.40	5.05	7.50
20	3.10	3.40	3.80	4.20	4.90	7.30
50	1.80	2.15	2.35	2.60	3.00	4.35
100	1.50	1.80	1.90	2.12	2.38	3.25
250	1.40	1.65	1.70	1.80	2.05	2.80

High-grade unbranded stock
Duration

Quantity	5 mins	10 mins	15 mins	20 mins	30 mins	60 mins
10	1.85	1.97	2.10	2.30	2.62	3.64
50	.99	1.01	1.05	1.13	1.25	1.65
100	.88	.90	.91	.99	1.08	1.41
500	.80	.81	.82	.88	.96	1.25
1000	.79	.80	.81	.85	.90	1.24
2000	.77	.78	.79	.83	.88	1.24

Figure 17.9 Rates of a video production company

THE MAKING OF 'THE OLD MAN AND THE SILENCE'.

<u>Brief History of Odessa Films.</u>

Odessa Films is a limited company set up to produce independent films and provide professional experience for talented amateur film/video makers wishing to further their experience within the medium.

Odessa Films produce original work, therefore production staff are sought for their interest and skill in:

Script writing	Art direction
Storyboarding	Direction
Producing	Lighting
Sound	Music
Sound effects	Photography – video and stills
Acting	Continuity
Set design/construction	Costuming
Make-up	

And all other areas of the film-making process.

Odessa Films has just completed its first film titled 'The Old Man and The Silence'. The film is a low-budget, 25-minute drama shot and edited on broadcast video tape at a cost of £8,000.

The film allowed 20 people to gain professional film-making experience in their own specific area of the production process. The crew consisted primarily of students following media-related courses throughout the country.

The main equipment used on the film is as follows:

<u>CAMERA</u>

Sony BVW400AP kit.

Broadcast high resolution, hyperhad FIT camera docked to BVV5 Portable with playback adaptor and shooting kit.

Cost £325 per day.

Additional camera lens – Canon J8 x 6 wide angle.

Cost £260 per week.

<u>LIGHTING</u>

ARRI 2 x 2 kilowatt Blonde Lighting Kit.

Cost £90 per week.

ARRI 4 x 800 watt Red-Head Lighting Kit.

Cost £75 per week.

<u>EDITING EQUIPMENT</u>

3 Machine Pro-Beta edit suite. (One mch c/w DMC slow motion facility.)

Sony BVE 910 edit controller, Sony DFS 500 vision mixer with Down Stream Keying and trail and lighting boards. Soundcraft BVE 100 audio mixer, Sony CD player and 3 head cassette playback, plus Sony DPS 7 sound processor with audio delay. All vision and audio effects can be programmed from the edit controller with transitions/FX recorded within the Edit Decision List. A separate PC with Sony EDL can supply list management.

Cost £350 per day.

'The Old Man and The Silence' took seven days to shoot, working entirely on location within Hornton Church and the surrounding countryside. The editing process took a further seven days.

Finance for the project was raised by selling shares in Odessa Films, with each share selling at a price of £100. Odessa Films are currently marketing 'The Old Man and The Silence', and the hope is that it will reach a broadcast medium. In the meantime, Odessa Films are targeting film festivals in this country and in Europe. Also, 'The Old Man and The Silence' will be used as a marketing tool to raise finance for a second project.

Figure 17.10 Publicity material showing production costs

Figure 17.11 A studio set for a quiz programme

Identify relevant technical requirements for production

During the initial stages of developing a programme, there will be a series of meetings to discuss basic requirements such as lighting, set design, props, sound, costumes and make-up, etc.

Studio sets

One of the first decisions that a producer has to make is whether to use a studio or to shoot on location. If a complicated set is required, involving several rooms inside a large Victorian house for example, then it may be better to find a real house and film inside. However, if one set is to be used week after week, then it will be worthwhile to build it in the studio. There are obvious advantages to using a studio. They have been designed to have good acoustics and to make setting up the lighting easy. They will have flat, even floors and a sound-proof gallery from which the producer can control the crew and the talent. It is almost always more cost-effective to shoot in a studio than on location.

Not all of the technical equipment found in a television studio is used in every production, so to keep it safe from damage and to avoid wasting space and cluttering up the studio, different types of cameras, mikes, stands, cables and so on will be stored elsewhere and booked for a production.

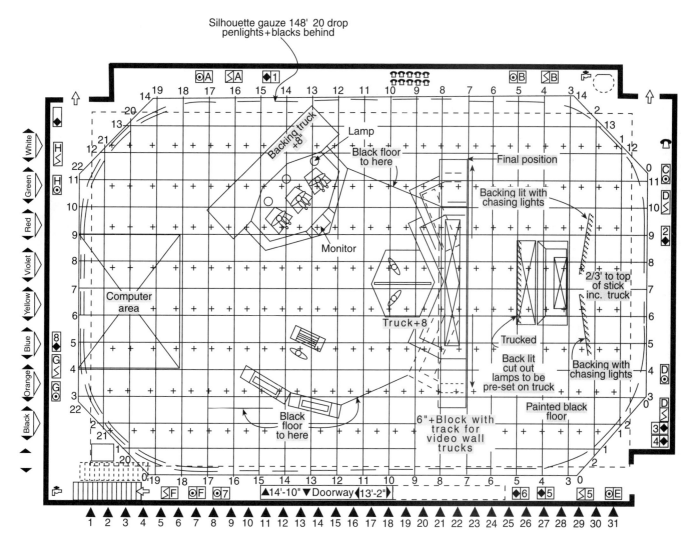

Figure 17.12 A studio floor plan

A **floor plan** is a drawing of the studio on a scale of 1:50. It is similar to a map. The walls are clearly numbered, with wall one being next to the production gallery. A superimposed grid indicates which part of the floor is useable, so that gangways and exits are free for personnel to walk along and through. The grid too is numbered around the edge, so that it is easy to locate any position. Although these numbers will appear on the walls or floor of the studios, the grid itself does not! The floor plan shows where camera cables, microphones and speakers can be plugged in and the position of scenery hoists. Onto this plan will be marked the camera positions, sound booms and the various parts of the set.

Activity

Draw a floor plan to scale of the studio or any room where you will be filming. Remember to mark in doors, power points, camera positions and so on.

Drama rehearsals are not held in the studio where the actual filming will take place. This would be too expensive. It is up to the floor manager to find a suitable location called the **Outside Rehearsal Room**, where the floor plan can be marked up so that the actors can practise. Different-coloured PVC tape is used to indicate where walls, doors and windows are. The director and cast will **block out** the basic moves and work out camera positions.

Lighting

After the initial planning meeting, the lighting director will work out a **lighting plot**. This shows which lights are needed and where they should be positioned. On a scale of 1:50, a floor plan shows where the **lighting barrels** (the bars on which two lamps can be suspended) and the scenery or sets are situated.

The individual lights used are known as **lamps** or **luminaires**. Most studio lamps use halogen bulbs which give very consistent light. Lamps can be mounted on floor stands but usually in studios they are suspended from tracks or grids or moving gantries on the ceiling. These systems make it easier to change the position of lights from one production to the next.

On the lighting plot are drawn all the lamps needed to light the set and the direction in which they are to point. It is also indicated if **gels** are to be used. Gels are coloured filters placed in front of the lamp which alter the **colour temperature**. Although not always noticeable to the human eye, there is a difference between the colour of daylight and the colour of artificial light. Their temperature, measured in degrees K (Kelvin), is not the same. Daylight colour temperature is around 5,400 degrees K and is a blue light, whilst artificial tungsten light is around 3,200 degrees K and gives off orange-coloured light.

So a blue gel will make artificial light look like daylight whereas an orange gel will do the reverse. A frost gel softens the light by diffusing it.

A general purpose light is a **fresnel**, which gives a soft-edged beam of light that can be made narrow (spotted) or wide (flooded). Moveable flaps around the lights, called **barn doors**, can control the direction and pattern of light and restrict the width of the beam as well as hold gels in place.

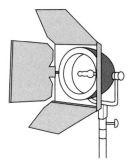

Figure 17.13 A fresnel light with barn doors

Figure 17.14 A three-point lighting plot

Techniques

How lighting is used is very important. If a lamp is positioned wrongly, for example straight into the face of a newsreader, the person will look washed out and there will be a large shadow on the wall behind. Outside, it is often better to shoot early in the morning when the sun is at a low angle so that shadows give depth to the picture.

Here are two examples of basic lighting techniques. If *one person* is speaking to camera, a **three-point lighting plot** can be used. Two hard lights are positioned, one in front to one side, and one behind the subject. These are known as the **key light** and the **back light** respectively. The key or main light is positioned at an angle of 45 degrees to give the nose a slight shadow. A weaker **fill light**, positioned to the front and on the other side from the key light, lights up the other side of the subject's face and gives a softer light which gets rid of any harsh shadows. The back light gives depth and it makes the subject stand out from the background. It has to be carefully positioned so that it does not shine into the camera.

If there are *two subjects* to be lit, then a technique called **upstage cross lighting** is used. Again, only three lights are necessary but both fresnel spots work as both key and back lights.

The strength of each light is balanced by controls on a **dimmer board**. How much lighting is needed depends on the sensitivity of the cameras, the size of the studio (including its height) and the mood required according to the type of programme. A **lumen** is the quantity of light emitted per second and a **lux** is the metric unit of illumination in which studio lighting levels are measured.

Activity

Using as a basis the floor plan you have already prepared, draw to scale a lighting plot for the room or studio you will be using.

The lighting plot is a fairly basic drawing, so when it comes to filming, adjustments are often needed; this is called **fine lighting**. In the case of drama, the lighting director will attend, along with the sound supervisor and the technical co-ordinator, a **technical run-through** in the Outside Rehearsal Room. The actors will run through the various scenes in the order in which they will be shot rather than according to the storyline. This gives the technical crew a chance to see where problems may occur and to mark in extra details.

For **location work**, lighting can be more of a problem. In a studio all lighting is artificial and controlled. On location a balance between natural and artificial light has to be achieved.

If there is insufficient light, one of the following will be done:

- the subject is moved to where there is more light
- the lens aperture is opened up

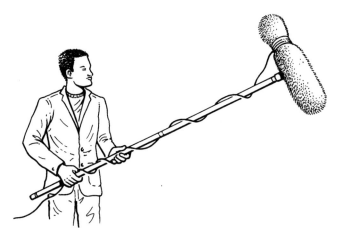

Figure 17.15 Fishpole with Dougal

- more room (local) lights are switched on
- the team brings their own lights.

Portable lights (run off either the mains or a generator) might be needed for both indoor and outdoor work. These are mounted on tripods, whose height can be adjusted. These lights can give a narrow **spot** or a wide **beam** of light.

There are two types of lights used:

- **redheads** – in a red casing, which give out 800 W of light
- **blondes** – in a yellow casing, which give out 2 kW of lighting.

Sound

Besides the floor plan and lighting plot, you will need an **audio plot**. This will detail the position of microphones and where the boom operator will stand at certain times. It may also mention other sound sources, such as for the theme music or sound effects.

Sound is an important part of most moving image productions. Some of the different types of microphone have been described in Chapter 13. Some types are particularly useful in film or television as they are either unobtrusive or invisible.

Gun or **rifle microphones** are common for both drama and electronic news gathering, studio and location work. They are unidirectional and are often fitted to a **boom** or **fishpole** so that they can be moved quickly out of camera shot and from one actor or presenter to another. If you are using a microphone on a boom be careful that it does not cast a shadow. For outside work, a fluffy cover called a **Dougal** is often put over the microphone to prevent noise from the wind.

The **Lavalier** or **tie clip microphone** can be clipped to clothing up to approximately 50 cm from the mouth. It is useful for presenters but less so for actors because of the cable connecting it to a mixer. It may also pick up on body movements.

The **radio microphone** allows for complete freedom of movement as there is no cable. It is a cordless microphone which has a small transmitter (which can be fitted in a pocket) and receiver. There is a problem if used near military bases or airfields because it might pick up other signals.

A **conference microphone** is useful for picking up speech from small groups of people around a table, as it is omnidirectional. A **PZM (pressure zone** microphone) or a **boundary microphone** are also good in this situation as they are flat and can be placed unobtrusively on a table.

Whenever you are out on location, it is worthwhile recording some **wildtrack** (a few minutes of sound without pictures), because it may be useful at the editing stage to cover any gaps in the synchronised soundtrack. Every location, whether in a street or a park or in a building, has its own unique mixture of sounds.

Activity

Close your eyes and listen carefully to all the different noises you can hear – however faint – during the space of two minutes. Make a list and compare it with the list of noises others in your group have heard.

Other requirements which you will need and should be aware of at this stage are sound and vision mixing and editing facilities. You will need to decide now what special effects and titling (including captions) you are going to use so that you can book equipment. So to plan your budget and the schedule effectively, you will need to understand the techniques and capabilities of equipment outlined in Chapters 18 and 19.

Identify personnel and allocate relevant production roles

Roles in television and film may differ, depending on the scale of the production, so that sometimes two jobs are combined or people with similar duties may have different names or report to different people. Some of the jobs listed below are concerned mainly with planning or with production, or post-production; others will see a project through from beginning to end. Some people will find that their work centres around the studio floor or the offices; others will mainly work in the **control room suite** which is above and overlooking the actual studio. The suite has three areas: for sound control, for lighting control and the main production control area known as the **gallery**.

Production team

A large studio or television company will have an **executive producer** who is in overall control of both the director and the producer. In television, especially in news and magazine programmes, overall responsibility may be assumed by a **programme editor** who may look after a whole series and not just an individual programme.

The **director** has overall responsibility for achieving the artistic and creative objectives. She or he will decide on the basic content and its treatment, appoint personnel and acquire funding. The director will have had experience, often acquired in the theatre, of working with actors. A director will also supervise the **scriptwriters** and research team and the administration. In film, there may be as many as three assistant directors with different duties.

The **producer** is the person who heads the production team and knows how to interpret the idea behind the production in practical terms. She or he will have strong powers of leadership, and will perform a mixture of management and operational roles. In television, the producer and the director may be the same person.

The **assistant producer** helps the producer in scriptwriting and researching and may direct some sequences.

The **production associate** may work for more than one producer (for example in the BBC) and is responsible for budgets.

These two people are not to be confused with the **production assistant (PA)** who helps the director – not the producer – with the administration: booking equipment, producing camera scripts and cards. At one time in film, the PA to the director was traditionally a woman, because of the secretarial skills needed. A PA has to prepare all the character generator copy so that titling and credits can be made. During recording or transmission, the PA will follow the script carefully, call shot numbers and time the various sequences and take continuity notes. He or she will try to keep the director on schedule. A PA will often co-ordinate activities. There may even be a second PA to do some of this or a **continuity person (CP)**. By continuity, we mean the checks that take place to ensure that sequences shot out of order follow on smoothly. For example, the same props must remain in the same position, or the weather has to stay the same during a single scene lasting ten minutes that has actually been shot over three days.

The **production manager** is more likely to be found in film and is a deputy producer. She or he may stand in for the director and assist with the artistic side of things, but is mainly responsible for the day-to-day problems of filming: running rehearsals, finding locations, choosing music, etc. The production manager will work out the production schedules and act as floor manager in a television studio. For a large production, there will be a separate **location manager**, **production secretary**, accountant and assistant.

A production manager is more likely to work in drama and light entertainment and the assistant producer in other areas.

The **floor manager (FM)** relays instructions from the director to actors, talent and crew through the use of hand signals. She or he ensures that rehearsals start on time and is responsible for the health and safety of not only actors and crew but also of the studio audience if there is one. The **assistant floor manager (AFM)** helps the floor manager in the studio but also has a lot of duties on location. These include organising props, writing rehearsal schedules, arranging transport and noting script changes. The **floor assistant (FA)** gives the calls for artists, make-up, costumes, the band, etc. and puts up names on dressing rooms. The FA makes sure that everyone gets to the right place on time.

Even small programmes may need three or four **research assistants** to find out about people, check information or locate pictures, etc. A **casting director** will search out and audition actors for drama productions.

Along with the director and the production assistant, there will be two other people working in the production **gallery**. The **vision mixer (VM)** works in television and video production – but not in film – and mixes the pictures coming in from the different cameras in the studio and adds effects. Sometimes there is a **video effects supervisor** if a lot of special effects (such as chromakey) are being used. The **videotape recorder operator (VTRO)** has to work out how much tape needs to be stocked for production and post-production. He or she will route and check audio and video signals.

Also in the gallery will be a videotape engineer, **technical co-ordinator (TC)** or **technical operations manager** who will ensure that there are no technical hitches or communication problems. He or she is responsible for any VT (videotape recordings) used during a production and will sort out any minor problems with the camera crew.

Camera crew

The **camera operators** generally work directly under the director, and have a **senior camera person** or a **camera supervisor**. They have to familiarise themselves with the script, the set and their camera cards.

Camera assistants are otherwise known as **grips** (who move the cameras and operate the dollies and cranes), **clapper-loaders** (because they are responsible for preparing the clapperboard) and **focus-pullers** (they ensure the correct lens is on the camera and that the camera can get the shot in focus). They do a number of administrative and practical jobs such as looking after the equipment, ensuring that there is sufficient video film and, on location, possibly driving the camera crew around.

The **video engineer (VEG)** is responsible for the maintenance of the studio cameras and the studio floor monitors.

Sound and lighting crew

The monitoring of sound takes place in a separate room, the sound control room where the **audio director** or **sound supervisor**, with possibly one or two **sound assistants**, is in control. On the studio floor, a **microphone boom grip** and **operator (MBG or MBO)** must become familar with the camera positions and the movements of actors so that they know where to place and move the microphones. **Sound operators** or **recordists** are responsible for recording wildtrack when on location. A **grams operator** plays in, on cue, sound effects and music which can be mixed with the actors' voices.

The **lighting director (LD)** organises what lighting is needed and draws up the lighting plot, and is considered to be part of the camera crew. They have to make aesthetic, creative choices and also technical decisions. The LD is assisted by the **lighting and vision supervisor (LVS)** who remains in the lighting gallery or lighting/vision control to operate the lighting console. The lighting desk is, in the majority of studios, operated by computer. The LVS will sometimes have an assistant who will control the exposure of the cameras. The **studio engineer** is responsible for sorting out the colour balance on individual cameras, so that they all match up with one another. In film the LD is sometimes known as a **cinematographer** or **director of photography**.

303

The **lighting technicians** (sometimes referred to as **sparks**) or **electricians** will not only work for the lighting director to wire or set up lamps, but may also check any cabling or wiring from any other equipment that is being used, such as amplifiers used by rock groups or standard lamps used in a play. They need to have a head for heights as they will have to work many feet up amongst the lighting grids. In film, the chief lighting technician is known as the **gaffer** and the second electrician as the **best boy**.

Designers, costumes and props

The **set designer** will have been involved with the project from its early stages. Unless the set is computer generated, it will have been erected by a **scene crew**, including **painters** and **carpenters**. **Set dressers** will add props. **Production operatives** used to be people who made final adjustments to the sets and moved anything that needed moving, but now their duties have been extended to include autocue operations or even vision mixing.

Graphic designers can have a wide range of jobs from producing titling, designing animation, drawing diagrams and maps, and making props such as newspapers or passports. They are no longer responsible for producing the captions which appear at the bottom of the screen identifying presenter or interviewees. This is the job of the **caption generator operator**.

It is not only for drama, but for current affairs and quiz programmes, that **make-up artists** and **hairdressers** will be needed. The make-up for some actors can take a long time to prepare. For example, it takes about two hours to do the make-up for the mechanoid Kryten, in the science fiction TV series *Red Dwarf*. Using a technique called prosthetics, a mask is moulded and glued onto the actor's face.

The **wardrobe master/mistress**, **costume designers**, **costume assistants** and **dressers** (who do the laundry and help actors change) are essential for any drama production.

The **properties master/mistress** has to choose and assemble all the various items needed to dress the set, which can be just about anything from a telephone to a vase or even animals! This is not always an easy task, especially if there is to be a close-up, for instance of an eighteenth-century newspaper, because it must look authentic if the real thing is not available.

Some productions will need specialist help, such as **animators**, **stunt people** and **special effects staff**.

Talent and other roles

The people who appear on camera i.e. the **talent** – **actors**, **presenters**, **interviewers** and **interviewees**, **contestants**, **guests**, even the audience – all have to be organised. A regular magazine programme, such as the lunchtime *Pebble Mill* programme, has a member of staff allocated to recruiting an audience. Sometimes people write in asking to watch a programme being made, but this person also regularly phones local organisations, such as wine clubs, senior citizens' groups or even some colleges, to ask if they would like to bring along a group of people to sit in the audience. When the audience arrive, they need to be given refreshments, told where to leave their coats, where the toilets are, etc. Magazine and sit-com programmes that use a live audience also need to provide an entertainer to 'warm up' the audience before filming begins so that they feel ready to clap and laugh.

Presenter is the term given to people who 'front' a show; they are often hired for their personalities. **Announcers**, sometimes called **continuity announcers**, read the links between programmes. These can inform the viewers about the schedules or what sort of programme it is they are about to watch, refer to delays or changes, and interrupt a programme if there is an emergency. They can give a 'house style' to a television channel, through their choice of words and tone of voice, hence the word *continuity*.

Especially when there are large groups of people around, such as audiences and film extras, it important that there are **security officers**, **safety officers** and even **medical help** available.

When on location, it is also essential that catering facilities are organised. If a large camera crew and dozens of actors and extras arrive in a small village, the local pub or village shop will not be able to cope with the demand for food. To save time and money, and to keep up the spirits of the crew and cast, it is essential that everyone is fed good nourishing food at the appropriate time.

In the film world there has always been a term for the general dogsbodies, who are known as gofers or **runners**; this is the traditional entry level for the industry.

Post-production roles

Some people come into their own in the post-production stages. The **video** or **film editor** (depending on which industry is involved) has one of the most creative as well as technically demanding jobs. There will usually be an **assistant editor** who logs shots and handles the original film, known as **rushes**. In film, **lab technicians** are needed to develop, grade and process film, or to duplicate and check videos.

The **sound dubbing editor** or **mixer** works on the edited soundtrack and will mix dialogue and sound effects and add the music to the final soundtrack. They may have to rerecord parts in order to fit the soundtrack to the pictures. Changes in recording levels will also have to be evened out.

Transmission staff with experience of telecommunications and computers make it possible for programmes to go on air. **Engineers** continually monitor and correct the signals coming in from other stations and sources and all outgoing signals. They will also repair, service and maintain equipment.

The list of peripheral jobs in moving image production seems endless: there are **accountants**, **lawyers**, **marketing** and **sales personnel**, **secretaries**, **receptionists**, **cleaners and drivers**. The person who stores copies of films or television programmes for posterity is known as an **archivist**.

Activity

Make a list of the personnel you will need for your moving image production and allocate individual roles. Explain why certain people have been chosen for particular jobs.

If you have chosen to make a live studio production, here is a list of the minimum personnel you will need. Depending on the size of your team, some people may have to perform two jobs:

- producer/director
- floor manager
- lighting director
- two camera operators
- sound director/operator
- props/costume/make-up personnel
- talent!
- vision mixer
- video recorder operator.

Reconnaissance of recording locations

The importance of a **recce** and the detail needed to be included in a report have already been stressed in

Chapter 8. The characteristics and problems associated with any individual studio or location have to be recognised and the effect they might have on production needs to be acknowledged. It might be the most wonderful location in aesthetic terms, but if it is too expensive, or takes too long to get a crew there,

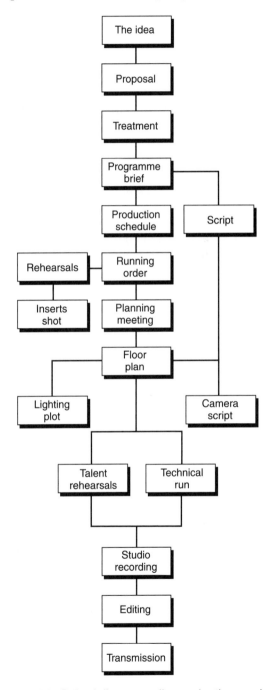

Figure 17.16 Scheduling a studio production such as a quiz or magazine programme

then it will have to be abandoned. The **British Film Commission** is a professional body that can find suitable locations for filming in Britain and is the first point of contact for foreign film crews wanting somewhere suitable to shoot their latest epic.

It cannot be emphasised too much that risk assessment is an essential part of the recce. For example, if you are filming on a boat or up a mountain, what safety harnesses will be needed? If you are planning to use firearms – even replicas – in a place where you might be spotted by the public, whom should you inform?

The recce is all about anticipating problems before they arise and then thinking of how they can be solved.

Activity

Carry out a recce for your own production, using a report form as suggested in Chapter 8 (page 190) or one you have devised yourself. The main points to cover are:

- visual suitability
- audio qualities
- risk assessment
- permissions
- feasibility, in terms of accessibility and so on.

Be honest with yourself. Have you chosen the first place that sprang to mind, or did you consider other locations?

Organise the production schedule

Scheduling is about dates and times. It's about the **logistics** of getting the right people and equipment together in the right place at the right time to produce quality work in a safe, non-stressful environment. It is about organising personnel so that everyone is aware of their responsibilities. It is about organising the budget so that money doesn't run out halfway through the project, meaning that it has to be abandoned.

Figure 17.16 is a diagram showing the process for a TV studio production, such as a quiz or magazine programme, from beginning to end.

The schedule for a daily news programme will be much tighter; see Figure 17.18 on the next page for an example.

Below we discuss in more detail how the production of a studio drama might be organised. Some tasks may be done simultaneously.

Planning stage

1 The producer has an idea or is approached by someone with an idea. A treatment is prepared.
2 The producer buys the rights to a book, commissions a script or chooses an existing script and gets copyright clearance. The length of the production is assessed and slots for commercial breaks may need to be considered.
3 A budget is created.

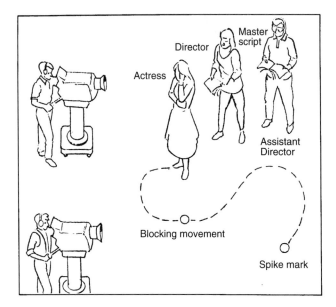

Figure 17.17 A blocking plot

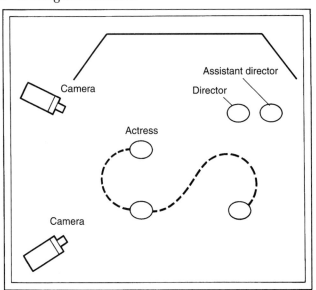

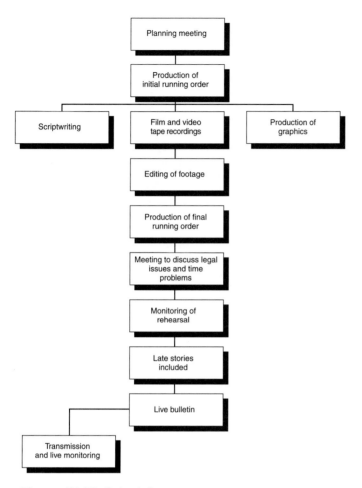

Figure 17.18 Scheduling a news programme

4 Production facilities, i.e. studios, are booked.
5 A director and other team members are chosen.
6 Auditions for the actors are held and should be videotaped to see how well they perform in front of a camera.
7 The set is designed and approved by the director.
8 Costumes and make-up designs are agreed and props are acquired.
9 A master script and floor plan is created. This may include storyboards and the **blocking plot**. This shows all the sets and, through the use of colour-coded circles and arrows, the movements made by the actors (see Figure 17.17).
10 The shot lists and camera cards are created.
11 The audio and lighting plots are drawn up.
12 Titling and credits are designed.
13 There is a maintenance check on equipment such as cameras.
14 Rehearsals are carried out, including a technical run-through.

15 The **running order** breaks down the programme into sequences. It shows the name of the sequence, who and what is in it, details about vision and sound and its duration. These sequences can be shot in order of convenience, rather than the order viewers will see them on the screen. So scenes using the same actors or the same set may be shot after each other.

Case study

Compare the running order for *Pebble Mill* with that of *Tellystack* (see Figures 17.19 and 17.20).

Production stage

16 There are crew and cast calls – this might be either a joint meeting or separate meetings. This covers facilities in and out of the studio and any other arrangements. The production schedule shows the dates and times when different personnel, including the audience, are needed and these are precisely stated. The budget is an important part of scheduling.
17 Because of their use of a lighting plot, the BBC will set up the lighting first, before installing a set into a studio, but not all companies do this. The lamps are installed or **rigged** by electricians.
18 The scenic painters and crew move in to do their work.
19 The camera crew will get the cameras out of the store and set them up on the chosen mountings, dollies or cranes. They will cable them up to the designated electricity points. They may need to rig a **tele-prompt** or **auto-cue**. This is the device put onto the front of a camera next to the lens, which scrolls up the words a presenter has to say. Anne Robinson uses a tele-prompt in the programme *Points of View*. It means she doesn't have to memorise a script, and it looks more natural than reading from sheets of paper.
20 The props are added to the set, along with glasses of water, flowers, etc. by the **dressing crew**.
21 Meanwhile the sound crew will start setting up and testing microphones. They may provide **earpieces** for talent. These are tiny devices hidden in the ear, which enable the wearer to hear any instructions the director may need to give from the gallery. This is known as **switched talkback**.
22 The videotape operator/engineer will prepare the deck and select tape.

Item	Area	Contributors	Dur
1. Titles	VT Seq 1	Opening titles **Applause** + Alan entrance	00.40
1a. Opening (01.10)	Area chat Cams 2+4 S/F	Alan open the show + Intro music (1) + S/F	00.30
2. Music (1) (06.05)	Area music Cams 1+2+4+5 VT Seq: 2 S/F's	**Applause in** "Overture" (L.U. Orchestra) + poss VT or S/F's **Applause out**	04.55
3. Intro	Area chat Cams 4+3	Alan intro music (2)	00.20
3a. Music (2) (07.45)	Area music Cams 1+2+4+5	**Applause in** "Mack & Mabel" (L.U. Orchestra + Vox x 2) **Applause out**	01.20
4. Intro	Area chat Cam 3	Alan intro	00.20
4a. Jerry Herman (1) (KPA) (14.55)	VT Seq: 3	VT – Jerry Herman **(No applause)**	06.50
5. Backref/ Intro	Area chat Cams 3+4	Backref + intro **Applause in**	00.20
5a. Music (3) (18.35)	Area music Cams 1+2+4+5 VT Seq: 4	"Movies were movies" (L.U. Orchestra + Vox) + poss VT old footage **Applause out**	03.20
6. Jerry Herman (2) (25.55)	VT Seq: 5	VT – Jerry Herman (2)	07.20
7. Music (4)	Area music Cams 1+2+4+5	"Look what happened to Mabel" (L.U. Orchestra + Vox) **Applause out**	03.00
Walk across (28.55)	Area chat Cam 3	Caroline walks across to chat area to join Alan + Howard	
8. Chat (33.55)	Area chat Cams 2+3+4+5 S/F's	Alan + Howard McGillin + Caroline O'Connor chat + S/F's **Applause**	05.00
9. Jerry Herman (3) (37.00)	VT Seq: 6	VT – Jerry Herman (3)	03.04
10. Music (5)	Area music Cams 1+2+4+5	**No applause! No lighting change** "I won't send roses" (L.U. Orchestra + Vox x 2) + Caroline enters/reprise "I won't send roses"	02.30 01.50
(41.30)		**Applause out**	00.10
11. Thanks/ intro	Area chat Cam 3	Alan thanks above + links to	
11a. Showbiz quiz/ trail	VT Seq: 7	Alan live OOV VT – Showbiz quiz + Announce winner +	01.20
11b. Trail/ payoff	Area chat Cam 3 VT Seq: 8	Alan live OOV VT – Trail tomorrow + close show	00.25
11c. Credits (43.35)	Area chat/music Cam 5 Aston Band	Band play reprise + Aston closing credits + Applause out of programme	00.25

Guests		Arrival	Researcher	
Howard McGillin	(1)	08.00	Anya Francis	(72)
Caroline O'Connor	(2)	08.00	Anya Francis	(72)
The Orchestra of "Mack & Mabel" (21 persons)	(12) (4) (7)	08.00	Belinda Essex	(71)
Alan Titchmarsh	(8)			

REHEARSAL SCHEDULE

08.45	Rehearse overture
09.25	Rehearse movies were movies – Howard
09.45	Rehearse I won't send roses – Howard/Caroline
10.10	Rehearse Mack & Mabel – Howard/Caroline
10.25	Rehearse Look what happened – Caroline
10.45	Block show
11.00	Rehearse live trail
11.05	Live TX trail (30")
11.06	Block show
11.30	Dress dome of the musics
11.40	Audience in
11.55	Rehearse live trail
11.59	TX live trail (15")
12.05	TX live prog
12.50	End TX
12.55	Record opening/links/trails for Anthony Quinn
1.20	Wrap

Figure 17.19 Running order for *Pebble Mill*

23 The person responsible for continuity prepares to take notes.
24 Lighting is checked using a stand-in.
25 Camera operators check that they can communicate with the gallery.
26 Rehearsal of actors, cameras and audio.
27 Master script is updated.
28 The scene is recorded.
29 The producer confers with the director on the acceptability of **takes**.
30 Checks are made with the continuity person.
31 Steps 16 to 30 will be repeated for each new scene.
32 Director calls for a **wrap** and **strike**, which mans that recording is over for the day.
33 Videotape is rewound and accurately labelled.

TELLYSTACK SCHEDULE: FRIDAY 28TH JUNE 1996

Camera line-up...0900/1000
Camera rehearsal 1000/1300
Lunch..1300/1400
Camera rehearsal 1400/1730
Check line-up/make-up & wardrobe........................1730/1800

Record pilot..1800/1900
Evening meal 1900/1930
Check line-up, make-up & wardrobe........................1930/2000

Record promo 2000/2200
Clear as required...2200
Part lighting de-rig...2200/2300

TELLYSTACK PROGRAMME RUNNING ORDER

1.	VT	Opening titles
2.		Paul's entrance & intro
3.		Contestant intros & chat + music sting
4.	VT	Hero clip
5.		TV Hero entrance & chat
6.	Comp	Round one: channel control + music sting or FX + time up FX + applause FX
7.		Prize trail + link to telly tease question
8.	Aston	Telly tease question
9.	VT	End of part one animation **Tape stop & reset**
10.	VT	Part two animation + applause FX
11.	Aston	Answer to telly tease
12.		Paul – welcome back
13.		Round two intro + music sting
14.	Comp	Round two – talent search + music sting + time up sting + applause FX
		Tape stop and reset
15.		Paul – interview TV Hero + applause FX
		Stop tape & reset
16.	Comp	Round three – final stack
17.		Prize award
18.		Wrap & goodbye
19.	Aston	Closing credits

Figure 17.20 Running order for *Tellystack*

Post-production

34 The producer arranges the scheduling of editing time.

35 The master script is reassembled into the intended order of the drama rather than shooting order.

36 The audio director supplies music and sound effect tracks.

37 Log forms of the videotapes and the tapes themselves are handed over to the producer.

38 The director does a rough cut edit.

39 This is reviewed with the producer and audio director.

40 The final edit is made, and music and sound effects are added.

41 The edited master tape is labelled and the record tag removed to prevent accidental erasure of the tape.

Activity

Working as a team, draw up a schedule for your own productions. It should be as detailed as the above list, but remember to add dates and times.

Case study: *Tellystack* schedule

UK Gold have commissioned 130 *Tellystack* shows (see page 287). Each show is half an hour long which, after taking commercial breaks into account, totals 24 minutes and 30 seconds. As we said earlier, it is more economical (assuming that everything else is equal) to produce something using sets that are straightforward and that can be left up or broken down easily. The producers have made decisions which reflect the need to economise but still to produce a quality product within the constraints of its 'fitness for purpose'.

The filming of the series is done in blocks. The aim is to produce five shows per day. These are then stored on video tape ready for broadcasting. This means that considerable 'economies of scale' can be achieved. In other words, if the set has to be erected, and talent made up with hair groomed etc., and the director and production crew hired, it makes sense to produce as many shows in a day-long session as is possible. Like any production line, the larger the scale of production, the cheaper will be the cost per unit.

As mentioned above, *Tellystack* was commissioned by the cable television channel UK Gold. It is produced at Carlton studios in Nottingham by the production company Zenith North, using a combination of Carlton staff, Zenith North staff and freelance personnel.

Zenith North make use of the Carlton facilities. The budget specifies how much money is available for the various parts of a production. This affects how the show is compiled. In the case of *Tellystack* there is, in effect, no post-production, with editing taking place as and when needed.

If the director is not happy with anything, either because someone has stumbled over their words, or because a contestant looked very glum or nervous, the director Ian Bolt will stop the filming and use the 'talkback' (intercom) to ask the VT Engineer (Adrian Huckfield) to wind back the tape and **pickup**, if possible, from a certain point. If it has to go back to the beginning then it is a **retake**. To make a clean edit the pickup has got to be from a point where it is technically possible to do so without it showing on screen. Adrian will try to pickup from the point asked or else will advise as to where he thinks the pickup could go from.

The show needs to give the impression that it is fast and spontaneous. In actual fact, during the making of the film there will be numerous stops and starts as they reshoot a particular part of the action. This could be the result of a mistake by the presenter, the contestants, the question master, any of the production crew or a computer fault. The director, for example, is continually giving out instructions to the cameras. A lot of this direction involves knowing and anticipating what will happen next. For example, the director will know that after finishing a certain sentence, the presenter will move, say, to the right of the set. He will, therefore, need to prepare the designated camera for this move so that Paul Ross does not suddenly go out of focus or out of frame.

The archive clips to be used are all carefully logged by the VT Engineer. This is so that the producer and director know how much archive footage is going into the show, and therefore how much time is needed for studio filming.

The specification for this series was prepared in May 1996, the first pilot took place on 28 June 1996 and a complete series was made in July of that year, ready for transmission!

Evidence assignment

You and your team should submit two scripts, one for a fictional programme and one for a non-fiction programme. These production/shooting scripts should use standard layout. You should also include storyboards. This work could be based on, and develop further, the scripts produced for Unit 2 Element 4 (Chapter 8).

The scripts will be accompanied by:

- the programme brief for both productions
- minutes of meetings between the client and your production team
- a list of resources and technical requirements for both productions
- a production schedule
- an evaluation of your contribution within the team.

Notes on research, recces and legal, ethical and representational issues should be stored in your production handbook.

Chapter 18

Production – record moving images

There are a lot of practical skills involved in this element but, although the technology may seem sophisticated, you will soon learn to master the basics. Some of the theory and techniques of stills photography apply also to moving image production, so it will be helpful if you refer to the section on how to use an SLR camera in Chapter 6 (page 140).

You need to become familiar with the various pieces of equipment, their controls and their capabilities, so that you can use them confidently and effectively. Both in this element and the next it is vital that you read the manufacturers' instruction manuals for your particular items of equipment so that you are aware of their individual features and how they work.

You will need to practise the different filming techniques several times before tackling a major assignment. It is advisable to build up a portfolio of the different camera shots, both in the studio and on location, and it is a good idea to experiment with lighting. You should always work from a script or storyboard, and it is important that you sometimes work from a colleague's script so that you learn how to interpret someone else's ideas.

Select appropriate equipment for recording and operate according to industrial practices

Recording context

By the recording context is meant not only the place where film or video is shot (e.g. studio or location, interior or exterior) but the type of programme for which it is shot.

If you are planning a new sports or news programme for the Midlands, then the new West Midlands Television Centre in the heart of Birmingham will be the ideal recording context for you! It has cost £15 million to build and is due to become operational in 1997. Central to its activities will be a large regional production studio but there will also be two more studios for news and sport, eight edit suites, production control, a graphics department, transmission and library facilities. It will, naturally, have the latest technology and equipment.

Students, of course, usually have to settle for far less. However, if you know your equipment well, are aware of its capabilities and have thoroughly planned your production and practised all aspects, then you should end up with a video you can be proud of. Central to your work will be a **camera** (see below).

Film and video

At this stage, you should be aware of an important distinction. We often use the expression 'filming' and 'videoing' interchangeably. But there are important distinctions between them, stemming from the original technology of the film and television/video industries.

The pioneers of motion pictures were Thomas Edison in the United States and the Lumière brothers in France at the end of the last century. Warner Brothers introduced sound films between 1926 and 1930. Colour films using Technicolor's three-colour system date from the 1930s.

A motion picture or **film** is a series of still photographs on film, projected in rapid succession onto a screen by means of light. Because of an optical phenomenon, known as **persistence of vision**, the viewer has the illusion of smooth and continuous movement. A **film camera** works on the same principle as the SLR camera. It makes rapid exposures of people or objects in motion. However, after each exposure, the **35mm film** is moved on by an accurately controlled electric motor, from the supply reel onto the **take-up reel**. Sound is recorded separately.

After shooting, the take-up reel holds the **rushes**. These then have to be processed in a laboratory and, as in still photography, changed from a negative to a positive image. Then the film is ready for viewing and editing. These days the shots or **takes** can be reviewed as they are filmed by electronically feeding the viewfinder image into a video monitor. When the film is edited, it is physically cut and rearranged.

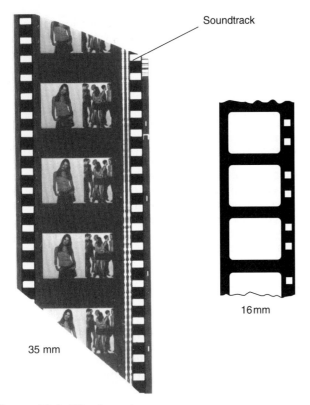

Figure 18.1 Film formats

The film is shown using a motion-picture **projector**, which is capable of reproducing sound in synchronism with the visual images.

The standard format for film is 35mm because this gives a high-quality picture but it is very expensive. Some systems, such as IMAX, use 65mm and this is also used widely when there are a lot of special effects. Early amateur cine films used 16mm format because it is much cheaper and even today some professional producers (e.g. for commercials) use this format for that reason and the quality is still sufficient. However, cinema movies, commercials for national television and TV series are still produced on 35mm film.

Television

Television relies on the same phenomenon as film, i.e. that the human retina retains an image for a brief time after it has actually disappeared. TV broadcasting is an electronic system which transmits images to receivers that can project these images onto a picture tube or screen, and which can also recreate sound. In the case of television, parts of a picture are displayed on the screen so fast that a viewer sees them as a complete picture. Between 25 and 30 pictures per second give the illusion of movement. In a television set, an electron beam scans across the screen in horizontal lines (625 lines per picture in Europe, 525 lines per picture in the US). New technology has meant that the tube in modern sets has been replaced by an electronic chip.

Video equipment

The **videotape camera** records and reproduces an electronic signal containing audio and video information. The lens system focuses the image onto a light-sensitive surface in the camera head. Originally this would have been a camera tube but, these days, the light sensor is an electronic chip called **CCD** (charged coupled device). The electronic signal can be stored on **cassettes** of magnetic tape and played back on **video cassette recorders** (VCRs) or transmitted via cables or even satellite through a control unit onto our television screens. This technology is used in television studios and also now for the home market. The way in which videotape is edited is explained in Chapter 19.

Cameras

There are basically two types of cameras – lightweight cameras, such as **camcorders**, and the even smaller **palmcorders**, which are compact and portable, and **studio cameras**, which are heavy duty and mounted on dollies and pedestals (see below). Despite their names, both can be used for studio and for location work. Most schools and colleges use camcorders to record video footage.

Tapes

There are a number of tape formats. Most domestic video recorders and the larger portable video cameras use **standard VHS tapes** (VHS stands for **Video Home System**). These tapes are the sort you can buy from high-street shops and supermarkets to record programmes from your TV. If you rent or buy a film or video, this is the quality of tape you will get. Their advantages are that they are of a reasonable visual quality and will play for up to 4 hours (or even 8 if the video player has a long-play facility). A disadvantage is that the actual tape tends to be thinner so they break more easily with heavy use.

A better picture quality is available on **Super-VHS** but these are more expensive. You will also be unable

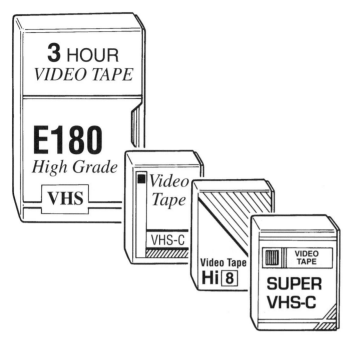

Figure 18.2 Different sizes of video tapes

VHS-C and **Super VHS**-C are tapes designed for the very small cameras; the C stands for compact. They will play for only 30 or 45 minutes (twice as long if you use the long-play facility when recording). An adaptor is needed to play them on an ordinary video player. This is a rectangular-shaped device, the same size as a standard cassette, into which the compact tape is placed.

Video 8 and the improved version, **Hi8**, are aimed at professional users, as is reflected in the price. They both have very good sound quality and Hi8 in particular has a very high picture quality. Video 8 was developed by Sony for the camcorder market and is particularly popular with small independent film-makers. Instead of one and a half-inch tape, 8mm tape is used, at the same time allowing a much longer running time than the compact cassettes, especially when in long play.

to play back these tapes on a standard domestic video player. You will have to copy them first onto a standard tape.

Parts of a camera

Figure 18.3 is a diagram showing the basic parts of a camera.

Through the **viewfinder**, you will see the images which are being recorded. The viewfinder tube only shows you the images in black and white when playing back what you have just recorded. This

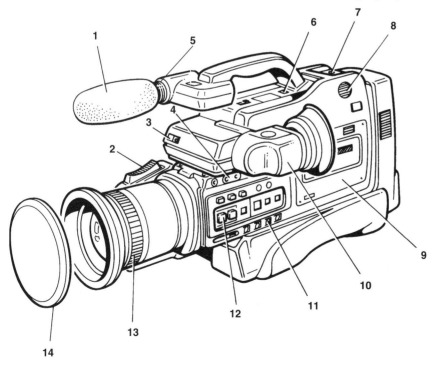

1	Stereo microphone
2	Zoom buttons
3	White balance sensor window
4	Iris close open/shutter –/+ button
5	External microphone socket (MIC)
6	S-VHS system selector switch (S-VHS ON/AUTO/OFF)
7	Tape eject button (TAPE EJECT)
8	Built-in speaker
9	Cassette compartment
10	Viewfinder
11	Date/Time button (DATE/TIME)
12	Still/Strobe button (STILL/STROBE)
13	Focus ring
14	Lens cap

Figure 18.3 Parts of a video camera

record-review/picture search function is useful for checking that you have shot useful footage but you should remember that, when using batteries rather than the mains supply, the rewind and fast forward mechanism will discharge the battery more quickly.

The **lens** adjusts the focus of the image, making it sharp or soft. It also controls the size of the image through the angle and focal length.

The **aperture** or **f-stop** determines the shutter speed of the camera. Shutter speeds can vary between 1/50 and 1/10,000; the high speed is best for recording fast action sequences. The image viewed through the lens is focused onto the camera tube, which is light sensitive.

The **white balance**, sometimes called **auto-white** or **colour balance**, adjusts the proportions of the amount of red, blue and green in the picture to suit the lighting conditions. It can be pre-set by pointing the camera at a white surface and operating the control. Modern camcorders, with an auto mode, control exposure and white balance automatically.

The **power zoom** is operated by a rocker switch which allows you to zoom, i.e. move in or out on a subject from a close-up to a wide angle, establishing shot. This is another function, however, which uses a lot of power; something to remember if the camera is using batteries.

The **auto date** and **time** inserts onto the video when the filming took place. This should generally be switched off. Many a student video has had to be reshot because it was only noticed at the editing stage that some sequences were shot with the date and time appearing in the corner!

Some controls are concerned with light. A **manual iris control** or **back-light button** opens up the lens aperture to give a foreground subject the right amount of exposure. This prevents your subject appearing as a black silhouette when shot against a bright background such as a window. On the other hand, a low light helps you to film in locations where lighting is poor. A DC light can be mounted on the front of a camcorder and is useful when fixed lighting would get in the way or be too difficult to set up. There are many special effects that can be found on modern cameras which let you **strobe**, **superimpose images**, and add **tracer**, **stills** and **wipes**. **Auto-faders** let you fade sound and vision whilst recording.

Sound is recorded through the **integral microphone** but there will also be a sound extension socket so

that auxiliary microphones, which may give better or different sound quality, can be added.

Some cameras have built-in **character generators** which let you add titling to the video, but it is better to do this at the editing stage if you have the equipment. Others have a **time function** facility where a timer records short sequences at regular intervals so that slow events or actions, such as plants growing or clouds passing, can be speeded up.

Of course, the most important button is the **record button**!

Activity

Locate the various parts of the camera you will be using. Practise the various shots suggested in Chapter 8 (see page 194). Find out what effects it can do, but remember, it is generally better to add special effects at the editing stage. Then fill in a video skills sheet similar to the one below in Figure 18.4.

Video Camera Skills	Student name	Date	Staff Signature
Connecting to mains power			
Inserting/ejecting battery			
Inserting/ejecting video tape			
Starting/stopping 'record'			
Using the 'standby' button			
Using the 'fade' button			
Using 'macro'			
Focus control (manual & auto)			
Inserting auxiliary mic			
Connecting to TV monitor			
Charging battery			
Fixing to tripod			
Tripod movements			
Close up			
Extreme close up			
Medium shot			
Wide angle			
Pan and tilt			
Pan and tilt + zoom to CU			
CU, pulling to WA and pan			
Pull focus shot			
Connect tripod to dolly			
Tracking shot using dolly			

Figure 18.4 Video skills sheet

Other features

Studio cameras, especially those used for television programmes, have other capabilities as well: for example, large zoom lenses which include an extender lens giving a wide range of angles. They also have **filters** which can be clamped into the front of the lens or contained within the camera head itself in a filter-wheel. Some filters have a similar purpose to those used in still photography. A **neutral density (ND) filter** enables a camera to operate in very strong sunlight. A small lens aperture can cut out excess light but a better picture quality is maintained by using a filter. **Corrective filters** perform the same task as the **white balance** on smaller cameras, as they compensate for a change in lighting e.g. from artificial to natural lighting. There are also **special effects filters**, such as star filters which can create patterns around the main image, or image diffusers which produce multiple images that can be rotated. However, because of the increasingly sophisticated use of computer technology, it is now better to add special effects at the editing or vision mixing stage.

Supporting cameras

Figure 18.6 A tripod

Whatever type of camera is used, it is vital to keep it steady whilst recording, to avoid camera shake showing on your video production. If your camera is hand held, you should grip it firmly and with your elbows tucked in, as with a stills camera. You may find it helpful to kneel or sit; otherwise stand with your legs slightly apart so that your weight is distributed evenly. Use a car roof, walls or table, etc. as supports.

There are a number of ways that a camera can be supported, and all but the smallest cameras have a fitting on the bottom so that they can be mounted on one of the following:

■ **monopod**
This is the cheapest type of stand, as well as the lightest, and gives vertical stability.

Figure 18.5 A monopod

■ **tripod**
This is a stand with three legs which can be extended independently to cope with uneven ground. These tripods are usually made from aluminium, which is very lightweight, so that they are easy to carry. Some tripods have a spirit level so that you can check your shots are level.

■ **rolling tripod or dolly**
For studio work, where there is a smooth, even floor, it is useful to have a more heavy-duty tripod fitted to a base with castors. This improves stability although

Figure 18.7 A rolling tripod or dolly

315

the height of the camera will be fixed. A command for a camera to move towards a subject is *dolly in* and away from a subject is *dolly out*.

■ **pedestal**

This is standard equipment in larger studios. Besides being extremely stable, it enables the height of the camera above the floor to be altered smoothly. A heavy central column is controlled, usually pneumatically, by two steering wheels. The top one guides the direction and height of the camera and the bottom one locks the camera into position.

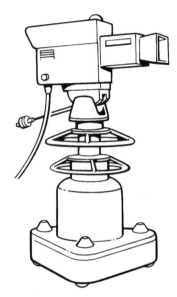

Figure 18.8 A pedestal

■ **camera crane**

In large-scale productions, directors often require an elevated viewpoint so that action can be shot over

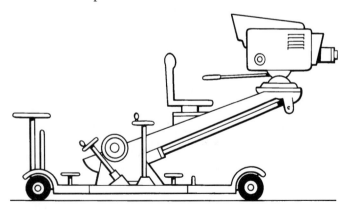

Figure 18.9 A camera crane

the heads of crowds or scenery. The large academy crane consists of a boom or crane-arm fixed to a wheeled platform. This means that a camera crew of three is required: the camera operator, who sits on the boom itself behind the camera, a boom operator and a tracker who steers the crane. Smaller motorised cranes need a crew of only two.

■ **steadicam**

This is a stabilising system for hand-held cameras which suspends a camera in a harness so that it is unaffected by gravity. This is now standard within the film and television industry and is especially useful in news gathering and taking footage whilst on the move.

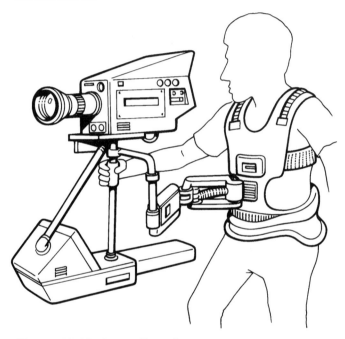

Figure 18.10 A steadicam harness

■ **car mount**

It is very difficult to hold a camera whilst filming from a car, so clamps are used to connect the camera to the car door.

Vision mixer or switcher

In live television productions, an essential piece of equipment is the **vision mixer** or **switcher**, which is located in the production control area or gallery. The output from all studio cameras, VCRs, caption scanners and so on is connected to the **inputs** of the unit. In television, the **output** is connected via distribution amplifiers to the transmission monitor.

In most media departments the output is connected to another VCR so that a student production is recorded onto cassette.

The function of the vision mixer is to cut, mix, fade up or out, superimpose and provide special effects. This will be explained more fully in the editing section in Chapter 19.

Microphones

Sound is an extremely important part of the recording process, consisting of speech and music. With some productions such as music or instruction videos, the complete sound-track can be added, i.e. dubbed on, afterwards, but mostly it will be recorded at the same time as the pictures. The different types of microphone and their uses have been listed in Chapter 13 and in Chapter 17 (page 301). In the studio, the audio signals will be sent direct to the sound control room. On location, it will be necessary either to record sound – whether speech or wildtrack – onto the video or onto a separate sound recorder.

All cameras have their own integral mikes but where possible you should use auxiliary mikes.

In the sound control room, the signals from a mixing desk will be monitored using:

- **headphones**, or preferably **loudspeakers**, which must be of a high standard in order to check the quality and balance of the sound.
- a **volume unit (VU) meter**, which is cheap, or the more accurate **peak programme meter (PPM)** designed originally for the BBC. These will check that there is no distortion and that the levels

(shown in decibels) will not overload amplifiers or transmitters, etc.

Loudspeakers are used in studios for a number of reasons:

- **monitoring** in the sound-mixing area
- **studio foldback** – this is when different sound sources are fed to loudspeakers on the studio floor
- as a **public address (PA) system** if there is a live audience, so that they can hear what is going on and they know when to laugh and/or clap
- for **intercommunication** between crew and talent and the production gallery.

Lighting

Lighting has already been described in Chapter 17 (see page 300). You should have access to portable lights with which to experiment but you will also find it worthwhile to visit your local theatre to see how lighting is operated from a desk and the different effects of soft and hard beams and filters and gels.

Connectors and cables

Besides the main pieces of equipment, you will need a variety of cables and connectors. Some have already been described in Chapter 13, as they are also used in audio, such as the different types of jacks,

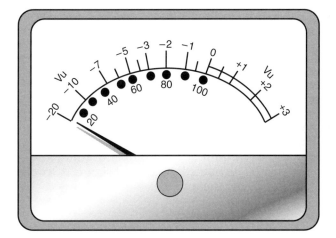

Figure 18.11 A VU meter

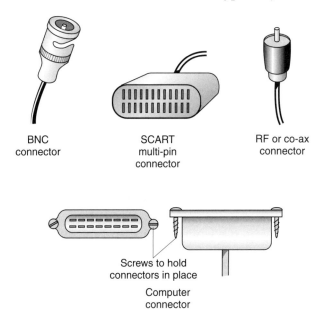

BNC connector

SCART multi-pin connector

RF or co-ax connector

Screws to hold connectors in place

Computer connector

Figure 18.12 Different types of connectors

phono, XLR and DIN plugs. Some others are used for video work (see Figure 18.12).

- a **BNC connector** can carry a video signal. Its design allows it to be securely screwed into its socket.
- a **SCART multi-pin connector** is a large multi-pin connector found on television sets, VCRs and computers. They have approximately 20 pins so can carry the variety of signals passed between these pieces of equipment.
- an **RF** or **co-axial connector** carries a combined audio and video signal from an aerial or from a camera to a TV receiver or VCR's antenna (aerial) socket.
- a **computer connector** has screws to fasten the computer securely to other equipment such as printers or editing equipment.

Activity

Look at the back of an editing suite. Do not remove any of the leads! Make a list of all the different connectors and identify which pieces of equipment they link together. Then use the correct cables to link together a television and a video camera and a television and a VCR.

In a studio all cables should be clearly labelled. Sometimes it is necessary to change input leads so that other sources, such as a DAT recorder or an extra video camera, can be used. However it is good practice to inform the studio technician or teacher of what you are doing and to put back leads into their original configuration when you have finished.

There are two types of **cables** used for cameras:

- a **multi-wire cable** which can connect the camera to VCR, mixer or television, usually used in schools and colleges
- a more substantial **multi-core cable** which in studios routes the camera to the **central control unit (CCU)**. This one cable provides power, synchronisation signals and intercom facilities as well as carrying the audio and video signals.

There are various other types of cable, their use depending on the length needed and the quality required. Multi-wire or multi-core cable is only suitable for up to 300 metres whereas **co-axial** or **tri-axial cable** goes for up to approximately 1300 metres. The lightest and strongest cable which can be used for distances over 4000 metres without interference is a **fibre-optic cable**, made from strands of glass fibre.

Adaptors and batteries

Before connecting up equipment, you should read the instruction manual. For instance, all electrically powered equipment is designed to be used with a particular form of supply, i.e. AC (alternating current) or DC (direct current). Electricity voltage can vary between different countries: it could be 120 volts or 220 or 240. Some equipment is adaptable and can be powered from different sources, but you should always read the manufacturer's instructions as otherwise you could seriously damage an expensive piece of kit and possibly endanger yourself or others.

A **transformer power pack**, such as those used by computers and many musical keyboards to connect them to the mains, will transform mains electricity down to a low voltage direct current suitable for that piece of electronic equipment.

An adaptor enables you to use a number of devices from a single source. So if you plug a **four-way** extension lead into a wall socket you will be able to use four different pieces of equipment rather than one. However, the combined load must not exceed the rating of the source of supply, for example 13 amps for the 240 volt AC supply which is standard in the UK.

When on location, you may not have access to a mains power supply. Fortunately, portable video equipment uses **batteries**, which can be recharged using the appropriate charger unit. However, you should remember that power is used up from the moment you switch on and that zooms and lights, for example, can quickly exhaust the battery. So you should always remember to take spare, fully charged battery packs with you.

Power can be saved by using a **standby control**; some video cameras have an auto switch-off if the unit has not been used for several minutes.

Batteries should not be stored in extreme temperatures; if they are left out in the sun they will lose their charge quickly. Old batteries can discharge themselves, so do not be surprised if a battery you knew was recently fully charged seems to have little voltage in it – it may have come to the end of its life cycle. There is a limit to the number of times a battery can be recharged; it is a bad sign if it seems to recharge very quickly.

Activity

Book all the equipment you will need to make your own moving image production. Include not only cameras and lights, but also tripods and smaller but essential equipment such as batteries and cables. You can use the form below or design your own.

Video Equipment Booking Form

Student name..

Date ....

Time From: ....   To:..............................

For what purpose do you need the room or equipment?

Equipment needed:

Room needed:

If filming on location have you informed a member of staff?

Has equipment been returned?

Has room been locked where appropriate?

Has all equipment, including microphones and lights, been switched off?

Have camera batteries been put on charge?

Have there been any problems with the equipment?

Figure 18.13 Video equipment booking form

Record material and produce a field footage log in accordance with scripts

Many of the creative and practical working practices for camera, sound and lighting have already been described in this unit and in Chapter 8. However, there are some visual and aural instructions you should also know about.

Figure 18.14 Floor manager's hand signals

During live productions floor managers will have received instructions from the producer or director in the production gallery through their headphones (**cans**). They will need to relay some of this information to the crew, performers and possibly the audience. They do this through the use of hand signals. Figure 18.14 shows a few examples.

Just before recording the programme, the director/producer will say '**silence on set**'. He or she wants to know that:

1   all the artists are in position

2   all crew on the floor are ready

3   the lighting is working

4   the sound crew are ready to go

5   the technical co-ordinator has started running the videotape to record and can report that the machine is up to speed. This is known as **tape pre-roll**. The director gives two cues, 'ready to roll tape' and 'roll videotape'.

The clock starts running and the floor manager counts down from 10 seconds. The VT clock was specially designed for television; it is placed in front of a camera which identifies the tape.

At the count of 5, the production assistant joins in and also counts down to zero. A fraction of a second before zero, the producer/director says 'Go grams' (i.e. the music will start) and 'Fade up 1' (camera 1) or 'Cue her/him or 'Fade up VT3' (if there is an inserted clip).

During rehearsals and transmission the director's assistant will also be giving information over the talkback to the crew. Below are some expressions they might hear on a current affairs programme where some archive film is being inserted. It is more usual now to hear the insert referred to as **VT** (**videotape**), but sometimes the film insert is called **TK** (**telecine**). If any 35mm or 16mm film is used then a **telecine operator** is needed. **Telecine** is the device used to convert film into a video signal.

Shot 199 on 2 ... 1 next – camera 2 is shooting and camera 1 is to prepare for shot 200.

Stand by film – the film insert is being lined up.

On 1 ... film next – camera 1 is on air and the film is ready.

Run film ... counting down 8–7–6–5–4–3–2–1–zero – the film is cued in and the leader tape is run, zero indicates the footage is being played.

On film for 4 minutes 5 secs – the duration of the insert is always given.

One minute left on film. Out words '... they have now left the country'. Coming to shot 212 on Cam 2 – the camera crew will now have sufficient warning that the film clip is ending and that camera 2 will soon be on air.

30 secs ... 20 ... 10 ... 5–4–3–2–1–zero – this is the out-cue; the DA counts down the end of the clip and then camera 2 will be on air.

Shots 245, 246, 247 are cut – this is a reminder that three shots have been deleted from the script.

Extra shots 334A and B – this is a reminder that additional shots have been added to the script.

Shot 452 and 4. Stand by music and roller – camera 4 is taking shot number 452, the audio tape will play the theme music and the captions will be scrolled.

Stand by for retakes – the crew must wait whilst the recording is checked and decisions made as to whether some scenes need reshooting.

We have a clear – the recording is checked and is satisfactory.

Here are some other terms you will find useful:

Stand by – a verbal command that the director is ready to start filming.

Opening shots please – the director wants to see the first shots on each camera.

Turnover – the director wants the recorder switched on.

Running – this is the response of the recordist: the cassette machine is in record mode but on pause.

Back to the top – repeat the scene or the rehearsal again.

Camera right or camera left – if you refer in this way to a camera, you describe the direction as if you are in the same position as the person operating the camera.

Set – the camera operator has adjusted the white balance, is in focus and has framed the image. The camera is on pause.

Action – the director calls this, the camera will come off pause and, two seconds later, the performance will start.

Hold it – an instruction to the floor manager to stop the rehearsal or recording. If an individual camera movement is to be stopped the following command is used.

Steady it there – stop the camera move.

Freeze – the talent should stop quite still.

Wind him/her up – an instruction to the floor manager to indicate to an interviewer that the interview should end in 15 seconds.

Stretch it – go more slowly, there is time to spare.

Kill her/cut her – there is no time left, she must stop immediately!

You should work to 3 – you should face camera 3.

Go grams – means start the music, you might also hear '**go tape**' or '**fade up sound**'.

Super – superimpose another picture.

Lose – get rid of the superimposed picture.

Go wider – zoom out.

Tighten your shot – zoom in slightly.

Kill the dog – remove the dog from shot, the animal is being too obtrusive (or any other item).

Hold the cat – keep the subject, i.e. the cat, in shot as it moves.

Tighten them up – ask a group of people to move closer together.

Freeze – the production crew and cast must remain where they are whilst continuity notes are made.

A wrap – a good take is on tape and another shot can be started.

Pick-up shots – this is any additional footage not specifically asked for in the script that could be inserted during editing in case there is an awkward cut, similar to wildtrack in audio.

Cut – the director calls this to stop the recording.

A strike – the final stage of a location shoot when all equipment is disassembled and packed away for removal. The shooting environment is put back in order.

You should use a **clapperboard** when filming. The board should be held in front of the camera at the beginning of each shot: read out the shot and take number, and then drop the clapper arm.

Figure 18.15 A clapperboard

If you decide to use the clapperboard at the end of the shot, rather than the beginning, it should be held upside down.

If you want to indicate that you are not recording synchronised sound, then hold the board in front of the camera without clapping.

Figure 18.16 The clapperboard is held upside down at the end of a shot

Activity

Practise using a clapperboard and the verbal commands. At first you will feel awkward, but it will eventually help the team to take the work seriously and save time in the studio.

The **source tape** is the original footage. This will later be edited onto a **master tape**.

Keeping a log

The **location** or **field footage log** is a record of all filming done on location. It will list the identification number of each spool of film or video cassette. It will have dates and timecode, it will contain notations about each shot and take and the duration of each take. Knowing the reasons for retakes is useful. It can then be used as the **editing cue sheet**.

Time code (sometimes called **SMPTE**, see Chapter 19, page 329) is a control track on videotape which displays hours, minutes and seconds (so 11.15 22 is 11 hours, 15 minutes and 22 seconds). It can have a frame number at the end too, such as 10.08.55.20. It can show the real time or start at 00.00.00.00. It is useful for editing to have a copy of the videotape made with the time code visible.

A good series of notes also helps the director to know what has been shot, what still needs to be shot, what

Film: Return of the Killer Sheep						
Spool	Scene	Take	Shots	Timecode	Dur	Comments
1342	30	1	244-265	214355	1'16	boom in view
1342	30	2	244-269	214523	1'18	OK
1342	30	P/UP 1	269-370	214649	0'35	James dropped sword
1342	30	2	272-370	214822	0'20	Alice said ship instead of sheep
1342	30	3	272-370	214902	0'22	OK

Figure 18.17 A field footage log

may need a retake and which shots will fit together well.

Activity

Even when you are only practising video, you should get into the habit of keeping a log. Use a form similar to the one in Figure 18.17.

Issues relating to content considerations

Most legal and ethical issues will have been resolved before the production stage but, especially in live television programmes, documentaries or the news, or interviews in shows, unforeseen circumstances may cause a dilemma.

These are the **legal and ethical considerations**:

- defamation
- copyright
- discrimination
- representation
- confidentiality
- privacy
- accuracy of sources
- exploitation
- sensationalism.

For further details about these read the Legal and Ethical appendix.

Activity

Below are some hypothetical problems you may meet when directing a production. Identify the legal or ethical issues (from the list given above) and discuss with your team what you might do. Could these situations have been avoided in the first place?

1 You are making a programme about nursing as a career. You have arranged to go to the local hospital on a certain day but, when you get there, only female staff are available for interview.

2 A studio guest has been giving a very funny account of her life. Suddenly she starts making comments about an actor and a politician which you know to be untrue.

3 During the run-through of a children's sports quiz, which is to be broadcast live, the music which accompanies some activities seems very dull. The floor manager suggests using some music by Blur which she has on CD.

4 The filming of a studio discussion on racism has been scheduled, to be included in a documentary. Unfortunately, on the day of filming British Rail has cancelled the trains from Bristol to London because of a fault on the line. As a result the two guests invited to represent the Black community phone in to say that they will be at least three hours late because the motorway traffic is very heavy.

5 A news bulletin reports on an aircrash in which it is said that 200 of the 300 passengers are dead. As it is being read on air, another report comes in saying that only 50 are dead.

6 The script for a crime programme exaggerates the details about a series of murders. The presenter reads it out in a style which might frighten elderly viewers.

7 You notice that the interviewer on a sports programme addresses most of the questions to the young female athlete rather than to the older male.

8 All of the runners on the film set, most of the dressers and even some of the grips are students from a nearby university. The producer says that this is good work experience.

9 An investigative documentary is being made on a councillor accused of fraud. He refuses to speak to the presenter, so he is filmed over the wall from the neighbour's garden.

10 A televised talent competition for stand-up comedians is being filmed during the daytime. All the studio audience, who have to vote for the winner, are retired people.

Follow safe working practices at all times

Working practices have to take into consideration all of the following:

- production team
- audience
- general public
- equipment
- videotapes or film.

For full details of risk assessment and health and safety issues, read the special appendix.

Other points to note with regard to safe working practices, include the following:

- A **slate** is a video recording device which labels the **leader** of each videotape take. Leaders, sometimes called **academy leaders**, give the title of the production, the producer/director, the date, the take number and the videotape code. Between this information and the take they will have a portion of video black or colour bars. A take begins with the slate and ends when the director says 'Cut' or the clapperboard is seen.
- The **record button** is a circular red insert plug on the bottom of professional video cassettes. Removing it prevents erasure.
- Recorded tapes should not be left near a magnetic field, for example on a loudspeaker, or on the floor of a tube train as the electric motors underneath the floor produce a strong magnetic field.

Activity

Make sure all your tapes are clearly labelled with your name, course title, title of the production and the date, and stored in a cover, also clearly labelled. When you have made a master copy you should remove the record button or tab, which will prevent it being recorded over and erased.

Evidence assignment

Working in a team, you should record the two scripts planned and researched in Unit 5 Element 1 (Chapter 17).

The rushes (unedited footage) should be submitted, supported by a production log and the scripts.

You should record in your production handbook your choice of equipment and how safe working practices were followed. Any legal, ethical and representational issues arising at this stage should be noted.

Chapter 19

Post-production – edit moving image products

Film and video editing is as creative a process as scriptwriting or camera work. It requires a great deal of mental skill and patience in selecting and structuring. As mentioned earlier, large-scale movies for the cinema and some commercials and series for television are still produced on film, which can be physically cut and sections can be re-ordered. However, television stations now rely on videotape. When they want to use film in a production, it is converted using telecine.

Most students will be recording using video rather than film cameras, so this unit will be looking in detail at how to edit videotape. To avoid confusion, the original footage from the cameras is referred to as the rushes, rather than the master or source tapes, and the final edited version of the footage is known as the *edit master* rather than the record tape.

Log recorded rushes and select footage

The editor needs the shot and slate details for film and the cassette number and time code and number of shots and takes for video. There should also be a resumé of the content as well as the start and finish points of the dialogue. Continuity notes and field logs, which include information on the moves of the actors and cameras, are helpful. (Look back at Figure 18.17 on page 322.)

Activity

You can use a form similar to the one in Figure 19.1 to log your shots. Use either a time code or counter number to identify takes. Remember that all your cassettes will need to be identified, preferably by the use of a number.

When the shots have been logged according to their relevance and technical quality, then decisions can be made about what footage will be used for the master edit.

Script title			Page No.	
TIME CODE	VISUALS	SHOT	AUDIO	

Figure 19.1 Log sheet for shots

If you have already compiled a good footage log it will be very useful at this stage. Some sections which have already been identified as unusable can be rejected without watching them again. However, you will need to become very familiar with the material that may be suitable, so it will not be enough to play this footage through once. It is a long process, but taking care at this stage will make the actual editing much quicker.

In drama production, the editor will also need a copy of the script. This should be marked with the slate number and indications of where takes start and finish. This marked-up version is sometimes called the **tramline script**.

Selecting footage

Both sound and visual images have to be taken into consideration when choosing which shots to use and which to reject. If a number of takes have been done, then the best can be chosen. The selection should be justified on the following grounds:

- relevance to the narrative
- technical quality.

Relevance to narrative

Extra footage, such as cutaway shots, may have been recorded in anticipation that inserts may be needed to add interest. In the pre-production stage, a **cutting order** may have been produced which shows how shots were intended to go together. In the process of filming, however, directors can be struck by inspiration or a change in circumstances, and different footage is the result.

In the early days of film, entire scenes were shot with the camera in one position with a fixed lens. What viewers saw was similar to what they would have seen if the action had taken place on a theatre stage and they were sitting in the audience. These days, the viewer sees a variety of shots: sometimes we see the action through the eyes of the protagonists, sometimes we are like a 'fly-on-the-wall'.

Activity

Choose any five minutes of a silent movie. (Choose an action sequence rather than a romantic interlude!) Count and describe the shots. Do the same for a modern film, preferably of the same genre. Compare the results.

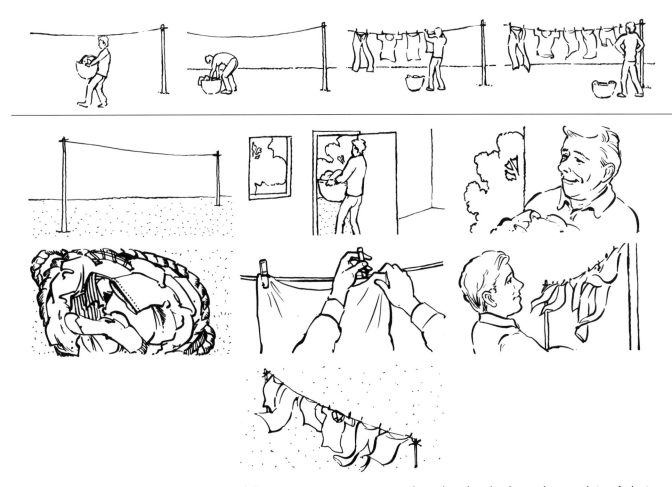

Figure 19.2 Old and modern versions of the same sequence – nowadays the view is shown in a variety of shots

Technical quality

Any of the following can spoil a take:

- there is dust on the lens or even a hair
- the shots are unsteady
- the wrong type of shot was taken (MCU instead of CU)
- the focus is poor
- the lighting was not adequate or there was too much light
- actors or presenters can't be heard.

If sound quality is poor, the visual images may be usable but the audio track may need to be replaced.

Continuity

Continuity must be checked. This applies to sound as well as visual images. These are the kinds of problems you need to look out for.

- In a period drama, for example, one set in the Victorian era, are there items in view that shouldn't be there – such as aircraft, electricity pylons or wristwatches?
- If someone has a scar, is it still there in subsequent scenes?
- If parts of scenes are filmed at different times, have props been replaced in the same position? Are actors wearing the same clothes, such as the same coloured tie or pair of shoes? If actors are eating a meal, is the food exactly the same?

Changing weather conditions and the time of day or even month can also affect continuity. In the course of a scene, does the weather change suddenly from rain to sun? Are there sometimes long shadows and sometimes short ones, showing that one part of the scene was shot in the morning and one at midday? Does any scene start in early spring and finish in mid-summer?

Activity

How good would you be as a continuity assistant? Look at the two pictures of a set in Figure 19.3. The actor made a mess of his lines so the scene was cut and a new take was made of the middle section. However, there are seven problems with continuity. Can you spot what they are?

However, remember that although a director can order a retake if there are continuity problems in drama, this is not possible with some documentary or news material. You can't ask a boxer to repeat a knockout blow on his opponent because you want a better shot. Existing footage may have to be included.

Activity

Mark on your log which shots are relevant. Which can you match up with your storyboard and script? Mark also those which are of a good enough quality.

Figure 19.3 Can you spot the differences?

When you start making video productions you may well find at this stage, if you are being critical of your work, that you need to refilm some sequences.

Organise and secure additional material as appropriate

At this stage you should also collect together the following material which you may be using in the final edit: music, titling and credits, graphics and rostrum shots.

Music

It is impossible to overestimate the importance of background music in a film or the theme tune of a television series. Sometimes the music has become a hit in its own right, for example 'Take your breath away' from the film *Top Gun*. It can really enhance the mood as well as give a feeling of continuity to what might otherwise be a series of disjointed shots or **jump cuts**. (A jump cut is where certain steps in a movement or activity are left out: for example, a man pours a cup of tea, we see him stir the sugar in the cup and lift it to his lips, and next, we see the empty cup on the saucer.)

Activity

Make a shortlist of five pieces of music which would be appropriate for your production. Give the reasons for each choice in terms of mood, period, style, nationality, etc. Also note down who owns the copyright.

Titling and credits

Some cameras and editing suites can have small character generators fitted to them with which you can write titles and credits and **scroll** them onto the screen. Fonts, however, tend to be very limited and the lettering may only be possible in black. Titling generated on a computer, such as the Amiga, is by far the best option. The software is capable of combining a wide selection of fonts, changing their size and slant, underlining words and producing them in an infinite number of colours. This work should be started long before the post-production stage.

Activity

Prepare your titles and credits. Choose a font which reflects the mood, period and style of your production.

Graphics and rostrum shots

These have been described in Chapter 17. Imaginative camera work can give life to stills and add interest to programmes such as historical educational programmes or news stories, where current footage may not be available. You should also read the print and graphics section in Chapter 6 on how to prepare artwork.

You may, in addition, need to organise a script and an artist to record a voice-over, and make a list of possible **special effects** using a vision mixer or digital effects unit. (These are described below on page 332.) But beware of being tempted into adding too many special effects, such as strobe or paint, and remember that they should never be used in an attempt to cover up poor camera work.

Activity

Introduce at least two graphic and/or rostrum shots into your non-fiction production.

Sequence the selections into an edit decision list

The **edit decision list** is sometimes known as an **editing script** or a **paper edit**. This is a list of the shots in the order they are required. The beginning and end of each shot will be identified, either through a description (of the visual image or of words spoken) or through a code number. You will have identified earlier on which are the good shots and how they match up with the narrative as outlined in the script. Now you have to make a final decision on how they are going to be used, where they will be cut and whether, for instance, cutaways will be inserted. Good editing emphasises what the director thinks is important: it guides the audience towards significant parts of the narrative.

Continuity also has to be considered at the editing stage. There must be continuity of movement. For

Title: **Fine Days**		Format: **VHS**	Date: **12/4/96**
Counter start	Counter finish	Details (content, take no. etc.)	Comments
0325	0336	L/S of Jane on swing	not properly in shot (CUT)
0337	0350	L/S of Jane on swing	OK
0351	0451	M/S of Jane on swing zoom out	OK
0452	0515	M/S of Jane sitting still on swing	Wrong expression on face (CUT)
0516	0530	L/S trees	unsteady (CUT)
0531	0600	L/S trees	OK
0610	0608	Track M/S Jane walking past fountain	wobbly (CUT)
0609	0613	Track M/S Jane walking past fountain	OK
0614	0620	L/S of fountain zoom in	OK
0621	0625	CU of fountain	OK
0626	0627	M/S of Jane in woods	child walked into shot (CUT)
0628	0637	M/S of Jane in woods	

Figure 19.4 An edit decision list

instance, if someone is walking along the street from right to left but this is followed by a close-up of feet moving from left to right, the audience will be confused. It is difficult to relate the two shots.

Another fault to avoid is **crossing the line** (see Figure 19.5). For example, if you are filming a hockey game,

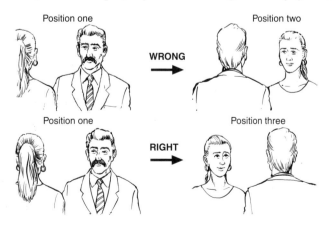

Figure 19.5 How to avoid 'crossing the line'

all cameras should be on the same side of the pitch, although they can be facing opposite goals. Shots taken from the other side would disorientate the viewers. Similarly, in an interview or conversation between two people, shots from differently positioned cameras should always be edited to show them on the same side of the screen.

This is called a **shot/reverse shot**.

Some shots do not follow each other at all well. Try to avoid:

■ cutting between two similar shots – there should be a marked change of angle or distance
■ going from very wide to close-up
■ cutting to a shot that is moving.

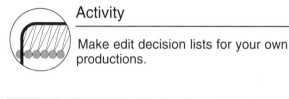

Activity

Make edit decision lists for your own productions.

Edit material according to the edit decision list

Equipment

For the most basic editing you will need:

■ the tape containing your camera shots
■ a blank videotape to be the edit master
■ one VCR to play back the rushes
■ one VCR to record this material onto the edit master
■ two television monitors so that you can monitor what both VCRs are playing.

Don't forget to book the equipment for an adequate length of time!

A **video cassette recorder** records in the same way as an audio cassette recorder. Patterns of magnetic signals are put onto a strong plastic ribbon or tape, which has **metal oxide** on one side, by the **recording head** which is an **electromagnet**. This is why a tape can be ruined, and its material erased, by leaving it near other equipment, such as loudspeakers, which have their own magnetic field.

Because there is so much information which needs to be put on a videotape, it is wider than an audio cassette tape and runs at 15 ips (inches per second) whereas audio runs at 7.5 ips (although this too can run at 15 ips for higher quality).

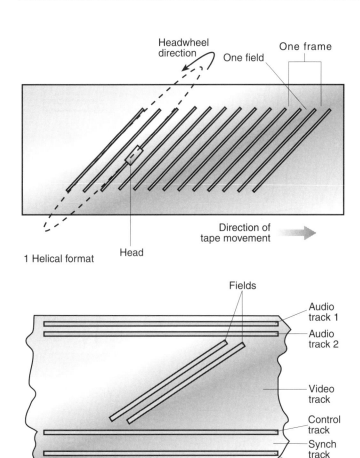

1 Helical format

2 Videotape tracks (SMPTE)

Figure 19.6 Video recording

The recording machines now used in the broadcast industry are **helical** tape machines. These lay down slanting video tracks which contain **fields** of information, for example about the picture and about synchronisation. Two formats commonly used in broadcasting are called SMPTE (Society of Motion Picture and Television Engineers) and U-Matic. The sound and control tracks run horizontally along the tape.

In film editing, rushes are physically cut, re-sequenced and the same tape spliced back together. With videotape, editing is done electronically: material from a number of tapes is put into order and electronically transferred onto another tape. This process of copying information from one tape to another is known as **dubbing**. The original tape is a **first-generation tape**. A copy or edited version on another tape will be a second-generation tape. Each

generation will be of poorer quality than the previous one in terms of both picture and sound.

The edit decision list will tell you which shot needs to be worked on first. The beginning and end of this first shot are known as **edit points**, and finding them on the tape with the rushes is known as **cueing up**. This shot can be dubbed onto the blank cassette and the same process repeated for the next shot. Then you review the master edit tape. If you are satisfied, the process can be continued.

If you are using such a simple set-up, without an editing controller, it is important that you pre-roll the machines for a few seconds, i.e. get them running to speed, before pressing the record button at the desired point.

In the example in Figure 19.7, shot 3 is wanted first and then shots 1, 4 and 2 from the rushes.

Most editing suites, however, will include other equipment. **Three-machine editing** is most usual, where two source machines VCRs – are linked to the edit VCR via a controller.

Basically, there are two types of edit: **assemble** edits and **insert** edits.

Assemble editing

The editing process explained above is an example of assemble editing. A number of shots are joined together, one after another in the correct sequence. Audio, video and control tracks are copied over together. However, you would be unable to go back to the start and add titling sequences or insert graphics, because the control track originally dubbed

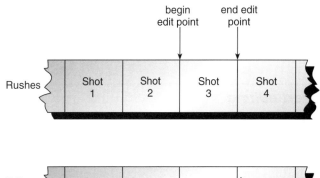

Figure 19.7 Edit points

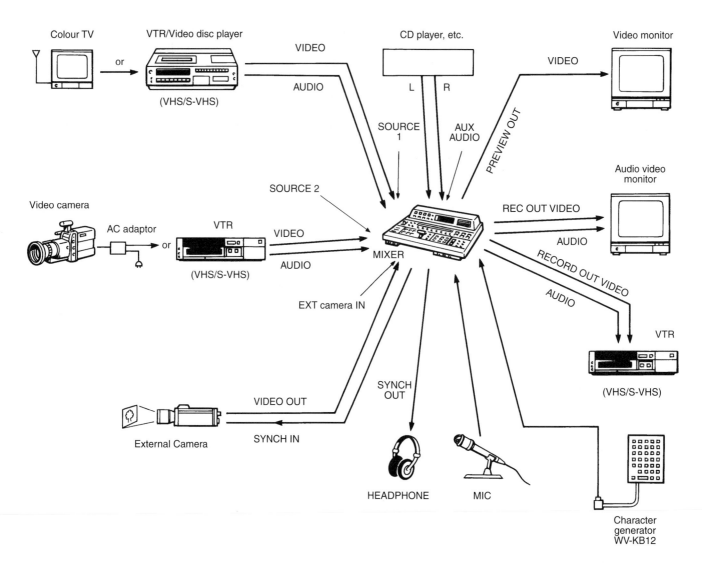

Figure 19.8 Editing system

will be erased and there will be distortion between edits.

Insert editing

In insert editing, a control blade is laid down first by using a vision mixer to record black onto the entire length of the tape. This adds control track pulses from the synch generator. This control track will remain unerased even when new material is added and the result will be a smoother set of edits.

New material can therefore be inserted over the old. For example in a cookery programme, a chef such as Delia Smith (the **talking head**) describes how to

Figure 19.9 Adrian Huckfield at Central TV Nottingham in the post-production area

Original rushes

Shot 1 Flour	Shot 2 Butter	Shot 6 Delia talking	Shot 7 Mixing ingredients	Shot 20 Baked cake

Assemble edit

Shot 20 Cake	Shot 6 Delia talking	Shot 1 Flour	Shot 2 Butter	Shot 7 Mixing ingredients

Insert edit

Shots 1 and 2 overlaid

Shot 20 Cake	Shot 6 Delia talking	Shot 7 Mixing ingredients

Figure 19.10 Insert editing for a cookery programme

make a cake. To make it more visually interesting, shots of the ingredients are shown whilst she is talking. These images can be inserted without altering the audio track.

An edit controller uses SMPTE.

Off-line editing

This can be described as a **rough edit**, pre-edit or work print. It lets you see what the cuts look like in order to finalise the edit script. It is usual in the industry for a small format tape – three-quarter inch tape – to be used instead of one-inch tape and also cheaper editing machines, as quality does not matter in this instance. It gives you the opportunity to take a little more time to experiment with the way in which different shots are to be joined.

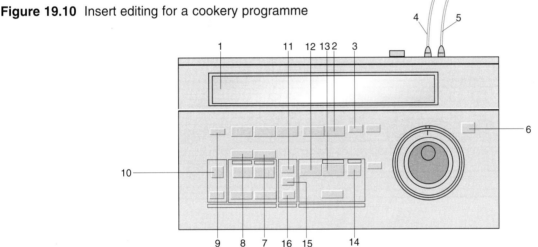

1 Multi-function Display
The operating conditions are displayed in this window.
2 Pause/Still Button
Press the Pause/Still Button to stop the tape temporarily. When this button is pressed during playback, the tape will be in the Still Playback mode. Press it again to restart the tape movement.
3 Record Button
Press the Record Button to start recording.
4 Connection Cable to the Playback VTR
Connect this cable to the editing socket of the playback VTR.
5 Connection Cable to the Recording VTR.
Connect this cable to the editing socket of the recording VTR.
6 Jog/Shuttle Button
Press the Jog/Shuttle Button to activate the Jog Dial and the Shuttle Ring.
7 Recorder Button
Press the Recorder Button to operate the recording VTR.
8 Player Button
Press the Player Button to operate the playback VTR.

9 Counter Reset Button
Press the Counter Reset Button to reset the tape counter of the VTR selected with the Player or Recorder Button.
10 Programme Button
Press the Programme Button to set editing start and end points, and also to change and clear editing start and end points.
11 Assemble Button
Press the Assemble Button to perform an assemble editing.
12 Preview Button
Press the Preview Button to preview preset editing operation.
13 Edit Start Button
Press the Edit Start Button simultaneously with the Preview Button to start editing.
14 Stop Button
Press the Stop Button to stop the editing operation.
15 Insert Button
Press the Insert Button to perform an insert editing.
16 Audio Dubbing Button
Press the Audio Dubbing Button to perform an audio dubbing.

Figure 19.11 An edit controller

331

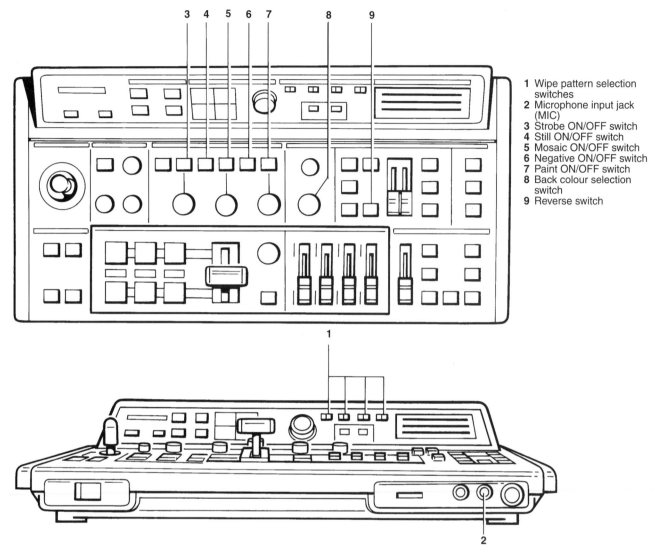

1 Wipe pattern selection switches
2 Microphone input jack (MIC)
3 Strobe ON/OFF switch
4 Still ON/OFF switch
5 Mosaic ON/OFF switch
6 Negative ON/OFF switch
7 Paint ON/OFF switch
8 Back colour selection switch
9 Reverse switch

Figure 19.12 A vision mixer

On-line editing

The time code from the rough edit is used to select material from the original rushes to use for the master edit tape.

Non-linear editing systems

The development of digital editing systems, such as 'Avid' and 'Lightworks', has resulted in **non-linear** or **random access** editing. If you make your video on an analogue system and then discover you have left out a vital two-minute sequence, which should be there at the start, you will have to do the editing all over again. There is no way you can slot it in, even using insert editing, without losing two minutes of other material. However, in a non-linear system, the material is digitised and can be manipulated and placed in any order. You could start editing a programme from the end if you wanted to!

Vision mixing

A **video switcher** or **vision mixer** is central to a TV studio. It allows you to choose material from a number of visual and audio sources (cameras, VCRs, computers, audio tape and CD players, etc.) and add effects.

There are three basic methods for introducing and leaving shots or changing from one shot to the next: cuts, fade-ins (or fade-outs) and dissolves or mixes. They work like this:

- **cuts** – the picture changes instantaneously from one view to the next
- **fade-ins** – a blank (usually black) screen becomes brighter to reveal a picture (see Figure 19.13)

Figure 19.13 Fade-in

- **fade-outs** – the reverse of fade-ins (see Figure 19.14)

Figure 19.14 Fade-out

- **dissolves** or **mixes** – one picture gradually has another superimposed and the first picture is faded out to be replaced by the second picture (see Figure 19.15)

SCENE 1: INPUT A ⇨ SCENE 1 and SCENE 2 ⇨ SCENE 2: INPUT B

Figure 19.15 A dissolve or mix

- **wipes** – a new picture moves across the screen to replace another (see Figure 19.16)

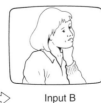

Input A ⇨ Wiped picture ⇨ Input B

Figure 19.16 A wipe

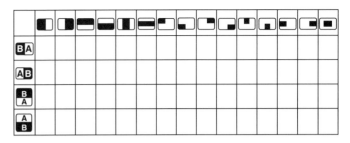

Figure 19.17 Wipe patterns

Even simple vision mixers can have many different wipe patterns. The wipe can be from right to left, up to down, or a mixture of both (see Figure 19.17).

If the wipe is halted halfway through, the effect is a **split screen** as in Figure 19.18. Other special effects include **strobe** and **mosaic**.

Figure 19.18 A split screen effect

Activity

Practise these different effects on any footage that you have recorded. Which do you think are most suitable for:

- TV drama
- the news
- a quiz
- a sit-com
- a documentary
- a romantic film
- an adventure film?

Some, of course, will be useful for any production, but have you ever seen a fade-in for the news?

Chromakey

Chromakey (**CSO**) is a very common special effect. In chromakey, a particular colour (usually blue) is chosen. When the system detects that colour in the main source, it will replace it with material from a second source. For example:

Camera 1 (source)

Figure 19.19 Newsreader with chromakey window in background

1   Source 1, a camera in the studio is filming an actress waving her arms about in front of a blue curtain (the chosen chromakey colour)

2   Source 2 is a VCR showing an aerial picture of a field.

3   The chromakey system detects the blue curtain and replaces it with the field which is shown on a third screen and is recorded onto another VCR. The effect is a picture of a girl flying. If the girl was wearing anything blue, then that too would be replaced.

It is not recommended that red is used for the chromakey colour, as shades of red appear in people's skin tones.

This effect is not only useful for fantasy films but also for non-fiction productions, such as the news and sports. Consider the following example.

Camera 2 (fill)

Figure 19.20 The Eiffel Tower in place for the chromakey window

Programme

Figure 19.21 The combination of two sources

1   Source 1 can have a **chromakey window**. The example in Figure 19.19 shows a newsreader.

2   The report is about Paris, so source 2 shows the Eiffel Tower in the top right-hand corner (Figure 19.20). It is important that the tower appears precisely where the window is.

3   In the resulting combination of the two sources, the chromakey system enables the Eiffel Tower to be shown in the corner of the screen (Figure 19.21).

Activity

If you have a chromakey system installed, try two similar effects. You could video the sky, rather than go for an aerial shot, and a local building rather than the Eiffel Tower!

Digital video effects

Digital video effects (**DVE**) produced using computer technology can either be added to the vision mixer as separate units or built in. The range of effects produced is limitless. Images can be distorted or objects can be made to fly round the screen. Objects can be exploded and reassembled.

Here are a few examples:

- **Rotation** – three-dimensional shapes, such as cubes can be rotated.
- **Flip** – this makes the first picture appear to be some sort of page which is being turned from the corner or moved out of the way to reveal another picture.

- **Push** – this is a very similar effect to a wipe, except that a second picture actually moves onto the screen and the first moves over as it is pushed off.
- **Compression** – here a picture is made longer, higher or smaller. This device is very useful when chromakey windows are being used, as a picture can be altered to fit in the window.

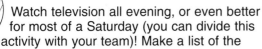

Activity

Watch television all evening, or even better for most of a Saturday (you can divide this activity with your team)! Make a list of the various digital effects used and which programmes they appear in.

Audio dubbing

You may not be happy with the original sound-track or you may want to add music or a voice-over. With a stereo VCR the original sound-track can be erased and replaced with new material or one channel can retain the original sound-track while the other adds extra audio sounds. Sound can be added from another audio source, such as a mixing desk connected to the record VCR, or a microphone can be inserted into the record VCR itself.

If you are producing a drama, you may decide that the original quality of the sound fluctuates too much between shots. However, it will not be easy to have your actors re-record the dialogue and dub it, as it will be hard to make it synchronise with their lip movements.

Synchronised sound

This is a system which uses time codes to control the starting point and speed of various pieces of editing equipment so that they are **synchronised**. Sound can be lifted off a videotape onto a multi-track recorder. It can be manipulated and improved and mixed with other sound effects or music before being placed back with the video pictures in perfect synch. Any special effects and music on the new track can then be added.

Prepare edit master for playback

At the end of the production stage, you should protect your tapes from being erased by removing the tab or record button. The tapes should be clearly labelled and **cued**, i.e. left in the position where the programme or production begins playing. They should be stored in a suitable place, neither too hot nor too cold, and well away from any equipment which might demagnetise them.

Evidence assignment

Your team should produce two edit masters, labelled and cued for playback. The tapes should be accompanied by:

- an edit decision list
- a log of recorded rushes, with comments on their technical quality and relevance in terms of content
- a record of any material additional to the script that was needed.

335

Chapter 20

Review and evaluate moving image products

When reviewing and evaluating the work done for this unit, you should look not only at the end product, but how you and your team worked together. You should identify your personal strengths and weaknesses in various roles and your contribution to the productions.

Present finished products to an audience

There are two ways to present your work:

- through a **live screening**
- through the circulation of **duplicated cassettes**.

The audience should be:

- the client
- the target audience.

The client is the person or organisation that has commissioned the work. In college activities this role is either carried out by your tutor or, possibly, by an outside organisation.

It is important to bear in mind all the time that the work has to fulfil the client's **specifications**. Whether in industry or in education, it is the **fitness for purpose** that is of prime consideration. Artistically, the goal may be to achieve the highest standards, but this may not always fit with the budgetary constraints of a commercial organisation. This is why you must continually liaise with the client to ensure that the work stays on target in terms of time, money, and all the other resources agreed in the product specification.

The advantages of a live screening will be that you can assess feedback instantaneously and note audience reactions including body language. It is easy to arrange a viewing in class time, but then students may not be your target audience. The reaction of individuals may also be affected by the opinions and attitudes of others in a group (**group dynamics**), particularly if they are in the same peer group. Advice on how to make presentations is given in Chapter 28.

Duplicating cassettes means that it is possible to select an audience sample who can watch the product when they want to, in the environment of their choice. But it is expensive and time consuming to copy cassettes and the quality may deteriorate with another generation of tapes.

Analyse audience feedback on products

Feedback from an audience can be collected through interviews, discussion groups, questionnaires and so on. You will find it helpful to read Chapter 24 here and also Chapters 12 and 16. These describe different methods of collecting information and how to analyse it.

Your research should be as objective as possible. The questions you ask should cover the content and the technical quality. A discussion might centre around the following questions:

1 Did the audience understand what was going on in the film or programme? Specific questions could be used to test their comprehension, such as 'What was the main point that the presenter was trying to make?' or 'What was the argument about in this episode of a soap?'

2 What did the audience think was the purpose of the production – to entertain, inform or persuade? Specific questions could be along the lines of 'What did you find funniest in the comedy?' or 'Would this advertisement have persuaded you to buy Bonzo dog food?'

3 What did the audience like most about the production? Specific questions could be 'Did you like the theme music?' or 'What did you think of the presenter?'

4 What was their lasting impression of the production? You could ask questions that would test people's memories, for example 'How many people were in the room?' or 'What did the stage set for the quiz look like?'

5 How original or topical did the audience think the production was? Another way to test this would be to ask them if they have seen a film or television programme which reminds them of yours.

6 What did the audience think of the technical quality of the production? Were they able to hear everything that was being said? Was the background music too loud? Did they think that the editing cut too quickly from one shot to another? Were some scenes too dark? Was enough colour used, or was the production rather dull?

7 What did they think about the length of the programme? Was the programme too short? Would they like to see another episode?

8 The opportunity should be given for your audience to say if they disliked anything in particular. A constructive form of criticism could be obtained by asking them what they would change if they were making the programme.

The information and responses you collect will help you to assess how commercially viable or popular your product is likely to be if released on the open market.

Activity

Decide which methods you are going to use to collect audience feedback. Organise and carry out the research and draw valid conclusions. Do you and the team agree with the audience feedback you have collected? Were their attitudes and opinions expected?

Present the findings to the client.

Evaluate finished products

The success of the product needs to be carefully evaluated – not only by an audience but by yourself. Only you and your team know what result you were aiming for. You should assess whether the original camera work was weak, if the camera script was not followed or if you ran over the budget or the deadline.

Activity

Design an assessment form to cover the points listed below and allow room for extended comments. Some issues to consider have been suggested, but you can add to these.

You could score each item out of five *or* grade it poor, below average, average, good, excellent. This can then be turned into a report to the client. Such an evaluation form is useful for supporting or explaining audience feedback to a client and also prior to assessing how well the project was completed.

Evaluation issues

Visual technical quality
Camera work
- Were the shots steady?
- Were the shots sufficiently varied in terms of LS, MCU, high and low angle, and so on?
- Did you shoot enough material?

Lighting
- Was the set lit sufficiently and appropriately for the effect you were trying to produce?
- Did changes in natural lighting affect outdoor filming?

Graphics and effects
- Are the titling, typefaces and effects (for example, extrusions, perspective, colour, scrolling) appropriate for the material?
- Could you have used more rostrum shots to explain situations?
- Do effects (such as mosaic, negative, fades) clarify and enhance the narrative structure, or are they used to compensate for poor camera work?

Mise-en-scène
- Does the combination of camera work, lighting, effects, scripts and props work?
- Does everything fit together?

Editing decisions
- Were these decisions guided by creativity or to patch up poor material?
- Were there alternative ways you could have edited the production?
- How much did the specified length of the product affect editing decisions?

Quality of editing
- Does the editing clarify and enhance the narrative structure?
- Do shots follow on cleanly or are there jump cuts?
- Is continuity maintained?

Audio technical quality
Microphone technique
- Are microphones in view when they shouldn't be?
- Have you used the appropriate microphones for the situation?

Sound levels and mixes
- Can you hear all speech clearly?

337

- Can different people be heard at the same volume, unless intended otherwise?
- Is background noise too loud?

Music and sound effects
- Do these reinforce the mood or the purpose of the work?
- Does the theme music grab the viewer's attention?
- Does the theme music suggest the genre of the work?

Editing
- Did you get rid of any unnecessary coughs, splutters or wrong dialogue by editing?

Content
- Did it meet the proposal?
- Did it use the correct codes and conventions for this genre?
- Does it show originality?
- Is it aesthetically convincing?

Assess own and team's role in the production process

It is not just the product itself but your working practices which need to be assessed. You have to look at how well you yourself performed and also how effectively you functioned as part of a team.

Evaluation forms for the individual and team projects have been given in Chapter 12 (pages 243–4). In that section there is also an in-depth discussion on the feedback process, which it would be worth looking at again now.

It can be difficult to be objective about your own performance and that of other people. It is not enough to state that you enjoyed being an editor or scriptwriter, camera operator or presenter. You must identify what particular aspect you enjoyed for each job, and how effective you were. For example, think about the following questions:

- Did you enjoy working in a team or do you prefer working on your own?
- Were you a leader or a follower?
- Were you on time for production activities?
- Were others ever held up by you?
- Could you accept criticism?
- Could you produce high-quality work first time, or did you need to have several attempts?
- Do you want to do the same job again?

List your strengths and weaknesses in relation to specific tasks.

Activity

Design an assessment sheet along the lines of the evaluation above, but list the different roles in the production process. Fill in this assessment form yourself and then ask the other members of the team each to fill in a similar form about you. Compare the results!

Justify completed moving image product and compare with another product

If you have produced a commercial TV show or a documentary or news programme, you can compare it with similar ones of the same genre on BBC or independent television. You should compare their **purpose** and the **target audience**. It will, however, be very difficult in practice to compare the **resources** available, especially in terms of equipment, budget or personnel, because of the sensitive nature of commercial information. Nevertheless you will be able to compare your product with a professional one in terms of:

- **Style**
  Humorous, serious, sophisticated, fast or relaxed pace, surreal or realistic, colourful or sombre, emotional or objective?

- **Format**
  Does your programme follow the same formula or narrative structure as others of the genre? Is it the same length? Has it similar presenters or talent?

- **Representation**
  Does your work represent events, issues or people in a similar manner? This part of the evaluation should cover more than stereotypes.

Commercial television is generally taken to mean any service that is not public sector, i.e. the BBC. In this sense it is termed 'independent'.

A commercial operation implies an organisation whose basic function is to make money. This will generally apply to the term *independent,* hence the mainstream bodies – ITV (Independent Television), IRN (Independent Radio News) and ILR (Independent Local Radio). However, some independent media producers are non-commercial because they are community or charity orientated, i.e. non-profit making.

Sometimes the term independent can be used more narrowly to imply an alternative or small-scale product, such as an experimental low-budget documentary or Indie music.

This unit will end with a case study of a community TV channel that operates on a small budget with mostly amateur staff. It is the type of organisation that a student can join in order to gain experience of the world of television.

Case study: Diamond Cable 7

Diamond Cable 7 is the community television service for the Leicester area. Although Diamond Cable Communications is a private, commercially run organisation, the role of Cable 7 is to involve the community in planning and producing their own programmes. Jenny Ludlam, Channel Manager, sees the Cable 7 role as a facilitating one: 'We provide the opportunity for local people to get involved with the way things are run and what is produced. Many of the programmes are made by volunteers who have come up with an idea that we have supported.'

These volunteers are both private individuals and local organisations. Altogether they total approximately 150 budding film-makers, presenters and camera crew. Besides the channel manager, they are supported by two full-time and three part-time technicians, and two administrators, all based at Cable 7's Leicester studios. These Cable 7 staff run regular monthly training evenings where volunteers learn about Cable 7 and how to use the equipment to make their own programmes.

The channel carries nine hours of new programming each week, including a weekly live broadcast *Cablelive* every Thursday evening at 6.30pm. It also produces *Filbert Focus,* the regular monthly feature from Leicester Football Club.

A planning meeting takes place every week to discuss and plan the schedules, and talk about any problems or developments. Figure 20.1 shows a typical week's scheduling.

Study the schedule. What does it tell you about the kind of service that Cable 7 is promoting?

Most popular of all the programmes is *Woodside Waifs,* a weekly feature on lost and abandoned animals filmed by Cable 7's Eric Sauzier. Together with the RSPCA, Cable 7 compiles a programme in which a number of animals are introduced to the camera each week with a profile on each given by RSPCA staff. It is a good

Diamond Cable 7 Programmes for week commencing June 3rd	
Thursday 6th, Friday 7th and Saturday 8th June	
6.30pm	CABLELIVE
7.10pm	WOODSIDE WAIFS Scraggy ragamuffins need tender loving care.
7.30pm	ROUNDABOUT Penny Heard with lots to do in Leicester.
7.45pm	FIT BITS Lyz Ankers gets you fit for Summer.
8.00pm	SATRANG Our weekly look at the local Asian scene.
8.35pm	STUDENT CUTS Students from Leicester University look at the local art scene.
9.00pm	CHEZ LESTER More capers from the infamous boarding house.
9.10pm	BEDTIME WITH PARISS A Bedtime story with a difference!
9.15pm	FILM DE MONT More work from the media students' file.
9.30pm	SOKKIT The team visit the radio station Leicester Sound.
10.00pm	Close
Sunday and Monday 9th and 10th June	
4.30pm	THE WORLD OF THE GREYHOUND Top dog action from Peterborough.
5.00pm	Women's football tournament.
7.00pm	Close

Figure 20.1 Part of a week's schedule for Cable 7

example of the role the channel plays in the community.

Altogether the channel works with over one hundred organisations, including educational establishments, community groups, charities, emergency services, sports clubs, museums and local authorities.

When Cable 7 is not broadcasting programmes, a text service called '7 text' is displayed with news and views, advice and information on local events. There is no charge for this service or for the Classified Ads section if the article for sale costs less than £100. In addition, the channel also offers advertising opportunities to local firms, either in a static form on the text or as a full commercial during the programming schedule. BBC Radio Leicester is played alongside this text service.

For one afternoon a week, staff and animals at the RSPCA's Woodside Animal Centre become stars of the small screen. They write and present *Woodside Waifs* which appears on the local community television service – Cable 7. The programme already has a dedicated following, turning staff into recognisable faces at local supermarkets.

Woodside Waifs has been on the air for just over a year and during that time staff have developed into polished performers, says Suzie Graham, manager of the animal home. 'When we first started we were petrified, and if you watch the early programmes we were awful. But as time has gone by everyone has become far more relaxed because it is a weekly event.'

A feature on the animals in need of re-homing is the focal point of the show. Every week staff decide which of the animals will appear before the cameras. They write the script which gives a history of the animal and the kind of home they are looking for. This has proved to be an extremely effective way of finding suitable new homes. 'We don't just give the audience information about the animal,' says Suzie. 'We explain exactly what is needed to take care of the animal in question. The programme is very good from an educational point of view.'

As well as dealing with individual animals, *Woodside Waifs* covers local and national animal welfare issues. Other items include a guide to animal behaviour, pet care tips and wildlife rescues.

The programme is very much a joint venture and while Cable 7 supplies the camera crew and gives advice, it is up to Suzie Graham to come up with new ideas and decide the shape programmes should take.

This ideal opportunity to provide a regular showcase for animal welfare was presented by the producers of Cable 7 who were looking for community-based programmes to broadcast. They want to give a voice to people within the local community, and staff at Woodside have proved that they can produce the goods in a professional and entertaining manner.

Cable 7 has been up and running for two years and at the moment reaches only the people living in and around central Leicester, but with time the station hopes to expand. And when this happens, the local RSPCA will have an even greater chance to keep animal welfare in the spotlight.

Figure 20.2 All about *Woodside Waifs*

So how do Cable 7 and the community interact in practice? If local organisations or individuals have ideas they have to produce a proposal. This allows people the opportunity to present their idea formally for consideration. At the same time it enables the channel manager to assess the idea in terms of its suitability for community broadcasting, or indeed any broadcasting. Jenny Ludlam has editorial control of the output. Apart from the legal and ethical considerations discussed in the Legal and Ethical appendix, she will also have to decide whether a subject is suitable for community broadcasting. For example, the subject should not be concerned with promoting the interests of a commercial concern or something which may cause offence.

---

1. **Why do you want to produce a programme?**

Please tell us your reasons for wishing to produce a programme, what you hope to achieve and why community TV is the best medium for you:

We want to produce a programme to show people what the YMCA is really like and change the often distorted view they have of us. Next year is our 150th birthday, so we have lots of celebrations and interesting events for them to watch. The YMCA exists for the community, so community TV is the obvious medium to use.

2. **What is your programme about?**

Describe the general content of your programme and how it will look: studio shoots/interviews/video inserts/remote shoots. Please be as specific as you can, particularly if you are thinking of doing a series. Use a separate sheet if necessary.

The programme will show what happens at the YMCA, all the activities, events, general information etc. and all the special events planned for our 150th birthday. This will all be filmed on location. There will be interviews with members of the YMCA and people who use us.

3. **Who do you want to watch your programme?**

Please state the age and interest of your target audience.

From 0-80: every member of the community, although many areas of the YMCA particularly appeal to the under 25s.

4. **Do you want your audience to respond to your programme? If so, how?**

Indicate phone-in/competition/visits/mail, etc.

There will be competitions and visits for response throughout the series of programmes.

5. **How much time are you prepared to commit?**

Making programmes takes a great deal of time and commitment – your time! How much are you willing to spend on your programme?

Whatever is necessary for the success of the programme.

6. **Extra publicity for your programme**

Your programme will be publicised within Cable 7, but it is up to you to publicise the programme outside the Channel. We need to see copies of press releases/posters/fliers/programmes, etc. before they are sent out. Also please give us copies of any press coverage/publicity letters you receive.

---

7. **How long will your programme be?**

Less than 5 mins.___ 10 mins.___ 20 mins. ✓
30 mins.___ 60 mins.___ Any other length *or 15 mins*

8. **What facilities will you require?**

Please indicate if you need film crew/equipment only/studio/edit facilities:

Camera man; sound man; editing.

9. **When, if at all, will your programme be out of date?**

The special features – 1 month; but general footage, 12 months.

10. **Additional programme information**

If you wish to add any other points not covered by the above please do so here:

Figure 20.3 A Cable 7 programme proposal

The proposal shown in Figure 20.3 is typical of the kind of programme that Cable 7 supports.

Although it is a business, Diamond Cable supports the community focus of Cable 7 because it provides good publicity – it promotes Diamond Cable as a company that is interested in the community. It is, therefore, prepared to cover the overheads such as heating, lighting, telephone, rent and rates. It also provides a yearly operating budget of £172,000, of which £142,000 is spent on salaries, with £30,000 for operating costs, which includes the servicing and repair of three vehicles.

How appropriate would either of your productions be for broadcasting through Cable 7? Draft a letter to Jenny Ludlam explaining how your work would be suitable for this channel, or how it could be adapted, and where it would fit into the schedules of Cable 7.

Evidence assignment

Play your moving image productions to an audience. Record feedback from the audience and analyse the findings.

Write a report evaluating each product in terms of:

- how much it kept to the original proposal
- whether the content used accepted codes and conventions
- its relevance for the target audience
- topicality, entertainment value and originality
- technical quality, including camera work, lighting, visual effects, microphone technique, sound levels, accuracy of editing, etc.
- audience response.

The report should also assess the effectiveness of the planning and production processes, and evaluate your own performance within the team.

Details of the methods used for audience testing can be kept in your production handbook. This work may also be used as evidence for Unit 6 Element 4 (Chapter 24).

Producing Moving Image Products: Unit Test

1 Which of these productions is most likely to involve contingency planning?
  a a television soap
  b a horror film
  c a televised horse race
  d a cinema commercial

2 Details about which of the following will be contained in the programme brief for a quiz programme?
  a the names and addresses of members of the audience
  b a recce report on lighting and sound
  c the projected budget for talent
  d the results of the pilot programme

3 Who will have to agree the programme brief for an adventure series on commercial TV?
  a the audience for the pilot
  b the TV company directors
  c the production team
  d the advertisers

4 Which of these is an example of content research for a documentary on the Olympics?
  a the names of the winning international athletes
  b how long it takes to produce animated sequences
  c when a well-known sports commentator is free
  d which type of microphones will be best on location

5 For which of these would you be expected to produce a camera card?
  a an interview with a lawyer as he or she leaves the courtroom
  b an interview with the winner of a cycling competition
  c an interview with an accident victim in hospital
  d an interview with a guest on a chat show

6 Which of these is most likely to use a storyboard?
  a an advert
  b a chat show
  c a news bulletin
  d a weather report

7 Which of these is most likely to describe an establishing shot?
  a CU   **b** LS
  c MS   **d** ES

8 Why does a camera operator find a camera card useful?
  a it contains the dialogue and actors' movements
  b it shows what the other cameras are doing
  c the camera can be programmed to follow it
  d it is a shortened version of the shooting script

9 Which of these shots is typical of rostrum camera work?
  a an aerial shot from a plane
  b a close-up of an actor
  c a zoom in on a still
  d a medium shot using strobe

10 Decide whether the following statements are true or false:
  i cel animation is produced using a computer
  ii animation is used only in children's programmes

  Which answer below is correct?

  a **i** is true and   **ii** is true
  b **i** is true and   **ii** is false
  c **i** is false and   **ii** is true
  d **i** is false and   **ii** is false

11 On an hourly average, which of the following would probably be the cheapest to produce?
  a a sit-com
  b the main evening news
  c a horror film
  d a period drama

All of the items below help a production team set up their equipment. Use them to answer questions 12–14.

a the recce
b the lighting plot
c the audio plot
d the floor plan

12 Which of the above would you consult to find out how to position a microphone for a studio discussion?

13 Which would you consult to alter the position of a lamp suspended from a gantry?

14 Which would you consult to find out the position of the scenery hoist?

15 What colour gel will make artificial light look like daylight?
a yellow
b blue
c red
d orange

16 Which light would you use to get rid of shadows on a newsreader's face?
a a fill light
b a back light
c a key light
d a cross light

17 Which of these microphones should not appear in the camera shot?
a a tie-clip mike for an outside broadcast
b a boom mike in a drama
c a radio mike at a sporting event
d a conference mike for a studio discussion

18 Who is responsible for helping the director with administration and keeping him or her on schedule?
a the assistant producer
b the producer
c the executive producer
d the production assistant

19 Which of the following works in the production gallery?
a the floor manager
b the focus puller
c the vision mixer
d the clapper loader

20 What tells the floor manager the sequence of activities in the studio on a particular day?
a the running order
b the treatment
c the camera card
d the cue sheet

21 When the lighting is poor, which control will open up the lens aperture?
a the power zoom
b the manual iris
c the viewfinder
d the tracer

22 What will help you make a smooth tracking shot in the studio?
a a steadicam
b a dolly
c a monopod
d a tripod

23 During a recording session in the studio, which of these commands will the director give first?
a go grams
b we have a clear
c action
d turnover

24 What should a field footage log contain?
a the production budget
b the recce report
c the number of shots and takes
d the names of the camera operators

25 When is a paper edit done?
a before the master edit
b as the film is shot
c after the master edit
d during the master edit

26 What is the name used for the beginning and end of the shots to be dubbed on to another tape?
a dubs
b inserts
c cue ups
d edit points

27 On the main evening news, which of the following types of edit do you expect to see?
a dissolves
b cuts
c mixes
d wipes

28 What can compress a picture to fit in a 'window' in the corner of the screen?
a the vision mixer
b chromakey
c a DVE unit
d an edit controller

29 Which of these is a rough edit?
   a an on-line edit
   b an assemble edit
   c an off-line edit
   d an insert edit

30 Which of these editing systems needs to be digital?
   a linear
   b off-line
   c random access
   d three machine

All media research is conducted for one of two main reasons: either to expand knowledge generally or to solve particular problems or needs. Students, teachers, sociologists and members of the general public may perhaps study the media for the first reason.

This unit is, however, concerned mainly with the second type of research. It will look at both products and

audiences and the methods by which information about them is collected and interpreted. Professionals within the media industries, governments wishing to control the media, and people with financial interests in the media are amongst those who have definite objectives or reasons for instigating research and using the data to support their own purposes.

Investigate the use of audience research in the media

This chapter looks at the five main reasons for carrying out audience research. These are: to assess existing media products, to develop new products, to market media products, to assess the effect of media products, and to control media products. There are two main types of research, quantitative and qualitative, each with strengths and weaknesses. There are various bodies that engage in research.

Activity

Choose a magazine. What do you know about it? In particular, can you answer the above questions without doing any research? You will probably need to have completed more of this unit and also some of Units 1 and 8 before you have the skills and knowledge to do this easily. Try identifying what makes the magazine typical of its genre and what makes it different from its rivals.

Principal uses of audience research

Research is the systematic collection, recording, analysis and presentation of data or information for a purpose. Research can sometimes be called 'study' or 'survey', 'investigation' or 'enquiry'.

Information may be found from living humans through interviews, questionnaires, diaries or case studies, or it might be found in books, magazine articles or reports. Research might last a day, it might take months. It might cost very little or it might cost thousands of pounds. In this unit you will be looking at professional examples of research and how to conduct your own research about media products you have made or used.

Assessment of an existing product

Researchers first need to analyse the product in question. What exactly are its contents? How is it made? What is its history? How and why has it developed? Who owns the product? What sort of people produce it?

With such background knowledge the researchers can then begin to look at how the product is *used*. They will want to know its success in terms of popularity and in financial terms. This will be based on precise information: how much does the product cost to make? How much does it cost to buy or use? How big are the profits or losses? Are there fluctuations?

But most of all the researchers will be looking at audience or consumer attitudes and behaviour. At the very least they will want to find out how many people use the product and how often. At a more complex level they will research how the product is used by people and their conscious and subconscious opinions, feelings and expectations concerning the product. They will investigate what sort of people the consumers or audience are.

This is known as **demographics**. The age and sex of a person are the two most obvious questions asked, but also of interest to advertisers are the areas in which they live, what type of education they have had, their employment status, their lifestyle, their shopping behaviour, their marital status, if they have children and how many, the type of house they live in and how long they have lived there, and their income.

Grade	Social class	Occupation
A	Upper middle class	A successful professional, administrative or managerial person or someone with private wealth; generally an older person, e.g. a director of a large firm, a senior civil servant.
B	Middle class	Intermediate managerial, administrative or professional person; e.g. junior solicitor, young doctor, lecturer, journalist
C1	Lower middle class	Junior management, supervisor and clerical staff; sometimes called 'white-collar workers'; e.g. secretary, small trades person, salesperson
C2	Skilled working class	Skilled manual worker who has possibly served an apprenticeship or had a significant period of training, sometimes called a 'blue-collar worker'; e.g. shop assistant, garage mechanic, lighting assistant
D	Working class	A mainly manual worker, generally semi-skilled or unskilled; e.g. cleaner, porter
E	Lowest level of subsistence	State pensioner, widow, casual workers, the unemployed and those reliant on social security schemes

Figure 21.1 Social classes

Particularly from questions on occupation or employment, the **social grade** is assigned to a household. Figure 21.1 shows an example of how this is achieved.

Activity

Fill in the accompanying questionnaire on newspapers (Figure 21.2). Compare the results with a friend's. How many of your answers are the same? What differences are there?

The researchers may want to find data that will give some indication of how long the product will remain popular or financially viable. A media product such as an encyclopaedia may have a shelf life of several years, whereas a new rock music CD may be popular for just a week or so.

NEWSPAPER SURVEY

The purpose of this survey is to investigate people's newspaper reading habits.

It would be helpful to us if you complete and return this simple questionnaire.

1   What is your age?
    12–17 ☐   18–23 ☐
    24–29 ☐   30+ ☐

2   Are you:
    Male ☐   Female ☐

3   How often do you read a newspaper?
    Daily ☐   Twice weekly ☐
    Weekly ☐   Once a fortnight ☐
    Once a month ☐   Never ☐

4   Which of the following daily newspapers do you enjoy reading?
    You may tick more than one box

    The Daily Express ☐   The Sun ☐
    The Daily Mail ☐   The Daily Mirror ☐
    The Star ☐   The Guardian ☐
    The Times ☐   The Independent ☐
    The Daily Telegraph ☐
    Any others (please name) ....

5   Do you read a *Sunday* paper? If so, which one?
    ....

6   Which part of a newspaper do you *always* read?
    You may tick one or more boxes

    The front page ☐   Sports pages ☐
    TV listings ☐   Cartoons ☐
    The problem page ☐   The car page ☐
    News stories ☐   The horoscope ☐
    The editorial ☐   Advertisements ☐
    The business page ☐   The fashion section ☐
    Travel pages ☐   The cookery section ☐
    Births, marriages and deaths ☐
    Any other ....

7   Which of these do you read *first*?
    ....

Thank you for completing this questionnaire. Please return it to: R. Moss by 27 February 1997

Figure 21.2 Newspaper questionnaire

In assessing existing products it may be necessary to find out more detailed information, such as why some TV programmes remain popular for so long or why some products come back into fashion.

Case study – Batman and Robin

Superheroes are always popular when times are disturbed and social order is threatened, so it is no surprise that Batman first appeared as a cartoon character in *Detective Comics* in 1939, just before the Second World War. Although he is a superhero, in contrast to Superman he is an ordinary human being who trains until he is well equipped physically and mentally to fight the master criminals. He has independent means and moves in high circles of society. Batman became a star of radio, too, and appeared in films in 1943 and 1948.

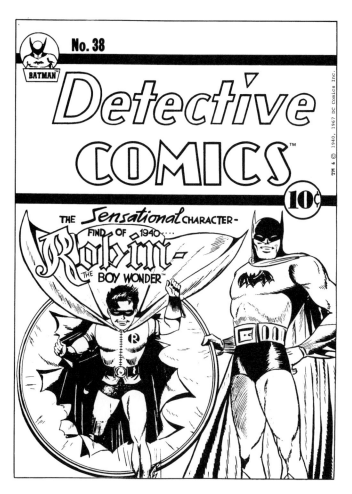

Batman, Robin and all related indicia are trademarks of DC Comics © 1967. Used with permission. All rights reserved.

Around 1960, the appeal of the cartoon was declining. Then a television series recreated Batman and gave a new pop-style image which updated him. It is interesting to note that this was again a period of some social unrest in America and the period of the Vietnam war.

The product was also adapted to the sexual mores and sensitivities of the period. The television adaptation of Batman attempted to avoid accusations of homosexual overtones in the Batman and Robin relationship by installing an aunt in the Wayne household. The sales of Batman comic books also revived. The 'dynamic duo' retired in 1969 so that Robin could go to college.

However, this was not the end. Warner Brothers revamped the image of Batman yet again in comic books before releasing a blockbuster film in 1989. Conglomerate ownership helped make the film part of a product line of toys, clothes and other spin-offs. In this process of 'synergy', a film feeds off the record label: two soundtrack albums were produced, musical artists, satellite and cable divisions and merchandising. Michael Keaton and Jack Nicholson were the two stars, and they made large amounts of money on merchandising and production deals. The sequel *Batman Returns* (1992) was followed by the even more successful *Batman Forever* in 1995.

Existing media products may need to be modified if they are to remain successful. Either their content, design, price or availability may need to be altered. Researchers will have to investigate the consumers and audiences. What do they want? What do they need?

Society is always changing, and new fashions and trends come and go. Education has an important effect on people. Can they read, can they use computers? What is their attitude towards other people? As each generation of Western children becomes more sophisticated, their expectations of the media rise.

The economic situation in a country also profoundly affects how it uses different media products. Wealth enables people to spend more time and money on certain media products, such as the new multimedia. During the American Depression of the 1930s the big musicals became very popular at the box office: people wanted escapism to compensate for their dull, drab lives.

The political attitude of a government, or political events such as wars, can also influence how consumers react to media products. During the Falklands War the British public accepted and perhaps even expected a higher degree of racist comments about Argentineans than would have been acceptable before or since. In a country such as China, where the media are still tightly controlled and until recently choice of products has been limited, media producers are less concerned with competition and the need to change or develop products.

Development of new products

The media are well known for the high turnover of their products, whether these products are records, novels, films or TV programmes. Producers are always on the lookout for new ideas.

Sometimes a completely new form of media product appears, such as CD-ROM, the Internet, interactive videos and digital radios.

There are two main areas to research, the **market-place** and the **proposed product**. The researcher will begin by doing the research listed above, assessing the strengths or existence of rival products. Can a niche in the market be identified for another new product?

Case study

Cross Counties Radio is a company hoping to win the new radio licence for Hinckley. The questionnaire in Figure 21.3 formed part of their research into the need for a new product.

The second area of research will take the form of a **feasibility study**. It is vital for accurate information to be collected on how much the product will cost to develop, produce, distribute and launch. Without these details an idea is unlikely to attract the financial backing that will enable it to be turned into reality. Or, if the idea is developed, it may fail to make a profit – or even worse, drain a company of its finances, as has happened with some films and multimedia packages.

A **sample** or **prototype** of a new product may be used in a trial run in order to test its potential and see how audiences or consumers react. Films have previews after which considerable changes may be made.

The first *Police Academy* film was not originally made with Eddie Murphy in the starring role. It was only after the film was completed and played to a select audience that the decision was made to remake the film with Murphy in the lead.

A new TV series may have a **pilot** episode to see whether the public will enjoy it.

Marketing of media products

Marketing, too, is concerned with assessing existing products and developing products. It is also concerned with distribution, advertising, promotion and public relations. It needs to know when is the correct time to bring out or relaunch a product. When will be the best time to schedule a programme or advertisement to go out on air?

Effective marketing plans need to be created. All these activities are based upon research and are dealt with in depth in Unit 7.

Good research will enable producers to demonstrate their position in the market-place. Advertisers who wish to place advertisements on TV or radio, or in newspapers and magazines, need to be persuaded by hard facts and figures that the target consumers for their product are the same type of people who will be viewing or listening to programmes in which the ads are inserted, or who read the articles near to where the ads are placed.

Besides maintaining existing customers or audiences, research will identify new markets.

Activity

You have to plan an advertising campaign for a pop video you have made. What sort of information would you need to find?

Assessing the effects of media products

The development of the mass media – from the first newspapers, to TV and later the Internet – has aroused interest in sociologists, psychologists and educationalists. There has been much debate on the effect of TV on children's reading, and the effect of violence in films on teenagers. There is a lot of interest into how influential the new multimedia can be in helping people to learn in schools and colleges.

Owners and governments are deeply interested in the effects or influence media products have on individual people and entire populations. Audiences and consumers can behave in an active or a passive fashion and this is discussed in detail later on.

PUBLIC RESEARCH FORM FOR CROSS COUNTIES RADIO

Name .... Home town/village ....

Postcode .... Telephone number..

Age: Under 14 .... 15–24 .... 25–34 .... 35–44 .... 45–54.............. 55+...................

Which of these radio stations do you listen to? (Tick appropriate boxes)

	Every day	Every other day	Twice/week	Once/week	Never
BBC ONE FM					
BBC RADIO TWO					
BBC RADIO THREE					
BBC RADIO FOUR					
BBC FIVE LIVE					
BBC RADIO LEICESTER					
BBC CWR					
LEICESTER SOUND					
MERCIA FM					
CLASSIC GOLD					
BRMB FM					
KIX 96					
HEART FM					
CHOICE FM					
VIRGIN 1215					
ATLANTIC 252					
OTHER........					

1   Please tick which times during a typical *WEEKDAY* that you listen to radio:
    6am–9am.... 9am–12noon.... 12noon–3pm.... 3pm–6pm.... 6pm–9pm.... 9pm–12m'night.... 12m'night–3am.... 3am–6am....

2   Please tick which times during a typical *WEEKEND* that you listen to radio:
    6am–9am.... 9am–12noon.... 12noon–3pm.... 3pm–6pm.... 6pm–9pm.... 9pm–12m'night.... 12m'night–3am.... 3am–6am....

3   With relation to the output of a new community radio station, would the following interest you:

	Very interested	Fairly interested	Not interested
LOCAL NEWS COVERAGE			
NATIONAL NEWS COVERAGE			
LOCAL TRAVEL INFORMATION			
LOCAL EVENTS COVERAGE			
AN EMPLOYMENT PROGRAMME			
CLASSICAL MUSIC			
COUNTRY MUSIC			
ROCK MUSIC			
DISCUSSION/DEBATE			
A PHONE-IN			
A TEENAGE/YOUTH PROGRAMME			
HOLIDAY ADVICE			
A COOKERY PROGRAMME			
A GARDENING PROGRAMME			

Figure 21.3 Local radio questionnaire

Controlling media products

Media products can be controlled from within the organisation that owns them, and from outside.

Information is power. From multimedia moguls to proprietors of small print shops, owners need to know everything about their product and that of their competitors if they are to survive in the cut-throat world of media. They also need to know who is working for them, and if their work ethos and viewpoint coincide with that of the company. Research can support their editorial policy.

A government that can control the media has a powerful weapon. From the inception of newspapers, many governments have recognised the need to control their content. During the Second World War, the radio became a powerful medium for propaganda, a position which has been taken over by TV since the 1960s. Some governments like research studies that show the negative effects of the media on the public. They need to prove that films or music, for example, can be harmful to people. This can then justify legislation to control them. Of course the media can fight back!

During the early 1990s, after a number of tabloid newspaper reports on scandals in the royal family, there were threats of new laws to control the press. The government claimed that it was raising press standards and protecting the public. Newspaper editors claimed that the government was trying to curb the freedom of the press. Government research was based around the Calcutt Report and the recommendations of a number of committees. Research by the press included uncovering alleged scandals about various government ministers.

Activity

Imagine that you are a dictator. Recently there have been several books in circulation, some of which are by foreign authors, saying how corrupt you are.

Discuss with your colleagues what laws need to be introduced to enable you to control the publishing industry. At present the people in your country are tolerant of foreigners, but the country is going into an economic decline. What information would you need to collect to justify your actions?

Principal methods of media research

There are two main types of research, **quantitative** and **qualitative**.

Quantitative researchers collect facts and figures and study the relationship of one set against another. The chosen research method can cope with very large samples and data can be easily input and analysed by computer. The results can be quantified, shown using graphs and diagrams, and conclusions drawn. The questions asked by researchers can be answered by a simple 'yes' or 'no', or by a number. Examples are:

- Do you own a video recorder?
- How many people visited the cinema last year?
- How often do you see a film in a year?
- How expensive is it to rent a video?

Qualitative researchers are more concerned with understanding the opinions, attitudes and behaviour patterns of groups of individuals. Their aim is not a statistical analysis but explanation of a situation or event. The results are more likely to be presented in essay form. The questions asked by these researchers will usually require more thought and time when answered and analysed. Examples are:

- Why did you buy a video recorder?
- What effect did horror movies have on people last year?
- What do you like about visiting the cinema?
- Which type of films do you like the most?

Activity

You and a colleague are doing research on newspaper readers. You ask your partner four quantitative questions and then your partner asks you two qualitative questions. Write down the answers. Which piece of research was finished more quickly?

Examples of research methods

There are a number of methods used in media research. These include:

- *Surveys* – Questionnaires, interviews.
- *Diaries* – Members of a sample group record their reactions to media products.
- *Reviews* – These may be in books or magazines, and give opinions on media products. Figure 21.4 shows a clipping.

The Brady Bunch Movie

USA 1995

Director: Betty Thomas

Los Angeles, 1995. The city is a loud, violent mess, but for the Bradys – architect Dad Mike, homemaker Mom Carol, and their six kids, Greg, Marcia. Peter, Jan, Bobby and Cindy – it's still 1975. Little Cindy visits next door neighbour and amoral real estate agent Mr Dittmeyer to retrieve lost mail. As the Bradys are the only family on the street who won't sell their home to make way for a mini-mall, Dittmeyer holds onto a $20,000 property tax bill in the hopes they will be forced out...

When it was announced that Hollywood was going to bring television's *The Brady Bunch* to the big screen there were loud rumblings that it would be a colossal commercial bomb to match the *The Coneheads* or *The Beverly Hillbillies*, especially as *The Brady Bunch*'s audience is a very specific one. Since it originally aired in North America between 1969 and 1971 – and then enjoyed constant re-runs throughout the 70s and early 80s – this cheesy sit-com never really appealed to the then-teenage Baby Boom generation, and had petered out before the kitsch savvy 'Generation X' could claim it as their own. It's the in-between generation, those who watched the show as impatient, yearning pre-teens, who ....

Figure 21.4 An extract from *Sight & Sound*

- *Documentary evidence* – Annual reports, viewing figures, etc.
- *Observation studies* – For example, a researcher may sit in on a group of young children and watch how they react to a violent TV programme.
- *Case studies* – The researcher uses a particular individual or institution as an example of a certain pattern of behaviour.
- *Physical tests* – For example, measuring the heartbeat response to visual stimuli.
- *Simulation exercises* – Similar to role play, a situation is set up as near as possible to real life but in a controlled environment where behaviour can be observed.
- *Focus discussion groups* – An appropriate sample of people is gathered together to discuss a specified topic. Sometimes this can take the form of a listening panel.

Activity

List which of the above research methods you have used in school projects or lessons.

Strengths and weaknesses of research methods

Which is the best research method to use? That depends on the circumstances. Sometimes a combination of methods is needed.

The two methods used most often are **questionnaires**, which are typical for quantitative research, and **interviews**, typical of qualitative research. What are their strengths and weaknesses?

Questionnaires

A questionnaire can cope with a large sample of people. Many people like answering questionnaires. The questions are usually quick to answer and the results can be analysed quickly by computer. Then the results can be easily understood through graphs and diagrams, and data can be interpreted in broad conclusions. Respondents can remain anonymous. This is a cheap method for large samples, especially if not posted. A questionnaire needs relatively few staff to run. These are all strengths of the questionnaire method.

Weaknesses of the method include the fact that a questionnaire cannot explain audience behaviour or attitudes. it is also hard to check whether questions are answered honestly and correctly. The return rate of questionnaires by post is low, and it can take a long time for questionnaires to be returned.

Interviews

In an interview, detailed questions can be asked and clarification of the questions and answers is possible. Therefore motives and feelings can be investigated. Interviewers can tailor the questions to the individual: irrelevant questions can be omitted, others added. In this way unexpected information can emerge. A friendly personal approach is possible, and the response to questions is instant. These are all strengths of the interview method.

Weaknesses of the method include the fact that only comparatively small samples are practicable, and the method is time-consuming for both interviewer and interviewee. Appointments may need to be made, and well-trained interviewers are needed. It can be time-consuming to analyse the results and present data, and this is work that is not suitable for clerical staff. Further weaknesses of the method are:

- Interviewees may react negatively or over-positively to the personality of the interviewer.
- Interviewees may expect something in return for their time, such as a payment or a free gift.
- A comfortable location may need to be found for the interviews.

The effective use of resources

For students, interviews are cheap to conduct, whereas a postal or telephone survey is expensive. Reproducing a questionnaire can also be expensive for a student. However, *professionally the opposite is true*. Interviews take time, and if staff are paid by the hour then costs can escalate dramatically – particularly if the interviewers are highly trained and qualified.

Ultimately the effectiveness of any research method depends on whether it can produce the information that is needed to meet research objectives.

Activity

1 You work for an advertising agency and you need to find out where to place an advert for a particular model of car. What research method will you use, and why?
2 Your friend is a university student who has to do a project on the influence of advertising on young people. What research method would be most effective, and why?

Surveys and diaries

As will be discussed later in this chapter, some media research bodies carry out their research using surveys and diaries.

Social surveys are carried out when a researcher wishes to gain statistical information from a large number of people so that generalisations about the population at large can be made. The emphasis is on **facts** – quantitative information based on questionnaires – though interviewing is often included to support the evidence. The strength or weakness of any survey depends both on the size of the sample used and on whether the sample is representative of the audience or consumers to be studied.

Asking people to keep a diary can be a means of gaining detailed information on their behaviour, such as listening or viewing habits. Again, it is important that an appropriate sample be chosen. It may be necessary to give some incentive such as a free sample or money to encourage participants. Some people may find keeping the diary up-to-date irksome and boring, and they may forget to fill it in. Clear guidance must be given if they are to complete the diary correctly with the right data. It is a time-consuming method for the sample, even if it only runs for a day!

Activity

Keep a diary of your own media habits over 24 hours. Note down when you listen to the radio, watch television or read a newspaper or magazine, etc. Did you have any problems in collecting the data? For how long do you think you would have to run this experiment before a recognisable pattern emerged? Do you think it would be easy to analyse the results?

Observation studies and simulation exercises

Observation methods involve a researcher gaining membership or access to a group of people so that their behaviour can be studied in its natural context without disturbance. There are two ways of doing this:

- When the observation is **covert**, the subjects are unaware of the researcher's identity and purpose.

Figure 21.5 Observation methods may be covert or overt

■ When the observation is **overt**, the researcher's real identity is known but possibly not the real reason for the research.

The longer the observation study lasts, the less the subjects are likely to notice the researcher.

Observation methods have, for example, been used to assess the effects of TV violence on young children. In an experiment, young children were shown some TV programmes and then their subsequent behaviour towards dolls was noted – the children acted out the violence in the programmes on the dolls. It is an excellent method for noting detailed individual behaviour and gaining unexpected data.

It is possible to raise some criticisms of the method. First, samples are small; and secondly, it is hard to assess the effect of the presence of the researcher in the group. In the example just given, the children may have reacted in the way they did to draw the attention of a 'stranger' in the group. There is also an ethical problem in the covert method of observation.

Sometimes it is not possible or convenient to observe people's behaviour in its usual context, such as in their home. Then a simulation exercise, possibly involving role play, may be set up. The simulation may involve physical testing – a person's heart-rate may be monitored, for instance, whilst they watch a horror programme. Once again, a weakness of this method is that only small samples can be used cost-effectively, and the results may not be representative.

Discussion groups

Individual interviews have already been discussed. It is possible for group interviews or discussion groups to be effective, but this will depend on group dynamics and the skill of the researcher in controlling the flow of discussion.

One advantage of this technique is that more conversation will flow and more ideas will be generated because the group members will respond to each other and the researcher can become more of an observer. One disadvantage is that one or a few people may dominate the discussion.

The makers of Guinness have used focused group discussions in the development of their advertising campaigns. On one occasion, people were asked to draw what they thought Guinness represented to them.

Case studies

Case studies are important because they can give detailed examples of events that have happened or situations that have occurred. The facts are already known and conclusions can be drawn. The main problem lies in assessing whether the case study is typical or complete. A case study is useful for supporting other research, such as a survey, and for bringing life to a report.

The use of secondary data

All the methods discussed above can be considered to provide **primary data**. However, of equal importance is **secondary data**. (Both primary and secondary research were looked at in Chapter 5.) This can involve the study of records and documents, both historical and secondary, newspapers and magazines, reports, books, including biographies. The worth of this evidence can be assessed by the following:

■ *The age of the data* – Is it still relevant, or have social, economic or technological changes made it outdated?

- *The qualifications of the author* – Are they experienced or renowned in this field of study? What are their professional qualifications? Does the publisher usually publish books on this topic?
- *The purpose of the documentary evidence* – Has it been written to entertain, or is there a serious reason behind it? Has it been sponsored by any body with a vested interest in this subject? Research funded by a film company on the effects of horror movies on teenagers may be biased.
- *The reviews* – If you are researching film, TV or radio programmes there are often reviews in magazines or newspapers that can give useful information. Film critics, for example, have considerable experience in their area and their viewpoint and judgement can be informative.
- *The quality of the research* – How big were the samples on which the evidence is based, and were they based on a good cross-section? How reliable are the case studies, or are they merely anecdotal? Does evidence from other sources support the research?

Activity

List which combinations of research methods would be suitable in the following cases, and give reasons for your answer.

1 Finding out how popular a particular film is, and why.
2 The effect of a series of health programmes on older people.
3 Which parts of a newspaper are read most, and why.
4 The influence on children of TV advertisements for sweets.

Practical considerations

It is valuable experience for students to contact research and media organisations for themselves. However, responses can be mixed. The authors of this book sent a letter to organisations when researching for this unit – it is reproduced in Figure 21.6.

This was a general letter to gain an initial response. Nearly every organisation replied, some to arrange future meetings. Sometimes the information given was enough in itself, sometimes it was apparent that the organisation had encountered similar requests and had already prepared publicity material.

At other times we used a longer letter to request specific information – see Figure 21.7. Many students when asking for information are too broad in their

---

HINCKLEY COLLEGE

24 January 1996

London Road, Hinckley, Leicestershire LE10 1HQ.
Tel: (01455) 251222
Fax: (01455) 633930

Principal: Ifor Jones

Dear Sir/Madam,

My colleague Sue Warr and I have been commissioned by Heinemann Educational to write a textbook for the:

GNVQ Advanced Qualification in Media: Communication and Production.

At present we are gathering case study material.

We are keen to stress the importance of research in the media and wonder if you would be kind enough to provide us with some information on your organisation. We would very much like to be able to give an impression of how it works and the types of jobs and activities that take place. Because it is a student textbook we would like to be able to use some research findings and explain how they were gathered and the uses to which they were put. In addition we would welcome any advice you could give us on sources of information for our book.

If you feel you could be interested in your organisation being cited in a textbook case study I would be most grateful if you could contact me at the above address.

Yours faithfully,

P Morrissey

Pete Morrissey
Media Programme Manager

DIVISION OF DESIGN AND PRODUCTION

Figure 21.6 A general letter for first approach

demands. The more specific (i.e. narrow) the request for information, the more likely it is that someone will find the time to reply. So don't write to a magazine company asking what influence do they think articles about sex have on young people, if that is your chosen area for research. Be more precise. Possibly direct your letter to the 'agony aunt' rather than to the editor. Briefly explain your research objectives. Ask for the titles of any recent articles that have been controversial. Ask what proportion of letters from readers are about sex.

London Road, Hinckley,
Leicestershire LE10 1HQ.
Tel: (01455) 251222
Fax: (01455) 633930

9th May 1996

Dear Tony,

Re. Media Studies Textbook

You may recall my contacting you regarding the textbook that I and my colleague Sue Warr are writing.

I am particularly interested in the way Radio City markets itself. Identifying two broad but overlapping market segments is the basis for intended analysis and I would like permission to use parts of your Media Pack to illustrate this. In addition I would be grateful if you could provide a little more information, firstly on how this market research was carried out, and secondly on how you continue to meet the demands of the target audiences identified, e.g. what kind of questions do you ask when carrying out audience telephone research?

For example, could you highlight the non-music differentiation between the two services, e.g. is the news more in-depth on Gold? Is there more "serious" comment/discussion? Is there any difference in the sports coverage? etc.

In addition, I would like to emphasise the essentially commercial nature of the station's activities. Any (non-sensitive!) information on how the station runs as a business (e.g. sales, commercial production and sponsorship), including plans for the future, would be a great help.

Finally, could you give a brief outline on how the music selection works?

If you are able to help and there is any particular text or artwork you feel should be included in this book, then I would be glad to take your advice.

Yours sincerely,

P Morrissey

Peter Morrissey
Media Programme Manager

Figure 21.7 A follow-up letter

If you are lucky you will get a reply. But remember, media producers are swamped by students' letters and are very busy. Always keep a copy of your letter – at the very least you can use it as evidence for your key skills in communication!

Activities of industry research bodies

Investigation of the size and make-up of audiences for the mass media is itself a major service industry. At its most basic it provides numbers – how many readers, listeners or viewers there are. Deeper research splits these data into class, gender, age, occupation, area, etc. A further layer of research seeks more in-depth, qualitative information that explains consumer behaviour.

A number of official research bodies provide data relating to the following types of media industry:

- broadcast (TV and radio)
- print (newspapers, magazines, books)
- outdoor (posters, billboards on fixed sites and on public transport)
- cinema and video.

Print and graphics media

There are two major official bodies for audience research for newspapers and magazines. Superficially they provide the same sort of information, but they have a different bias. One concentrates on distribution and purchasing information, and the other focuses on who the readers are and how they use the products.

The **Audit Bureau of Circulations** is a body that monitors the publishing industry. It provides certified *circulation* figures for newspapers and magazines. It has three main divisions – one for the consumer press, one for the business press, and **Verified Free Distribution** which checks distribution claims of publishers of free newspapers.

The Bureau (usually known as ABC) was founded in 1931 as a non-profit-making organisation by the forerunner of the Incorporated Society of British Advertisers. Its main objective remains to assist media owners and buyers in the effective buying and selling of advertising space, by the collection and dissemination of accurate information about the circulation figures of newspapers and magazines. It is the UK's only independent system for the validation of circulation and exhibition attendance data.

ABC is managed by a full-time staff, governed by a general council of 28 people consisting of permanent and elected members representing advertisers, agencies and publishers.

In addition to independently audited circulation figures, ABC publishes:

355

Average Issue Readership – All Adults

	TOTAL		MALE		FEMALE		15–44		45+		ABC1		C2DE		MAIN SHOPPER	
		SEX					AGE				SOCIAL GRADE					
WEIGHTED SAMPLE	19625		8586		11039		9424		10201		9816		9809		13432	
ESTIMATED POP. (000s)	44722		21737		22986		23424		21298		21562		23160		28227	
	000	%	000	%	000	%	000	%	000	%	000	%	000	%	000	%
Daily morning newspapers – 6 days																
The Sun	10001	22	5637	26	4364	19	6162	26	3839	18	3020	14	6981	30	5728	20
Daily Mirror	6876	15	3741	17	3135	14	3485	15	3391	16	2146	10	4730	20	4088	14
Daily Record	1959	4	1044	5	915	4	1169	5	790	4	584	3	1375	6	1141	4
Daily Mail	4544	10	2294	11	2250	10	2043	9	2501	12	2940	14	1604	7	2814	10
Daily Express	3328	7	1738	8	1590	7	1414	6	1914	9	1970	9	1358	6	1984	7
The Daily Telegraph	2554	6	1434	7	1120	5	1001	4	1554	7	2197	10	358	2	1578	6
Daily Star	2063	5	1409	6	654	3	1431	6	632	3	532	2	1531	7	1085	4
Today	1710	4	914	4	795	3	994	4	716	3	780	4	930	4	1021	4
The Times	1391	3	799	4	593	3	750	3	642	3	1215	6	176	1	892	3
The Guardian	1314	3	726	3	588	3	857	4	457	2	1108	5	206	1	851	3
The Independent	1003	2	624	3	379	2	679	3	324	2	848	4	155	1	618	2
Financial Times	743	2	572	3	171	1	447	2	296	1	673	3	70	–	433	2

Figure 21.8 An extract from NRS data

- a breakdown of circulations by types
- cover prices and subscription rates
- publishers' terms of control
- a geographical analysis
- profile audits.

Each ABC return is published as a *Certificate of Circulation* which forms a guarantee for newspapers and magazines to show advertisers and clients.

The *ABC Review* is published twice a year and is currently split into two volumes, one covering UK national daily and Sunday newspapers, UK regional morning, evening, Sunday and paid-for weekly newspapers, consumer magazines and specialised journals. The second volume covers international and world regional newspapers.

ABC provides information as the industry-accepted standard to *British Rate and Data* (BRAD) – see later. An example of ABC data can be found in Figure 23.7 on page 386.

National Readership Surveys is the leading organisation for measuring the *readership* of major newspapers and magazines. It was formed in 1992 to replace JICNARS (Joint Industry Committee for National Readership Surveys).

Every month the NRS provides data for the 12 months' fieldwork completed four weeks earlier. Each month this continuous survey takes a 'snapshot' of that readership, and at the end of the year the 12 months' data will show an average of what the readership was like six months previously.

To be included in the figures for readership, someone must have read a daily newspaper every day, a weekly newspaper within the last seven days, and a monthly publication within the past four weeks. Other figures show the coverage of publications by a certain type of reader, and the growing popularity of new titles and profiles.

These demographics are very useful for advertisers. The information they provide includes details of age, sex, social grade, area, education, employment status, lifestyle, shopping behaviour, household composition, income, marital status. Figure 21.8 shows a small extract.

Outdoor advertising

Posters on transport, billboards and panels can play an important part in an advertising campaign, little or large, cheap or expensive. Outdoor sites are also taken to mean those in shopping centres and car parks.

Data on the effectiveness of this type of advertising can be difficult to collect, especially qualitative data or even accurate quantitative data. People may remember having seen a certain advert on a billboard but might find it hard to recall how often they have seen it. Contact with posters is random and unintentional.

Although in Britain there are 130 000 poster panels at 70 000 sites, these are distributed unevenly, and

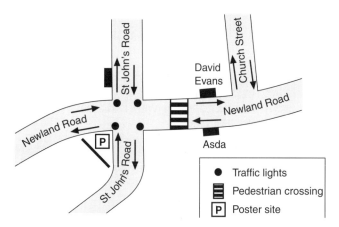

Figure 21.9 Sketch map of a poster site

both pedestrian and vehicular traffic around them is hard to assess. How much attention people are paying is even more tricky to determine. A poster may be in a busy place such as Picadilly Circus in the heart of London, but more people may look at a poster by a bus stop or traffic lights in a medium-sized town because in London there are so many other things demanding people's attention. Here are the organisations that have attempted to deal with this problem.

The **Outdoor Advertising Association** (OAA) has as its members all the main contracting companies and many smaller ones.

The **Joint Industry Committee for Poster Audience Research** (JICPAR) includes representatives of the media owners, the advertisers and the advertising agencies. It also includes representatives of the poster specialists who select sites and organise campaigns for buyers.

A system known as *OSCAR* was launched in 1985 which gives a listing and classification of all UK poster sites. The model was created by Audits of

Vehicular visibility	Pedestrian visibility
■ Distance at which visible ■ Angle to road ■ Competition from other panels ■ Deflection from line of sight ■ Degree of obstruction ■ Height of panel from ground ■ Illumination	■ Proportion able to see the panel, as judged by the fieldworker ■ Competition from other panels ■ Illumination

Figure 21.10 Visibility factors in the OSCAR system

Great Britain (AGB) and the research was carried out by NOP Market Research Ltd. Each researcher or fieldworker had to draw a map of the location of the poster, and collect information about the local population, the type of residential area, traffic flow, proximity to shops etc. A number of factors were identified against which a site could be scored (see Figures 21.9 and 21.10).

Every six months an *OSCAR Digest* is published, giving information on the number of panels by size owned by different companies, and the audience scores categorised by size of poster and vehicular and pedestrian audiences. This is a very useful tool for manufacturers and advertisers. There are two main limitations, however. The surveys rely heavily on the judgement of individual fieldworkers, and the data take so long to collect that they cannot take into account seasonal fluctuations such as holiday traffic.

Audio-visual media

Television

Set up in 1980, the **Broadcasters Audience Research Board** (BARB) produces statistical research on television audiences. It is owned jointly by the BBC and ITV, but its board of directors includes members from IPA (Institute of Practitioners in Advertising), Channel 4 and BSkyB, representing satellite broadcasters. This organisation compiles television ratings figures.

The sample or panel of homes is selected through the Establishment Survey based on a random sample of over 43 000 interviews conducted continuously throughout the year and structured by postcode areas. This tries to ensure that the panel is representative and up-to-date with a variety of viewing habits, TV equipment ownership, family composition and demographics.

The audience size is measured via a sample of 4500 computer-linked homes in which meters are installed. If a home has more than one TV then meters will be attached to all of them. When members of the household select a programme to be viewed, the meter records their presence and which channel is chosen. Each household also has a gadget similar to a TV remote control with numbered buttons. Each member of the household over the age of four, and even visitors, are allocated a number which they press when they start and stop viewing and these data are also collected by the meter. All the information is automatically retrieved nightly by a computer using the telephone system.

The use of video recorders has also had an effect on the measurement of audiences. Some households use VCRs for 'live' viewing because it gives a better picture, so a separate meter is attached to the VCR. The viewing of a programme previously recorded at home is known as 'time-shifting'. It is difficult to interpret data about time-shifting as some recorded programmes are never watched, some may be watched several months later, and some may be watched repeatedly. The contents of a pre-recorded tape such as a rented video cannot be identified, so these tapes are registered as 'other playback'.

BARB estimates that the response rate from the panel is almost 99 per cent accurate. Three weekly specialist reports are issued as a result.

- The *Network Report* summarises information of live and timeshift viewing figures for each of the main channels. It gives numbers of people watching specific programmes and programmes at certain times. Advertising agencies, advertisers and network controllers and programme schedulers are particularly interested in these figures. Figure 21.11 shows an example.

TOTAL TV (HOURS)	15.5	20.0	19.8	19.20
BBC1	6.2	7.1	6.6	6.07
BBC2	1.0	1.5	1.5	1.45
ITV	6.9	8.4	8.0	7.41
C4	1.4	1.8	2.0	2.43
OTHER		1.2	1.7	1.84
YEAR	**1990**	**1991**	**1992**	**1993**

Figure 21.11 BARB figures in the **Network Report**

- The *Astra Report* gives viewing statistics for cable and satellite. Again, advertisers, advertising agencies and producers want these statistics. Figure 21.12 shows an example.
- The *BBC Report* has a different emphasis because the BBC carries no advertising, and most of its output is mainly networked rather than regional. However, producers and managers still need to know the success of their product and how the 'competition' is doing.

BARB issues a weekly press release giving the hours of viewing for each channel and listing the audience sizes of the most popular programmes.

SKY 1		Millions viewing (including time-shift)
1	SIMPSONS (SUN 1800)	1.17
2	VOYAGER (SUN 1500/2001)	0.71
3	STAR TREK NXT GENRTN (TUE 1704/2159)	0.66
4	STAR TREK NXT GENRTN (WED 1703/2200)	0.52
5	SIMPSONS (FRI 1800)	0.49
6	BEVERLY HILLS 90210	0.47
6	SIMPSONS (TUE 1803)	0.47
8	STAR TREK NXT GENRTN (FRI 1703/2201)	0.46
9	STAR TREK NXT GENRTN (THU 1704/2203)	0.43
10	SIMPSONS (WED 1800)	0.40

SKY MOVIES		
1	POLICE ACADEMY FILM	0.97
2	THE CROW (SAT 2201)	0.96
3	MURDER ONE	0.44
4	GUNMEN	0.43
5	MRS DOUBTFIRE (MON 1801)	0.39
6	NO ESCAPE	0.35
7	BENEFIT OF THE DOUBT	0.33
7	SUMMER RENTAL	0.33
9	PELICAN BRIEF	0.30
10	HOT SHOTS! PART DEUX (SAT 1001/2000)	0.28

SKY SPORTS		
1	FOOTBALL (MON 1800)	1.48
2	FOOTBALL MATCH	1.09
3	FOOTBALL (TUE 2000)	1.00
4	FOOTBALL (SUN 1300)	0.81
5	FOOTBALL PREVIEW	0.68
6	DARTS	0.46
7	FOOTBALL INTRO (SUN 1200)	0.45
8	SKY SPORTS CENTRE (TUE 2215)	0.37
8	SKY SPORTS CENTRE (MON 2215)	0.37
10	FOOTBALL INTRO (WED 1900)	0.33

Figure 21.12 BARB figures in the *Astra Report*

BARB also publishes information showing audience profiles (e.g. Figure 21.13) and equipment ownership data.

What is *not* measured by the meter system is how well the programmes are bring watched, or indeed if the set is actually being watched at all, the motivation for watching or the reactions of the viewers.

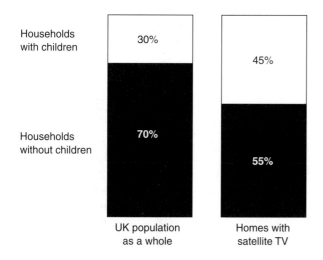

Figure 21.13 BARB figures for one audience profile in 1996

However, BARB does offer an 'audience appreciation' service which is completely confidential to the subscribing broadcaster. The service began in 1994 and consists of a regional panel of 3000 adults over the age of 16 which meets weekly. A 1000-strong panel of children between the ages of 4 and 15 meet every four weeks. Panelists have to keep diaries about what they watch, how much they like the programmes, and what they think of content and presentation.

Radio

Radio Joint Audience Research (RAJAR) is a body created in 1992 to research audience figures for both the BBC and independent radio companies. It replaced JICRAR (Joint Industry Committee for Radio Audience Research). The results of its research are issued as quarterly summaries in three parts. Unlike the BARB it does not include statistics on children. Only people over the age of fifteen are included.

The **weekly reach** (see Figure 21.14) is the number of people who listen to a radio station for at least five minutes in the course of an average week. It is given as a number expressed as hundreds of thousands of people. The number next to it tells what percentage of the total population are listening.

In the next column the total hours for listening are averaged. 'Per head' is the total figure averaged across the entire adult population of the UK. 'Per listener' is the total figure averaged across all those who listen to the station for at least five minutes per week (i.e. the weekly reach). The 'share of listening' is a percentage of the total listening time for all radio.

Cinemas

After a decline in the 1960s and '70s, cinema attendances are now increasing again with the

	Adult (15+) population (000s)	Weekly reach		Average hours		Total hours (000s)	Share of listening (%)
		(000s)	(%)	Per head	Per listener		
BBC NETWORK RADIO							
Radio 1	46957	11197	24	2.1	8.9	99909	11.8
Radio 2	46957	8429	18	2.3	12.9	109155	12.9
Radio 3	46957	2576	5	0.2	3.7	9508	1.1
Radio 4	46957	8430	18	1.9	10.5	88818	10.5
Radio 5 Live	46957	4405	9	0.4	4.6	20428	2.4
NATIONAL REGIONAL							
Radio Scotland	4147	911	22	1.4	6.3	5741	8.1
Radio Ulster	1220	403	33	2.9	8.8	3540	19.6
Radio Wales/Cymru	2335	549	24	3.1	13.1	7187	17.8
LOCAL							
Local radio	37040	7388	20	1.8	8.9	65429	9.6
GLR	9829	381	4	0.2	5.3	2021	1.1

Figure 21.14 RAJAR figures for individual BBC services in one quarter of 1994

	Total (000s)	5–6 (%)	7–11 (%)	12–17 (%)	18–24 (%)	25–34 (%)	35+ (%)	Male (%)	Female (%)	ABC1 (%)	C2DE (%)
Population	52119	2	7	7	12	17	55	49	51	42	58
Selected mainstream releases:											
The Little Mermaid (U)	2225	6	24	15	11	25	19	40	60	57	43
Cyrano de Bergerac (U)	450	–	–	9	26	38	27	59	41	70	30
Home Alone (PG)	5099	1	13	23	29	15	19	49	51	51	49
Robin Hood: Prince of Thieves (PG)	6026	1	13	19	23	18	26	53	47	58	42
Dances with Wolves (12)	2798	–	–	14	17	24	45	47	53	60	40
Naked Gun $2\frac{1}{2}$: The Smell of Fear (12)	2434	–	–	31	35	21	13	57	43	54	46
Sleeping with the Enemy (15)	2390	–	–	13	39	26	22	39	61	55	45
Terminator 2: Judgment Day (15)	4536	–	–	17	36	31	16	60	40	52	48
The Silence of the Lambs (18)	4453	–	–	–	37	31	32	53	47	59	41
Selected art film summary	986	–	–	7	25	39	29	54	46	65	35

Visits by certificate August–October 1991	% of visits	7–11 (%)	12–17 (%)	18–24 (%)	25–34 (%)	35+ (%)	Male (%)	Female (%)	ABC1 (%)	C2DE (%)
U	8	24	8	5	30	33	43	57	57	43
PG	33	16	22	21	17	24	51	49	55	45
12	14	–	25	16	23	36	46	54	60	40
15	32	–	15	38	27	20	59	41	52	48
18	13	–	–	42	40	18	55	45	52	48
All visits	100	7	17	27	25	24	53	47	55	45
Multiplex visits	52	7	15	34	24	20	53	47	54	46

Figure 21.15 A CAVIAR survey of cinema profiles in 1991

advent of the new multiplexes. There is also an increasing demand for videos for home rental, and a need for a supply of films to show on TV and on the satellite and cable channels. Advertisers such as Pearl & Dean and RSA Advertising, film and video distributors and film production companies need accurate audience data.

The **Cinema Advertising Association** (CAA) is the best-known source of UK admissions data. It was established in 1989. Gallup, on behalf of CAA, collect information directly from cinema operators such as Odeon, Showcase and Warner, over the phone on a weekly basis. These circuit cinemas account for 80 per cent of UK admissions. A sample is taken from the independent cinemas who form the remaining 20 per cent of the market.

This information is quantitative: it merely gives information on how many people are attending a certain film and no details on who they are or what sort of people they are.

Cinema and Video Industry Audience Research (CAVIAR) is a body sponsored by CAA and represents the interests of advertising agencies, distributors and retailers. Its survey relies on interviews and a questionnaire to find out more

detailed data on audiences, not only for cinema and videos but also for TV (terrestrial, satellite and cable) and newspapers and magazines. Its main survey is carried out between October and November each year. It is based on a sample of approximately 31 000 covering all age groups over the age of five years. The interviews are conducted face-to-face. Figure 21.15 shows an example.

An extra survey, CAVIAR Film Monitor, is carried out every month on a sample of about 4000 people over the age of seven. This asks about their attendance at 24 films currently on release.

Activity

Now that you have studied the information on research you should test your knowledge by attempting this crossword.

ACROSS
2 A method of research that can give qualitative information
5 See 1 down
7 See 6 down
10 See 1 down
12 Initials of the official body researching radio audiences
13 See 3 down
14 Group of people asked to fill in a questionnaire for NRS

DOWN
1 (and 5 and 10 across, and 9 down) What BARB stands for
3 (and 13 across and 11 down) Leading organisation for measuring the number of people reading the major newspapers
4 What BARB installs in some homes
6 (and 7 across) Number of listeners who tune into a given radio station over a period of 7 days
8 Sort of information the CAA collects

Activities of independent research agencies

What precisely makes a research agency independent? They can be considered independent:

■ if they are independent of government control or the official agencies described above
■ if they are independent of commercial interests or other external influences.

Activity

As you read through the following descriptions of organisations, decide into which of the above categories they fall.

There are three main groups to study:

■ commercial research organisations
■ academic research bodies
■ campaigning organisations.

There is in fact a Market Research Society, founded in 1946, which is the UK's professional association for individuals involved in compiling or using market, social or economic research. This body monitors and develops the profession in order to maintain standards, build up public and business confidence and improve theoretical and practical work. It publishes a Code of Conduct, which helps to ensure that research is conducted in accordance with the principles of data protection encompassed by the Data Protection Act.

The MRS also issues rules relating to confidentiality and the special care to be taken when interviewing children. It is also concerned with education, and issues qualifications administered by De Montfort University. It has a certificate, the equivalent of NVQ Level 3, and a Diploma run by the Leicester Business School. It has regular publications, including a quarterly *Journal* and *Research Abstracts*.

Commercial research organisations

There are many of these; this is a growth area. Often they do work for the official research agencies such as BARB and RAJAR mentioned above.

For example, **RSL Media** is a company capable of conducting large-scale surveys on behalf of 'syndicates' of media owners with a common research requirement. RSL collects qualitative and quantitative data and can call on 1350 trained interviewers. RSL states its aims as:

■ to address problems individually, within the context of the total media market-place
■ to supply authoritative data on which to base management and marketing decisions
■ to gain insight and understanding through qualitative research
■ to measure behaviour through reliable quantitative surveys
■ to understand and reflect dynamic changes in the market-place, whilst maintaining the benefits of consistent trend data
■ to use the company's experience and understanding of how the various media work, and the attention to detail required to research each individual audience

Asian Businessman Readership Survey (ABRS) measures the readership of international, pan-regional and national business titles among senior businessmen and women in selected establishments in eight South East Asian countries.

European Business Readership Survey (EBRS) has been produced bi-annually since 1973. The 1993 Survey covers a universe of 300,000 senior business individuals in 47,000 establishments in seventeen European countries, and is sponsored by the *Financial Times*, other international and national publications and advertising agencies.

Pan European Survey (PES), sponsored by international titles, measures readership among high-status men and women in Europe who qualify on the grounds of income, occupation and education.

Pan European Television Audience Research (PETAR) measures cable and satellite viewing across six European countries. The universe includes all those aged four and older within cable/satellite homes.

RSL Media also conducts numerous multinational surveys among specialist markets such as **Chief Executives** and **International Financial Managers**.

All these surveys contain a vast amount of data which helps senior management identify the right audience for a particular product.

Figure 21.16 Some international studies by RSL Media

■ to remain at the forefront of technological developments, and provide cost-efficient solutions.

The company has done work for major research organisations in the UK, such as BARB and RAJAR, and has also undertaken international studies as listed in Figure 21.16. More details of one of these studies, repeated every three or four years, are shown in Figure 21.17.

Some of RSL's work is published and available to the public.

RSMB Television Research and **AGB Television** are two further companies that won contracts in 1991 to supply data to BARB. RSMB is a subsidiary of Millward Brown who replaced Gallup in compiling the Top Ten music charts. AGB is a subsidiary of Taylor Nelson Audit of Great Britain plc, an early pioneer in metering TV audiences. RSMB is responsible for such things as sample design and control systems, and AGB for the design supply and maintenance of metering equipment.

BRAD (British Rate and Data) gives, in monthly editions, 400–500 pages of information on where adverts can be placed and how much they cost. Everything is there – the national and local press, TV

Asian Businessman Readership Survey (ABRS)

Universe covered	Heads of functions in eligible establishments in Hong Kong, Indonesia, South Korea, Malaysia, Philippines, Singapore, Taiwan and Thailand
Universe size	194 409 heads of functions in 40 295 establishments
Survey method	Telephone screening, then postal survey
Sample size	6247
Survey data	Readership of international and national business titles; business decisions and responsibilities; air trips, etc.
Sponsors	*Asian Wall Street Journal, Asia Inc., Asiaweek, Business Week, The Economist, Far Eastern Economic Review, Financial Times, Fortune, Newsweek*

Figure 21.17 Specification of one of RSL's studies

and radio, cinema, posters, bus-shelters, parking-meters, litter-bins and transport advertising.

Opinion polls

Newspapers, especially the tabloids, like to include information from opinion polls by companies such as **MORI** and **Gallup** to report on public opinion about any topical issue, from the serious to the trivial. The increasing reportage of opinion poll findings after the 1945 General Election was a noticeable innovation in the media's coverage of political issues. Typically such a poll is designed to illustrate public opinion on a topical issue and consists of a breakdown of responses from a sample, to preset questions. Some researchers have expressed the concern that the published poll may actually influence the voters.

The Gallup organisation has had international recognition since the 1930s as being a leading company in the field of public opinion polling. In the example in Figure 21.18, Gallup has researched audience reaction to a televised interview with Diana, Princess of Wales.

Besides polling public opinion, Gallup's activities also encompass the entire field of marketing, media, advertising and management. Through Gallup Worldwide it covers 20 of the world's largest nations, containing 60 per cent of the world's population. The organisation collects data not only through questionnaires but also through interviews and other techniques.

Academic research bodies

Academic research is often considered to be the most independent of all because individual lecturers tend to choose their own areas of study. This may not necessarily be true, as most educational establishments are under considerable financial pressure and therefore more likely to be open to influence from governments and organisations.

Any university or college with a media department will do research on audiences, whether by staff or students. However, some are better known than others and have had their research published or their data used by bodies such as BARB or political parties. The work of David Morley, who has done research at the University of Birmingham and later at Goldsmiths' College, has already been mentioned in Chapter 4.

University research projects are listed in a publication called *Current Research in Britain,* published by Cartermill International Ltd. All large reference libraries have a copy of *CRIB.* This tries to ensure that research is not duplicated. Figure 21.19 shows an example from *CRIB.*

Some noteworthy departments are:

> Henley Centre
> Media Group, Glasgow University
> Goldsmiths' Media Research Group, London University
> Centre for Mass Communication, Leicester University
> Centre for Contemporary Cultural Studies, Birmingham University
> Communications Research Centre, Loughborough University
> Media Research Group, Portsmouth University
> Centre for English Cultural Tradition, Sheffield University

PRINCESS DIANA INTERVIEW

1 Did you watch, or hear or read about, the television interview with the Princess of Wales?

	Today
Yes, watched	73
Yes, heard/read	32
No, neither	7

(All following questions based on those aware)

2 As a result of seeing the interview, or reading or hearing about it, do you think more or less of the Princess than you did before?

	Today
More	46
Less	10
Same	43
Don't know	2

3 As a result of seeing the interview, or reading or hearing about it, do you think more or less of Prince Charles than you did before?

	Today
More	2
Less	36
Same	60
Don't know	2

4 Do you think she should have given the interview or not?

	Today
Yes	74
No	20
Don't know	6

5 Do you think the interview was on balance a help to the Monarchy, or do you think it did it still further damage?

	Today
Help	18
Further damage	44
No effect	29
Don't know	9

6 Do you think the Monarchy and the Royal Family will still exist in the next century?

	Today
Yes	68
No	20
Don't know	12

7 In your view, is Prince Charles fit to be King?

	Today
Yes, is	45
No, is not	46
Don't know	9

8 In your view, should the Royal Family 'skip a generation', with Prince William becoming King in Prince Charles's stead, or not?

	Today
Yes, should	43
No, should not	46
Don't know	11

9 If Prince Charles does become King, should the Princess become Queen?

	Today
Yes	41
No	47
Don't know	12

10 In view of Monday night's interview, should Charles and Diana divorce?

	Today
Yes	58
No	24
Don't know	18

11 What do you think was the main reason the Princess gave the interview: to exact revenge on the other members of the Royal Family, as a cry for help or simply to put her case on the record?

	Today
To exact revenge	14
A cry for help	17
Put her case on record	77
None of these	2
Don't know	1

Figure 21.18 Gallup's Diana questionnaire

Project title	The media coverage of sport with special reference to the Olympic movement
Investigator(s)	Halloran JD, Professor
Institution contact	Sreberny-Mohammadi A, Professor (Director)
Department	Centre for Mass Communication Research
Institution	University of Leicester
Institution Address	104 Regent Road, Leicester LE1 7LT
Telephone no.	01533 523875
Subject area	Media Studies
Keywords	Media
	Sport
	Olympic Games
Included in volumes	Social Sciences
Project start year	1993
Expected end year	1996
Reference no.	28850

Figure 21.19 An entry from *Current Research in Britain*

The Glasgow University Media Group was set up with a grant from the UK Social Science Research Council. The group has published research findings that have won considerable attention and not unexpectedly drawn fire from the media under investigation. By 1982, the Group had published three major works on the way that TV handles the news. First came *Bad News* (Routledge & Kegan Paul, 1972) which exploded the generally held image of broadcasters being substantially more objective and reliable in news reporting than the press. The group monitored all TV news broadcasts over a six-month period in 1975. *War and Peace News* (Open University Press, 1985) looked at media coverage of the Falklands War, the miners' strike and Northern Ireland.

In the 1980s a mythology was created by the newspapers about the policies of Labour-led councils, particularly those in Greater London – the catchphrase was 'the loony left'. Accusations arose from rumours that were simply not true, such as the banning of the nursery rhyme 'Baa Baa Black Sheep' by Haringey Council, on racist grounds. A study of this campaign of 'disinformation' was conducted by Goldsmiths' and the findings were summarised in an *Open Space* TV programme on BBC2 in March 1988. The researchers found no substance in the press allegations, but the rumours had far-reaching effects on public opinion.

Campaigning organisations

There are two types of pressure groups:

- those which act to protect their members' interests
- those which aim to promote a cause which will be in the general interests of society.

They vary not only in the focus of their concern but in the degree or influence they exert. In some cases a government may consult relevant pressure groups before introducing or amending legislation or policies, and some groups enjoy relatively easy access to government ministers.

The **International Broadcasting Trust** (IBT) is an independent, non-profit-making television production company specialising in making programmes about developmental, environmental and human-rights issues for UK and international broadcast. It was established in 1982 as an educational charity and comprises over 60 member organisations – development agencies, environmental groups, churches, trade unions, educational bodies, race and immigration bodies – whose common concern is to use TV as a means of promoting greater discussion in the UK about its relationships with developing countries and the world community.

According to the Director of the IBT: *'Television matters enormously. Survey after survey shows that the majority of people now get most of their information about the rest of the world*

INTERNATIONAL BROADCASTING TRUST

from their TV sets. So if we are to increase the level of public awareness of global issues – and we plainly must as a matter of urgency – then we have to take the role and impact of television extremely seriously.'

The intention is that the programmes will be an educational resource as well as informative to the general public. The Trust publishes and distributes literature to enable educational groups to follow up issues in greater detail. In the first programme, Jonathan Dimbleby took a critical look at public and mass media attitudes to developing countries.

The **International Institute of Communications** (IIC) is another independent, non-profit-making association that provides a forum in which communications professionals from around the world can meet to discuss and debate issues in telecommunications, broadcasting, digital media and information technology. The IIC has 1200 members in more than 70 countries, some of whom are government policy-makers, managers, researchers and academics. The association discusses how the new technology can cause economic, social and cultural changes. It holds regular conferences and six times a year publishes the magazine *Intermedia*.

Article 19 is a global pressure group, centred in London, using electronic media to monitor state censorship around the world. The group derives its name from the United Nations Declaration of Human Rights, Article 19, which asserts that 'Everyone has the right to freedom of opinion and expression ...'. Computer databases have been established by Article 19 on the current state of freedom of information, press laws, official secrets legislation, codes, cases and practices in all countries.

ARTICLE 19
INTERNATIONAL CENTRE AGAINST CENSORSHIP

The staff of Article 19 comprises regional researchers and consultants who are experts on particular countries or freedom of expression themes. On the team are:

- a law programme director, whose mandate is to promote the highest standards for the protection of freedom of expression and to provide practical assistance in challenging restrictive laws and practices
- a UN consultant, who promotes their work at UN level
- a campaign and publicity coordinator
- a publications section
- a fundraising and administrative section.

A recent study by Article 19 looked at how election broadcasting in Malawi was monitored. The publication *Forging War* investigated how the media in Serbia, Croatia and Bosnia had been used by the various governments, and how the media had to struggle to maintain any sort of independence.

Campaign for Press and Broadcasting Freedom is a UK organisation founded by John Jennings in 1979 as a broad-based non-political party pressure group, dedicated to making Britain's media more open, diverse and accountable. Specifically the campaign has worked for the right to reply, a freedom-of-information law, and more community-based and alternative newspapers. The Campaign publishes a bimonthly bulletin, *Free Press*.

Campaign for Freedom of Information was founded in 1984 and is funded by grants from the Joseph Rowntree Charitable Trust, the Consumers' Association and other donations. Its main aim is to establish and maintain people's rights of access to information. For example, the Campaign wishes to give journalists greater protection of their sources. Some annual awards have gone to media people. Their work has made an impact on the national media, with Campaign staff appearing on various programmes including Channel 4's *News* and *Dispatches*, the BBC's *Newsnight*, and also on radio in *Today* and *Radio 5 Live*. Articles have been published in the *Guardian* and the *Independent*.

The **National Viewers' and Listeners' Association** originated in 1963 as a clean-up TV campaign started in Birmingham by Mary Whitehouse and others. She felt that television was attacking and undermining Christian civilisation. The movement later renamed itself the National Viewers' and Listeners' Association (NVLA). Over the years, the movement has succeeded in gaining access to practically every forum in which the issues of broadcasting are discussed. It has been active as a moral watchdog in other arts, especially the theatre and publishing, and wants to strengthen the Obscene Publications Act.

The National Viewers' and Listeners' Association has been actively involved in:

- *monitoring programme content and publishing regular reports which have helped to stimulate public and parliamentary concern, especially as to the cumulative effects of violent entertainment upon society*
- *providing timely information to the government and lobbying members of Parliament*
- *securing effective legislation to outlaw child pornography, 'video nasties' and indecent displays*
- *numerous television and radio programmes stimulating public debate on these key issues*
- *effective reform of the law on obscenity to curtail pornography and media obscenity*
- *developing links and exchanging information with like-minded organisations at home and abroad*
- *campaigning to establish the Broadcasting Standards Council*

■ *pressing for a European agreement on programme standards in an era of direct broadcasting by satellite.*

The basis of NVLA thinking is that of traditional Christian ethics, the belief that chastity and the family underpin all that is best in Western society and that such values are constantly under threat and have to be protected.

The **All Party Media Group** is a parliamentary group. Its purpose is to serve as a forum for the discussion of public policy as it affects the media.

It does not aim to be a campaigning body but it does seek, by enabling regular and detailed contact between members of both Houses of Parliament and key industry figures, to improve the quality of debate on the media in Parliament. Its 80 members are drawn from all political parties and they can attend over 50 meetings a year. SONY Broadcast and EMAP Media help to fund the cost of administration.

There are many other pressure groups that interact with the media, though they are not directly concerned with media issues. Examples are Greenpeace, Amnesty International and the World Wide Fund for Nature. These organisations publish their own magazines and access TV programmes – so in a way they have a concern about how audiences react, otherwise they may lose their power to raise money.

Other bodies

There are certain organisations that do a lot of research into the media and audiences, such as UNESCO, but which do not fit neatly into any of the categories listed above.

The **Independent Television Commission** (ITC) is a body set up by law to regulate commercial television. It does do regular research on audiences to support its work. Its annual survey looks at such subjects as swearing, sex and sex-role stereotyping in adverts and programmes.

The **British Broadcasting Corporation** (BBC) has many research departments, which are not concerned merely with production research. The main one concerned with audience research in the UK is the Broadcasting Research Department (BRD). In fact, the earliest television audience surveys were conducted by BRD, using street interviews to elicit day-after recall of TV viewing, and this continued until 1981. One of the main methods now used to collect data is panels to measure listener reactions.

Members of the public are recruited at random to sit on the panels.

Another example of such a section is BBC Worldwide Monitoring. This was established on the eve of the Second World War to monitor overseas broadcasts. It was set up at the request of the government to assess the use being made of radio as a propaganda tool. Today, its Summary of World Broadcasts in *World Media,* a weekly publication, covers developments in radio, television, satellite communications, cable and news agencies from around the world. Figure 21.20 shows a brief extract.

International Broadcasting Audience Research (IBAR) is an important main part of the BBC's World Service relating to audience research outside the UK. IBAR has been researching overseas since 1944 and at any given time is working on about 70 projects. Its mission statement says:

We want to make an effective and recognised contribution to the development and achievement

Figure 21.20 An extract from *World Media*

of World Service's objectives. We shall do this by providing an in-house consultancy which does professional research in a creative and fulfilling environment, maintains a productive dialogue with its clients, and strives to improve understanding of the people to whom the World Service broadcasts.

IBAR consists of two sections. The first does research and the second listens to, responds to and reports on the half million or so letters and phone calls from listeners reaching World Service each year. This research is necessary to monitor performance and to produce programmes and schedules that will meet the needs of rapidly changing audiences. The resulting data and reports are stored in the IBAR library. A quarterly newsletter gives brief results of recent surveys as well as in-depth feature articles.

Activity

Identify the research bodies you might approach for the following projects.

1 You need to compare radio listening habits in Africa with those in the UK. You have little money to spend on research.
2 You work for a broadsheet newspaper and want to publish the public's reaction to media coverage of the 'mad cow disease' (BSE) scare.

3 You are a journalist working in an authoritarian state and need advice and support on how to cope with the censorship laws and still be able to inform your readers adequately.
4 You need to know approximately how many people can listen to local radio in Azerbaijan.

Evidence assignment

In teams of four or five, compile a file relating to audience research for and by the media industries. The file should contain the following information, using diagrams, examples and lists with notes wherever possible:

■ an explanation of the principal uses of audience research
■ an assessment of the strengths and weaknesses of audience research methods
■ explanations of the roles and practices of official and independent research bodies and agencies.

Publicity materials from various bodies can be included. However, individual organisations should be approached by only one person within the class. Letters should be kept in your portfolio as evidence of communication skills.

Explore the relationship between media and audiences

Media producers, advertisers, governments, pressure groups, anthropologists and sociologists are all intensely interested in how media products can affect the behaviour and attitudes of readers, listeners and viewers. Is their influence harmful or beneficial? Can people be influenced without being aware of it? Are the effects short or long term? Are certain people more susceptible? Or do people largely ignore the media messages by which they are bombarded?

The term 'audience behaviour' covers a wide range, and refers to either individual or group behaviour. It implies acceptance or rejection of the media message, or whether people buy or use the media product. It implies abstract concepts of behaviour such as change of attitudes or ideas as well as more concrete behaviour such as changing voting patterns, watching more TV or reacting with violence.

Comparing models of audience behaviour

Controversy surrounds the way the media affect us and how they can do this. Sociologists and psychologists are concerned with the media's influence on our education, personal lifestyles, consumer behaviour and opinions on political issues. These experts are concerned with how the media may affect the behaviour of children and induce violence.

There are two main schools of thought, *passive* and *active*. Followers of the passive school believe that

Figure 22.1 According to some, the media can be like a drug

large numbers of people absorb media messages and react in predictable ways. Followers of the active school think that we as individuals exert a lot of control over how we use media products, and are less affected by them.

The passive approach itself can be split into two different types of models. One type describes the so-called 'hypodermic needle' effect. The other type is based on the stimulus–response effect.

Passive theories

Why 'hypodermic needle'?

The hypodermic needle theory implies that the media are capable of mass manipulation – that a large proportion of the population accept and believe the messages given in newspapers and films, or on radio and TV. The image of the hypodermic needle does not intend to convey the feeling that we are immune to the media, but rather that we the public have been drugged by them. We are unable to prevent media messages from being injected into our brains. It is sometimes knows as the 'bullet' theory. Just as we cannot prevent the bullet entering our body, neither can we defend ourselves against the media. This idea has been used to support claims that certain sectors of society are vulnerable to the media and should be protected. It thus justifies the use of censorship.

There is evidence to support the theory:

- One of the earliest cases, often cited, was *The War of the Worlds* radio broadcast in 1938. Orson Welles' radio production of the science fiction story by H.G. Wells convinced nearly a million Americans that their country was being invaded by Martians.
- Contemporary audiences can be just as gullible. Every April Fools' Day, many viewers believe spoof TV programmes. The BBC's *Panorama* programme managed to convince some viewers that spaghetti grew on trees!
- Followers of soaps have been known to believe that the characters are real. Actors who play villains have been verbally and sometimes physically attacked in the street.

Figure 22.2 *The War of the Worlds* convinced many listeners that Martians had landed

- Santa Claus is another example of how millions of people, in this case children, can be persuaded to believe in a myth, partly through books and films. The actual image of Father Christmas has also been influenced by the media.

Propaganda

Propaganda is used in a deliberate and systematic effort to manipulate other people's beliefs and attitudes. The propagandist will set a goal and will then select facts, arguments and symbolic images to support this. Contrary facts may be distorted or omitted. Adolf Hitler used the media as a tool to spread propaganda during the 1930s. He used films to support his idea of a Teutonic master race, and newspapers instilled in Germans a fear of the Jews.

In recent years, every major industrial firm, every government, political party, pressure group, social and religious movement has developed a team of propaganda experts – usually called researchers, public relations experts, lobbyists, information specialists or spin doctors! Such people recognise the ability of the media to promote the ideas and image of the organisation for which they work. In 1984 the Republican Party in the United States spent over $25 million on promoting their presidential and vice-presidential candidates in the media. In Britain, political leaders have become very aware of their TV

image – Margaret Thatcher as Prime Minister was advised to change her hairstyle, clothes and accent.

Activity

Find recent examples in the press where pictures or stories might be trying to influence your viewpoint. This could be a political article or one about a war in some part of the world.

Do other members of your group feel the same way about the coverage? Is there an obvious bias, or is there subtle persuasion through choice of words and images and the way in which they are put together to make you think in a certain way about the situation?

Imitation

Although the word 'passive' implies inaction, these models of behaviour also try to explain how the influence of the media can result in action. One example is imitation.

Psychologists after the Second World War showed considerable interest in the ways in which communication occurs and its effects. **Behaviourist** or social learning theory implies that children learn to respond in a certain way by the observation of adult behaviour around them, and by the reaction of adults towards their own behaviour. Children copy adults. If they act in a certain way they are rewarded. Television or films are now sometimes seen as taking the place of role-model parents. The result is that children (or vulnerable adults) copy the actions seen on TV or in films.

Figure 22.3 Have 'video nasties' contributed to 'moral panic' in society?

This belief that children or teenagers can be negatively influenced by popular media products, such as films or pop music, occurs regularly. There is a 'moral panic' in society generally, usually orchestrated ironically enough by the press. An example of this is the early public reaction to the hip-swivelling Elvis Presley in the 1950s or to 'video nasties' in the 1980s and 1990s.

Stanley Cohen, in his 1973 book *Folk Devils and Moral Panics* (London: Paladin), analyses the media treatment of fights between Mods and Rockers at British seaside resorts in the 1960s. He quotes from a *Daily Express* article of 19 May 1964:

> *There was Dad asleep in a deckchair and Mum making sandcastles with the children when the 1964 boys took over the beaches of Brighton and Margate yesterday and smeared the traditional postcard scene with blood and violence.*

Cohen argued that the media isolates groups of individuals and gives them an identity. Others imitate and this leads to increased levels of deviance and confirms in the public's mind the stereotypes created by the media. This *deviance amplification* has been seen since in the media treatment of glue-sniffing, drugs, teenage alcoholism and heroin abuse.

Critics of the power of the media consider that over-exposure to scenes of violence and death can **desensitise** viewers or readers, who can see such images without feelings of horror or distaste.

Case study

The charity Oxfam used to show pictures of starving children in advertisements, but in a later campaign changed this approach to show photographs of smiling children. It was considered that the public had ceased to be shocked and had begun to ignore the normally distressing images, and so were not donating as much money.

Find some examples of charity advertisements. What approach do they take? For example, do they aim to shock you into giving money, or make you feel that you can make a difference?

Catharsis

The passivity of audiences also incorporates the idea of catharsis. The 'couch potato' media consumer experiences the world *through* the media. Such a person not only gets the same emotional feelings as the actors on screen or the characters in a book, but also shares a physical release such as a violent outburst or sexual activity.

Stimulus–response theory

By the mid-1950s, psychological interest settled largely on the persuasive aspects of various types of messages.

Stimulus–response theory states that people become *conditioned* to react in a certain way after receiving a stimulus. The stimulus could be a film, resulting in violent behaviour, or it could be an advert, persuading someone to buy a product. The 1957 bestseller *The Hidden Persuaders* by Vance Packard brought to the attention of the public the techniques by which advertisers manipulate the public.

Advertising can be considered as a commercial type of propaganda. Just as an electoral campaign aims to make people change their voting habits, so an advert also wants to control our behaviour. Modern adverts have changed from their Victorian predecessors. They are now unlikely to give detailed lists of the virtues of the product and the names of people who recommend it. In fact many modern adverts tell you nothing about the product – they provide only its name and an image. (Look again at the examples of newspaper advertisements in Chapter 2.)

Case study

One brand of jeans dramatically increased sales because of its clever use of a series of popular songs. The music was absorbed into people's minds, creating a link between a pleasurable experience and the ownership of this brand of jeans. The stimulus was strengthened by the songs appearing in the charts.

How many songs can you name that have entered the charts after being used in a TV advertising campaign?

We can all of us live without most of the products advertised on television or radio. The adverts attempt to create needs in us that we didn't know we had. Advertisers rely on this stimulus–response effect for the success of their campaigns.

Activity

Make a list of the adverts you like the most on television. Have you ever bought any of

these products? Did you need that particular brand or would another have been as good?

Discuss with your friends what is fashionable to wear at the moment. How do you know this? Is it because you have seen similar clothes on models or people featured in a magazine or on a TV programme? Have you ever bought clothes with a designer label or logo? Do you think you were influenced by the media in your choice?

Positioning audiences

In Chapter 4 the way in which narrative structure is used to position audiences was noted. In fact, it is not merely the narrative which positions us but the entire media product, whatever its genre or medium. Psychologists have suggested that these media products are constructed in such a way that responses are limited – the audience or consumers are guided in the direction of the **dominant**, **preferred** readings. This can be done in the case of television advertising, not only by the advert itself – what the actors say and the images shown – but also by where the advert appears in the schedules.

Sometimes, the way in which media products 'talk' to us and make assumptions that we are a certain type of audience is called **mode of address**. For instance the news presenter on the BBC's early-evening news talks to us as if we are responsible, law-abiding adults. We are encouraged to assimilate the BBC viewpoint over what is acceptable and good in our society. This news gives the dominant reading that, for example, drugs are bad, nurses are good, the government may be poor but the Queen Mother is wonderful. In contrast, a programme such as *The Clothes Show* addresses us as individual people who are interested in our personal appearance, in fashion, spending money, being young and up-to-date. Mode of address implies that if people are treated in a certain way then they will react in a predictable manner.

On the other hand, some theorists believe that positioning will only *reinforce* existing attitudes and behaviour rather than convert others. The

hypodermic needle theory is a **one-step flow model** of communication – the mass media communicate directly with a mass audience. In the **two-step flow model**, something mediates or intervenes between the sender and the receiver of the message. For example, sixteen-year-old Fred has parents who do not swear, but Fred hears a lot of swearing in a popular television comedy. According to the one-step flow model, Fred will imitate this behaviour and also start swearing profusely. However, according to the two-step flow theory, the influence of Fred's family will counteract or mediate the television message that swearing is generally acceptable, and Fred will not swear profusely.

The two-step flow model is derived from the work of Lazarsfeld, Berelson and Gaudet (1994) which acknowledges the importance of the social context in the way audiences interpret media messages. Their work was based on research around the 1940 American presidential election. It concluded that the decisions of the voters were not significantly influenced by the mass media. People tended to stay with the parties they grew up with and floating voters paid even less attention to the media than those with stronger political leanings.

Social conditions do change. For instance, family and work conditions are less static now, and there are more floating voters. Fewer people vote for the same political party throughout their lives.

However, some theorists, such as Graeme Burton in *More than Meets the Eye,* have claimed that certain products such as magazines can create their own readership. It could be argued that a TV cult programme such as *Red Dwarf* has 'created' an audience for itself.

Challenges to the passive theories

The passive theories have been challenged. Critics claim that most people are now too sophisticated to believe everything they are told. Cultural, economic and social influences are of equal if not greater importance in shaping people's behaviour and attitudes.

Many sociologists believe that mass communication influences attitudes and behaviour only if it confirms the status quo – that is, what people already believe in or want. Even if they do not switch the TV off, people tend to ignore a party political broadcast if it is not for the party they already support.

In Western society we are bombarded by so many media messages that they can act like 'counter propaganda'. There is such an overload of communication that people are becoming alienated from the message.

Activity

When you read a newspaper, do you read all of it or only certain parts? Make a list of the sections you read. It may help if you refer to Figure 21.2 on page 346.

What other things do you do whilst watching television? Do you, for example, eat a meal, or read a magazine?

Compare your lists with those of a friend.

The influence of any media product is lessened if we do not give it our entire attention. If we go to the cinema, we generally give the film our full attention. There is little conversation and nothing else to see as we sit in the dark. This is an example of the media being used as a **primary activity**.

If someone reads a magazine whilst eating their tea and occasionally talking to someone else in the room, then reading the magazine has become a **secondary activity**.

Listening to the radio is often a **tertiary activity**! In a factory or whilst driving, the main preoccupation of the listener is with operating equipment or steering the car. Then the radio programme is often background sound.

In 1985, Marplan carried out research on 20–34-year-olds which compared their memory of an advert for an item of men's toiletry seen at the cinema with that of a similar group who saw the advert on TV. The results showed that the percentage of people who could recall part of all of the advertisement at the cinema was considerably greater than those who saw it on TV – see Figure 22.4.

	Cinema	Television
Sample size	200	97
Seeing the advertisement	85%	68%
Recalling the product		
Spontaneous	7%	1%
Product-group prompted	20%	3%
Brand-prompted	47%	11%
Total recall	74%	15%

Source: CAA/Marplan 1985

Figure 22.4 The results of a Marplan survey

Activity

List examples of how you have used various forms of media recently. Have they been primary, secondary or tertiary activities?

Active theories

All of us make decisions on how closely we pay attention to media products. We also make our own interpretations of them depending on our age, gender, individual experiences, tastes, social and cultural background and level of understanding.

- A magazine article on current trends influenced by 1960s music and fashion could be fresh and exciting to a young teenager. It might have a different – possibly nostalgic – appeal to someone in their forties who may be mildly amused by the way that fashions repeat themselves.
- A television programme on eating disorders might be interesting to both teenagers and doctors, but they will probably have different reasons for watching it. The teenager may have a subjective viewpoint (suffering from anorexia?) and need to know that he or she is not alone. The doctor may have a more impersonal, objective viewpoint and be interested in the research behind the programme and why young people are affected by eating disorders.
- Cultural differences, too, can alter our perception of a product. A kiss in an Indian film can be as daring as nudity in a Western film.

Besides our family, the most powerful influence on our choice of media products and how we use them is that exerted by our **peer group**. Teenage girls can enjoy the short stories and cookery articles in *Woman's Realm,* and women in their fifties may love to read the fashion articles and the problem page in *Nineteen*. But neither is likely to become a regular subscriber because of peer group pressure.

Uses and gratifications theory

Because of our individual social and psychological make-up, the mass media cannot influence all of us all of the time in the same way, as is implied by the passive theory. The factors outlined above will affect what media products we use and how much we are affected by them.

The basis of an active theory such as the 'uses and gratifications theory' is that we are not 'used' or controlled by the media but that we use media products for our own purposes and to fulfil our own needs. Those needs can be divided into two categories, personal and social.

- A **personal** need is something you want to do that will satisfy you as an individual. You may be feeling stressed, so you listen to music on the radio. You may have an interest in dolphins, so you watch a wildlife programme on TV.
- A **social** need is when you want to do something that confirms your position within society. Many of your friends like going to the cinema for a night out and you want to go with them. You listen to the football results so that you know what's happening and can chat about it with your friends.

Obviously the gratification of a social need may also gratify a personal need.

 Activity

Make a list of the different reasons you had for:

a going to the cinema to watch a film this month
b watching the television one evening this week
c buying a magazine.

Was it because you were bored? Were you asked out by someone? Are you a fan of the stars? Do you do these things out of habit? Do you always go to that type of film? Do your family always watch this programme? Or were there other reasons? Try to identify which reasons are personal and which are social.

Find someone in the class who has been to see a similar film, watches a similar programme or buys the same type of magazine. Compare your reasons. Were they the same?

This exercise is worth doing outside the classroom, with people outside your peer group, such as parents, children or people in different types of jobs.

The different uses and gratifications of media consumers have been described by Blumler and Katz in *The Uses of Mass Communication* (1974). They defined the four broad needs of TV viewers as:

1 **diversion** – an escape or emotional release from everyday life and problems
2 **personal relationships** – being able to talk to your friends and colleagues about what you have seen
3 **personal identity** – comparing your lifestyle and situations with those of a character on TV

4 **surveillance** – gaining information about the world around you, and events.

As individuals we need companionship. We need enjoyment and amusement, the confirmation that we belong to and understand the society in which we live. We want to know what is going on in the world and that others share our opinions of other situations and people, whether real or imaginary. Sometimes we may want advice or guidance about what our behaviour or tastes should be. *Every media product fulfils a number of these needs.* In the activity above you were asked to identify reasons for going to see a film. You perhaps put down as one main reason 'It sounded exciting', but you probably identified more than one reason for going.

Comparing the theories

An active theory is obviously useful for describing the complex way in which media products and their audiences can interact and how individuals respond. But it ignores the basic concept of mass media – that the same message can be transmitted to millions of different people in a number of different ways and be understood by them.

In trying to compare the active and passive theories, it is possible to over-simplify and lose their meanings. They both make valid points and it is not a question of believing in either one or the other.

- A **passive** theory describes how large numbers of people, a 'mass', consume a variety of media products like television and newspapers. It looks at human psychology and suggests that this determines how they absorb information and affects behavioural patterns. It acknowledges the strength of peer group pressure as well as the pressure of society at large. Based on case histories, it suggests that there is a simple reaction to media messages; we believe what we hear or we buy what is advertised.
- An **active** theory describes how the individual is affected by media products. Later theories have also suggested that the flow is not just one-way and that consumers influence, as well as are influenced by, the media. Active theories look at social influences on individuals and how they behave in small groups. Experiments have been used to explain the complex reaction of the media on consumers.

Published evidence on models of audience behaviour

The background to these models of audience behaviour has been outlined above. Cultural and academic groups, politicians, sociologists, psychologists, teachers and the medical profession have all published books or papers on the various models. Not all of it is easy to understand.

However, two excellent treatments of the subject are: *Media Sociology* by David Barrat (Routledge, 1986) and a chapter entitled 'Audience' by Gill Branson in *The Media Studies Book,* edited by David Lusted (Routledge, 1992).

Gill Branson's chapter bibliography (or list of references) is annotated; that is, she gives an indication of how useful each publication is. Extracts from her bibliography and that in David Barrat's book are shown here as Figures 22.5 and 22.6.

1 Clive James, The *Independent*, 22 May 1987.
2 See David Morley, *The 'Nationwide' Audience* (London: BFI, 1980), especially Chapters 1–4 for a succinct account of this and other dominant ways of thinking about 'the audience' for the media.
3 See Jane Root, *Open the Box* (London: Comedia/Channel Four, 1985) and the first programme of the series it was written to accompany (available through the BFI Film and Video Library) for a lively account of the imagery and extremes of the 'effects' case. For a helpful discussion of the 'video nasties' panic, see Julian Petley, 'A nasty story', *Screen*, vol. 25, no. 2 and Annette Kuhn's reply, *Screen*, vol. 25, no. 3.
4 *Video, Violence and Children* (London: Hodder & Stoughton, 1985) by the so-called Parliamentary Group is a recent example of such work. See also David Lusted, 'Feeding the panic and breaking the cycle', *Screen*, vol. 24, no. 6, for a critique of the area.
5 Len Masterman gives an account of one such theorist, Dallas Smythe, in his chapter on 'Audience' in *Teaching the Media* (London: Comedia/M K Media Press, 1985).
6 See John Caughie, 'On the offensive: TV and values', in David Lusted and Phillip Drummond (eds), *TV and Schooling* (London: BFI, 1985).
7 For a clear account of the earliest, news-centred work around 'agenda setting', see Dennis McQuail and Sven Windhal, *Communication Models for the Study of Mass Communications*, pp. 62–4 (London: Longman, 1981).

Figure 22.5 An extract from Gill Branson's annotated bibliography

Curran, J. (1977) Capitalism and the Control of the Press 1800–1975. In J. Curran, M. Gurevitch, and J. Woollacott (eds) *Mass Communication and Society.* London: Edward Arnold.
Curran, J. (1982) Communications, Power and the Social Order. In M. Gurevitch, T. Bennett, J. Curran, and J. Woollacott (eds) Culture, *Society and the Media.* London: Methuen.
Curran, J. and Seaton, J. (1981/1985) *Power without Responsibility: The Press and Broadcasting in Britain.* London: Fontana (second edition 1985).
Curran, J., Gurevitch, M., and Woollacott, J. (eds) (1977) *Mass Communication and Society.* London: Edward Arnold.
Dyer, R. (1977) Stereotyping. In R. Dyer (ed.) *Gays and Film.* London: British Film Institute.
Eco, U. (1981) *The Role of the Reader.* London: Hutchinson.
Eysenck, H. and Nias, D. (1980) *Sex, Violence and the Media.* London: Granada.
Ferguson, M. (1983) *Forever Feminine: Women's Magazines and the Cult of Femininity.* London: Heinemann.
Fiske, J. (1982) *Introduction to Communication Studies.* London: Methuen.
Fiske, J. and Hartley, J. (1978) *Reading Television.* London: Methuen.
Fiske, J., Hartley, J., O'Sullivan, D., and Saunders, D. (1983) *Key Concepts in Communication.* London: Methuen.

Figure 22.6 An extract from David Barrat's bibliography

It is very important when doing research to be able to evaluate material. We live in an age where we can rapidly become swamped by the amount of data and information available to us from books and screens, from libraries and from our homes. We need to be able to assess quickly the value of individual items.

How can published evidence be evaluated? There are a number of considerations.

The area selected for investigation

What exactly is the book or article about? It may be a general study, a broad overview of radio or television audiences. Or perhaps it may be a report covering a narrow field such as the effect on male cinema-goers of film posters in a bus station in Leeds.

You may be looking for a book or article which will introduce you to a subject, or you may be seeking precise information to support your own work. Many a promising title may prove to be not quite what you are looking for. So you will have to investigate further than the front cover.

The date

Published work may be of interest even if it is 100 years old. However, we live in a rapidly changing world, so *conclusions* drawn about people then – 20 years ago, or even last year – may not be true of our society now.

For example, 50 years ago radio had an enormous impact on the lives of the average person during the Second World War. It boosted their morale and provided many of their information and entertainment needs. Times have changed. We are at present not at war, and there are many more ways for the population to gain information, including TV and the Internet. There are more alternatives for entertainment, including computer games and videos. Technology has changed the audience. We are now far less likely to listen to the radio as a family, as happened 50 years ago.

The qualifications and bias of the author

It is important to be able to recognise the background of the writer, particularly if the published evidence is of an academic nature. Someone who has a doctorate will have had considerably more general research experience than someone who has never attended a university. The subject area of the degree is also significant – whether the writer is a scientist, a sociologist or a psychologist. Henry Smith BSc may have a first degree in information technology, Jane Brown MPhil a master's degree in literature, and Gareth Jones PhD a doctorate in anthropology. You need to know.

The publisher and the place of publication

The publisher's name can indicate the status of a book. Certain publishers issue certain types of books. Ladybird, for example, is renowned for easy-to-read children's books, Heinemann is noted for its textbooks. The place is also important. Is this an American or a British book? For which audience was it intended? These details can also indicate the scope of the evidence.

The topics covered

If there is an abstract or summary of the work, then this can save you time. It should be apparent how useful a document will be to you without having to read all the way through it. If there is an index, this too will be useful.

How large is the topic to be investigated? If it is too large, then research is likely to be very superficial. If it is too small, and the research objectives too specific, then the conclusions may not be valid for anything other than this particular group.

Is the evidence appropriate for the topic, or has the writer included other material that, although interesting, may be irrelevant? Is the research original – has new research been done, or does the writer rely on other researchers' work?

Who commissioned the work and why?

Sometimes a government or a commercial business can sponsor research, and university researchers too are eager to get funding in this way. But this must be considered in assessing the conclusions of the evidence. Has the research been leaning towards proving rather than disproving an opinion of the sponsor?

Methodology

How were the data collected? Were the research methods used appropriate for the task? (See Chapter 21 on quantitative and qualitative research.) How accurate are the data? How large was the sample group? How well trained were the interviewers? Are the case studies anecdotal rather than the product of face-to-face interviewing?

The quality of the work

It is essential that the reader can see that the conclusions of the writer are drawn directly from the

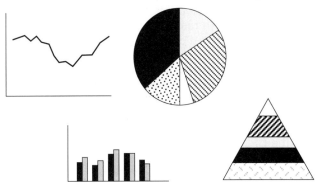

Figure 22.7 Illustrative material can aid in understanding a complex issue

data, and that the writer has not jumped to conclusions. Has the writer been objective or subjective?

The presentation of the work is important too. Illustrative material such as graphs, charts and diagrams can explain a complex situation better than many paragraphs of text.

Case study

Some of the research done by David Morley was mentioned in Chapter 4. Reread it to remind yourself of the purpose of the following piece of research on how a TV audience responded to the *Nationwide* current affairs magazine programme. What follows is an evaluation of his published evidence based on the active theory of audience behaviour.

■ *Area selected for investigation.* This is a narrow field of investigation. It does not attempt to cover all genres of television or the reactions of all sections of British society.

■ *Date.* The research was carried out between 1975 and 1979 and was published in 1980. The material is dated. Both TV audiences and the TV product, a magazine programme, have now changed. The expectations and the sophistication of both have changed. So a different response might be expected from later research.

■ *Qualifications of the author.* Morley has done prestigious work at several universities, including Birmingham and Glasgow, and held the position of Reader in Media Studies at Goldsmiths' College, London, in the 1980s.

■ *Publisher.* The British Film Institute (BFI) is renowned as a reputable publisher of media books. The evidence is not only published in Britain but is based on research done in Britain, so it is particularly relevant to British students.

■ *Topic covered.* He restricted his study to how a TV audience responded to the *Nationwide* current affairs/magazine programme. His objectives were well defined, he investigated narrative structures and how individuals from different backgrounds interpreted media messages. He wanted to prove that this was an active not a passive process.

■ *Who commissioned the work?* The work was funded by the BFI, so no obvious bias is likely.

■ *Methodology.* Videotapes of two *Nationwide* programmes were shown to two different groups. Then the samples were interviewed. There was a very limited sample group and the test period was very short. The responses might have been different

if the groups had been shown a series of programmes and their changes in attitude over a period of time noted.

■ *Quality.* Morley produced a detailed book with diagrams. Even so, it is not always easy to understand by the lay person. The vocabulary is complex and aimed at university students with a sociological rather than a technical media background.

Morley's work has been criticised because, although it recognises how the programme was constructed and the way in which the viewers decoded its meaning, the work actually ignores the process of *how* groups of people decoded the messages.

Another criticism is the smallness of the sample groups. There should have been a **control** group. A control group is a sample who go through the testing process and are used as a check on the original group. Another control would have been to show the groups a different type of programme to check their responses.

Morley's categorisation of groups is also suspect, being rather simplistic. Two white working-class apprentices in their twenties may have very different personalities, backgrounds and experiences. He relies heavily on class as being a meaningful category.

However, the broad, overall conclusion of the work with regard to dominant, negotiated and oppositional readings does seem to be valid when the evidence is read, and has been supported since by other writers.

Activity

a Choose one of the other books or articles mentioned above and evaluate its importance.

b Try to find published evidence which supports passive behaviour. It might be useful before you do your evaluation to read the following notes on how to set out a list of references.

Compiling a list of references

It is very important when you do research to cite or acknowledge the work or ideas of other people. Not only is it unethical not to do this, but you may also be breaking copyright laws.

Researching an assignment in a library or elsewhere means you are drawing on other people's ideas. The easiest way to acknowledge your sources is to use a list of references. This also helps to establish your argument and allows others to check and assess your sources. You can also use references in other people's work to find further information for yourself.

Sometimes it is convenient to photocopy something you find interesting or useful. This is allowed up to a point. As a student you can photocopy up to 5 per cent of a book, or one article from a periodical, *provided this is for your own use in your studies.*

Your references can be compiled using either a 'name and date' system (sometimes referred to as the Harvard system) or a 'numeric' system. The text below refers to someone else's work by citing the name and the year of publication:

> More people watch television on Monday (Smith, 1991).

The list of references would then have an entry, in alphabetical order:

> Smith, J. (1991) *British Viewers' Watching Habits,* Routledge, London.

In a numeric system your text would refer to a work by using an indicator, as in

> More people watch television on Monday [1].
> or More people watch television on Monday[1].

The list of references would then have an entry, in numerical order:

> [1] Smith, J., *British Viewers' Watching Habits,* Routledge, London, 1991.

The above examples cite a book. If the work is an article in a periodical, the reference list entries might be

> Jones, S. (1991) 'Who watches TV anyway?', *Media,* vol. 3, no. 2, pp. 3–6.
> or [1] Jones, S. 'Who watches TV anyway?' *Media,* 1991, vol. 3, no. 2, pp. 3–6.

It is very important when you do research to cite or acknowledge the work or ideas of other people. Not only is it unethical not to do this, but you may also be breaking copyright laws.

Assessing debates on the influence of the media

A debate is a discussion or argument about an issue or event, which can be in the past, present or future. For a debate to take place, there must be at least two people with different viewpoints or attitudes, but there can be several sides to a debate. A debate can cover a large or a narrow topic, and it may take place in public or in the home.

Debates about the media are very commonplace, and there is almost always controversy. Where does it come from?

- In *academic circles,* as we have seen above, there are different theories evolving all the time. GNVQ students, too, can contribute to the debate – it does not have to be left to the lecturers!
- *Politicians* argue that new laws are needed to control the media. They also argue about how politics and politicians are represented in the media.
- *Media producers* sometimes encourage controversy, because it creates publicity for their products. Or they may argue for greater freedom in which to operate.
- *Media professionals* – official bodies such as the British Board of Film Classification, owners of media corporations and manufacturers of new media equipment – want to have their say.
- *Other professionals and specialists* such as teachers, the police, doctors, psychiatrists or religious leaders are concerned about the effects of media products on society.
- *The public* may initiate debates with any of the above groups.

So these debates take place in a variety of places – in the classroom, at home, in Parliament, in the press and on TV and radio. They will sometimes be formal, in the form of a university thesis or a letter to the editor, or informal as in a radio phone-in or playground discussion. They may be verbal, such as a speech in the House of Lords, or written as in a student essay. All are important and ultimately influential.

These are the main areas where students can find out about these debates:

1 **Written materials.** Go to the local library. The librarian will be able to help you track down books, reports, etc. Parliamentary speeches are collected in *Hansard.* Newspapers, both tabloid and broadsheet, and magazine articles will provide ample sources of materials. Many libraries now have past issues of newspapers on CD-ROM to make searching easier.
2 **Aural materials.** There are regular documentaries and news reports on television about the influence of the media. Personal interviews with any of the people mentioned above will provide useful source materials.

Activity

Look at the list of media issues below. Which ones can you remember hearing about and where? Think of two more to add to the list.

Lack of control over satellite TV
Violence in films and on television
Swearing on TV and in films and videos
Sex in TV programmes
Religious influence in scheduling of TV programmes
Blasphemy in comedy programmes
Violence in computer games
Pornography in magazines
Pornography on the Internet
Censorship of films and videos
Freedom of the press
Influence on politics by the media
Influence on the media by politicians
Influence on voters
Manipulation by advertisers
Influence of media images (e.g. thin supermodels)
Role models in the media (e.g. pop star behaviour)
Influence on public opinion by news reporters
Influence of the media on children
How too much TV can affect children's reading
The connection between popular music and drugs
How female roles and behaviour are influenced
The success or value of individual films or programmes
The future of various media industries
The effect of comics on young boys.

Case studies

The authors of this book compiled the above list of issues by studying CD-ROM editions of newspapers. If you do a similar search you will find a lot of letters and articles over a period of a few weeks, and then a particular debate may disappear from the pages for a while only to resurface later. Figure 22.8 shows an example of part of an article from a compact-disc edition of *The Times*.

Activity

Build up a portfolio of various debates and how they affect individuals or groups in the UK and other countries. Where did the debates appear? On TV or radio or in the press? Summarise each debate and then assess it by considering the following points:

a the identity of the participants
b the aims of the participants
c how the views are presented
d what model of audience behaviour they exemplify
e how great they believe the effect of the media is on an audience.

Responding to a selected media text

Some active theories have been developed by sociologists who are interested in how groups with different lifestyles and experiences – such as retired people or schoolchildren – react to the media. This can result in **stereotyping**.

Other theories take a psychological approach in looking at how the different mental make-up of groups such as men and women or young and old people can affect how they are influenced. It is a similar debate as to what makes a child develop in a certain way: is it its genetic inheritance, or how it is brought up? Other psychological approaches look at attitudes and prejudices: where they come from and what can change them.

For more information on this topic refer back to pages 103–4 in Chapter 4.

It has been discussed earlier in this Unit how a number of factors can affect communication. These include age, sex, class, occupation, interest groups, etc.

Activity

Set up an experiment. Find a sample of people, preferably of mixed ages and sex, who are prepared to watch the news on TV and the weather report. You may choose to do this in the classroom with a recorded video of a news programme, and have a discussion afterwards; or you may wish to ask different families to watch the news in their homes and write their responses in a diary. It is up to you how you organise your research.

Collect the following information, following a consistent pattern.

a Record what they expect or anticipate from the programme. What motivations do they have towards watching news programmes?
b Afterwards record the reactions of the audience, their attitudes and opinions. Do any of the reports make them change their behaviour? How much attention did they give? What did they think of the presenter?

The Times and *The Sunday Times* Compact Disc Edition

SOURCE: *The Times*   DATE: 20 August 1993   PAGE: 10

India's censors lose battle of the blouse

From Christopher Thomas in Delhi

INDIAN film producers, who are in constant battle with government censors, have won a fight to save the lyrics of a slightly risqué song entitled What's Beneath the Blouse? The controversy has turned it into a hit.

An estimated ten million cassettes of the song are in circulation after a long battle highlighting the government's capricious attempts to control the nation's most popular and powerful medium.

Not everybody is happy with the outcome. A lawyer in Delhi was outraged when he heard his six-year-old daughter singing it, and has filed a suit alleging that the lyrics are obscene.

The second line of the song says: "There is a heart beneath my blouse." This answer to the question posed by the title seems to have saved it from the axe. Shakti Samanta, chairman of the censorship board, said: "Taken in the context of the film and the song's second line, we did not find the lyric offensive."

The barriers of official tolerance are constantly being pushed back, if modestly, under pressure from audiences demanding more than the tired old song-and-dance formula. Indian cinema has become a vehicle for social commentary, tackling issues such as political corruption, dowry and women's rights. It makes the government jittery.

A measure of prurience has crept in, too. Gyrating women with uncovered legs are routine fare, much to the outrage of traditionalists. A number of recent films have hinted at, and even portrayed, young love, a daring subject in a country where most of the young film-goers are expected to have marriages arranged for them.

A popular theme is love between a rich heroine and a poor hero, improbable in this class-obsessed society. The girl has even been known to run away from home to live with her man.

This portrayal of women as independent and strong-minded is an increasing, if small, trend, although women are still usually portrayed as submissive.....

Figure 22.8 Some newspaper articles can be read from CD-ROM. © Times Newspapers Limited 1993

c Analyse your findings. What similarities and differences can you find between individuals? Are you able to make any generalisations?

d Assess how the conditions of the experiment may have affected this piece of research. Consider the size of the sample, the reality of the simulation if it took place in the classroom, the time allotted to the feedback. Identify any problems that arose and how you would change them in future experiments.

Evidence assignment

You should compile a report explaining and comparing models of audience behaviour.

Include a discussion of two published pieces of evidence about models of audience behaviour.

This could be an individual written report, or a recorded discussion intended to be included as part of a magazine programme for BBC Radio 4.

The report or discussion should also assess current debates on the influence of the media on audiences.

You should carry out research to find out how individuals and groups respond to a media text of your choice. This can also be used as evidence for Unit 6 Element 4 (Chapter 24) or linked in with the research done for Unit 1 Element 4 (Chapter 4).

Chapter 23

Analyse and interpret published data

You should be aware now of the extent of audience research that is being carried out by a wide variety of individuals and groups, and how this may be done for either commercial or social reasons. By looking at what has happened in the past, newspaper editors, advertisers, programme schedulers and film financiers hope to predict what will happen in the future.

Data are the raw materials collected by researchers, generally taken to mean quantifiable facts and figures, lists of information, graphs, diagrams and statistics. Some data can be anecdotal or descriptive, however. It is up to you to weigh up the value of such evidence and check to see whether it is supported by data from other sources.

Data on the consumption of media products

Data on the consumption of media products is found everywhere. Some of it is freely accessible to the general public – you can find statistics on the front of your newspaper (see for example Figure 23.2), in magazine articles and in popular books such as the *Guinness Book of Records*. This information is generally included for its entertainment value or for advertising purposes.

Some media organisations such as the BBC and *The Guardian* produce special publications giving facts and figures about their work. They see this as being beneficial to the community, as a form of education, and good publicity for their particular product.

Activity

Find examples of sources of data freely available to the public. Make notes about where the information was found and the reason for its inclusion in a publication.

Some data are designed to be used by people with a specialist or professional interest in the media. They may be students or people working in one of the various industries. Books and professional journals contain facts and figures. Figure 23.1, for example, shows year-by-year data on cinemas from *Film Year Book*. Figure 23.3 is an article on home-interest magazine publishing from *Marketing Week*.

Chapter 21 you read about the sort of information collected by official research bodies and independent research agencies, and why it is needed. Some of these sources of information are not freely available to the general public, sometimes because of their cost.

	1989	1990	1991	1992
Box office grosses (£m)	2260	2610	2955	3223
Average UK admission prices (£)	2.35	2.66	2.90	3.11
Index at constant price (1980 = 100)	97	100	103	100
Screens taking advertising	1432	1552	1642	1805
Regional film theatres	33	36	38	43
Multiplexes (5 plus screens)	29	41	57	63
Number of multiplex screens	285	387	510	556
Number of single screens	341	349	328	338
Total screens	1550	1673	1777	1848
Average US admission prices (US$)	4.44	4.75	4.90	5.06
Index at constant prices	112	115	115	115

Figure 23.1 UK cinema screens, admissions, box-office gross and average ticket prices

Source: *Screen Digest*/CAA/BFI

These sources are not comprehensive – others can be added which are accessible by you, such as your local authority, the borough or county council archives, public and academic libraries. The media regulatory bodies discussed in Chapter 30 – such as the Press Complaints Commission and the Radio Authority – may also respond to specific queries. Sometimes the data you collect may be anecdotal or descriptive, sometimes it may be statistical or graphical.

The data from the official research agencies is likely to be accurate, up-to-date and detailed, because of the scale of the organisations and the frequency of their research. The publications discussed above, aimed at the public or a general market, often base their information on examples of data provided by the official organisations such as BARB or ABC.

HINCKLEY
Herald & Journal

Wednesday, November 6, 1996   **30p where sold**   Delivered to 35,733 homes - VFD Jan 1 - June 30, 1996   **VFD**

Figure 23.2 A newspaper masthead with Verified Free Distribution (VFD) information for advertisers

MAGAZINE WATCH

What does the future hold for the home interest sector of the magazine market? Quite a lot, if recent growth in circulation is anything to go by.

The home interest magazine sector has enjoyed phenomenal growth over the past ten years.

In 1984, there were only four titles: *Homes & Gardens, Ideal Home, House and Garden* (which have all been published since 1920) and *World of Interiors*, launched in 1981. Combined average monthly sales stood at around 600,000 copies.

By the end of 1994, the number of titles had grown to 13 and circulations had tripled to nearly 2 million. It is the newer titles that account for almost all of this growth in copy sales: *Country Living* and *Country Homes and Interiors*, both launched in the mid-eighties, on their own account for more than 300,000 copies.

But the really explosive growth has come from two more recent titles: the five-year-old *House Beautiful*, which has established itself as market leader with an average sale of 320,000 (January to June 1994), followed closely by IPC's *Homes & Ideas* at 295,000.

Indeed, *House Beautiful's* publisher, National Magazines, felt that its successful formula had been followed rather too closely by *Homes & Ideas* and took legal action against IPC. It is clear, though, that *Homes & Ideas* has succeeded in expanding the market rather than simply grabbing share.

Most of the leading titles consistently attract large volumes of advertising. The majority of this, not surprisingly, is from manufacturers of household durables, furnishings and accessories, trying to reach either the core "home-centred" readers, or those who turn to these titles for advice or inspiration on an important project such as new carpets or curtains. The presence in most titles of an index of advertisers bears witness to how active the readers are in gathering information.

It is this high level of reader involvement which has led to an increasing number of potentially lucrative spin-offs, ranging from "reader offers" and book publishing to reader events, which include the highly successful Country Living Fair at IPC's recent At Home exhibition.

These activities can make a major contribution to profitability, and the more popular brands in the market have not been slow to recognise this. *House Beautiful* added a new dimension recently, with the launch of a branded range of wallpapers.

So will the home interest sector continue to grow at the same rate, and if it does, where will the growth come from?

With less than ten per cent of households buying a specialist home interest magazine, there is certainly plenty of scope for growth. It is likely that the new economics and techniques of publishing will encourage new ventures to highlight and expose niches in the same way as for smaller existing titles.

However, the recent success enjoyed by both *House Beautiful* and *Homes & Ideas* will surely have the major publishers investigating the feasibility of further titles aimed at this end of the market.

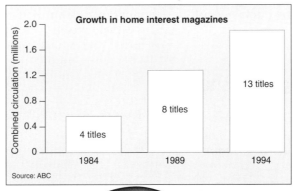

Growth in home interest magazines

Combined circulation (millions)

4 titles — 1984
8 titles — 1989
13 titles — 1994

Source: ABC

Figure 23.3 A market analysis from *Marketing Week*

Individual media producers also collect and analyse their own data. But such company information, especially when it relates to marketing and budgets, tends to be secret, particularly when it is recent and might be of use to a rival company.

WE REACH

7 out of 10

HOMES & BUSINESSES
IN OUR CORE AREA

70% of homes in the
Harborough area read our
newspapers

Figure 23.4 Blowing the company trumpet to attract advertisers

Companies also collect other information which, whilst not secret, is aimed at potential advertisers or professionals within the media industries. Figure 23.4 shows a simple example, issued by the publishers of the *Harborough Mail.*

Analysing and interpreting published data

Some data tell us how much a product is used. Look at the various sets of statistics in Figure 23.5, from **NRS Ltd.**

These figures measure readership, which is *not* the same as the number of copies sold. Within a household, although only one copy of a newspaper or magazine is bought, the whole family may regularly read parts of it. Advertisers are as interested in what *type* of person is reading a publication as in how many copies are sold. Note that in this example the number of readers is estimated in thousands and based on people over the age of 15 years.

Activity

Answer the following questions by using Figure 23.5.

a   How many people read the *Independent* in the six-month period in 1992?
b   Which was the most popular tabloid?
c   Which broadsheet was read by the largest group of people in professional jobs (ABC1)?
d   Did more men or women read the *Financial Times*?
e   Which newspaper is most popular with people over the age of 45?
f   How many men read the *Sunday Mail*?
g   Which Sunday newspaper did most women prefer to read?
h   Was the paper with the highest number of readers a daily newspaper or a Sunday newspaper?
i   Did the *Sunday Express* or the *Sunday Telegraph* attract the *least* number of working-class readers (C2DE)?
j   Which Sunday paper were readers in their twenties or thirties most likely to look at in 1992?

For many purposes, such as an editor wanting to know how to adjust the contents of a publication to match the profile of the readership, or particularly advertisers wishing to identify a specific target group, this information is not detailed enough. So in Figures 23.6A–D the data look at the profile of the main shopper in the family (female) and what she reads. This female group is further segmented by age, size of household, social grade, working status, area, income and children.

	TOTAL		SEX			SOCIAL GRADE			AGE			
			MEN		WOMEN		ABC1		C2DE		15–44		45+
UNWEIGHTED SAMPLE	15724		6819		8905		8360		7364		7867		7857
EST. POPULATION 15+ (000's)	45300		21857		23443		19641		25660		24067		21233
	000	%	000	%	000	%	000	%	000	%	000	%	000 %

Daily morning and evening newspapers – Adults

	000	%	000	%	000	%	000	%	000	%	000	%	000	%
Sun	10114	22	5669	26	4445	19	2636	13	7478	29	6212	26	3903	18
Daily Mirror/Record	9897	22	5352	24	4545	19	2695	14	7202	28	5202	22	4696	22
Daily Mirror	8022	18	4392	20	3630	15	2148	11	5874	23	4117	17	3904	18
Daily Record	1942	4	996	5	946	4	565	3	1377	5	1126	5	816	4
Daily Mail	4696	10	2388	11	2308	10	2890	15	1806	7	2249	9	2447	12
Daily Express	3946	9	2129	10	1816	8	2131	11	1815	7	1664	7	2282	11
Daily Telegraph	2715	6	1499	7	1215	5	2260	12	455	2	1095	5	1620	8
Daily Star	2523	6	1649	8	874	4	573	3	1950	8	1745	7	779	4
Today	1630	4	960	4	670	3	763	4	866	3	1009	4	621	3
Guardian	1483	3	856	4	627	3	1122	6	361	1	941	4	541	3
Times	1137	3	698	3	440	2	930	5	207	1	631	3	507	2
Independent	1136	3	671	3	465	2	928	5	208	1	734	3	402	2
Financial Times	678	1	468	2	210	1	611	3	67		422	2	255	1
Any national morning	28107	62	14623	67	13485	58	12205	62	15902	62	14448	60	13659	64
London Ev. Standard	1286	3	679	3	606	3	877	4	409	2	810	3	475	2
Any reg. morn/eveng	14921	33	7755	35	7166	31	6418	33	8502	33	7578	31	7342	35
Any reg. evening	12683	28	6620	30	6063	26	5248	27	7436	29	6689	28	5995	28
The Word	12625	28	6607	30	6019	26	5064	26	7562	29	6345	26	6280	30

Sunday newspapers – Adults

	000	%	000	%	000	%	000	%	000	%	000	%	000	%
News of the World	12554	28	6519	30	6036	26	3512	18	9042	35	7687	32	4867	23
Sunday Mirror	8940	20	4507	21	4433	19	2721	14	6219	24	4987	21	3953	19
People	6262	14	3245	15	3017	13	1748	9	4514	18	3115	13	3147	15
Mail on Sunday	5863	13	2903	13	2959	13	3666	19	2197	9	3314	14	2549	12
Sunday Express	5082	11	2654	12	2428	10	3043	15	2039	8	2131	9	2951	14
Sunday Times	3477	8	1919	9	1557	7	2636	13	841	3	2109	9	1368	6
Sunday Post	3155	7	1565	7	1590	7	1011	5	2144	8	1317	5	1838	9
Sunday Mail	2302	5	1213	6	1089	5	745	4	1557	6	1333	6	969	5
Sunday Telegraph	1851	4	987	5	863	4	1452	7	399	2	832	3	1019	5
Observer	1619	4	886	4	732	3	1262	6	356	1	839	3	780	4
Sunday Sport	1311	3	1037	5	274	1	316	2	995	4	1069	4	242	1
Independent on Sunday	1211	3	680	3	532	2	947	5	264	1	830	3	381	2
Any national Sunday	31519	70	15801	72	15717	67	13687	70	17832	69	16565	69	14953	70
Any natn/reg Sunday	31770	70	15929	73	15841	68	13766	70	18004	70	16658	69	15112	71
Any regional Sunday	842	2	483	2	359	2	302	2	540	2	427	2	415	2

Figure 23.5 Specimen newspaper statistics for one six-month period in 1992, produced by NRS Ltd

		TOTAL		AGE						SIZE OF HOUSEHOLD			
				15–24	25–34	35–44	45–54	55–64	65+	one	2 or more	3 or more	4 or more
UNWEIGHTED SAMPLE		16233		970	3336	3367	2722	2458	3380	2733	13500	7205	4152
EST. POPULATION 15+ (000's)		19685		1534	4001	3612	3217	2734	4587	3378	16307	9416	5371
		000 %		000 %	000 %	000 %	000 %	000 %	000 %	000 %	000 %	000 %	000 %
Prima	6	1922 10		181 12	601 15	477 13	307 10	204 7	151 3	153 5	1769 11	1179 13	715 13
Good Housekeeping	6	1832 9		62 4	317 8	389 11	381 12	285 10	397 9	259 8	1573 10	890 9	505 9
Woman & Home	6	1785 9		59 4	215 5	283 8	347 11	368 13	513 11	302 9	1483 9	762 8	421 8
Family Circle	6	1663 8		58 4	308 8	426 12	356 11	247 9	267 6	178 5	1485 9	946 10	597 11
Cosmopolitan	6	1268 6		263 17	426 11	242 7	199 6	83 3	55 1	168 5	1100 7	693 7	399 7
Ideal Home	6	1260 6		86 6	297 7	289 8	229 7	191 7	168 4	144 4	1115 7	652 7	378 7
BBC Good Food	6	1196 6		51 3	245 6	279 8	229 7	207 8	185 4	151 4	1044 6	573 6	323 6
Homes & Gardens	6	1195 6		30 2	175 4	234 6	269 8	203 7	283 6	217 6	978 6	500 5	259 5
Essentials	6	1013 5		144 9	312 8	215 6	160 5	101 4	81 2	70 2	942 6	583 6	347 6
Vogue	6	987 5		171 11	217 5	190 5	176 5	101 4	131 3	125 4	862 5	491 5	280 5
She	6	902 5		134 9	258 6	176 5	139 4	115 4	80 2	105 3	797 5	503 5	302 6
House & Garden	6	811 4		39 3	175 4	162 4	164 5	134 5	136 3	102 3	709 4	363 4	208 4
Clothes Show Mag	6	701 4		201 13	175 4	131 4	111 3	44 2	40 1	57 2	645 4	436 5	233 4
Country Living	6	647 3		29 2	112 3	166 5	132 4	102 4	106 2	77 2	570 3	328 3	181 3
Mother and Baby	6	641 3		137 9	270 7	91 3	79 2	46 2	18	17 1	624 4	453 5	282 5
Living Magazine	6	558 3		28 2	98 2	160 4	132 4	76 3	65 1	50 1	507 3	325 3	203 4

Figure 23.6A NRS data for selected women's monthly periodicals in 1992

		TOTAL		INCOME OF CIE (HOH/CWE)						WITH CHILDREN		
				I £3750 or under	II £5270	III £7320	IV £9150	V £12880	VI £17880 or over	0–15 years	0–4 years	0–23 months
UNWEIGHTED SAMPLE		16233		3104	1761	1529	2287	4315	2590	5288	2399	1054
EST. POPULATION 15+ (000's)		19685		4315	2252	1878	2835	4886	2434	6148	2836	1297
		000 %		000 %	000 %	000 %	000 %	000 %	000 %	000 %	000 %	000 %
Prima	6	1922 10		233 5	178 8	145 8	311 11	631 13	340 14	877 14	402 14	167 13
Good Housekeeping	6	1832 9		229 5	158 7	161 9	258 9	513 11	451 19	568 9	225 8	95 7
Woman & Home	6	1785 9		274 6	237 11	222 12	259 9	454 9	286 12	419 7	161 6	78 6
Family Circle	6	1663 8		214 5	175 8	165 9	245 9	495 10	289 12	609 10	212 7	80 6
Cosmopolitan	6	1268 6		154 4	91 4	106 6	170 6	341 7	277 11	428 7	210 7	92 7
Ideal Home	6	1260 6		156 4	87 4	103 5	189 7	410 8	280 12	449 7	215 8	97 8
BBC Good Food	6	1196 6		123 3	102 5	95 5	176 6	368 8	282 12	374 6	172 6	73 6
Homes & Gardens	6	1195 6		157 4	109 5	112 6	178 6	344 7	259 11	302 5	105 4	44 3
Essentials	6	1013 5		107 2	90 4	85 5	162 6	333 7	173 7	415 7	201 7	88 7
Vogue	6	987 5		140 3	89 4	74 4	106 4	250 5	239 10	282 5	122 4	44 3
She	6	902 5		117 3	78 3	82 4	123 4	240 5	194 8	334 5	167 6	72 6
House & Garden	6	811 4		80 2	66 3	65 3	113 4	258 5	198 8	240 4	113 4	52 4
Clothes Show Mag	6	701 4		100 2	40 2	65 3	83 3	187 4	116 5	223 4	99 4	45 3
Country Living	6	647 3		62 1	45 2	48 3	77 3	218 4	163 7	187 3	69 2	27 2
Mother and Baby	6	641 3		136 3	36 2	65 3	103 4	174 4	90 4	381 6	307 11	204 16
Living Magazine	6	558 3		53 1	43 2	52 3	101 4	161 3	124 5	202 3	68 2	21 2

Figure 23.6B NRS data for selected women's monthly periodicals in 1992

		TOTAL	London	Midlands	Lanca-shire	York-shire	Southern	East of England	Wales & West	Central Scotland	North East
UNWEIGHTED SAMPLE		16233	2738	2583	1867	1463	1472	1198	1461	1143	920
EST. POPULATION 15+ (000's)		19685	3875	3159	2413	1941	1796	1398	1596	1230	996
		000 %	000 %	000 %	000 %	000 %	000 %	000 %	000 %	000 %	000 %
Prima	6	1922 10	363 9	302 10	229 9	229 12	175 10	145 10	172 11	93 8	86 9
Good Housekeeping	6	1832 9	475 12	251 8	186 8	118 6	210 12	141 10	163 10	85 7	56 6
Woman & Home	6	1785 9	370 10	280 9	149 6	163 8	216 12	136 10	184 12	88 7	66 7
Family Circle	6	1663 8	387 10	250 8	146 6	157 8	174 10	149 11	137 9	84 7	68 7
Cosmopolitan	6	1268 6	374 10	180 6	133 6	110 6	113 6	96 7	84 5	76 6	47 5
Ideal Home	6	1260 6	265 7	214 7	122 5	121 6	105 6	98 7	110 7	70 6	48 5
BBC Good Food	6	1196 6	322 8	186 6	137 6	94 5	124 7	85 6	74 5	45 4	50 5
Homes & Gardens	6	1195 6	269 7	220 7	109 5	88 5	128 7	101 7	111 7	46 4	44 4
Essentials	6	1013 5	215 6	167 5	104 4	104 5	93 5	87 6	81 5	50 4	40 4
Vogue	6	987 5	330 9	162 5	89 4	66 3	94 5	59 4	67 4	40 3	33 3
She	6	902 5	266 7	176 6	91 4	57 3	83 5	74 5	55 3	28 2	31 3
House & Garden	6	811 4	218 6	129 4	81 3	53 3	86 5	68 5	64 4	33 3	35 4
Clothes Show Mag	6	701 4	190 5	116 4	88 4	53 3	51 3	49 4	52 3	47 4	30 3
Country Living	6	647 3	125 3	128 4	46 2	42 2	82 5	60 4	81 5	13 1	15 2
Mother and Baby	6	641 3	155 4	88 3	58 2	60 3	65 4	46 3	58 4	41 3	30 3
Living Magazine	6	558 3	144 4	87 3	60 2	43 2	61 3	51 4	40 3	27 2	21 2

Figure 23.6C NRS data for selected women's monthly periodicals in 1992

		TOTAL	A	B	C1	C2	D	E	Full-time	Full/prt time
UNWEIGHTED SAMPLE		16233	679	3133	4982	3100	2154	2185	4124	7748
EST. POPULATION 15+ (000's)		19685	549	2857	5100	4817	3258	3105	4698	9005
		000 %	000 %	000 %	000 %	000 %	000 %	000 %	000 %	000 %
Prima	6	1922 10	46 8	302 11	618 12	518 11	293 9	146 5	621 13	1145 13
Good Housekeeping	6	1832 9	142 26	506 18	512 10	365 8	184 6	124 4	513 11	963 11
Women & Home	6	1785 9	67 12	392 14	508 10	449 9	207 6	161 5	419 9	816 9
Family Circle	6	1663 8	56 10	309 11	510 10	414 9	235 7	139 4	482 10	935 10
Cosmopolitan	6	1268 6	44 8	269 9	501 10	242 5	142 4	70 2	547 12	841 9
Ideal Home	6	1260 6	82 15	273 10	377 7	310 6	122 4	96 3	389 8	732 8
BBC Good Food	6	1196 6	72 13	327 11	372 7	222 5	131 4	71 2	394 8	677 8
Homes & Gardens	6	1195 6	80 14	323 11	354 7	221 5	122 4	95 3	326 7	613 7
Essentials	6	1013 5	33 6	172 6	325 6	258 5	152 5	74 2	372 8	628 7
Vogue	6	987 5	69 13	227 8	329 6	172 4	107 3	83 3	334 7	559 6
She	6	902 5	45 8	203 7	299 6	186 4	95 3	75 2	325 7	542 6
House & Garden	6	811 4	65 12	237 8	220 4	151 3	81 2	56 2	228 5	427 5
Clothes Show Mag	6	701 4	18 3	105 4	246 5	157 3	118 4	57 2	256 5	435 5
Country Living	6	647 3	50 9	215 8	199 4	107 2	38 1	39 1	177 4	329 4
Mother and Baby	6	641 3	8 1	62 2	170 3	183 4	110 3	109 4	138 3	281 3
Living Magazine	6	558 3	26 5	138 5	185 4	115 2	66 2	27 1	200 4	352 4

SOCIAL GRADE columns: A, B, C1, C2, D, E. WORKING STATUS columns: Full-time, Full/prt time.

Figure 23.6D NRS data for selected women's monthly periodicals in 1992

Activity

Examine the data in Figures 23.6A–D and answer the following questions based on the 1992 figures.

a Which magazine was a woman who earned £14 000 a year with a three-year-old toddler the most likely to choose?
b Would a part-time factory worker in London prefer to read *Woman & Home* or *Family Circle*?
c Where did women live who preferred *She* magazine to *Vogue*?
d Which magazine did middle-aged women in professional jobs like best?
e Would someone in her early twenties have been more likely to read *Clothes Show Magazine* or *Cosmopolitan*?

The **Audit Bureau of Circulations** supplies different information. Its figures reveal how many copies of a newspaper or magazine are sold, their price and other details about the product itself. Figure 23.7 shows a small sample relating to general consumer magazines.

Activity

Examine the data in Figure 23.7 and answer the following questions. The statistics cover a six-month period.

a Which was the most expensive publication?
b Which were weekly publications?
c Which had the largest circulation?
d Which had the largest circulation overseas?
e Which had the highest subscription figures?

Examples of data collected by **BARB** have been given in Chapter 21 (see Figures 21.11 and 21.12). The weekly viewing figures (Figure 23.8) are vital for people within the TV industry, especially for those organising the schedules.

Magazine title	Group class code	No. of issues during period	Basic cover price at end of period	Average net circulation per issue — Total	UK/E = United Kingdom & Eire / OC = Other countries	Newstrade and other single copies	Single copy subs sales	Multiple copy sponsored subs sales	Regular multiple copy sales	Issue-specific multiple copy sales
Life & Work	702	6/6	£0.60	66016	UK/E 65689	1113	407	–	64169	–
					OC 327	–	101	–	226	–
Live & Kicking	802	6/6	£0.99	137618	UK/E 137302	137302	–	–	–	–
					OC 316	316	–	–	–	–
Living	875	6/6	£1.30	111328	UK/E 109483	105192	4230	4	15	42
					OC 1845	1653	190	2	–	–
Loaded	776	6/6	£2.20	127677	UK/E 126202	124241	1958	3	–	–
					OC 1475	1386	89	–	–	–
Looks	875	6/6	£1.50	227681	UK/E 221175	221019	156	–	–	–
					OC 6506	6402	104	–	–	–
Loot – London's Noticeboard	179	130/6	£1.20	25383	UK/E 25383	25383	–	–	–	–
					OC –	–	–	–	–	–
Loot – The Northwest Noticeboard	179	78/6	£1.00	22085	UK/E 22085	22085	–	–	–	–
					OC –	–	–	–	–	–
Manchester Guardian Weekly N. America Sales	343	26/6	£0.60	26052	UK/E –	–	–	–	–	–
					OC 26052	2626	23256	170	–	–
Manchester UNITED Magazine	759	6/6	£1.95	133267	UK/E 128138	121236	6812	–	–	–
					OC 5129	3356	1773	–	–	–
Marie Claire	875	6/6	£2.00	455109	UK/E 423723	403777	18546	76	151	1173
					OC 31386	29467	1899	20	–	–
Melody Maker	712	26/6	£0.75	60540	UK/E 54641	54426	212	3	–	–
					OC 5899	4817	1041	41	–	–
Men's Health	551	3/6	£2.25	114975	UK/E 114975	108056	6919	–	–	–
					OC –	–	–	–	–	–
Mizz	802	13/6	£0.80	183818	UK/E 183292	183025	267	–	–	–
					OC 526	496	30	–	–	–

Figure 23.7 ABC data for selected consumer magazines

Channel	Average weekly viewing (hrs:mins) per person	Share of total viewing (%)	% reach Average daily	% reach Average weekly
ALL/ANY TV	30:11	100.0	84.8	96.1
BBC1 (incl. Breakfast News)	9:51	32.7	71.7	94.3
BBC2	3:26	11.4	44.3	85.9
TOTAL/ANY BBC	13:17	44.0	76.3	95.2
ITV (incl. GMTV)	10:49	35.8	69.7	93.9
CHANNEL 4/S4C	3:10	10.5	43.5	85.1
TOTAL/ANY COMM.TV	13:59	46.3	75.2	94.9
Other viewing	2:55	9.7	15.7	22.8

Figure 23.8 BARB data for hours of viewing, share of audience, and reach (including time-shift)

Activity

Examine the data in Figure 23.8 and answer the following questions.

a For how long did the average person watch BBC2?
b Did people watch BBC or commercial TV the most?
c What percentage of the population watched TV every day?
d Which channel attracted the highest percentage of the population to view over the space of a week?

Although Figure 23.8 gives a good overview, more detailed statistics are needed to be useful in planning programmes and scheduling. Once again BARB supplies the data (Figure 23.9).

Activity

Examine the data in Figure 23.9 and answer the following questions.

a Which channel did people in Yorkshire prefer to watch in December?
b In which two regions did the share of viewing for BBC2 remain constant for the two months?
c In how many regions does BBC1 have a higher share of the audience than ITV?
d In which region did Channel 4/S4C lose 0.8 per cent of the share of viewing in December as compared to November?

Information is also needed about the individual programmes and the audiences they attract – see Figure 23.10.

	ITV Dec (%)	ITV Nov (%)	Channel 4/S4C Dec (%)	Channel 4/S4C Nov (%)	BBC1 Dec (%)	BBC1 Nov (%)	BBC2 Dec (%)	BBC2 Nov (%)	OTHER VIEWING Dec (%)	OTHER VIEWING Nov (%)
London	31.7	33.7	9.9	10.6	36.5	33.6	12.7	12.2	9.2	9.8
Midlands E&W	36.1	40.9	8.8	9.3	34.4	29.5	10.8	10.5	9.9	9.9
North West	35.5	39.5	9.9	10.1	34.0	30.4	11.1	10.7	9.6	9.2
Yorkshire	36.8	40.4	9.9	9.9	33.8	30.1	11.2	10.8	8.4	8.7
C. Scotland	36.6	40.2	10.4	11.1	33.5	30.3	11.2	10.8	8.3	7.5
Wales & West	34.4	37.8	8.4	8.9	36.3	32.4	11.4	11.4	9.5	9.5
South & S. East	34.7	38.3	9.2	9.5	35.3	31.9	12.4	11.9	8.4	8.4
North East	32.4	36.5	10.6	11.4	35.0	31.2	11.1	11.1	10.9	9.8
East of England	33.8	38.0	8.7	9.1	35.9	32.3	11.1	11.2	10.6	9.4
South West	36.0	38.3	9.1	9.2	36.7	33.9	12.1	12.2	6.0	6.4
Ulster	41.0	43.8	9.2	9.4	29.4	27.0	8.8	8.5	11.7	11.2
Border	35.8	39.3	11.1	10.6	33.9	30.8	10.6	10.5	8.6	8.8
N. Scotland	35.5	38.5	9.5	9.4	33.8	31.2	10.2	10.1	11.0	10.8

N.B. These data are based on the hours of viewing to ITV, Channel 4/S4C, BBC1 and BBC2 received from each region's designated transmitter only, together with all hours of viewing to satellite, cable and other channels reported within the region.

Figure 23.9 BARB data for share of viewing by ITV region

| DAY: Friday 5 January 1996 | | | | Indiv 4+ | | | Housewives | | |
Programme title	Start	Dur	000's	TVR	Share	000's	TVR	Share
BUSINESS BREAKFAST	06:00	60	35	0.3	13.8	19	0.4	17.0
BREAKFAST NEWS	07:00	133	137	1.0	13.0	56	1.1	12.4
KILROY	09:13	47	215	1.5	18.9	115	2.3	20.6
NEWS & WEATHER	10:00	6	201	1.4	16.4	97	2.0	15.7
CAN'T COOK WON'T COOK	10:06	25	276	2.0	22.0	140	2.8	23.6
GOOD MORNING	10:31	29	207	1.5	15.8	97	2.0	15.9
NEWS & WEATHER	11:00	5	172	1.2	14.1	56	1.1	9.6
GOOD MORNING	11:05	55	194	1.4	14.7	71	1.4	11.6
NEWS & WEATHER	12:00	7	185	1.3	13.2	80	1.6	11.9
PEBBLE MILL	12:07	45	164	1.2	10.3	75	1.5	10.4
NEWSROOM SOUTHEAST	12:52	8	223	1.6	12.5	112	2.3	13.7
ONE O'CLK NWS/WEATHER	13:00	30	467	3.4	24.2	248	5.0	27.2
NEIGHBOURS	13:30	23	947	6.8	45.2	458	9.3	46.3
BANACEK	13:53	72	427	3.1	23.7	243	4.9	27.9
TIME KEEPERS	15:05	25	145	1.0	8.0	76	1.5	9.0
LITTLEST PET SHOP	15:30	24	171	1.2	7.7	79	1.6	8.8
LOOK SHARP	15:54	15	266	1.9	10.2	64	1.3	6.8
POPEYE	16:09	10	319	2.3	11.6	81	1.6	8.4
JULIA JEKYLL/ H. HYDE	16:19	16	412	3.0	14.1	106	2.1	10.3
MASK	16:35	22	574	4.1	16.9	167	3.4	13.5
NEWSROUND EXTRA	16:57	14	654	4.7	17.9	229	4.6	16.9
BLUE PETER	17:11	26	1011	7.3	24.6	368	7.5	23.5
NEIGHBOURS	17:37	23	2056	14.8	42.6	825	16.7	43.0
SIX O'CLOCK NEWS	18:00	30	1193	8.6	23.0	591	12.0	29.0
WEATHER NEWS	18:30	3	1175	8.4	22.9	565	11.4	28.1
NEWSROOM SOUTHEAST	18:33	28	1085	7.8	21.0	525	10.6	25.3
COP AND A HALF	19:01	89	1030	7.4	17.2	363	7.3	14.0
QUESTION OF SPORT	20:30	30	1391	10.0	21.8	551	11.2	20.3
NINE O'CLOCK NEWS	21:00	27	982	7.1	16.1	383	7.8	14.1
NEWSROOM SOUTHEAST	21:27	4	1135	8.2	18.6	481	9.7	17.3
WEATHER NEWS	21:31	3	1434	10.3	23.4	618	12.5	21.8
BACKDRAFT	21:34	130	1605	11.5	30.7	653	13.2	28.0
A LENNOX... IN THE PK	23:44	60	296	2.1	11.3	116	2.4	10.1
MIDNIGHT FEAR	24:44	87	147	1.1	16.7	67	1.4	17.1
CLOSEDOWN	26:11	2	17	0.1	3.8	8	0.2	4.0

Figure 23.10 BARB's weekly BBC1 audience report for Friday 5 January 1996

Activity

Examine the data in Figure 23.10 about BBC1 programmes for Friday 5 January 1996. TVR are the television ratings for individuals. This is the number of individuals viewing, given as a percentage. So if 164 000 people over the age of four years are watching, that is 1.2 per cent of all people over the age of four. However, if 167 000 people are watching who are housewives, the TVR will be higher, at 3.4 per cent. Answer the following questions.

a Which programme had the largest number of viewers?

b Which programme went on for longest?
c Which programme did housewives watch the least?
d What percentage of viewers were watching at 17.11?
e Was the programme *Midnight Fear* more popular with housewives than with the population generally?

As explained in Chapter 21, the statistics from RAJAR tell us how many listeners and potential listeners there are to the various radio stations. The data in Figure 23.11 are for BBC stations from one quarter in 1994.

	Adult (15+) Pop'n (000's)	Weekly reach (000's)	Weekly reach (%)	Average hours Per head	Average hours Per listener	Total hours (000's)	Share of listening
BBC NETWORK RADIO							
Radio 1	46957	12283	26	2.4	9.2	113090	13.3
Radio 2	46957	8987	19	2.3	12.2	109395	12.9
Radio 3	46957	2380	5	0.2	3.5	8426	1.0
Radio 4	46957	8517	18	1.9	10.3	88012	10.4
Radio 5 Live*	46957	4275	9	0.4	4.2	17803	2.1
NATIONAL REGIONAL							
Radio Scotland	4147	867	21	1.4	6.7	5775	8.2
Radio Ulster	1220	356	29	2.8	9.5	3367	19.4
Radio Wales/Cymru	2335	541	23	2.9	12.5	6780	16.6
LOCAL							
Local Radio	36858	7864	21	1.9	9.0	71152	10.5
Radio Berkshire	612	56	9	0.4	4.5	253	2.5
Radio Bristol	1162	284	24	2.1	8.6	2431	12.0
CWR	472	37	8	0.4	5.3	197	2.4
Radio Cambridgeshire	550	116	21	1.9	9.1	1052	10.5
Radio Cleveland	685	115	17	1.4	8.3	952	8.2
Radio Cornwall	397	156	39	4.6	11.8	1832	22.6
Radio Cumbria	373	124	33	3.2	9.7	1206	17.9
Dorset FM	171	26	15	1.0	6.8	178	5.8
Radio Derby	563	182	32	3.1	9.6	1741	16.1
Radio Devon	872	218	25	2.8	11.1	2422	15.2
Essex	1116	245	22	2.3	10.5	2566	11.8
GLR	9829	384	4	0.2	3.9	1499	0.8
GMR	2033	276	14	1.2	8.9	2463	7.1
Radio Gloucestershire	348	67	19	1.5	7.6	506	8.2
Hereford & Worcester	467	101	22	2.2	10.3	1034	12.3

*Radio 5 Live launched on 28 March 1994, one week after the start of the quarter. Results shown are for the whole quarter.

Figure 23.11 RAJAR data for BBC radio stations in 1994

Activity

Examine the data in Figure 23.11 and answer the following questions.

a Which station broadcasting to all the population had the largest weekly audience?
b Which local radio station could be heard by the largest number of people?
c Which local radio station was actually listened to by the most people?
d Which regional station did people spend the most time listening to?
e Which local radio station was performing the best in getting a high percentage of the population to listen in?

The **Cinema Advertising Association** (CAA) collects data about cinema audiences, so that advertisers can plan effective campaigns. Figure 23.12 shows an example of some information (published with NRS).

Activity

Examine Figure 23.12 and answer these questions.

a Which age group went to the cinema most?
b If you were a teacher or a doctor were you more or less likely to go to the cinema than if you were a shop assistant or unemployed?
c Did men go to see films more often than women?

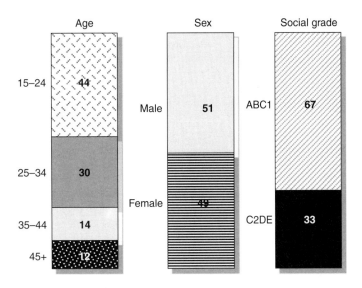

Figure 23.12 CAA/NRS audience profile (percentages)

- by age
- by sex
- by housewives (female, main shopper)
- by social grade
- by weight of ITV viewing
- by the age they finished education
- by marital status
- by number of children in the household.

The statistics in Figure 23.13 cover the first 20 weeks of a year and relate to adults in the age range 25–34. The *average admissions* are shown in millions. The *cover figures* are percentages of the population. The *frequency* column shows the average number of times cinemagoers had been to the cinema during the year. The *cinemagoers* line at the bottom of the table gives the percentage of the population in that category who ever go to the cinema.

Again, a more detailed breakdown of the statistics is needed for them to be useful to advertisers. Figures are given for a number of demographic groups:

Activity

Examine the data in Figure 23.13 and answer the following questions.

	Adults 25–34		Men		Women		Female main shopper		Women with children		AB		C1		C2	
No. (pointer)	81		82		83		84		85		86		87		88	
Population	9101		4643		4458		4081		2767		1859		2623		2258	
Wks	Adm (m)	Cover	Freq	Cover	Freq	Cover	Freq	Cover	Freq	Cover	Freq	Cover	Freq	Cover	Freq	Cover	Freq
1	2.30	6.0	1.08	6.7	1.08	5.3	1.07	5.0	1.06	3.6	1.04	9.9	1.08	7.2	1.08	4.3	1.06
2	4.60	10.6	1.22	11.6	1.25	9.5	1.19	9.1	1.16	6.7	1.12	17.3	1.24	12.7	1.24	7.8	1.17
3	6.90	14.4	1.35	15.6	1.40	13.1	1.30	12.6	1.26	9.4	1.18	23.2	1.39	17.0	1.39	10.8	1.26
4	9.20	17.6	1.47	18.8	1.54	16.2	1.40	15.6	1.35	12.0	1.25	28.1	1.53	20.5	1.53	13.5	1.34
5	11.50	20.4	1.58	21.6	1.68	19.0	1.49	18.4	1.44	14.3	1.30	32.3	1.67	23.6	1.66	15.9	1.42
6	13.79	22.9	1.69	24.1	1.81	21.5	1.58	20.8	1.52	16.5	1.36	35.9	1.80	26.3	1.79	18.2	1.50
7	16.09	25.1	1.80	26.3	1.93	23.7	1.67	23.0	1.60	18.5	1.42	39.1	1.93	28.7	1.91	20.2	1.57
8	18.39	27.2	1.90	28.3	2.05	25.8	1.75	25.1	1.68	20.3	1.47	42.0	2.05	30.8	2.03	22.2	1.63
9	20.69	29.1	2.00	30.1	2.17	27.7	1.83	26.9	1.76	22.0	1.53	44.6	2.18	32.8	2.15	24.0	1.70
10	22.99	30.8	2.10	31.8	2.28	29.5	1.92	28.7	1.84	23.6	1.58	46.9	2.30	34.6	2.26	25.7	1.76
11	25.29	32.4	2.19	33.4	2.39	31.1	2.00	30.3	1.92	25.1	1.64	49.1	2.42	36.3	2.37	27.3	1.82
12	27.59	33.9	2.28	34.9	2.50	32.6	2.08	31.7	1.99	26.5	1.69	51.1	2.53	37.9	2.48	28.8	1.89
13	29.89	35.3	2.38	36.2	2.60	34.0	2.16	33.1	2.07	27.8	1.75	52.9	2.65	39.3	2.59	30.3	1.94
14	32.19	36.6	2.47	37.5	2.71	35.3	2.24	34.4	2.15	29.0	1.80	54.6	2.76	40.7	2.69	31.7	2.00
15	34.49	37.9	2.56	38.7	2.81	36.6	2.32	35.6	2.22	30.2	1.86	56.1	2.88	42.0	2.80	33.0	2.06
16	36.79	39.0	2.65	39.9	2.91	37.7	2.39	36.8	2.30	31.2	1.91	57.6	3.00	43.2	2.90	34.2	2.12
17	39.09	40.2	2.73	40.9	3.01	38.8	2.47	37.8	2.37	32.3	1.97	58.9	3.11	44.4	3.00	35.4	2.18
18	41.38	41.2	2.82	42.0	3.11	39.9	2.55	38.8	2.44	33.2	2.02	60.2	3.22	45.5	3.10	36.5	2.23
19	43.68	42.2	2.91	42.9	3.21	40.8	2.63	39.8	2.52	34.2	2.08	61.3	3.34	46.6	3.20	37.6	2.29
20	45.98	43.1	3.00	43.9	3.31	41.8	2.70	40.7	2.59	35.0	2.13	62.4	3.45	47.6	3.29	38.6	2.35
Cinemagoers		67.2		69.0		65.4		65.3		59.0		81.8		76.3		63.7	

Figure 23.13 CAA/NRS detailed cinema audience profile

a Were women with children less or more likely to go to the cinema than women without children?

b After how many weeks does it begin to be noticeable that professional men attended the cinema more often than those in junior management?

c On average, how many times a year did the main shopper in the household go to the cinema?

d How many million people had attended the cinema by the end of the 20 weeks?

e What percentage of women with children never went to the cinema?

Anecdotal evidence

The data we have looked at so far have been factual, obtained from quantitative research. But data can also be anecdotal, from qualitative research. You can find examples of this in many newspapers. Anecdotal data about audience behaviour is based on people's personal experiences or on cases they know personally.

Here are edited extracts from an article in *The Times* in 1995:

> *Louise Maguire, manager of the recently opened Café Cyberia Internet Centre in Edinburgh, says people are becoming addicted to the chat-line facility that allows them to converse terminal-to-terminal: 'People get engrossed. It has to do with the curiosity and the novelty of speaking to someone in Canada or Australia.'*

> *David Newton, a cyberguide at the café, says MUDS (multi-user dungeons) can be highly addictive.*

> *Dr Prem Misra, a senior consultant psychiatrist in Glasgow, has treated a number of computer addicts. 'It can cause mental or emotional strain,' he says. One of his worst cases was a teenager who spent at least 12 hours working on programmes or playing games.*

Each of these extracts is interesting but inconclusive until placed alongside the others. The varied backgrounds and qualifications of the interviewees gives breadth and weight to the argument that computers can be addictive.

Activity

Figure 23.14 shows an edited extract from an article in *The Guardian* in April 1993. Discuss what attitudes or opinions about computer games these statements would reinforce.

I'd like to play all the time

When eight-year-old Neill Moore returns home from school, the first thing he wants to do, he says, is play with his Super Nintendo. Like millions of youngsters, he was given the game for Christmas and the Nintendo console is permanently strapped to the television set in the family home in west London.

'I like playing Nintendo because I like the characters and the action. My favourite games are Street Fighter 2 and Super Mario World. I would like to play all the time but I have to ask my mum and dad before I can use my machine,' says Neill, who attends the George Tomlinson school in London.

Before he can play with his Nintendo, Neill has to complete his homework. The amount of time he spends playing is strictly monitored by his mother. 'Sometimes my mum will not let me play but I play a lot more during the weekends. At times, I play for up to five hours, especially if my dad is alone with me in the house,' he says.

Neill says that playing video games has not made him violent. 'The games are not bad for you because they help you learn things and they are fun. When I am in the playground I play Street Fighter with my friends and we act out the scenes.'

Khim Kharaud, 7, owns a hand-held Nintendo console bought for her by her parents. She does not play every day and when she does, the maximum time her mother allows her is half-an-hour. 'I don't like playing with it that much because I think some of the games are boring,' she says. 'They are all about fighting and after a while it is very easy to play them and get a high score. I only wanted a Nintendo because I felt left out. Sometimes I would rather play with my friends. Sitting in the house and playing Nintendo can get a bit boring.'

According to a book by Eugene F. Provenzo, called *Video Kids Making Sense of Nintendo*, video games encourage sexism, violence and racism in children. Women are typically cast as victims and foreigners as baddies. 'I don't think that's right,' says 13-year-old Jaspal Bhatti who owns a Super Nintendo and a hand-held console. 'They are just games and they are exciting. I don't think anyone believes that they are true. I like to play them because they are better than watching television.'

Nicholas Scott, 11, owns a Sega Mega Drive which he bought himself. He has three games and says that his favourite is Sonic Hedgehog 2. 'I play for about three hours per week, sometimes with my friends or sometimes alone. I play my Sega because I get bored at home and like to entertain myself.' Nicholas says that before he can play, he has to ask his mum. If he had his way, he would like to play more with his Sega.

Nicholas adds: 'I would like to play an hour extra each week. My mum controls the amount of time I can play but she doesn't really like my Sega machine. She hates the noise it makes.'

Nicholas admits that playing video games sometimes distracts him from his homework. 'Sometimes I come home and start playing my Sega. I leave my homework too late and I don't feel like doing it because I would rather be playing.'

Nicholas, who goes to school in Pimlico, south London, agrees that some of the games can make children aggressive. 'Some of the games show you violent moves which you can later practise on your friends. I don't find myself becoming aggressive but some of my friends do. They start fighting and think they are in a video game. I don't own any aggressive games but I sometimes borrow them.'

Figure 23.14 Anecdotal evidence about computer games

A case very often quoted about the influence of 'video nasties' on children is that of murdered two-year-old Jamie Bulger. His killers were said to have watched the video *Child's Play 3* before the crime took place. Two boys aged 11 were convicted of his murder in 1993. The trial judge said: 'It is not for me to pass judgement on their upbringing, but I suspect exposure to violent video films may in part be an explanation.' David Alton MP claimed that there definitely was a link between the 'cult of mutilation as entertainment and sadistic crime'.

Activity

Ask an older person (over the age of 60), possibly a relative, what difference having a television has made to his or her life. Compare your quotes with those of other people in your group. Can you build up a picture of the changes television has made to older people? For instance, do they talk less to their families? Do they sit down less often to have a meal at the dining table?

One of the problems with anecdotal evidence is that people's memories can be inaccurate or incomplete. They may not be typical, they may be biased for some reason. This sort of data is useful to support more factual research and to give colour, but should not be used on its own.

Case study

In the article reproduced here as Figure 23.15, statistics are given but there are also quotes from teenagers giving their opinions about adverts in magazines. The statistics are based on professional research.

Teen mags are alive and kicking

CHRIS BOULDING

The generation gap is alive and well, and its survival is helped by the plethora of teenage magazines on the market. Their readership wants to be told that their parents are wrong. "Some people write in a way that makes you think these people are all right...some people will write and you'll think: 'Oh no, typical grown-up's view,'" says Duncan, aged 15.

And if proof were needed, only three per cent of all magazines read by 11- to 19-year-olds are read in the presence of parents, according to Youth Facts 4, EMAP Youth Group's latest study. Sixty per cent are read "on my own".

For kids, the medium is very much the message. Nearly a quarter of teenage magazines are read to "keep in touch with the latest things", while another 51 per cent are read for the most resonant of adolescent reasons – because the kids have nothing else to do, or are bored.

Almost half (46 per cent) of magazines are read within the sanctity of the bedroom; this figure increases with titles that teenage girls think their parents would disapprove of.

For boys, however, the picture is somewhat different. Computer magazines – the staple diet of teenage boys – are far more likely to be read and discussed at friends' houses.

Advertisers have to negotiate their way around these reading habits to get to the naked consumer. Unfortunately, teenagers are very resistant to advertising's obvious aspirational deals.

"It's a balance between trying to strike a chord with them and not have them think: 'What are they trying to make us do?'" says Millward Brown client services manager Sarah Harris.

Although three-quarters of teenagers claim to find the advertising in their magazines useful, they can be very frustrated by seeing the same ad too often. "When I first saw it, I thought 'Oh, what's this?' But then it was in every magazine and you can get bored with it," says Helen aged 15.

According to EMAP, all brands themselves fall into an "acceptability continuum". First there are the "undesirable" brands, which could ruin a teenager's life, such as wearing Marks & Spencer's socks to a rave party.

Then there are the "inconspicuous" brands that are more widely used: they say nothing about you as an individual. More acceptable are the so-called "safe" brands – such as Nike and Naf Naf – which will guarantee acceptance among your peer group. And last, there are the innovative "new" brands, involving risk and credibility.

Magazines can convert the level of brand on the acceptability continuum into another, claims Harris. The best example of this is Adidas, which produced a range of sports wear in the seventies with its classic white stripes down the side. The clothes began to appear in magazines and very quickly became necessary purchases.

Figure 23.15 *Marketing Week* on teenage fashion

Identifying trends in media consumption

Trends are noticeable changes in behaviour or attitudes that show a continuous increase or decrease over a period of time. Here are some examples:

- Children are watching television for fewer hours per day now than they were five years ago.
- Public opinion shows that more adults believe that there is too much violence in films.
- Fewer people bought *The Globe* newspaper in 1996, than in 1995 and 1994.

A graph, such as that in Figure 23.16, is a good way of showing a trend.

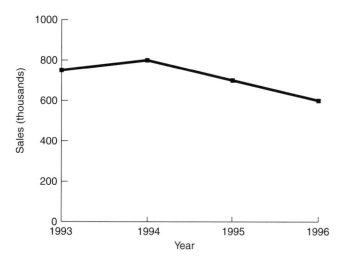

Figure 23.16 Sales figures for *The Globe* newspaper

To identify a trend, you need a set of statistics taken at certain points over a period of time. One set of statistics, such as those in Figure 23.17, cannot reveal a trend.

Even two sets of figures may not reveal a trend or can be misleading, as in Figure 23.18A which shows viewing figures at two points for an imaginary soap called *Media Life*. From this graph it could be imagined that the show is slowly increasing its audience figures. However, a larger set of figures can tell a different story. Figure 23.18B reveals that the soap is actually losing viewers. A change in storyline and bad weather, making people stay in, temporarily boosted figures in December, but the underlining trend for this programme is downwards!

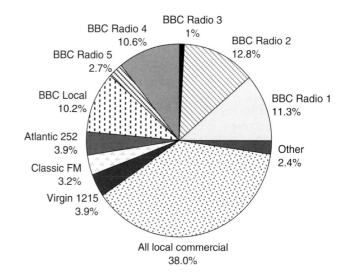

Figure 23.17 RAJAR data for radio audience shares in one quarter of 1994

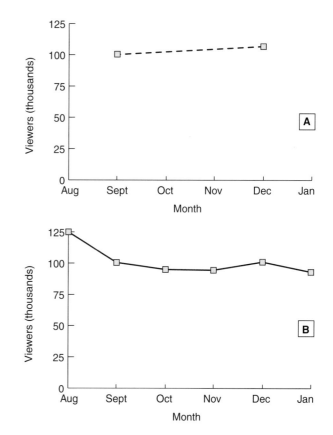

Figure 23.18 A graph drawn from only two points can mislead

Specific trends

Researchers are interested in observing various specific trends showing the interaction between products and markets. These include **quantity of consumption**. For example, a research study by Cinema and Video Industry Audience Research (CAVIAR) between 1985 and 1995 revealed that there had been a steady increase in the number of people watching films at the cinema.

Activity

Look at Figure 23.19, which shows projected figures for satellite and cable TV. What trend do they predict, and why?

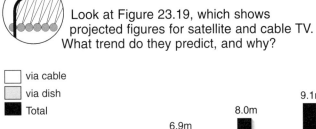
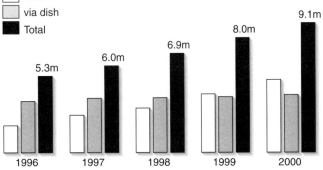

Figure 23.19 Satellite and cable TV projections by Zenith Media in 1995

Another specific trend of interest is **quantity of consumption by market segment**. Often it is not the *total* market that media producers, and especially advertisers, are interested in, but rather a certain group of media consumers, such as women or professional people.

Activity

The data in Figure 23.20 relate to female viewing figures. What trends are identifiable and why?

TOTAL TV	26.8	27.0	26.3	25.8	26.9	28.1	26.67	26.11
BBC1	9.9	10.0	10.0	9.5	9.5	9.8	9.24	8.96
BBC2	3.0	2.8	2.6	2.4	2.6	2.8	2.59	2.66
ITV	11.7	11.8	11.5	11.7	12.2	12.7	11.90	11.69
C4	2.2	2.4	2.2	2.2	2.6	2.9	2.94	2.87
	1987	1988	1989	1990	1991	1992	1993	1994

Figure 23.20 BARB data for network average weekly hours of terrestrial TV viewing by women

Another specific trend is in **changing objects of consumption**. Researchers are interested in knowing whether people are switching from one form of media to another (e.g. from radio to television) or if they are changing from one product to a rival. Figure 23.21 shows the number of new consumer magazines entering the market over a long period. In some years there were a lot of new magazines, but in 1992 and 1993 many publications lost so many readers that they were unable to continue.

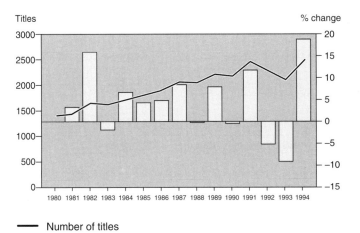

— Number of titles

□ % change yr/yr

Figure 23.21 BRAD data for growth in consumer magazine titles

Activity

It is generally assumed that people are deserting traditional cinemas for the new multiplex cinemas. Study the data for 1991 and 1992 in Figure 23.22. Can you see any evidence of such a trend in these statistics? Which age group may be abandoning the traditional cinema? Are they turning to the multiplexes or are they taking out home videos instead?

Age group	Multiplex visits		Non-multiplex visits	
	1991 %	1992 %	1991 %	1992 %
7–14	13	14	17	20
15–24	44	45	33	38
25–34	24	24	25	18
35+	19	17	25	24
Total	*100*	*100*	*100*	*100*
Male	53	50	53	50
Female	47	50	47	50
ABC1	54	55	56	57
C2DE	46	45	44	43

Figure 23.22 CAVIAR data for multiplex and non-multiplex visitors

Another specific trend is in the **changing market profile of a market segment**. By comparing the type of data, such as that collected by NRS over a number of years, trends in the behaviour of women or men of different ages or social background (etc.) can be observed.

Quality trends

Data are not only about the quantity of media products consumed, but also their quality. The **Broadcasting Standards Council** (BSC) monitors the portrayal of violence, sex and matters of taste and decency in broadcast material and logs the number of complaints received about programmes on television, radio, cable and satellite services relating to these areas. This is a statutory body created under the 1990 Broadcasting Act. Its three member panels are changed regularly during the course of the year. By comparing data from different reports a pattern can possibly be observed of how many complaints there are and if the nature of the complaints is changing. Figure 23.23 shows one such complaint and the outcome of the BSC's investigation.

Reasons for changes in media consumption

There are many reasons why media products increase or decline in popularity. Upward or downward trends in their consumption may be observable after a matter of weeks, or a continuous trend may take years to observe and explain.

Casualty

BBC1 Saturday 13 January 1996, 8.05–8.55 pm

The complaint

Seven viewers complained of an incident in which a schoolgirl had a broken bottle thrust into her face, causing serious injuries. They considered that the incident was too violent for showing before the Watershed, especially in a programme known to be watched by many children.

The broadcaster's statement

The BBC said that 'Casualty' had established a reputation for the frank depiction of injuries reaching the Accident & Emergency department and for setting the traumatic experiences surrounding them in a personal context which often conveyed a moral message. On this occasion, the assault on the 16-year-old Ayesha had been the 'punishment' inflicted on her by her brother for posing for a 'girlie' magazine. It had led to her rejection of him and shown up the consequences of the value system which had prompted his action against her. The BBC had given careful thought to the incident and had preceded the transmission with a warning pointing to a 'vicious and brutal attack'. The BBC said that some viewers had believed the sequence included the actual moment at which Ayesha had sustained her injuries, although this was not so. However, it was aware that the incident had exceeded the expectations of some viewers and for that it expressed its regret.

The BSC's finding

The full Council considered that the sequence, even allowing for the omission from it of the actual moment of impact, had been too violent for showing in a pre-Watershed placing. It therefore upheld the complaints.

■ **COMPLAINT UPHELD**

Figure 23.23 How the BSC reports on complaints

There are basically two possible reasons for a change in consumption.

Either

- the product has changed, or
- the audience has changed.

These two factors will always be interlinked, which can make describing why a trend has occurred rather complex. A product such as a TV soap may decline in popularity during the summer months because the storylines have become less interesting, but the drop in viewing figures may also be explained by the number of viewers who are on holiday or working and relaxing outside in the garden.

Sometimes, whilst the trend for the entire market of a product may increase, there may be a decline hidden within this, whereby a segment of the market is no longer 'using' the product. Consider an imaginary case. The total readership of *Men's Weekly* has steadily increased over three years from 185 000 to 264 000. This is good, but those figures do not show the fact that readership amongst 25- to 35-year-old males in a professional bracket has dropped from 87 000 to 50 000. This could be significant information for manufacturers of upmarket products normally advertising in the magazine, and worrying for the editor who wants to encourage this group of readers to become the regular purchasers of the future.

Activity

Drawing on your own personal experiences, discuss in your group whether a decline in listening figures for BBC Radio 1 could be due to:

- the quality of the programmes
- competition from other radio stations
- competition from other media such as television, cinemas or computer games.

We next consider the factors contributing to a rise or a decline in consumption.

The price of a media product

The cost of a media product to a consumer includes:

- the purchase price of a television, radio, video player, computer, etc.
- the purchase price of a newspaper, magazine, video, etc.
- a ticket price for entrance to a cinema
- the cost of hiring a video
- travel costs to get to a cinema or video shop
- television licence fee
- satellite or cable subscriptions
- delivery charges.

A change in any of the above is likely to affect how much that product is used by that consumer.

Generally speaking, if the price of a product drops more people will buy the product; if it rises fewer people will buy it. In the 1990s there has been a prolonged newspaper war with the prices of tabloids and some broadsheets sinking into the 20–40 pence bracket. In order to maintain market share, let alone increase sales, a newspaper has to remain competitive.

Offers of subscriptions at reduced price (twelve copies of a monthly magazine for the price of ten) can also improve sales. Many people are looking for value for money and will switch to a product that seems to offer it.

The spending power of the majority of people within a country is determined by how well the economy is doing. If taxation and ordinary living costs are low then people will have more money in their pockets to spend on luxury items such as glossy magazines, computer systems, video players, etc.

Activity

Look at the data in Figure 23.24. showing the number of televisions and video players owned by people in this country. Make a survey of how many televisions, radios and video recorders are owned by you and the rest of the class and your families. How typical are you, when you compare the results with the data in Figure 23.24?

TV households penetration (%)	1990	1991	1992	1993	1994	1995
TV ownership and reception capabilities						
2 sets	32	34	35	36	36	37
3+ sets	13	13	15	17	16	17
Colour TV	95	92	96	97	97	98
Teletext	32	34	40	48	52	57
Remote control	59	63	69	75	81	84
VCR	59	62	65	72	74	76
All cable						
Homes passed	7.7	9.3	10.8	14.4	18.3	23.3
Homes connected	1.6	1.9	2.5	2.9	3.8	5.0
Broadband cable						
Homes passed	3.0	4.5	7.0	10.2	14.6	20.8
Homes connected	0.5	0.9	1.5	2.1	3.1	4.4
All direct-to-home satellite systems						
Direct-to-home satellite dishes/SMATV	4.3	7.2	11.1	10.0	12.6	13.6

Figure 23.24 BARB data for TV and VCR ownership over a period

Certain sectors of Western society are becoming increasingly affluent and are prepared to pay high prices. This is shown by the number of people, especially young people, who are prepared to pay for designer-label clothes. They are not always interested in 'value for money'. So sometimes, setting a high price can encourage certain sections of the market to buy the product if this indicates that the product is exclusive and desirable. When some people find extra money in their pockets, they will spend it on glossy lifestyle magazines, such as *Vogue,* as they want to identify with the lifestyles shown in them.

Activity

What is the most you would ever spend on a magazine? Have you ever switched to another magazine because your usual choice became too expensive? Compare your response with those of others in the group.

Certain sections of society will always have more spending power than others. At the beginning of the twentieth century it was the adult wage-earning population who determined the nature of media products. Especially catered for were moral and political viewpoints and tastes of the affluent middle classes. In the 1950s and 1960s a new market emerged. Teenagers had money in their pockets and were eager to spend. The 1980s saw the rise of the senior citizen with a good pension to spend and the prospect of a long and active old age. They are prepared to spend on expensive television sets and

Figure 23.25 People buy glossy magazines to identify with the lifestyles depicted

glossy magazines. Advertisers are keen to sponsor or advertise in media products which appeal to this group.

Increased competition may lead to a drop in price and, for example, increase the circulation figures of newspapers overall. But the sales of individual newspapers may actually suffer and certain titles be forced out of circulation.

The price of a product is also determined not only by how many people buy it but also by the cost of raw materials. The increasing shortage of cheap newsprint has caused a lot of problems for the newspaper industry: they either have to pass this cost on to the purchaser or make it more expensive for people to advertise in their product. Not only raw materials but also wages have significantly affected the cost of a product. Quality programmes such as dramas or documentaries are expensive in the amount of time and people needed in the planning and research stages. It is much cheaper to make quiz and chat shows. At the moment these also attract high audience figures, but in the long run people may tire of them and viewing figures will drop.

Economies of scale enable manufacturers to drop unit costs if more people buy their product. Raw materials are cheaper if bought in bulk. This is obviously true for print publications. The situation is more complex for audio-visual products. A programme made for the BBC will cost the same to make if it is seen by one region or seen by the whole nation. What will make the programme profitable is the number of sales it makes to other networks or to overseas TV stations. If more networks buy programmes, viewing figures will increase.

New technology such as DTP systems and lightweight cameras can also reduce costs by producing things more cheaply and quickly, and again more will be sold.

The availability of a product

The consumer now has more choice of media products than ever before. It is often said that we live in a shrinking world, made possible by the improvement in transport and telecommunications. Major British newspapers can be bought in all the main cities of the world, British television programmes are seen everywhere, and in Britain viewers can see American or Australian programmes every day of the week.

The development of cable and satellite TV has increased choice enormously for the viewer. There are now more radio stations than ever before. Even a small newsagent will stock dozens of titles of magazines and many newspapers. If people cannot collect their newspaper then it can be delivered. Supermarkets and petrol stations make print products readily available.

As mentioned before, increased availability of television and radio stations, and an increase in the number of titles of individual print publications, may lead to an increase in overall viewing and listening figures but not necessarily to an increase for an individual title or programme.

Advertising

What will increase the consumption of an individual product, whether it is a programme or a station, a film or a magazine, is advertising. This is an industry in itself. Advertising not only brings a product to the attention of the consumer, it creates a demand, it suggests to the consumer that there is a need in their life waiting to be satisfied. How advertising works for media products is studied more closely in Chapter 27.

Activity

Identify instances when any sort of advertising, either posters or TV/radio/magazines/newspaper adverts, encouraged you to:

■ see a film
■ watch a TV programme
■ buy a record, cassette or CD
■ hire a video
■ listen to a radio station
■ buy a book, newspaper or magazine.

Make a list of both the product and how it was advertised. Compare this with lists of other members of your group.

Social influences

Peer-group pressure

At different stages of our lives we seek an identity, and we do this in a number of ways, quite often by trying to be like other people of either our own age or background, with similar tastes, opinions and attitudes.

Everybody conforms to a certain extent to their own age group, especially when it comes to what is clearly visible, namely fashion. Most students, even if they are mature students, know that if they came into college wearing a suit or high-heeled shoes they would set themselves apart from the group. They would probably feel slightly odd. Most of us don't want to feel like that and wear clothes that establish us as part of the group.

Peer-group pressure can also encourage us to buy certain magazines, watch some programmes rather than others, and listen in to a specific radio station. In other words, peer-group pressure can change the consumption of media products.

Activity

Which of the following have you done recently because of the influence of your peers?

■ seen a film
■ watched a TV programme
■ bought a record
■ hired a video
■ listened to a radio station
■ bought a book, newspaper or magazine.

Compare your list with those of others in the group.

Family influence

Even more influential than our peers can be our family, in terms of which media products we use and how often we use them. Young people seldom buy their own daily newspaper, but they do perhaps occasionally read the one at home bought by their mother or father. Unless you have a television of your own, your viewing habits will also be defined by the rest of the household.

Activity

Discuss the following in your group:

a When you were between the ages of ten and fifteen, who in your family made the following decisions:

what television programmes to watch?
what newspaper to buy?
which videos to rent?

b Was there any form of censorship exerted by your family? This could vary from open disapproval to banning of certain programmes or magazines.

c Was there a newspaper that you read, or TV and radio programmes that you watched or listened to, because someone else had bought the paper or chosen the programme?

Socio-cultural influences

The mass circulation of newspapers would never have occurred without a population that was literate. **Education** improves our ability to understand and appreciate some media products and creates a need for information. We now live in a society where jobs can be hard to find and keep, so there is pressure put on those both in and out of employment to keep up-to-date and gain new qualifications. Educational programmes, magazines and newspaper supplements are now produced not only for children but also for adults who want to continue their education for various reasons throughout their lives. The popularity of Open University degrees over the last two decades demonstrates this trend.

Figure 23.26 Open University courses are supported by many TV programmes

Some educational programmes are broadcast through the night for people to video or watch. Here is an example of early-morning programmes scheduled for Wednesday 19 June 1996:

12.30	The Learning Zone: Art in 14th century Florence
01.30	The Psychology of Addiction
02.00	Nightschool TV: Technology
04.00	BBC Focus: Health and Safety at Work
04.15	Find out about BBC Focus
04.30	Disability Today
05.00	Voluntary Sector Television
06.00	Open University: Water by the Volume
06.25	Pathfinding in the Brain
06.50	Velocity Diagrams

At the weekend BBC2 currently has educational programmes running from 6.00am to 12.15pm on Saturdays and from 6.15am to 9.10am on Sundays. There are, of course, schools programmes and educational programmes for young children on the other terrestrial channels as well as on BBC2.

Activity

Make a list of all the educational programmes scheduled for one weekday within a 24-hour stretch on each of the terrestrial TV channels. What percentage of the total output of each channel can be considered educational? This is certainly more than there would have been twenty years ago. What reasons can you give for this?

Society is always changing, and it has been argued in many quarters that we are living in an increasingly dangerous and violent society. Many people prefer to find entertainment in their own homes rather than venture onto the streets. The controlled environment of the multiplex seems safer than the cinema in the centre of town, even though it means travelling in a car to an out-of-town entertainment complex.

There are other reasons, however, why multiplex cinemas have become popular and revitalised attendance figures for films, despite the high prices of tickets.

Activity

In a group, discuss different reasons for the growing attraction of multiplex cinemas and then list the reasons in order of priority. Consider such things as: a good evening out; other activities such as bowling and restaurants nearby; the buildings are smart and comfortable; a good atmosphere for families; a wide choice of films; a safe environment; easier to park than in the town centre.

Changes in population can affect media products. After the Second World War there was a baby boom, but now the proportion of teenagers is dropping significantly whilst the proportion of elderly people is increasing. This affects the type of programmes and the number of print publications produced for these age groups.

Changes in population are sometimes the result of immigration. Radio stations have emerged to cater for different musical tastes or have included speech-based programmes in a different language. BBC Radio Leicester targets the Asian population in its programming. Newspapers and magazines have also responded to the possibility of attracting new customers: the *Leicester Mercury,* for example, has a special Asian edition.

Channel 4, like BBC2, was set up to broadcast programmes of special interest to minority groups, including gay people, disabled people, ethnic minorities, religious groups, etc.

Activity

a Find as many examples as you can of programmes on radio or television that cater for minority groups.

b There have been calls from prominent members of the clergy and senior politicians for a return to Christian moral values. If there were a major response to this appeal in society, what effect do you think the movement would have on:

■ the output of radio stations?
■ the scheduling of television programmes?
■ the contents of newsagents' shelves?
■ the genres of videos for hire?

The amount of time people spend watching television or reading magazines depends on the **leisure** time they have. Since the 1950s, people have expected paid holidays and free weekends. Some people have more leisure time because they are unemployed. There are now TV programmes aimed at men during the daytime, whereas 20 years ago daytime viewing was for very young children and housewives.

Soap operas were traditionally aimed at a large female audience, but now the viewing figures show a large male audience too. BARB data for 1 January 1996 showed that 26 per cent of male viewers and 38 per cent of female viewers watched *Coronation Street;* 14 per cent of male viewers and 15 per cent of female viewers watched *Neighbours;* and 25 per cent of male viewers and 33 per cent of female viewers watched *EastEnders.*

Sport has always been popular for people to watch or follow through the media. There has been an important trend in recent years for people to join in sporting activities and to keep fit, partly as a result of government reports on the poor health of the nation as the result of lack of exercise. This has been reflected in the increase of sports coverage on

Figure 23.27 Male daytime viewing is increasing

television, but probably the main reason for the increase in sports coverage is the improvement in the way that games are shown, with action replays, close-ups, explanations of the action, etc. Television shows mainly major popular sports such as football and horse-racing. Minority sports such as sumo wrestling or women's hockey, even if they attract a lot of supporters, get very little coverage. Magazines have been more responsive in covering not only minority sports but obscure hobbies.

Major **events in society** can also cause a big increase in viewing figures. This could be something like a royal marriage – or a royal divorce. Or it could be a war. During the Gulf War, more people switched on to more news programmes to watch the action as it unfolded in the desert.

At one time it seemed that radio would fall out of popularity because of the invention of television, and it is undoubtedly true that BBC radio has lost many listeners. However, radio and television are not always direct rivals because they fulfil different needs. For example, people working in factories or at home, travelling in their cars or jogging round the block can listen to radio but not watch television.

Quality of the product

The quality and content of all media products can dramatically affect their appeal. There is always a need to change, in order to appeal to a new generation of consumers.

An example is the breakfast show on BBC Radio 1 which was losing listeners steadily until Chris Evans became the presenter. Audiences can become bored with a product. A magazine such as *Woman's Own* has changed its middle-class image to appeal to a younger, less affluent reader.

Viewers respond well to a mixture of the familiar and the novel. A well-known character in an unusual storyline with a wedding or murder at the end is guaranteed to keep viewers hooked for weeks.

New technology

New technology and its effects are described in detail in Chapter 31. Developments have improved the quality of products as well as enabled them to be produced more quickly and cheaply. Desktop publishing (DTP) has meant that small magazines and other small print publications are now

Figure 23.28 Niche publishing is now made possible by DTP

commercially viable. The new ranges of small video cameras and computers have enabled numerous small production companies to be set up who now make a large number of the programmes that fill up the schedules of the many channels now available to the viewer.

Improvements in physical appearance or sound – such as thicker paper in a magazine or stereo sound and realistic colour in a television – encourage greater consumption. The whole of the Western world now expects modern products which reflect the fact we live in a technological age – whether it is clothing, kitchen appliances or cars that are being bought. If the product shows a concern for the environment then so much the better. The customer has become more discriminating and discerning.

There are now more media products than ever before, and finding a niche for a new product can seem daunting. There is a possibility that the Western market is becoming saturated with products. The need to remain financially competitive can result in inferior products which ultimately consumers turn their backs on. It is very cheap to produce quiz shows to attract large audiences, but very expensive to produce period drama which may have an enthusiastic but smaller audience. Advertisers may be interested in sponsoring the former but not the latter, so the result will be that good products are replaced with inferior ones. There may be the potential to send hundreds of new TV channels into people's homes, but if they are all offering the same diet of programmes then their variety actually becomes very limited.

Evidence assignment

Choose a specific area for investigation concerning how a media product is used by a target audience. For example: How much do women watch sports programmes on Saturday television? Or which newspapers do young people read to find out about employment prospects? You decide.

Identify the sources where information can be found about the consumption of the chosen media product. These sources can include official statistics or articles from magazines, television reports or newspaper stories.

Analyse any statistics you may have found to determine whether there is a growing or declining trend in consumption.

Evaluate the accuracy or usefulness of the data or information you have collected, and draw conclusions.

Your work should be shown to the group in the form of a ten-minute presentation. Examples of excerpts from the product should be shown and OHTs or flipcharts used to explain the data, with pie charts or graphs. Chapter 28 gives advice on making presentations.

Chapter 24

Carry out audience research

In earlier production units you will have done research into the planning stages. Afterwards you will have evaluated the product. That evaluation will have needed to look at whether the production process was completed on time, whether the quality was satisfactory and whether it complied with the brief. This chapter now looks at the success of a product (either professional or made by you) in terms of its reception and use by a viewer, listener or reader. Was it informative, entertaining, persuasive? Did the consumers want to read, watch or listen to further examples of the production? Did they think it was value for money?

Principal objectives of audience research

The more clearly and concisely a researcher can define the aims and objectives of his or her research, the more effective it will be in terms of results and the more economical it will be in terms of resources. These days there is as much danger of collecting too much information or the wrong sort of information as there is of not finding enough.

Objectives must be clear and focused (i.e. well defined) and must be achievable within certain constraints. What *precisely* do you want to know? Is it:

- people's use of a product?
- people's attitudes towards the product?
- people's future intentions towards the product?
- explanations for all of the above?
- all about the users or potential users?

Case studies

These are all examples of research topics chosen by students on their own products and on commercial media products.

An evaluation of a children's story written by the student
Audience feedback on a student video
Gender stereotyping in adverts
The effects on readers of photographs accompanying hard news stories
The need for some teenage magazines to be censored
How public attitudes to the emergency services are affected by TV programmes such as The Bill, London's Burning *and* Casualty

There are several clear stages to any research project:

1 Sometimes the topic or subject to be studied is called a **hypothesis**. The researcher makes an assumption in the form of a statement and then sets out to prove or disprove it. This can be a useful starting point. Here are some examples produced by students:

CHRIS: *Some TV programmes are aimed at a male market.*
ELIOT: *TV dramas such as* London's Burning *and* Soldier, Soldier *influence the way people feel about the public services.*
ADRIAN: *Hard news stories with pictures are more influential than those without.*
PETER: *Sport on TV encourages young people to participate in sports activities.*
DEAN: *Without music on TV the dramatic impact of programmes would be significantly weakened.*
ADAM: *Layout and font are more significant than content in persuading a reader to buy a certain newspaper.*
LISA: *Magazine readers are more influenced by adverts showing a human image than by those showing an inanimate object.*
HAYLEY: *Some magazines are inappropriate for the age of the reader.*

2 Once the area of research has been chosen, then a list of more precise objectives can be defined. These objectives should be:
- To analyse what the media product is
- To identify the consumer/audience
- To discover how often the product is used
- To find out how the product is used by the consumer/audience (e.g. what parts of the newspaper are read, whether a listener gives all of his or her attention to the radio)
- To find out what the consumer/audience feels about the product.
One student chose as his hypothesis 'There is too much imported TV on our screens'. He drew up the objectives shown in Figure 24.1.

RESEARCH OBJECTIVES AND FEASIBILITY STUDY

The hypothesis I have chosen to research is 'There is too much imported TV on our screens'.

To clarify some of the wording used when I say 'imported TV', I am referring to programmes that originate from outside the European Community, such as American sitcoms and Australian soaps. When I say 'our screens' I mean being shown on UK terrestrial TV (i.e. BBC, ITV and Channel 4).

I will, by means of quantitative and qualitative research, endeavour to find answers to the following:

a How much imported TV do people *think* there is?
b How much imported TV is there *actually,* and what percentage of total TV is this?
c Are there any restrictions in place that limit the amount of imported TV shown?
d Why do some people prefer imported TV to our own home-grown material?
e Why do people watch TV soaps/sitcoms?
f What model of audience behaviour best applies to these viewers?
g How and why did TV soaps develop?
h How popular is imported TV in terms of viewing figures?
i Is the cost of imported TV related to the amount on TV, especially in the daytime?

Figure 24.1 One student's objectives set out clearly

3 At this stage it is worthwhile brainstorming questions around the objectives.
4 It should now become clearer what type of research methods will be most appropriate: questionnaire, interviews, case studies, a visit to the library, etc.

Case study

Here is how and where this student decided to carry out the research he had identified above:

'I hope to be able to employ a mix of the different methods of research, and answer most, if not all of the questions. I think most of the questions can be answered, some more easily than others. I am planning to use a wide range of research techniques/tools,

depending on what sort of answers the questions demand.

a How much imported TV do people *think* there is?
I will find out how much imported TV people think there is primarily by means of a *questionnaire,* and I will also ask this question when conducting my interviews. This is very feasible; as long as I get sufficient questionnaires back this should be fairly easy to establish.

b How much imported TV is there *actually,* and what percentage of total TV is this?
I will find out how much imported TV there is, and has been, on our screens by a number of methods. I will study a typical day's TV listing, from the *Radio Times,* and see how much of the day's TV is imported. I will also look in the annual BBC and ITV reports to see how much imported TV they show. The facts are there, it's just a matter of translating them. This is one area where some form of graphical representation may be beneficial.

c Are there any restrictions in place that limit the amount of imported TV shown?
To see if there are any restrictions in place I will write to the relevant regulatory body. In the case of ITV and Channel 4 this will be the ITC. I will also study any documents that the ITC and BBC publish. This too is feasible. I hope to receive a useful reply from the ITC, otherwise I can research this question through published material.

d Why do some people prefer imported TV to our own home-grown material?
Why some people prefer to watch imported TV is a qualitative question that will involve a unique, personal reply. I will try to investigate this when I do my interviews, as the answers may be long and involved.

e Why do people watch TV soaps/sitcoms?
This is one of the questions I will ask in my interview. I will also conduct a literary search into TV soaps to see whether anyone has published a theory on the topic, or if they have thrown up any ideas on the subject.

f What model of audience behaviour best applies to these viewers?
After studying why people watch TV soaps/sitcoms I should be able to match this with one of the media theories on audience behaviour.

g How and why did TV soaps develop?
To research the history of TV sitcoms I will locate and study books written about this topic. I will also make use

of the CD-ROM to see whether any newspaper articles have been written about the topic recently.

h <u>How popular is imported TV, in terms of viewing figures?</u>

To see how popular imported TV is should be a relatively easy task. I will study past and present BARB viewing figures, and see how many people watch these programmes.

i <u>Is the cost of imported TV related to the amount on TV, especially in the daytime?</u>

This question really has two parts: how much does imported TV cost, and does this relate to the amount shown on TV (i.e. if it is fairly cheap per hour do the TV companies use it as 'filler' to pad the daytime scheduling?). The first part regarding cost might be difficult, if not impossible to establish. The second part, about cost and amount on TV, will probably be more difficult to prove/disprove conclusively. I may have to use my own personal judgement on this issue.'

Activity

Choose two areas of audience research, one on a media product you have made yourself and one on a similar product professionally made. Decide whether you want to find out how the product is used, or attitudes towards it, or a mixture of both.

- List your research objectives
- List where you will find information.
- Indicate whether this is quantitative or qualitative research.

Developing methods and instruments for conducting research

Effective research will mix both quantitative and qualitative research methods. Whether you use focus groups or case studies, or whether you define the media consumers by lifestyle groupings as described in Chapter 5 or as ABC1C2DEs as explained in Chapter 21, depends on what precisely you are trying to find out.

The two main methods used in research are questionnaires and interviews. If the correct information is to be collected, a questionnaire needs careful designing and interviews must be planned.

Designing a questionnaire

Activity

Read through the questionnaire in Figure 24.2. Would you find it easy to answer? How many mistakes can you find?

PLEASE FILL IN THIS QUESTIONAIRE

NAME

AGE

ADRESS

TELEPHONE NUMBER

INCOME

WHAT WORK DO YOU DO?

HOW OFTEN DO YOU WATCH TELEVISION?

    OFTEN   SOMETIMES   NEVER

PUT A NUMBER BETWEEN ONE AND FIVE BY EACH PROGRAMME TO SHOW HOW MUCH YOU LIKE IT

   COMEDY DOCUMENTARIES FILMS NEWS SOAPS

HOW MANY TIMES HAVE YOU WATCHED A PORNOGRAPHIC FILM ON TV?

DO YOU OR YOUR PARTNER DECIDE WHICH PROGRAMMES TO WATCH?

WHEN DO YOU WATCH TELEVISION?

   MORNING AFTERNOON EVENING

WHAT PROGRAMMES DID YOU WATCH WHEN YOU WERE YOUNG?

WHO IS YOUR FAVOURITE TV PRODUCER?

DO YOU WATCH BBC1 AND CHANNEL 4?

DO YOU AGREE THAT ADVERTS INFLUENCE WEAK PEOPLE?

WHAT WOULD YOU DO IF YOUR CHILD BECAME VIOLENT AFTER WATCHING AN ACTION FILM?

WHY DO YOU THINK THAT THE QUALITY OF TV IS DECLINING?

THANK YOU FOR COMPLETEING THIS QUESTIONNAIRE

Figure 24.2 An unsatisfactory questionnaire

Avoiding design problems

■ The appearance of the questionnaire in Figure 24.2 is the first problem. It would be better to use both lower and upper case, and instructions should be in a different font from the questions themselves so that they are more obvious.

Good spacing between questions would help both the reader and the person collating the data. Boxes for answers look much neater than dotted lines. Numbering the questions and allowing space on the right of the sheet would also be helpful when it came to analysing the results.

■ It is best to start a questionnaire with a brief sentence to explain its purpose. Always use language that is clear, simple and friendly. This questionnaire could have started:

Please could you spend a few minutes filling in this questionnaire about TV viewing habits, for a student project.

This is better than:

I am a second-year GNVQ advanced student doing an assignment for Unit 6 and I am researching the hypothesis that television adversely affects people.

■ The questionnaire fails to say how it should be filled in. It needs instructions such as:

Tick only one box unless otherwise indicated.

■ *Personal details.* A strength of questionnaires is that they can be anonymous, which encourages people to answer truthfully. This one starts off badly. Not only does it ask for the respondent's name but also their address, telephone number and income! All questions should be relevant. How necessary are these? It could be argued in this case that occupation and income can have some bearing on people's viewing habits, as can where they live – but these questions are too direct. For instance, it would probably be adequate to establish the region or district in which someone lives rather than their complete address and telephone number.

However, some basic information has been omitted that would be useful, such as the gender (male or female) of the respondent.

Age is a standard and useful question. However, it is less offensive and also easier to analyse if categories are given:

What is your age?
Under 20 ☐

20–29 ☐
30–39 ☐
40 or over ☐

Be careful not to use *overlapping categories* such as 10–20, 20–30, 30–40 and 40+. In this case which boxes should 20- and 30-year-olds tick? The data collected may not be accurate enough.

What work people do can be relevant to the questionnaire, but again it is more helpful if categories are given:

Clerical worker ☐ Professional person ☐
Factory worker ☐ House person ☐
Unemployed ☐ Teacher ☐ Other ☐

The 'Other' category is often useful. There is always someone who wants to give an answer you haven't thought of!

■ *How often do you watch television?* The options for this question are ambiguous. What is meant by 'Often' or 'Sometimes'? Both of these can vary a great deal between individuals. Again it would be better to give precise categories, such as:

Under 5 hours a day ☐
Between 5 and 10 hours a day ☐
Over 10 hours a day ☐

■ *Put a number between one and five ....* The instructions for the next question are confusing. Does the respondent put 5 or 1 for the type of programme that gives the most satisfaction? Is the respondent supposed to 'rank' the programmes giving 1 for the best, 2 for the next favourite, 3 for one fairly liked, 4 for one not really enjoyed and 5 for the type most disliked? Or can he or she give a score of 3 for all of them?

■ *How many times have you watched a pornographic film on TV?* Some people might consider this to be an offensive question. It also seems to presume that they *will* have watched a porn film. If sensitive questions have to be asked, then it must be apparent to the respondent that they are relevant, and it is better if they are positioned towards the end of the questionnaire and not near the beginning.

■ *Do you or your partner decide ....?* This question makes the assumption that the respondent has a 'partner'. It also has to be considered whether it might be preferable to say husband, wife, friend or other member of the family.

■ *When do you watch television?* An instruction is needed here to indicate whether one or more categories can be chosen.

- *What programmes did you watch when you were young?* This involves a lot of thought and time to be answered. Some people might list the names of 50 or more programmes, others might list just half a dozen different genres. How would you analyse the information?

- *Who is your favourite TV produc*er? Here is an expectation of knowledge that most people would not have.

- *Do you watch BBC1 and Channel 4?* This is an example of a linked response. It is OK if the person watches both channels, but what if they only watch BBC1 or only watch Channel 4? Should they tick the box?

- *Do you agree that adverts influence weak people?* This is a leading or biased question. It suggests or implies that adverts can influence people, especially weak people.

- *What would you do if your child became violent …?* This is a hypothetical question. The respondent has to imagine an answer. Any data collected would be purely subjective, an opinion rather than a quantifiable fact. The value of a question of this kind is dubious.

- *Why do you think that the quality of TV is declining?* There is a similar sort of problem here. The researcher is asking the respondent to speculate. How would you analyse the information?

- *Thank you ….* Although the researcher has remembered to thank the respondent, he has not explained to whom the questionnaire is to be returned, by what date and where to.

- Finally, the spelling in the document has not been checked! There are three spelling errors.

Administering a questionnaire

After designing your questionnaire, it is essential to *pilot* it. This will test how long it takes to answer. The shorter the questionnaire, the more likely that people will fill it in. A trial run will check that all the questions and instructions are clear. Your guinea-pigs will soon tell you if they find any of the questions offensive or irrelevant, and if they are too difficult or time-consuming. They may also suggest other questions that could be added.

After photocopying or printing the questionnaire, you are ready for distribution. It is always an advantage to hand questionnaires to people personally and wait for them to be completed. Postal

surveys are not only expensive but the response rates are generally low, even if a stamped addressed envelope is included. It is also usual for a covering letter to be enclosed which involves more time and expense.

Professional research agencies keep careful records of when and where questionnaires were distributed and the date they were returned. Although these questionnaires may appear to be anonymous, there is sometimes a coded number in them which acts as a tracking system.

Activity

Figures 24.3 and 24.4. show two examples of questionnaires designed by students. One aims to find out whether magazine readers are more influenced by adverts showing a human image rather than an inanimate object. The other is a survey about imported TV programmes.

a Try answering the questionnaires in Figures 24.3 and 24.4. Which did you find easiest to do, and why?
b As a group, design four short questionnaires on your newspaper-reading, TV-watching, radio-listening and cinema-going habits. Limit yourselves to a maximum of ten questions for each questionnaire.
c Design a questionnaire for your own chosen research project.

Conducting interviews

It can be very time-consuming to run an effective questionnaire. To do research through a series of interviews requires even more skill and time. The most important thing is to make sure that you are asking the right people the right questions in the right way.

You could ask the people you have chosen to interview identical questions to those in the questionnaire. However, the interview situation is the ideal opportunity to collect qualitative rather than quantitative information. It is a chance to explore not only behaviour but the reasons behind it, and opinions and attitudes. With a questionnaire, the researcher already has a clear idea of the sort of answers that will emerge. With an interview, new and unexpected data may be recorded.

Who are you going to interview? The selection of respondents and interviewees will be dealt with more fully later in this chapter. However, you will need to know general details about their age, career, lifestyle,

QUESTIONNAIRE

I would be most grateful if you could assist me by completing the following questions.

What is your gender?
Male   Female
☐   ☐

What is your age?
12–17   18–23   24–29   30–35   36+
☐   ☐   ☐   ☐   ☐

Which of the following images do you prefer to see in an advert for perfume or cologne?

Sexy female ☐	Sexy male ☐
Non-sexy female ☐	Non-sexy male ☐
Houses ☐	Cars ☐
Scenery ☐	Animals ☐
Female figure ☐	Male figure ☐

Which magazines do you read?
JUST 17   TV HITS   BEST   VOX
☐   ☐   ☐   ☐

WOMAN'S WEEKLY   SUGAR   RADIO TIMES
☐   ☐   ☐

NME
☐

OTHER   ....
         ....

How often do you read a magazine?

Once a month   4 times a year   Twice a year
☐   ☐   ☐

Weekly
☐

Thank you for completing this questionnaire; it is most appreciated.

Once completed please return to Lisa Rose, Hinckley College, Media Studies, by 20 January

Figure 24.3   A student's questionnaire on magazine advertisements

Questionnaire on imported TV

As part of an assignment for a GNVQ Advanced Media course I am currently undertaking research by a number of means, including this questionnaire, into people's viewing habits and general attitudes towards imported TV, such as Australian soaps and American sitcoms.

*Please tick only **one** box per question, unless instructions state otherwise.*

(1) Are you male or female?
☐ Male   ☐ Female

(2) How old are you?
☐ 5–10 yrs   ☐ 11–16 yrs   ☐ 17–22 yrs
☐ 23–28 yrs   ☐ 29–34 yrs   ☐ 35–40 yrs
☐ 41–46 yrs   ☐ 47+yrs

(3) What percentage of what you watch on ITV & CH4 do you think is foreign-made?
☐ 0–24%   ☐ 25–49%   ☐ 50–74%   ☐ 75–100%

(4) Which channel, in your opinion, shows the most imported TV?
☐ BBC1
☐ BBC2
☐ ITV
☐ CH4

(5) What was the last film you watched on TV?
....

(6) Please list below any five TV programmes that you can think of
#1:..
#2:..
#3:..
#4:..
#5:..

(7) Do you prefer to watch:
☐ Australian-made films
☐ American-made films
☐ European/British-made films
☐ Others (please state) ....
☐ No preference?

(8) Please tick the boxes if you watch any of the following programmes.
(You may tick more than one box)
☐ Neighbours   ☐ Home & Away
☐ Shortland Street   ☐ Prisoner Cell Block H
☐ Roseanne   ☐ Home Improvement
☐ You Bet Your Life   ☐ The Ricki Lake Show
☐ NYPD Blue   ☐ Bakersfield PD
☐ Fresh Prince of Bel Air   ☐ Hangin' with Mr. Cooper
☐ The Cosby Show

(9) Please look at the attached programme guide for yesterday. Highlight all the programmes you watched, on any channel.

Thanks for filling in this questionnaire. The time and trouble you have taken to do it is much appreciated!

Please return this questionnaire to John Dickson before Monday 3rd February 1997 either in person or by post to: 12 Cavendish Street, Nuneaton, Warwickshire, CV11 5BG

Figure 24.4 A student's questionnaire on imported TV programmes

etc. If you are interviewing children, then permission should be obtained from the parents or whoever is in charge of them such as a teacher, youth leader or crèche manager.

The next step is to design the questions. This will give you some idea of how long the interview is likely to last. It will give a structure to the interview and keep the research to the point.

You should start with some general questions to the interviewees about themselves to set them at ease, including some chat to explain what the interview is about. Unlike with questionnaires, you will be able to use open-ended questions where the answer will be more than a simple 'yes' or 'no'. Sometimes, however, you will find that people are not giving full enough answers and you should be prepared to use some prompts.

Your questions should follow each other in a way that will make the interview seem like a conversation rather than an interrogation. It is better that the interviewees do not see a copy of the questions beforehand or their replies may lack spontaneity. You should prepare a few phrases to close the interview, such as '... and one last question...'. Don't forget to thank your interviewees, even if the answers have been disappointing.

Sometimes it helps to bring with you an example of what the interview is about. For example, if you are researching magazines, then it might be a good idea to take along a few copies of different magazines to stimulate conversation.

Next you can begin to think of the time organisation of the interviews. Remember that people are giving up their time to help you so you should try to fit in with their arrangements as much as possible. You will get a better response if you avoid 'grabbing' an interview when, for instance, someone is having a ten-minute teabreak in the middle of a busy morning. It is important that you and they are relaxed and can talk without interruption. That is why the location for the interview is also very

Figure 24.5 Do not forget to thank your respondents

important. You will not feel like having an extended, friendly discussion if the room is uncomfortable, lacking in privacy or difficult to find.

How are you going to record the information during the interview? It helps to maintain an informal atmosphere if you don't need to be continuously writing. One of the best ways is with a tape recorder. You should ask the permission of the interviewees before using it. Initially interviewees may be reluctant but usually after a while they forget their self-consciousness. If it is impossible to use a tape recorder for any reason, then some form of shorthand is necessary. Don't try writing down complete sentences – that would destroy the flow of the conversation.

To be a successful interviewer you need lots of practice. You need a friendly personality but not one that will influence how the other person thinks or will inhibit what they say. It is not only our words that affect people, but how we say them, our body language, how we look at people, even the way we dress.

Activities

a You and a partner are researching violence on TV. One of you is to interview a young child and the other an adult. Between you write down ten questions for each interviewee. Do the questions differ? What differences would you expect to find in the running of the two interviews?

Carry out the interviews and compare the results.

b Arrange a series of interviews for your own chosen research project.

Focus groups

Focus groups are valuable not only at the ideas stage of media production but also in assessing audience feedback. They are excellent for finding out people's opinions and attitudes. Many people become less self-conscious when talking with a group of people in a friendly atmosphere than when in an individual interview situation.

It is common practice in the film industry to invite along a selected audience to preview a film before it goes on general release. Students, too, should use this method to help them evaluate their own work. Groups are cheap to run and, if well organised, can give more detailed and interesting feedback than either a questionnaire or an individual interview.

In a discussion group, individuals are encouraged to talk freely about a chosen topic. This could be about the content of a particular newspaper or radio programme. The ideal size of a focus group is between five and ten people. Too small a group and the discussion might be limited in its scope and the difference of ideas that emerge. Too large a group and some members will be too nervous to speak. It is also inadvisable to choose people who are too different in age or background. Neither should you choose people to whom you are too close, such as friends or relatives. They might find it hard to be unprejudiced or honest about the quality of your work.

The group should be given sufficient time beforehand to read the newspaper or magazine or to listen to the programme in a comfortable, quiet environment.

The group should then discuss the topic sitting informally around a coffee table rather than in a circle. Someone needs to be 'in charge' to direct the conversation, or else people may start talking about something completely different. It is a good idea to plan beforehand some ideas to be discussed, such as the style of a radio presenter or whether the print in a magazine was easy to read.

This is a situation where it may be better to record what people say, either on video or on a cassette, so that the information can be analysed in detail afterwards. Unless you are very skilled it can be extremely difficult to follow several people talking together and write down what they are saying. You will also miss valuable clues about the group's body language.

Afterwards the results are analysed by making a list of the main points covered. Any particularly relevant quotes are written down. Then sometimes generalisations can be made or conclusions drawn.

Activity

Practise running a focus group discussion for ten minutes. Choose an existing media product such as an advert or a cartoon strip and find out what people like and dislike about it. Record the discussion and analyse the results.

Choosing a research methodology

As noted earlier, most research involves choosing two or three methods in order to be detailed and reliable. You may decide to do a literature search and observation studies, or a questionnaire plus case studies, or diaries, interviews and a collection of critical reviews. In making your decision on how to do the research the following should be taken into consideration.

Time

The most important factor to consider when doing research is time. Researchers must work to a series of *deadlines*. It is very easy to get side-tracked down one particular avenue of investigation and lose sight of overall objectives. It is essential to set out a schedule at the beginning. This should be realistic and not under-estimate the time it will take to, for instance, organise interviews or get back replies from a questionnaire.

Activity

If you wanted to conduct three 20-minute interviews, with a retired person, a small child and another student in your class – how much time should you allocate for this task? An hour would definitely not be enough. In a group, brainstorm all the things which mean adding on extra time to that hour, such as finding rooms, contacting the senior citizen, obtaining permission from the parent of the child, planning the questions, etc.

If you have a month or so to spend on a particular piece of research then there are a number of methods you can use, such as a questionnaire or asking people to keep diaries. You will also be able to use a larger sample. If, however, the research has to be completed within a few days, then consider a library search or an interview session with a few people.

Professional research organisations such as RAJAR work to very strict deadlines. Their clients need data on a regular up-to-date basis. They would have no use for data that took a year to arrive, no matter how in-depth and complete the research was.

Money

Financial resources are less of a consideration for students than for professional researchers. A student has to pay for paper, pens and possibly postage and photocopying. In a commercial organisation the main item of expenditure is staff wages, and research can rely heavily on having relatively few but highly trained staff to plan a project and analyse results, and a large number of people to collect data and enter it on a computer.

A research organisation will also have building overheads, computer time and facilities, postage and telephone bills and printing costs to consider. BARB collects data from special meters and these are expensive to install and maintain.

Human resources

Professional organisations use well-qualified staff. Interviewers in particular need to be intensively trained if they are to be effective. Interviewers who carry out research over the telephone need to have a suitably friendly voice. Those who conduct face-to-face interviews need to be aware of how body language can affect the responses. Other employees will be needed who have computer skills to input data and collate the results.

Materials

Superficially, questionnaires demand the most resources because of the quantity of paper used and the amount of computer time. Sometimes, special equipment is needed such as the meters used by BARB. For interviews, tape recorders and microphones are useful, or a video camera if you are doing an observation study.

 Activity

Assess the feasibility of your chosen research project. Consider human resources, financial resources, materials and time.

Choosing an appropriate sample of respondents

A general rule is that the greater the size of the sample tested, the more accurate the results will be. However, a questionnaire sent to 100 people might be better than one sent to thousands if for the second survey the sample was unrepresentative or inappropriate.

■ If research aims to show the TV viewing habits of the entire population of the UK, then a cross-section of the population should be sampled. This will include males and females, children and adults, from all different backgrounds and areas.

■ If research is investigating why women like to read the local newspaper, then there is little point in sending questionnaires to children or men or to people who do not read the newspaper.

Population (or **universe**) is a word with a special meaning for statisticians. It actually refers to *any* group from which a sample is taken. So a population could be:

■ the students in a college
■ the audience for a film
■ all TV programmes made by the BBC
■ all the people who subscribe to satellite TV.

The **sampling frame** is a list which identifies members of a population. It could be:

■ the names and addresses of all subscribers to a magazine
■ the names of radio programmes produced in one year by a particular station.

Refer back to Figure 21.17 on page 362, which gives an example of a universe and a sample.

 Activity

Define the sample of people you would choose for

a an interview to find out what people find most useful about the traffic reports on local radio
b a questionnaire on the influence of TV adverts on a Saturday afternoon.

Sampling techniques

There are five common sampling techniques.

In **systematic sampling** you choose what proportion of your target group you want to interview or to receive a questionnaire. It might for example, be 1 in 4, or 1 in 10, or 1 in 1000. Then you would go down the list of the sample frame picking out every fourth, tenth or a thousandth name or item to be tested.

In **simple random sampling** the people or products in a sampling frame are given a number which is drawn at random, possibly by computer, or as in the National Lottery.

In **stratified sampling** the sample frame is divided into groups. In the case of an audience this could be into different age groups, or in the case of films into genres. A percentage of each group is chosen for the survey depending on what percentage of that group is in the sampling frame.

For example, if there are 140 000 people watching a TV soap under the age of 18 and 60 000 people watching who are 18 or older, then these figures are translated into percentages of 70 and 30 per cent respectively. A random sample is then taken based on these percentages, so 70 young people and 30 older people might be asked to fill in a questionnaire.

Multistage sampling is usually carried out for large surveys when the sample frame covers the entire population of the country or the whole geographical area. If the BBC wants to find out about people's opinions on current affairs programmes for radio, they might identify a sample group by dividing the country into a few large regions, then into local regions, and finally a few chosen smaller area streets are chosen at random (see Figure 24.6).

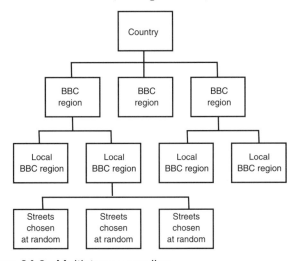

Figure 24.6 Multistage sampling

Quota sampling is the method many professional researchers and most students use because it is easy to carry out! A set number of people are used from the sample frame, as in:

- 10 readers of tabloid newspapers who are female
- 25 people aged 20 to 40 who went to the cinema last week
- 60 people aged 20 to 35.

Activity

Choose a sample of respondents for the questionnaire and interview designed for

your chosen research project. Try to use a cross-section of people that will meet your research objectives, rather than people who are readily available such as your friends or other students who may not be representative.

Obtaining and logging relevant information

As research progresses it is essential to track what has been completed and how much relevant data has been collected. Precise record-keeping is essential and planning will help to ensure that deadlines are met.

- Keep an index or list of different areas of investigation, as subject headings. File relevant information under these headings. You may need to cross-reference material that is useful for two different areas.
- Notes should be taken on any relevant books or articles, films or radio and TV programmes. Write down the bibliographical details.
- Doublecheck that quotations are accurate.
- Discard irrelevant information or data.

Using charts

Quantitative information has to be stored and organised. A **tally chart** is a good way of recording either observed data or information from questionnaires. Every time a questionnaire is returned, a mark is put for each positive response on to one master questionnaire sheet. Then when the survey is complete all the marks are counted up to show the **frequency** of answers for each possible answer (see the example in Figure 24.7).

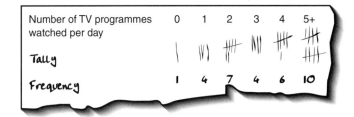

Figure 24.7 A tally chart

Results from tally sheets can be converted into a graph, pie charts or bar charts, as in Figure 24.8. Pie charts are good for showing the proportion of each

413

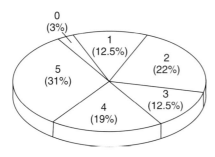

Figure 24.8 Data in Figure 24.7 shown as a pie chart

group of people to the whole. In the example the total number of respondents is 1 + 4 + 7 + 4 + 6 + 10 = 32. The tally for 'no programmes watched' is 1, so the pie segment for this category is 1/32, which is 3.1 per cent. In degrees it is $1/32 \times 360 = 11$ degrees. Similar calculations are done for the other five tally figures.

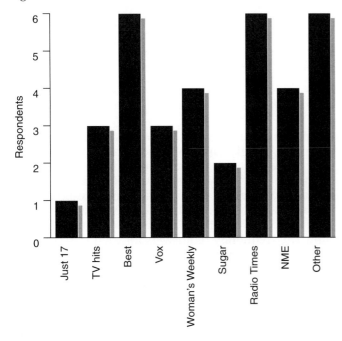

Figure 24.9 Data gathered from the questionnaire in Figure 24.3: magazines read by female respondents

Bar charts are good for showing the overall pattern of distribution of the numbers of items in each group (see Figure 24.9). When a bar chart is constructed so that the area of each bar is proportional to the number of items in that group, it is called a **histogram**.

Graphs can show straight lines between points, or curves. The latter are better for showing steady growth.

Drawing valid conclusions from research findings

A frequent problem with research is that too much information is collected! It is very easy to be side-tracked, especially when interviewing, into collecting material that may be interesting but is irrelevant as far as the research objectives are concerned.

Case study

The student conducting research on imported TV programmes (Figure 24.4) went back to his original research objectives and made brief notes about relevant research findings. Then he wrote more fully on the different aspects such as audience behaviour. Subsequently, in an evaluation of the research, he started drawing some conclusions. These he presented to an audience in a talk. Here are some extracts from his written work.

AUDIENCE BEHAVIOUR

From the BARB figures, from my own questionnaire's results, and from my interviews, it is plain to me that these imported programmes are very popular. This is easy to ascertain as the data are quantitative and so you can see it in black and white. A more difficult question to answer is *Why are they so popular?* This demands a qualitative reply and a questionnaire is not a good means of getting any answers to this. Books are okay as far as they go, but probably the best way to get an honest reply is in an interview situation. From my interviews it became clear that all soaps, but in particular imported ones, are watched for sheer escapism.

If you've just had a horrible day at work, perhaps got drenching wet from the rain on your way home, you can turn on the TV and get *Home & Away,* where it never rains, everyone's in summer clothes, having 'barbies', going to the beach and where everyone's problems usually get solved with a happy ending. If you tell an Australian person you watch *Neighbours,* you'll probably be asked why, because many say it's the worst programme they've got.

Consequently the theory which best describes people's attitudes towards this particular type of media is the main active one, *uses and gratifications.* This theory is based on the belief that the people who watch have certain needs (or uses) which they seek to satisfy (or gratify). The main needs are:

- **Diversion** – Escape or emotional relief from everyday life.
- **Personal relationships** – The show encourages companionship via its characters and sociability through discussion.
- **Personal identity** – Making comparisons with people or situations in the show.
- **Surveillance** – Seeking information about the world we live in.

This theory, though, assumes that individuals carefully plan what they watch. If one of your family is watching *Neighbours* in the living room and you happen to be sitting there, the chances are you'll watch it too, even if you're not really paying too much attention.

EVALUATION OF RESEARCH

I think that although I may have had preconceptions about how much imported TV there is, I think that I approached the research into this subject with an open mind, ready to accept the facts. I think that I dealt with the facts to hand in a professional, unbiased manner.

One of the first and most important facts I learnt about this topic from my research is that Channel 4 and ITV companies are regulated by the Independent Television Commission, or ITC, as to the percentage of transmission time that can be made up of 'foreign' programmes. In the age of 'Europe', foreign in this case means non-EC. Programmes can be exempted from this rule, however, if they are of a cultural or educational nature.

Up to midnight, overseas programmes can account for no more than 14% of total programming. After midnight no more than 25% of transmission time can be taken up by non-EC, non-exempt programmes.

Also the amount of overseas material permitted per year should be no more than 4 hours per week on average during the so called 'peak' viewing times:

Mon–Sat	6.30–10.30pm
Sun	7.15–10.30pm

The most recent data I have available, for the year 1991, indicates that both ITV and Channel 4 were well within these limits, showing on average just 2.5 hours per week during peak times.

So in a nutshell, although people often complain about the number of Australian soaps or American sitcoms on TV, this is in fact regulated to, in my opinion, very high standards.

There have also been fears that the import of these programmes jeopardises UK-produced programmes. According to recent BBC Broadcast Research data during 1993/94, the percentages of new (i.e. excluding repeats shown) UK-made programmes shown at peak times were:

BBC1	77%
BBC2	62%
ITV	75%
CH4	57%

I was quite pleased with the amount of data I located and studied for this project. I managed to find numerous books about soaps and imported TV both at the college's own library and at the main town library in Nuneaton. I also used the ordering facility for books kept at other libraries in the county.

By thinking of keywords such as 'American', 'soaps', 'imported' I was able to retrieve quite a few relevant articles from the information contained on the newspaper CD-ROM discs. The search also threw up lots of stories which were of no use, so these were discarded. I have highlighted the sentences in the print outs [not included here] which are particularly significant.

As I've previously stated, a lot of TV that is imported comes in the form of soap operas. As this was a major area, I researched the history of this type of programme as well as trying to find out why they are so popular. The answer to the question *Why are they popular?* can be found in the pages of this folder.

I also found out that soap operas are so called because when they first started on the radio in the 1920s they were aimed particularly at a female audience (fact) in the hope of selling them the latest soap (washing) powder. The length was originally only 15 minutes but later changed to 30 and in some cases 60 minutes. The transition from radio to television didn't come about until the late 1950s when the viewing public became disenchanted with the previously popular quiz shows.

Case study

It is also useful at this stage, before you begin your own investigations, to look at how a professional piece of research is put together and presented. What follows are edited extracts from a paper read by R.M. Worcester and B. Gosschalk (respectively chairman and managing director of the research company MORI, London) at a conference in America in 1994. The research concerns the British public's attitude to crime. First they establish why the research is of interest:

Context
Britain is obsessed with crime. Crime now occupies more space in the newspapers and gains more coverage in the broadcast media than ever before and competes for the splash in broadsheet newspapers as well as the tabloids. Qualitative research reveals that violence is the issue which people cite most frequently when asked what it is they dislike about life in Britain today; quantitative research confirms that crime/law and order, violence and vandalism are regarded as among the most important issues facing Britain today, coming only after unemployment.....

Notice the way in which they use statistics to support their interpretation of the facts:

Fear of crime has grown substantially over the past seven years. In particular, the fear of having one's home burgled (+17% to 77%), of being mugged (up 14% to 52%) and of having possessions stolen (also up 14%, to 38%) show significant increases in fears cited by the public in a 1994 MORI survey for Reader's Digest compared with the same questions asked seven years ago.

Then they discuss the role of television in people's lives:

The role of television
The broadcasting industry in Britain, as in many other countries, has grown significantly over the past decade. Technology developments in the 1980s led to the growth of new media channels and equipment accessible to the consumer market: cable and satellite television, video recorders, teletext and substantially increased television output all increased the competitiveness in this area. These developments have given more choice and more control over home entertainment to television viewers.

Survey research has monitored the growth in multi-set households, to the point where two in three own at least two television sets, ten percentage points higher than in 1991, while one in four have at least three sets in the household. Homes with children are substantially more likely to have more than one set; more detailed analysis shows that those in households with children aged 10–15 are most likely to have three or more sets (48%), compared with those with younger children (27%) or those without children in the home (23% – source: Independent Television Commission).

They reveal who has funded their research and cite other research done in this field:

Violence on factual television
The inter-relationship between television, violence and young people lay at the heart of the major study which the Broadcasting Standards Council (BSC) commissioned MORI to undertake in the summer of 1993 on the subject of violence in non-fictional programming.

The BSC's remit since its establishment in 1988 has been to deal with violence, sexual conduct and matters of taste and decency. The study's focus was the depiction of violence in television news, current affairs, reconstruction programmes and documentaries. The objectives of the survey were to assist the Council when reaching decisions on complaints, and to give guidance to broadcasters and programme-makers.

An extensive qualitative study had already been completed by Dr David Morrison of the Institute of Communications Studies at the University of Leeds, and these findings played an important part in the development of the quantitative survey....

They explain how their research was carried out so that the accuracy of the research can be assessed:

Methodology
The questionnaire was piloted in two stages. The first stage was a dynamic pilot at a central location in Cambridge. Six interviews were conducted, each observed by a researcher from the Broadcasting Standards Council or MORI. On the basis of these interviews and a discussion involving the researchers and the interviewers, the questionnaire was modified, and immediately retyped. A second set of six interviews was conducted, again with the researchers from MORI and the BSC observing. After further discussion and modification three more interviews were conducted. The client and the MORI researchers were thus able to appreciate the problems and dynamics of the interview and worked closely as a team to address the issues raised – a good illustration of cooperation to improve a complex study.

A draft questionnaire was now prepared for the second, more extensive stage of piloting. At the second stage the questionnaire was piloted in-home with the general public, selected with particular emphasis on the elderly and DE social classes, to ensure that no difficulties in question wording or comprehension would be encountered during the survey.

For the quantitative study, the first part of the questionnaire was split into two versions and administered to matched sub-samples. MORI interviewed a representative sample of 1296 adults aged 16 and over in 52 constituency sampling points in Great Britain from 4 to 22 September 1993. Quotas were set for video owners, as well as a 40-cell interlocking demographic quota, and a booster sample of satellite receivers was interviewed.

They report on the main findings, giving figures and interpreting these facts.

Key findings

.... When asked which of the three issues caused them most concern, the majority (56%) cited violence. One in four said bad language caused them most concern, while 15% said none of the three issues caused them particularly concern. Gender was the most important attitudinal discriminator, with women more likely to be concerned about each issue. This is particularly true with regard to concern about violence (see Table 4).

Table 4: Issues causing most concern: demographic variables

	Violence	Bad language	Sex	None of these
Total	56	24	12	15
	(%)	(%)	(%)	(%)
Male				
18–24	37	14	6	44
25–34	49	23	5	29
35–44	48	29	5	21
45–54	58	27	9	10
55–64	53	32	12	12
65+	52	38	10	8
Female				
18–24	60	18	7	19
25–34	70	17	3	12
35–44	70	23	12	3
45–54	70	27	15	5
55–64	51	30	23	3
65+	57	24	34	2

NB. Multiple answers permitted

They comment on difficulties that the researchers had:

The pilot study had shown how difficult many people found it to distinguish between violence on television in general, on the one hand, and violence in factual programmes on the other. This caused the researchers considerable difficulty in designing the questionnaire. The bottom line is that people think violence is violence, regardless of its source.

The most detailed part of the paper concentrates on giving data relating to the heart of the topic; i.e. violence on TV and the effects on behaviour:

Table 5: Attitudes to violence on television and effects on behaviour

	Strongly agree %	Tend to agree %	Neither/ DK %	Tend to disagree %	Strongly disagree %
Violence on TV simply reflects the state of society	24	51	7	14	4
Violence in factual TV makes people more ready to accept violence in real life	17	41	11	23	8
Watching violence in factual programmes has made me behave much more carefully	21	46	15	14	4
Violence on TV has made people unnecessarily afraid	13	43	11	27	6

Table 6 Attitudes to violence on television

Question: Violence on factual TV can make people more or less upset depending on the circumstances. Do you think people tend to be more or less upset if ...?

	% saying 'more upset'
The victim is particularly weak and vulnerable	85
The victim is someone like your own friends and neighbours	80
The reporter sounds genuinely upset about the violence	61
The music increases the dramatic effect	56
The violence is shown in a completely realistic way	44
The programme is of special interest to you	41
The violence is necessary to make it really clear what happened	35

	% saying 'less upset'
The victim deserves to be punished	42
You are told beforehand what is going to happen	42
You have seen it often already	39
The victim is partly to blame	38
The sounds are edited out	35
It is happening in another country	29

NB Omits answers below 25%

The facts are interpreted and conclusions drawn:

Younger people were less likely to feel threatened by violence and to believe that violence on factual television leads people to be more accepting of violence in real life.

Two in five say they feel differently about violence in factual programmes compared with fictional violence; just over half say they do not. The main reasons for feeling different relate to the reality of violence on factual programmes and a widespread sense that fictional violence is unnecessary, or exaggerated, or simply for entertainment. The study tested the hypothesis raised in the qualitative phase with a series of questions exploring whether people perceive different circumstances as having a more or less upsetting effect on the viewer. Table 6 shows how clearly the public differentiates between varying situations.

In particular, people find violence on factual television more upsetting if the victim is weak or vulnerable, or

someone like their own friends and neighbours. Production features can also impact on attitudes; for example, the dramatic effect of music and the degree of sympathy in the reporter's voice both affect the response of viewers. On the other hand, knowing in advance what is going to happen, and believing the victim deserves to be punished, led to a feeling of being less upset. In the qualitative research many participants commented on the frequent re-runs of the Rodney King beating; quantitatively the survey found the frequent exposure led to two in five feeling less upset by violent scenes.

The qualifications of the authors are given. You should note that they draw not only on research done by MORI but on other books and journals.

Robert M Worcester is Chairman of MORI (Market & Opinion Research International), Visiting Professor of Government at LSE (London School of Economics and Political Science) and at the Graduate Centre for Journalism at City University, London. An American, he is a past president of WAPOR (1982–84) and is an Editor of the *International Journal of Public Opinion Research.* He is the author of *British Public Opinion: A Guide to the History and Methodology of Opinion Polling.*

Brian Gosschalk is Managing Director of MORI. An Oxford honours graduate, he is a Member of the Council of WAPOR and is co-editor of *Political Communications and the British General Election of 1992.*

References
1. MORI survey for *The Times* of London, January 1994

2. Gunter, B. and Svennevig, M. (1988): *Attitudes to Broadcasting Over the Years,* London: John Libbey & Co.

3. Lee, R. (1975): Credibility of newspapers and TV news: *Journalism Quarterly,* 55, pp. 282–287

4. Gunter, B., Sancho-Aldridge, J. and Winstone, P. (1994): *Television: The Public's View 1993,* London: John Libbey & Co.

5. Millwood Hargrave, A. (1993): *Violence in Factual Television – BSC Annual Review 1993,* London: John Libbey & Co.

Evidence assignment

You should conduct at least two pieces of audience research relating to media products made during the course. One should investigate attitudes and the other the consumption of a media product. This can also provide evidence for Element 4 of Units 3, 4 and 5 (Chapters 12, 16 and 20), Element 2 of Unit 7 (Chapter 26), Element 2 of Unit 6 (Chapter 22) and Element 4 of Unit 1 (Chapter 4).

The purpose of the research could be:

- for planning a new product (e.g. What similar TV programmes do viewers watch, and why?)
- for evaluating the success of your product (e.g. What did your readers like about your print product, and why?)
- for making a marketing plan (e.g. How much are people prepared to spend on a new magazine and what will encourage them to buy it?)
- for investigating how narrative structures can affect how audiences understand the meaning of a text (e.g. What do you think was the main point of this video? Would you have found it easier to understand if the information/story was presented in a different way? What did you like/dislike about the characters/presenter?)
- for describing how individuals and groups respond to a selected media text (e.g. Do parents notice their children behaving more aggressively after watching cartoons?)

In the research you should:

a   state clearly your research objectives
b   assess the feasibility of your investigations, considering the resources needed
c   explain why you chose certain research methods
d   describe how you developed research instruments such as questionnaires
e   give details of the sample chosen
f   log information and data as they are obtained
g   analyse the findings
h   draw conclusions from your research.

A summary of this research can be added to your production handbook.

Investigating and Carrying Out Audience Research and Analysis: Unit Test

Audience research looks at people's attitudes and behaviour. Below are some examples of areas that might be investigated. Use them to answer questions 1–3.
  a which parts of a newspaper are read
  b which newspapers women buy
  c how much people are prepared to spend on a paper
  d who else reads a newspaper besides its purchaser

1 Which of these areas of investigation will help someone planning a new newspaper to find out if there is a gap in the market for a new, upmarket paper?

2 Which will help to find out how many consumers use a product?

3 Which will help to decide what type of contents to include in a new publication?

4 Which of the following questions is an example of quantitative research?
  a why do you go to the cinema rather than rent a video?
  b how many romantic films have you seen this year?
  c how have horror films affected you in the past?
  d what makes you laugh in comedy thrillers?

5 Which method is best for obtaining statistical information?
  a simulation exercises
  b case studies
  c focus groups
  d questionnaires

6 Decide whether each of these statements is true or false.
  i it is easier to interview people than to design a good questionnaire
  ii interviews are usually better than questionnaires for collecting qualitative information about individuals

Which of the answers below is correct?

  a i is true and   ii is true
  b i is true and   ii is false
  c i is false and   ii is true
  d i is false and   ii is false

7 Which of the following would make interviewers or observers **least** effective?
  a they talk all the time
  b they write down what they see or hear
  c they remain unbiased
  d they cannot come to a conclusion

8 What could be a major problem with any case study, e.g. one about a magazine producer in a study of media ownership?
  a it might not provide enough statistics
  b it might not be typical
  c it might not be interesting
  d it might not have the producer's permission

9 Which of the following information can be found from the Audit Bureau of Circulations?
  a the age of readers
  b the addresses of newsagents
  c the cost of a magazine
  d the type of adverts in newspapers

10 Which of the following information can be found in National Readership Surveys?
  a what sort of person buys the newspaper abroad
  b weekly circulation figures
  c how many people read books, magazines and newspapers
  d the shopping behaviour of readers

11 The *Hamley Herald and Journal* is a free newspaper. Which organisation checks its distribution figures?
  a VFD
  b OAA
  c NRS
  d CAA

12 For which of the following are statistics produced by the Broadcasters Audience Research Board?
a television, film and video
b terrestrial, cable and satellite television
c all television and radio stations
d British and international viewing figures

13 Which group of people is excluded from the RAJAR listening figures?
a people living in Scotland
b people who listen to commercial radio stations
c children under the age of sixteen
d people who listen to a station for under an hour per week

14 Who commissions research on posters?
a JICPAR
b JICRAR
c CAVIAR
d MORI

15 How does the Cinema Advertising Association get its admissions data?
a by issuing questionnaires to the public
b by phoning cinema operators
c through interviews with the film industry
d through observation studies of audiences and adverts

A lot of research into audience behaviour is carried out by independent organisations. Below are some examples. Use them to answer questions 16–18.

a the public's views on whether television gave too much coverage of the World Cup
b statistics on how many people have not renewed their satellite subscriptions
c reports on how much young children are influenced by bad language on television
d the number of hours people listen to BBC rather than commercial radio

16 Which of these would you expect to be carried out by an official research body such as RAJAR?

17 Which would be carried out by an opinion poll organisation such as Gallup for a tabloid?

18 Which would be carried out by a pressure group such as NVLA?

19 A model of audience behaviour cites the effect of propaganda on the masses as evidence to support its theories. What is the name of the model?

a uses and gratifications
b activist
c influential
d hypodermic needle

20 What does the active theory claim?
a that the media deliberately control us
b that we do not all react to the media in the same way
c that we are unaffected by the media
d that we don't pay attention to the media

21 What do we mean when we talk about the dominant reading of a documentary by a viewer?
a the viewer understood what was said but disagreed
b the viewer believed the message intended by the producer
c the viewer concentrated whilst the programme was on
d the viewer was able to interpret the message in his or her own way

22 When we are evaluating a book about the influence of the Internet on children, which of the following is most important to consider?
a the age of the book
b where the book was published
c the length of the book
d the cost of the book

23 What do the figures below show?

Hours per week spent by women watching TV								
	1987	1988	1989	1990	1991	1992	1993	1994
BBC1	9.9	10.0	10.0	9.5	9.5	9.8	9.24	8.96
BBC2	3.0	2.8	2.6	2.4	2.6	2.8	2.59	2.66
ITV	11.7	11.8	11.5	11.7	12.2	12.7	11.90	11.69
C4	2.2	2.4	2.2	2.2	2.6	2.9	2.94	2.87
TOTAL TV	**26.8**	**27.0**	**26.3**	**25.8**	**26.9**	**28.1**	**26.67**	**26.11**

a fewer women are watching TV
b women are watching C4 less
c the average woman spends less time watching TV
d television is becoming less popular in Britain

24 Which of the following is the best way to show a trend in consumer figures?
a a pie chart
b a tally chart
c a line graph
d an ideogram

25 One study calculates that in 2005 the average number of hours of television watched by each person per day could be the same as now. However, the overall number of hours watched by all viewers could be less than now. What is the most likely interpretation of these results?
a television has become too expensive
b the results are inaccurate
c people have become bored with television
d the population has dropped

26 What is most likely to increase the sales of a glossy magazine for one week?
a placing a poster outside the shop
b giving away a free gift
c dropping the price by 10p
d a special offer on subscriptions

27 What can a newsagent do that is most likely to increase the sales of a children's comic?
a change its position on the shelf so that it is near the sweets
b drop the price by five pence
c advertise it on local radio
d personally recommend it to parents

28 You are carrying out research on how often students listen to radio. What essential information should be included in a questionnaire?
a a promise of anonymity
b details about yourself
c where and when the form is to be returned
d how the information given will be analysed

29 Which research method for monitoring audience behaviour will require the least resources, in terms of staff and money, for collecting the data over a long period of time?
a questionnaires
b interviews
c focus discussion groups
d asking people to keep diaries

30 The sampling frame for British people who watch BBC2 is:
a all the people who watch BBC
b the names and addresses of people who watch BBC2
c all members of the population
d the name and address of every member of the British population

All media products are intended for an audience. Sometimes that audience will seek out the product or stumble on it by accident, but successful media producers will actively market the product and draw it to the attention of potential users. They will not want its success to rely on chance encounters or the whims of the public. The media is a highly competitive business and vast resources are spent on marketing. The ways in which producers create and keep audiences are described below.

You will be expected not only to understand what is involved in the marketing of professional media products, but also to be able to construct and carry out a marketing plan for one of your own media products. You will find the research techniques described in Units 2 and 6 to be helpful as well as Chapters 12, 16 and 20 in the production units. If you have also studied Chapter 22 (audience behaviour) in Unit 6, you will have a good basis for developing and implementing your own marketing strategy.

Chapter 25

Analyse the role of marketing in the media

This chapter looks at what media companies aim to do in order to market their product effectively and how they achieve these aims. It considers what is meant by marketing and discusses the various methodologies employed by professional businesses. There are case studies of the various methods used by media producers and how they choose and mix their marketing activities.

Aims of marketing

Many people think that marketing is basically advertising and selling. These are certainly part of it but marketing is something much more. Advertising and selling are concerned with disposing of the product once it is made. Marketing, however, starts much earlier – at the strategic planning stage.

The key factors involved in marketing are:

- **anticipating audience needs** – finding out what customers will want, even before they realise they want it!
- **satisfying audience expectations** – this entails knowing the likes and dislikes of the customers; how they want to use products and where they want them; what price they are willing to pay.
- **generating income or profit** – making money is essential for all commercial products, if only to cover the cost of wages and materials in order to finance further products. Media producers funded by the state or charitable organisations may not need to make a profit but will have to verify that money has been spent wisely. They will also have to show that the product offers value for money

for the funding body in terms of its purpose, propaganda or profile raising, etc.

- **maximising benefit to the organisation** – in addition to making a profit or striving to be cost effective, marketing should also enhance the image of the organisation itself.
- **managing effects of change and competition** – organisations and their products need to anticipate changes in the market-place or to respond to economic and political changes.
- **utilising technological developments** – it is vital that organisations stay in touch with their markets. Huge improvements in technology, particularly information technology and telecommunications, have vastly improved market research techniques through the gathering and processing of marketing information. Marketing and advertising can be targeted far more precisely than was possible previously. Advertising for numerous products, including magazines and newspapers, music CDs and computer software, are now found on cable and satellite channels.
- **enhancing audience perception of the product** – the consumer should be convinced that this is a desirable, quality product that can be identified with their lifestyle.
- **enhancing audience perception of the organisation** – it is not only the product itself but the organisation that produces or distributes it which should have a high status with the user. So, for example, the BBC promotes itself through trailers of forthcoming series as a producer of quality period drama generally.

This may seem straightforward enough, but it is in fact difficult to get right. Sometimes a seemingly well-researched idea – which ought to satisfy all of the above – will flop, whereas something else will be a surprise success.

Activity

The BBC soap *Eldorado* proved to be an expensive failure, whereas the adult comic *Viz* has been a runaway success. With a partner, draw up a list of other successful and unsuccessful media products.

Consider the list of points above and make a note of how you think the products you have named met or failed them.

The Chartered Institute of Marketing gives us the following definition:

> *Marketing is the management process responsible for identifying, anticipating and satisfying customer requirements profitably.*

If we look at this definition more closely we can identify certain key words.

First, the word **management** is used. This shows that marketing is very important and is therefore something that senior members of an organisation should be responsible for.

The words **identify** and **anticipate** indicate that research is needed to find out what people want, *before* the product is made. And **profitably** reminds us that giving the customer what they want should be achieved while maximising benefit to the organisation.

A key phrase is **anticipating audience needs**. In order to be successful, media products need to reach their target audience or consumer. Matching up the target audience with the product is the basis of marketing. Therefore the needs of different audiences have to be explored.

Maslow's hierarchy of needs

Abraham Maslow was a psychologist who developed a theory of human needs. In 1954 he proposed that

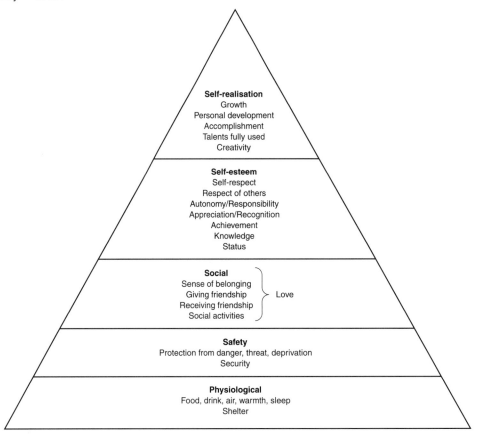

Figure 25.1 Maslow's hierarchy of needs

people have various levels of physical and psychological needs and these tended to be structured in a hierarchy, as illustrated in Figure 25.1.

As you can see, we start with very basic, physical needs, such as food and shelter and security, but as these are satisfied people yearn for other forms of fulfilment, such as the love and respect of others, until they read the highest stage which is self-fulfilment (Maslow called this self-actualisation). Different media products satisfy these different levels of needs.

Maslow's theory has also clearly influenced how advertisers target their audiences. People are categorised in a variety of different ways. Chapter 5 describes pyschographic groupings, dividing people into mainstreamers, aspirers, succeeders and reformers. Another method used by researchers is socio-economic groupings, which makes use of the A, B, C1, C2, D and E classification (as explained in Chapter 21).

Activity

Working in small groups of three or four, choose a film, a TV programme, a newspaper and a magazine. Discuss what type of needs they fulfil. Then suggest which sort of lifestyle group and which socio-economic group they are intended for.

Customer utility

Products can be divided into two categories: tangible and intangible. This unit covers the audio-visual, print and new media industries. Media products are often *intangible,* i.e. a service, rather than a physical product. For example, you go to watch a film, or you listen to a radio show. However, you can often end up with a *tangible* product, such as when you buy a video or CD or a magazine. It does not really matter whether the product is tangible or intangible, what is important from the customer's point of view is whether they will obtain **utility** (also referred to as *benefits* or *satisfaction)* from the product.

It is the concept of customer utility that is really at the heart of marketing. Marketing is a **customer-orientated activity**. It is the identification and even anticipation of customer needs that drives the marketing concept.

Concepts of change

The world is constantly changing, in terms of populations, tastes and fashion and expectations. When the telephone, for example, was first invented, it was thought of by many influential people as nothing more than an amusing gimmick. Since then it has revolutionised communication and is thought of more as a basic necessity rather than a luxury, and certainly not as a toy. Similarly, in Tsarist Russia the development of cinematography was given very little credence by Nicholas II. When the Communist revolution swept through this huge empire, their leaders Lenin and Trostsky understood the immense propaganda value of this organ of mass communication. They harnessed its power to reach out to the diverse millions of people with all their different languages, dialects and customs.

As well as social and cultural changes, there are also political and economic developments, which all add to the immensely complicated patterns of changing behaviour and attitudes.

Thus if people and markets are constantly changing, then businesses should also change. The dynamic outside environment means that organisations cannot afford to become static. Instead they too must be dynamic in order to keep up with changes and even anticipate them. It is the flexible, innovative organisations that are able to stay ahead and deliver utility to the customer.

Marketing activities used by media industries

The main marketing activities include the following:

- **research** – about the product; about the audience/consumer
- **communication** – this includes advertising, public relations, sales promotion and direct selling
- **product design** – for new products; for updating existing products
- **pricing** – considering what the customer can afford; relating to how much the product costs to make
- **sales packaging** – this is the overall physical image of the product. Media products such as TV channels, videos, radio stations, newspapers and so on are all 'packaged' by the way they are presented to us with their logos, jingles, page layouts, and in fact their 'house style' generally

■ **dissemination** – product awareness and understanding. It is important to know what the product is about and where to obtain it.

Obviously media products can be very different and so the way they are marketed will also vary. For example, marketing a pop video will be different from marketing a TV current affairs programme. Therefore the mixture of activities that make up marketing will be different. This is called the **marketing mix** and it consists of the following 'ingredients':

Product, Price, Place and Promotion

This is often referred to as the four Ps. However the four Ps have now been joined by the letter S for 'service' as this takes into account the importance of after-sales support. The 4 Ps involve the following factors:

■ **product** – design, style, colour, packaging and presentation
■ **price** – discounts and promotional offers
■ **place** – wholesalers, retailers, stock levels, transportation, distribution and access
■ **promotion** – personal selling, advertising, publicity and PR (public relations).

Case study: *New Woman*

In this case study we will look at the marketing mix (i.e. the four Ps) for the magazine *New Woman*.

Product – This is a glossy magazine. It is more upmarket than, for example, *Woman's Own*. It is aimed at women between the age of twenty and forty who have either a full- or part-time job. These women are fairly affluent with money to spend on leisure activities, fashion and make-up. Although articles do cover serious issues, they tend to be less intellectual or demanding than those in a magazine such as *Marie Claire*. The sexual content of the magazine is high. The editor has stated, 'the sex features we run are funny, informative, realistic, supportive, often voyeuristic, but never exploitative (which is more than can be said of the way some newspapers approach women and sexuality)'. There are 170 pages in the September issue and there are sections on health and beauty, men, living and fashion. The many adverts are mainly concerned with fashion and health products.

As is typical with general-interest magazines for women, the front cover has a close-up photograph of the face of a beautiful young woman.

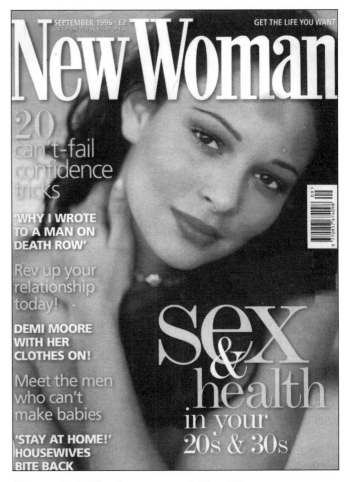

Figure 25.2 The front cover of *New Woman*

Place – It can be purchased at newsagents, supermarkets, garages, etc. Also direct through the post.

Price – £2.00 or £24 for a year's subscription, including postage. In September's issue there is a special offer, a reduction of 10 per cent for the 12 issues and a free gift.

Promotion – The September issue had a free gift, i.e. two mini paperback books of erotic fiction, specially commissioned and produced for the magazine.

Using this analysis as your starting point choose another media product (for example a new TV or radio programme, computer software or a magazine) and identify the 4 Ps.

Market research

When marketing, the first move is to identify what is needed (or wanted) and the customers who need this. The way that companies try to keep ahead and anticipate trends is through **marketing research**.

There are numerous activities classified under marketing research. Broadly speaking the research can be classified as either primary or secondary research. (You should look at Unit 6 for more detailed information on research methods.) Primary research takes place when there are no previous data to work from so the information needed has to be gathered from scratch. Secondary research relies on already existing data.

The data are gathered by experiment, observation or survey. In large organisations marketing research will be part of a **marketing information system** which also includes research carried out on competitors and on the economic, political and legislative environment.

In practical terms, research is carried out by taking a sample of the **population**. In research terms, the word 'population' means the whole of something from which you take a sample. It can literally refer to the human population of a geographical area, which could be the whole country or perhaps a city or county. On the other hand it could mean, for example, the number of homes with satellite dishes, or the number of poster sites in a certain area. The population is sometimes referred to as the **universe**.

Market research is needed for the decision-making process. You must ask the right questions, from the right population sample and draw the right conclusions. Marketing is a **strategic** activity. This means that it is of central importance and should be part of the overall business plan of an organisation. A marketing information system is therefore needed to obtain a picture of the economic, political, cultural and legislative environments within which an organisation's target markets reside.

Sources of information

Unit 6 gives you information on the various organisations concerned with audience research. Other information that can affect the decision-making process can also be obtained from more general sources and should not be overlooked. These include the following.

- *The A–Z of UK Marketing Data* gives information on products by area, market size, etc.
- *British Business,* produced weekly by the Department of Trade and Industry, gives statistics on UK markets.
- The Office of Population, Censuses and Surveys

provides statistics on population, occupation and economic groups. It is based on counties.
- HMSO (Her Majesty's Stationery Office) produces a whole range of publications useful to the marketer. Among them are *Annual Abstract of Statistics, Monthly Digest of Statistics, Economic Trends, Social Trends, Regional Trends, National Income and Expenditure, General Household Survey, Family Expenditure Survey, OECD Main Economic Indicators.*
- *BRAD* (British Rate and Data) gives details of all magazines (general, specialist and trade) including circulation figures, advertising rates, names and addresses, etc.

In addition there are the *Yellow Pages* and *Thomson's Local* directories which are useful publications to start with.

Market segmentation

It is time now to introduce the idea of **segmentation**. Markets can and should be broken down into smaller markets, which we can call market segments. This means that there are often products which can be **differentiated**. Take the video market for example. This can be broken down into lots of different market segments. The demand for these can come from young people, the middle-aged, elderly, rich, poor, male, female, etc. Markets can also be segmented geographically, or by personality type (psychographic), ethnicity, etc. Therefore the product can be differentiated into, for example, SF, western, crime, thriller, chiller, horror, romance, in order to match the particular market segment at which it is aimed.

Newspapers are another good example: a newspaper tries to differentiate itself from other newspapers both by its content and its image. A mass circulation paper will, ideally, try to appeal to as much of the market as it can. In other words, it will get as many and as broad a section of people as possible to read it. However, there will still be a core market which will be the main target for the marketing efforts of the newspaper.

Activity

Papers are classed as either popular or quality, alternatively called tabloid or broadsheet because of the size of the paper. However, there are also tabloid-sized papers that do not fit into either category. An example of this would be the now defunct *Today.*

Make lists of all the national daily newspapers, categorising them as popular, quality or mid-range. Identify their core markets. In other words, what kind of people read each of these papers?

Newspapers also have different sections within them which appeal to different people.

Activity

Make a list of the different reasons why people buy a newspaper. It will help if you refer to Unit 1: Investigating the Content of Media Products.

Test marketing is a form of research. The idea is to provide a product or service for a limited period of time, a limited area or a limited number of people. In other words, a sample. It allows you to find out whether people really are prepared to pay for your product or service and whether you are asking the right price.

Communication

This refers to how the organisation and the product itself communicates with the public. The numerous forms of communication include advertising, public relations, sales promotion and direct selling.

Advertising

This form of communication includes film posters, TV ads, etc. Chapters 27 and 28 deal with this in depth.

Activity

Over a week collect examples of advertisements for media products. You will need to record TV and possibly radio ads, as well as collect print ads. This material will be useful for Chapters 27 and 28.

Public relations

All media organisations need to consider their public image. Some organisations are large enough to justify having specialist PR departments. The BBC and some newspapers, will, in addition, have their own education departments, which are a form of PR. Many organisations will be associated with sports sponsorship or charitable causes.

In addition to dealing with the public, some organisations may be large enough to have a specific Press Relations function which covers dealings with the press, radio and television. This will often involve issuing press releases, but could also involve giving interviews and statements, including press conferences.

Case Study: Grotbags

In June 1991, Central Television sponsored a special needs concert held at Hinckley College. This took the form of a variety show performed by people with special needs themselves. The television company had a department which would give grants for community projects within the region. The money donated by Central paid for scenery, make-up, transport, prizes, etc. Central also arranged for Grotbags, a popular character from children's television, to star in the show. This was also good publicity for a new TV programme based on a character in her show called Norman the Nettle.

Figure 25.3 Grotbags at the concert

Figure 25.4 Concert ticket

Can you find an activity, event or organisation that your local newspaper or radio station supports?

Public relations is also about how the staff of an organisation, whether a receptionist, cinema attendant, reporter, camera operator or researcher, deal with the public in the course of their duties. The staff performing these duties are all representatives of their organisations and therefore need good communication skills when dealing with clients and the general public. In some roles they will require a high level of sensitivity. For example, the receptionists or telesales staff on a local newspaper have to deal with announcements of births, marriages and deaths and need to display politeness, tact and possibly sympathy whilst authenticating facts and asking for payment.

Public relations can also be damaged by prejudice and stereotyping, and by the poor personal behaviour and appearance of staff.

Activity

Choose a job role such as DJ, cinema box office clerk or video sales assistant. Make a list of six ways in which a person in that role could damage the organisation's image and six ways in which it could be improved.

Sales promotion

This aspect of media communications differs from advertising in one very important way. Advertising brings the customer to the product; for example, you see an advert for a film and as a result you go and watch the film. Sales promotion, on the other hand, brings the product to the people. Examples of sales promotions are free gifts and samples, special events and discounts and special offers (e.g. subscribe to a monthly magazine for a year and pay only for ten editions).

Competitions and sponsorship of events and organisations are also forms of sales promotion. In addition, merchandising promotes the product. For example, a film or band will often be promoted by the sales of tee-shirts, music, key rings, pens, wallcharts, etc.

Activity

What merchandising would you select to promote the video you have made (or plan to make) for Unit 5?

Direct selling

This takes place when the product is sold directly from the producer or distributor to the customer, without going through a shop or other agency. Examples of this would be mail-order catalogues for music CDs or audiotapes.

Product design

Product design needs to be continually re-assessed to cater for the changing tastes and needs of consumers, the economic climate and new production techniques. Products can quickly develop a dated look and their image can therefore suffer. New design can help to give a new lease of life to a product. Just about any feature of a product can be changed. This could include, for example, the size of typeface for a magazine, or the length of a sitcom. (See the key design features in each of the production units.)

Case study: *Punch*

The satirical magazine *Punch* reappeared in September 1996 after an absence of four years. The front cover (see Figure 25.5 on the next page) was remodelled using the successful style of the *New Yorker* magazine. This new image signalled the changes in both appearance and editorial style that have taken place within its covers. The use of better-quality paper, colour and graphics brought it more in line with other magazines. A move towards the more explicit humour that characterises *Private Eye* and *Viz* aimed to refresh the product for those who remembered the old *Punch* whilst at the same time attracting a new generation of readers.

Pricing

This is part of a product's marketing strategy. It means that there is a policy behind the price-setting for the product.

Most consumer products have to cover production costs and make a profit. However, for commercial media producers production costs are not covered by the sales of the product itself. Instead, most income

Figure 25.5 The cover of the new *Punch*

depends on advertising and sponsorship. For example, the *Leicester Mercury* would cost twice as much without its advertising income, and *The Guardian* might cost £5 instead of 45p.

There are numerous factors to take into account when considering a product's price. A very important issue is the price of similar rival products. However, products do not always compete on price. Some organisations will instead compete on after-sales service, quality or (as you will read below) on the image of the product.

A product may not even have to make a profit. It may be produced as a public service or even as a **loss leader** to help promote itself or its producer and win market share. In these circumstances the price may not even have to cover production costs.

Aspects of pricing

Other aspects of pricing policy include subscription and club membership. These help an organisation's financial and production planning by giving a more definite indication of how much of the product they will sell in a particular time period. If a magazine, for example, knows how many regular subscribers it has it will be able to cut down on wasteful excess production. Savings can then be passed on to the subscriber in the form of a reduced price. In addition, by offering discounts (such as 12 monthly issues of a magazine for the price of 10) to consumers who, for example, subscribe for a year and pay in advance, the consumer becomes 'tied in' to the product and also helps the producer's cash-flow.

Price can also be considered as a form of communication because the cost of a product makes a statement to the consumer, not only about the product itself but also about its image. Some products, such as perfume and designer clothes, like to give an image of luxury or exclusivity. This is reflected in the price, which can have far more of a profit margin built in than the actual production materials justify. Consumers expect (and often want) to pay over the odds for such items as it implies that they are part of the lifestyle suggested by the product. (For example, advertising for Stella Artois lager maintains that it is 'reassuringly expensive'.)

A significant number of women who buy *Vogue* magazine, for instance, cannot afford the lifestyle (clothes, make-up, holidays, restaurants and so on) promoted within it. However, they enjoy the luxury of the magazine itself.

Sales packaging

This is part of the product mix, along with size. The need is to make the product stand out. It is also part of marketing communication as it signals something about the product.

Dissemination

There are two aspects to be considered here. One involves **informing** the consumer about the product and the other concerns the **distribution** of that product.

How is the consumer informed?

- advertising
- promotions

- 'word of mouth' from other customers. Peer pressure is a powerful force in this respect and can be the deciding factor in watching, for example, a soap series or buying a computer game
- sales personnel, whether in shops or through direct selling, are vital to the dissemination of the product
- publicity, both from the producer and from other sources, such as film critics, reviews and reports and gossip columns.

How is the product distributed?

- do you use a transport system and, if so, do you have your own vehicles, or use others such as the Royal Mail as carriers?
- do you despatch direct from where the product is actually produced (e.g. where the magazine is printed or the CD is manufactured), or do you stock it in different depots or warehouses?
- will the product go direct to the customer's home or premises, or to a retail outlet?

You can read more about distribution under **place** (see page 426) which is part of the 'four Ps' of the marketing mix. Examples can also be found in the *Leicester Mercury* case study on page 445.

Marketing principles

There are certain **marketing principles** which apply to all products, whether media-related or general. These have to be taken into consideration if the product is new or if it is in competition with other products. Sometimes products have to be adapted in order to appear original. Conversely they may also have to be adapted to bring them in line with a current trend.

Product life-cycle

Like people, products are born, they grow up and develop. They take on certain characteristics, develop a personality, change into something a little bit different (or even a lot different!), and eventually die.

Development | Growth | Maturity | Saturation | Decline

Figure 25.6 Graph to show product life-cycle

The duration of the life-cycle varies according to the product. Some products last longer than others: Horlicks has been around for decades, while other products, such as chart-orientated pop songs, have only a short life expectancy. Indeed some products, like most pop music and fashion garments, are conceived with the assumption that they will be replaced by another music or fashion product after a relatively short time.

Activity

Think of a TV programme that was a cult hit for a short while and another that has been popular for a decade or more. Can you suggest reasons for changes in the latter that can explain its survival?

Consider the drink Lucozade, for example. Originally this was produced and sold as a medicinal drink for sick people. It came in large glass bottles and was associated with illness. This image never changed and it began to lose sales. It has since been successfully marketed as an athletic, young person's drink. It comes in cans or small bottles and is associated with health. Since then it has gone further and appeals as a fun, youthful drink. The ads are more surreal but are basically competing more directly with Coke and Pepsi with their use of energetic music, and colourful images of youthful people having a seriously good time.

This marketing process is called **re-positioning**, because Lucozade was placed into a different market segment: youth and vitality. This does not mean that only young, fit people buy it. Indeed, it is also bought by the not-so-young and not-so-fit, because what they are actually buying is an image which makes them *feel* good.

It is this **image** that is so important in the marketing of a product, and so difficult to get right. Even when it is right it rarely stays that way. Images go out of date quickly and if the organisation is not continuously monitoring its product the product itself can easily develop a stale image. Again, this can be constantly seen in the transient worlds of fashion and popular music.

It cannot be assumed that products will go on indefinitely. Therefore a product has to be monitored, changes made, and new ones developed in readiness to take over. This steering of a product, and monitoring and updating it, is termed **product management**.

Product portfolio matrix

A useful way of looking at a product's position in the market is called the Product Portfolio Matrix, which was developed by the Boston Consulting Group. It is sometimes referred to as the Boston Box. It divides products into four categories, as shown in Figure 25.7. As you can see, a Star product has high growth and a high market share; Cash Cows are successful products which have reached maturity and now provide a steady income; a Problem Child is a product with potential but which is encountering difficulties and a Dog product is one which has very little going for it in terms of growth or market share. It may, however, still provide a source of profit but is obviously on the way out and not a candidate for investment.

Case study: Pop music

Some performers may still be popular on the live circuit but no longer sell the quantity of records that make them attractive to record producers.

Examples might be:

- star product – Oasis
- cash cow – Paul McCartney
- problem child – Dodgy
- dog product – Gerry and the Pacemakers.

Relative market growth

Market share	High	Low
High	STAR	CASH COW
Low	PROBLEM CHILD	DOG

Figure 25.7 The Product Portfolio Matrix

Products can and often will go through the different categories in the matrix. Today's *rising star* for example, will most likely become tomorrow's *cash cow*. The cash cow can then be used to support another star financially or perhaps a *problem child* if the 'problem' is finance.

Trends in the market-place

Product performance and changes in the market-place are analysed for developing trends. Product life-cycle strategy can concern either a plan for new products to come on to the market at certain appropriate intervals, or for changes, whether in content or image (or more likely both) to an existing product. Again, Lucozade is a classic example of this.

Media celebrities, such as film and pop stars, are often invented or re-invented in this way. For example, the 1960s pop band the Monkees were 'manufactured' for a zany TV series as America's answer to the Beatles. Members were chosen for their appearance and personality rather than their musical or acting abilities and had never played as a group before appearing in the TV series.

Media marketing of film

If we take a media product such as a film, we can see how the principles of marketing apply at all stages of its production and distribution.

Initially there is an idea, but to turn this idea into a film takes not just hard work and creativity, it also takes money – and usually lots of it. Therefore, the idea must be **viable**. This means it should be a good commercial proposition and not just good artistically. The film will need financing, either by a film studio or banks, and the financial backers will have to be convinced that it is a worthwhile investment.

In order to make a viable film the producer must have an identifiable **target audience** in mind which will be sufficient to cover the costs. As a rule of thumb, a film should **gross** (that is, revenue before expenditure is subtracted) two and a half times what it costs to make in order to be reasonably sure of making a profit.

Therefore, the first stage of marketing, the market research, needs to be carried out in order to establish the target audience. Once this has been achieved, the scripts are written and the actors and actresses chosen. As part of the marketing strategy, big star names are often used to **promote** the film.

After the film has been made the next stage is **distribution**, which brings together the film and the potential audience.

What makes you want to go and see a film? Think of some films you have been to see recently. What was it that made you want to see them? Below are some possible reasons for being influenced. How do they match up with your reasons for films you have seen?

- the actors and actresses
- the director
- the posters
- the film title
- TV advert
- radio advert
- newspapers and magazine advertising
- promotional 'trailers' at a cinema
- friends' recommendations.

The chances are there was more than one reason although one will probably stand out.

It is usually the film distributor who is responsible for marketing the film both to the public and also to the **exhibitors**. Prints of the film have to be made and these cost around £1000 each. Therefore a film being exhibited in 100 cinemas across the country would cost £100 000 before it could actually be shown.

The distributors identify the target audience. Even though this would have been done at the pre-production ideas stage, it would still be necessary to evaluate the final product and make adjustments as necessary.

Advertising

An advertising campaign is then aimed at the target audience. You should note that advertising can be classed as either **direct** or **indirect**. Adverts such as TV and radio commercials, posters, and classified and display ads in newspapers are direct advertising, whereas features and interviews are ways of indirectly advertising a product to the public.

For example, if the film was to be an adaptation of *Coronation Street,* the target audience would be from their late twenties onwards and with an emphasis on women. It would be advertised on mainstream TV chatshows (indirect advertising) and the press, including such magazines as *TV Times, Radio Times, Titbits, Weekend* and *Woman's Own.*

How would you advertise a film like the *Police Academy* series? Identify the target audience and the types of TV programmes, radio shows, magazines and newspapers where you would be most effective in reaching that audience.

The **television** is the most popular medium but it is also the most expensive for advertisers. High-budget films are, however, often advertised, usually by using a 'trailer'. The advert is scheduled to reach its target audience. For example, a film about the late Formula One racing driver Ayrton Senna would probably be advertised during a sports programme.

Radio is a far cheaper advertising medium and has its own strengths because it can promote the film by playing the soundtrack. In fact, the soundtrack often becomes a product in its own right, with its own merchandising, as well as helping to promote the film. In addition, local radio is also useful for attracting the audience, not only to the film itself but to its local venue.

The **poster** campaign is central to the advertising campaign. The artwork is the 'key art' and is used in the various posters and TV ads to give a unifying image. The posters will have catchphrases (known as **tag lines**). The writing (copy) will also consist of quotes from critics and list the achievements of the members of the cast or production unit.

As well as advertising to the public the distributors also have to attract the attention of **critics**. One way is to release a press pack which contains stills (photographs) from the film with details about the cast and film crew, a synopsis (brief summary of what the film is about), and any titbits that will help to stir up curiosity.

For example, during the filming of *Psycho* (Paramount, 1960) it was rumoured that its producer and director, Alfred Hitchcock, was trying to buy up all the copies of the book on which the film was based, so people would not know the ending. Whether this was true or not, it still had the desired effect of making people curious and thus providing more publicity. For this Hitchcock needed the press and the other media to help create the need to see the film. Another publicity stunt was to claim that all members of the cast had to swear an oath of secrecy. Again, he relied on the press to publish these stories and thus publicise the film. Yet another technique was to play a recording of Hitchcock's voice to the audience as they left the cinema asking people not to reveal the ending of the film, 'because it's the only one we've got' – thus making the audience itself part of the publicity campaign.

The press would also be invited to preview showings of the film and to press conferences, or even exclusive interviews with the stars.

Further promotion of the film will take place using **merchandise**, such as tee-shirts, toys, costumes, etc. The film *Batman* generated Batman and Robin outfits, ranges of confectionery products, posters, cards, snacks, etc. and is but one example of how big-budget films are promoted through other products, often in association with other organisations, such as McDonald's.

'Going to the movies'

When we look at the reasons why people go to see films, we should consider reasons that may not be to do with the film itself. It can also be about where it is being shown and the whole image associated with a visit to the movies.

Cinemas have changed considerably in recent years. Although they are still to be found in the centre of our towns and cities, the multiplex has proved itself very popular with cinema-goers. This is because a multiplex cinema has a large number of screens (usually eight to ten), with a strong emphasis on comfort and attractiveness. It is often part of a larger recreational environment where people can eat at a burger or pizza bar and play arcade games or 10-pin bowling. There may also be a restaurant and shops. In business terms this is called **external economies of scale**.

To help market their products, exhibitors will stagger the start times so that if one film is sold out a customer can choose another. A film product can be **positioned** or re-positioned by placing it at particular cinemas, or moving it from one area to another or, for example, from a larger to a smaller auditorium as it moves through its **product life-cycle**. The film can still continue to make a profit and thus maximise its returns to investors but it no longer needs the same resources.

The size of the auditoria is also part of **segmenting** the market, by providing films for both mainstream and more minority tastes and the appropriately sized venues to cater for this demand.

The aim of a multiplex is to cater for as much of the total market as possible and to do this by **differentiating** the film product and **segmenting** the market for these films into different audiences.

Marketing approaches used by media producers

In this section you will be looking at how different organisations market their particular products. You will notice a variety of marketing activities which have been chosen to provide a 'mix' for different occasions and time-scales. These may or may not vary according to whether the product is audio-visual or print-based.

Case study: Radio City

Radio City is a Liverpool-based commercial station broadcasting throughout Merseyside, the North-West of England and North Wales. This gives it a potential audience of over two million people. It actually consists of two radio stations: 96.7 City FM and Radio City 1548 AM.

Before the Broadcasting Act of 1988 many stations used to broadcast on more than one frequency, usually on FM and AM. This act, however, stipulated that these stations would have to release one of the frequencies

Figure 25.8 City FM presenter Tony Snell

for other purposes. Some stations came to agreements with other organisations so that they could use the AM frequency. This is the case with Leicester Sound, which gave up their FM frequency to Sunrise Radio, which is an Asian network based in London.

Most stations, however, decided to make use of this extra facility to create another service, which meant they could target their programmes more precisely. This is the strategy that Radio City adopted. In other words, they segmented the market for radio in their region and offered a differentiated service on the AM frequency.

The market is segmented demographically so that Radio City offers a service to two overlapping age groups. City FM plays music from the 1980s and 1990s, with strong news and sports coverage, and aims this at the 15–40-year-old market segment. Radio 1548 AM plays hits from the last five decades aimed at the 35–55 age group.

A radio station has to run as a business. It does not just consist of the presenters (DJs or 'jocks' as they are often known). These people, of course, are a vital part of the product; they reflect, and also shape, the 'personality' of the station.

Figure 25.10 Flyer for a nightclub promotion

Figure 25.9 Radio City promotions

But a commercial radio station needs money. In order to have money it needs listeners. This is because advertisers pay radio stations so that they can have their adverts played to the station's audience. The bigger the audience, the more money the radio station can expect to charge advertisers. The promotions and sales teams generate the awareness, interest and therefore the income. Without this there would be no station.

In order to obtain listeners the station must find out what people want. They carry out research to identify their target audience and then continue to carry out regular research in order to keep this audience and indeed expand it by widening its appeal. (See Unit 6 for more information on how radio research is carried out.)

All activity at the station is co-ordinated through a central administration system called **traffic**. The term 'traffic' comes from the flow of activity in a commercial station which is routed via Sales, to Programmes and then to Accounts. The person responsible for coordinating this is known as the **Traffic Controller**.

The listeners and the advertisers are both, in effect, customers for Radio City's 'products'. The marketing campaign is therefore aimed at both parties.

Promotional material targeted at the public includes posters, stickers, newspaper advertising and, of course, 'promos' broadcast by the station itself, as well as its roadshows and outside broadcasts from public events and shows.

Presenters behind the desk at clubs, as well as other 'celebrity' appearances, all maintain a high station profile and generate interest and loyalty.

Promotional material aimed at the advertisers is generally more detailed, and is supported by audience statistics.

RADIO CITY HEADLINE FIGURES (RAJAR QUARTER 4 – 1995)			
	Reach	*%*	*Avg Hours*
Total Radio City:			
Adults	660 000	36	13.6
96.7 City FM:			
Adults	501 000	27	13.3
ABC1s	208 000	29	11.0
C2DEs	292 000	27	15.0
Men	264 000	30	13.8
Women	267 000	25	12.8
Radio City 1548 AM:			
Adults	268 000	15	8.7
ABC1s	97 000	13	4.6
C2DEs	171 000	16	11.0
Men	131 000	15	8.4
Women	137 000	14	9.0

Figure 25.11 Radio City audience figures

Potential advertisers are provided with a folder or brochure, often called a 'media pack' which presents the results of audience research. Radio City now issues these on CD. Basically, the idea of an advertiser's

Figure 25.12 Radio City advertising

media pack is to sell the station to the advertisers by highlighting its strategy of keeping in touch with the community. The station seeks to demonstrate that it is providing the service which people want by showing that they are continually monitoring and reappraising the situation.

Once the airtime has been sold the station can actually produce the advert through its commercial production unit called Creative Services.

In marketing terms this is an example of giving a 'valued-added' service because the station is offering a

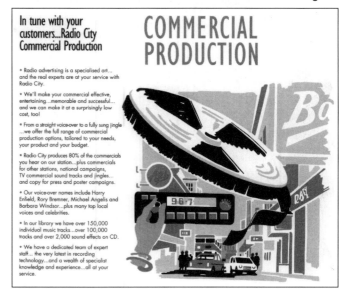

Figure 25.13 Promotional information on Radio City Commercial Production

Figure 25.14 Radio City's presenter Debi Jones

Radio City use a computer programme called **Selector** to help them produce their music mix. They first have to input the parameters regarding the target audience, such as the age group, sex, time of day, etc. The programme then prints out its selection of music keeping those parameters in mind. Additional conditions can be built-in; for example, the programme controller can stipulate that slow records are not played 'back-to-back' in the morning breakfast period.

News and comment can also be differentiated by giving it a local flavour. Radio City builds in a campaigning angle to its news, with regular extended bulletins and special documentaries. In addition to the news there is also the *City Action Desk* so that, with the help of their radio station, the audience can become involved in local issues.

Sports, weather and traffic news can, of course, be easily tailored to a local or regional audience. The

NEWS

All the news...round the clock on 96.7 City FM and Radio City Gold...bulletins on the hour and every 20 minutes at drive times ...plus newsbreaks for all the hot stories

• With a strong and experienced local team, and the national and international network of IRN - the radio subsidiary of ITN - wherever it happens, whenever it happens, Radio City News has it covered.

• The fastest, most comprehensive local news service is on Radio City...with the City News Team on the road in the radio cars to cover the action as it happens... and constant coverage of everything that really matters in the region.

• National and international news comes from the unbeatable Independent Radio News Service...with reporters and correspondents all around the world... a satellite service backed up by all the hot stories from Britain's Press Association.

• City News has a campaigning side, too - with regular extended bulletins and special documentaries covering issues of great importance to the region.

• Up to date and specially researched weather forecasts...the latest travel news... the best service around comes from City News.

NO WONDER THE NORTH WEST TUNES INTO RADIO CITY FOR ALL ITS NEWS!

Figure 25.15 Promotional information on Radio City News

'package' i.e. providing the advertising message itself and not just the advertising medium (i.e. radio airtime).

A good radio station has a 'personality', that is, certain characteristics and features which make it different and individual. All the ingredients of a station's output, such as the music mix, the news, comment, sports, traffic reports, combined with the personalities of the presenters, all blend together in successful stations to give that particular sound which identifies it to its followers and encourages listeners generally to identify with it.

In marketing terms this is known as **brand awareness** and it is continually cultivated by radio stations.

Let us start by looking at the music mix. This is a crucial area of activity and one that is continually being researched and monitored. A station chooses its music selection to fit in with a particular time of day and the audience that is listening in at that time. If their research shows that at a certain time of day the audience is mainly women then they will play the music that their research indicates that women prefer.

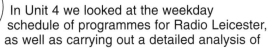

In a region famous for its sporting success, Radio City's coverage takes all the prizes...with all the local national and international action as it happens... in-depth analysis, discussion and phone-ins too

• Peak audience on the year-round Saturday afternoon show is over 70,000 - that's higher than the average home gates of our three major teams combined.

• Regular drive time bulletins keep the North West up to date with all the latest sports news and views.

• Live match commentaries follow the fortunes of Liverpool, Everton and Tranmere...Saturdays and midweek...plus all the goals and results from round the country, as they come in.

• Rugby, cricket and the other national sports get top coverage, too...and we don't neglect minority sports, local leagues and special events.

• Radio City has reporters on the spot wherever the sporting action is in the North West.

Figure 25.16 Radio City Sport

amount of coverage of these areas is determined by the audience research findings.

With sport it is the depth and immediacy with which it is broadcast to the listeners that is important. With this in mind Radio City have lines connected directly to the Everton and Liverpool FC football grounds and these

Figure 25.17 City FM's sports presenters are given a high profile

are simply plugged in for instant live coverage. Sport is an important ingredient in the programme mix and is therefore given a high profile on Radio City. The sports presenters are given the same kind of celebrity profile as the music 'jocks'.

To help listeners to identify with their particular sound the stations will develop their own **jingles** which act as an aural logo, promoting the station and perhaps a particular presenter.

Now write a report which summarises the marketing activities for Radio City. Your summary should be structured, using headings and sub-headings, etc. derived from marketing terminology.

Case study: Radio Leicester

In Unit 4 we looked at the weekday schedule of programmes for Radio Leicester, as well as carrying out a detailed analysis of the *Talkback* programme in particular. We can now return to this schedule and examine it in terms of its programme mix and the marketing plans for improving the position of each of the programmes within that mix.

Liam McCarthy, the managing editor of Radio Leicester, wants to increase the market share of listeners to the station and to the individual programmes. He and his staff have identified certain marketing strategies, including a number of areas for improvement.

There are certain points which you should note that will help you understand the information:

- **reach** means the actual number of listeners to a programme
- **share** is the numbers listening to a particular programme during a certain time slot as a proportion of all those listening to radio during that period
- **programme briefs** are short summaries of programmes and their aims. The ones discussed here are either quotes or paraphrases from the station's marketing plan.

1 Good Morning Leicester

Programme brief *Good Morning Leicester* has a pivotal role as a 'flagship' programme. It is relatively popular, with a crucial position as the first programme on the schedule. Its aim therefore is to set the standards in journalism and production quality; these are then used as a benchmark for the rest of Radio Leicester's output.

A key objective is set out in the words of the marketing plan:

'to set "today's" news agenda rather than repeating that of yesterday. GML should use a variety of innovative story treatments to provide a unique news and information service for the county, one that is not afraid to set its own agenda – or stray from the national news agenda when appropriate. It must be relevant to existing listeners and yet attract additional listeners to the station and place a high priority on information services, traffic and travel news and an event diary.'

The results of **market research** gave the following audience information:

- each week 112 000 people tune in to Radio Leicester between 6 and 9am
- there are 31 000 exclusive listeners in this timeband, i.e. they do not listen to Radio Leicester at any other time
- the average listener to this show is tuned in for 59 minutes.

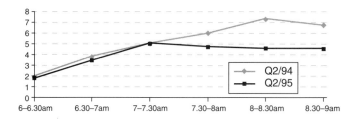

Figure 25.18 Year-on-year changes in reach 1994 to 1995

In 1994 to 1995 the early programme held its position but the 7 to 9am section of GML declined. Analysis of the audience data revealed that 7am is the 'switch-off' point.

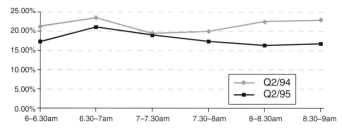

Figure 25.19 Year-on-year changes in share 1994 to 1995

In 1994 to 1995 share fell over most of the programme time slot, and particularly in the 7 to 9am period. The marketing objectives for 1995/6 therefore addressed the problems of a falling reach in the 7 to 9am period and a falling share across the 6 to 9am period.

First, the scheduling was changed. There were originally two programmes occupying the period from 6 to 10am. These were combined into a single programme of three hours' duration (6 to 9am) which also meant an earlier, 9am start for the *Talkback* programme.

To accompany the scheduling changes, plans were also put in place to change the style and content of different parts of the *Good Morning Leicester* programme. These were the areas identified for improvement:

1 Increase the speech content of the first hour (6 to 7am) by innovative development of feature materials.
2 Improve the quality of the programme between 7 and 8am in order to retain listeners at the switch-off point (after the 7am news). Listeners are generally loyal and do not change stations as much as they change TV channels. However, if they do switch stations it may be difficult to get them back. With this in mind the marketing plan needs to maintain the **reach** (the actual number of people listening) during the 6 to 7am slot whilst at the same time increasing the percentage **share** of the market.
3 Keep 'breaking' stories fresh and dynamic, so that they carry forward through GML and into *Talkback*. A breaking story is one that is still developing. The marketing plan recognises the importance of maintaining listener interest by keeping them up to date with fresh angles and developments on an unfolding story. If listeners feel they are being kept in touch with a story and it is interesting, they are unlikely to start trying to obtain reports about it from another station.
4 Be creative with the programme format, and avoid 'format traps'. For example, always providing a light item at 7.55am can become a little too predictable for some listeners. Sometimes, a change can be a welcome surprise and stops the programme from getting stale.
5 Ensure all reporters are briefed by the programme producer so there is not a 'hotch potch' of styles. Whilst it is important to give personality to a programme, broadcasters do need to maintain an identifiable sound.
6 Boost the impact of the programme at 7.40 and 8.40 after the sports news, on the basis that this is a key switch-on point for younger listeners.
7 Establish a daily 'Thought for the Day' strand. (This had previously been a regular feature which has now been brought back by popular demand.)

2 Talkback

Programme brief We have already given an idea of the content and style of this programme. The following extract further defines the product and gives it a 'personality' which people can identify with.

'It is important that this programme is seen as a platform to develop stories which have been run in other sequences. Talkback must have a wide variety of story treatments with a range of round-table discussions, radio car inserts and, where possible, outside broadcasts. To ensure the programme remains flexible it is vital that the programme is live.

Overall the programme should sound surprising, lively and humorous – serious when appropriate but not necessarily sombre. It should be the listeners' champion and friend.'

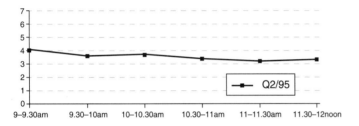

Figure 25.20 *Talkback* reach

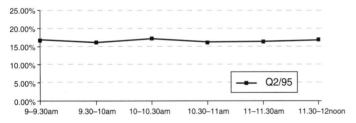

Figure 25.21 *Talkback* share

The objectives for 1995/6 were to maintain the audience inherited from *Good Morning Leicester* and to arrest the decline in listeners during the period of the programme.

The station planned to make use of the earlier, 9am, start (mentioned earlier) to attract additional younger listeners by providing guests who would address issues of interest to a wide range of people. In order to do this the programme would include topics such as house buying and child care, whilst not ignoring the older

listeners by providing coverage of, for example, retirement issues such as pensions.

The programme recognised there is a need to give an even more accessible flavour to the programme, ensuring that listeners feel able to contribute throughout.

Talkback also differentiated itself by covering more news and topical issues (that is, issues that are in the news at the moment), whilst the *Midday Programme* concentrated on features such as health, travel and the environment. However, there was always overlap between the programmes in terms of the topics covered, which is why it is the style of the programme, and not just the content, that is important.

3 Midday

Programme brief The *Midday Programme* has a consumer-led brief, offering accessibility to the audience for help and advice in a wide range of areas. Included in the programme is the lunchtime news sequence from 1pm, although breaking stories can and should appear at any point within the three-hour programme.

There should be an emphasis on 'real people' and personality presentation. An important feature of the programme is the opportunity to provide 'in depth' interviews with interesting local people which, in 25 minutes, will do more than scratch the surface. The programme also includes a variety of light features, including 'flash-back', 'all abroad' and a general knowledge competition.

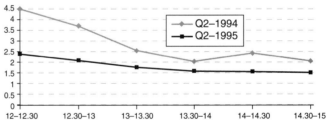

Figure 25.22 *Midday* year-on-year changes in reach 1994–1995

There was a decline in reach compared with the same quarter of the previous year (see Figure 25.22).

Share fell dramatically although this was now less obvious in the latter stages of this timeband (see Figure 25.23).

Objectives Obviously the station needed to arrest the decline in the number of listeners over lunchtime. The plan was to do this by **differentiating** it from *Talkback*

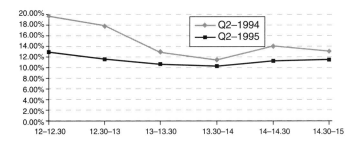

Figure 25.23 *Midday* year-on-year changes in share 1994–1995

because it was felt to be too similar. Therefore more production support was allocated in order to strengthen the programme content.

The programme started a 'pets phone-in', with a vet to answer people's concerns about their animals, and sports updates. In addition, the programme continued to develop the 'light touch' features such as 'all abroad' in which listener's friends and relatives who live abroad are contacted.

4 Mid-Afternoon

Programme brief The afternoon programme, with a new shorter format, should be concentrating on developing outside broadcasts. This time slot offered the opportunity for Radio Leicester to be seen to broadcast from a wide range of locations – not only events but also places of employment, hospitals, colleges and community projects, etc. Given the younger age profile of the audience at this time of day the programme has a family feel and has an opportunity to develop some, but not too many, regular features of family interest.

It is also recognised that between 4 and 5pm it is important that this sequence should reflect the move towards 'drivetime' (i.e. the rush-hour), with increased bulletins and, where necessary, carrying 'breaking' stories.

A crucial change took place in how the audience figures were calculated. Figures for the Asian Network were

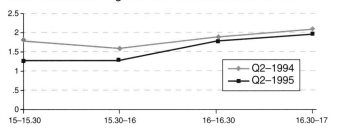

Figure 25.24 *Mid-Afternoon* year-on-year changes in reach 1994–1995

included in the 1994 calculations but were excluded from 1995. The year-on-year changes in reach (see Figure 25.24) therefore indicated a very good performance. It is vitally important to qualify bare graphs and figures with information of this kind, otherwise it can give a misleading impression.

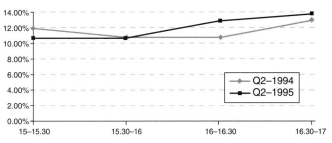

Figure 25.25 *Mid-Afternoon* year-on-year changes in share 1994–1995

Share was bettered year on year, although poor inheritance from earlier in the day will have prevented an even stronger performance.

Objectives for 1995/6 included the following:

- consolidate the strong audience performance
- continue to offer programming that will retain the relatively young mix of audience at this time
- ensure there is a wide coverage of geographical and editorial areas in the form of outside broadcasts
- draw new listeners.

5 Leicestershire Tonight

Programme brief *Leicestershire Tonight* is not a direct copy of the *Good Morning Leicester* format. It is a programme in its own right and is there to reflect the day's main local, national and international news, in addition to originating its own ideas. The staffing for this programme means that it should carry a large proportion of live material. It is important that *Leicestershire Tonight* should carry a complete service of local information

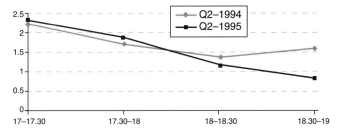

Figure 25.26 *Leicestershire Tonight* year-on-year changes in reach 1994–1995

provision, including traffic and travel news, and also diary events and programme trailing.

Year-on-year reach figures indicated that the programme did well (see Figure 25.26) although the final hour was suffering. Strengthening the 6 to 6.30pm slot, given the size of the car audience, could pay some further dividends.

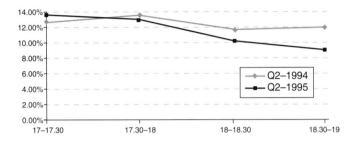

Figure 25.27 *Leicestershire Tonight* year-on-year changes in share 1994–95

Share held steady in the first hour of the programme although this slot did not compare favourably with the 20 per cent share enjoyed at breakfast. (See Figure 25.27).

Objectives for the programme included:

- develop the speech content between 6.00 and 6.30pm
- reflect the importance of the car-listening audience during this programme
- be imaginative with the programme running order and not slavishly following predetermined formats
- consider the stories covered at 5.40pm and 6.40pm after the sports bulletins, to attract listeners who primarily tune in for sport
- draw listeners across from *Good Morning Leicester*. This involves 'cross trailing' which particularly targets the 30 per cent of GML listeners who do not listen to Radio Leicester at any other time.

Activity

Using the information given in the two case studies, identify how the marketing approach for the public service station Radio Leicester differs from that of the independent station Radio City.

We have seen how ILR (Independent Local Radio) is mainly music-based and looked at Radio City as an example of this. We have also examined Radio Leicester as an example of the BBC's policy of an 80

per cent speech-based output. We can now, however, consider a radio station that makes substantial use of both talk and music in its programming mix.

Case study: Catalunya Radio

Catalunya Radio is based in Barcelona. it is the national radio of the autonomous region of Catalonia in Spain.

Figure 25.28 Radio Catalunya's logo

In Chapter 13 we looked at a programme schedule for Radio Catalunya. The variety of programmes show how the station differentiates its broadcasting for the target audience of the various market segments. But the differentiation goes much further than this. Catalunya Radio actually consists of four channels, each of which broadcast for 24 hours per day.

Catalunya Radio itself is designated as Channel One. As we saw on the schedule, it is a mixed channel which broadcasts mainly information, news and talk programmes but also includes light music shows.

Radio Associaco de Catalunya (Channel Two) is a light, pop-rock music channel aimed at a young audience. Catalunya Musica (Channel Three) broadcasts classical and what they term 'contemporary serious' music. Catalunya Informacio (Channel Four) is a dedicated news channel.

The radio station cannot operate with purely commercial motives. Together with the state television channel, Televisio de Catalunya (TV3), it forms a public broadcasting service called the Catalan Broadcasting Corporation. It is financed by the Catalan government and answerable to the Catalan parliament, which in turn is answerable to the Catalan people. It therefore sees itself as the voice of Catalunya and its people.

The Catalan people were not allowed to have an identity separate from the Spanish until the death of Franco and the end of his dictatorship. Catalans have a different culture, customs and language from other regions of Spain. The radio has therefore tried to reflect the interests of the region and its people by scheduling a diverse range of programmes and separating into different channels.

From the detailed schedule of Channel One, and the descriptions of the other three channels, we can see that the station covers the main market segments. Geographically, the whole country (Catalunya) of six million people is covered; Channel One alone has an audience of 600 000 – giving it the number one spot in audience rankings. The broadcasts actually extend beyond the Catalan region and into Catalan-speaking areas of Valencia, the Balearic Islands, Aragón and Southern France.

You have been asked to market Catalunya Radio. List the factors that will affect your marketing approach. Using the information given in this chapter, compare the task of marketing Catalunya Radio with that of marketing Radio Leicester.

Case study: The *Leicester Mercury*

The *Leicester Mercury* carries out extensive **marketing activities** in order to provide a **differentiated** product to a **segmented** market. Its research provides it with detailed data on the market, i.e. the potential readership of the *Leicester Mercury*. The examples in Figure 25.30 show how it profiles the whole market by age and sex (demographics) and by socio-economic groupings.

The *Leicester Mercury* is owned by Northcliffe newspapers, which in turn is owned by the *Daily Mail*. It is the sixth largest regional daily, with an approximate circulation of 120 000 and readership of around 317 000 per day. Although there has been a slight drop in circulation, there has been an increase in readership and this is a trend which is fairly typical. This readership **penetration** constitutes approximately fifty per cent of the adult population of Leicestershire.

It costs approximately 52p to produce one copy of the Mercury yet it retails (sells to the public) for 27p. How can they afford to do this? This answer is **advertising**. The main source of income is the sale of advertising space to private individuals and to businesses.

If you look at a local 'paid for' newspaper you will find that approximately half the space is given to advertising. This is also the case with the *Leicester Mercury*. Advertising is the reason that most newspapers are able to survive. It is so important that at the page planning stage it is the space for adverts that is reserved first, and the news stories are planned around this, as you saw in Chapter 9.

In order to make itself attractive to advertisers, the *Leicester Mercury* needs to make itself attractive to readers. The more people who read the paper, the more

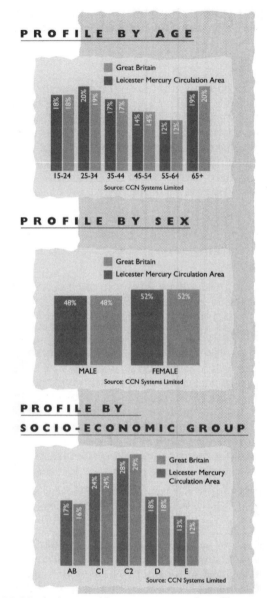

Figure 25.29 *Leicester Mercury* rate card profiles

advertisers will be prepared to pay so that they can reach those readers. This is why the paper is prepared to invest so significantly in marketing activities. They need to find out what people want and need from a paper so that they can then provide for these needs. In other words they are giving **utility** to the customer so that it becomes, as the paper's own objective states, 'part of people's lives'.

We can now look at how the *Leicester Mercury* uses the **marketing mix** in order to achieve this objective of becoming part of people's everyday lives, i.e. the four Ps of product, place, promotion and price.

Marketing mix for the Leicester Mercury

Product

It has to be remembered that the *Leicester Mercury* is a product which, like all products, requires product management. Over the past ten years there has been a massive change in the needs and expectations of customers and newspapers have to adapt to this. We have already discussed how, in this dynamic environment, the product is continually under review. This is carried out by market research. As we have seen, this is divided into **field** and **desk** research. Field research makes use of a variety of research methods. One **quantitative** method is the use of **tracking sites**, where 700 people a year are monitored.

Another, **qualitative**, example of field research is the use of **focus groups** in which in-depth interviews are used to find out what people would like in their newspapers.

Focus groups showed that there was a distinction between older and younger readers. The older readership was concerned about having more readers' letters, more 'nostalgia' pieces about times gone by, and wanted accuracy of reporting and high standards of spelling and grammar. There was also a demand for more news of a very local kind and more focused features, for example, regular in-depth consumer reviews.

Younger, more occasional, readers wanted something entertaining to read and easy to find their way around, with an attractive design and presentation.

This survey resulted in a number of changes. For example, the paper introduced *The Week,* which is a 'what's on' entertainment guide to the East Midlands with plenty of features and reviews, strong use of colour and an easy-to-follow format. In addition, there are now more 'lifestyle' articles such as 'Shelf Life', which is a consumer-based page, 'Green Life' that looks at environmental issues, and 'School Life', focusing on education. Sports coverage – which was already quite substantial for a newspaper – was also increased significantly. The publicity for this was supported by a prominent poster campaign on buses and poster sites and in programmes and displays at sporting events.

Desk research is carried out using the census and other sources of information. These include surveys such as those carried out by media research organisations which give demographic and socio-

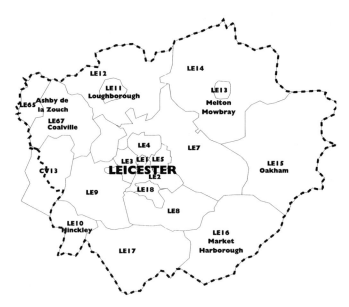

Figure 25.30 *Leicester Mercury* circulation area

economic data (as illustrated in Figure 25.29). There are also readership surveys which compare circulation figures with competitors, and their data are compiled in-house in order to make comparisons with the *Mercury's* own previous sales performance.

The core product, the *Leicester Mercury* newspaper itself, is **differentiated** to cater for different market **segments**. First, it is differentiated in terms of geographical area and time of day. There are 10 editions printed per day: three are for the city and come out at 10.45am, 2pm and 5pm; one caters for the city's large Asian community and the others serve the different districts of the county (see Figure 25.30).

In this way the paper can target its appeal more precisely. Customers can read about very local issues concerning their district, and businesses can target those same customers more precisely with their advertising.

The contents of the paper are differentiated to appeal to different reader interests. There are regular feature pages for fashion, weddings, farming life, property, business, holidays, countryside, leisure and sport. Some are published on specific days; for example, 'Weddings Fair' can be found on Mondays, whilst 'Business Life', a pull-out section printed, like the *Financial Times,* in pink, can be found in Tuesday editions. Again, this develops a link between the paper, customers who read it and customers who advertise in it. If somebody is planning a wedding, then they will (hopefully) buy the *Mercury* on Monday, whilst any business selling wedding products and services will try to target those potential customers by advertising in the Monday editions.

Besides its core product, the *Leicester Mercury* also produces a variety of supplements, special editions and weekly free papers. Supplements include *The Week* (entertainment guide) and the *Property Guide,* whilst special editions have been based, for example, on aircraft, car and train classics. Then there is the *Sporting Green,* produced specifically to cover this ever-popular area. These all have the function of appealing to people's interests and continually making and reinforcing the image of the *Mercury* as the place to turn to whatever your needs and interests.

Figure 25.31 There are many editions of the *Leicester Mercury*

Place

The *Mercury* is sold in 900 retail outlets, including 44 Mercury Shops. These shops actually form another company whose primary aim is to promote the sale of the newspaper. However, their secondary purpose is to make money through the sale of a variety of merchandise such as cigarettes and confectionery.

The promotion of the newspaper is carried out through the use of the fascia board and other advertising décor which 'frames' the shop, free delivery of the paper and prime positioning of it within the shop. This close interaction within another organisation involved with the same product – although at a different stage of production – is known as **vertical integration**.

In addition to the Mercury News Shops, the product is sold in other newsagents, garages, supermarkets, off-licences and the eighteen news vending sites in Leicester city centre.

The free papers of the Leicester Mail Group (mentioned above under *Product*) are delivered to a quarter of a million households every week. The distribution of the Mail Group has been developed to complement the *Leicester Mercury*. Advertisers can purchase a package of spaces both in the paid-for and free papers. We have seen that the *Mercury* is read by 50 per cent of the adult population of Leicester. The *Mail* has a penetration of 70 per cent, achieved because it is free, delivered to the door and highly targeted via 13 micro editions.

Promotion

The core product is promoted on a daily basis by the newspaper sales executives, who provide the direct contact with retailers. Visits are made about three times a week for large concerns and once a month for smaller outlets. There are four city and five county areas, each with their sales rep. They have four main tasks:

1 *To visit shops and other retail outlets and ensure they are maximising their sales opportunities.* The rewards can be substantial (as you can see under Price below) so it is important to make these visits and encourage growth where appropriate.

2 *To make quick evening calls to top up supplies and ensure that the bill posters are displayed.* In this servicing role they are supported by a team of nine part-time merchandisers who work between 4.30 and 6.30pm to ensure that no outlet runs out of copies.

3 *To check that a high profile of the* Leicester Mercury *is maintained, both*

inside and outside the retail outlet. For instance, the reps check the positioning of the newspapers: are they at a suitable height and in multiple places? They also look at the paper's position in relation to other products on sale. So they may ask the proprietor what sells well in their shop. If the answer happened to be crisps, then the rep would encourage the paper to be placed close to the range of crisps on sale.

They also advise on numerous promotional material such as stickers, banners and posters used to frame shop doorways and windows and place on their fascias.

4 *To deal with any problems and queries.* Whatever the query, the sales executive wants to appear encouraging and positive as it helps to promote the *Mercury*'s image and provides a supportive 'feel good' environment for the retailer.

In addition to home deliveries via newsagents, there is also direct delivery where the delivery

Figure 25.32 There are 13 targeted editions of the *Mail* free weekly newspaper

teams are employed by the *Mercury* and have team leaders who collect the money on the doorstep. This in itself constitutes a market segment which returns a profit and maintains the paper's profile.

An important means of generating sales is the substantial and 'on-going' canvassing operation. This involves cold calling on the telephone and on the doorstep. There is generally a special offer, such as free copies or a free gift, to encourage people to place a firm order for a certain period. The Newspaper Sales Department maintains a database of addresses linked to newsagents. It is an expensive operation but generates 20 000 new orders a year.

Other promotional activities are the events, such as roadshows and exhibitions, which the *Mercury* either organises, sponsors or has a presence at. Annual events organised by the newspaper include the *Leicester Mercury* Historic Transport Pageant and Vehicle Parade which is the largest event of its kind in the country, two holiday exhibitions, a fashion show, the Business show, the Wedding and Home Show and the Leicestershire Ploughing Match and Agricultural Machinery Show.

The paper also sponsors the *Leicester Mercury* Race Night at the racecourse, the Best Kept Village competition, Crimebeat and Operation Jackdaw (in conjunction with the county's police force), as well as supporting major musical, drama and literary festivals.

Through Mercury Travel, thousands of readers take their holidays with the newspaper each year, whilst many others participate in its events, enter in-paper competitions or purchase one of the many items of merchandise which are often specially generated and collectable.

The intention of these promotional activities is to encourage people to refer to the product. Therefore a high profile must be maintained with poster sites and the sides of buses, special offers, merchandise such as pens and special edition vintage model cars, holidays, and tips for the home. They all become linked with the *Leicester Mercury* which helps their strategy of making it a 'part of people's lives'.

Price

We have already seen that the *Leicester Mercury* retails at 27p per copy. The price to the retail outlet is approximately 18p which is roughly a 30 per cent discount. Therefore an outlet selling 600 to 700 copies per night is making £15 000 profit each year, and is a lucrative trade which the sales executives encourage with incentives. The retail pricing policy is that it is sold at the set price of 27p and that the newspaper itself is made more valuable in terms of what it offers so that people get more for the same money.

Activity

Investigate your local newspaper and list its activities under the headings of the marketing mix. Compare their marketing approaches to those of the *Leicester Mercury* as discussed in this chapter.

Evidence assignment

Compile a report on the marketing activities of media industries. This could be produced as a brochure or pamphlet. The work should be word processed, and the information should be organised in a clear and attractive manner with appropriate headings and choice of fonts. Illustrations and diagrams should be included. The report can also be used as evidence for Unit 2 Element 2, Chapter 6.

The report should start with a general explanation of the aims of marketing. Then, under the following main headings, you should give examples from the different media industries:

Research:
- product design
- pricing
- sales packaging
- investigating audiences
- investigating competition

Communication:
- advertising
- public relations
- sales promotion

Distribution channels:
- direct selling
- wholesalers and/or retailers
- networks
- agents.

You should conclude the report with a comparison of the marketing approaches used for two products from different industries. For example, you could choose to compare the marketing mix for a magazine and a radio show, or for a newspaper and a TV documentary series.

Prepare marketing plans for media products

A marketing plan will give details of the various marketing activities to be carried out, when they will be undertaken and how they will be mixed. It will give details of time-scales and who will be responsible for different activities.

You may find it difficult to get up-to-date or detailed information for this unit. Companies can be sensitive about revealing what they usually consider to be a commercial secret. For example, you are unlikely to obtain easily the business plans of Microsoft or Virgin. Some material is, however, in the public domain. Advertising rates and subscription prices are generally available, and public services such as the BBC publish annual reports and publicity material which contain marketing information.

Introduction

A marketing plan should include the following:

- a review of the current situation. The company and the product should be described. The market-place and competitors should be identified
- aims and objectives should be clearly summarised. These may be long term but should also include objectives which can be achieved over the next twelve months
- a list of how and when these objectives can be achieved. The resources needed to redesign the product or run an advertising campaign should be identified
- the procedures for monitoring progress and providing feedback should be given.

Marketing plans will have a similar purpose and structure whether they are for a newspaper or a radio station, cable TV or film, the music industry or the new interactive media (CD-i or the Internet).

Market research data for selected media products

Market research will need to cover the following:

- **sales trends** – these will consider the entire product, or parts of a product, the entire

audience/consumer group or sections of it, such as women or children
- **changes in the market share** – it should be noted if competitors are doing better or worse, or if new rival products are appearing. **Competitor activities**, which can also include mergers and takeovers, can affect market share dramatically
- **customer behaviour** – research into media audiences is very complex and carried out on a vast scale. Knowledge of **customer preferences**, of their buying patterns for print publications or **patterns of consumption** for audio-visual products, will be highly significant.

Marketing services

All of these aspects have been dealt with in depth in Unit 6, which also showed us some of the organisations, for example NRS, ABC, BARB and RAJAR, that are involved in monitoring audiences. There are, however, even more specialised services available, not least of which is in the area of advertising. But these services will still make use of the data supplied by BARB and RAJAR, as will the media outlets themselves, who can compare their popularity with rivals. With radio, the station can see from the half-hourly intervals where they are most popular and unpopular.

Register-MEAL is a company which provides the industry standard for advertising expenditure measurement. The company was created from the merger between MEAL (Media Expenditure Analysis Ltd) and the Media Register. The parent company, Neilson, is the world's largest marketing information group.

The company measures the amount of money spent on advertising each of the different 'brands' (goods or services, for example, kitchen furniture, holidays) in all the different media organisations in the country. All the information is input and collated on database.

The *Leicester Mercury* uses a variety of different sources for its market research data, including the County Council which carries out population surveys to help plan future service provision for the county. The *Mercury* also uses private organisations that are nationally recognised sources for the newspaper industry such as JICREG (Joint Industry Committee for Regional Press Research) and RSGB (Readership Surveys of Great Britain). In addition, the paper makes use of the MOSAIC database owned by CCN.

Lifestyle classification systems

MOSAIC is what is known as a 'lifestyle' method of grouping people. We have already seen that there are different ways by which people can be classified for marketing purposes. For example, there are the socio-economic and psychographic categories.

Lifestyle groupings are a type of psychographic profiling but are much more detailed and sophisticated. They classify people by their spending and saving habits, types of clothes and houses, what they watch, read and listen to, religious beliefs and political leanings, etc. These go towards compiling profiles of particular 'types' of person.

The MOSAIC classification divides people up into 12 lifestyle groups, each with sub-groups. Like all lifestyle classification systems they tend to use colourful descriptions to 'paint a picture' of the type of person the advertisers can target. This 'picture' includes the percentage of the population in that category and what is considered to be a 'typical' example of the kind of place these groups of people are likely to live in.

For example the L2 (Lifestyle 2) group is called 'Suburban Semis' and contains 11.0 per cent of the population. Its sub-groups are named 'Green Belt Expansion' with 3.4 per cent and a typical location is given as Canvey Island. 'Suburban Mock Tudor' (3.2 per cent, Redhill) and 'Pebble Dash Subtopia' (4.4 per cent, Bexleyheath) make up the rest of this grouping.

Another lifestyle classification system is ACORN, owned by CACI Ltd, which again divides the population into groups such as 'Wealthy Achievers' and 'Prosperous Pensioners'. They also compile a 'change' profile of the population to keep marketers abreast of the changes taking place within society. For example they classify 19.4 per cent of the population into a category which they term 'continuing decline'. It contains sub-groups (types) such as 'many more single parents, greater social stress'. On the other hand they classify another population group as 'rising affluence' constituting 12.1 per cent of the population. An example of a 'type' within this group would be 'maturing areas, more home owners and pensioners'.

Case study

As part of the *Leicester Mercury* student project described in Unit 3, students had to investigate the market-place in which their product would be distributed. Because the newspaper is already an established 'going concern' students did not have to carry out market research to the extent that has been described here. Neither would they have been expected to conduct research at this kind of standard and detail as it requires a high degree of training and experience, a high level of sophisticated resources and a great deal of financial backing.

However, the students were expected to be aware of the market research data and how it is used to identify and target particular market segments. The *Leicester Mercury* therefore delivered workshops to the students at an early stage of the project on the specialist companies and techniques they use, and how the product is marketed.

A large amount of market research data was obtained and used, along with the students' own 'content analysis' to get an idea of the type of publication they would be in partnership with, and its market. **Content analysis** involves a sift through the pages of a number of editions, preferably over a week, to get an idea of the product and its audience. This provides information on what kind of stories are covered, the amount and type of advertising, the number and type of photographs, etc. These all give an indication of the paper's target audience.

Students also looked at the appearance of the paper to gain an impression of the image it wanted to convey. This is indicated stylistically by the masthead, headlines and general layout of the pages. You can read more about this in Chapter 3 and in Unit 3. In addition, the tone of the editorial content and particularly the 'comment' will also be an indication of the type of paper and its market.

Activity

Choose one of the products you have made for Unit 3, 4 or 5. Collect information about:

- sales, viewing/listening/readership data
- customer/audience preferences and behaviour
- competitor activities.

You will have to work as part of a team, because this research will need to be detailed. You may be collecting statistical (quantitative) or anecdotal (qualitative) information. You may investigate professional competitors (in which case you may be collecting information from video shops or software houses – or their outlets – for example). However, you may be part of a simulation exercise, in which you treat the products made by other student groups as the competitors.

Ensuring that data is sufficient, up-to-date and accurate

If a media organisation, such as the *Leicester Mercury* or Radio City, or indeed the student project team, are to proceed to the stage of developing a marketing plan, they must be confident that the market research is good enough for them to formulate that plan properly.

The research data should cover: the sales trends, changes in market share, customer behaviour, buying patterns, customer preferences and competitor activities. The following information comes from market research carried out on behalf of the *Leicester Mercury*.

Sales trends

The chart in Figure 26.1 is aimed at showing advertisers that they can place their ads with confidence because there is a strong regular readership 'committed' and 'loyal' enough to pre-order the paper. The figures show an upward change in this mode of sale.

A COMMITTED LOYAL READERSHIP

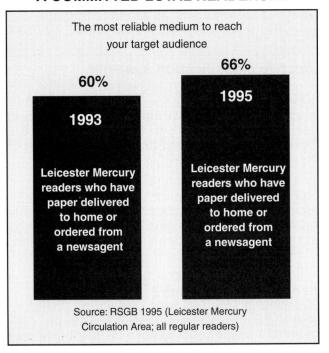

Figure 26.1 Sales trends for the *Leicester Mercury*: mode of sale for 1993 and 1995

Changes in market share

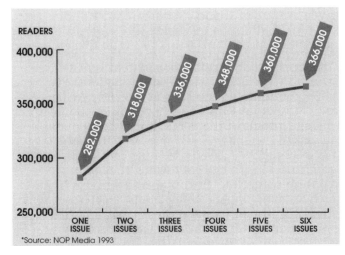

Figure 26.2 Readership of the *Leicester Mercury* in 1993

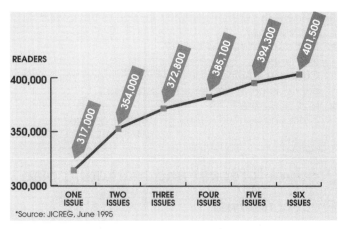

Figure 26.3 Readership of the *Leicester Mercury* in 1995

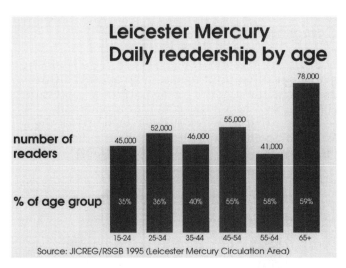

Figure 26.4 Readership of the *Leicester Mercury* by age

The two charts in Figures 26.2 and 26.3 show how unduplicated readership grows by advertising more frequently. This is because different people read the *Mercury* on different days. The market research company has calculated the numbers of readers who can be reached by advertising from between one and six days.

By comparing the figures we can see that there has been an increase in readership, whether it is comparing an average day or an average week, between 1993 and 1995.

Customer behaviour

Research carried out into customer behaviour may give valuable information. For example, the *Leicester Mercury* found that, on any given day, nearly half of the adult population in the circulation area read the *Leicester Mercury* and that more than four out of ten of all *Leicester Mercury* readers do not read a national daily newspaper. Research also revealed that the average time spent reading the *Leicester Mercury* is over half an hour.

Buying patterns

Information on customer buying patterns could include, for the *Leicester Mercury,* an analysis of customers' age groupings. For example, the bar chart in Figure 26.4 shows that the greatest number of readers is in the 65-plus age group.

Customer preferences

For the purpose of marketing its advertising space, the *Leicester Mercury* will want to find out how people make key decisions about important purchases such as cars and houses, or if they need to employ a tradesperson, or need to find or change jobs. Figure 26.5 shows that of all those expressing a preference in the *Leicester Mercury* circulation area, nearly three-quarters chose the *Mercury* when it came to buying or selling a car; 70 per cent chose the paper to look for a new job and a large majority turned to it for buying or selling their home.

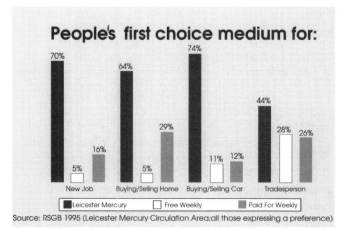

Figure 26.5 The choice of medium for important purchases or decisions

Competitor activities

The *Leicester Mercury*'s competitors in the advertising market are other print media, radio and TV. Figure 26.6 shows the result of research into the success of competitors. The *Mercury* could show potential advertisers that there is a strong preference for the *Mercury* in comparison with television, radio and other print media.

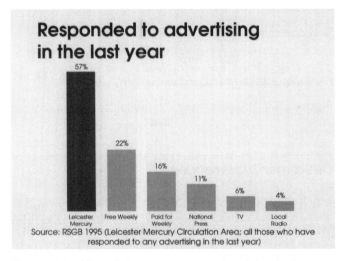

Figure 26.6 People's response to advertising in the *Leicester Mercury*

The data obtained for this research was the most up-to-date available. The total sample was sufficient, consisting of interviews with 715 adults with quota controls on gender, working status and age to ensure a representative sample. The interviews were across 55 sampling points, which were selected using random location procedures as laid down in the JICREG guidelines.

Activity

Look at the data you have collected in the previous activity. Ask yourself these questions:

■ **Is it sufficient?**
Have you collected quantitative and qualitative information?
Did you research an appropriate sample?
Have you researched the product and the audience/consumer?
Have you used a number of information sources?

Is there enough information for you to draw valid conclusions?
■ **Is it current (up-to-date)?**
Is it timely?
Currency may be within one week or one year. This depends on the **fitness for purpose**.
■ **Is it accurate?**
Have you verified it through another source?

Product forecast and marketing plan

Product forecast

A **forecast** is a way of determining how much demand there will be for a product. This allows you to plan the resources for your marketing campaign for that product.

You can make use of different techniques to forecast demand. These generally require market research information and usually involve complex mathematical models that are calculated by computer. One approach, called the **Delphi technique**, relies on expert opinion to predict the demand, based on informed knowledge of the product and the market. In its proper form the technique requires several experts to give their opinion on a certain scenario. The responses are pooled together into a combined scenario which is fed back to the experts, who then revise it, give further comments and feed it back. This goes on until a consensus is reached.

Another approach, called **Time-series analysis**, examines past data and uses it to calculate future demand. An example is to look at past sales trends and extrapolate them to predict future trends.

Case study

In the *Leicester Mercury* student project Time-series analysis was used to examine the sales figures for the 'parent' product (the newspaper). Students were therefore confident that there would be widespread dissemination of their product, based on these figures. The readership figures could therefore be justifiably used in the students' advertising campaign.

The sale of the product on campus was a different proposition. The whole point of Time-series is that it is based on past performance and, because this project had not been carried out before, there were no hard data that were directly applicable. Forecasting was therefore based on a combination of the Delphi technique, which in this case relied on the *Mercury* staff to give estimates, supported by Time-series data on the sales figures for the Hinckley area.

To anticipate demand students researched the market, i.e. college students and staff. A survey was carried out, asking the following questions:

- Do you buy the *Leicester Mercury* regularly?
- Do you know how much the *Leicester Mercury* costs?
- How much do you spend on snacks at college each day?
- If you were offered 50p worth of snacks, a 10 per cent discount to a hairdresser/clothes shops/record store, and half-price admission to a club *plus* a copy of the *Leicester Mercury*, all for 27p, would you take it?

This not only helped to forecast demand but it put the publicity campaign in motion.

Marketing plan

A marketing plan is a formal and carefully researched and structured report that covers marketing activities (research, communication, timing), product design, pricing, sales packaging and dissemination. It analyses all the issues that may affect the company's future business so that it can maximise profits in different circumstances. The marketing plan of the *Leicester Mercury* student project is described in the following case study.

Case study

Objective   The *Leicester Mercury* student project had as its objective to produce a professional, four-page supplement to be inserted into the *Leicester Mercury*. The supplement would primarily operate as a promotional tool for potential students. It would also, however, need to consider its other audiences, i.e. advertisers and parents.

Review of current situation   The market research showed that the *Leicester Mercury* is read by a wide cross-section of the population in terms of age, sex and socio-economic grouping. However, the target audience had the lowest percentage readership.

The supplement was an insert into the main paper. Therefore there was not that much opportunity for visually attracting audiences. However, because it was part of a much bigger publication, sales and

distribution were already covered by the *Mercury*'s existing system.

There were no existing outlets on the college site for the sale of the paper. General student interest did not appear to be very high. There was no regular student magazine.

Procedure   The task would be achieved by carrying out the following activities:

- *research* into the market and the parent product
- *communication* – broadly speaking, marketing communication takes place in all marketing activities except perhaps market research
- *product design*, which communicates a message in much the same way as does the content
- *pricing* – setting a price for the paper and for the various sizes of advertising space (there could be discounts for bulk buying or for prompt payment)
- *content* – researching and writing stories which would appeal to the target audience. These would take a 'human interest' angle and make bold use of photography to create interest in the text.

Advertising sales   This aspect involved the development of an advertising plan. The details of this are reproduced in Chapter 27. But the main aspects were as follows:

- research and produce a hit-list of potential advertisers
- obtain list of college suppliers
- produce a sales letter
- produce a telephone script
- produce sales packages
- produce an information pack for advertisers (containing details of advertising rates).

Decision on editorial–advertising split   The normal split is 50:50. Students were a little concerned that this only leaves two pages for editorial. The amount of advertising that would be sold was an unknown quantity, and it was acknowledged that there was the possibility of not selling enough advertising so that the ratio would become a problem. It was, however, decided to monitor the situation and not allow more than 40% advertising.

Promotions   Advertising and sales are part of the promotions mix, which is itself part of the overall marketing mix. The other ingredient in the promotions mix is **word-of-mouth**, probably the most effective form of advertising. The newspaper sales team would need to generate visible interest, particularly on the day of the sale, with people carrying the distinctive carrier bags and eating their way through the free gifts. People are naturally sceptical and will walk past even if they are told something is free, because they will be wondering 'what's the catch?' Satisfied customers need to be on hand to testify that it is a good offer.

The plan involved developing a strategy for obtaining promotional goods and material from companies.

Developing a distribution and sales system   Again, these are channels of communication. They all give potential customers a certain message and must therefore be considered in terms of their image and appearance.

Timing is important because you not only have to consider what to sell and where to sell it, but also when is the best time. For example, with the *Mercury* project the students aimed at a distribution date which supported a college promotional campaign. They also had to consider the times of day for selling from particular outlets. An obvious example would be to set up a vending operation, such as a stall outside (or inside) the college diner, to take advantage of the lunchtime trade.

Resources   The necessary resources included a sales office with a direct-line telephone. It was also important to allocate production roles to individual students in order to maximise human resources, and to book the production facilities that would be needed at the *Leicester Mercury*.

Monitoring and control   Marketing should normally be an on-going company activity which requires regular reviews, known as **marketing audits**.

However, even in the 'one-off' situation which this plan was designed for, it is vital that regular reviews should be carried out. These should take the form of frequent meetings which take account of what is a dynamic situation. It may be that there is a need to make changes to resource allocation, including individual roles, time-scales may need to be altered, approaches to customers modified (see Chapter 27); the objectives may even be modified because of difficulties or perhaps because new opportunities have arisen. As with all production activities, these meetings should be minuted.

Activity

Design a marketing plan for your chosen product. This should take the form of a formal report with appropriate headings and sub-headings. It should contain statistical information, financial details (costs and revenues) and a time-scaled schedule. The resources needed should be identified.

Make a forecast, based on your research, on how well your product will be received by a particular consumer group.

Product development based on a marketing plan

Justifications for product development should discuss the reliability of research data and forecasts and highlight the potential financial return.

As we saw above, **research data** should be up-to-date, accurate and fit for their purpose. **Forecasts** can then be made, based on some solid information, rather than just relying on hunches and guesswork.

Financial returns

Professional media producers have to justify their marketing plans to their financial backers, who may be a bank or a parent company. Many producers tend to 'play safe' for a number of reasons. It may be because their main interest is in producing a profit and so they continue with a tried and tested formula. They may also be restricted in what they do by their financial backers, who are generally conservative and whose overriding concern is with getting their money back. (Some people within the British music industry claim that it is declining because accountants working for the major record companies insist on safe releases by known major performers and bands rather than risk investing in new groups and soloists.)

Activity

What effect do you think an overriding concern with financial considerations can have on, for example, film-making and musical recordings?

Product development

The development of any product will involve either modification of an existing product or innovation.

Modification is the adaptation of, or improvement on, an existing product in order to create new markets or expand current ones. An existing product's modifications should extend its **product life-cycle**.

Innovation is a more radical change than modification. It implies inventiveness and creativity, and results in a completely new product.

Any product, whether existing or new, should be innovative in its approach to marketing in order to be competitive. The following are examples of modifications to existing products where new marketing plans would be needed:

- change of size (or length) – such as a broadsheet newspaper changing to tabloid size
- change of frequency – for example, a soap opera broadcast every weekday instead of three times a week
- change of quantity – for instance, the print run of a free newspaper is increased
- change of content – such as a radio station replacing part of a music programme with a phone-in slot
- change of style – e.g. a magazine makes its editorial comment features more light-hearted
- change in materials – for example, an adult comic changes to glossy paper
- change in format – for instance, a musical re-release is made available only on CD
- change in target audience – e.g. a newspaper introduces a section for young people.

The justification for introducing such product modifications may include the following:

- to save on production costs
- to sell to more people
- to reach more people
- to reach different people
- changes in technology (for example, many home music centres no longer have turntables)
- changes in materials available (for example, a world shortage of newsprint)
- changes in fashion and taste
- cultural changes (such as people's perception of what is decent/acceptable may alter with time or events)
- changes in the legal framework (e.g. film classification or libel laws)

- to adapt to the economic climate (for instance, what people can afford)
- changes in how people use a product (e.g. different working patterns affecting the numbers of radio listeners at different times of the day)
- the increased demand for up-to-the-minute information
- the activities of new or existing competitors
- identification of a growing or shrinking market (e.g. a growing demand for teen magazines or a decline in local newspaper advertising).

Activity

Suggest, with justifications, creative ways in which your chosen product could be modified if market conditions were to change.

Evidence assignment

Design a marketing plan for one of the media products you have made. The plan should cover these activities:

- research
- communication
- timing
- product design
- pricing
- packaging
- dissemination.

Include details on the market research data you have collected, and how the validity of the data was checked.

Prepare a product forecast which includes ideas for how and why the product could be developed and modified.

Make a presentation of the plan to the client.

Produce drafts and treatments for advertisements

The advertising campaign is an important part of the overall marketing plan; it has been called 'the conspicuous part of marketing'. The term *campaign* is used because businesses do not usually advertise as a 'one-off' but instead plan for a series of advertisements. This makes good sense because different types of people need to hear or see the same thing several times and often in differing ways, in order to get the message.

Sales promotions and direct selling, merchandising and some publicity may not strictly speaking be regarded as advertising, but they are referred to within the unit as they can form an integral part of an advertising campaign.

Identifying an appropriate advertising approach for media products

First of all, it may be helpful to consider some definitions of advertising.

An advert is a type of mass communication which aims to promote the sale of a product or service. An advert is a message or series of messages about a product or service. The message is intended to inform and influence the behaviour and attitudes of people. These messages are carried in the media which are often but not always (in the case of media products or services) owned and controlled by people other than the advertiser. Even the BBC carries advertising for its own media products such as the *Radio Times,* videos of drama series, books about and based on programmes, fact sheets, music cassettes and CDs, and so on.

Use of a marketing plan

Why are advertisements used? The answer to this question may include the following:

1 Many people need to be informed about a new product, special offer, price change or improvement.

For example: it would be impossible for *The Times* newspaper to inform all its readers and potential readers personally that the price is to be reduced. A TV advert can do this more efficiently and cost effectively.

2 People need to be informed quickly about a new product, special offer, price change or improvement.

For example: film companies cannot wait for the reputation of a new film to be established by word-of-mouth. This would be too slow. A film poster will do the job more quickly and accurately.

3 The customers or audience are not located in one place but are scattered over a region or are even in different countries. Personal selling would not be economic or even feasible.

For example: information about a new classical music album available on CD will reach a high percentage of the target audience through a radio advert on Classic FM.

4 Advertising is useful when it is difficult to identify customers.

For example: there is a fanzine for a new rock band. The names and address of readers will not be available as the product is new so an advert in a music magazine may be the answer.

5 The distribution chain is long and customers are remote from the producers. Advertisements enable the producer to send a message direct to the consumer or audience. Other people in the chain, such as retail outlets, may distort or even give unfavourable information about the product or promote a rival product.

For example: the newsagent selling a local paper does not know that there is always a special feature on Wednesday about buying cheap secondhand cars and recommends a specialist car magazine to a customer. An advert on local radio when people are driving to work could point out this feature effectively.

6 An advert is very effective in arousing initial interest, excitement or awareness in a product or service. It can help create new markets.

For example: a music teacher wants to give some lessons on modern music. She or he may be totally unaware of the existence of a CD-ROM which gives information and pictures of musicians and allows excerpts of music and instrumental sounds to be heard which would be ideal material. An advert in an educational magazine could create the link between product and customer.

7 An advert brings not only the product itself but the brand name to the attention of the consumer or audience and keeps it there. It sustains interest in a range of products and services by one company.

For example: watchers of Disney Films would soon get annoyed if a salesperson rang them up or mailed them continually to ask if they had seen the latest Disney film, visited Disney World or bought some Disney merchandising. Television adverts can, however, keep the name in the public's mind.

8 Frequent adverts can give 'post-purchase reassurance'. This makes the consumer feel that they have bought the right product. It reinforces a customer's relationship with a product.

For example: News of the World readers may feel pleased to see regular adverts on television for this newspaper. It makes them feel that they are buying something popular and acceptable, with a high profile.

9 When the advertising message is an emotional appeal, aimed at influencing people's lifestyles rather than giving factual information, then an advert is usually more appropriate.

For example: there is a new magazine for women which has a high proportion of erotic stories and sexual advice. A potential reader is more likely to buy the magazine after seeing a poster than if approached by a salesperson.

10 Adverts are effective with products that have an obvious selling point, which does not need a salesperson to give a personal explanation to the consumer or audience.

For example: a trailer for a new drama series can give information about when it will be on television.

11 Adverts can help the salesperson by introducing and reinforcing messages. A successful advert will invite further enquiries about the product or service.

For example: adverts for services on the Internet in magazines may not give sufficient technical details to satisfy readers but will arouse initial interest and clearly list the main points.

12 Regular adverts will bring the product or service to the attention of a new generation of consumers or audiences.

For example: teenagers will give up reading some comics as they grow older, so the publisher will need adverts aimed at young children to attract a new readership.

13 An advert may enable a producer to sell direct to the customer.

For example: large retailers may want to stock only magazine titles with a large readership, so specialist magazines with a small circulation may need to place an advert in another magazine informing customers of how they can subscribe direct in order to obtain copies.

It can be seen from the points above that advertisements are useful for two purposes:

■ **short-term objectives**, such as informing people of a change of price
■ **long-term objectives**, for instance keeping the brand name in the public's mind.

A marketing plan will help to make it clear where, when and how advertisements should be used.

Activity

Make a list of the advertising objectives which could apply to the media product you have chosen to market. Identify which are short-term and which are long-term objectives.

Where can adverts be placed?

Adverts are all around us, in all kinds of locations, including:

■ newspapers – local, regional and national
■ magazines – lifestyle and specialist
■ terrestrial, satellite and cable TV
■ local and national radio
■ the cinema screen
■ the Internet
■ display material in shops
■ posters
■ flyers
■ a variety of products, for example beermats, keyrings, carrier bags and so on.

They can take the form of trailers, display or classified adverts, advertising features, press releases, teletext pages, sponsorship, retail brochures, etc.

Activity

In small groups, make a collection over the space of a week of a representative sample of the media adverts you come into contact with. Try to gather audio-visual adverts as well as those from print publications.

Approach

The marketing plan will outline what **approach** will be most appropriate for the specified media product in terms of:

■ the choice of **medium** i.e. where the advert should be placed
■ the **message** to be selected i.e. what information or image needs to be given.

Decisions about both of these will need to be justified in terms of:

■ their relevance to the target audience
■ their relevance to the product
■ the content of the advertisements
■ the resources needed to produce and disseminate the advertisements.

Target audience

The first thing to be considered is relevance to the target audience. The marketing plan has already defined the **target audience**. They may have been classified into lifestyle groupings or into socio-economic groups. The more precisely the consumer is identified, the easier it is to address a particular message to her or him. As a general rule it is better for an advert to make a strong impact on a small audience than to give a weak message to a much larger group.

For example, a TV producer may want people who are teenagers or pensioners, who are unemployed or from a professional background, to watch a new soap. However, an individual advert will be more effective if it is aimed at teenagers, for example, or at adult males, or women teachers, because the vocabulary used in either advertisement will be unlikely to attract or hold the attention of all groups in the same way.

 Activity

Look at the adverts you have collected. For which types of audience are they most relevant? What is it about them that appeals to a certain target audience? Consider vocabulary, images, music or sound.

No advert appeals to everyone. When considering the population as a whole, a single advert is never going to be 100 per cent successful. An advert carries

information and is a means by which people can be persuaded to change attitudes or behaviour. However, it will lose its impact if it is seen or heard by people who are hostile, indifferent or ignorant with regard to the product or service.

In Britain **subliminal** advertising is banned. This is when an advert subconsciously influences the behaviour of the viewer or listener without them being aware of this. For example, images of drinks and a desert scene are inserted into a video so quickly that the viewer does not realise that he has seen them but they are recognised by his subconscious and the viewer will respond by wanting a drink.

The diagram in Figure 27.1 indicates how attitudes can potentially differ even amongst people of a similar age group or of the same gender or ethnic background.

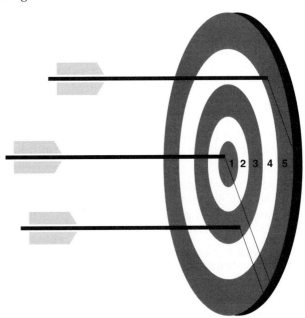

Figure 27.1 Attitudes of audiences

Key to Figure 27.1

1 These people will be definite members of an audience or consumers. They need little or no persuasion. It is enough for the advert to inform them about when a programme can be viewed or where a magazine can be bought. They are active in seeking out products and services. They will say, 'I am buying the *Daily Mail* today.' They know what they want.

2 These people intend to be members of the audience or consumers. They have a good attitude towards the product, but may need additional persuasion or information to turn an intention into behaviour. This type of person may think something is a good idea but gives priority to other things. The advert may need to include a special offer with a closing date to make them act. This type of person will say, 'If I get time I'd like to go to see that film next week.'

3 The majority of the population may have an attitude of indifference towards a product or service. These are the 'don't knows', or the 'don't cares', in other words, the silent majority. They are existing without the product or service and have no real need for it. It is possible to change their attitude but an advertising campaign rather than a single advert will be more effective. The campaign may succeed by creating a need, appealing to emotions and people's wish for a different lifestyle rather than using adverts which give information. This sort of person might say, 'I'm not interested in a new car magazine, I'm happy with the one I buy every month.'

4 A certain proportion of the population may be positively hostile towards what is being offered. Except for a miracle, they are unlikely to become customers, not in the short term at least. Their feelings and views may be irrational – based on ignorance, prejudice or misinformation – or their attitudes may be based on good reasons or personal convictions. It is not worth the time and effort for these people to be targeted by the advertiser. These people will say, 'Producing this car magazine on glossy paper is wasting the earth's resources and is full of advertising for vehicles which are polluting the world' or 'This film has too much sex and violence and is corrupting the morals of society.'

5 These people may share all the attitudes and behaviour patterns of any of the above but are unable to use or buy the product because they cannot possibly afford it or they will never have sufficient time or a purpose for using it. They too are not worth targeting.

Activity

Look again at the adverts you have collected. Are they aimed at people who are already members of the audience or consumers? Or at people who intend to use or buy the product or service? Or at people who are at present indifferent towards the product?

Choice of medium

A number of factors can affect the choice of medium:

1 Which medium is most likely to reach the largest number of the target audience?
If the product is a new computer game for children, and the target audience is all children between the ages of six and twelve, then the answer will be an advertising slot on children's TV on a Saturday morning. If the product is a new pop video, an advert on MTV will reach a high proportion of the target audience.

Whether you are a professional media producer or a student on a simulation of a marketing exercise, you will need to organise market research to confirm that your target audience does listen to, watch or read your chosen medium. This will need to be done in some detail. It is not enough to know that someone watches ITV regularly or buys the *Sun*. You will need to know precisely what time of the day they are viewing or which section of the newspaper they read. Otherwise, they may still miss your advert if it is positioned on the wrong page or scheduled at the wrong time.

In Britain, the most important media for advertising are the press and television. Radio is perceived as being less important here, whereas in the United States radio advertising has a far higher profile. However, in India, where relatively few people have their own television sets, millions go to the cinema so cinema advertising is far more powerful.

2 What is the cost of reaching this target audience?
For most target audiences, the largest number will be reached by advertising on prime-time TV when some programmes attract millions of viewers. Placing a full-page advert for a new film in the leading tabloid newspaper will also be effective because the circulation figures are so high and cover hundreds of thousands of people from all walks of life. What will prevent many producers from advertising on television or in national newspapers is the cost. In a summer campaign, Central television tried to persuade viewers that it is cheap to advertise on TV (see Figure 27.2).

But small media producers cannot afford to advertise on national television. It will be more cost effective to advertise in a specialist magazine, or on local radio, where they can still reach a significant number of the target audience (see Figure 27.3).

459

Prices per Spot for the Central Full Region

	10 SEC £	20 SEC £	30 SEC £	40 SEC £	50 SEC £	60 SEC £
T00	125	208	250	333	415	500
T01	250	415	500	665	830	1000
T02	500	830	1000	1330	1660	2000
T03	750	1245	1500	1995	2490	3000
T04	1000	1660	2000	2660	3320	4000
T05	1250	2075	2500	3325	4150	5000
T06	1500	2490	3000	3990	4980	6000
T07	2000	3320	4000	5320	6640	8000
T08	2500	4150	5000	6650	8300	10000
T09	3000	4980	6000	7980	9960	12000
T10	4000	6640	8000	10640	13280	16000
T11	5000	8300	10000	13300	16600	20000
T12	6000	9960	12000	15960	19920	24000
T13	7500	12450	15000	19950	24900	30000
T14	9000	14940	18000	23940	29880	36000
T15	11000	18260	22000	29260	36520	44000
T16	13500	22410	27000	35910	44820	54000
T17	16000	26560	32000	42560	53120	64000
T18	19000	31540	38000	50540	63080	76000
T19	22500	37350	45000	59850	74700	90000
T20	27000	44820	54000	71820	89640	108000

Local Advertiser Packages

Central West	10 SEC £	20 SEC £	30 SEC £	PRODUCTION
5 SPOT PACKAGE	3500	5810	7000	Still
10 SPOT PACKAGE	6500	10790	13000	Still
15 SPOT PACKAGE	9990	16590	19980	Live Action
Central East	10 SEC £	20 SEC £	30 SEC £	PRODUCTION
5 SPOT PACKAGE	2000	3320	4000	Still
10 SPOT PACKAGE	3000	4980	6000	Still
15 SPOT PACKAGE	4995	8295	9990	Live Action
Central South	10 SEC £	20 SEC £	30 SEC £	PRODUCTION
5 SPOT PACKAGE	2000	3320	4000	Still
10 SPOT PACKAGE	3000	4980	6000	Still
15 SPOT PACKAGE	4995	8295	9990	Live Action

Figure 27.2 Central TV rates for adverts

Total Audience Package 0600–2400	£28.00
Daytime Package 0600–1900	£39.00
P1 0600–0900 Mon–Fri 0900–1200 Sat–Sun	£54.00
P2 0900–1200 Mon–Fri 0600–0900 Sat–Sun	£46.00
P3 1200–1500 Mon–Sun	£26.00
P4 1500–1900 Mon–Sun	£28.00
P5 1900–2400 Mon–Sun	£9.00

Price in £'s   These are pre-payment rates

Above rates apply for 30-second commercials. The following rates apply for other lengths

10-second	–30%	50-second	+70%
20-second	–20%	60-second	+100%
40-second	+35%	60-second	+pro rata

Figure 27.3 Leicester Sound rate card

3 Does more than one type of media need to be used to run the advertisements?
New television programmes, films, magazines and so on sometimes use a combination of posters and trailers and display ads to promote themselves. For example, the *News of the World* regularly advertises on weekend television but also places advertisements in other newspapers.

4 Does the choice of medium suit the particular product?
An advert for a colourful, glossy, new fashion magazine could look rather dull in a newspaper which reproduces only in black and white. A music album released by a new band would be best supported by an audio-visual advert so that their music can be heard.

It is also vital to consider which *section* of the chosen medium is most appropriate to use. You may have decided that newspapers are the best choice for you to advertise in. However, you must then consider which newspaper. So the *Financial Times* would probably not be the best place for an advertisement about a TV series of daytime programmes for the unemployed!

WHY RADIO?

Radio	works
Radio	reaches more people
Radio	goes where people go
Radio	is fast – immediate and flexible
Radio	generates customer flow
Radio	reaches new potential customers
Radio	is personal
Radio	appeals to the emotions and thought processes
Radio	is remembered
Radio	is very cost effective
Radio	is exciting
Radio	maintains sales and revenue momentum
Radio	commercials are 'front page' commercials
Radio	sells by word of mouth (just like you) – it's the best recommendation you can have
Radio	is the most intrusive medium in the world
Radio	stays with the shopper through the entire decision-making process
Radio	builds and maintains loyalty
Radio	helps you keep ahead of others in your line of business (getting your unfair share of the market)
Radio	helps you combat other business categories
Radio	builds employee morale
Radio	targets specific groups
Radio	combats the curve of forgetting (repetition building reputation)
Radio	is first for information
Radio	offers a bonus weekend audience
Radio	will boost the image and prestige of your business

52% of listeners are tuned in to commercial radio

Figure 27.4 Reasons for the effectiveness of radio advertising

All the media are eager to attract advertisers, as the resulting revenue forms a major part of their income. Figure 27.4 shows some reasons given by a commercial radio for why advertising on radio is effective.

The **Radio Advertising Bureau** was founded in 1992 by the UK commercial radio industry to act as the central marketing department for the media, totally independent of the airtime sales departments. The RAB is a trade marketing body, addressing the needs of national advertisers and agencies rather than listeners. The organisation is funded by a levy on all national radio advertising, which enables it to be

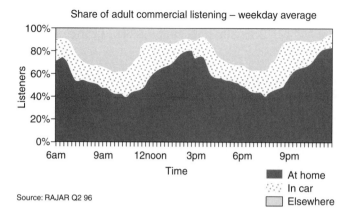

Source: RAJAR Q2 96

Figure 27.5 Listening by location: all commercial radio

impartial in its advice and recommendations and to carry out research, such as that shown in Figure 27.5.

The mission statement of the RAB explains its purpose:

'To contribute to the achievement of significant market-share growth by the radio industry in total, by actively managing the development of an improved climate of familiarity and favourability for radio as an advertising medium amongst advertisers, their creative and media intermediaries alike.'

Newspapers also like to prove how they can promote sales – see Figure 27.6.

THE BENEFITS OF NEWSPAPER ADVERTISING

1 Develops an even flow of trade.

2 Captures new customers.

3 Keeps the advertiser's name constantly before the public.

4 Ensures a fair share of business.

5 Promotes faster turnover and helps overcome expenses.

6 Helps keep staff constantly employed.

7 Reaches potential customers economically.

8 Gives full descriptions, economically and with flexibility.

9 It is a vast market-place.

10 The reader seeks classified, display seeks the reader.

Figure 27.6 Advantages of newspaper ads

Activity

Brainstorm all the possible advantages of:

1 producing cinema ads
2 running a poster campaign.

Relevance to product

What is being advertised and what is the best way to do this?

We looked above at what medium might be the most appropriate. Now we can look at the **selection of messages**.

What needs to be included?

In other words, what information, mood, emotion or image needs to be put in the message?

It has been estimated that on average we are exposed to 1200 advertising messages each day! We obviously do not concentrate on all of these or are even aware that we have seen or heard them. Our brains select what to ignore and what to notice.

In order to advertise effectively you must select one clear, simple, uncluttered and directed image of the product or information about the product that is most likely to interest or excite the customer. This selected idea then become the **USP** (Unique Selling Proposition) which lies at the heart of the campaign.

The USP may be:

- this film is exciting
- the Internet brings you up-to-the-minute news
- this newspaper is for the thinking woman
- this comic is educational for children
- this magazine is cheap
- this TV programme is good entertainment for all the family.

Products may well have more than one selling point: a magazine may be cheap and colourful, a TV programme may appeal to teenagers and women, a film may be wonderfully romantic, have major stars and be based on a classic novel. However, it is usually better to focus on one selling point at a time for an advert.

What is the best way to convey this message?

The following aspects will all have to be considered:

- words
- visuals
- music/sounds
- arrangement of these within the advert
- positioning (scheduling) of the advert.

Two more aspects – the **content** of adverts and their **treatment** – will be dealt with in detail below (see pages 464–6).

Resource requirements

In choosing which approach will be most appropriate, the deciding factor will be the **resource requirements** – human, financial (commercial effectiveness), time and materials.

Human resources

Who is needed to produce the adverts?

- The **advertisers** are the companies producing products or services. We are considering here almost exclusively companies making media products. A few media organisations may produce some of their own adverts internally, but others will seek help from outside the organisation.
- The **media** are the newspaper and magazine publishers, TV and radio stations, transport authorities, etc. who carry the ads. They may also be responsible for the actual production of the adverts themselves.
- **Advertising agencies** are companies specialising in the development and production of advertising campaigns for a variety of clients.

A typical team needed for an advertising agency would include:

- the account manager – deals directly with the client
- the account planners – decide on strategy and the general creative approach
- a product/brand manager – is responsible for one particular product or group of products, which prevents a brand from becoming neglected
- an advertising/promotions manager – will deal with other aspects of the campaign, such as specific promotions, and may give advice on packaging and display
- creative people (art director/copywriter/visualiser)

– these write and design ideas for adverts
■ market researchers – who research the product, the market, and the media which will carry the adverts.

A typical advertising agency performs the following services for clients:

1 plans marketing and advertising strategies and plans how the budget will be spent
2 writes copy
3 prepares artwork, layouts and storyboards
4 may buy in artwork and services of other specialist production companies, for example animation experts for a TV ad
5 selects the appropriate media
6 contracts for time and space in the media to show the adverts
7 checks bills and pays media
8 organises merchandising and promotional events to the trade
9 researches market, media, copy and results
10 manages public relations activities.

Financial resources

Examples of rate cards for adverts have been shown in Figures 27.2 and 27.3 in this chapter. Advertising agencies receive a commission from the media owners of approximately 15 per cent.

Time needed

All activities have to be carefully scheduled. It is essential that a product such as a film is released at the correct time of year. A good time for a children's film to be released is during the school holidays, especially at Christmas. A TV series on holiday destinations is possibly best in the spring, when people are planning their holidays.

The publicity to advertise such products also needs to be carefully timed. If people are informed too far in advance they will forget; if too near, they will have arranged to do other things. A campaign will need to build in strength over a period of time. So some products have been introduced by a series of enigmatic posters and then more details slowly given over a period of weeks or even months. This arouses and sustains public interest.

The process of scheduling of the adverts, and the various people involved is dealt with in more detail below (see page 467).

Materials needed

An advert is a short or small print and graphics or audio-visual product. The production materials needed have been identified in the production units 2, 3, 4 and 5.

Activity

Identify the resources you will need for the ideas you have listed above, for an advertising campaign to support the media products you have made. You will need to:

1 make a list of people who will have roles in the advertising team
2 agree a budget with the client (who may be your teacher)
3 make a list of the materials you will need, including equipment and locations.

Content issues relevant to the selected approach

The advertising approach should take account of the numerous legal, ethical and representational issues raised when producing an advertising campaign. This is dealt with in the appendix covering legal and ethical issues.

Not only individual adverts but advertising itself is criticised for the following reasons:

1 it is a waste of money and world resources and adds to the price of the product
2 it forces people to buy things they do not need
3 it encourages people to spend money they can ill afford
4 it appeals to less sociable emotions such as envy and snobbishness and encourages materialism.

The Advertising Standards Authority was set up in 1962 by the advertising industry. It operates a voluntary code of practice called 'The British Code of Advertising and Sales Promotion Practice', which covers the contents of all forms of advertising in newspapers and magazines, cinema commercials, posters, direct mail, and sales promotions. It does not cover television and radio ads, these are monitored by the Independent Television Commission and the Independent Radio Authority.

Product placement

The ITC Code of Programme Sponsorship guidelines forbid the inclusion of a product or a service within a programme in return for payment or other valuable consideration to the programme-maker or ITC Licensee.

Programmes can use 'real' products, even if supplied free of charge by a manufacturer, as long as they are not over-prominent. Product placement is allowed on American television. Manufacturers will also pay thousands of pounds for their product to be used in films.

Activity

Watch a TV soap or situation comedy. How many examples of 'real' products can you see, such as cars, food, drinks, shops?

The ASA code states that all advertisements must be legal, decent, honest and truthful. They must not offend people, or downgrade competitors, and they must not deliberately misinform.

Activity

Can you find any adverts which you think may not be legal, decent, honest or truthful?

The laws you should be aware of in this context are:

- Copyright Design and Patent Act 1988
- Race Relations Act
- Equal Opportunities Act
- Trades Descriptions Act

Listed below are the ethical issues you should consider:

- **Social issues** can be :
  - avoidance of crime
  - unemployment
  - improvement of education
  - police force
  - public health

- **Events** can be :
  - sporting
  - live show
  - political conference

- **Ideas** can be:
  - political
  - environmental
  - cultural
  - religious.

Activity

Discuss how much media adverts stereotype. Suggest one idea for an advert which uses either women or men in traditional roles and one idea for an advert that reverses these roles.

Ideas for advertising media products

A good advert will follow the AIDA principle and should:

- **Attract**
- **Interest**
- arouse **Desire**
- create **Action**

Activity

Choose three adverts for different media products which you consider effective. Identify which parts of them follow the AIDA principle.

We have looked in earlier production units at where ideas for media products come from. Ideas for adverts can be found from a similar variety of sources. They can offer representations of different lifestyles or they can be pure fantasy; they can be funny or inspire fear. Sometimes, other media products themselves can provide inspiration. So a cartoon character from a Disney film could successfully 'star' in an advert for a children's comic.

Case study

Study the film posters in Figures 27.7 and 27.8.

Disclosure

Both the photographic images and the prominent positioning of the actors' names in *Disclosure*

Figure 27.7 Poster for the film *Disclosure*

Figure 27.8 Poster for the film *Goldeneye*

emphasise the stars as the main selling point. From the picture itself, the expression on the faces, you cannot tell what the story is about. The small print underneath gives some indication, but this is of secondary importance to the fact that Michael Douglas and Demi Moore are starring in the film. The advert is aimed at fans of these two people.

Goldeneye

This poster emphasises the genre of the film: this advert is targeted at lovers of action movies. Prominent here is the gun and the face of a young attractive healthy male. The women are less prominent. The graphics of fire, cars, fighter planes and the man running, all underline the potential excitement. The name of the actor here is unimportant, but the name '007' is prominent.

Activity

Look at all the adverts you have collected. Can you identify the main selling point of each, i.e. the USP?

Make a list of the selling points of your own media product.

Which do you think is the best point and why?

Different types of adverts

Here are some examples of different types of adverts:

1 those that give **information** about a product, for example: *Cheapo* magazine costs only 90p
2 those that promote a **lifestyle**, for example: rich successful people read *Social Climber* magazine
3 those that evoke an **emotion**, for example: Do you remember how magical Christmas was when you were a child? Then you'll love the new film *Santa came to stay*
4 those that promote a **brand name**, for example: *Squirrel* is the latest in a line of successful horror films made by Talker Brothers.

Activity

Look at the list of four types of adverts described above. Can you make the different angles apply to your media product?

Brand image

The basis of a brand is a name. But other features combine with this to create an image such as visual design, colour, typography, house style and slogans. The brand image is what the logo symbolises about the range of products or services; the brand image conveys the emotions and understanding of the range of products that are created by the sight of the brand name.

The following are examples of **brand names**. They are always printed in different forms of advertising (from posters to carrier bags) using the same font and usually the same colour (see Figure 27.9).

This enables the product to be remembered and easily identified. It provides strong links between advertising and other forms of promotions. Giveaways, such as balloons or stickers, will use the brand name.

Figure 27.9 Brand names are always printed in a recognisable style

New products can be introduced under an existing, well-established and regarded brand name. Sometimes the name of a film director has the status of a brand name, for example Steven Spielberg (*ET, Back to the Future*, etc.) or Bertolucci (*Stealing Beauty, Last Tango in Paris*). Occasionally, it is possible for a media producer with a successful brand in one sector to enter another sector with a different product, e.g. Virgin (Virgin record shops, Virgin Radio, Virgin Atlantic and Virgin Finance).

Target audience

All ideas for advertising have to be based around the **target audience**. If you have completed Units 2 to 5, you will have looked at how ideas for different products are generated and what appeals to certain groups of people and their expectations, in terms of

Figure 27.10 Radio stickers use brand names for easy identification

colour, typography, zany images, pace, quality of voice and accent, etc.

You will need to make a decision about whether your selling point is a *lifestyle* (e.g. 'intelligent people listen to Radio PBM') or some piece of *information* about the product ('you can rent videos cheaper from Videohouse').

Packaging

An advertising agency will take a good, hard look at the packaging of a product – its overall **look**, for instance at the cover if it is a book or magazine, the case if it is a video or CD-ROM. These may be included in the adverts themselves if they are particularly attractive or striking. With student work, you may need to consider this aspect before proceeding to the adverts proper.

Activity

Brainstorm some ideas for both print and graphics and audio-visual adverts for your media product, considering the target audience, medium and selling point. These may be based on current or historical events, stars, current buzz words, cartoon characters, famous paintings, fairy stories, etc. The list is endless!

When you have sketched out the ideas you should discuss them with the client.

Perhaps the most important thing to remember about your advert is that it should be **memorable**. Techniques for this are explained below; see pages 470–74 which deal with drafts and treatments in detail.

Preparing a schedule for the campaign

A schedule is a time-scale within which certain activities should be carried out. A schedule can be planned at the first team meeting.

In order to prepare a schedule for the campaign the following decisions will need to be made with the agreement of the client.

- **What activities have been chosen?**
  These should include newspaper adverts, press releases, merchandising, etc.

There should of course be a mixture of activities.

- **Which media will be used?**
  Television or radio commercials.
  Posters or adverts in magazines.
  What areas or types of audience should these media cover?

- **Timing**
  When will advertisements be made and when will they appear?
  When should promotional leaflets be distributed?

- **Frequency of advertising**
  How often will a magazine need special promotions?
  How frequently should commercials be heard on the radio?

Figure 27.11 is a flow diagram which shows the usual order of activities for planning a schedule.

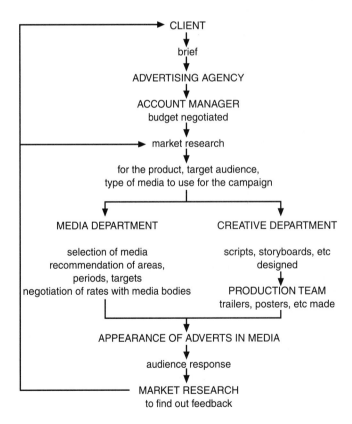

Figure 27.11 Schedule for planning an advertising campaign

467

Film campaign

Here is how an advertising campaign for a film might proceed.

- **Press advertising**
  This is mostly done through newspapers and usually starts two weeks before the film opens.

- **Television advertising**
  Trailers will appear on terrestrial television about a week before the opening night, but this is very expensive and so is done for high-budget films only. Satellite and cable television also show trailers for lower-budget films.

- **Radio advertising**
  This is a popular way to advertise films, especially if they have a good soundtrack, such as in *Top Gun*, that might make the charts.

- **Posters**
  These are often the heart of the advertising campaign and will be designed and produced long before the film is finished, ready for distribution in the weeks leading up to the film's release.

- **Publicity**
  High-quality black and white stills of the stars and the sets are produced whilst filming, for later release to the press. These can then be sent in the **press kit** to magazine and newspaper journalists. Also included in the press kit are details of credits, biographies of the stars and production crew, especially the producer and director. Journalists in television and radio also receive EPKs (electronic press kits), which contain video clips, audio clips and interviews with the stars and crew.

- **Trailers**
  Short teaser trailers of 30 seconds are played in cinemas up to six months before the film's release. Longer trailers are played in the cinemas between seven and five weeks before the film is shown.

- **Preview screenings**
  The press will be invited to a pre-release screening so that they can write reviews and publicise the film by word of mouth.

For more detail on film advertising, publicity and promotions, you are recommended to study the *Movie Mogul* pack detailed in Chapter 17 page 295.

Activity

You have to arrange the dates for the advertising campaign for a new blockbuster film for children to be released at Christmas. Write a schedule, giving precise dates for the activities listed above.

Case study

The *Leicester Mercury* student project sales team developed their advertising campaign as part of the project marketing plan. The advertising approach needed to be relevant to the product and relevant to the target audience. This involved the team in identifying what were several target audiences. These were organisations which:

- in the past advertised in the *Mercury* and would do so again at an attractive price
- may or may not already advertise with the *Leicester Mercury* but are involved with the college
- may or may not advertise in the *Leicester Mercury* but wish to reach the student and youth market.

The students had to find a marketing approach that was relevant to the product because it matched the expectations of the *Leicester Mercury* readership, whilst remaining appropriate for the younger audience it was targeting.

Advertising plans for the students' newspaper had to take into account the different target audiences identified. Attracting potential advertisers so that they can advertise in a print product requires a different approach from that used for attracting readers to that product. There were, therefore, two distinct campaigns: one to sell the *newspaper* and the other to sell *advertising space* within the newspaper.

The students researched potential advertisers and set up a database. They stored details of all responses, including 'not interested'. Much can be learned from negative responses. It is worth reflecting, for example, on why the organisation said no and whether anything could be learnt from it for future approaches.
All responses should be discussed at regular team meetings. If you are not achieving much success you can look at your approach and decide whether it is appropriate. Are you getting past the secretary when you make your telephone calls? Do people come out with all kinds of excuses that you have no answer for? These kinds of issues need to be dealt with and, where necessary, plans modified as a result.

The students started looking for potential advertisers among those organisations in existing contact with their college. First of all they produced a sales letter. Remember that it is vitally important that all marketing communications, such as sales letters, telephone calls and information packs, are produced as professionally as possible. This is the first contact with your potential customers and it is the first impression that lasts the longest.

Telephone script

- I would like to speak to Mr Brown – would you put me through please?

    Who's calling?

- Gary, representing Hinckley College.

- Hello Mr Brown – I'm Gary from Hinckley College –

- I'd like a couple of minutes of your time please …

- Are you aware of Hinckley College?

- Are you aware that we cater for students from 15 years of age upwards?

- Would you say that a large portion of your client base are students – or the younger age group?

- How do you currently attract the younger clients into your business?

- You obviously understand the value of the younger market.

- If I could show you a credible method of attracting new younger clients – you'd be interested – wouldn't you?

- The Hinckley College are putting together a supplement promoting the college itself and encouraging students from further afield.

- The supplement will be inserted into all editions of the *Leicester Mercury* – giving you a potential reach of over 317 000 readers on one day.

- The *Leicester Mercury* is a paid-for newspaper – it's daily and it is the largest provincial newspaper in the city and county.

- By sponsoring the Hinckley College supplement you will achieve the following:
    - You will be reaching your target market – they are the people with disposable income
    - You will be demonstrating an interest in education
    - Good for your image and credibility!
    - 12 months' shelf life – unique opportunity – a once-off
    - At least 00 companies are already sponsoring the supplement – they understand the value of reaching and supporting students.

- So what I can do for you is to include your company name and logo – at the base of page 1 – for **just** £00 and by doing so you will ensure over 317 000 are exposed to your company within this highly prestigious educational supplement.

- Do you have a logo available to be included in the Sponsorship List?

- Thank you for your business – and good luck.

Figure 27.12 Telephone script for *Leicester Mercury* student project advertising campaign

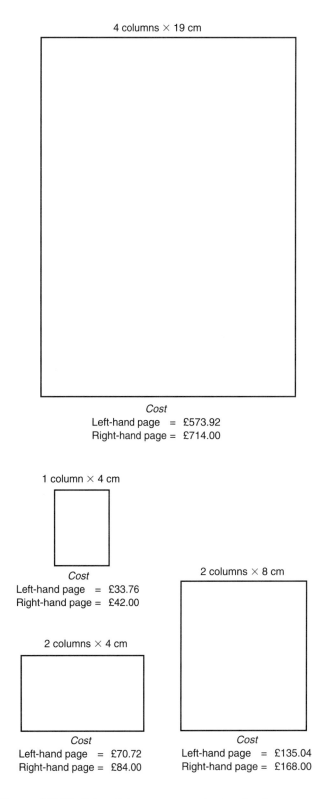

Figure 27.13 Advertising space and rates for the project

The students decided to send out the sales letter first and then follow up with a telephone call. Figure 27.12 shows the telephone script they produced for these calls.

A sales package was produced, detailing the different sizes of adverting space on offer and their cost. Cost of newspaper advertising depends on certain specifications:

- the **size** of the advert, which in turn is determined by the price per column centimetre
- the **position** in the paper: for example, right-hand pages are more expensive because the eye sees them first. Also a front page advert will cost more than one of the same type in the inside pages
- the **amount** of advertising space that a customer buys. There could be discounts or specially negotiated rates for large amounts or for regular customers
- the **type** of advert required: will the customer provide 'camera-ready' artwork (artwork that is ready for printing without any work needed on it) or will they want the ad designed? Does the customer want colour or monochrome?

The information pack for advertisers contained details of advertising rates, with background information about the organisation or project. It tried to anticipate questions by, for example, giving a list of benefits and particularly USPs (Unique Selling Points).

The advertising sales team of the *Leicester Mercury* student project drew up a list of activities and, where appropriate, gave deadlines and allocated responsibilities. This is the list of the type of activities that they identified:

- produce a database of potential customers
- set up a mail-merge facility and produce a form letter
- list the selling points
- produce examples of advertising space and costs
- produce 'thank you' letters
- write a telephone script
- obtain office space and telephone

On the next page is an excerpt from the schedule they devised.

The team were involved in other activities besides those listed. They found, for example, that they often had to make telephone calls just to find out the name of the person they wished to write to. In addition, not everything can be planned or foreseen. For example, the team had to re-negotiate some of the advertising agreements and, with the page design team, redesign the pages because the *Mercury* changed its size halfway through the project. However, careful planning and scheduling enabled the team to work in a structured and organised manner.

Remember that it is good marketing policy to follow up orders with a 'thank you' letter (see Figure 27.16). It keeps customers informed about the project and helps to create a good working relationship for the future: successful marketing is all about **repeat business**.

Drafts and treatments for advertising media products

The details of how to prepare specifications, briefs, drafts, treatments, scripts and storyboards for media products have been described already in the production units and you should refer to those sections again now. Here we will discuss general principles for designing adverts and how to transform the ideas you have into a product.

Most people generally read a newspaper for the news not the adverts, or listen to a radio station for the music rather than the commercials. So an advert must gain the reader's, viewer's or listener's primary attention; it needs to command their concentration against other influences. It must sustain interest and not be boring. But above all it must be **memorable**.

Benefits of advertising with us

*Your advert will be seen by over 317 000 people.

*Our rates are just 75% of current 𝔐ercury prices.

*Your advert will be in **all** editions of the 𝔏eicester 𝔐ercury.

*The supplement will attract a large number of student readers, these are the people with disposable income.

*You will be demonstrating an interest in education.

*This is an annual publication, so it will stand out from the rest of the 𝔏eicester 𝔐ercury.

*We aim to promote this edition of the 𝔏eicester 𝔐ercury across Hinckley & neighbouring areas.

Figure 27.14 Extract from the information pack for advertisers

Wednesday 24 January

Mark	Set up mail-merge database on the computer. Write a form letter.
Team	Meeting with Gary (editor) to decide on advertising/editorial split. Decide on costing structure for advert.

Thursday 25 January

Dominic	Size last year's adverts and look up phone numbers relating to advertisers.
Vicky	Look up 50 businesses in *Yellow Pages.* Write down their names, addresses and phone numbers.

Friday 26 January

Vicky	To look up another 25 addresses.
Mark	Check on available admin. help from college staff.
Dominic	Visit library to check facilities.

Monday 29 January

Mark	Meeting with Roger Crossley (Vice-Principal) to arrange an office and a phone. Discuss college's commitment to advertise.
Dominic	Make a flip chart showing the overall strategy.

Tuesday 30 January

Vicky	Research companies that might want to advertise with us.
Mark	Make a presentation to Tim Cowen, Annemarie Shillito and Barbara Hastings at the *Leicester Mercury.*

Thursday 1 February

Vicky	Phone companies to get names of people to contact.
Mark	Liaise with admin. staff to organise printing letters and envelopes.

Friday 2 February

Dominic Vicky &	Phone companies to get names of people to contact.
Dominic	Visit shops in Hinckley town centre to get contact names of potential advertisers.

Monday 5 February

Mark	Print out letters. Collect labels from Moira Reid (college staff).

Wednesday 7 February

Mark	Liaise with Chris Turner re production of examples of adverts.
Vicky	Use a DTP package to produce an information/price sheet and size/cost guides to give advertisers.
Dominic	Add names of more potential advertisers to database.

Thursday 8 February

Mark & Mike	Devise a written advertising agreement for advertisers to sign. (See Figure 27.15.)
Mark & Mike	Visit clients in Hinckley.

Friday 9 February

Vicky & Dominic	Visit clients in Hinckley.

Wednesday 21 February

Team	Visit clients.
Vicky	Telephone canvassing: cold calling.

Thursday 22 February

Dominic	Cold calling.

Mark Pearson/Mike Sewell
c/o Pete Morrissey
Hinckley College,
London Road,
Hinckley,
Leicestershire
LE10 1HQ
☎(01455) 251222

Advertising Agreement

Thank you for agreeing to advertise in our feature. The following details must be confirmed before publication.

The four-page supplement will be printed in all editions of the *Leicester Mercury* newspaper on one day, in the week commencing Monday 25 March 1996.

All advertisements need to be received at least one week prior to the publication date.

Please note the publication will be in Black & White print only.

Invoices will be despatched after publication.

Agreed details

Name _____

Company name _____

Size of advert _____

Placement _____

Cost _____

Origin _____

Proof required? _____

Voucher copy required? _____

I, the undersigned, have read, and agree the details listed above are correct. I also understand that usual *Leicester Mercury* conditions of acceptance for advertising* apply.

Signed _____ Date _____

*Written copies of which are available on request.

Figure 27.15 An example of an advertising agreement

Vicky & Mike	Visit clients.
Mark	Plan page layout and do percentage/ratio percentages.

Friday 23 February

Team	Telephone canvassing and visits.

Tuesday 5 to Friday 8 March

Team	Collect copy. Liaise with design team.

Monday 11 March

Mark	Meeting with *Mercury* staff.

Tuesday 19 to Thursday 21 March

Team	Show adverts designed at college to the clients.

Our Ref: : MDP/21/B
March 1996

Dear

On behalf of my advertising team, and indeed all the students who have been involved in this project, I would like to thank you for advertising in our *Leicester Mercury* feature.

Our page layout team are presently in action putting the four pages together and the final product will appear in the *Leicester Mercury* on Tuesday 26 March 1996. We will provide you with a copy on the day of publication.

The experience we have gained in dealing with your business has proved invaluable. It has given us an interesting insight into the world of print advertising and commerce as a whole. Situations can be taken from text books, but far more experience is gained from working on a real project.

We realise that, without your support, our feature could not be published. The publication of your advert will not only promote your business but also serve to demonstrate your interest and willingness to work closely with education.

Thank you again for your support and we hope your advertisement benefits the business.

Yours sincerely

Figure 27.16 A thank you letter keeps the customer informed

The following are some of the various techniques used in the different types of media to do this.

- **Appropriate words**
  The vocabulary should be that used by the target audience. Short words (e.g. Help! No!) can grab the attention – whether they are written or heard – far more than a longer sentence. Slogans, buzz words and familiar phrases are also useful. The catchphrases on posters are known as **tag lines**.

- **Repetition**
  Important information, such as a telephone number or the name of the product, is often repeated in audio adverts. Sometimes, in the case of television commercials, an advert for a particular product is shown at the beginning of a commercial slot and again at the end with slight variations – it may be shorter or have a different ending.

- **Striking pictures**
  Images, whether still or moving, can be stunningly beautiful or shocking, but they should stay in the viewer's or reader's mind.

- **Large print**
  One or two words using a large typeface will focus the attention more than a paragraph in small print.

- **Bright colours**
  Red or yellow are colours that 'pull' the eye and can give significance to words or images. The choice of colours and how they relate to each other is important. Too many colours can look fussy and confuse the message.

- **Unusual layout or structure of material**
  You don't read an advert like a page of text. For instance, a good designer will direct the eye so that it moves around a poster gathering information in a certain order. To avoid boredom, try arranging the images in a poster or the arrangement of shots in a storyboard in an unusual way. Use strange camera angles or unexpected edits to make your advert stand out from rival adverts. Avoid arranging all text in a straight line and centring everything, including the graphics.

- **A well-known personality**
  The human form is always a strong image to attract attention and it is a familiar ploy to use famous actors or celebrities to promote a product (sometimes just using their voices can be enough, for example on radio or TV adverts).

- **Familiar music**
  Adverts for programmes on television, radio or for films will generally use their theme music. The music will have been chosen in the first place because it supports the genre and enhances the emotions and action found in the product. Adverts for newspapers and magazines, however, often use music with which the public is familiar, and which also reflects the quality of the product. Often this is classical music, as publications try to show that they are patriotic or have traditional values.

- **Narrative structure**
  Adverts can be based on stories and events, true or fantasy (for example, Jack and Jill went up the hill to listen to radio AZ). A series of adverts can follow the storyline of a soap (as exemplified in

Figure 27.17 An enigmatic poster can arouse interest

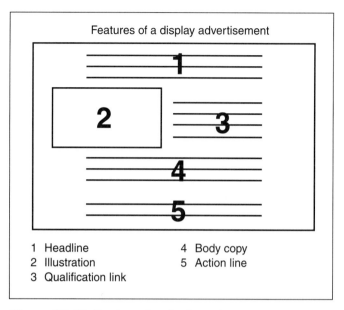

Features of a display advertisement

1 Headline
2 Illustration
3 Qualification link
4 Body copy
5 Action line

Figure 27.18 Design of a display advert

the series of Gold Blend coffee adverts which followed the romance of two people as they made frequent cups of coffee). An enigmatic advert which puzzles the audience can also be used to arouse interest and sustain it, as the person who sees or hears it wonders about what it means. Usually an enigmatic poster is part of a series: each successive poster will clear up the mystery a little further.

Activity

Which of the adverts you have collected use these techniques?

Which of them could an advert for your media product use?

Display adverts

The design of posters was discussed in Unit 3, so we will now look at how to design a display advert.

The main features of a display advert are: headline, illustration, qualification link, body copy and action line (see Figure 27.18).

The **headline** should not be the name of a company, shop or product. It is better for a headline to be based on one of the following:

- describe the advantages of the product – what it does, how it is easy to use, for example, '*Do-it-Yourself*, the new programme on Sundays, will help you tackle those awkward jobs about the house with ease'

Figure 27.19 Overlapping images can be an effective technique

- promise benefits, for example, 'Read *Do-it-Yourself* magazine and save money'
- mention the consumer or audience, for example, 'Just bought a house? Read our section on do-it-yourself in the *Daily Worker'*
- arouse curiosity, for example, 'Have you got to do it yourself?'

One or two **illustrations** will bring life to the advert. Try altering their size, position and angle to see what different effects you can create. It is sometimes effective to overlap images, as in Figure 27.19.

The **qualification link** expands upon the headline and explains the meaning of the advert. The **body copy** gives the main message of the advertisement, and gives details of the product or service on offer (see Figure 27.20).

Figure 27.20 In this advert the body copy gives information and the action line tells the reader what to do next

This advert also has an **action line**. An action line encourages the reader to act on the advert, buy this magazine, watch this programme, subscribe to this satellite channel – *now!*

Activity

Analyse the two adverts shown in Figure 27.21 on the next page. In the Internet leaflet, how many of the 'rules' above does it follow? Notice its interesting shape – it folds down to a small square. Compare the style and content with the *New Internationalist* advert beneath.

Activity

Do a rough or draft for a display advert for your media product. What publication do you intend it to appear in?

Audio-visual advert

We shall now look at an advert for an audio-visual product.

Film trailers, whether seen in the cinema or preceding a film on video, have to be memorable because there will usually be a lapse of time before the viewer rents another video or goes to the cinema again. Trailers are shown next to other films aimed at the same target audience.

Activity

Make a list of trailers preceding the main film on a rented video. What do they have in common?

The most important information to communicate is:

- the genre
- the title.

The standard trailer will consist of brief clips from the film with a voice-over. These excerpts are carefully chosen: the viewer must be intrigued but not completely satisfied! Viewers must be made to feel that they have to see this film or rent the video and find out what happens. The narrative structure of a trailer is therefore always open.

Figure 27.21 Two different styles of advert

Case study: Film trailer for *Mask*

For instance, the trailer for the film *Mask* is a good example of one that wants the viewer to remember the genre and the title. A teenage target audience is less likely to be impressed by or remember other details. The name of the film's director or producer is therefore unimportant and so are the names of the actors. Even the identity of the star, Jim Carrey, has a low profile and is mentioned only in conjunction with the fact that he has starred in *Ace Ventura,* another popular film.

The trailer can be divided into four sections:

1 the background to the action is given   72 secs
2 something dramatic happens   12 secs
3 the subsequent action is shown   99 secs
4 information about the film is given   5 secs

Each section is constructed from a number of clips, which are sometimes accompanied by dialogue from the film soundtrack and sometimes use a male voice-over and added music soundtrack.

The genre is fantasy, and the fairy-tale nature of the film is established from the start by the opening words of the voice-over.

This long first section gives us insight into the main character and his lifestyle. The music is largely responsible for indicating that there is a lot of slapstick humour in this film. It is zany and jolly and its pace suggests action.

The short second section begins with the voice-over saying: 'All that is about to change'. The viewer sees enigmatic images, and will have to watch the film to have them explained.

The quick editing of clips in the third section, the pace and the style are comparable to techniques used in pop videos, which confirms that this is a film to be enjoyed by young people. There are a lot of special effects

sequences in this section. The music is louder and, like the hero, more assertive.

In the final section, the voice-over tells us: '*Ace Ventura*'s Jim Carrey **is** the Mask'. We see the main character in close-up, then the distinctive yellow title spins onto the screen.

The last few seconds show the credits for the film, with details of the producer, name of film studio, when it was made, etc.

Activity

Analyse the construction of a film trailer. Then choose a film of the same genre on video. Identify clips which you would use to construct a video trailer following the same narrative structure. Write a voice-over that would accompany the clips. Choose a suitable piece of music for the background that would be typical of the genre. When you have a storyboard plus soundtrack on video, this is known as **animatics**.

Evidence assignment

Use the marketing plan you developed in Element 2 (Chapter 26) for one of your media products, as the basis for an advertising campaign.

Create a portfolio of roughs, drafts and treatments showing your approach to the campaign. This may be centred around posters or advertisements in newspapers and magazines, or on radio or TV. You should include explanations for your choice of message.

The portfolio should also contain a schedule which will take into consideration the choice of media for the adverts, their timing and frequency.

Present drafts and treatments for advertisements

When a project is commissioned it is good practice for checks and assessments to be made at certain key points along the way. These points are sometimes referred to as 'milestones'. Milestones serve a very useful purpose because they allow the client and the producer to come together and ensure that the project is still 'on track' and that the client is getting what was requested, or changes to the specification meet with approval. Therefore the presentation of drafts and treatments for advertisements is a very important stage in their production.

Checks on the work done so far are also useful for testing out the ideas on a sample audience. Modifications can then be made and the ideas continuously refined until a consensus is reached. Advertising agencies know that they need to keep in contact with their 'account' i.e. the client (whether an individual or an organisation). If they do not it can lead to all kinds of misunderstandings and, possibly, the loss of valuable business.

Drafts and treatments

It is always good practice to 'steer' a project through with both parties involved, and resolve any problems before they get out of hand. It would be far more expensive in terms of time, money and business reputation to discover what the client really wanted after the job has been completed. After all, many clients are not exactly sure of what they want to convey or how they should convey it. This is where the advertising agency or representative is able to give advice and present several different ideas or variations of the same idea in the form of drafts and treatments. These are rough impressions of an advertisement. The **treatment** refers to the way in which an advertising message is put across. Will it be humorous or serious? Bright, cheerful, zany, 'way out', austere? What visual means will you use to give these impressions? You have to consider whether to use colour and if so which colours or monochrome (black and white). You have to decide whether you

Ad agency manager

Client

Figure 28.1 Ideas for advertising treatments can vary greatly

will use actors or perhaps cartoon characters. Does the advert need illustrations, such as explanatory diagrams?

If the advert is audio-visual you have to think about the sound as well as the images. Will you make use of music and, if so, what kind? We know that music influences how people feel. You will have to choose the music (and/or sound effects) carefully in order to create the right mood and atmosphere.

When a client asks an advertising agency to carry out a piece of work, the 'account' will be handled by an account manager who will in turn assemble a team – including a graphic artist. The graphic artist will produce some roughs, or thumbnail sketches, and these can be presented to the client to see what they think before the job moves on to full production.

Design a presentation in an appropriate form

The form of the presentation

Presenting the drafts, etc. to a client can take a number of different forms. The 'client' may be one decision-maker to whom the agency has to sell the idea, or it could be a roomful of decision-makers. This will therefore affect the **form** of the presentation.

You will need to ensure that you will have an audience for the presentation. You therefore need to send out details such as the time, place, content and duration. This in itself is a form of advertising and should take the form of a personal invitation.

The invitation should be personalised, preferably by putting the person's name on the letter or invitation card, or at least by addressing the person in a term which makes him or her feel part of an exclusive group of people.

On what basis will you select your audience? Of course, it may be your clients in which case the decision regarding who will be invited will already have been taken. However, if it is your peer group, will you make it an open invitation, or will you invite a representative sample of the target audience?

If you do have to send out invitations, ask the invited person to respond, perhaps by returning a tear-off slip – although you may want it to appear more personal than that.

When you have your audience you will need to ensure that the seating plans are appropriate for the style of presentation. You need to make sure that the audience can see not only you and the illustrations, but also each other if this is appropriate. A horseshoe shape is generally the best configuration in this case.

Tone and manner of spoken delivery

The way in which you express yourself will be determined by a variety of factors concerning the type of audience and type of material. Issues affecting how you will interact with the audience will also involve decisions concerning the use of **visual** or **audio-visual** material to illustrate content. The two principal factors you should consider are:

- who is the audience? In reality this may well be your peer group, although members of the peer group can assume particular roles.
- how large is the audience? Is it just one or two persons or is it a large gathering?

It is these two factors which will determine how formal the presentation should be. There may be only a single person to present the work to but it may still involve a formal presentation if that person is an important decision-maker and his or her company (or yours) prefers it that way.

Other factors which will affect the tone and manner of delivery are the age, sex, ethnicity and beliefs of the audience and the kind of relationship (informal or formal) that you have with them.

The type of language will depend on the age and experience of the audience and their familiarity with the product and with the vocabulary used. Be wary, for example, of using jargon which can confuse and alienate. You should also be wary of the complexity of your language if the audience are very young or from an environment that is not usually exposed to it.

It is better to use short words and short sentences to put across your ideas. These may well need to be supported by illustrations. We all know the saying that a picture is worth a thousand words.

You can also say or illustrate the same point again but in a variety of different ways. Much the same point can be brought home to an audience by stating it verbally, by seeing it in writing and by looking and listening to it on tape or screen. This reinforces the message but without it becoming repetitious and tedious. In addition, another presenter can provide that variety when giving the same message. He or she will also add general variety by alternating the delivery of the presentation.

In any presentation concentrate on summarising a few key points and emphasise them.

Venue

When planning the presentation you need to check out the venue. This will probably be a room or hall. You may need to use an amplifier and microphone so that people can hear you clearly.

It will also help your voice, and that of the other speakers, if a glass of water is kept available. This is common practice for anyone involved in debates, meetings or public speaking and you will usually see glasses of water on desks and tables during television interviews and talk shows, etc.

Your event may include providing refreshments and even a buffet. In this case ensure that a variety of drinks is available, including water; not everyone wants tea and coffee. If any food is provided there should be a choice for those who are vegetarian.

If the presentation involves a walk-around exhibition with stands, you may well need to give visitors some direction in the form of notices and by making yourself and others available to help and show people around.

It may help to make the presentation more interesting if you deliver from two or three positions on a stage or presentation area. You can then leave each stage of the proceedings still in place rather than taking it down to replace it with the next part. This means you can refer back to examples easily as they are still in view. You do of course have to be careful not to block out the audience's view.

Wherever you deliver from, you have to decide whether to sit or stand. Sitting tends to look less formal but it may be hard for your audience to see you. Even if you can be seen you also want to be the focal point of the presentation. After all, these are *your* ideas so you should take a prominent place in the proceedings. Standing is therefore the best position although under certain conditions you could sit on something high, like a table, thus giving the impression of being in control but without being too formal.

You should encourage questions, although you may wish to structure the presentation so that you take questions at certain times. Try not to leave it only to the end for people to become involved. The aim is to give the audience ample opportunity to express their opinions and ask questions.

Delivery

You should, of course, be friendly but at the same time business-like. Avoid being over-familiar. If the audience does not know you then they probably won't like it. If the audience does know you (e.g. if they are your peer group) then being too familiar with them will create too carefree an atmosphere, which is not conducive to the professional business of promoting your product. In fact it is not easy presenting to your peer group. You, or they, may be tempted into not taking it seriously. You may be embarrassed about making an effort.

Use your judgement to make the odd amusing remark to put people at ease. It is not appropriate, however, to turn the proceedings into a stand-up comic routine. This would have the effect of detracting from the professionalism and purpose of the event. Also, if you do use humour, be sensitive to people's feelings and beliefs. Not everyone may appreciate supposedly light-hearted remarks which could result in offending and alienating someone.

Basically you will need to show sensitivity and awareness when dealing with your audience.

It is you, therefore, who will have to judge *how* to deliver your presentation. You should, however, bear in mind that regardless of the form of the presentation, the main purpose is to communicate your ideas convincingly to the audience and to allow the audience to communicate with you.

Type of material and use of equipment

To be effective, you will not only show design sketches, etc. but also prepare a justification for the ideas, and be able to say how they would work.

Depending on the numbers in the audience and the complexity of the ideas, you will have to decide what equipment and materials you will need to support the presentation.

It is important when planning your use of equipment to become familiar with it. This requires practice. An OHP (overhead projector) may appear quite straightforward but there is still a certain amount of skill and dexterity required in order to be able to use it confidently. You need to know how to focus it and how to move it to adjust the size of the image. You can also use it creatively by overlaying different OHTs (overhead transparencies) or animating the display by moving about cut-up sections of transparency.

Check-list for using audio-visual aids

- Check that the equipment actually works after it has been moved into the position you want. This is very important when using an OHP as the filament in the bulb is very brittle and can break easily when hot. You should leave an OHP for about fifteen minutes after it has been used to allow the bulb to cool down.
- Ensure that all electrical leads are taped down so they do not trip up you or anyone else. (See Health and Safety appendix.)
- Ensure that the OHP is positioned so that the transparency is projected clearly and can be seen by an audience. Avoid placing it where you or the OHP will obscure the screen.
- Check the rest of the room and re-arrange seating if necessary. Are there blinds or curtains to prevent glare?
- Do not overload the OHT with information. Instead use it for headings and 'bullet' points. You can then talk around these points, using short briefing notes to support you (see Figure 28.2).
- Prepare and use briefing notes. These are short notes to help you with your talk. You can keep them on numbered cards or paper, using one for each point and writing on one side only. These precautions should help to prevent you from getting into a muddle.

MANDATORY UNITS

1 Investigating the content of media products
2 Planning and research for media production
3 Producing print products
4 Producing audio products
5 Producing moving image products
6 Investigating and carrying out audience research and analysis
7 Investigating and carrying out media marketing
8 Investigating media industries

Figure 28.2 An overhead transparency should not be overloaded with information – this is sufficient

- Try not just to read from the cards or from the OHT. It sounds more natural if you can say things in your own words. It is better to use the briefing notes, OHTs, etc. as 'prompts' for your memory and as a means of structuring your talk. The structure could be something like this:
  - introduction
  - main issues
  - specific examples (with handouts?)
  - question and answer
  - summary and conclusion.

Of course the format could be different, perhaps with **handouts**, video clip, tape/slide images, etc. shown first. However, the main point is to introduce the situation, which could be a problem to be resolved, give specific examples and then give resolutions, allow time for questions, then summarise the main points and give a conclusion.

- You do not have to reveal all of the OHT at once. It may be better to reveal your points one at a time and keep a sheet of paper over the rest of the transparency. This will help to keep the audience concentrating on the point you are making at the time instead of reading ahead.
- Interact with your audience. Ask them if they can see the screen, flip chart, etc. and whether they can hear you properly.
- Avoid looking down at the OHT or briefing notes. Try to look from the OHP to the audience alternately.
- Speak a little more slowly and steadily than usual but put some inflection in your voice so that it doesn't sound dull. Resist the temptation to speak too fast, which often happens when people are nervous. (See Chapter 3 for vocal techniques for radio broadcasting which would be applicable here.)
- Look at the audience, but don't stare. Move your eyes steadily around without lingering on anyone for too long, and look at people's foreheads rather than their eyes.
- Make use of colour and size to give emphasis to your slide. The techniques will be the same as for page layout in Chapter 11.
- Use a pointer and remember to point at the OHT, rather than the screen. If you point directly at the screen, the projector will enlarge the silhouette of your arm and obscure the information on the screen.
- If you are using a television and video, make sure you know how to operate it. This means ensuring that you know what channel it should be on and where the play, stop and pause buttons are. Also ensure that the videotape is lined up at the correct

place, otherwise you will end up fumbling about. You are trying to influence people so it is not a good time to look disorganised and amateurish.

The same points obviously apply to a cassette player, slide projector or any piece of equipment or material. Remember, it is better to build in some practice time rather than risk wrestling with a piece of equipment in front of lots of quizzical eyes, making you hot and bothered just when you don't need it.

Non-verbal communication

When you are giving a presentation you should remember that it is not just what you say but the manner in which you say it and your overall appearance that is important. This in itself is a form of communication called NVC (**non-verbal communication**).

An obvious form of non-verbal communication is a person's appearance. Whether we like it or not, we are judged (and also judge others) on appearances, particularly if people are meeting for the first time. First impressions do count for an awful lot and people will often have very little to go on at first apart from the way you look.

The details of your appearance will to a large extent depend on the product. Hair and clothing should be appropriate and not clash with the image of the product that you are trying to project. If the advertising campaign is for a new zany teen band then perhaps you can afford to dress in a more extrovert manner. This, however, may extend only as far as wearing a bright shirt or jewellery. Even if it is appropriate to dress casually you should still ensure that you are clean and tidy. Remember that you are in the public eye – so pay particular attention to hair, nails and shoes because audiences have a knack of noticing these.

The way we stand, walk and gesticulate all communicate messages to observers. Folded arms can indicate defensiveness, while open palm gestures show friendliness. Holding your hand over your mouth can mean that you lack confidence in what you are saying, or even that you are not being completely honest. There are numerous other examples of how our 'body language' can reveal our true feelings.

Apart from suggesting that you are nervous or unsure of yourself, gestures such as continual pacing up and down, scratching and covering your mouth with your hand can be irritating and off-putting to an audience. Try to keep control of your movements and channel your nervous energy into a positive gesture, such as occasionally stretching out your hands to the audience.

Presentation check-list

Use this check-list when preparing to give a presentation:

- **The audience**
  who are they and do you know them?
  what age are they?
  how many are there?
  do they know each other?
  what is their state of mind (e.g. interested, nervous, hostile)?
  are they comfortable?
  can they see and hear the presentation?

- **The content**
  introduce yourself
  introduce the topic
  state the purpose of the presentation
  give general situation
  give specific details/examples
  summarise what you have said
  seek feedback by encouraging questions, perhaps by having someone in the audience briefed to initiate the process. Perhaps also give out questionnaires.

Make sure that you thank the audience at the end.

Present drafts and treatments to an audience

In this section we will look at how to present drafts and treatments to an audience. The drafts and treatments will come from a campaign to advertise the product you made in Units 3, 4 or 5.

Before you start you should try to relax. The presentation is a performance, so you have to ensure that psychologically you feel good about what you are proposing and how you are presenting it. The best way to feel confident is to make sure some thorough planning has been put into the project. If you have paid attention to detail and followed the check-list then at least the presentation of the proposed product will be correct. Even if the advertising drafts are not accepted uncritically, the main purpose is to find out whether the drafts should be taken forward into production.

At the beginning of the presentation you should check that people are comfortable and are able to hear you. When you show them some written text, whether on a screen (overhead projector, slide projector or TV monitor) or on a handout to be distributed, give the audience time to read it. Do not carry on talking while they are reading.

While you are delivering your message you don't necessarily have to stay in the same place. Indeed it is helpful to check on whether the audience can see an illustration or text, or whether they can hear a colleague, by moving to the back of the audience. But be careful, as walking behind people whilst they have to face the front can make them uneasy.

If you are asked a question that you cannot answer, then be honest and admit that you are not sure but state that you will find out. You and your advert designs will lose credibility if you start to bluff. In fact you should inform your audience early on in the presentation that you will be taking names and addresses of people who would like more information.

Describe key aspects of the product to the audience

You should refer to Chapter 27 to ensure that you have a clear grasp of the general concepts associated with this area.

Key aspects

The **choice of medium** is a crucial consideration when advertising a product. There is little point in a media product such as a local radio station or local newspaper being advertised on national television. Although it would reach the **target audience**, it would also reach just about everyone else in the country – most of whom would not be interested. The cost would be extremely high without the advertising being effective.

The *Leicester Mercury* is a regional newspaper distributed mainly in the county of Leicestershire. The medium for advertising it should therefore be one that covers the same area. It is a general-interest rather than a specialist product, so the student supplement produced by the *Mercury* student project could be advertised on local radio, such as Leicester Sound or even the community-based stations. It could also be advertised on posters, including those used on the college site.

The **purpose** of the advertising was to encourage students to purchase a product that the majority of them would not normally buy. This was done by raising awareness of the content (special student feature) and publicising the free gifts.

In order to give examples of your **treatment of the material** you could show various key aspects of the advertising draft and their treatment. This will form part of your **rationale for advertising decisions**. In order to show the key aspects you should deconstruct the advert.

Deconstruction of the advert

It is useful to break down any advertising draft into different components. This could be, for example, a rough of a poster, or a recording of the voice you envisage using for a radio advert.

You can show the component parts of the whole advertisement in order to emphasise their part in the overall message.

Figure 28.3 An advert for a print product

Imagine if you had to present the ad shown in Figure 28.3 to your audience for them to comment on your ideas.

You might want to emphasise that the human subject is well to the right of centre in this image. People read from left to right so the eye is dragged across the page to the 'celebrity' and then back to the text. Or perhaps you want to show the depiction of the thought bubble. Does this give it a 'young' cartoon-style look and at the same time parody the ad? Maybe you want to show the prominence of the price and how it is the only other part of the image that is in the same colour as the name of the product.

You could crop the ad in order to emphasise these aspects. Do this by cutting up the image into the parts you wish to highlight, masking the parts you don't want revealed with card, paper or masking tape or by using an OHP or video camera to enlarge/zoom in on key aspects. You are deliberately not showing the rest of the ad at this stage so that the audience can concentrate on the parts you want to highlight.

You could also draw attention specifically to your use of colour by overlaying your image with different coloured transparencies to show how the meaning can change with a change of colour.

Seek feedback from the audience

It is imperative that you obtain feedback from the audience during the presentation so that their comments can be taken into account when carrying out modifications to your drafts and treatments.

In the *Leicester Mercury* student project the feedback comments on the advertising poster (see Figure 28.4) were collated and are summarised below. The main comments and criticism concentrated on the need to place the emphasis in an advertising message on the benefits to the purchaser:

- The word 'free' is given the most prominence. It was a good idea to place the emphasis on the benefits to the purchasers and less on the name of the newspaper. However, the main benefits, i.e. the details of what is free, should be more obvious. Instead, the headings 'Hinckley College' and 'Leicester Mercury' are made more apparent than the word 'snacks'. This puts the emphasis in the wrong place because neither of the organisations carry sufficient weight with the target group (college students) to justify placing the emphasis on their name. Instead the emphasis should be placed on the benefits of the free snacks, as well as some very brief but eye-catching comments which could refer to the content of the student section of the paper.

There were also several other adverse comments which had to be taken on board:

- There are no graphic illustrations to attract the eye.
- It is not ideal to centre all the features (text etc.) on a page. This tends to make an advert too

---

Tuesday 26 March

Special Feature produced by

Hinckley College students

FREE

SNACKS WITH EVERY

PURCHASED

Available from:

Canteen, Information Centre & Business Block

Figure 28.4 An advertising poster for the *Leicester Mercury* project

regular and therefore uninteresting.
- The language and overall appearance of the advert is rather dull and uninteresting.
- Some members of the audience felt that the meaning was unclear regarding the 'special feature'. This could have been illuminated by additional information on the content of the feature.
- There is no angle or 'hook' to arouse and sustain interest. The hook could be a slogan or a picture with certain associations – perhaps simply a bag of crisps, or something that conveys excitement or interest, such as a comical or dynamic character.

The use of a celebrity, such as a Harry Enfield type, would have worked well on this type of advert. Harry Enfield has produced a series of successful ads for a savoury snack food, which is based on his 'Self-righteous Brothers' characters. Students would have identified more with some humour such as this.

Evaluate the presentation

Materials and visual aids

Consider these general points:

- Did the amount of material fit the time allocated for the presentation?
- Did you have cue cards to help you remember points?
- Were your visual images large enough for all the audience to see?
- Did you use a range of equipment and materials in order to give variety and add interest to your presentation?
- Were the equipment and materials used appropriate for the message you were communicating?

Other points for evaluation

When evaluating the presentation you should consider:

- **Fitness for purpose**
  Was there a more effective way of communicating with the target audience? What was the cost of the presentation? Did it keep to budget? Did the expenditure justify the choice of medium or could it have been done more effectively, and perhaps more cost-effectively, by using, for example, a leaflet?

- **Response**
  How many responded to the invitation to come to the presentation?
  How many actually turned up?
  How much interest did the material generate?
  Are the ideas on target or will they have to be re-worked?

- **Resources**
  Were sufficient resources allocated to the presentation?
  Could it have been improved by staging it in a different venue?
  Was the time and duration of the event suitable?

It is now time to look at the effectiveness of your contribution and that of the whole team.

If you were nervous you should try to analyse why. How much confidence did you have in the drafts? Did you feel happy about the proposals and did you feel confident in producing them?

 Activity

Try working your way through the check-list below.

Present drafts and treatments for advertisements

Self-evaluation check-list

Your name ....

Name of your product ....

Evaluate your performance in each of the following areas, using this scale:

5 = excellent, 4 = good, 3 = average, 2 = below average, 1 = poor

- attendance ☐
- time-keeping ☐
- reliability in completing tasks ☐
- meeting deadlines ☐
- self-motivation ☐
- appearance ☐
- professional behaviour in dealing with audience ☐
- ability to work in a team ☐
- ability to motivate others ☐
- relationship with staff ☐
- coping with pressure ☐
- use of initiative ☐
- use of equipment ☐

(Use the check-list items as prompts in making extended comments.)

Comments

Group evaluation

Now, as an individual, use the next form to carry out an evaluation of the whole group's performance. Again, you should use the 1 to 5 scale.

Present drafts and treatments for advertisements

Group evaluation check-list

Your name ....

Name of group ....

Evaluate your performance in each of the following areas, using this scale:

5 = excellent, 4 = good, 3 = average, 2 = below average, 1 = poor

- ■ team spirit and attitude ☐
- ■ attendance ☐
- ■ time-keeping ☐
- ■ reliability ☐
- ■ organisation ☐
- ■ effectiveness ☐
- ■ relationship with staff ☐

Comments

Evidence asignment

You are to present your ideas for an advertising campaign as developed in Element 3 (Chapter 27), to an audience.

The presentation should be organised so that:

- ■ the main points are clearly communicated
- ■ material is delivered in a structured way
- ■ you speak in an appropriate tone and manner so that everyone can hear and understand
- ■ equipment such as OHPs and video players are used effectively
- ■ feedback is obtained during the presentation.

Afterwards, submit an evaluation of the presentation, considering:

- ■ its suitablility for the audience
- ■ whether it fulfilled its purpose
- ■ whether resources were used efficiently
- ■ audience feedback.

Investigating and Carrying Out Media Marketing: Unit Test

1 Which of these marketing activities comes first?
   a writing and making adverts
   b designing the packaging
   c researching the product and consumer
   d scheduling the advertising campaign

2 Which of these is a marketing activity for a magazine?
   a supervising the print run each month
   b researching feature articles
   c deciding if the cover price should change
   d writing copy and taking photographs

3 Packaging is an important marketing activity for videos. What will indicate the house style of a series of videos about wildlife?
   a the length of its programmes
   b the style of the covers
   c the cost of the videos
   d the names of presenters

4 Effective market research on the success of a new television satellite channel would be carried out by interviewing:
   a the general public
   b all people who watch satellite television
   c all people who watch this particular channel
   d a sample of subscribers to this channel

5 When the people who might listen to a new radio programme are divided into groups such as students or women, this is known as:
   a market segmentation
   b product differentiation
   c population sampling
   d market specialisation

6 Which of the following is an example of test marketing?
   a a permanent reduction in the cover price of a comic
   b a free gift given away with a magazine
   c a pilot programme for a new quiz show
   d a questionnaire sent out with a newspaper

7 A magazine wishes to increase its circulation figures. Which of these is an example of a sales promotion?
   a direct selling to the public
   b redesigning the front cover
   c adverts on television or radio
   d a special discount

8 Which of these items in a newspaper is intended to have a long product life cycle?
   a a hard news story
   b a feature article
   c a strip cartoon
   d an advertisement

9 When a product such as a comic is altered to appeal to a different age group, this is known as:
   a re-positioning
   b rescheduling
   c re-segmenting
   d restructuring

10 What is a product which has reached maturity and provides a steady income called?
   a a problem child
   b a cash cow
   c a star
   d a dog

11 Which of these is an indirect form of advertising for a film?
   a a poster outside the cinema
   b an advert in a national newspaper
   c an interview with the stars on radio
   d a commercial on television

12 On the bottom of the poster for the film *Alien* it says 'In space, no-one can hear you scream.' What is the correct term for such a catch-phrase on a film poster?
   a the synopsis
   b the ident
   c the caption
   d the tag-line

13 On a radio station such as Radio 1 or Atlantic 252, which of the following is most responsible for creating 'brand awareness' in listeners?
  a the style of news reading
  b the music mix
  c the age of the presenters
  d the number of adverts

14 If the market share of a newspaper increases, what does this mean?
  a it is selling more newspapers than its rivals
  b other publications have gone out of business
  c it is selling more newspapers than last month
  d it has more readers than previously

15 Sometimes a television programme likely to have few viewers is scheduled between two popular programmes – this is known as a hammock. Why is it done?
  a to spread good programmes out evenly throughout the day
  b to persuade viewers that it is not worthwhile switching over to another channel
  c to encourage people to watch both of the popular programmes
  d because it is too expensive to have three popular programmes in a row

16 Which of these is an example of desk research?
  a holding small focus groups
  b interviewing the public
  c using BARB statistics
  d issuing questionnaires to consumers

17 How can a **newsagent** best improve sales of a magazine?
  a alter its position so it is more prominent on the shelf
  b reduce its price
  c talk to customers about it
  d stock more copies

18 A marketing plan for a new comic must include:
  a names and addresses of writers and cartoonists
  b artwork and copy for advertisements
  c a schedule of when different activities are to take place
  d a copy of the first issue of the comic

19 Consumers can be divided into different categories. Which of the following would be typical of the descriptions used in lifestyle groupings:
  a B2 workers
  b radio listeners in Scotland

  c male householders
  d spendthrift students

20 Read the following statements about marketing plans and decide whether they are true or false:
  i a marketing audit will be carried out at the end of the campaign
  ii the marketing plan will include a budget

  a **i** is true and **ii** is true
  b **i** is true and **ii** is false
  c **i** is false and **ii** is true
  d **i** is false and **ii** is false

21 The marketing plan may propose changing the style of fonts used on the front cover of a magazine. What would be the most likely reason for this?
  a to save on production costs
  b because of changes in technology
  c to fit more information on to the page
  d to attract a different type of reader

22 Which of these would be a long-term objective of an advertising campaign for videos?
  a to inform the public of where to buy the videos
  b to increase sales by dropping the price
  c to maintain brand awareness
  d to ensure that people know where to enquire about the products

23 Where would an advert be placed to reach the largest number of young people?
  a in a popular national tabloid newspaper
  b on prime-time television
  c on posters in town and city centres
  d on commercial radio in the evening

24 In an advertising agency, the person who deals with the client and is in overall charge is called:
  a the account manager
  b the market researcher
  c the art director
  d the copywriter

25 Product placement in television programmes is forbidden by the:
  a ASA
  b ITV
  c APP
  d ITC

26 The advert for a new magazine states: 'People in control read Powermad Magazine.' What is the advert trying to do?
- **a** give information about the product
- **b** promote a lifestyle
- **c** evoke an emotion
- **d** promote a brand name

27 In the AIDA principle what does the letter I stand for?
- **a** investigate
- **b** intention
- **c** invite
- **d** interest

28 The film *Revenge of the Killer Sheep* is due for release in June 1997. When will the main trailer be seen in cinemas?
- **a** April 1997
- **b** June 1996
- **c** January 1997
- **d** June 1997

29 What is the name given to the part of a newspaper or magazine advert which explains the meaning of the advert?
- **a** the action line
- **b** the qualification link
- **c** the headline
- **d** the body copy

30 When preparing text for an OHT, what is the **most** important thing to remember?
- **a** use headings and bullet points
- **b** make it colourful
- **c** it should be word processed not hand-written
- **d** it should use drawings and diagrams

The media are the fastest growing and fastest changing sector in our society. This is not only because of technological developments, from personal computers to satellites, but also because of their influence on so many people – from children and shoppers to politicians. The tentacles of the media stretch into all corners of our lives, through entertainment and education, through information and communication services. Whatever employment you eventually end up in, it will be difficult to escape the power of the media. That is why this qualification is so useful! This unit is not just about working in the media but working with the media.

New products are arriving all the time and there is continuous change to existing products. There are many different trends; for example, the proliferation of small local products or the creation of multinational media conglomerates. It is essential to look at not only media

in Britain but world-wide, from what are sometimes called the media-saturated Western countries to the growing markets of the developing world. Satellite television and the Internet ignore national boundaries. It is important to know who produces and controls the media and why.

It is very difficult in today's world to predict anyone's career. You may not wish to enter the media after the course as, for instance, a journalist or camera operator – you may instead want to go into associated fields such as advertising, personnel or public relations; or you may wish to continue studying for a sociology or business degree; you may want to be a teacher. However, it is important that you are aware of the employment opportunities and training necessary in this highly competitive and sophisticated world.

Chapter 29

Investigate ownership and control in media industries

This chapter is concerned with the ownership and control of media companies. Because of the rate at which the media are changing, some of the information in this chapter may well be dated by the time this book is published, but it will give you a starting point! Magazine and newspaper articles will give you current information on changes and new developments in the media industries. One way to stay up-to-date is to read regularly the specialist magazines such as *Broadcast* or *Sight and Sound*. Each week, Monday's *Guardian* newspaper has a pull-out section devoted to the media.

Principal UK media producers and the types of organisations involved with media products

Introduction

In the last decade, the number of media products has increased enormously. The question of who owns whom and who controls what has become ever more complex. These two aspects – ownership and control – are not necessarily the same. Governments may exert considerable influence on the production, content and distribution of media products through legislation and the establishment of regulatory bodies. To make

the matter more confusing, what may seem to be a large, independent company may be only a subsidiary of an even bigger conglomerate! For example, the *Nottingham Recorder* is published by the Nottingham Group, which is owned by Northcliffe Newspaper Group, which in turn is part of the *Daily Mail* and General Trust whose management company is Associated Newspapers.

There has been a proliferation of small companies but there is also a significant number of extremely large companies who have interests not only in the media but in other areas. It is these large, influential producers we shall look at first. Later in this chapter we discuss the *types* of organisations involved in media – private enterprise, public service and so on (see pages 510–12).

The following reference books will be useful for research in this area:

- *Benn's Media Guide*
- *Willings Press Guide*
- *The Guardian Media Guide*
- *Kompass*
- *Kelly's Directory.*

Different media producers

There are thousands of media producers in the UK; some are large companies with international sales and a wide range of products, some are small local companies with only one product. In this chapter we shall start by concentrating on the major producers and their products and services. You will find that some organisations have products aimed at local, national and international markets. *The European* newspaper and *Vogue* are examples of publications found around the world, whereas a newspaper such as *The Aldershot News,* although produced by a big company (the Guardian Media Group), has a far smaller, local market.

Most of the producers listed below are private, commercial companies, or independent producers, but there are some influential public bodies such as the BBC or HMSO.

Some independent producers have a cultural or community commitment or are committed to avant-garde or experimental work. Sometimes this is then distributed or broadcast by larger organisations. Their work has also become more influential and available to the public because they need not rely on the large newspapers to print their work or the main TV channels to broadcast their moving image productions. The rise of cable, the mushrooming of radio stations and the ability to produce a cheap newspaper by desktop publishing has meant that it is easier for such work to reach an audience.

These groups may be funded by local authorities or regional arts boards. The European Social Fund has also financed a number of media projects. This is described in more detail below.

Print producers

First we shall look at producers in the *print* industry. This includes newspapers, magazines, comics and books.

Newspapers

The Media Organisations appendix shows a list of seven major companies and the newspapers they sell in the UK. They produce a variety of tabloid and broadsheet newspapers, both daily and weekly. Figure 29.1 shows their share of the market.

As the information in the appendix shows, many of their newspapers have been in circulation a long time. There have always been, and still are, two main reasons to own a newspaper:

■ to make money
■ to influence people and events.

In the early days, newspapers tended to be run by aristocratic landowners and they were often started for political reasons. The proprietors had financial and editorial control. Gradually, newspapers came to be run by companies with boards of directors, and the need to be commercially viable became more important.

You will find it helpful at this stage to read or revise the section on newspapers in Chapter 3, which describes the different types of newspapers and their content and gives a brief history.

Activity

List the newspapers given in the Media Organisations appendix under two headings, **Tabloid** and **Broadsheet**. The easiest way to do this is to visit a newsagent. The *Daily Express* and *Daily Mail* have been described as mid-range tabloids. What do you think is meant by this?

For the next part of the Activity, work in a group. Each student should look at one or two newspapers. Compare their content in terms of:

■ **content and style** – how colourful are they? How large are they, in terms of number of pages? What is the proportion of adverts to news, and what type of adverts are carried?

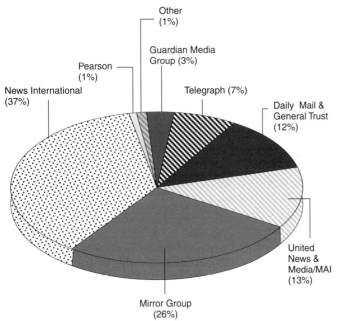

Figure 29.1 Newspaper companies and their share of the market

■ **political bias or persuasion** – for example, *The Sun* is considered to be right-wing, whereas *The Guardian* would claim to be taking the centre ground in politics, although it would be fair to say that it is believed to be more inclined towards left-wing politics. *The Morning Star* is the best-known socialist newspaper.

DAILIES	1985	1990	1995
1 Sun	4,065,000	3,936,000	4,080,000
2 Daily Mirror	3,253,000	3,907,000	2,603,000
3 Daily Mail	1,828,000	1,669,000	1,788,000
4 Daily Express	1,875,000	1,560,000	1,279,000
5 Telegraph	1,221,000	1,086,000	1,066,000
6 Daily Star	1,434,000	919,000	738,000
7 The Times	480,000	432,000	647,000
8 Today		581,000	566,000
9 Guardian	487,000	431,000	400,000
10 Financial Times	229,000	288,000	294,000
11 Independent	–	414,000	294,000
SUNDAYS			
1 News of the World	4,787,000	5,038,000	4,744,000
2 Sunday Mirror	3,211,000	2,911,000	2,560,000
3 People	3,090,000	2,589,000	2,066,000
4 Mail on Sunday	1,605,000	1,890,000	1,959,000
5 Sunday Express	2,405,000	1,729,000	1,403,000
6 Sunday Times	1,258,000	1,187,000	1,253,000
7 Sunday Teleg.	690,000	592,000	692,000
8 Observer	746,000	568,000	464,000
9 Ind. on Sunday	–	363,000	327,000

Figure 29.2 Average daily circulation figures for individual national newspapers

Figure 29.2 shows the circulation figures for individual newspapers over the past decade.

Activity

Study the figures above and use the Media Organisations appendix to answer the following questions:

1 Which daily newspaper has increased its circulation the most?
2 Which Sunday newspaper has declined the most?
3 Which have more sales – daily or Sunday newspapers?
4 Which newspaper owned by United News and Media has the largest circulation?
5 Which newspaper owned by News International has the smallest circulation?
6 Which is the most popular tabloid?
7 Which is the most popular broadsheet?
8 The *Daily Mail* is now more popular than the *Express*. Which had the bigger circulation in 1985?

9 Which is the newest Sunday newspaper?
10 Who owns two of the most popular Sunday newspapers?

Local newspapers

Very few local newspapers are owned now by small companies. In fact less than one-fifth can be considered independent; 60 per cent are owned by the companies listed below. They tend to concentrate on certain areas, such as Scotland or the South.

■ **Trinity International Holdings**
This company (based in Chester) is the largest owner of regional newspapers. It has 1300 titles with a weekly circulation of 12 million.
■ **Northcliffe Newspapers Group**
■ **United Provincial Newspapers**
■ **Reed Regional Newspapers**
■ **Westminster Press**
■ **Midland Independent Newspapers**
■ **Eastern Counties Newspaper Group**
■ **Emap.**

In Leicestershire, examples of independent local weeklies are *The Hinckley Times* and the *Rutland Times*.

Other papers are owned by larger newspaper companies, for example:

■ The *Leicester Mercury* is produced by the Leicester Mercury Group which is part of the Northcliffe Newspapers Group
■ The *Harborough Mail* is produced by Welland Valley Newspapers which is owned by Emap
■ The *Ashby Times* belongs to Trident Midland Newspapers Ltd.

Activity

Find out who produces your local newspaper. Does it belong to one of the companies listed above, another group, or is it independent?

Magazines

Thousands of different magazines are published; some are sold over the counter, some are posted to subscribers. Some are large and glossy with two hundred pages, others may be significantly smaller and printed on poor-quality paper. Some have a readership of thousands, others may have a circulation of under a hundred. Some are available internationally, others only locally.

There are approximately 10 000 different magazine titles available in Britain. Only about 2,500 can be described as 'consumer'; the rest are trade, business and professional publications. The development of the magazine industry has been described in Chapter 3. It must be emphasised, however, that this is a growth industry, with possibly 200 to 300 new titles appearing every year, whilst others disappear.

Activity

Write down the names of what you think might be the 20 most popular magazines. Look on page 493 to see if you have guessed correctly – the answer is given in Figure 29.3.

But who actually owns these magazines? The Media Organisations appendix shows a list of the major magazine publishing companies, with examples of their publications. Some of these companies publish a wide variety of general-interest magazines, others will publish only technical journals whilst some will produce a single publication.

Activity

Make a list of all the magazines and comics read by you or your family and friends. Who publishes them? What types of magazines are they? If they are not included in the list given in the Media Organisations appendix, then you will find the information in the magazine itself, probably on one of the first few pages.

Book publishers

In the book trade there are thousands of publishers, but about 50 of them account for over half of all UK book sales and many of these publishers are part of bigger conglomerates. The independent sector is being reduced in size all the time. In 1995, for example, André Deutsch was bought by the VCI Video Group.

Some publishers specialise in books for a particular age group, others in books on a specialist subject; they may concentrate on cheap popular fiction in paperback, or educational books in hardback. As you will see, some publishers make their money selling a few titles, while others have to produce hundreds of books to equal them. Town-centre bookshops still have a significant share of the sales market, but

increasingly books are sold in a number of less traditional ways:

1 in supermarkets
2 through book clubs
3 direct through the post
4 book 'parties' or personal visits by sales people
5 in electronic format.

Activity

In 1995, Hodder Headline announced that they were planning to expand the number of titles they produced by 50 per cent and target outlets such as supermarkets and petrol stations. Can you find examples of companies who are selling books using other such strategies?

The Media Organisations appendix shows some examples of well-established companies, with different characteristics and their products. Use it to help you carry out the following Activities.

Activity

1 Find a book published by Usborne. What is it about its format which makes it appealing to children?
2 Enquire at home or at friends' houses. Do they own any publications by Reader's Digest? Have they ever received any literature through the post advertising Reader's Digest books or magazines? What special offer or incentive was there to make an order?
3 Compare Macmillan with HarperCollins. One company is privately owned, the other belongs to a larger organisation and is extending into other areas. Discuss the advantages and disadvantages of this in terms of survival, cashflow, competition and so on.
4 Who now owns the company which publishes this *GNVQ Advanced Media* textbook? Does your college library have any other books from this series? If so, compare their covers, content, layout and size. How similar are they and how typical are they of similar textbooks on the market?
5 Two other highly successful and innovative publishers are **BBC Books** and **Penguin**. Research these two companies yourself, by writing to the publishers and consulting *The Writers' and Artists' Yearbook*.
6 Draw a bar chart showing the financial success of the publishers in questions 1–5 above. You can start your chart by using the information given, but you can add to your data by looking up information about other publishers in *The Writer's Handbook*.

Top-selling Magazines		
1	Reader's Digest	1,673,306
2	What's on TV	1,633,010
3	Take a Break	1,508,000
4	Radio Times	1,463,942
5	TV Times	1,015,141
6	Bella	981,000
7	Woman	812,211
8	Woman's Weekly	798,177
9	Woman's Own	795,293
10	TV Quick	728,000
11	Prima	618.870
12	Viz	571,295
13	Best	564,233
14	Chat	541,423
15	Good Housekeeping	518,435
16	People's Friend	479,582
17	Hello	476,551
18	Candis	476,400
19	Cosmopolitan	460,582
20	BBC Good Food	438,715

Figure 29.3 Circulation figures for the top twenty magazines

Audio and audio-visual producers

In the following section, we shall be looking at the **audio** and **moving image** industries. Figure 29.4 shows the structure of broadcasting in the UK.

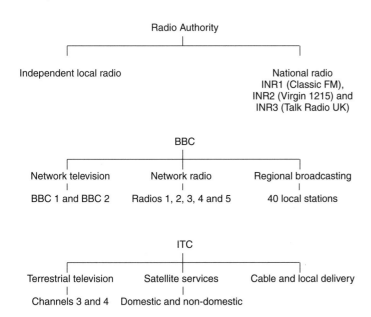

Figure 29.4 Structure of broadcasting

Within the **audio** industry there are two main areas to consider:

- the radio industry
- the music industry.

Radio

As described in Unit 1, in the UK, radio is shared between the BBC and the independents and is broadcast on four wavebands.

- short wave (SW) 3956 KHz – 26.1 MHz
- medium wave (MW) 525 KHz – 1605 KHz
- long wave (LW) 148.5 KHz – 283.5 KHz
- VHF/FM 88M – 105 MHz

Both public service radio (i.e. the BBC) and independent private radio may offer a national, regional or local service.

First we will look at **national** stations.

The BBC

The BBC is a **public corporation** set up in 1927 to provide a television and radio broadcasting service at home and abroad. A **Charter** establishes the Corporation in law, and sets its objectives and constitution. The **licence** from the Home Secretary is a statement of the terms and conditions under which the BBC can broadcast. The main restriction on the BBC is that it cannot carry advertising.

There are 12 **BBC governors** who lay down broad policy guidelines, select the director-general and other senior staff, and are responsible for maintaining programme standards. Theoretically, they are appointed by the Queen but in reality the Prime Minister advises on the appointments, which are for five years. The governors' responsibilities are shared in Wales, Scotland and Northern Ireland with national broadcasting councils. They are supported by the BBC General Advisory Council. The governors give general advice but the day-to-day decisions are taken by the board of management. The chairman of the board is currently Marmaduke Hussey, former director of Times Newspapers. There is also a board of management under John Birt, the director-general. Figure 29.5 shows the structure of the BBC.

The BBC broadcasts five national radio stations. Figure 29.6 shows an analysis of network radio output for 1992.

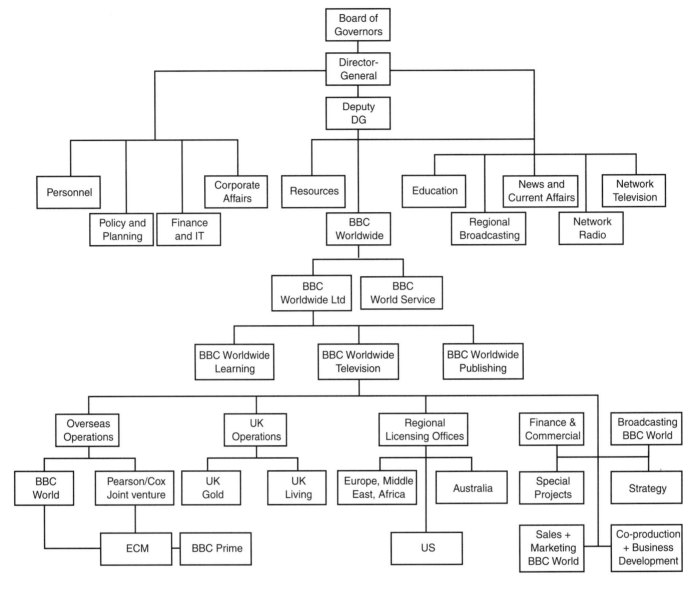

Figure 29.5 The structure of the BBC

 Activity

Look at the analysis in Figure 29.6 and answer the following questions:

1 Which station has the most light entertainment?
2 Does Radio 4 or Radio 5 broadcast more current affairs programmes and news?
3 Which station has no religious programmes?
4 Which stations have educational programmes?
5 Which station has the second highest number of programmed hours for sport?

Here are more details about the individual stations:

■ **Radio 1** (97.7–99.8) Controller: Matthew Bannister
This station attracts the most listeners – over 11 million. It plays all types of popular music and is aimed at a young audience, early teens to early thirties. Intensive marketing, which included a major replacement of presenters in 1995, improved listening figures dramatically.

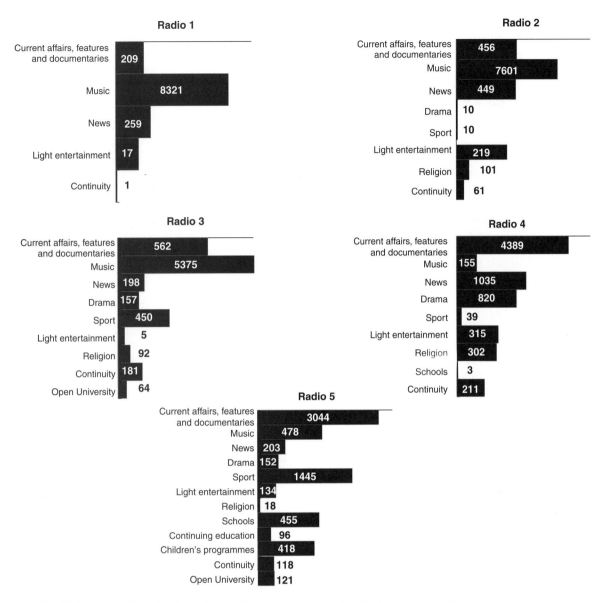

Figure 29.6 Network radio output analysis of programme content in hours per year

BBC publicity describes it as:

'The network at the cutting edge of popular music. Plays the charts but boldly seeks out new bands. Live roadshows around the country. Live concerts and sizzling summer festivals. Street sounds. Free range presenters. Spiky humour. News with a beat. Serious talk about the issues of the 90s. Dramas with a sharp edge. Quirky. Adventurous.'

■ **Radio 2** (88.1–90.2) Controller: Frances Line This is also a popular station, with nearly 9 million listeners. It broadcasts middle-of-the-road popular music and a proportion of speech programmes and is aimed at an older age group than Radio 1.

Described by the BBC as:

'Inviting, companionable, engaging. With a wider range than you think. The best in jazz, musicals, rock, gospel, rhythm and blues, country, folk, popular music and popular classics. Lots of it live. The BBC Big Band. The BBC Concert orchestra. A greater variety of music on Radio 2 than on any commercial station. Presenters who connect with

their listeners' lives. Phone-ins, quiz shows and information on leisure interests and health issues. Frequent news headlines.'

- **Radio 3** (90.3–92.4) Controller: Nicholas Kenyon
This station mainly broadcasts classical music, both old and new. It has a listenership of approximately 2.5 million, which makes it the least popular of the BBC's national stations.

BBC publicity points out that this station is:

'Britain's classical music patron, commissioning the classics of the future. Opera from New York. Music festivals around the UK. Weekends and seasons with a theme. Explorations of leading classical music cultures. Live concerts. Jazz. Classic drama. A celebration of culture on a symphonic scale. Not just the highlights: 70 per cent of the music played on Radio 3 is in the form of complete works.'

- **Radio 4** (92.5–95.9) Controller: Michael Green
This is a speech-based station and appeals to the same age group as Radio 2, with nearly the same number of listeners. It is renowned for its drama, commissioning 200 new plays every year.

The BBC describes this station as follows:

'Reports the news, analyses the issues, quizzes the politicians, prays, gardens, cooks, plays cricket, travels, farms, tell jokes, goes to the theatre, gets letters from America, reads bedtime stories, plays music for people on desert islands and finds its way through a moral maze. A kaleidoscope of information. Thought-provoking, opinion-forming radio.'

- **Radio 5 Live** (909 kHz) Controller: Jenny Abramsky
Since 1992, when the information in Figure 29.6 was published, the content of Radio 5 has changed. Originally intended to have an educational bias, this station now broadcasts mainly sport, news and current affairs.

BBC publicity describes Radio 5 in the following terms:

'Where news and sport come first, 24 hours a day. Breaking the news stories as they happen. Asking the questions at press conferences. The eyes and ears of the nation. Plus entertainment news, health, the environment, education and live interviews with newsmakers and athletes. Live sport and full match commentaries. Football, racing, athletics, rugby, golf, tennis, fishing. Live radio, up all night from around the UK and the world.'

Activity

Listen to two programmes from each of these five stations. Briefly describe their content and style. How typical are they of the stations as described above?

The BBC also provides national radio stations for **Wales** (BBC Radio Cymru), **Scotland** and **Northern Ireland** (BBC Radio Nan Gaidhal). These services reflect the cultural traditions and interests of each country through their selection of news and current affairs, music, sport and drama.

The **BBC World Service** broadcasts radio in English and 38 other languages. It is estimated that it attracts 130 million regular listeners. It is especially valued for its news bulletins.

Independent national radio

The 1990 Broadcasting Act empowered the Radio Authority to give licences for three Independent National Radio (INR) Networks:

- **Classic FM** 99.9–101.9
This plays popular classical music; its presenters have a far more personal and informal approach than Radio 3. It has become the country's largest commercial radio station.

- **Virgin** 1215
This plays contemporary adult music, rock and pop.

- **Talk Radio UK**
This is a speech-based programme notable for its phone-ins. Many consider that it has not lived up to expectations. Some presenters (nick-named 'shock-jocks') hoped to attract listeners by their outrageous comments.

In addition, **Atlantic 252** (252LW) can be considered a national radio station. Because it operates from Ireland, it does not need a British government licence, yet it reaches two-thirds of the country.

Activity

Listen to each of the above stations and compare their output in terms of style and content. What adverts are broadcast and who is their target audience? What does this say about the type of listener to this station?

The Radio Authority has given five **regional** radio licences for independent stations. The intention was to increase listener choice, so these stations were not intended just to play music. These licences have been granted to the following:

- **Century Radio** – easy listening and country music.
- **Galaxy Radio** – classic and contemporary dance music as well as regional news.
- **Heart FM** – easy listening adult music.
- **JFM 100.4** – soul, jazz, R&B, blues and news.
- **Scot FM** – a mixture of speech-based programmes and contemporary music for adults.

BBC local radio

The BBC has forty local radio stations serving local communities. Although music is played on their programmes at key times of the day, speech predominates. Their style is described by the BBC as 'authority with warmth. A clear alternative to other local radio'.

Independent Local Radio (ILR)

There are approximately 180 commercial stations throughout the UK, and the number is increasing annually. As with local newspapers, many local radio stations are owned by larger companies. The main owners of local radio stations are shown in the Media Organisations appendix.

Activity

Use the Media Organisations appendix to identify who owns your local radio stations. Analyse their content and style. Who is the target audience?

When the words **cable** and **satellite** are used most people think of television, but there are some radio stations too that now use this technology. Here are some examples:

- **Satellite**
  - *Asda FM* This is a national in-store radio station transmitting to Asda shops throughout the country.
  - *CMR (Country Music Radio for Europe)*
  - *UCB (United Christian Broadcasters)*
  - *Virgin Radio*
- **Cable**
  - *Fashion FM* This is another in-store radio station, operating in Oxford Street, London.

- *Radio Phoenix* A Welsh hospital radio station.
- *Sunrise Radio – Europe* This belongs to the Sunrise Group, which broadcasts news, information and music to Asian communities.

Activity

Listen to your local BBC station and your local commercial radio station. Compare programmes going out at the same time in terms of style and content.

Radio news

The BBC has its own news staff, but most commercial radio stations and hospital radio stations use news bulletins provided by **IRN** (**Independent Radio News**). This in turn gets the news from ITN or Reuters. Some sports news is provided by Sportsmedia Broadcasting.

The main rival to IRN is Network News based at Chiltern Radio.

Music industry

The media and the music industry are inextricably entwined. The former publicises the latter; radio produces charts which promote record sales, newspapers write about musicians, magazines give reviews, television can show us live performances. It is hard to imagine television and radio without music – there would be no music programmes, no theme tunes, no backing music.

What are the different aspects to consider in the music industry?

- Musical composition
- Live performances – concerts and tours
- Recorded performances – on television and radio
- Making recordings – on vinyl, CDs, cassettes, videos
- Controlling how music is used by the other media – in films or for adverts
- All types of music – classical, popular, jazz, etc.
- Publication of sheet music
- Music equipment and systems – DAT recorders, mini-disc
- Musical instruments – violins to synthesizers
- Music journalism
- Music education.

Like any other media industry, its activities include research, development, production, A&R (artists and repertoire), sales, distribution, marketing, etc. Music is one of the UK's biggest export industries: in 1995 it netted foreign earnings of £571 million, most coming from royalties for live performances and broadcasts.

British contemporary popular music has a strong reputation world-wide and it is estimated that British artists account for 24 per cent of the world market and 17 per cent of US album sales. The music industry world-wide, which includes publishing as well as record sales, amounts to £24 billion.

In the UK, at the beginning of the 1990s, it looked as if the pop record industry might be in decline because of the growth of television, radio and video games. Classical music, in comparison, was booming. However, in 1995, 200 million albums were sold and figures from the British Phonograph Institute in 1996 showed a 12 per cent growth at the beginning of the year. The 'Britpop' phenomenon, including bands such as Oasis, Blur and Pulp, brought new talent to the scene. Their success took even the record companies by surprise. Parlophone, who issued Blur's *Parklife,* expected sales of 150 000 – instead, the album sold 1.2 million in the UK alone.

No other industry has such a fast turnover of product lines. Consider the recording industry: 700 new products may appear each week, few will make a profit, most will be lucky to sell a few thousand copies and will be fortunate to be stocked for as long as two months on a shelf!

In the 1990s, as in other industries, there have been take-overs and the streamlining of music businesses. For example, in 1992 Thorn EMI took over the Virgin label for £560 million. As this book is being written, Thorn is splitting from EMI and there is speculation that this last remaining British record company (whose artists include the Beatles, Queen and Blur) may be bought by the Canadian drinks giant Seagram, by Sumer Redstone (owner of MTV), by Rupert Murdoch's News Corporation, or by the Disney Corporation.

Record companies

There are two main types of record company:

- majors
- indies.

There are, however, two main goals for any recording company: to be successful and to be profitable. **Major** recording companies tend to be run by accountants, who are reluctant to take risks, which is

why there are so many re-issues of formerly successful albums on CD. These backlist releases were spread out over a number of years so that maximum publicity could be given to each star as they were re-released.

This is particularly true of classical music. For example, in 1995 the record company BMG produced a collection of all of the RCA recordings of the violinist Jascha Heifetz, which amounted to 65 CDs!

Recording is horrendously expensive, so companies want to be certain that the thousands spent on promoting a group or artist will be recouped. Here are some approximate costs of how much it takes to sign on a new band:

Costs	£
The advance for the band and their manager	175 000
Recording costs	150 000
Marketing	150 000
Video for the single	75 000
Slot as support band for a major artist on tour	25 000
Promotion to get radio airplay	15 000
Press trips	5 000
Total	£595 000

On the other hand, the cost of recording and marketing an established artist is relatively cheap in relation to the profit to be made from sales and associated activities. It may have cost Warner Brothers an initial investment of over $2 million to put an album by Madonna in the charts, but she has earned the company $1.5 billion in sales!

The big companies have been accused of stagnating the market by not developing new talent. Major companies have, however, been interested in investing in the development of new formats; they have been encouraged by the success of CDs, which first came on the market in 1982.

The following major companies operating in the UK are **multinationals**:

- EMI
- CBS
- Warner Music
- BMG
- Polygram.

The size of a multinational's operations in a country depends on the:

- size of the local market
- availability of promotional and retail outlets
- number of local artists.

Case study: Polygram

Polygram (owned by a Dutch electronics giant) includes Polydor, Phonogram, Island, A&M, London and over eighty other labels.

Besides the recording industry, Polygram is diversifying. Their Digital Compact Cassette system started a format war with the Sony Minidisc. They also set up a distribution company for small movies (with a $10 million budget or less) in partnership with Universal, and they bought a 51 per cent share in Interscope (makers of *The Hand That Rocks The Cradle*). The company has production deals with Jodie Foster and invests in the massive Chinese market.

The **independent** recording and publishing companies (**indie labels**) seek out and develop new, unknown bands, who may play more progressive, experimental music. As a result, more adventurous and creatively fresh records are produced. These small publishers act as talent scouts for the music business. The companies themselves are small and generally limit themselves to one or two artists or one type of music. If a group is successful, they will franchise their rights to a major company (for example, Sony now owns 49 per cent of the Oasis label Creation).

Case study: XL Records

The independent XL Records started off with a tiny budget in the early 1990s. They found, promoted and recorded The Prodigy. The media ignored the band completely until both their first album *Jilted Generation* and their single *Firestarter* reached number one in the charts. Their world-wide sales amount to 5 million.

Activity

Make a list of bands which have moved from an indie label to a major recording company.

Music retailers

There are four main outlets for recorded music:

1 Large high-street chainstores, such as Woolworths and W.H. Smith (which between them accounted for nearly half of all record sales in the UK in the early 1990s).

2 Large high-street specialist record shops, for example Our Price, Virgin, HMV. (Virgin were able to promote their own label in their shops and EMI could do the same, as they bought HMV.)

3 Small independent record shops.

4 Mail-order record clubs, such as Britannia Music Club.

Activity

Discuss how much the music press, television and both BBC and independent radio influence the recording industry.

Television, film and video

The UK **television**, **film** and **video** industries are small in comparison with those in other parts of the world (for example, the number of films produced in Britain is tiny compared with the number emerging from the giant Indian film industry). But they are nonetheless important because of the quality and innovation of their products.

Terrestrial television

Like radio, television can also be international, national, regional and local. There are three types of television to consider: terrestrial, cable and satellite. Television viewing is Britain's most popular leisure pastime: about 93 per cent of households have a colour television set and about 66 per cent have a video cassette recorder (VCR).

The BBC

In the eyes of many people, not only in this country but abroad, the BBC is perceived to be the world's leading broadcasting organisation for both radio and television, producing quality programmes which fulfil its original purpose to inform, educate and entertain. There are two television channels which reach approximately 20 million licence-paying households in Britain. Since its inception, rival television channels have emerged and the BBC has had to reassess its position and become competitive. Figure 29.7 shows an analysis of the output of the different BBC channels.

Activity

Study Figure 29.7 and answer the following questions.

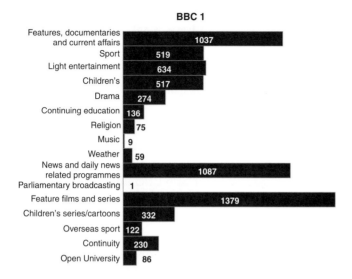

BBC 1

Category	Hours
Features, documentaries and current affairs	1037
Sport	519
Light entertainment	634
Children's	517
Drama	274
Continuing education	136
Religion	75
Music	9
Weather	59
News and daily news related programmes	1087
Parliamentary broadcasting	1
Feature films and series	1379
Children's series/cartoons	332
Overseas sport	122
Continuity	230
Open University	86

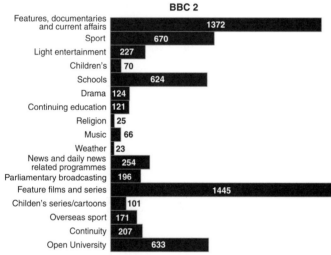

BBC 2

Category	Hours
Features, documentaries and current affairs	1372
Sport	670
Light entertainment	227
Children's	70
Schools	624
Drama	124
Continuing education	121
Religion	25
Music	66
Weather	23
News and daily news related programmes	254
Parliamentary broadcasting	196
Feature films and series	1445
Childen's series/cartoons	101
Overseas sport	171
Continuity	207
Open University	633

Figure 29.7 BBC Network television output analysis in hours per year

1 Which channel has most overseas sport?
2 Which channel has most education programmes?
3 Where will you find most children's cartoons?
4 Which channel has most sports coverage?
5 Which channel shows the most feature films and series?

This is how the BBC now describes its broad objectives:

With the television programmes commissioned and scheduled for BBC1, **the network of broad appeal,** *and BBC2,* **the channel of greater risk and innovation,** *we aim for distinctiveness while still serving a broad range of viewers. Throughout*

its existence, the BBC has had to strike the balance between popular appeal and special interests.

Even our most popular programmes must offer something distinct – a platform for new talent, programmes that families can watch together and which reflect the realities of life in different areas of Britain, our cultural mix, as well as a range of viewpoints representing our changing society.

Activity

Look at the BBC viewing schedules for a weekday. Discuss in a group which programmes you would consider to be innovative, which have broad appeal, which offer new talent and which represent special interests, different viewpoints and the cultural mix. Do your conclusions support the statement above?

We can look in more detail at the two BBC channels:

- **BBC1**

  As we have read above, BBC1's brief is to provide a wide range of quality programmes of different types for a national audience. How well does it succeed?

  It does have some extremely popular fictional programmes attracting millions, such as *EastEnders* and *One Foot in the Grave.* However, 47 per cent of peak-time output consists of non-fiction programmes on wildlife, consumer issues, science, news and current affairs, compared with 27 per cent on ITV. Of course, some of these factual programmes are also extremely popular, such as the *Antiques Roadshow, Tomorrow's World* and *Wildlife on One.*

- **BBC2**

  This channel broadcasts programmes that are not mainstream, such as opera, modern dance, drama or comedy by new writers, live studio performances by new bands. Its programmes are often more controversial.

The BBC retains a strong commitment to education, with programmes for everyone from pre-school children to adults. About 90 per cent of schools make regular use of BBC School Television. Continuing education and training programmes are targeted at adults. The strategy is to provide television and radio programmes supported by magazines, booklets, fact sheets, audio recordings and videos. Recently the BBC has strengthened its partnership with the Open University by introducing the night-time service called *The Learning Zone.*

The home of BBC television since 1960 has been Television Centre at White City in West London, but there are also three network production centres in the regions, which are listed below. The BBC aims by 1998 to make a third of its programmes in the regions. BBC Scotland, Wales and Northern Ireland also make programmes specifically for viewers in these areas. In recent years there has been a dramatic increase in the number of programmes made by independent producers.

The **BBC regions** are:

- **BBC Midlands and East** – the regional HQ is in Birmingham, with centres also in Nottingham and Norwich.
- **BBC South** – the regional HQ is in Bristol, with centres also in Elstree, Southampton and Plymouth.
- **BBC North** – the regional HQ is in Manchester, with centres also in Leeds and Newcastle.
- **BBC Scotland** – the national HQ is in Glasgow, with centres also in Edinburgh, Aberdeen and Dundee.
- **BBC Wales** – the national HQ is in Cardiff, with centres also in Swansea and Bangor.
- **BBC Northern Ireland** – the national HQ is in Belfast.

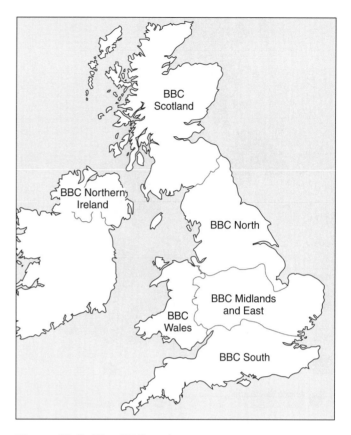

Figure 29.8 The BBC regions

Activity

Make a copy of the map shown in Figure 29.8. Mark in the regional headquarters with a triangle and the other centres with a square. How evenly spread are they over the UK?

These different TV centres produce individual daily news programmes, such as *Midlands Today* or *Look North.* Identify which region you come under and the name of the daily news programme you watch.

The BBC is renowned for its coverage of **news and current affairs** (NCA). On breakfast television, there are almost three hours of business and general news to start the day, and there are full bulletins at 1 pm, 6 pm and 9 pm with short summaries between these times. NCA has a budget of £180 million and over 2 000 staff. In 1993–94 the BBC funded ten new journalist posts, and regional news has improved in quality and length.

Independent television

The BBC lost its monopoly of television in 1955 when ITV started broadcasting. Like radio,

commercial television relies on revenue from advertising for funding, and the various ITV companies are answerable to shareholders and advertisers. They are not free from regulation, however, and are answerable to the ITC (Independent Television Commission).

The **ITV Network Centre** was established as a result of the 1990 Broadcasting Act and became operational in 1993. Its director is currently Marcus Plantin. It is owned by the ITV companies and its main functions are to:

- commission new productions, either from the companies themselves or independent producers
- purchase programmes
- schedule programmes.

We will consider ITV, ITN, Channel 4 and Channel 5 in more detail here.

- **ITV (Channel 3)**
  There are 15 regional Channel 3 independent television licensees, and one which provides national breakfast-time programmes. They are listed in the Media Organisations appendix and

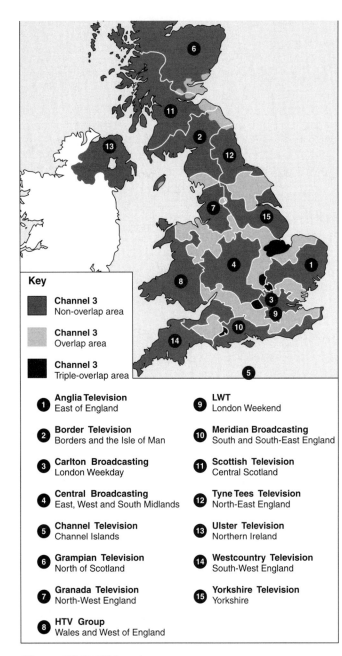

Key

■ **Channel 3**
Non-overlap area

▨ **Channel 3**
Overlap area

■ **Channel 3**
Triple-overlap area

① **Anglia Television**
East of England

② **Border Television**
Borders and the Isle of Man

③ **Carlton Broadcasting**
London Weekday

④ **Central Broadcasting**
East, West and South Midlands

⑤ **Channel Television**
Channel Islands

⑥ **Grampian Television**
North of Scotland

⑦ **Granada Television**
North-West England

⑧ **HTV Group**
Wales and West of England

⑨ **LWT**
London Weekend

⑩ **Meridian Broadcasting**
South and South-East England

⑪ **Scottish Television**
Central Scotland

⑫ **Tyne Tees Television**
North-East England

⑬ **Ulster Television**
Northern Ireland

⑭ **Westcountry Television**
South-West England

⑮ **Yorkshire Television**
Yorkshire

Figure 29.9 ITV regions

the areas they cover are shown in Figure 29.9. Licences were awarded by competitive tender in 1991 for a 10-year term commencing in 1993. In their bids, ITV companies had to show that they were capable of providing high-quality, diverse and original productions. They had to prove that their services would include adequate news coverage, regional production, training, provision for the deaf and hard of hearing and blind or partially sighted, and party political broadcasts.

Activity

Which of the regional network programmes mentioned in the Media Organisations appendix have been broadcast in your area? Can you identify other programmes currently on your screen which have been made by another regional TV company?

■ **ITN (Independent Television News)**
This organisation provides the national and international news service to Channel 3. Its programmes have to be transmitted live and simultaneously by all the regional Channel 3 licensees. It also provides the news for Channel 4 and for Independent Radio News (IRN). Each regional company also produces its own news programme covering local events and issues, for example *Wales Tonight* or *London Today*. Its services include:

– News at Ten
– Channel 4 News
– Early evening and lunchtime news
– Morning and afternoon bulletins
– The Big Breakfast News
– Into the Night
– World news for airlines
– ITN videos.

Activity

Identify your region on the map shown in Figure 29.9. Which news programme does it produce?

■ **Channel 4**
Channel 4 was launched in 1982 and is a combination of public service broadcasting and commercial television. It has a statutory duty under the 1981  Broadcasting Act to provide information, education and entertainment and to appeal to the tastes and interests of audiences not served by other UK television channels. It is intended to be more adventurous, experimental and innovative than Channel 3 and it has a distinctive character. It makes very few of the programmes its transmits, but commissions them from independent production companies. The chief executive of Channel 4 is Michael Grade.

Until the end of 1992 the channel was funded by a subscription levied on the ITV companies in return for which they had the right to sell airtime on Channel 4. In 1993 Channel 4 started to sell its own airtime.

In Wales, the Channel 4 frequencies are used by **S4C (Sianel Pedwar Cymru)**, which broadcasts on average 32 hours per week in the Welsh language, mainly during peak hours, and the rest of the time reschedules Channel 4's programmes in the English language.

- **Channel 5**
  This new channel should come on air in 1997. Delays may be caused because there is a need for viewers to have their VCRs retuned.

There were four contenders for the channel's licence. They included:

- UKTV, with a bid for £36,261,158 (backers were CanWest Global, Mirror Group, Scandinavian Broadcast System, SelecTV, The Ten Group).
- Virgin Television, with a bid for £22,002,000 (backers were Associated Newspapers, HTV, Paramount, Philips, Virgin, Electra).
- New Century television, with a bid for £2 million (backers were Granada group, TCI, BSkyB, Polygram, Really Useful Group, Kinnevik, Goldman Sachs, Hoare Govett).

The winner was:

- *Channel 5 Broadcasting* with a bid of £22,002,000 (backers were Pearson, MAI, CLT, Warburg Pincus Ventures).

Teletext

This is the name for the pages of written information that can be received by some television sets fitted with decoders. The copy gives a wide range of information about TV listings, leisure, finance, sport, travel, etc. and also includes summaries of international and regional news. The two main services are:

- **Teletext Ltd**
  This company took over from Oracle and provides a teletext service for channels 3 and 4. It is owned by the *Daily Mail* and General Trust.

- **Ceefax**
  This is the teletext for the BBC. It also provides a subtitling service for the deaf and hard of hearing.

Cable and satellite television

Satellites (in a fixed position) deliver television and radio services either direct to dish aerials on the sides of buildings or homes, or to a cable network central receiver for local distribution. Satellite, which uses a transmission system called MAC to transmit, actually provides a better picture than the technology used by terrestrial television.

Over three million people have a satellite dish, and more than a million households are connected to cable. Nearly all satellite channels are available on cable, but the reverse is not true.

The ITC describes a cable system as:

'a network of cables. In Britain, these are almost always installed in ducts below roads or footpaths. They radiate from a central control point (called the head end) to homes and businesses in a town or group of towns or, in London, a group of boroughs. The systems use mainly coaxial cable but usually employ optical fibre in the trunks. A cable system is primarily a means of delivering television to the home. The cable system is connected to viewers' existing TV sets, usually through a set-top box provided by the cable operator. The cable systems currently being designed can carry between 30 and 45 channels.'

The companies that own the satellites or lay the cables are not the same companies who provide the programmes or services. Every satellite can send out a number of channels and these are leased to individual companies.

An ITC licence is required for both of the following services:

- **Non-domestic satellite service**
  This is when a satellite service is transmitted or **uplinked** from the UK to individual dishes in this country and to all member states of the European Union and some other European countries not in the EU.

- **Licensable programme service**
  This is when a programme service is provided by someone in the UK via a cable system. Community television services fall into this category. Local cable television programming is sometimes referred to as **narrowcasting**.

Satellite ownership

The three main TV satellites are owned by companies based in France (**Astra** and **Eutelstat**) and America (**Intelstat**).

BSkyB is the most successful British company and owns the following channels:

Sky Movies   Sky Movies Gold
Sky News   Sky One
Sky Soap   Sky Sports
Sky Sports 2   Sky Travel
The Movie Channel

There are over 60 other non-domestic satellite services with licences from the ITC. Examples of these channels are:

The Adult Channel
Cartoon Network
The Children's Channel
The Chinese Channel
The European Family Network
International Shopping Network
The Learning Channel
MTV Europe
Middle East Broadcasting
Muslim Television Ahmdiyya
The Parliamentary Channel
QVC The Shopping Channel
Satellite Information Services – Racing Facts
Setanta Sport
Sell-a-vision Shopping
The Travel Channel
UK Gold
UK Living
Visual Arts
World Health Network

Activity

Study the list shown above. What sort of programmes do you think these channels would carry? What type of people would be interested in these satellite services? If you wish to carry out further research into individual channels, their phone numbers are in the *Guardian Media Guide* or in the *ITC Factfile*, which also includes their addresses.

Cable ownership

The cable companies are sometimes called multiple systems operators (MSOs). The table shows the major MSOs who laid the cables and own the cable systems:

	Number of homes connected	Homes in the area still unconnected
TeleWest	301,802	1,404,131
Comcast	151,293	547,710
Nynex	130,377	687,923
Videotron	95,558	446,966
Bell	75,873	340,460
Telecentenial	64,813	254,826
General Cable	56,574	275,318
CableTel	20,735	134,766

Activity

The table above shows that TeleWest has installed cable in the most homes and CableTel in the least. Convert the figures into percentages to show what proportion of homes in each company's area are receiving cable. Who has been most successful in persuading homeowners in its area to have cable?

Here is some information about the companies who own the approximately 132 franchises for cable systems. Many of these are North American.

- **Bell Cablemedia**
  Franchises are in London, Leeds, Norwich and East Anglia, Harrogate, York, Worcester, Wearside.

  Subsidiaries: Encom Cable ITV and Telecommunications, Fenland Cablevision, Jones Cable Group, Norwich Cablevision, Peterborough Cablevision. Owned by Bell Canada.

- **Diamond Cable**
  Franchises are in Nottingham, Newark, Mansfield, Grantham, Melton, Grimsby, Lincoln.

  Owned by Diamond Cable USA with European Cable Partners (72.4 per cent) and McDonald Family Trust.

- **BT Cable TV Services**
  Franchises are in Westminster, other parts of London, Milton Keynes, Washington. Subsidiaries: BT New Towns Systems, Westminster Cable, Barbican Cable, Irvine Cable, Milton Keynes Cable.

  Owned by BT (i.e. this is a UK company).

Over 60 licences for cable channels have been awarded. These include

The Afro-Caribbean Channel
Airport Television
Black Music Television
CNN International
Cable Video Store
EZTV Youth Entertainment
Ebony Television
The Education Channel
Havering Community Channel
Interactive London News Network
Performance – The Arts Channel

Royal Opera House Channel
Videotron Home Shopping

Activity

Look at the names in the above list. What type of services do you think are being offered? How do they compare with the satellite channels?

Identify which cable company operates in or near your area and in neighbouring large towns. Find out what channels are on offer. You can do this by contacting the Cable Association or consulting the list in the *BFI Film and Television Handbook*. Note down the name of the cable company, the name of the franchise holder and the name of the owner.

Independent television producers

From the beginning, Channel 4 had a high proportion of programmes made by independent companies. Now, because of the 1990 Broadcasting Act, BBC and the Channel 3 companies are also expected to have 25 per cent of their programmes made by independent producers.

There are now hundreds of these production companies around the country, for example:

■ Hat Trick Productions (*Whose Line Is It Anyway, Drop the Dead Donkey, Delia Smith's Cookery programmes*)
■ Channel X (*Jonathan Ross Presents, Jo Brand Through the Cakehole*)
■ The Mersey TV Company (*Brookside*)
■ SelecTV, which incorporates Alomo, Clement Le Frenais and Witzend Productions (*Lovejoy, Birds of a Feather, The New Statesman, Pie in the Sky, Goodnight Sweetheart, A Class Act*).

Case study: Carnival

Carnival (Films & Theatre) Ltd is one of the UK's leading independent **production** companies. It was founded in 1978 by producer Brian Eastman. Carnival produces drama for the cinema, television and theatre. Recent box office hits included *Shadowlands* and *Under Suspicion.*

Carnival has also produced programmes for all the major channels.

■ For ITV:
Poirot
Jeeves and Wooster

Forever Green
Anna Lee
Head over Heels

■ For Channel 4:
The Big Battalions
Porterhouse Blue
Traffic

■ For the BBC:
Bugs
Blot on the Landscape

The company has won many British and international awards and nominations, including Oscars, Emmys, Baftas, Tonys and Oliviers!

Working individually or as a group, over the space of a week, note down the names of any production companies which appear in the credits at the end of a programme. How many can you collect?

Once made, television programmes need to be sold. Some companies are specifically set up to promote and distribute both network and independent productions.

Case study: Pavilion International Ltd

Figure 29.10 The Pavilion Logo

Pavilion was formed in 1978 and is now a leading independent television **distribution** company. It specialises in the distribution of factual and drama programmes throughout the world, and represents Channel 4 television as one of their distributors of documentary and educational programming. They distribute for ITN, TV3 Spain, SVT Sweden, independent productions for the BBC and for over 100 independent production companies, including Australian producers.

In addition to this, the company is also involved in two other specialist areas:

■ PSI – a jointly owned company with Associated Newspapers which sells sports programmes
■ Independent Wildlife – which is involved in co-production and sales of natural history and environmental programmes.

Pavilion sells to over 100 countries on five continents and exploits the rights to broadcast television, satellite, cable, home video, in-flight entertainment and educational markets. The seven major markets are UK, USA, Australia, France, Italy, West Germany and Japan. They promote programmes at trade events, such as Monte Carlo or the London Programme market.

Pavilion can also co-develop ideas with broadcasters and independent producers via a subsidiary company, Harlequin Films and Television.

Film

What makes a film British? Is it because it was made in Britain, or financed by British people, or because the stars or the producer are British? The BFI defines a UK film as one produced or co-produced by a UK production company, or made in the UK by an overseas producer. But as investment in UK films continues to fall, the UK lags behind Germany, Italy and France in the number of films made on home soil.

Country	Numbers of films (incl. co-prods)	Investment ($m)
Belgium	8	9.97
Denmark	14	25.71
France	152	550.01
Germany	67	–
Greece	18	7.68
Ireland	6	33.32
Italy	106	227.4
Luxembourg	4	1.9
Netherlands	16	–
Portugal	16	3.9
Spain	53	99.4
UK	59	159.38

Source: Screen Digest/BFI

Figure 29.11 EC film production 1993

Figures 29.12 and 29.13 shows lists of UK feature films produced in 1993, and their producers.

Now look at Figure 29.14 for the list of Top 20 films at the UK box office in 1993.

Activity

How many of these films have you seen, and how many of the film distributors have you heard of? How many of the production companies have you heard of? What conclusions can you draw about UK film production?

Title	Production company(ies)
Backbeat	Scala Prods, with Royal Films (Germany), Channel 4 and Polygram
Begl	Beg Productions Ltd/Robert Golden
Beyond Bedlam	Metrodome Films backed by Business Expansion Scheme
Blue	Basilisk with Uplink (Japan)
Boy Meets Girl	Kino Eye
A Christmas Reunion	Y Wennol
Dead Lucky	Cross Sound Prods
Deadly Advice	Zenith/Mayfair
Death Machine	Fugitive Features/Entertainment/Victor (Japan)
Decadence	Vendetta Films/Schlemmer (Germany)/DeLuxe (Luxembourg)
Four Weddings and a Funeral	Polygram/Channel 4/Working Title
The Funny Man	Nomad Pictures/Redman Entertainments
Glastonbury The Movie	Videodrome
The Higher Mortals	Children's Film Unit
Intimate With a Stranger	Independent International Pictures
Ladybird, Ladybird	Parallax Pictures/Channel 4/UIP
London	Koninck/BFI/Channel 4
Midnight Movie	BBC/Whistling Gypsy
The Priest and the Pirate	Video in Pilton
The Prisoner	BBC/Distant Horizon
The Queen of Clubs	Santana/Vital Productions
Seaview Knights	Seaview Knights Prods backed by Business Expansion Scheme
Second Best	Sarah Radclyffe Prods/New Regency
Shallow Grave	Figment Films/Channel 4
Shopping	Impact Pictures/Polygram/Channel 4
Sister My Sister	NFH Films/British Screen Finance/Channel 4
Staggered	The Big Nowhere plc backed by Business Expansion Scheme
To Catch a Yeti	String of Pearls
Tom and Viv	New Era/UGC-DA/ITC/Entertainment/British Screen/IRS Media
UFO	Busybrave/Polygram
Welcome to the Terrordome	Non-Aligned Productions
Widow's Peak	Jo Manuel Prods/British Screen

Source: Screen Finance/Screen International/BFI

Figure 29.12 UK feature film production 1993

Title	Production company(ies)	Other participating country(ies)
The Adventures of Priscilla, Queen of the Desert	Specific Films/Latent Image	Australia
Amateur	Zenith/UGC	USA/France
Au Pair	Teliesyn/Hermes Film	Germany
Before the Rain	Aim Productions/Vardar Film/Noe Productions	Macedonia/France
The Bishop's Story	De Facto Film and Video/K-Films/B-Film/Cinegal	Eire/France
Borderline	Forever Films/Mythos/Greek Film Centre	Greece
A Business Affair	Film and General/Osby Film/Connexion/Cartel	France/Germany/Spain
Camilla	Skreba/Shaftesbury Films	Canada
Draum Spel	Unni Straume Filmproduksjon/Trust/Nordic Film and Television Fund	Norway/Sweden
In Custody	Merchant Ivory/Likproof	India
The Life and Extraordinary Adventures of Private Ivan Chonkin	Portobello Pictures/MK2/KF/Trite/Fandango/Channel 4/ European Co-Production Fund	Czech Republic/France/ Russia/ Italy
Loaded	New Zealand Film Commission/BFI/British Screen/Channel 4/ Strawberry Vale/Movie Partners	New Zealand/Germany
Mesmer	Levergreen/Satel Film/Accent Films/Filmstudios Babelsberg	Austria/Canada/Germany
Moondance	Lodge Prods/Little Bird/MFG	Eire/Germany
Nostradamus	Allied Entertainments/Vereinigte Film	Germany
The Phoenix and the Magic Carpet	Magic Carpet Films/Smart Egg Pictures/Zoran Films International	USA
A Pin for a Butterfly	Skreba/Heureka/British Screen/Channel 4	Czech Republic
Playmaker	New Era/Steinhardt-Baer	USA
The Prince of Jutland	Woodline Films/Allarts/Films Ariane/Kenneth Madsen Filmproduktion	Holland/Denmark/France
Le Roi de Paris	Adventure Pictures/Rio	France
The Seventh Floor	Portman Entertainment/Sogovision/Channel 10	Australia/Japan
Sirens	Sarah Radclyffe Productions/Samson Productions/British Screen/Australian Film Finance Corporation	Australia
Sista Dansen	Sandrews/Shibsted Film/Metronome	Sweden/Denmark/ Norway
That Eye the Sky	Working Title/Entertainment Media	Australia
A Time for Witches	Mark Forstater Prods/Casting Service Film/Elnor/Odra-Film/Max-Film	Poland
War of the Buttons	Enigma/Les Productions de la Geauville/Fujisankei	France/Japan/Eire
Words Upon the Window Pane	Pembridge/Northpro/British Screen/Calypso/DeLux	Eire/Germany/Luxembourg

Source: Screen Finance/European Film File

Figure 29.13 UK co-productions 1993

Film studios

There are still British film studios at Pinewood and Shepperton. Work at these facilities has shown signs of increase, with blockbusters such as Luc Besson's $75 million *The Fifth Element* and Philip Noyce's *The Saint* using them. Even the studios at Elstree re-opened in June 1996 for a Stanley Kubrick film, *Eyes Wide Shut,* starring Tom Cruise and Nicole Kidman. Third Millennium Studios plan to develop an old aerodrome in Hertfordshire as a new production complex and there is also currently a proposal to build a £225 million film and TV theme park in West London. This is to incorporate a working film studio, the first to be built since 1945.

Cinemas

Films are shown or **exhibited** through chains of cinemas. There are nearly 2 000 cinema screens in the UK, about 700 of which are at **multiplexes**. (This may sound good, but France, Germany and the USA have far more screens per head of population.)

Cinema attendance in Britain fell to very low levels

	Title	Country	Distributor	Box Office (£)
1	Jurassic Park	US	UIP	46,564,080
2	The Bodyguard	US	Warner Bros	14,665,069
3	The Fugitive	US	Warner Bros	14,002,047
4	Indecent Proposal	US	UIP	11,885,752
5	Bram Stoker's Dracula	US	Columbia	11,548,429
6	Sleepless in Seattle	US	Columbia	9,417,608
7	Cliffhanger	US	Guild	9,219,405
8	A Few Good Men	US	Columbia	8,416,625
9	Aladdin	US	Buena Vista	8,167,165
10	The Jungle Book (re)	US	Buena Vista	7,415,989
11	In the Line of Fire	US	Columbia	6,817,821
12	The Firm	US	UIP	6,816,581
13	Forever Young	US	Warner Bros	6,787,327
14	Sommersby	US	Warner Bros	6,668,012
15	Home Alone 2: Lost in New York	US	Fox	5,663,186
16	Demolition Man	US	Warner Bros	5,628,613
17	Under Siege	US	Warner Bros	5,422,549
18	Much Ado About Nothing	UK	Entertainment	5,133,502
19	Groundhog Day	US	Columbia	5,098,267
20	Made in America	US	Warner Bros	4,999,057

Source: EDI

Figure 29.14 Top 20 films at UK box office 1993

in 1984, when there were only 54 million admissions, but have risen to twice this level in the mid-1990s. Because there are comparatively few screens, small British productions have less chance of exhibition. Films distributed by the major studios account for about 80 per cent of admissions.

Look at the table in Figure 29.15. Notice how the number of UK films on wide release declined during the 1980s and is beginning to pick up again now. A more depressing figure is the number of UK films which are never released.

Year	Wide release (%)	Limited run or selected release (%)	Unreleased (%)
1983	51.3	46.2	2.5
1984	50.0	44.0	6.0
1985	52.8	35.9	11.3
1986	55.8	41.9	2.3
1987	36.0	60.0	4.0
1988	29.5	61.2	9.3
1989	33.3	38.9	27.8
1990	29.4	47.1	23.5
1991	32.2	37.3	30.5
1992	38.3	29.8	31.9

Source: BFI/Screen International/Screen Finance

Figure 29.15 UK film releases

The first multiplex was a cinema-disco (The Point) opened at Milton Keynes in 1985. The largest British multiplex now has 14 screens, but there are plans to build 'category killers', as they are known in the US – sites that have between 20 and 24 screens which wipe out opposition within a twenty-mile radius.

Who owns the multiplexes? The following companies own and control about half of the screens in the UK:

- MGM (along with 90 former Virgin sites, was bought out by ABC in the summer of 1996)
- Odeon
- UCI
- Warner Bros
- Showcase.

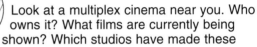

Activity

Look at a multiplex cinema near you. Who owns it? What films are currently being shown? Which studios have made these films? Are there any UK productions?

Identify the advantages and disadvantages of multiplex cinemas; consider choice, travel, costs, the proximity of other leisure activities. Refer to Chapter 25 for more information on multiplexes.

Video

Video rental shops boomed in the 1980s, but now face increasing competition from cable and satellite television. Blockbuster Video is the world's largest video retailer. They are improving turnover by the sale and rental of video games and CD-ROMs. Figure 29.16 shows a table with the distributors' shares of UK video transactions in 1993.

Company	%
Warner	19.5
CIC	16.2
Columbia TriStar	15.2
Guild	11.1
Buena Vista	10.5
Fox Video	10.4
Entertainment in Video	7.1
First Independent	3.2
High Fliers	1.4
Polygram	1.4

Source: BVA/MRIB

Figure 29.16 Distributors' shares of UK video rental transactions 1993

Market share by volume	
Company	%
Buena Vista	16.6
Polygram	12.9
BBC	11.5
Warner Home Video	9.4
Video Collection	8.1
CIC	6.3
Fox Video	5.7
Columbia TriStar	3.4
Pickwick	2.5
Source: CIN/BVA	

Figure 29.17 Video sell-through

Besides rental, big profits are made by selling videos, an activity known as **sell-through**. Only 30 per cent of feature films account for this market; popular sellers are children's videos, comedies and music videos. Look at the table in Figure 29.17; notice the success of the BBC.

However, the American film studios and distributors are supreme in film and video rentals and sales in the UK, and the main studios also have valuable deals with BSkyB. British and European films cannot compete against these giants.

Animation

In recent years there has been an increase in the number of successful cartoon films made in Britain, due to the pioneering work of British animators using 3D and computer animation. Channel 4 and S4C have invested £2–3 million per year in animated films for both children and adults. *Creature Comforts* by Aardman Animation and *Manipulation* by Danile Greaves won Oscars in the early nineties.

Other producers of well-known cartoons include:

- The Britt Allcroft Company (*Thomas the Tank Engine and Friends, Magic Adventures of Mumfie*)
- Cosgrove Hall Films (*Dangermouse, The Wind in the Willows, Count Duckula, The B.F.G., Noddy, Avenger Penguins*)
- Fairwater Films (*Sid the Sexist, The Shoe People, Cheese and Crackers*)
- FilmFair International (*The Wombles, Paddington Bear, Huxley Pig, Gingerbread Man, Asto Farm*)
- Grasshopper Productions (*The Mousehole Cat, East of the Moon*).

Activity

Discuss why you think that animation is a developing industry in the UK compared with feature film production. Consider costs, production skills and technology.

New media

What part does the UK have in the production of **new media** products and services such as the Internet, interactive multimedia, and CD-ROM production?

The Internet

The Internet is a global network which links together computers belonging to individuals, businesses or organisations and also enables them to access databases.

A comparison has been made between the Internet and commercial television in the 1950s: all advertising and news, and no programmes! The Internet has been criticised as an advertising medium, however. Listeners can hardly avoid hearing the adverts if they are tuned in to a commercial radio or TV station, but on the Internet, users consciously have to look up adverts.

Below are a few examples of gateway companies which sell access to the Internet:

- BBC Networking Club
  E-mail: info@cityscape.co.uk
  Web page: http://www.bbcnc.org.uk

- Pavilion Internet
  E-mail: info@pavilion.co.uk
  Web page: http://www.easynet.co.uk

- PC User Group
  Web page: http://www:ibmpcug.co.uk

Multimedia is the mixing of stereo sound, still or moving images and text by means of a personal computer. The images are seen on the computer screen. When the user can choose what is seen and heard, and manipulate the order of the material, this is known as **interactive media**. Games run on Amigas or Ataris are a form of multimedia, but there are more serious uses, as in making sales presentations or describing a complex process, such as a heart operation. Microsoft, Bill Gates' company which launched Windows software, was a pioneer in this field. Some publishers now bring out their reference works on CD-ROM, for example dictionaries and encyclopaedias. The format (basically a CD player connected to a PC to produce sound and pictures) can make educational material look like fun. Music reference works are particularly successful, as you can hear the music and not merely read about it. Philips CD-i system was an early example of an interactive multimedia system.

Penguin published its first electronic novel in November 1995. BT started interactive TV trials in East Anglia in June 1996, offering home banking, movies-on-demand and interactive advertising.

Examples of UK CD-ROM publishers include:

- First Information Group plc
- Jane's Information Group Ltd
- SilverPlatter Information Ltd.

Examples of UK multimedia systems manufacturers are:

- Broad Knowledge Systems Ltd
- Pioneer High Fidelity (GB) Ltd
- Sterry Communications Ltd.

Skillset quotes the following figures for the types of organisations employing multi-media staff, based on research by Recruit Multimedia, a leading employment agency:

Organisations employing multimedia staff

Specialist design and presentation houses	22%
Book and magazine publishers	20%
Dedicated multimedia production houses	19%
Corporates (major UK and international companies)	18%
Financial services (e.g. chartered accountants)	10%
Others	11%

For more information on the Internet, interactive multimedia including interactive television and CD-ROM production, see Chapter 31.

Ownership patterns among principal UK media producers and their effect on products and consumers

By now you will have realised that many companies own or belong to other companies, and many of the larger companies have interests in different parts of the media or even outside the media.

In the UK, there are millions of business organisations, ranging from those owned and run by one person to giant corporations. They can be classified under the following headings:

- private enterprise
  i.e. sole proprietor or trader
  partnerships
  joint-stock companies
- co-operative enterprise
- public enterprise.

The type of business is usually decided by the amount of money needed to set up and run the business successfully and enable it to grow. All businesses need **capital**, i.e. money, to operate. **Fixed capital** is the money needed to buy furniture or equipment (known as **assets**) which last a long time, such as a printing press or a mixing desk. **Working capital** is the money used for everyday expenditure, such as buying film or travel expenses.

Private enterprise

A **sole trader** or **proprietor** is the owner of a shop or commercial business, run by one person. There may be assistants or other staff, but the ownership rests in the hands of one person. The owner retains personal control and receives all the profits from his or her hard work and initiative. This type of business is usually set up using the owner's savings and through loans from banks, friends and relatives, etc. Traditionally, sole traders have been most common in sectors of the economy where personal service is important, such as retail, and these can also be found in the media, for instance a small independent record shop, or a desk-top publisher.

Partnerships occur when a number of people, between two and twenty, combine to provide capital jointly for the **firm** (this is the term used rather than company) and share the profits. Partners tend to specialise in different areas of the business, for example, one person may have creative ideas, the other accountancy skills. In the past, partnerships have often been between professional people, such as lawyers or dentists, where not a lot of capital is required in comparison with a manufacturing business. In the media, partnerships have been set up in the new media industries where people with ideas have needed financial backing. The advantages of a partnership arrangement are that more skills, expertise and money are brought into the business and responsibilities are shared.

Sleeping partners are people who provide capital but do not work or have much to do with the running of the firm. The Partnership Act of 1907 enables a person to become a 'limited' partner, so that if the firm goes bankrupt, he or she loses only the money invested in the firm, rather than being responsible for the repayment of all debts, which is the case with unlimited liability.

There is also another important trend in the media industries and that is towards **co-productions** where companies work together and/or put up the finance for a specific project. This style of partnership is increasingly found in television and film, where two companies come together for one particular film or programme. One company may provide the capital, and the other the equipment and staff.

Case study: Channel 4

Channel 4 has co-financed many productions, including *The Madness of King George* and *Four Weddings and a Funeral*, the latter in association with Polygram Film Education. This was the most successful British film ever, in commercial terms, with enormous box office returns. It had a budget of somewhere between £1 and 2 million, generous by British standards.

A **joint-stock** company is a business where the capital is raised by the sales of shares and the profits are distributed to the shareholders, i.e. the investors. The Limited Liability Act of 1862 means that if the company should go bankrupt, the shareholders lose only the money they invested in the company. This greatly encouraged investment in industry at the time and continues to do so. At meetings, each shareholder has one vote per share, so major shareholders can outvote people with few shares.

There are two types of joint-stock companies:

- **Private** – they must have between two and 50 shareholders. Their shares must be sold privately and not to the public. These are more numerous than public companies but on average are much smaller. They are often family firms who need extra capital but want the family to retain control of the company. The **directors** (usually the major shareholders) who run the companies must give permission before the shares can be sold to any one else. These companies, known as **corporate bodies**, have the initials 'Ltd' after the name. **Limited** means that there is limited liability. If the company goes bankrupt because it has too many debts which it cannot meet, the shareholders or owners are not personally responsible in law to pay the money owed. Liability is restricted to the company assets rather than to private individuals. A private limited company can offer shares only to business associates, family and friends.

- **Public – a PLC (public limited company)** raises its money on the Stock Exchange, which means the public can buy shares. These companies must have at least two directors and a minimum of seven shareholders (there is no maximum number). The shareholders sell the shares when they want to without having to ask the directors. This is a good way of raising large amounts of capital but leaves a company vulnerable to take-overs. It cannot prevent a number of small shareholders from selling their shares to one person or company. If that person or company succeeds in buying 50 per cent or more of the shares then they will gain control. Richard Branson's company Virgin started off as a small record company, but going public enabled it to raise large sums of capital to expand into other areas such as airlines, cinemas and financial services.

Activity

From the information about UK media producers gives above, identify the companies in the Media Organisations appendix which are limited and those which are PLCs.

A **co-operative enterprise** is a business organisation where the plant, equipment and stocks of goods are owned collectively by those with a direct interest in the articles sold or services provided. There are both consumer and producer co-operatives. In the latter case, profits go to the workers (the producers) not to shareholders. Co-operatives are often started with ideological motives. In December 1995, the daily paper for the shipping industry, *Lloyd's List and Shipping Gazette,* was sold by Lloyds to its staff, as a co-operative enterprise.

Case study: Magnum Photographic Agency

Magnum is a co-operative photographic agency founded in 1947 in New York by, amongst others, a Frenchman, Henri Cartier-Bresson, a Hungarian, David Seymour (originally Szymin) and a Pole, Robert Capa (originally Friedmann). They formed the co-operative in order to control what assignments they did, how their pictures were used, and to retain copyright in their work. There was a famous exhibition of their work in 1990, recorded in a book *In Our Time: The World As Seen By Magnum Photographers.* They are noted for their coverage of civil unrest, war and famine

511

in all corners of the world. Capa was killed in Vietnam in 1947 and Seymour was shot and killed in Egypt in 1949, but their work is carried on by a new generation of photographers.

Public enterprise

At the beginning of the 1980s, 11 per cent of the UK's output was from the nationalised industries. These can be defined as public corporations whose boards of directors are appointed by the government, but who are not civil servants and are engaged in industrial or other trading activities. The Post Office and its sub-division, British Telecommunications (which became British Telecom in 1981), fell into this category. The BBC, which is discussed in detail later, is also a public, national service.

Most nationalised industries have now been **privatised**. Arguments for privatisation, i.e. against public enterprises, include:

- they are too large, requiring huge management structures, leading to inefficiency and overspending
- lack of competition means that such organisations have a monopoly – they can charge what they like and do not have to worry about the quality of their work
- they are vulnerable to political interference.

As noted above, some organisations belonging to the public sector may have objectives that vary from a private sector organisation. They may wish to provide a service to the community rather than make money. Public corporations, local authority enterprises and other forms of public ownership are generally funded by the state through various types of taxation (e.g. the BBC is partly funded by the licence fee).

Activity

What arguments can you find *against* privatisation which will justify the continuation of national institutions such as the BBC?

Types of take-over

Vertical integration has been a common business practice for many years. It occurs when a company takes over another which works at a different stage in the production line, e.g. a film studio buys a multiplex cinema.

Horizontal integration, on the other hand, occurs when the two companies are at the same stage, for instance one film studio buys another film studio.

Take-overs by large companies of small ones in the same line of business are also usual, for example a regional newspaper buying up smaller ones.

Mergers occur when two companies which are of equal importance and/or financial value join together.

Case study

In spring 1995, the cross-media ownership rules (see below and Chapter 30) were relaxed by the British government. In early February 1996, MAI merged with United News and Media. At the heart of MAI's media interests were the ITV franchises Anglia and Meridian, plus a large stake in Channel 5 and links with Time Warner. United's main interests lay in newspapers (the *Daily Express* and *Sunday Express*), exhibitions and information services operating worldwide.

Lord Stevens of United became chairman and Lord Hollick of MAI became chief executive of the new group. United shareholders got 50.7 per cent of the company and MAI shareholders got 49.3 per cent. Together they made a media group worth £2.9 billion.

Media analysts expect the companies to make significant savings by pooling resources. However, the main reason could be that MAI wanted to protect itself from being taken over by Carlton or Granada.

Stephen Armstrong wrote in *Broadcast* magazine: 'One signal of what might be in Hollick's ten-year plan is his admiration for the Disney Empire and its sheer breadth of supply. He wants to be one of the new breed of "lifestyle suppliers" – an all-encompassing media brand that can give you your TV, radio, newspapers, house, books, records, cruise ship holidays, theme park thrills and, of course, films.'

Details of ownership can often be found on labels on the media products themselves, as well as on any

Heinemann Educational
A Division of Reed Educational
& Professional Publishing Limited

Registered Office
Quadrant House, The Quadrant,
Sutton, Surrey, SM2 5AS

Registered in England 3099304

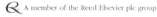 A member of the Reed Elsevier plc group

correspondence the companies may send to you. Companies always give their **registered address** on their company letter-headed notepaper. No matter how many different branches a company might have, there will only be one registered address. You can write to the company secretary at the registered address to ask for copies of annual reports, and these will give details of holding companies, subsidiaries, etc.

Activity

Choose a cross-section of books, CDs or cassettes, and magazines and identify from their covers which company made them and if there is a parent company.

Cross-media ownership

Cross-media ownership, such as that described in the case study above, is a growing trend. It is sometimes called **convergence**.

In America, there was a collapse of audiences for the terrestrial TV channels ABC, CBS and NBC when cable arrived, so now big companies like Granada, Channel 4, Carlton and Associated Newspapers are being advised by strategists to look ever more closely at cross-media relationships. Maybe the BBC will ally with BSkyB?

Cross-media ownership has been made easier by new ownership rules in the UK, including:

■ an increase in the number of radio licences that can be held by one organisation (35 rather than 20)
■ allowing terrestrial broadcasters to have controlling interests in satellite and cable companies as long as they do not exceed 15 per cent of the audience share
■ abolition of the 50 per cent limit on combined Channel 3 holdings
■ allowing newspaper companies with under 20 per cent of national newspaper circulation to control radio and TV companies, with up to 15 per cent market share in a locality
■ newspaper mergers not to be referred to the Mergers and Monopolies Commission unless they exceed a circulation of 50 000 (it was 25 000 before)
■ regional newspapers, however, not to be allowed to own local TV or radio licences if they control 30 per cent or more of the region's circulation.

Activity

How do these rules help media companies, and how do they intend to protect the public?

Expansion

There are many reasons for companies wanting to grow bigger. They may expand for any of the following reasons:

■ It gives them more opportunities to make a profit. They can maximise benefits by sharing distribution costs. They can combine market share and not compete against each other.
■ It can help their existing business (perhaps the new business can distribute or promote the product).
■ It enables them to survive if their present area of work is declining.
■ It provides better economies of scale (more purchasing power and cheaper production costs).
■ It makes them more influential or powerful (they can pressurise governments).
■ It stops rival companies from becoming bigger.
■ New technology and multi-skilled staff bring the industries together (journalists can work for both television and radio).
■ Improved communications networks can be set up (computer databases and telecommunications).
■ They are under pressure from shareholders.

Activity

Decide which of the needs listed above will be best satisfied through:

■ vertical integration
■ horizontal integration
■ expansion into non-media areas.

Effects of expansion

The trend towards larger companies and increased competition, and how this will affect public interests, has become the subject of much debate, both in and out of Parliament.

Heritage Secretary Virginia Bottomley stated in 1996:

'We are the communications and broadcasting heart of Europe … Our broadcasting policy is designed to protect the strength of the domestic

market by allowing the development of more broadly based media groups which have the ability to harness the potential of digital broadcasting and other new technologies ...

... The Broadcasting Bill sets out a new media ownership regime. The reform of the media ownership rules supports the Government's wider deregulatory initiatives and benefits important industrial sectors. UK media companies will be able to merge and develop across sectors of the industry. This will underpin the commercial viability of UK companies and help us along the road to bringing about the information society ...

... The media ownership proposals will help media groups make the necessary investments in technology and services. This is not a dogmatic belief in "big is beautiful". It is an acceptance that the long-term risk investments, which will have to be made if British companies are to deliver a wider range of quality consumer services, will require companies which are more broadly based than the current legislation allows. In short, if British companies are to compete and survive, they will have to grow ...

... The media ownership proposals ensure continued competition and plurality of ownership, preserving regional voices and production. We want competitive broadcasters serving viewers, not marauding monopolists. Broadcasting is too powerful and pervasive a medium to give control to any one organisation.'

However, there were politicians and media representatives who argued against this speech, suggesting that the deregulation would create monopolies, that smaller organisations would be taken over, and that the result would be less choice not more.

These were some of the questions raised:

■ Granville Williams (Campaign for Press and Broadcasting Freedom): 'Rupert Murdoch's media empire grows ever more dominant in the UK! Why did the government duck the challenge of legislating for the divestment of some parts of his media interests, however small, to ensure a more level playing field for other media groups?'
■ John Birt (BBC): 'How can we best reconcile the need for universal availability of major sports events – including national and international competitions – with the proper interests of sports rights holders and subscription networks?'
■ Gus MacDonald (Scottish TV): 'Scottish, Welsh and Northern Irish viewers and licence payers

make up about 17 per cent of UK audiences. Yet producers outside England supply barely one per cent of programmes in the peak-time schedules of UK networks. Will new legislation encourage our London-based broadcasters to be more British?'

Activity

Identify the problems raised by Granville Williams, John Birt and Gus MacDonald. Do you think they are justified? Can you suggest any other reasons why multinational conglomerates might not be a good idea?

Case study: News International Corporation

We have already seen that News International is the largest newspaper owner in Britain. Rupert Murdoch's company also owns or has a major stake in the book publisher HarperCollins (an international group) and the satellite channel BSkyB (40 per cent)

In addition to this:

■ In Australia he owns:
 – Channel 7 (15 per cent)
 – many newspapers and publishers

■ In Germany he owns:
 – Vox satellite and TV channel (49.9 per cent)

■ In America he owns:
 – a film studio, i.e. Twentieth Century Fox
 – a television station, i.e. Fox TV
 – a newspaper, *i.e. The New York Post* and the *TV Guide*

■ In Asia he owns:
 – Star TV (99 per cent) which covers India, China, Japan, the Philippines, Thailand and Hong Kong.

List the dangers there might be in one individual or company gaining control over such a wide range of media organisations world-wide. Consider both economic and political aspects.

We shall now look in more detail at an individual, large media company and how it has developed.

Case study: Pearson plc

Chairman and chief executive: Viscount Blakenham

Group managing director: Frank Barlow.

Main brands and subsidiaries:

■ **Leisure**
Alton Towers
Madame Tussauds
The Planetarium in London
Chessington World of Adventures
Warwick Castle

■ **Television**
Thames TV
Channel 5
Grundy International
SelecTV International
ACI
Phoenix

UK Living
UK Gold

■ **Publishing**
The Economist (50 per cent)
Addison Wesley Longman
Westminster Press
Mindscape
Financial Times
Penguin Books
Ladybird Books
Future Publishing

■ **Banking**
Lazard Brothers (50 per cent) (French, English and American banks)

■ **Property**
Lakeside shopping complex at Thurrock

The value of the Pearson group on the stock market has been estimated at £2.2 billion. Pearson is ranked 99 in the UK's Top 100 companies.

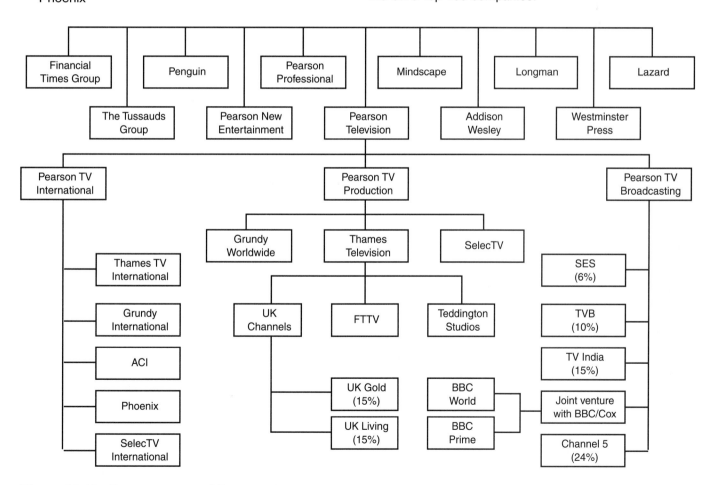

Figure 29.18 Group structure of Pearson plc

Background

The Pearson company started as a Yorkshire building firm called S. Pearson and Son in 1897. The Pearsons helped build the Blackwall tunnel and were involved in constructing railways all over the world. Various members of the family had other interests and so the company branched out into oil, merchant banking, publishing and engineering.

In the 1930s the family bought land and property, and joined the aristocracy, becoming known as the Cowdrays. One Cowdray became a Liberal MP and owner of British Airways. The third Lord Cowdray added Royal Doulton and the vineyards producing Chateau Latour wines to the company assets. He already owned the Westminster Press local papers and added the *Financial Times* group and Penguin and Longman.

In 1969, Pearson went public, and the name changed to Pearson plc in 1984. During this period, the company was streamlined and the less attractive businesses, such as Fairey Engineering and Doulton Glass Industries, were sold off. More take-overs of companies in publishing and entertainment, such as Addison-Wesley, the US publisher, opened up further markets.

In the 1990s, Pearson has become more of a leisure/media group, with an international reach. In 1994, the group moved into magazine publishing for the first time with the £52.5 million purchase of Future Publishing, which produces 30 consumer and computer magazines, including a title on the Internet.

Broadcasting

Pearson has also diversified into television and satellite broadcasting and has concentrated on its interests in publishing, business information, theme parks and interactive technology, selling off interests such as Royal Doulton. This is part of a long-term strategy, and investment has been huge.

The company is continually buying and selling within these areas. It has sold off its 14 per cent interest in Yorkshire–Tyne Tees and the 9.75 per cent interest in BSkyB which it had in the early nineties, but is rapidly developing its television division. Although mainly concerned with production, Pearson TV under its chairman Greg Dyke also has companies involved in distribution and broadcasting. In May 1995 the group acquired Grundy International (the company which makes *Neighbours*) for £176.3 million and US distributor ACI for £27.3 million. In November 1995, Pearson took a stake of 20 per cent in an American studio in Hollywood called Phoenix Pictures, which makes TV movies.

In 1996, there started a co-venture in an Indian channel with *The Hindustan Times,* Carlton Communications and

the merchant bank Schroders. Person is also planning to work closely with BBC Worldwide. The companies are already linked through UK Gold, in which Pearson has a 15 per cent interest and the BBC 20 per cent. The company is interested in buying MGM.

Figure 29.19 shows the present revenues of the company.

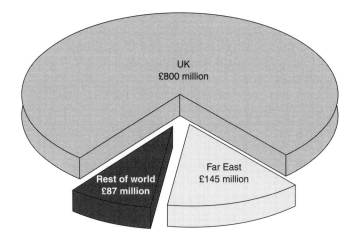

Figure 29.19 Pearson's revenues

The TV division is one of the company's main strengths. In 1995, the TV section tripled its profits, whereas profits for the whole company fell by £252 million. In May 1996 there were suggestions that the television division might be split off (demerged) from the rest of the group.

What caused the drop in profits for the rest of the company? There was a disastrous investment in the new media company Mindscape, a CD-ROM publisher in the US (cost: £330m), and losses of £46 million were predicted for the following year. Madame Tussauds and the *Financial Times* also had a poor year, with some job losses.

The company has occasionally seemed to be vulnerable to take-over. In the early 1990s, Rupert Murdoch's News International built up shares (15 per cent) in Pearson. To avoid any possibility of a take-over by this organisation, it looked as if Pearson and the Dutch company Elsevier were going to merge, but in the end the deal fell through and Elsevier merged with the publishers Reed. At this time, Pearson also made plans to buy the Mirror Group, but these too were dropped.

In February 1996, Pearson made a cash bid and bought HarperCollins Educational Publishing Inc., the US educational division of HarperCollins, from News International Corporation. It was suggested that this large investment wiped out profits and made Pearson less attractive to other companies. There have also been rumours of take-overs by Granada, the American cable and film company Viacom, and Michael Green's Carlton Communication.

Activity

Discuss the following questions about the Pearson company:

1 What other areas of the media could this company expand into?
2 How well is the company doing financially? Investigate its total sales, return on capital, earnings growth, sales increase, etc.
3 What advantages or disadvantages are there in products and services being owned by this conglomerate? Consider manufacturing methods, development, marketing, publicity, distribution, cost to the customer, quality and choice.

There are other large UK conglomerates, ranked among the top 1000 in the country, which besides their main media interests also have important non-media subsidiaries. For example:

■ News International
■ Reed International
■ Granada
■ Thorn EMI
■ *Daily Mail* and General Trust.

Activity

Investigate cross-media ownership in the UK company of your choice; you could choose one of the companies listed above. Find out about the background of the company, and what sort of companies it owns.

You can find information on them initially by consulting reference books such as *The Times 1000 1996* or *The Guardian Guide to UK Top Companies*. If you write to the head office of these companies they will send you their company report, which contains detailed financial data on their current success. Extra up-to-date information on who they are buying, or if they are in danger of being taken over, can be found by reading newspapers and specialist magazines such as *Broadcast*.

Non-media interests

Why do companies retain non-media interests? Basically, it's a 'don't put all your eggs in one basket' policy. If one area of the group is failing, then another part may be flourishing. Money can be siphoned away from one area to pay for another. Media companies can be very volatile. We have seen how Mindscape has proved a burden to the Pearson group.

But of course it can work the other way, with non-media organisations acquiring media interests. The BBC has made a long-term deal with a company called Flextech to create six new channels. Flextech was originally an oil services company but, by diversifying into the media, it has increased its value from £30 million to £670 million.

Not all media companies wish to diversify into non-media areas. They want to expand but may prefer to do so through vertical integration.

Case study: MVI Ltd

This company either owns or has a shareholding in the following companies:

■ *Pavilion* described above (see page 505)
An independent television distribution company.

■ *Carnival*
A leading independent drama production company described above (see page 505).

■ *Delta Ventures*
An audio-visual library and rights acquisition company created in partnership with the BBC and Gartmore. It has already acquired 50 independently produced movies.

■ *Harlequin*
A television programme packaging company, which can assist with television co-productions.

■ *PFM* (Production Finance & Management)
In association with major UK financiers, PFM provides competitive loans and management expertise for independent producers who have been commissioned from the ITV Network Centre.

■ *Talk Radio UK*
MVI is the largest shareholder in the consortium owning Talk Radio.

■ *Teletext*
MVI's partners are Associated Newspapers and Philips Electronics.

- *News World*
  A joint venture with Keighley Stoddart, this is a specialist conference exhibition company, targeted at the world's leading television news organisations, including Reuters, the BBC, CNN, ABC, CBC, and ARD.

- *Carousel*
  This organises events and sales promotion activities. It was involved in the BBC Children in Need 3-D week.

- *Neomedion*
  This is a specialist European media market consultancy, providing strategic intelligence and research resources to international media agencies, merchant banks and financial institutions, the European Commission and the European Parliament.

Make a list of ways in which each of these companies can assist the others.

Large media organisations and the consumer

The issues considered so far have been the advantages to the company of different types of ownership, such as increased market share, cheaper costs, etc. But what effect will there be on the consumer?

The main concern is with the adverse effects of cross-media ownership and commercialisation. These could include the following:

1 Undue influence – the values and ethos of a large media producer could be disseminated without much opposition. Other people may find it hard to get their viewpoints or opinions heard.
2 Less accountability and access by the public – how easy is it to control a multinational company? Whose laws do they obey?
3 Decreased choice – many smaller companies could be taken over and disappear, individuality and regional differences might be submerged under a corporate identity. Radio stations could all play the same type of music which attracts large audiences and appeals to advertisers, rather than catering for minority groups. Some think that this has already happened in the publishing industry, with the packaging of formula books and scripts for easy mass consumption.
4 Poorer-quality products – profitable products are not always those of the highest standard. Costs will be cut in order to remain competitive. For

example, television programmes which are cheap to make, such as game shows, will fill a lot of air time. There could be a lot more adverts to fund products.
5 Higher prices – if there is one company controlling a certain sector of the market, then it can fix prices to suit itself.

Influence of different revenue sources on media products

All companies need capital, i.e. **investment** to start their businesses. This can come from public funds, private individuals or companies (including banks). All companies need a flow of money coming into their businesses, i.e. **revenue**, which must exceed the money going out, i.e. **expenditure**, in order to keep the business going and pay for the materials and wages. This is known as **cash flow**. They must make enough in **profits** to cover expenditure and to pay tax. There must be enough money in hand to buy materials to make more products, and to pay back interest owed to people or organisations who have **invested** in the company.

After the initial investment from banks, or via partnerships, media producers can receive **revenue** for their products and services in a number of ways. However, the source of the money can influence the decisions taken about the production and distribution of a product. The case study below offers an example of the type of pressure that can be exerted on a producer.

Case study

Love is the Devil is a film in the planning stages. It is about the homosexual relationship between the artist Francis Bacon and John Deakin. The film was initially cleared by the lottery assessor of the Arts Council and the lottery advisory panel. But the Council's main board, chaired by Lord Gowrie, turned down the recommendation for an award of £380,000 towards the budget of £850,000. The British Film Institute is lodging an appeal against the decision. They are already disturbed that two other films, one about teenage prostitution and the other containing sexually explicit material, were also turned down when they applied for Arts Council funding. They claim this body is becoming too conservative.

Brainstorm what you think are the advantages and the disadvantages to media companies of having a private investor, rather than relying on what can be considered public funds.

We will now look in more detail at a variety of revenue sources and their potential effects on media products. The sources to be considered include the consumer, public funding, private investors and advertisers.

Revenue from consumers

The cover price

The quality and exclusivity of a print product is often reflected in its cover price, even though in the case of products carrying advertising this price does not cover production costs. If the cover price is too high, this will obviously affect circulation figures and, eventually, the survival or subsequent quality in terms of size, colour, type of paper used, etc.

In 1995 the Net Book Agreement (NBA) was abandoned. This meant that the retail price of books was no longer fixed by the publisher, and bookshops and other outlets could sell books at discount prices to create competition. The publisher Hodder Headline cut 50 per cent off the list price of John Le Carre's hardback novel *Our Game* and sold the book in supermarkets to stimulate sales.

There has also been a price war in classic novels, with works by authors such as Dickens and Hardy being sold for as little as one pound. Publishers have made this possible by using cheap paper and omitting editorial notes.

Sales of popular bestsellers and the classics have increased because of this price competition, but critics have claimed that this has been at the expense of new and less popular authors.

Activity

Discuss whether or not this dramatic use of price cutting is suitable for other areas of the media. If not, why not?

The price of videos, sound recordings, or programmes

Revenue is generated by the rental price or sale price of the product, either to an individual member of the public or to another media organisation. If the price is to be low, the original item will need to be produced cheaply or have sufficient numbers produced to justify selling the product at a bargain price. One division of the BBC, BBC Worldwide, received £305 million from overseas sales of its programmes in 1995 and aims to treble this figure over the next ten years. As more and more television channels are created, needing programmes to fill their schedules, there will be greater opportunities for producers to sell their programmes.

Cinema admission price

The admission price to a cinema will primarily reflect the surroundings in which a film is viewed. People will pay more for the extra facilities, generally of a high standard, offered by the new multiplexes. However, cinema owners will demand a constant supply of new and exciting Hollywood-type films to attract the film-goers they want, e.g. families, and young people with high disposable incomes.

Subscriptions

Whether for satellite television or for a trade magazine, the subscription system is popular with producers. In the case of publications, it helps them assess the amount of raw materials they should buy and the optimum size of their print run. In the case of television, it helps the company budget for buying or making new programmes.

Licence fee

The BBC relies on the licence fee paid by owners of television sets in the UK. This raised £1.75 billion in the year 1994/5. It enables the BBC to be less dependent on mass tastes or pressures from advertisers and sponsors. Not all their programmes have to be popular; the licence income enables them to network educational programmes as well as soaps. Both BBC television and radio are renowned for their high quality of drama; they can afford to make programmes that do not attract large audiences.

The licence fee system has, however, been criticised on a number of grounds:

- why should members of the public have to pay for two television channels and numerous radio stations they may never watch or listen to?
- money can be misspent in production without any accountability

■ the BBC is given an unfair advantage over commercial organisations offering a similar service.

Revenue from advertising

Commercial radio and television stations, newspapers and magazines rely on advertising for most of their revenue, rather than the cover price or subscriptions. However, adverts that are too dull or too long can alienate the reader, listener or viewer.

How often have you heard someone complain, 'this magazine is all adverts!' Advertising does influence the content of the product, because advertisers will want to see the newspaper or magazine include stories and feature articles that attract the type of reader who will buy their product or use their service.

Revenue from sponsorship

A substantial number of television programmes, from quiz shows to drama, are now sponsored by companies selling anything from drinks to electricity. There is generally a link between the nature of the product/service and the programme, for example the weather forecast has been sponsored by Legal and General, the insurance service.

Inevitably, the type of programme the sponsors want to see produced will be one that attracts large audiences of the sort that will buy their product or use their services.

In August 1995, News International were able to give away *The Times* free of charge for one day because of sponsorship by the Microsoft Corporation, who wanted to promote the launch of their new software, Windows 95.

Merchandising

As we noted in Unit 7, merchandising is an important source of revenue for many media organisations, from film companies to radio stations, from record producers to magazine publishers. It involves selling products related to popular media names, and can include almost anything from clothes and confectionery to toys and soft furnishings.

Funding from other organisations

Examples of such funding are given below. It is important that producers new to the media industry are aware of the different funding opportunities available to them, especially for moving image productions. There are, however certain criteria which need to be met before organisations such as the ones described below will allocate money to producers. For example, many need to work in a certain geographical area or make a certain type of product. This will have great influence on the resulting product.

There are a number of schemes to give **funding**, both public and private, for the development, production, distribution and exhibition of media projects. Funds fall into three main categories:

■ direct grants
■ production finance
■ reimbursable loans.

It is extremely rare for these funds to be available to students. Some of these grants deal with:

1 particular activities, such as production or distribution
2 certain groups of people, perhaps ethnic minorities or disabled people or those who live in a certain area
3 certain types of product, e.g. experimental films or art films.

The following organisations offer assistance with different types of funding.

Arts Council of England: Department of Film, Video and Broadcasting

This organisation supports the production of film and video within two areas:

1 documentaries on arts subjects (these are professionally made programmes by independent production companies)
2 films and videos made by artists.

Projects which they have supported include:

■ *Dance for the Camera* on BBC2, a series of 15-minute programmes made by choreographers and directors
■ *Synchro* (in association with Carlton television) – five-minute productions on black arts subjects. This had a budget of £10 000.

Sometimes, the awards can be small. The **Artist's Film and Video Committee** gives a budget of between £2000 and £9000 for film and video artists whose work is innovative and experimental, and has fine art at its background. On the other hand, the

Arts Council in conjunction with Channel Four Experimenta will give a budget of up to £25 000 for similar work on a larger scale.

The BFI (British Film Institute)

The BFI is an enormously influential organisation in the UK. It not only collects information about the film and TV industry and is powerful in the field of education and research, but it commissions and is involved in production itself.

BFI Production offers funding in three areas:

- **Low-budget features**
  If you send in a script or treatment, it will be responded to in four to six weeks. BFI will not totally fund a project but will offer partial funding. Projects should have a maximum overall cost of £450 000. BFI will act as a production base for larger films.

- **New Directors Scheme**
  This scheme aims to help film and video makers who are in the early stages of their careers or changing career. Up to five productions are made per year, with a budget of up to £30 000.

- **Productions Projects Fund**
  This fund supports innovative, low-budget films and videos in fiction, documentary and animation. It is particularly keen to support work in the regions. Most of the work is in co-productions, whose funding may reach £30 000.

British Council

This organisation can assist in the arrangements, financial and otherwise, for allowing both films and their makers to attend film festivals abroad.

Channel 4/MOMI Animators

Four professional residencies are offered each year to young or first-time animators. They are awarded a fee of £2500 and a budget of £1350 towards materials. They will have the opportunity afterwards to have their work commissioned for broadcast by Channel 4.

The Glasgow Film Fund

This fund offers production investment of up to £150 000 for feature films made in the Glasgow area or by producers based in Glasgow.

South West Arts

This organisation gives:

1. grants of up to £1000 to individuals
2. one-off major awards for collaboration with regional BBC or ITV companies
3. financial support for the exhibition of independent, arthouse, historic, experimental and community films and videos.

Welsh Production Fund

Part of the funding money (between £1000 and £10 000) from this organisation goes towards assisting the development of scripts, project packages, storyboards, pilots, etc.

The MEDIA programme

This programme is an initiative of the European Union. It aims to provide funding to develop skills needed in the industries as well as help for individual productions. Examples of two of their projects (of which there are about twenty annually) are given here:

- **European Scriptwriting and Film Analysis Certificate**
  This project runs workshops offering training to existing scriptwriters covering many genres, e.g. adaptations, originals, TV series.

- **MEDIA Salles**
  This is a project aiming to improve the business skills of film exhibitors. It trains and informs people in promotions and economic trends, etc.

In November 1993, the Department of National Heritage announced that it would continue to fund the ECF (European Co-production Fund) at the current level of £2 million until 1997. The fund is available for investment in feature films made by European co-producers and for investment in development work. It approves loans on commercial terms.

The Prince's Trust and the Prince's Trust Partners in Europe

This organisation helps young people under the age of 26 by financing projects and enabling them to run their own business in their chosen field.

The National Lottery

The contract to run the National Lottery was won in 1994 by Camelot. The BBC won the broadcasting rights, anticipating big Saturday night audiences, although ITV can broadcast the winning numbers simultaneously. A total of 28 per cent of the revenue has to go to good causes. At first, money was given only for capital projects (i.e. projects needing money for equipment or materials), but now applications can be made for help in putting on productions, and film producers in particular have begun to benefit from this. *Glastonbury – The Movie,* described in *The Guardian* as 'a cheap and cheerful summation of a typical Glastonbury festival', was the first film to be completed with the help of lottery funds.

The National Museum of Photography, Film and Television in Bradford announced a £13.25 million expansion in March 1996, helped by a large lottery grant of £6 million. The development will increase the museum's space by half, and will include electronic imaging, virtual reality galleries and a multimedia studio where members of the public can produce their own work.

It has been suggested however, that **tax incentives** (which, for example, encouraged the producers of *Braveheart* to film in Ireland rather than Scotland) would help the British film industry more than lottery money.

Activity

Brainstorm examples of products which use one or more of the above methods of funding. Which type of revenue would you expect to get for the media products you have made?

Expenditure for media products in relation to institutional context

Expenditure for media products covers research and development, production, marketing, distribution costs and sometimes the training of staff. It can include the following:

- wages (from the director to the cleaner)
- overheads (heating, lighting, water, rent)
- equipment (editing suites, presses)
- materials (newsprint, film)
- advertising (on television, in the local newspaper).

Besides the above, an organisation or company may also have to pay **interest** on investments to banks or shareholders, and **taxes**.

There are two types of taxation:

- direct taxes
- indirect taxes.

Corporation tax is an example of direct taxation. This is the tax which companies pay on their profits. Figure 29.20 shows the tax liabilities of one large media organisation.

	1995 £'000	1994 £'000
UK corporation tax at 33% (1994 – 33%)	21 268	35 048
Double taxation relief	(200)	–
Transfer from deferred taxation	(6325)	(6485)
Tax on UK dividends received	650	58
Overseas taxation	18 760	15 716
Tax relating to share of profits of associated undertakings	425	321
	34 578	44 658

Figure 29.20 Taxes levied on profit

Value Added Tax (VAT) is an example of indirect taxation. It is a tax on spending, and is currently levied at the rate of $17\frac{1}{2}$ per cent at each stage of production. For example, a magazine is subject to VAT when it is sold. The VAT paid on the raw materials and services that went into making it are reclaimed as a business expense by the publisher, so that the VAT is charged only on the finished product.

Case study

There was a series of price rises for newsprint in the period March to December of 1995, amounting to a 50 per cent increase. This halted the worldwide trend of the past decade towards larger newspapers with many supplements. More newspapers turned to tabloid format.

A number of effects could be observed in the American newspaper industry:

- *The Washington Post* cut back on foreign travel by reporters.
- *USA Today* cut back its news columns by 5 per cent.
- *The Wall Street Journal* laid off staff.
- *The New York Times* raised its cover price.

- California's *Orange County Register* reduced the width of its pages.
- *The Dallas Morning News* folded.

One of the worst hit UK companies was Rupert Murdoch's News International. Its weakest newspaper, *Today*, closed and the company was forced to cut the sizes of its print runs and the number of newspaper pages in March and April 1995.

Discuss which other media industries could be affected by world shortages of specific resources, both human and material.

Expenditure patterns

We have already looked at different types of businesses, and seen that small independent companies function differently from large conglomerates – for example they don't attract the same sort of investment. A massive injection of money is needed to develop new technology, so a small company is at a disadvantage. However, they can have advantages, in that they can be more flexible and responsive to changes in the market. Smaller companies can supply niche markets.

Flexibility can be achieved by both large and small organisations through the use of freelances. The wage bill can be dramatically reduced if full-time staff are replaced by part-time workers or people on short-term contracts who are only employed when needed.

The institutional context, size and type of an organisation will influence its spending patterns. Different types of organisations will have different priorities. A state-owned radio station may have to cater for minority groups, to entertain and educate. A commercial radio station needs to appeal to a certain type of consumer in order to attract advertisers. As a result, the commercial station may spend significantly more on marketing, the state-owned station on production.

Two media producers with the same aim, to make a large profit, may achieve it through different expenditure patterns. For example, a TV channel may wish to attract affluent, well-educated viewers. It might achieve this by becoming renowned for its drama. Therefore it will allocate a substantial part of its budget to producing high-quality plays. Another channel might wish to attract young people, and therefore allocate most of its budget to purchasing pop videos or covering sport.

Large firms are usually in a position to reduce the costs of production because of the economies of large-scale production. They can negotiate special deals, and by buying in bulk they can ask for a lower price. For example, a newspaper group can negotiate reductions in the cost of newsprint if it regularly buys enormous quantities.

The concept of economies of scale also applies to marketing and distribution. Large companies can spend huge sums on marketing, and particularly advertising. For example, the major film distribution companies can afford to advertise new blockbuster releases on television and in the national press. They will spend money on sending out a press kit containing publicity stills from the film, details of the cast and crew, etc. They will supply TV and radio with electronic press kits (EPKs) which contain clips and interviews.

However, the local press and radio are also important for publicising films and so smaller arthouses and independent producers can still advertise at a reasonable rate locally.

A large company which has many subsidiaries may decide from time to time to spend more on a certain area either to bolster up a weak area or to encourage growth in a certain sector.

Case study

Look at the figures below. Figure 29.21 shows the turnover of different sectors of United News & Media plc, a broadly based international publications, exhibitions and media group. The largest turnover is for magazines and exhibitions. However, Figure 29.22 shows that, proportionally, better profits are being made from advertising periodicals than from national newspapers.

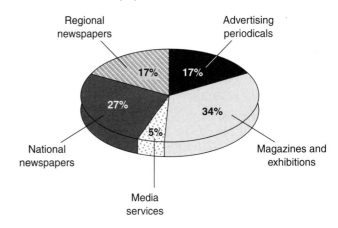

Figure 29.21 Percentage of 1995 group turnover, United News & Media

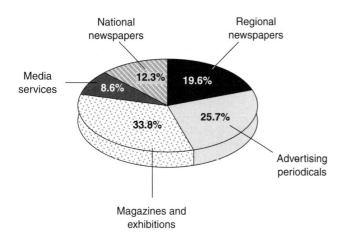

Figure 29.22 Operating profit by sector, 1995, United News & Media

Context

The wider context in which a media producer works is very important, because it undoubtedly affects the product. The context includes the following factors:

- the power of the state; whether it is democratic or authoritarian, and the extent of its control over the media
- the culture in which the media operate; is it technologically advanced, are there ethnic differences, how well educated are the public?
- the economic climate, including employment trends, the use of freelances rather than permanent staff, levels of taxation and interest rates
- trends within the media towards independent organisations and specialist services
- the underlying purpose of the producer, e.g. to make money or produce high-quality programmes
- the move away from characteristically national services and products to a global media network of interlinking products.

All of the above can influence the expenditure of the media industries. Both the film and music industries, for example, have been affected by the social and economic climate in which they operate. The rise of the multiplex cinema in out-of-town locations reflects the shopping habits and mobility of a large, affluent section of the population. The music industry has to cope with ever-changing technology, and has sometimes struggled to predict which format (vinyl, cassette, CD, mini-disc) will survive and be profitable. Small, independent record shops have struggled to compete with the purchasing power and marketing strategies of the high-street chain stores such as Woolworths and John Menzies, or the specialist high-street record shops such as HMV or the Virgin superstores. They can survive only by offering specialised services.

Activity

Choose an industry and make a list of the ways in which expenditure could be affected by the context (refer to the points above) in which it operates.

In earlier chapters we have looked at the production costs of individual products. We will now look at a large organisation, the **context** in which it is operating and in particular, its **financial organisation**, which has to take account of the future as well as the present.

Case study: The BBC

This organisation has been chosen for discussion as it remains a central part of the UK media industry with interests in publishing, new technology, and film production as well as television and radio. It is funded by the public, but is becoming increasingly commercial. However, as a public service provider the BBC cannot choose where to distribute its products. Instead, it is committed to providing its services throughout the country. Nevertheless it can make commercial decisions such as closing the network radio station in Coventry, CWR, because of the costs. It claims that the community is still provided for by another part of the BBC's local networks, WM (West Midlands), which according to the corporation delivers the same or a similar service.

We shall begin by looking at its revenue and expenditure in past years but will then discuss how it needs to change in order to survive financially and maintain its identity as a public service in our changing society.

Work through the case study by reading the BBC information and then answering the questions about it.

Look at the statement of income and expenditure for 1995–96 in Figure 29.23. Operating expenditure includes the cost of broadcasting, collecting the licence fee, and running the Open University Production Centre and commercial and other broadcasting subsidiaries.

	£m 93	£m 94	£m 95	£m 96
Income				
Licence fee	1 597.6	1 683.5	1 751.3	1 819.7
Commercial turnover (BBC Worldwide commercial activities)	204.3	238.9	305.1	338.4
Other income eg. renting facilities; programme rights	15.1	19.4	39.0	56.9
Open University Production Centre	11.8	9.5	12.3	11.9
Operating expenditure	1 823.7	1 829.4	1 987.4	2 151.6

Figure 29.23 BBC Home Services income and expenditure

Questions

1 What is the total income for each year?
2 What percentage of the income was raised by the licence fee in 1996?
3 In which year has there been the biggest profit?
4 Which source of income has not shown continuous growth?

Now that the BBC has to become more competitive, its commercial turnover is increasingly important (see Figure 29.24).

	£m 93	£m 94	£m 95	£m 96
Television programme sales	53.1	64.0	112.3	131.4
Magazine and book publishing	105.4	115.2	117.5	134.9
Videos, records and tapes	36.7	44.5	51.2	47.5
Other activities	9.1	15.2	24.1	24.6
Total	204.3	238.9	305.1	338.4

Figure 29.24 BBC commercial turnover

Questions

5 Which is the most profitable, the sale of television programmes, of books and magazines, or of videos, records and tapes?
6 Which area has shown the most growth?
7 Which area has not shown consistent growth?

All companies, including those in the public sector, have to pay tax on profits. The tax payable by the BBC is shown in Figure 29.25.

	£m 93	£m 94	£m 95	£m 96
Corporation tax	4.0	9.8	10.7	11.0
Deferred taxation (deferred to the following year)	(1.4)	(3.4)	(3.5)	(3.1)
Double taxation relief	(0.5)	(0.5)	(0.8)	(1.1)
Subtotal	2.1	5.9	6.4	6.8
Overseas taxation	1.9	1.8	2.9	3.1
Total	4.0	7.7	9.3	9.9

Figure 29.25 Taxation on the BBC

Questions

8 Between which years has taxation increased the most overall?
9 In 1996, what percentage of the total was overseas taxation?
10 Which has increased the most, corporation tax or overseas taxation?

Like private companies, the BBC has investments in various subsidiary companies. These are detailed in Figure 29.26.

	Holding of issued ordinary shares (%)
Subsidiaries	
BBC Worldwide Americas Inc. (registered in Delaware, USA)	100
Woodlands Publishing Limited	100
BBC World Service Television Limited	100
European Channel Broadcasting Limited	75
Associates	
European Channel Management Limited	45
Frontline Limited	23
Investments	
UK Gold Television Limited	20
Satellite News Corporation Limited	20

Figure 29.26 BBC subsidiary companies and investments

Questions

11 In which of these companies has the BBC the smallest share?
12 How many of the subsidiaries does the BBC own completely?

Cash flow can be a problem with companies, so it is important to keep some money in the bank. Figure 29.27 shows bank deposits.

	Cash at bank and in hand	Bank overdrafts	Unpresented cheques	Total
	£m	£m	£m	£m
At 31 March 1992	28.5	(3.9)	(37.9)	(13.3)
Change in the year	25.1	(4.4)	(10.0)	10.7
At 31 March 1993	53.6	(8.3)	(47.9)	(2.6)
Change in the year	33.5	6.1	(3.3)	36.3
At 31 March 1994	87.1	(2.2)	(51.2)	33.7

Figure 29.27 The BBC's short-term bank deposits and cash

Question

13 How much more did the BBC have in the bank at 31 March 1994 than it did two years earlier?

Creditors are people to whom a company owes money. These are detailed for the BBC in Figure 29.28.

	Group 1996	Group 1995	Home Services 1996	Home Services 1995
	£m	£m	£m	£m
Amounts falling due within one year				
Unpresented cheques	49.2	43.2	43.6	38.6
Bank overdrafts	–	7.7	–	5.4
	49.2	50.9	43.6	44.0
Trade creditors				
Programme creditors	56.5	76.8	56.5	76.7
Programme acquisitions	26.4	32.8	26.4	32.8
Salaries and wages	58.3	54.9	57.4	54.1
Residual copyright payments	33.1	24.1	–	–
Licence fee collection creditors	2.8	4.1	2.8	4.1
Other trade creditors	105.4	103.3	76.9	75.7
	282.5	296.0	220.0	243.4

Figure 29.28 The BBC's creditors

Question

14 How much was owed in copyright payments in 1996?

The BBC employs over 20 000 people full-time. If the staff are not paid, then production will soon come to a halt! Look at the staff costs shown in Figures 29.29 and 29.30.

	1996 £m	1995 £m
Salaries and wages (excluding redundancy costs)	613.7	604.2
Social security costs	53.8	53.7
Other pension costs – principal scheme	32.1	28.8
– other schemes	0.5	0.8
	700.1	687.5
Comprising:		
Home Services	655.7	645.3
BBC Worldwide commercial activities	37.7	35.8
Other activities	6.7	6.4
	700.1	687.5

Figure 29.29 BBC staff costs

The number of Governors who received remuneration (excluding pension contributions) in the following bands was:		
	1996 Number	1995 Number
£0 – £5000	5	–
£5001 – £10 000	1	5
£10 001 – £15 000	3	3
£15 001 – £20 000	1	3
£20 001 – £25 000	3	–
£40 001 – £45 000	–	1
£75 001 – £80 000	–	1
£85 001 – £90 000	1	–
	1996 £	1995 £
Board of Management		
Salaries and other benefits	2,364,659	2,276,411
Performance-related bonus payments	213,792	161,350
Pension contributions	190,689	191,192

Figure 29.30 BBC Governors' and Board of Management remuneration

Question

15 Have any savings been made between the two years?

The current context and future of the BBC

The current Charter for the BBC was issued in 1981. At that time there were few alternatives to BBC radio and television. However, since then the media world has altered dramatically. In the US, for example, the average household can receive over 50 TV channels and over 50 radio stations. The UK can claim, however, the highest level of television viewing and radio listening in Europe.

One trend points towards some newspapers, magazines, radio stations and TV channels offering general entertainment and information services to the masses.

Another trend in each of these media industries points towards specialisation for minority and special-interest groups. There will be increased competition to gain and retain a share of the audience or market, as audiences possibly shift between stations and channels and consumers drift from one product to another.

Media producers' share in the market will be reflected in the amount of advertising revenue they attract. There will be increased competition for public and private funding.

But it is not only the media world which has changed – so has society. Some people consider that British society has become more fragmented in recent years, into different social, economic, ethnic and religious groups. There is also the changing role of women to consider; far more are working both full- and part-time. The UK is now more involved in Europe, both politically and economically, and more people than ever before are travelling abroad and learning other languages. There is a strong interest in education and training, for all ages. People's expectations are also higher – they demand high-quality products and services. We now live in a technologically advanced society, with VCRs, computers, etc. in many homes.

How will the BBC survive in this climate?

The BBC will need to carry out sufficient research in order to predict social and economic trends. From its research the BBC has made financial projections, as shown in Figure 29.31.

In 1981, the BBC was part of a high-cost industry. Ten years on, some people claimed that they were overstaffed, had outdated working practices, poor industrial relations and inefficient management structures. The steps taken to improve this situation were described in the BBC publication *Extending Choice – The BBC's Role in the New Broadcasting Age* (see Figure 29.32).

- The industry is characterised by increasing flexibility of employment practices and conditions, use of freelance and contracted staff, and mobility.
- A number of broadcasters are choosing to separate the management of their broadcasting, programme production and resource activities to ensure appropriate managerial focus and financial discipline in each activity.
- They are increasing the proportion of their television programming that is commissioned from independent producers, in order to reach the legislated minimum of 25 per cent by 1993.
- There is growing use of externally supplied contractual services at all levels of the industry.

Figure 29.32 The BBC's view of the changing context of broadcasting

As with the newspaper industry, regulatory control has changed. In the past, the BBC's competitors too were subject to strict public service regulation; but now the ITC and Radio Authority are slackening their grip. Satellite channels already have greater freedom.

Do we need a public service broadcaster?

In France, the main public service broadcaster (TF1) was privatised in the mid-1980s and has been a

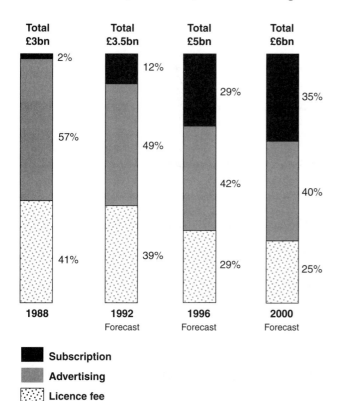

Source: BBC Policy and Planning Unit

Figure 29.31 The BBC's changing share of broadcasting industry revenues

commercial success. The other channels have been less fortunate. In Germany, the public service broadcasters ARD and ZDF have found it difficult to compete with aggressive commercial channels and have had to subsidise the licence fee with advertising. Canada and Australia are facing a similar situation. The one major exception is Japan, where NHK has adequate licence fee income and can support two terrestrial television channels, and also collects subscriptions for its two satellite channels.

It is argued that the BBC is not necessary. Commercial services are fully developed, offering a wide choice of programmes – many of which are of a high quality. In response to this, the BBC points out the different objectives of the two types of broadcasters and states:

> 'Commercially funded broadcasters quite properly set their priorities for programming and services against the overriding need to make a profit and generate a return for their shareholders. That is their obligation as commercial organisations ... these priorities require them to broadcast programmes that attract large or commercially attractive audiences ... and to limit their investment in programming to what the commercial market will afford.'

Publicly funded broadcasters, in contrast, have a primary obligation to the public. They do not need to make a profit or guarantee a return to shareholders. Their overriding public purpose is to extend choice by guaranteeing access for everyone in the country to programming services that are of unusually high quality and that are, or might be, at risk in the purely commercially funded sector of the market. People who watch only programmes for the mass market such as *The Generation Game* or *Eastenders* may argue that they don't want to pay for political documentaries or plays about homosexuals

---

The BBC's roles:
- Providing the comprehensive, in-depth and impartial news and information coverage across a range of broadcasting outlets that is needed to support a fair and informed national debate.
- Supporting and stimulating the development and expression of British culture and entertainment.
- Guaranteeing the provision of programming and services that create opportunities for education.
- Stimulating the communication of cultures and ideas between Britain and abroad.

Figure 29.33 Four main aims identified by the BBC

---

that appeal to minority audiences. However, the point about the BBC is that (like the National Health Service) it has the moral duty to provide a service for everybody – so that individual as well as the mass tastes can be satisfied.

In the future the BBC will have more clearly defined aims, as described in Figure 29.33.

What sort of organisation will the BBC need in the future?

Some people have argued that the BBC could be split up into independent units, each responsible for the different areas – education, news, entertainment, overseas services. The BBC, however, in its wish to remain united, argues for:

- a single coherent role and strategy for publicly funded broadcasting in Britain
- concentrated investment in specialist skills and expertise, at a level which could not be duplicated by a number of smaller organisations
- complementary scheduling of programmes across radio and television to ensure maximum choice for viewers and listeners, particularly at peak hours.

The effect of this unified structure on staff and resources will include the following:

- news and current affairs journalists will serve both television and radio, as part of a bi-media directorate
- regional journalists and production staff will operate across the media
- some activities such as education or religious programmes will be united under one roof
- comedy and light entertainment programmes developed on radio will be transferred to television and vice versa
- live music, sport, political coverage, etc. will be shared between television and radio
- staff will be trained to be multi-skilled, which will give them increased career opportunities and also increase productivity.

In an attempt to become more cost effective, the BBC has already made the following cuts:

- it cut its workforce by approximately 7000 in the seven years up to 1993
- it has reduced its property portfolio
- it has reduced its number of television and radio studios and outside broadcast units.

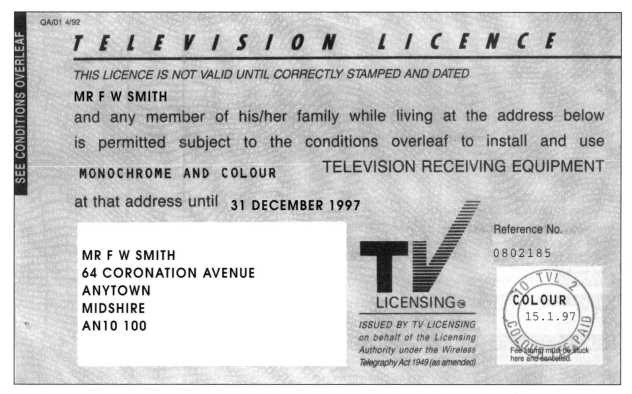

Figure 29.34 The TV licence funds the BBC

At present the BBC is funded by the licence fee (which currently costs £89.50 per year for colour television and £30 for black and white television). Some argue that this fee should be abolished. Why should the public pay for services it may not use? Why can't the BBC be supported by advertising and sponsorship?

In response to these arguments, the BBC says that:

- there is not enough advertising revenue to go around
- many people welcome a service that has no regular breaks for adverts
- the licence fee encourages the production of types of programmes that attract large audiences
- the licence fee works out cheaply for the viewer (see Figure 29.35).

The BBC will also ensure there are clearly defined roles for those in control (see Figure 29.36).

Producer choice

This concept is fundamental to the new philosophy of the BBC, and includes the following points:

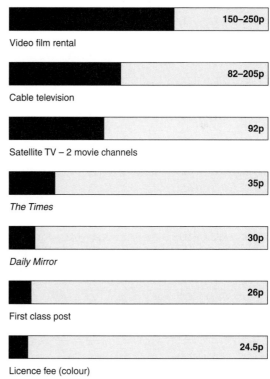

Video film rental — 150–250p

Cable television — 82–205p

Satellite TV – 2 movie channels — 92p

The Times — 35p

Daily Mirror — 30p

First class post — 26p

Licence fee (colour) — 24.5p

Figure 29.35 Comparative daily costs of colour TV licence fee

529

- The Board of Governors: regulating the BBC in the public interest; ensuring the independence of the BBC from political interference; and holding the Board of Management accountable for the performance of its executive task.
- The Board of Management: charged with the executive tasks of providing leadership and direction for the BBC; translating the BBC's mission into an overall strategy; and meeting an agreed set of quality and performance objectives.

Figure 29.36 Roles for the management of the BBC

- funds will be allocated to commission programmes that support the BBC's aims
- programmes will be commissioned either from BBC departments or from independent producers
- BBC producers will be free to use in-house resources (studios, camera crews, scenery, graphics) or use independent facilities
- this should reduce overspending and money saved can fund new projects
- the aim is for 25 per cent of programmes to be made by independent producers.

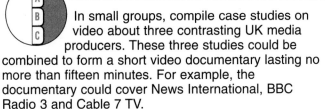

Evidence assignment

In small groups, compile case studies on video about three contrasting UK media producers. These three studies could be combined to form a short video documentary lasting no more than fifteen minutes. For example, the documentary could cover News International, BBC Radio 3 and Cable 7 TV.

Describe for each product:

- the content
- how and why it is made, distributed and sold or used.

Describe the owners:

- whether they are local, national or international
- whether they are private, independent or the state organisations.

The video should be shown as part of a presentation, which should start with a general description of:

- the ownership patterns in the UK – this information could be given through the use of OHTs or flipchart diagrams
- the main types of revenue and expenditure in media industries
- the context in which the various industries operate.

Investigate regulation of media industries

This chapter looks at the regulation of the media industries in the UK. It describes the legal and ethical framework in which the media operate and identifies the regulatory bodies relevant to the UK media industries. It considers how the ethos of professional institutions has an influence on the nature of media products. There is also a discussion on the balance between freedom of information, public interest and censorship.

Legal framework of the UK media

Deregulation

The main body of the 1990 Broadcasting Act is concerned with deregulation. The aim has been to keep broadcasting services as independent as possible. We can see this in the excerpts from the Act shown opposite. Particularly important are its references to media ownership.

The Act has made changes to the way in which independent television and radio is regulated and has introduced additional services. For example, the IBA (Independent Broadcasting Association) was replaced by the Independent Television Commission. The Cable Authority was made part of the ITC. The IBA's TV and radio transmission network was privatised and a new company, NTL (National Telecommunications Ltd), formed to transmit the programmes for the independent television companies, Channel 4, S4C and approximately 50 independent local radio stations.

The Act appears to guarantee the integrity of the BBC as a *service* (as opposed to a commercial operation) dedicated to quality and diversity. But there are no grounds for complacency. At the time of writing, the BBC's transmission services are about to be privatised. In addition, the World Service (called 'the brightest jewel in the BBC' by the BBC's chairman, Sir Christopher Bland), is under the scrutiny of the Director General, John Birt, whose restructuring plans for the service will break it up as a single international broadcasting entity.

These may or may not be precedents for some form of privatisation, in a climate where commercial

Ownership

- No holder of a regional Channel 3 licence can hold more than two licences (and not both London licences).
- If the holder of a Channel 3 licence holds two Channel 3 licences (or has an interest exceeding 30% in a second licence) he may not have more than 20% in a third licence.
- The holder of a licence to provide a regional Channel 3 service, or a national Channel 3 service or a Channel 5 service may not have more than a 20% interest in a body which is the holder of either of the other two categories of licence.
- No limits are set on the number of satellite service licences (called Non-Domestic Satellite Service licences) which may be held. But the holder of a satellite service may not have more than a 20% interest in a regional or national Channel 3 licence or a Channel 5 licence and vice versa. An exception is made where a Channel 3 or Channel 5 licensee replicates (i.e. simulcasts) his service by satellite, in which case he may hold a satellite licence for that service.

Cross-ownership. The basic rule is that no proprietor of a national or local newspaper shall be a participant with more than a 20% interest in the holder of a Channel 3 or Channel 5 licence, except in the case of local newspapers and regional Channel 3 services where their coverage area is not 'to a significant extent' the same. The rule also applies the other way round, i.e., limiting participation by the holders of Channel 3 or Channel 5 licences in bodies running newspapers. There are at present no restrictions on participation by satellite services in newspapers or vice versa.

Public telecommunications operators. A national public telecommunications operator with over £2 billion turnover may not hold a licence to provide a Channel 3 or Channel 5 service. No National Public Telecommunications operator may hold local delivery licences overlapping existing cable franchise areas.

Cross-media Ownership

In May 1995 the Government published *Media ownership: the Government's proposals*. The Government proposed to introduce primary legislation to: allow newspaper groups with less than 20% of national newspaper circulation to control TV broadcasters up to 15% of total TV market (defined by audience share), subject to a limit of two Channel 3 licences; abolish the rules limiting ownership between terrestrial television, satellite and cable broadcasters, except for those with more than 20% ownership by a newspaper with more than 20% national circulation; remove the 50% limit on combined Channel 3 holding in ITN; prevent concentrations in local media by preventing newspaper groups with more than 30% of regional or local newspaper circulation having control of a Channel 3 licence for the same region. The Government also set out a system for the longer term proposing definition of the total media market and the responsibilities and powers of the regulator. The ITC published its response to the Government's proposals in August 1995.

considerations have priority. It is the starting point for a debate on whether the BBC should be populist in its approach – providing what most people want, who pay their licence fees and so fund it – or should it be a *public service*?

Documentaries for example, are expensive to make, whether they are about a political scandal or about how other people live and other cultures or about wildlife. It is far cheaper to fill up air-time with popular game-shows or compilations made up from clips of old programmes.

The 1996 Broadcasting Act became law at the end of July of that year. It introduced sweeping changes in the way that the media operate, and seeks to ensure quality, diversity and choice for both producers and consumers.

Previously, a television company could not own more than two licences. This has been changed to allow a company to own more providing they do not exceed 15 per cent of the total audience share (share will be measured by the ITC). This 15 per cent rule also applies to radio.

Newspapers can buy TV companies and radio stations and vice versa, but again there is a ceiling on size. If a TV or newspaper group has more than 20 per cent of its total market then it cannot hold more than a 20 per cent interest in another medium.

Franchises

Deregulation has been concerned with how ITV franchises are allocated for the 10-year period following January 1993. Competitive tendering was introduced into broadcasting and included those outside of the then existing TV companies who wished to run a franchise. A franchise is a licence, granted by an 'owner' in this case the ITC, to an organisation (e.g. a TV company) to run the business for a certain period of time. The system of competitive tendering has been extended to new national radio stations and Channel 5.

The Act has also affected employment in the industry and led to other commercial consequences. As a result satellite companies have merged, the role of the publisher/broadcaster has taken shape (e.g. radio stations taken over by publishers), and training opportunities have declined.

DMWT (The Daily Mail and Western Trust) is in the process of acquiring 80 per cent of the independent local radio station Leicester Sound. Cross-Counties Radio, one of the major contenders for a

broadcasting licence to cover the Hinckley and Nuneaton area of the Midlands, is now in collaboration with Nuneaton newspaper the *Heartland Evening News* and sharing their office facilities.

In television the concept of 'Masthead TV' will become a reality if (as seems likely) the ITC relaxes the rules that have hitherto forbidden magazine publishers from having TV programmes based on their magazine titles. We should, therefore, be seeing television adaptations of, for example, *Smash Hits*, *Loaded* and *Vanity Fair*.

The financing of the BBC has been called into question. In addition, there has been a break-up of the listings duopoly: in other words, the *Radio Times* and the *TV Times* are now not the only magazines allowed to print what's on TV and radio, and many newspapers carry weekly listings of TV and radio programmes.

Cable regulations

Originally, under the 1984 Cable and Wireless Act, cable operators were able to run as many cable TV channels as they wanted within their own licence area. They were responsible not only for carrying the channels, but also for the content of the programmes. This created numerous problems when programmes originated from areas outside that of the then regulatory body, the Cable Authority. Programmes showing bullfighting from Spain or soft porn from Holland were found to contravene the 'good taste and decency' guidelines.

Since the 1990 Broadcasting Act, cable has been regulated by the ITC. You can read about the ITC in the Legal and Ethical appendix. The act now separates cable network franchising from programme licensing. A cable network owner can still carry channels from anywhere in the world but if these channels are not licensed by the ITC or its EU equivalents, then the ITC can ban them. A cable operator can also still run its own channels, but now each channel needs a separate licence.

It is now the channel provider who is responsible for content and not the cable operator, as long as the channel comes from an EU country or one that has ratified the Council of Europe Convention on Transfrontier Television. Nor can the cable operator be held to be responsible for any breach of copyright by the channel provider, if it has agreement for carrying the channel.

Defamation

This area of the law can be divided roughly into two parts: civil and criminal. Its purpose is to protect a person's private and professional reputation from unjustified attack. For example, someone could be financially ruined if it was stated in the media that the company he or she owns makes a shoddy or dangerous product. In 1989, the *Mail on Sunday* had damages of £470 000 awarded against it when it was found guilty of libelling a food retailer about food being used after the 'sell-by' date.

Libel is part of defamation law and takes place when the unjustified attack is written, published or broadcast in some way. A verbal defamation which is not written or broadcast is called **slander**.

You can probably see already that the law on defamation is a minefield for journalists and presenters. The law has to try to strike a balance between protecting an individual or organisation and letting the media inform the public about what is going on. For this reason the media do have defences that they can use in law. These include the following:

■ **justification** – as a journalist or other 'dealer in words', if you can prove that what you published is a fact then this is a complete defence
■ **fair comment** – if you can argue that what you have published was done in good faith and without malice because 'the public have a right to know', then, providing those comments are based on facts, they are classed as fair comment
■ **privilege** – the law recognises that some matters are of great public interest and the reporting of these matters should be protected against claims of defamation. Reports on parliamentary business, such as that contained in reports and White Papers, enjoy the protection of privilege. So do media reports on council business. A courtroom report will also enjoy privilege, providing it is a fair and accurate account.

National security

The **Official Secrets Act** was first introduced in 1911 and allows the media to be prosecuted for disclosing information about the security services, defence and the conduct of international relations. Up to 1989 it was an offence for someone working for the government to give information that *could* be damaging to the state, either (1) because the information itself was damaging or (2) the act of passing it on constituted a breach of trust. It was this second part of the Act (it used to be called section 2) that in 1984 led to a six-month prison sentence for a young junior clerk in the Foreign Office called Sarah Tisdall. She had passed on some photocopies of memos to the *Guardian* newspaper concerning the secret introduction of cruise missiles into Britain. Although it was acknowledged that the memos were not a threat, the prosecution argued successfully that she could do it again and then the result could be damaging.

The Official Secrets Act was therefore amended in 1989. Now, although the prosecution has to show that a journalist, for example, disclosed harmful protected information without lawful authority, in many cases *any* disclosure is classed as harmful. It is seen by many journalists as a 'catch-all' act which allows the government to hide behind the issue of 'national security' in order to protect itself from public scrutiny. Journalists and government workers cannot argue that they were acting in the public interest, and even if the material has been previously published they can still be prosecuted.

Another example of national security as part of the legal framework covers the **Prevention of Terrorism Act**. The broadcasting ban imposed under this act meant that, for example, the voice of Gerry Adams, the Sinn Fein Member of Parliament, was banned from being broadcast. Although his image could appear on TV, anything he said on radio or TV had to be read out by an actor! The ban has since been lifted.

Activity

Carry out research to find out about two famous legal cases in the 1980s: 'Clive Pontin' and 'Zircon'.

If you were an American journalist, what US law would give you an advantage over British journalists?

Copyright

Copyright is part of **intellectual property** law. If you write a book or a play, compose a piece of music or take a photograph, then *you* have ownership of that piece of work. Someone else cannot then make use of your intellectual property without permission and usually also payment. The main point about copyright is that it is automatic and *you* do not have to apply for it. However, it is advisable to keep a record, preferably with a solicitor, which proves that you created something before another party did.

You cannot copyright an idea – only the particular way of expressing it. It must actually be put on to paper, tape, disk or otherwise recorded. The 'work', as it becomes known, must be something than can be identifiable as consisting of artistic effort. This does not mean that you have to be a Michelangelo, only that some creative thought and effort went into the work. For example, writing your homework project will give you automatic copyright of that work.

Under the Copyright, Designs and Patents Act 1988, copyright applies to songs and instrumental music, books, articles, poems, films, radio plays, stage productions, etc. Even copying a particular typographical arrangement or reporting a speech can contravene copyright law.

The purpose of copyright is to protect the author of the work and, if sold, the owner of that work. However, the law recognises that society should not be deprived of the benefits of a work indefinitely and therefore puts a limit on the time that the owner and his or her descendants can benefit exclusively from it. The UK has now extended this copyright protection from fifty to seventy years, running from the end of the calendar year in which the author or creator dies.

A current case, as yet unresolved, concerns programme maker Edward Joffe, who claims that *The Little Picture Show,* produced by Carlton and Diverse Productions, is based on his *Video View,* and that he did not give his agreement to this.

You can read about copyright as it relates to performing rights in the Legal and Ethical appendix.

Photocopying of a work can take place for educational purposes providing that is not the work's purpose, e.g. a textbook. Any such copying should be restricted to 1 per cent of the work and does not apply if licences are available for the copying in question. Non-profit-making clubs and societies can make use of sound recordings provided that any proceeds are solely for the benefit of the organisation. A work can be used in public recitals or in journals, or cited in critical reviews, providing there is sufficient acknowledgement.

Under the 'fair dealing' provision of the Act, a work can be used for the purpose of reporting current affairs providing there is sufficient acknowledgement. In fact, if the 'reporting' takes place by means of a sound recording, film, broadcast or cable transmission then no acknowledgement is required. The BBC brought an action against BSkyB, who had used 'videograbbed' pictures of the BBC's World Cup coverage in a sports programme. The judge ruled that this was not an infringement of copyright because BSkyB were reporting current affairs.

A section of the Copyright, Design and Patents Act 1988 also deals with 'moral rights'. These are rights that remain with the author even if that author is no longer the owner of a work. The author is entitled to protection from derogatory representation of the work. For example, it would be an offence under this section of the Act if a publisher allowed a photograph to be 'doctored' (e.g. cropped, rearranged, collaged or juxtaposed) in a manner that brought ridicule to it, even if that 'author' no longer owns the photograph.

Identify regulatory bodies relevant to the UK media

There are a number of bodies which have been appointed to oversee the regulatory framework in which the UK media operate. They include: the Independent Television Commission, Radio Authority, British Board of Film Classification, Department of National Heritage and the Monopolies and Mergers Commission.

ITC and the Radio Authority

The Independent Television Commission (which replaced the Independent Broadcasting Association) awards licences to independent (i.e. non-BBC) broadcasters, including cable and satellite, and regulates their contents, including advertisements. The ITC's powers are derived from the 1990 Broadcasting Act.

For radio there is the Radio Authority which awards the licences and regulates the content of independent radio, including advertising. (See also the Legal and Ethical appendix.

British Board of Film Classification

This is an independent and non-governmental body which establishes the classifications for films. Its rules and classifications can be seen in Figures 30.1 and 30.2.

It is the local authorities (i.e. county councils and municipal councils) which decide whether a film should be shown in their area of jurisdiction. However, they do generally accept the standards and guidelines determined by the BBFC.

'U' (Universal) – Suitable for all
Contains no theme, scene, action or dialogue that could be construed as disturbing, harmful or offensive. Thus, the work could not be described as unsuitable for persons of any age. (The video-only 'Uc' category denotes particular suitability for young or pre-school children).

'PG' (Parental Guidance) – General viewing, but some scenes may be unsuitable for young children
Mild violence; occasional brief non-sexual nudity; bed scenes but no serious suggestion of actual sexual activity; limited scatological language, but no sexual expletives; no drug use or condoning of immoral behaviour unless mitigated by context (e.g. comedy); no undue emphasis on weapons (e.g. flick-knives).

'12' (Suitable only for persons of twelve years and over)
Implications of sex (within a relationship or in a humorous context); stronger language, but only a rare sexual expletive; more realistic violence limited in length and intensity, but no drug use.

'15' (Suitable only for persons of fifteen years and over)
Themes requiring a more mature understanding. Full-frontal nudity in a non-sexual context; impressionistic sex; more extensive use of expletives; mildly graphic violence and horror with some gore. Soft drugs may be seen in use, but not so as to condone or normalise. As with categories above, no details of harmful or criminal techniques, e.g. how to break into cars, pick locks, etc.

'18' (Suitable only for persons of eighteen years and over)
Themes requiring an adult understanding (e.g. complex sexual relationships, controversial religious subjects); explicit simulated sex (or in some educational contexts real sex); full nudity in a sexual context; unglamorised use of hard drugs when justified by characterisation or narrative; frequent use of sexual expletives; graphic violence, provided that it does not encourage sadistic pleasure or glamorise dangerous weapons.

'R18' (Restricted 18) – To be supplied only in licensed sex shops or cinema clubs to persons of not less than 18 years
Consenting, non-violent sex depicted with a degree of explicitness limited only by the law.

NB All decisions on category must strike a balance between precedent and the context of the individual film when taken as a whole

Figure 30.1 British Board of Film Classification guidelines

Symbols only, for use on:

Cassettes: front and spine of case
and top and spine of cassette
Discs: front of disc sleeve
and label on disc itself

Symbol plus explanatory statement for use on:

Cassettes: reverse side of case
Discs: reverse side of sleeve

 UNIVERSAL Suitable for all

 UNIVERSAL Particularly suitable for young children

 PARENTAL GUIDANCE General viewing, but some scenes may be unsuitable for young children

 Suitable only for persons of 12 years and over
Not to be supplied to any person below that age

Suitable only for persons of 15 years and over
Not to be supplied to any person below that age

 Suitable only for persons of 18 years and over
Not to be supplied to any person below that age

 RESTRICTED. To be supplied only in licensed sex shops to persons of not less than 18 years

Figure 30.2 BBFC certification symbols

The BBFC has been operating for over 80 years and was formerly known as the British Board of Film Censors. Its work now is more concerned with classification, particularly as the Board also covers films on video. The situation with video is slightly different as it is something brought *into* the home – you don't have to go *out* to the cinema to see it. Since being given the role of ensuring that a video on sale to the public is 'suitable for viewing in the home' the emphasis of the Board's work has changed from censorship to classification.

The BBFC has worked to gain the trust of the local authorities, Parliament, the public and other groups. In order to achieve this, it recognises that it is vital not only to be independent but to be *seen* to be independent. Therefore it does not accept any funding from the film industry. Instead, it finances itself from the fees charged for classifying films and videos. The BBFC seeks only to cover costs rather than to make a profit. It listens to the views of a range of organisations, including those from the industry itself, the media and pressure groups, but these organisations are not allowed to determine the standards applied by the Board.

a No film, other than a current newsreel, shall be exhibited unless it has received a certificate of the British Board of Film Classification or is the subject of the licensing authority's permission

b No young people shall be admitted to any exhibition of a film classified by the Board as unsuitable for them, unless with the local authority's permission

c No film shall be exhibited if the licensing authority gives notice in writing prohibiting its exhibition on the ground that it 'would offend against good taste or decency or would be likely to encourage or incite to crime or to lead to disorder or to be offensive to public feeling'

d The nature of the certificate given to any film shall be indicated in any advertising for the film, at the cinema entrance (together with an explanation of its effect), and on the screen immediately before the film is shown

e Displays outside the cinema shall not depict any scene or incident not in the film as approved

f No advertisement shall be displayed at the premises if the licensing authority gives notice in writing objecting to it on the same grounds as apply to the prohibition of films.

Cinema licences in London carry the following additional conditions:

No film shall be exhibited at the premises –

1 which is likely –
   a to encourage or to incite to crime; or
   b to lead to disorder; or
   c to stir up hatred against any section of the public in Great Britain on grounds of colour, race or ethnic or national origins, or sexual orientation or sex; or
   d to promote sexual humiliation or degradation of or violence towards women; or

2 the effect of which is, if taken as a whole, such as to tend to deprave and corrupt persons who are likely to see it; or

3 which contains a grossly indecent performance thereby outraging the standards of public decency

Figure 30.3 BBFC licensing agreements

However, the Board does try to work with the film industry and will advise on classification issues. If, for example, a production company or distributor wants to target a particular group, say the under-15s market, they can receive advice about what needs to be edited out in order for the product to be passed for showing to the target audience.

Although the Board has no legal status, there are important laws which have to be obeyed. These include the **Obscene Publications Act**, which requires that any material which 'corrupts or depraves' is refused a certificate. **The Cinematograph Film (Animals) Act** 1937 protects animals from mistreatment. Horses in battle scenes, for example, used to be brought down by tripwire, but this is no longer allowed. There are also the laws of **blasphemy**, **criminal libel** and the **Protection of Children Act 1978** to consider. In fact it is on the

protection of children that much of the Board's efforts are concentrated.

 Activity

Can you think of any film you have seen recently where you feel cuts should have been made? Why?

Department of National Heritage

This department is responsible for government policy concerning the media. As well as the media, the department has numerous other areas of responsibility such as libraries, galleries, museums, the arts, sport, the National Lottery and tourism. These are all dealt with in various sections called 'groups'. The group which has particular responsibility for the media is called the Broadcasting and Media Group.

The department oversees all government activity concerning the media. It drafts legislation such as the Broadcasting Act 1996 and makes provision for organisations such as the ITC, Press Complaints Commission, BBFC and others who provide the checks and balances that are needed to guide and regulate the mass media in a democratic society.

The department also negotiates the agreement with the BBC, and set out the terms and conditions by which the BBC operates.

Monopolies and Mergers Commission

As far as the media industries are concerned it is vitally important that no one organisation has too large a controlling interest over the extremely influential media of mass communication. This is becoming increasingly critical with the convergence of media forms, for example newspapers buying parts of TV stations and vice versa. A review of cross-media ownership therefore took place in the 1995 Green Paper, a Parliamentary discussion document which went on to become the 1996 Broadcasting Act.

A central concern of the Monopolies and Mergers Commission is how much of the media markets should be owned (i.e. controlled) by any one media company. It is the job, therefore, of the MMC to prevent companies from gaining so much control over a certain market that they are, in effect, monopolies. A merger that involves the acquisition of more than £70 million worth of assets or 25 per cent of the market is classed as a 'qualifying' merger. A qualifying merger is investigated by the Director General of Fair Trading, who advises the Secretary of State. The Secretary of State can then decide on one of the following courses of action:

■ refer the matter to the MMC
■ accept undertakings from the parties to the merger
■ clear the merger without reference to the MMC.

The following case study shows what happens when a matter is referred to the MMC.

Case study: Monopolies and Mergers Commission

In 1994 the MMC produced a report concerning the supply of films for exhibition in cinemas in the UK. The report highlighted a practice that was found to be 'against the public interest'. This practice involved leading film distributors (such as Columbia Pictures Corporation Ltd, 20th Century Fox Film Company Ltd, Warner Bros Distributors Ltd and Buena Vista International Ltd) insisting on lengthy minimum exhibition periods as a condition of supplying exhibitors with popular films.

The Director General of Fair Trading asked for undertakings from these organisations that they would come to an agreement which would not disadvantage smaller exhibitors.

The Director General subsequently reported to John Taylor, the Competition and Consumer Affairs Minister, that no satisfactory agreement had been reached. Therefore, in 1996, under the Fair Trading Act 1973, he made an order that exhibitors should not be required to show a film for more than two weeks if the exhibition period is within six weeks of the film's first showing in the UK, and for no more than one week subsequently.

The MMC judged that these periods were long enough for single-screen operators or those with few screens, as they needed to be more sensitive to consumer preferences (by changing the films more often) than multiscreens, which would always have a variety to choose from.

An example of the Secretary of State accepting undertakings is the 1994 acquisitions by Carlton of Central and London Weekend Television by Granada. In this case the Secretary of State for Trade and Industry Michael Heseltine accepted an undertaking that the parties to the mergers would bring their share of all TV advertising revenue to below 25 per cent.

Special provision for newspapers

In addition to general policy on acquisitions between parties, the Fair Trading Act contains special provisions relating to the transfer of newspapers between newspaper proprietors. These provisions spring from the report by the Royal Commission on the Press in 1962, and address concerns regarding the concentration of newspaper ownership and freedom of editorial expression. It is a criminal offence for a qualifying newspaper transfer to be made without the prior consent of the Secretary of State. In this instance, a qualifying merger is one in which the newspapers of the purchaser and those they intend to acquire add up to 500 000 or more paid-for copies per day of circulation. In the case of newspapers, any initial investigations required are carried out by the Department of Trade and Industry rather than the Office of Fair Trading.

However, a clause in the Act states that a reference to the MMC does not have to take place if a newspaper has a circulation per day of publication of less than 50 000 copies.

Ethical framework relevant to UK media

Law can be defined as a 'body of enacted or customary rules recognised by a community as binding' (*Concise Oxford Dictionary*) and it protects the ownership, control and practices of the media. Ethics, on the other hand, are moral principles, or rules of conduct, and ethical considerations are often linked to self-regulation in the form of professional codes of practices. These codes are designed to prevent unacceptable standards or irresponsible behaviour.

Press Complaints Commission

This body was created by the newspaper industry itself in 1991 and replaced the old Press Council. The Press Complaints Commission was established as a result of the Calcutt Report, which was commissioned by the government to investigate intrusions of privacy.

There were actually two Calcutt reports. The first, in 1990, emphasised self-regulation. In the 1993 report Calcutt decided that this had not worked and that the newspaper industry's self-interest took precedence over 'cleaning up their act'. He therefore recommended a statutory code of practice for journalists, a press complaints tribunal presided over by a judge, and making invasion of privacy (including bugging and the use of a telephoto lens) a criminal offence. The Chairman of the PCC, Lord McGregor, said that this constituted 'direct censorship' and was highly undemocratic. The government gave the first two proposals a cool reception but the third recommendation, concerning press trespassing, bugging, etc. could well become law in the near future.

The PCC is a self-regulating body, charged with enforcing the 1993 Code of Practice. This includes the following issues:

- **the right to reply**, which gives people or organisations the right to respond to criticism in the press. It is not enshrined in law and is a campaigning issue for the Campaign for Freedom of Information. Newspapers often do print apologies, but this is usually because of factual errors which could cause a libel action if not retracted.
- **'chequebook journalism'**, which really means bribing people to give a newspaper exclusive rights to a story. Although frowned upon it is not illegal.

The code also warns against printing 'inaccurate, misleading or distorting' material and states that newspapers should 'distinguish clearly between comment, conjecture and fact'. Other issues covered include privacy, use of listening devices, misrepresentation, harassment, discrimination and the interviewing or photographing of children.

Advertising Standards Authority

The ASA code of practice demands that advertising is 'legal, decent, honest and truthful'. This is discussed further in the Legal and Ethical appendix.

Film Makers Code of Practice

Until recently, film makers in London had to liaise with the separate boroughs who belonged to the Association of London Authorities. Their prime consideration was to the local population. Now the London Film Commission has taken over their role. Through their Code of Practice, they are concerned with promoting good relations between the film industry and the people who live and work in the locations used for filming. They will advise rather than dictate how film crews should behave in a

responsible fashion, for example, with regard to the hours when filming takes place or the reasonableness of asking people to remove their cars out of camera shot, etc.

National Union of Journalists

The NUJ operates a Code of Conduct concerning the way that its members conduct themselves in their professional roles (see Figure 30.4).

Journalists do not always enjoy the best of reputations and insensitive coverage of some high-profile disasters, such as those at Zeebrugge and Hillsborough, and royal family revelations have not helped their position.

Code of Professional Conduct

1 A journalist has a duty to maintain the highest professional and ethical standards.
2 A journalist shall at all times defend the principle of the freedom of the Press and other media in relation to the collection of information and the expression of comment and criticism. He/she shall strive to eliminate distortion, news suppression and censorship.
3 A journalist shall strive to ensure that the information he/she disseminates is fair and accurate, avoid the expression of comment and conjecture as established fact and falsification by distortion, selection or misrepresentation.
4 A journalist shall rectify promptly any harmful inaccuracies, ensure that correction and apologies receive due prominence and afford the right of reply to persons criticised when the issue is of sufficient importance.
5 A journalist shall obtain information, photographs and illustrations only by straightforward means. The use of other means can be justified only by over-riding consideration of the public interest. The journalist is entitled to exercise a personal conscientious objection to the use of such means.
6 Subject to justification by over-riding consideration of the public interest, a journalist shall do nothing which entails intrusion into private grief and distress.
7 A journalist shall protect confidential sources of information.
8 A journalist shall not accept bribes nor shall he/she allow other inducements to influence the performance of his/her professional duties.
9 A journalist shall not lend himself/herself to the distortion or suppression of the truth because of advertising or other considerations.
10 A journalist shall only mention a person's race, colour, creed, illegitimacy, marital status or lack of it, gender or sexual orientation if this information is strictly relevant. A journalist shall neither originate nor process material which encourages discrimination on any of the above-mentioned grounds.
11 A journalist shall not take private advantage of information gained in the course of his/her duties, before the information is public knowledge.
12 A journalist shall not by way of statement, voice or appearance endorse by advertisement any commercial product or service save for the promotion of his/her own work or of the medium by which he/she is employed.

Figure 30.4 NUJ code of professional conduct

On the other hand, many journalists have shown an enormous amount of courage and integrity in their coverage of dangerous war zones and unpalatable revelations. For example, John Pilger has brought us ground-breaking stories on the murderous Pol Pot regime in Cambodia (Kampuchea), atrocities in East Timor and, most recently, the brutal use of the local population as slave labour for a tourist railway in Burma. All of these implicated foreign governments and have made him less than popular with various authorities, including the British government.

Not all journalism concerns simply reporting hard facts. A large amount of journalistic output involves feature writing or documentary making, which rely on an interpretation of the facts, in turn giving rise to expressions of opinion. This is becoming more common as the nature of newspaper news is changing. News reporting is becoming so instantaneous that the newspapers are relying more and more on features and other entertainment sections to diversify and maintain sales.

Unfortunately there has been a general decline in the in-depth coverage of events and issues. Once something major or 'newsworthy' happens, such as the death of a teenager, allegedly from the use of recreational drugs, there is a huge hue and cry from the media, with all the TV and newspaper news and features dealing with it as if it were the only event in the world. Despite the vast coverage, there is usually very little real investigation and analysis; instead, there is a mainly emotional response, particularly from the popular press.

TV documentaries are also considered by many people to be suffering from this lack of quality investigative journalism.

In addition to the impact of technology and the public's apparent acceptance of these slipping journalistic and editorial standards, there is also the danger of legal action under the Official Secrets Act (or, more likely, under the Law of Confidentiality), or libel. The Broadcasting Act has also changed the status of some of the programme providers and slowed down the documentary output.

Even where there are documentaries, there is a trend towards the 'fly-on-the-wall' type, concerned with 'quality of access', which appear to have much in common with game shows; or the 'true confessions' type peeping into people's lives (compelling but cheap and tacky), rather than real attempts at a moral debate.

However, there are still good examples of investigative excellence on TV, such as *World in*

Action, Dispatches and *Cutting Edge*. Likewise, in newspapers, *The Guardian* continues its investigative tradition and every Monday carries analysis and comment on the media.

Professionalism and its influence on the nature of media products

The ethos of professionalism in this context includes practices involved in media production such as division of labour, 'house style' and working towards the stated aims of an organisation. These practices can have a self-regulatory effect. Professionalism is all about doing a good job – checking facts, meeting deadlines, carrying out tasks that have been agreed and being considerate and effective in your work.

House style

House style gives a media product, such as a newspaper, magazine, TV programme or radio station, a particular identity by which it can be recognised. It helps the product to stand out from other, similar products and can give employees a sense of pride and the reader or audience a sense of affinity with the particular publication or programme. For example, *World in Action* and the *News at Ten* on TV, and *Woman's Hour* on the radio, all have their own individual look/sound and 'feel', even though different producers are involved – they have to fit a particular pattern or style.

House style is a way of creating consistency in print products – in spelling, the use of abbreviations and in the use of certain words which may have alternative nuances or pronunciations. This gives the product an identity which helps it to be more easily understood and recognised. If a word was arbitrarily spelt or used differently within a print publication it would give an inconsistent and thus unprofessional impression, and be confusing for the reader.

To be successful, newspapers, magazines and books need to communicate effectively with their readers. As we saw in Unit 1, all forms of communication use a code which is developed and understood by the sender of the message and its reader. If the sender of the message starts to change the look or sound of those codes then the receiver will begin to notice inconsistencies which reduce the effectiveness of the message. It will create 'noise' in the communication system and the receiver will lose confidence in the accuracy of the message.

A **professional** media product must give its audience a sense of confidence. To gain that confidence the product should be consistent in the codes it uses. For example, which spelling do they use: goal or jail, connection or connexion, enquire or inquire; and do they mean the same thing anyway?

Other house-style decisions are made around the use of the suffix 'ize' or 'ise', in words such as recognise/recognize. Foreign words and place names also have to be given a single spelling, e.g. Czar or Tsar, Beijing or Peking. The use of capital letters can, in some cases, be open to interpretation, particularly where abbreviations are concerned. For example, some will be printed in lower case, such as Nato. Points between the letters are often not used, such as in UK, USA, UN and IBM.

Other areas of text where consistency is needed include the use of hyphens (e.g. take-off or take off), whether you use a person's full name and if you should include the title Mr, Mrs, Ms, etc. Many newspapers and news readers use the surname only, if it is a court case they are covering. Titles, such as military ranks or hereditary titles, and the way they are abbreviated, all need to have a consistent style established.

Professionalism

The **stated aims of an organisation** are a result of the development of a professional ethos regarding that organisation and the people who work there. As we saw above, the NUJ operates a code of conduct which journalists aspire to and which sets certain professional and ethical standards.

However, the more overtly commercial organisations will have a business ethos which may well be at odds with the beliefs of its individual members and may be challenged on ethical grounds by society in general. For example, an oil company may be more concerned with profits than with environmental safety, or a newspaper may be more concerned about circulation figures than fair and accurate **representation**.

 ### Case study

Many newspapers have a women's section, and the *Daily Mail* particularly promotes itself as a paper representing women's interests and viewpoints. Other papers such as the *Sun* and *The Times* have sought to emulate this in an effort to attract a greater share of the female readership. The women's sections claim to be *for* women but, critics argue, they are often really about making women's issues yet another saleable commodity.

In a criticism of these women's pages headed 'Blondes Forever Bubbly', Roy Greenslade argued in *The Guardian* (8 July 1996) that professional women in senior journalistic and managerial roles on newspapers are not really representing women's interests but are instead misrepresenting women whilst purporting to represent them. He wrote: 'For the *Daily Mail* women are a market to be exploited, not a reason for a crusade. (This also appears to be the case at *The Times*, which has imported female executives from the *Mail* with a similar brief.)'

The drive to increase sales may make it more necessary to reinforce old certainties and stereotypical assumptions about women instead of making serious attempts to challenge those attitudes in society.

In general, the article argues that the women's pages in the *Mail*, *Times* and *Sun* exploit and stereotype females, and by channelling women into that part of the organisation which is seen as their natural preserve is using professional women to continue 'a male agenda'.

Do you feel this criticism is justified? In order to answer this you will need to gather and assess evidence from these three newspapers, as well as other viewpoints. It would also be useful if you sought out the original article by Roy Greenslade.

Division of labour

To reiterate, professionalism in general means abiding by codes of conduct, endeavouring to carry out your duties to the highest standard and taking a pride in your work. To ensure this, work activities are usually developed into specialised functions and certain levels of competence that must be achieved in professional examinations or assessments. For example, journalists pass on their copy to sub-editors for editing and layout; camera crews put a director's vision into practice, whilst a producer will provide the resources and organising skills so this can happen.

Thus expertise is allowed to develop, which means an enterprise consists of specialised, professional staff operating within acceptable levels of competence.

Activity

During your GNVQ programme, you will be going on work experience. This is an important part of your education. It gives you the chance to observe working practices in industry or business.

How can you work in a professional manner? Make a list of your ideas, then compare it with other members of your group.

Below are some guidelines to consider with regard to professional conduct at work:

- Find out about the organisation. What products do they make or what services do they provide?
- Find out about your place in the organisation. Who do you have to report to?
- Know what your job entails. What will be your responsibilities and what will be your priorities?
- Make sure you understand the working practices and standards of the organisation you are working for.
- Make sure you are properly trained and equipped to do a job. Listen carefully to any instructions and write them down. If you don't understand something, then *ask*.
- Carry out tasks in the correct order. Don't leave jobs that look boring or difficult to the end.
- If you are working with someone else, make sure you do your fair share of the work.
- Always follow health and safety regulations. Look to see where the fire exits are. Never undertake any work which you think may be unsafe in order to please someone.
- Do not arrive for work tired from lack of sleep or under the influence of alcohol.
- Obey instructions about where and when you can smoke.
- If you are ill, telephone as soon as possible, so that your supervisor can make other arrangements for

duties to be covered.
- Wear suitable clothing – this may be either smart or protective clothing. Comfortable shoes are important!
- Be punctual. Keep to the set tea and meal breaks.
- Be polite and courteous. If you are having trouble with a task or in dealing with someone, then talk to your supervisor.
- Take responsibility for the work you do. Take a pride in completing a task to the highest standard, however boring or unimportant it may seem.
- Do not leave tasks unfinished. This means you have to be realistic about the amount of work you can do in a certain time. It is more professional to reject a task which is too difficult or will take too long than to fail in the attempt.
- Look out for challenges and opportunities!

Whatever job you eventually end up in, here are some further points to observe if you wish to be considered a professional:

- Keep abreast of developments in your chosen industry.
- Continually update your skills or train for more qualifications.
- You may need to join a professional organisation.
- You should be loyal to the organisation for which you work.

Balance between freedom of information, public interest and censorship

Censorship

Censorship laws mean that any book, play or article, etc. which is published or broadcast can be inspected to ensure that it does not contain anything which is immoral, blasphemous, obscene or seditious – and if necessary it can be suppressed.

Reasons for censorship may be on the grounds of political security, sexual mores, religious or public taste and 'decency'. They may be views which are held by the majority of people (and therefore part of the consensus) or a minority view which is imposed by a government or 'establishment'.

Issues of censorship are rarely clear cut. What may be acceptable to one person, for example, with regard to sex or swearing on TV, may be extremely offensive to another. So, for instance, many people feel that they should be able to see an exhibition of all of the late Robert Mapplethorpe's photographs;

541

others feel that some are pornographic and should not be displayed.

There was considerable secrecy imposed on the conduct of the journalists involved in reporting on the Falklands conflict and the Gulf war. The government defended this on the grounds of national security, and in the case of much of the material this would indeed have been the case. But there were numerous journalists who complained that material was also withheld which the public was entitled to see. More to the point, they asserted that withholding the material was more to do with preventing scrutiny of some of the government's secret actions, which could well be at odds with their publicly stated aims.

Propaganda

Although in Britain today most newspapers, and all mainstream television and radio stations, support what is known as 'the establishment', there is no explicit state control of the media as you would get in an authoritarian state such as Saddam Hussein's Iraq. Under such regimes the broadcasting and print output is carefully monitored and it is by maintaining a hold on these institutions (amongst other reasons) that the government holds on to power.

The power of the media is such that governments are sometimes tempted to try to control it, and use it as a vehicle to disseminate their own values.

In Rwanda in 1994 the country's radio network was taken over by extremists. They used it to spread fear and hatred of the Tutsi section of the population. These propaganda broadcasts incited members of the majority Hutus to carry out massacres against the Tutsi.

Nazi propaganda against the Jews in the 1930s was similar. Posters depicted Jews as sly, cunning and heartless. The image of the Jew presented to the German people was so de-humanising that one propaganda film even associated Jews with rats, showing images of the creatures running about and climbing over each other.

Leni Rienfenstahl's film *Triumph of the Will* was an all-embracing, uncritical celebration of Nazism. Using footage from the specially staged 1934 Nuremburg Rally, it is in fact the official record of this event. The film aligns itself wholeheartedly with Nazi ideals and seeks to engender these attitudes in its audience.

Freedom of access

One of the benefits of new technology (and, of course, also its disadvantage) is that it can circumvent the mainstream and official media communications and develop alternatives. This happened in the former Yugoslavia where an e-mail service called the ZaMir Transnational Network was established in cities such as Zagreb, Sarajevo and Belgrade to keep people in touch with each other within the former Yugoslavia and with the outside world. It helped counter the propaganda broadcasts and publications of Serb and Croat extremists.

New technology is making regulation more and more difficult as this extract from *The Times* (13 April 1995) illustrates:

'The Internet is giving extremists a previously undreamed of possibility for spreading racist and anti-Semitic propaganda... Bomb-making instructions and computer games, such as 'Achtung Nazi', in which the aim is to gas as many Jews as possible, are being posted on the worldwide computer link.'

Activity

Should society allow all beliefs to be represented and communicated by the media? Discuss this question with other members of your group.

Freedom of information

In all areas a balance has to be drawn between freedom of information and a realistic recognition that the public interest is not always best served by an unbridled freedom to disclose all information or permission to communicate any message or belief. It is worth noting, however, that in the USA people have much more access to government and company records than do people in Britain.

Censorship means deliberately vetting media output to the public and deciding what can or cannot be broadcast or written. It can be argued that stopping any piece of mass communication is censorship. However, in Britain bodies such as the ITC and BBFC carry out research into how the public feel about issues of taste and decency, etc. They publish their findings and encourage debate. This is different from an authoritarian state which controls media output in order to stay in power.

Article 19
The International Centre Against Censorship

Article 19 takes its name and purpose from Article 19 of the Universal Declaration of Human Rights.

Everyone has the right to freedom of opinion and expression; this right includes freedom to hold opinions without interference and to seek, receive and impart information and ideas through any media and regardless of frontiers.

Article 19 works impartially and systematically to oppose censorship worldwide. We work on behalf of victims of censorship – individuals who are physically attacked, killed, unjustly imprisoned, restricted in their movements or dismissed from their jobs; print and broadcast media which are censored, banned or threatened; organizations, including political groups or trade unions, which are harassed, suppressed or silenced.

Article 19's programme of research, publication, campaign and legal intervention addresses censorship in its many forms. We monitor individual countries' compliance with international standards protecting the right to freedom of expression and work at the governmental and inter-governmental level to promote greater respect for this fundamental right.

Article 19 has established a growing international network of concerned individuals and organizations who promote awareness of censorship issues and take action on individual cases.

Figure 30.5 Article 19 campaigns against censorship.

Freedom of speech, however, including freedom of access to the media, is not something about which we should be complacent. There are always people with vested interests (business, areas of government) who would prefer it if the public were happy with whatever is selected for them. Therefore a number of organisations monitor this situation and publicise and campaign against any erosion of our freedoms. A well-known example is the organisation **Article 19**, which campaigns internationally against censorship (see Figure 30.5).

Campaign for Freedom of Information (CFI) is an all-party body that argues for a freedom of information act and campaigns against what it sees as unnecessary official secrecy. It has already been successful in four areas concerning access to information. It would also like to see the repeal of the Official Secrets Act and its replacement with laws which can be used only when it can be shown that the security of the country has been seriously put at risk.

In tandem with its opposition to the Official Secrets Act, the CFI also supports the Public Interest Disclosure Bill, the aim of which is to protect employees and others who disclose information about serious malpractice. If this is successful it will encourage employees to try to exercise their moral right to disclose information, providing it is not motivated by any personal grievance or malice. Employees should try to resolve problems internally before going to the press, but in the final analysis, both the public and journalists should benefit from the right of disclosure.

Evidence assignment

There is to be a formal debate on regulation of the media industries.

Divide the class into two opposing groups. On the one side will be people representing each of the regulatory bodies. On the other side will be people representing media producers, such as owners of newspapers or film companies, and pressure groups within society such as Greenpeace.

The motion for the debate will be: 'It is not in the public interest for there to be so much regulation of the media industries.'

Individuals should each have an opportunity to speak, and they should explain the role and the viewpoint of the regulatory body, pressure group or media industry they are representing. They should discuss the nature of professionalism within their area.

Both legal and ethical issues, including freedom of information, tolerance, propaganda and censorship should be debated.

Write a report on the issues raised in your debate, describing the legal and ethical framework in which media industries operate, and explaining how the ethos of professional institutions influences the nature of media products. Include a list of the regulatory bodies relevant to the UK media and their roles.

Chapter 31

Explore the development of the media industries

This chapter considers what is meant by the 'media industries', including publishing, radio, audio-visual and new media. It looks at their development in terms of recent and emerging technologies and current economic factors. It also considers the sociocultural impact of developments in the media industries, including increased leisure time and greater literacy, and the meaning of media imperialism.

Recent and emerging technologies in media industries

The media industries to be considered here are publishing, radio, audio-visual and new media.

Publishing

Computerised typesetting

Until the development of computerised typesetting systems in the 1980s, typesetting was a skilled job, a traditional, male-dominated area of work and heavily controlled by the unions. But the introduction of word-processors, and typesetting machines that were very like WPs, led to enormous changes in the industry, including the break-up of the power of the unions and the loss of many jobs.

Journalists can now input their material directly, using a computer VDU (visual display unit), where it can be manipulated and edited. Direct input can actually take place from almost any location using a **modem** (a device which converts the computer signal to a telephone signal and back again). Obviously this has greatly changed the role of journalists, who can now be much more concerned with layout and the fit of a story on the page. Sub-editors call up the story file from the computer's memory and carry out any further alterations so that it is accurate and fits its allocated space.

Scanners are used to transfer pictures digitally on to the electronic page on the computer. Some scanners have an **optical character recognition** (OCR) capability which means that text that is scanned in

can still be treated as text and manipulated as individual characters on the screen (but it has not had to be keyed in). Photographs can also be sent by satellite and downloaded on to computer for incorporation into a newspaper page.

The copy is then phototypeset by sending it from the computer to a type of printer which prints out a photographic negative. This film negative is then placed on a printing plate. The printing plate is made of aluminium and is plastic coated. The plate is pre-sensitised with electrically charged particles. Ultraviolet light (a bright light) is shone through the photographic negative and activates the electro-static charge. Charged areas of the plate then receive the printed areas of the negative as an imprint on the plate. This has a chemical solution spread on it which creates areas which attract ink and repel water or vice versa. Grease-based ink and water mutually repel each other.

The plate is secured to the printing press and, in the offset lithography system, it picks up the ink from a 'bath'. The ink attaches itself to those areas of the plate that are not moistened with water. It then 'offsets' the page image on to a rubber cylinder called a blanket, which transfers it on to the paper.

Pages for photosetting can be sent by **facsimile** (fax) anywhere in the world, so the same publication can be produced simultaneously on different continents, i.e. information has become 'instant'. Alternatively, information can be sent directly from the sub-editor's screen by **e-mail** (electronic mail) to another computer anywhere in the world.

Publishing of all kinds has been revolutionised. It has become more easily accessible to the small business and home user by the development of **desk-top publishing** (DTP) which is based on digital technology, making use of computer, scanner and laser printer. (You can read more about DTP in Unit 3.) The printed page itself may soon be out of date, according to some people, with the increased availability of information on CD, CD-ROM etc. (see below).

Radio

The BBC's five national radio services are now able to broadcast in digital form, giving CD quality reception and freeing up more frequencies for the increasing number of services.

The BBC has played a pioneering role in new radio technology. **Digital Audio Broadcasting** was launched in September 1995. It will result in major improvements in reception and quality of sound, particularly on the move. The first mass-produced digital radio sets, home tuners and car radios will be available in 1997. DAB opens up the possibility of new programmes and services. The BBC service will carry the current five radio networks and also live broadcasts from both Houses of Parliament, plus live commentary of sporting events and programmes from the BBC World Service.

RDS (Radio Data Systems) is another new technology. Its most useful characteristic, at least for the motorist, is its ability to retune automatically, or 'autotune' as the BBC calls it. Other features are the travel information service which will interrupt a radio programme, cassette or CD, with a traffic report. There is also work going on to develop a car navigation system using the same satellite technology as used for shipping.

Audio systems and formats

CD (compact disc) is a form of digital recording. Each second of sound is sampled 44 000 times. The samplings are given digital codes which are then printed as minute reflective pits on the CD's surface. A laser beam reads the disc.

The CD has made vinyl gramophone records virtually obsolete. The sound quality is far better and the discs do not wear out or require much maintenance (although they do eventually corrupt). However, they are not used simply for music – they can also store vast amounts of text-based information.

See page 547 for a description of the MiniDisc format.

Integration of technologies

CD-ROM (Read Only Memory) carries text, pictures and sound digitally, which can be loaded on to the CD drive of a computer. Books and newspapers can be stored on CD-ROM and they are a crucial part of multimedia. For example, an encylopaedia such as *Encarta* is stored on disc and the information about a subject called up, not only in text but also in picture and sound form.

There is no interactive capability with these discs but they do help the user to visualise a topic, such as wildlife or musical composers, and also offer examples of their distinctive sounds.

Multimedia

Multimedia, as the name implies, means a number of different media used in conjunction with each other. This involves sound, text and vision, which can be carried, not only by computer disk and CD, but increasingly by telephone and satellite links.

Multimedia can also integrate and drive such equipment as computerised lighting and mechanical animation (animatronics). Electronic musical and sound equipment (such as synthesizers and samplers) can be integrated using MIDI (musical instrument digital interface) connections. Video cameras and VCRs can also be used to scan in still and moving pictures which can then be manipulated.

Interactive multimedia allows you to make choices and manipulate the contents of the software which could be held on CD-i (CD-interactive). In this sense it is 'non-linear', allowing you to delve into the package and move around in different directions, rather than having to follow a certain specified sequence.

Multimedia production software allows you to put all the different components of a production – sound, video, etc. – together into a presentation. The results can be impressive, but, particularly with interactive applications, it can take a prohibitively long time to put something useful together. The technology should not become an end in itself. So if you are planning to use multimedia techniques, ask yourself why you are doing it and whether it is fit for the purpose you intend. Would it be better just to use a book?

It is the CD's memory storage capacity that has really allowed multimedia to be a realistic desktop proposition. Multimedia needs huge amounts of memory and a single CD can carry the equivalent information of approximately 500 high-density (HD) computer disks. In addition, the storage capacity of CD is needed to make the carrying of video footage viable. One minute of audio or video would take up eight computer disks of memory.

The technical characteristics of the CD-ROM, with its ability to contain all the multimedia data (still pictures, video, sound, text and the computer program that drives it) make it vital to multimedia applications.

545

The biggest competition to CD are broadcasting systems (terrestrial, cable and satellite) which can send information in digital form directly into the home on optical fibre. The number of channel frequencies that can now be carried by these 'multiplexes' has increased dramatically. There is already scope for dozens of new radio and TV channels and some experts predict that it will explode to four thousand channels within your lifetime. The technical ability is already there, and in Europe there is already capacity for between 500 and one thousand channels. Think about all the programme-making that will be needed!

There is, however, another method of connecting directly with the home – using the home computer and the **Internet**. Broadcast-quality CD-ROM known as **DVD** (Digital Versatile Disk) can be downloaded via the 'net' on to the VHS recorder for the playing back on this new-generation CD-ROM (this is discussed further under the 'BBC Multimedia Centre').

On-line

BT (British Telecom) provides a direct-to-home digital link called ISDN, although this costs more than the normal telephone line. It is used by some radio stations for their remote studio links or for linking computers in different parts of the country. On-line services can deliver everything from interactive teaching to catalogues to the latest legal rulings.

Other high-capacity cable links are supplied by the cable TV companies. The advantage is that it allows 'inter-connectivity', which is not available on terrestrial or satellite broadcasts.

Inter-connectivity allows a two-way communication between the supplier and the user which means that information can be sent into the home and answers sent back. This will extend to the idea of **video-on-demand** (VOD), being developed by BT, which will allow households to order a particular programme to be sent down the cable to the home. It would be technically possible to fast-forward and pause, etc. as with a normal VCR. Terrestrial and satellite broadcasting cannot do this as they are not 'one-to-one' services in the same way as cable.

Before this, 'set-top' boxes will become available which can be connected to existing televisions. These will allow subscribers to unscramble digital signals and make use of 'pay-per-view' services.

Satellite

Satellite is a 'one-to-many' system, beaming down signals to satellite dishes on people's houses. It is also a one-way system, without the inter-connectivity of cable.

Once the satellite is in position and sending signals, it does not cost any more to provide it for additional homes. This is not the case with cable, which has to be laid to each home.

Internet

The Internet could be seen as an extension of e-mail (electronic mail), but is much much more. It is a huge source of information – mainly free. People 'publish' on the Internet, and advertise on it, as well as sending messages. It makes use of modems to contact computers all over the world. It works by sending the message via one or several **web sites** from where it is relayed to the web site nearest to its destination. Then it is passed to the computer terminal of the person you are contacting. Heinemann has a world-wide web site, and an increasing number of advertisers and organisations now give an Internet 'address'.

Messages can be sent and stored so that a receiver can download from the local hub and read the message on screen, or if two parties are connected at the same time they can communicate in 'real time'. Whilst large companies and academic institutions may have their own hub, individual users have to subscribe to one of the many commercial hubs (web sites), such as CompuServe or BBC Network.

A technological advance that will have implications for the Net is **voice recognition**. Improvements in this technology mean that people will be able to dictate to their computers without having to 'train' their voices or machines. Users will be able to speak in continuous (i.e. natural) form rather than using separate words. Not only will this be a good way of dictating, it will also voice-index libraries of material, whether books or film footage.

Voice recognition technology will, in addition, allow users to give voice commands to the digital media equipment in their homes and offices.

Electronic distribution is very flexible and will allow consumers to download a vast range of software, video and audio products into the home. The choice will be enormous, with thousands of channels to choose from.

The distinction between telephone, cable, TV, radio and computer is becoming increasingly blurred as these technologies converge and integrate; the method of delivery is different but the product is becoming similar. In the next 10 years all these facilities could be accommodated in a single machine, which could also combine your music centre. People may be able to interact with their digital TV sets in the same way as they interact with their computers. Similarly, computers will probably have a TV capability as well as the ability to download interactive multimedia educational and entertainment services.

The disadvantages of electronic distribution is that there is no tangible product. People like to have a CD case or a video box. In addition, there will be the expense to the user of having to store these transmissions in permanent form (if they so wish), on top of subscription charges and the cost of purchasing the actual 'product'.

Digital audio editing

Taking the concept of electronic communication and distribution a stage further, multimedia capabilities in the digital audio field mean that music can not only be created, but commercial music can be sent down the telephone lines and then modified to whatever is the user's preference. Songs could theoretically have an infinite number of variations, depending on users' choices.

Sound recordings can be captured in digital form, either on hard or floppy disk or on DAT (Digital Audio Tape). The recording and playback quality of DAT is at least as good as CDs. In addition there is DCC (Digital Compact Cassette) which is also high quality and can play ordinary cassettes. There is now the capability for writing CDs with CD production software, allowing sound, or other material, to be written to the CD.

Editing is carried out in 'non-linear' fashion by instantly accessing any part of the recording and removing, moving or mixing it with another sound. On computer screen, the composition is visually displayed and the editing carried out by cutting, moving and pasting the different parts of the recording. Software available includes Cubase, Notator for the Atari and PC, and Octamed on the Amiga.

The **MiniDisc** format was developed by Sony and is a convenient and high-quality digital playback format. Its quality is much better than cassette tape although the CD's quality is better. It did not seem to catch on when it was launched in 1992 for pre-recorded music, but appears to be enjoying a more successful second chance. For multi-track mixing and editing there is Yamaha's MD4 MiniDisc multitracker, which allows you to record, mix and edit tracks.

Non-linear (video) editing

This method of editing is now firmly established in the TV and video industries and is revolutionising programme making. It is faster and more flexible, allowing more experimentation. Various versions of the same programme can be made which allows producers and distributors to target and provide for their markets more specifically. Quite simply, programmes could be modified to fit the nine o'clock watershed by quickly making a more sanitised or child-orientated version of a story.

There are considerable employment implications for this, and you should refer to Chapter 32 for details.

The electronic newsroom and general broadcasting centres are developing rapidly. These will consist of a

Figure 31.1 Non-linear video programme production

network similar to a computer network, with a central 'server' sending out the video to be edited at digital video editing computers.

Avid have developed AvidNews as a tapeless newsroom. This will be combined with the disk camera it has also developed, to produce *tapeless broadcasting,* which is part of the **ENG** (Electronic News Gathering) concept. The convergence of video, sound and lighting technologies and their improvement and miniaturisation has resulted in the one-operator news team. The employment implications are obvious, and again are discussed fully in Chapter 32.

Sony, however, takes a more transitional approach to the move to digital and is working on developments that combine both videotape and hard-disk systems.

Computer animation

With paint and graphics packages such as PagePlus and CorelDraw, as well as the more industry-standard Adobe photoshop, computer animation has revolutionised graphics. Some drawing software enables the artist to draw the first and last frames of a sequence, and instruct the computer to create the frames in between. These can also be modified to create 3D productions. No longer are there hundreds of people drawing individual pictures for film cartoons: one person and a computer can do all the work instead.

Current economic factors and the potential economic impact of new technologies on media industries

The greater commercialisation of broadcasting services means that there are now an increasingly large number of organisations involved in these expanding markets.

Many of these organisations are not traditionally broadcasters or even traditional **media industries**. Indeed, broadcasting as we know it may be only a relatively small part of the market. Banking, home shopping and computer services, including entertainment and music, will all become players in this vast industry. Organisations like BT will become broadcasters and computer companies will compete with TV and film production companies to create and distribute programmes and other content.

Developments in audio-visual industries

The audio-visual industry is becoming globalised. This is likely to lead to large-scale restructuring, with huge media conglomerates forming and positioning to take advantage of media opportunities in all areas of the audio-visual industry, both at home and abroad.

Here are some recent examples:

- Disney buys ABC
- Viacom acquires Paramount and Blockbuster Entertainment
- MCI buys part of News Corporation
- Times Warner plans to merge with Turner Broadcasting Systems
- Microsoft forms partnership with NBC to develop a 24-hour news and information service.

There will be few British organisations which will be large enough to compete effectively on an international level. Already most cable companies are North American and large parts of our other media industries are owned by foreign companies.

Although such organisations obviously consider that the benefits to them will significantly outweigh the costs, these will nevertheless be astronomical. Terrestrial and satellite transmission operators have to re-equip for digital broadcasting. BT and other telecommunications operators are having to invest heavily in fibre-optic cable. There will have to be investments in the vast memory capacity needed to store all the films and other programmes that will be needed. These will be similar to libraries, but will actually be extremely powerful computer file servers for the viewer to select from.

Cable companies are already carrying out a vast programme of cable installation, which will have to continue and even increase. The equipment manufacturers will need to invest in new digital equipment and households will have to invest in new equipment to receive these digital services.

Sources of revenue

Revenue to pay for this will come from subscription charges and sponsorship. This is already taking place but will no doubt increase significantly. The general subscription will be supplemented by more specific 'pay-per-view' payments and 'video-on-demand'.

Advertising revenue is predicted as continuing to grow in a healthy fashion and this should only get better for the operators as advertisers are attracted to niche market audiences. There could even be interactive advertising.

The government's proposals for the use of new digital technology ensure that the BBC too will have access to digital frequencies. It opens up the prospect of new services aimed at specialised markets, such as pay-per-view, video-on-demand and possibly weather, traffic and shopping channels.

Funding of the BBC

There is a debate concerning the funding of the BBC. At present it is funded by the licensing fee. There is some discussion about whether there should be income from other sources, such as subscription charges for particular types of specialist programmes, sponsorship of sporting and artistic events by major companies or by advertising.

The BBC is opposed to advertising in its core programming on the grounds that there is ample evidence from other countries such as France, Germany and Canada, that trying to fund a public service partly with commercial activities does not work. It detracts from the quality of the programme making, which then means it is difficult to attract the level of advertising funding that is needed. On the other hand, if the BBC were able to balance public service and commercial activities, the quality of their programmes would mean that a substantial amount of the advertising revenue would come their way, to the detriment of the independent channels.

Despite this, the BBC states in its publication *Extending choice in the digital age* that it will:

> *'provide public services which will be funded primarily by the licence fee, linked since 1988 to the Retail Price Index'* (i.e. linked to the cost of living).

It also states it will maintain the BBC World Service and

> *'... will offer a range of commercial services which, in the words of the charter, can be "funded by advertisements, subscription, sponsorship, pay-per-view system or any other means of finance, whether for reception by the general public free of charge or available on individual demand or encrypted...."'*

The BBC asserts that its main responsibility is to its licence fee payers and it will always put services funded by the licence fee first.

Other sources of funding include non-commercial funding for programmes which have a 'distinct social, cultural, or educational value and for which commercial funding is unavailable or inappropriate'. Sources of this funding include the Open University, charities and revenue from the non-profit-making sale of tapes and CD-ROM and other support material for educational programmes to schools and colleges.

The BBC is also developing commercial funding to raise revenue from some programmes and services that will be additional to its core programming. To do this it has established BBC Worldwide Ltd for both the UK and international markets.

In addition, the BBC is engaged in trying to make efficiency savings of over £200 million to finance the new digital broadcasting and **new media** such as digital teletext, interactive programmes, web sites (for the Internet) and broadcast-quality CD-ROM (called **Digital Versatile Disk**). To this end the corporation has recently established a **Multimedia Centre** to develop the technology. It is financed by the licence fee but plans to become self-financing within a year.

Much of the development work has been farmed out to software houses under the concept of **producer choice**. This is where programme makers can use resources other than the BBC's to make programmes, and can employ independent services or facilities if they are cheaper or more appropriate. (See Chapter 29 for further details on producer choice.)

The CD-ROM products are being developed with an emphasis on interaction which gives the user so much choice, decision-making capability and interpretation of the events, that it calls into question the concept of authorship itself.

The medium to be used to reach the user are network computers, which are cheap Internet computers for the home with the software on DVD (Digital Versatile Disk), which will be the successor to CD-ROM. It has 25 times the capacity of CD-ROM and can carry broadcast-quality video.

The drawback of DVD is that you cannot record on to it. This was a deliberate policy because major film companies did not want broadcast-quality pirate copies of their films 'turning up at car boot sales'. Despite this, if a film is recorded on to VHS tape it can be played back at broadcast quality on DVD.

Internet income

Services that have been published on the Net include the cable sports channel ESPN, which is one of the few operators to charge for its web site, ESPnet Sports Zone, as does the *Wall Street Journal*.

But these are specialist services and can get away with charging a subscription. More web sites are planning to charge because the advertising revenue has not been sufficient to claw back their start-up costs.

Potentially the scale of the information available on the Internet is staggering, but accessing it can be problematic. WorldWide Web has techniques for carrying out searches and there are 'search engines' such as *Netscape*.

As present the 'Net' is rather disorganised, has lots of dubious users and is full of enthusiasts who revel in the jargon and obscurity of it all. However, there are large numbers of self-help groups and clubs which are useful and enjoyable for many people. It is becoming increasingly sophisticated, with more and more commercial organisations making use of it to promote and sell products and services. Record companies can send music samples to prospective purchasers and complete tracks can be bought and downloaded on to the home computer.

There is, however, still insufficient advertising take-up on the Net. Some commercial organisations do not feel that there are large enough numbers using the Net to justify the investment. Historically, the Internet has been seen as a source of free information, and there is a reluctance to pay for material on it.

Activity

How much do you think your household spends on media products in an average week? You should include newspapers, magazines, subscription TV, videos, cinema tickets, books and the TV licence fee (you will have to caluclate what this costs per week).

As a group, calculate the total spending by media category and present your information graphically.

Production, distribution and consumption

The world is 'going digital' and the effects on patterns of production, distribution and consumption are revolutionary. The vast numbers of new channels mean that consumer choice for subscribers will be massive as will the effects on how the consumers will use these products. With so many channels and the ease with which the consumer can switch between and dip in and out of them, the number of channels themselves becomes meaningless. A more realistic way of envisaging this is as a vast datastream, elements of which can be taken and combined with other parts.

With the 40 channels of live sports coverage from the 1996 Atlanta Olympics, a continuous choice of simultaneous events meant being able to cut from one sequence to another whenever you wanted, rather than waiting for the extracts of the different events to be shown when the terrestrial TV broadcaster decided.

Changing patterns of consumer behaviour

Consumption will become more 'niche-market' orientated, with channels for various kinds of music and sport, history, science fiction, games, children's activities, etc. Programmes will eventually be downloaded by consumers when they want them. Tickets for theatre performances and sports events will be purchased from the home and the downloading of films will have a serious effect on video shops.

Developments in publishing

In addition to developments in the audio-visual industry, there are significant changes taking place in publishing. A major problem has been the increased cost of paper.

But even more important than the price of paper is the competition from electronic forms of magazines and newspapers. There does not appear to be a serious danger of hard copy being superseded by electronic forms of magazines and newspapers in the foreseeable future. However, publishers do have to keep an eye on the market and on developing technologies, which is why they have diversified into CD-ROM and multimedia.

A good example of the convergence taking place within formerly disparate parts of the media is the cable TV programme *The Site*. Computer magazine publisher, Ziff-Davis now presents this one-hour daily TV show, whose subject matter is technology and the Internet. The show appears on NBC's cable service Super Channel and is owned by NBC and Microsoft. Here, three traditionally separate media industries involved in publishing, software and broadcasting have formed an alliance to produce a programme that benefits from the expertise brought to it from all three.

Another link-up between publishing and broadcasting comes in the well-established form of the 'tie-in' book. As the name implies, a TV series is tied in with a complementary print publication which discusses episodes, behind-the-scenes drama, plans for the future, trivia quizzes, interviews with the cast, etc. Some of these and alternatives are also available on the Internet.

Another print product that complements electronic media is the Internet-related magazine *Wired*. Although acclaimed as the bible of new technology, it is as much about lifestyle as technology, as we can see from the claims to be 'content with attitude' and 'smart media for smart people'.

The *Wall Street Journal* also has an 'online' edition and Times Inc.'s Massive Pathfinder Website has most of *Time*'s magazines 'online'.

Magazine publishing

There is now a vast array of magazine titles as publishers identify and fill niche-market gaps with specialist and hobby magazines, as well as those of general interest to readers. We could describe a certain variety – for instance *Hello!*, *Here!* and *OK!* – as 'chat mags'. These have one thing in common: they believe that most readers are endlessly fascinated by the most humdrum details about 'the stars'. They are uncritical, uncomplicated and unnaturally chirpy (note the use of the exclamation marks in their titles!).

A backlash against this type of magazine was launched in May 1996 with *Esquire*. Its remit is to be the opposite of most magazines. Instead of concentrating on the lives of celebrities it focuses on 'real people'. With other magazines, before a journalist can get to see a celebrity, the star's PR manager, agent or lawyer will often set stringent conditions on what questions can be asked and the kind of photographs that can be taken. *Esquire* staff feel that there are enough potential readers who are weary of this and it seeks to break this mould. It is based on 'real people' who come from all walks of life and whose ordinariness makes them interesting. It is too early to say whether they are sufficiently right to be successful.

Activity

Research the magazine market and identify a gap for a new type of general-interest magazine. Identify its target audience and its treatment (i.e. its paper quality, size, page design, appearance and image and the kind of content and advertising it would carry). Evaluate your choice, giving justifications.

There are also plans to launch Britain's first daily football paper. Although there is strong coverage of sport, and football in particular, in the press and although there are weekly papers such as the *Leicester Mercury*'s 'Sporting Green', there has not yet been a daily. In Spain there is *Marca* (owned by Pearson), *AS*, *Sport* and *El Mundo Deportivo* (although this daily is dedicated almost entirely to coverage of FC Barcelona).

There is some scepticism from the tabloid newspapers about the paper's chance of success. *The Sun*, for example, points out that they already produce about seventy pages of football in a week. There are also all the football magazines.

Activity

Do you think the market could support a daily football paper? Bear in mind that there are already two daily papers for horse and greyhound racing.

Film and animation

It should now be apparent that digitisation is the underlying technological force behind the changes in the media industries. The computer graphics industry is already prominent in DTP, multimedia, and video games. It is now the driving force in **special effects** in the film industry. Because so many films have special effects as their central component instead of the plot, it would be fair to say that computer graphics are driving the film industry, at least as far as the big action movies are concerned. Blockbusters such as *Twister* and *Independence Day* show that great special effects can be more important than stars or plot.

The huge success of *Toy Story* has brought about a similar level of interest in totally computer-generated features. The result is a meteoric growth in digital effects houses. Vast amounts of finance are pouring in to these animation centres and a shortage of talented animators means that film studios are chasing experienced animators with the same techniques (parties, hotel suites and large sums of money) as they use to court popular film stars.

Activity

Do you feel that special effects are taking the place of the plot as the most important part of a film?

Does it matter if films have sacrificed content for effects?

Choose a selection of films you have seen recently to support your argument.

Economic impact

The rapidly developing digital technologies are helping to give impetus to the acquisitions and mergers that are now gathering pace. Large profits are forecast, but this entails large levels of investment. This in turn affects ownership patterns, with large conglomerates forming to provide for the huge consumer markets they are creating.

However, mergers and acquisitions are not the only way to grow. New distribution networks for satellite and cable continue to expand and organisations can invest in these new delivery systems, as with Granada's involvement with satellite.

Consumption patterns will be driven by this new technology, but it may be the year 2010 before all our broadcasts are digital – it really depends on how soon more than 50 per cent of the population throw away their old TV sets and buy digital ones, complete with the other equipment required to receive pay

satellite and cable transmissions. Pay television, including interactive broadcasts and direct-dial film selection, will significantly alter consumer behaviour patterns.

For a discussion on the effects of all these changes on employment patterns, refer to Chapter 32.

Sociocultural impact of developments in the media industries

Leisure and literacy

Increased leisure time through the shortened working week, casualisation of labour (part-time and short-term contracts) and greater unemployment have meant that there is a massive market for consumers of audio-visual products.

There have also been great changes in social attitudes with regard to leisure choices. For example, many people would rather turn on the TV or play a computer game than read a book. TV and video, in particular, are seen as easy options for leisure time.

If we bear in mind that television has been with us only since the late 1950s, and the home computer since the 1980s, then we can see that the rate of technological change has been phenomenal.

In the time-span of a generation, people have become **media literate**, that is, sophisticated 'readers' of media products, particularly TV programmes. We can, usually effortlessly, recognise and interpret the codes and conventions associated with this mass cultural form.

This media literacy has developed at the same time as IT literacy, at least among the media generation. Computer technology, however, has not only involved games. Education has benefited from the use of computers to improve spelling, comprehension and mathematics. Students can use programmes for literacy and numeracy on a one-to-one basis, which is not as embarrassing as having to answer to a teacher in front of the rest of the class!

Media imperialism

The demise of Communism in Russia and Eastern Europe has meant that these countries have become lucrative new markets for Western consumer culture. They can be reached by satellite, the Internet, video, etc. because these know no boundaries.

These countries formerly did not share the values of the West: they were restricted in their exposure to world events and sheltered from their effects. However, they now have a media diet of mainly American imports, many of which have a level of violence and sexual explicitness which would not have been permitted before the momentous political and cultural changes that have taken place.

Not only Eastern Europe but also the Far East is becoming saturated by American cultural values, brought to them by Western-dominated media. These closely knit societies are now bombarded with images of greedy individualism and motiveless crime.

The USA has rich, well-developed media industries – films, advertising, TV, music, etc. – and it is perhaps inevitable that these will dominate indigenous or 'home-grown' media industries. Many cultures look to the USA and see affluence, freedom, desirable consumer goods and so on. The USA is therefore invited to export films, etc. which are readily received by other parts of the world. It is very much a one-way system, introducing the values and commodities of (American) consumer capitalism.

In the UK many commentators feel that different (lower) foreign standards of taste and decency will erode domestic standards. According to *The Times* (24 November 1993):

'The links between British broadcasting, film, the arts and culture are elaborate but fragile. They are seriously at risk from foreign investors taking control of British media with government blessing.'

Even domestic products are now often modelled on the breezy tone of American television.

In Russia, many of the 'Americanised' teenagers use American slang and bad language, because they think it 'cool' to do so. Most of them have never been to America, but America has been to them in the form of tough-talking police dramas, etc. Deregulation and the 'wired world' mean the globalisation of dominant cultural values through globalised media – and that means the globalisation of American cultural values.

France has always been concerned about the effects of foreign influence, including foreign words, on their language and culture. Now, as from the beginning of 1996 the country's 1500 music radio stations must play a minimum of 40 per cent of songs in the French language. If they fall foul of this they are liable to a penalty of a month off the air and a fine equal to 5 per cent of their annual revenue.

But perhaps it is not all bad news for countries trying to preserve some cultural identity. MTV has taken over the world, but at the same time it has been, to some extent, a two-way process. Non-American or British bands which did not traditionally get a hearing outside their own country are now given exposure on this phenomenally successful music channel.

Apart from audio-visual sources, governments are also extremely worried about some of the content that is carried on the Internet, such as child pornography and racist language. In addition, there may be political and philosophical ideas which these governments are afraid of. For example, *The Times* (13 April 1995) wrote:

'The Internet is a massive new communications system, a network without frontiers, without laws and with no one there to say that you cannot say that or you cannot see this. Suddenly governments are waking up to the realisation that this is an information highway without any way to police its users.'

In Iran and Saudi Arabia, for example, a ban has been imposed on much of the Internet's output. But even if countries wanted to ban the information on the Net it is extremely difficult to do so. There could be some ways of regulating it, such as making all computer owners register their computers and banning or restricting access to the Net without a licence. This, however, would be extremely hard to enforce.

Evidence assignment

In small groups, write an article of 800 words for a media magazine describing three cases where recent or emerging technological developments have affected different media industries. This article should include visuals.

The article should explain how economic factors have enabled the new technology to be developed, and how in turn the new technology has had an economic and sociocultural impact on the media industries and their audiences/customers.

You may be able to include in the article examples drawn from personal experience of new technology gained through work experience or industrial visits.

Investigate employment in the UK media industries

In this chapter we will be investigating employment and training in the media. Occasionally, on visits to media producers, students and teachers are told that jobs are getting harder to find, there is no job security nowadays, that the competition to get work is enormous, and that media qualifications are no use – experience is everything. This is a very pessimistic view. Although it may contain elements of truth, it is not an accurate reflection of the current employment situation in the media industries.

The 1990s have seen great changes in all areas of industry, from the media to manufacturing. But unlike the steel, coal or shipbuilding industries in Britain, the media are expanding and flourishing. It is true that some big institutions and companies may be declining and therefore will be difficult to get into, but there is a mushrooming of new companies, not only in publishing and broadcasting but in the associated areas such as advertising, computing, etc.

There are thousands of new exciting jobs that need young people with fresh ideas, a good overview of all media industries and their working practices, and who are able to adapt a variety of skills according to what is required. Later in the chapter we will be looking at how and why employment patterns have changed and what type of qualifications and training will be needed in the future.

Main functions carried out in the media industries

Within every media industry, there are four broad categories of job. These are:

- Origination – this begins with thinking up the ideas for a project, whether it is a television programme or a magazine article, and developing it. It includes making a budget and locating finance, liaising with clients and investors. It entails undertaking all the research, from interviewing to archive searches. It covers everything from the original designs up to later stages such as writing copy or filming and editing

and deciding how the material is to be structured (e.g. page layout).

- Production – this concerns the manufacture of the product, the means by which the material is turned into its final physical form (the newspaper or the record, the video or the transmitted radio programme). For example, the printing process comes under production.
- Distribution/transmission – this covers the means by which the product reaches the consumer, e.g. through newsagents or by satellite.
- Marketing – this area is concerned with all of the processes mentioned above, though different personnel may specialise in market research for originating the product, or in assessing the effectiveness of the distribution system.

Activity

1 In each of the production units (3, 4 and 5) and in the marketing unit (7), the various jobs in the different industries were described. From your reading of these sections, identify examples of jobs in each of the areas listed above.
2 You can find advertisements for media jobs in the *Guardian* newspaper every Monday. You will also find job advertisements on teletext (e.g. vacancies at the BBC are advertised on Ceefax or in specialist industry magazines (e.g. *UK Press Gazette* or *The Radio Magazine*). Collect representative samples of media jobs covering all of the categories described above.

Different types of job

There is a wide variety of possible occupations in the media, needing different types of people with different capabilities and personalities to do them. Some of these are technical jobs (e.g. sound engineer), others are management posts (e.g. producer), some demand creative skills (e.g. director) and others require practical ones (e.g. graphic designer). Work can also involve management of resources, for example financial (accountant), human (editor) or materials (print-room manager).

For some jobs, you have to work closely as a team, in others you need to be self-motivated and work on your own. If you work in a large company, you will have a clearly defined role and responsibilities. If you work on your own, or for a small company, you may have to turn your hand to anything as the need arises. If you are part of a small independent record company, you may have to set the microphones up, answer the telephone, plug the record, *and* scout for new bands.

Multimedia jobs

Multimedia is one of the newer media industries. Here, the ability to work in a team and to be computer literate is essential.

Skillset (a professional organisation concerned with training in the broadcast, film and video industry) gives a list of the jobs to be found in the multimedia sector and what skills and background are needed (see Figure 32.1).

Activity

Choose a job which interests you from each of the radio, television, newspaper or magazine industries. Describe briefly what the job entails and what sort of skills and personality would be needed.

Changes in employment

The trends in employment which can be observed in many British industries are reflected in the media also. As we shall see, some changes have taken place over a number of years, due to economic or social

---

Author/Editor/Content Provider:

Produces the text and makes it 'fit' the appropriate space. Requires some expertise in relevant software, e.g. 'Director' and the ability to design useable information. Many will also have programming skills and specialist knowledge of a subject area.

Animator:

Produces animation to illustrate appropriate text. Works closely with author and designer. Requires proven computer graphics skills, and animation training and experience. Many animators work as freelance contributors to individual projects.

Designer:

Creates the overall 'look' of the product. Requires proven CAD skills and a broad knowledge of relevant software. Often multi-skilled, able to perform complex image manipulation, etc.

Programmer:

Some programmers are very creative, lateral thinkers. It certainly helps! Requires high-level ability with both PCs and MACs. Languages include C++, Visual Basic, Windows.

Project Manager:

'Getting it done', co-ordinating, chivvying, understanding and sorting out problems. Broadly based software, management and communication skills.

Graphic Artist/Illustrator:

A creative graphic artist/illustrator who builds individual pages, using layout and design skills. Needs to be 'motivated to learn' any new software applications with particular expertise in Applemac systems such as Photoshop.

Operator:

Working on behalf of many members of a team, an operator needs to be very computer literate and familiar with many software packages. Many operators come from graphics backgrounds, and provide the basic, page by page, information that makes up a multimedia product. Operators rarely see 'the big picture' as they work on small elements of a project, which will later be combined with the work of others to produce the final piece.

Sound Technicians/Musicians:

Sound plays a critical role in multimedia and fitting the sound to the rest of the information 'rather like the piano accompaniment to a silent film...' takes great skill. Often from a sound recording background – good musicians, who can compose 'bites' are highly sought after. Many companies will use specialist sound providers once the visuals and text are complete. It is rare for sound specialists to be 'in' at the beginning of projects.

Multimedia Developer:

Involved in the development of an entire project, putting together text, images and sound, needs to be multi-skilled, familiar with the manipulation of text and images. Developers often work in smaller companies and need excellent team skills.

Multimedia Systems Analyst:

Very logical and analytical, ability to identify and communicate needs of different team members (and the client...), recommending appropriate hardware and software solutions.

Producer/Publisher:

Manages the business of the project – negotiating finance, organising staffing to meet the needs of the client. A manager with good creative skills.

Video Technician:

Making and/or editing video to match the text. Most will come from post-production backgrounds, and a thorough understanding of digitising video is essential.

Figure 32.1 Multimedia jobs

factors; others have taken place much more quickly, perhaps because of changes in legislation.

Overall the media is a growth industry. It is true that organisations such as the BBC are cutting staff (and using more external resources for production) and new technology means that a team of six can be replaced by two in some circumstances. But when you consider the number of new radio stations, the multiplicity of new magazines, the need for advertising and for people to provide programmes for the numerous cable and satellite channels, the organising of subscription TV, and the production of multimedia – employment prospects are good!

However, patterns of employment and working practices in the various industries are altering. The changes are outlined below.

1 Multi-skilling

Multi-skilling means that an employee can perform more than one job or can operate a range of related equipment.

The need for multi-skilling has arisen because many large companies and organisations such as the BBC have become (or are planning to become) much more streamlined. Because of the growth in small companies, there is a greater need for people to have management, particularly financial, skills as well as production skills.

When people are working in small teams, they need to be able to operate more than one piece of equipment. With the new, sophisticated lightweight cameras, a news crew can consist of as few as two people or even one person, who therefore must understand about both audio and visual recording techniques.

Activity

Think of a vacancy in a newspaper office or radio station for which you might apply. Make a list of the different skills you have learnt on this course which would make you a useful employee.

2 Transferable skills

You have transferable skills when you have a particular ability or knowledge which you can use in different areas. For example, if you are a skilled journalist, you could work for either television or audio. Anyone who is computer literate can be said to have a transferable skill.

All journalists in the BBC regions and local stations are now being trained in **bi-media** techniques, so that they can report on events for both radio and TV.

Activity

If you have completed most of the other units in this book, you will have found that you have been able to use some skills, both creative and technical, in more than one area. For example, interviewing techniques are used in newspaper journalism, television chat shows and market research. Make a list of other skills you have learnt, and the different areas in which they can be used.

3 More freelance work

When you start work, you are given a contract to sign which sets out the terms and the conditions under which you are to work, for example the number of hours, days off, etc. There are three types of contract:

- **Permanent or open-ended contracts**
  This is the 'traditional' permanent job that has no end-date stipulated. Someone with this type of contract can continue in the job until retirement, unless he or she is made redundant, the company ceases to exist or the person is deemed to have behaved in a manner which amounts to gross misconduct. Permanent staff have statutory employment rights with an annual salary, sick leave, holiday entitlement and usually pension rights.

- **Renewable fixed term contracts**
  Staff are taken on by a company or organisation for a fixed length of time. They may or may not (depending on the organisation) get paid holiday or sick leave entitlement. A contract that is regularly renewed is known as a rolling contract.

- **Freelance contracts**
  People working freelance are usually self-employed and may be on a fixed contract basis for any length of time, varying from a day to a year or more. They are responsible for their own tax, National Insurance and pension contributions. They may be paid for the amount of work they do (e.g. £250 for a magazine article) or they may be paid for a day's work (e.g. £250 for a day's filming).

Freelance workers are now very popular with employers, because they provide greater flexibility. If they are not permanent staff, then they also save money. At present it is estimated that 60 per cent of the broadcasting and film industry are freelances (about 15 000 people). Most staff are not on permanent contracts. Full-time staff are usually producers, administrators and marketing people. Even the larger production companies employ only between 50 and 100 people and only about 10 will be permanently employed.

A similar pattern can be observed in the newspaper and magazine industries, with full-time editorial staff supporting freelance photographers and journalists.

Freelance work can also be popular with freelance workers themselves, again because of the flexibility it offers. It means that people who (for a variety of reasons) either cannot or do not wish to work on a full-time permanent basis, can still work – often for a number of employers. As long as deadlines are met, freelance workers can arrange their hours to suit themselves.

4 Increase in part-time staff

Part-time staff may be on permanent contract but will perhaps work for only two or three days a week or work only mornings. This gives greater flexibility; for instance, a publisher may need a graphic designer and a copy editor. There may not be sufficient work for two people so the best solution is to have two people in part-time jobs.

Some enlightened companies also allow **job-sharing**. Here a full-time permanent job is shared between two people.

With both types of part-time work, employees now have the same rights as full-time members of staff, such as sick leave entitlement or maternity benefits. This has enabled many more women, particularly those with children, to return to work.

These changes have meant that many production companies in the media now have only a skeleton permanent staff. They call in part-timers or freelances or short-term contract staff as and when they are needed.

5 Increase in the number of people who work from home

Employees who work from home are also very popular with employers. They can save on expensive office space and all the other associated overheads. Sometimes, employers will provide equipment such as computers and telephones for staff, but this depends on the status of the worker. Home workers are less likely to be on permanent contracts, so this too can save a company money. There are also advantages to the employee, especially women with young children who need to spend a significant amount of time at home. Some people prefer to organise their day themselves and not to follow the office routine, unless they have the sort of job which means they have to be in contact with certain people on the telephone during the day. So if they like working early in the morning and late in the evening but want to take the afternoon off, they can. If they like working in peace and quiet, or with the radio on, they can and they do not waste hours of time getting to work.

6 Flexible working hours

The media have never operated on a '9 to 5' day. With newspaper presses working round the clock doing contract printing and radio stations transmitting 24 hours a day, more people in the media will be working anti-social hours, i.e. night shifts. This may suit many who want to avoid rush-hour traffic or have time off during the day.

Case study

Bill Bush is the support executive for the print department of a major regional newspaper. He has been in this position for 13 years. He is responsible for buying all the raw materials, compiling production figures and any other information needed by the accountants. His other major responsibility is for personnel and health and safety issues. He has one press room manager and four deputy print room managers to supervise operations and the machinery in the print room.

Bill started off his career as a wallpaper printer, and received his training and gained his qualifications through a formal apprenticeship. These days most training given at this particular newspaper is in-house. The presses are hi-tech and digital, with most people working from control rooms and in sound booths. Employees need IT skills and either an electrical or a mechanical background.

Case study

Here is how Barbara Jacobs, a writer, describes her career:

'In 1975 I had a serious bout of pneumonia which effectively finished my teaching career. I was told that if I carried on working as I had done I would be dead at 40.

'Since I'd been a "career" teacher, this was a massive blow, but the following year I saw an advert in *The Guardian* for writers for teenagers. It had been inserted by D.C. Thomson, publishers of *Jackie,* who were starting another teen magazine. I replied, enclosing a sample of my writing, along with 999 others! Fifty of us were interviewed and asked to do a further piece of writing, this time to order. My piece was bought. Two other interviewees sold their work, too.

'Thomson's wanted me to write first-person fiction, which is what I started doing in my spare time (by this time my husband and I had started a bookshop), but when my marriage failed at the same time as the bookshop, I started freelancing to try to support myself and my 5-year-old son.

'It was pretty grim. But I did reduce my rejection rate from 90 per cent (the average for a fiction writer) to 10 per cent by sending stories rejected by Thomson's to IPC teen magazines. In 1980 I sold 350 stories, working at the rate of 2 a day if I could.

'From there I moved on to writing serials and "emotional features", starting on *Just Seventeen* when it was launched, and wrote my first children's novel, then a series of teenage novels, one of which was a huge commercial success, and another of which won several awards.

'The editor I worked with most often, Lesley Robb of *Mates, Girl* and *My Guy,* asked me to do the problem page on *Girl* in 1986. I became "Alice". This led to my job as "Laura Downey", the agony aunt on *My Guy.* In that role I began to appear on television.

'At around the same time, the fiction editor on *Just Seventeen,* who was an astrology expert, as I am, was offered work as the astrologer on a new women's magazine. She didn't have time to do it, and passed it on to me. That was how I became "Carla Santini", the astrologer on *Me* magazine, for five years.

'Now, suffering from an identify crisis, I've brought all my work together under my own name. So it is as Barbara Jacobs that I continue to write and do television work, for over 70 hours a week.'

Activity

Compare the two case studies above. One worker is a full-timer in a large organisation and one works freelance from home. What advantages are there to their employers in each method of work? What advantages are there to the employee? Compare their training and education. How has this helped them in their careers?

7 Growth of small and independent production houses

There has been an increase in the number of staff employed in independent production houses or in small print and graphics companies. The number of independent television companies has increased dramatically over the past decade. Some concentrate on making certain types of programmes, such as comedy or drama. This trend will continue, especially with the BBC initiative of **producer choice**, where producers can choose to use facilities outside the BBC organisation for all or part of production. The ITV company Carlton has no production staff – all production work is contracted to outside companies. Similarly, BSkyB purchase most of their output from abroad, so staff are mainly administrative, such as customer service staff, and some engineering and technical personnel.

There has also been an increase in small print and graphics companies, largely because of the great technological changes in printing in the past 15 years. DTP and the latest range of photocopiers have enabled small companies to produce high-quality work. For example, look at the range of services now offered by Prontaprint (Figure 32.2), which has 256 franchises in the UK and Ireland.

8 Increase in the number of specialists

There is now a great need for specialists who can operate sophisticated equipment or who can offer a particular service. Some **facilities houses** can make complete programmes if they have sufficient studio space or staff, but most concentrate on providing equipment and specialist staff who are experts in a particular area such as animation, special effects, titling or editing. A single production, such as an action drama, may use several facilities houses.

An Ever Expanding Portfolio of Services

● **Studio Design Service**
To create the right look for your business.

● **Quality Business Printing**
Single-colour letterheads to full-colour brochures.

● **High-Volume Copying**
From a single document to collated multi-copies of large reports.

● **Colour Laser Copying**
Our skilled operators add value and give impact to your documents.

● **Presentation Services**
We'll output from your disks or design a complete presentation for you.

● **Short-Run Publishing**
As many personalised documents as you want, when you want them.

● **Binding and Finishing**
For a thoroughly professional finish to your documents.

● **Giant Colour®**
Large-format digital colour printing.

Prontaprint!

Figure 32.2 Services offered by Prontaprint

There is a similar trend in the print/publishing industry, with small companies or even individuals providing a particular service such as a sleeve design or illustrations.

9 Increase in the number of women employed

More women in society generally are now working in full-time or part-time jobs, and the number is increasing too in media jobs. Skillset figures show that in broadcasting and film 57 per cent of employees are female. However, it is true to say that in more traditional technical areas, such as camera, sound and lighting, there are still comparatively few women. They predominate in wardrobe, make-up, production support, and research.

Flexible working hours and short-term contracts appeal to a high proportion of women who want an interesting job but still want to spend a significant amount of time with their families.

10 Women reaching higher positions

More women are achieving managerial positions, particularly as producers, although their number does not proportionally reflect the number of women in the industries.

Activity

In Chapter 29 you were asked to find out who are the editors of our major national papers. What percentage of them are female?

11 Mobile workforce

People may have to travel more these days to work on projects. Traditionally, the main newspaper and broadcasting industries have employed people living either in London or in the South-east. Now the regions are developing their services and increasing their output. Small companies find it cheaper to move out of London. The market-place is now more global, the UK is drawing closer to the rest of Europe, and many companies are owned by a foreign conglomerate. Therefore more people may find that they will be expected to travel and work abroad at times.

12 Increase in the number of media-related jobs

Other industries and professions want to utilise media techniques and products to benefit their companies and organisations. For example, in education, many teachers and trainers (and not only those who actually teach media studies), use videos, computers and multimedia to support their lessons. Many manufacturing companies have their own in-house magazines or newspapers, and need skilled staff to produce these. They need people with media skills to help them give effective marketing presentations.

There is also rapid growth in areas such as advertising and personnel, all areas which need good communication skills.

13 Changes in the nature of employment

More jobs will rely on 'brainpower' rather than manual skills, as has happened in audio with digital editing replacing the cutting and splicing of tape. Creativity and organisational skills will be sought after.

14 More fluid organisational structures

Figure 32.3 shows an example of a traditional hierarchical structure in an organisation. It is clear who has to report to whom and individual responsibilities will be clearly defined. However, the trend in management is now for a flatter, more flexible structure where people work in teams and

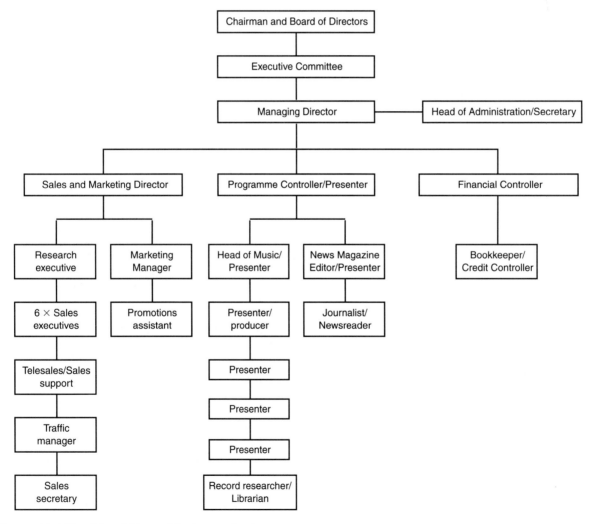

Figure 32.3 Traditional hierarchical organisation structure

may work for more than one department. This style of organisation is able to adapt more quickly to changing circumstances, e.g. when the workload in different areas fluctuates. Employees will operate in fluid teams that can be split up and reassembled to suit the needs of different projects.

15 Increase in the number of young people employed

This should cheer you up! The media need people with energy and fresh ideas, who enjoy using computers, travelling and working odd hours. Even in the BBC very few people are over 50, and a high proportion are under 30 years old.

Negative trends

However, some people are also predicting negative employment trends. These include the following:

■ **Fewer jobs in certain areas**
As mentioned before, these days some tasks can be handled by a small group of people instead of a large team. New technology, especially computers, has also put people out of work; for example, set designers – some sets are now illusions created by computers.

■ **Skill shortages**
A major reason for this could be the decline of the big institutions, such as the BBC. Small independent production companies will not be able to afford the time or staff to train. As a result, quality could decline.

■ **Low pay**
Because of increasingly tight budgets, working patterns in the media could become similar to those traditionally associated with the theatre, i.e. short-term contracts, and long periods of unemployment, resulting in low pay and a poor rate of annual income for most people.

■ **Fewer jobs for people from minority groups**
At present only about 3 per cent of employees in broadcasting are from an ethnic background. There have been initiatives, for instance by the BBC, to increase the number of people from minority groups to reflect British society, but there has been no significant change. The situation looks even bleaker for people with disabilities. The smaller companies which are taking the place of the larger institutions may find it difficult to adapt equipment and provide the facilities or suitable premises, for example for employees in wheelchairs.

Case study: How I entered journalism

Roger Williamson writes:

'At almost 41, I can now look back on nearly 20 years in the trade. Whatever branch of journalism you end up in, new recruits should always remember that the business is essentially one where you live by your wits, skill, imagination, timing and the amount of sweat you feel it's appropriate to put in.

'I used to write for university newspapers – features, classical music reviews, opinionated "think" pieces. You name it, I wrote it.

'After striving to secure a good first degree, I decided to bombard local newspaper offices. I spent two days in the reference library listing papers and editors in all the wonderful places I'd love to work as a reporter – Exeter, Stratford-upon-Avon, Newcastle, Harrogate, Bath. I must have sent off 30 letters and CVs. Not one replied with anything other than a promise to "keep your letter on file".

'Then the penny dropped. What would a born-and-bred Wiganer know about the daily life of a Devon fisherman? I must be a cod, the editor thought, reading my letter. Somewhat crestfallen, I copied the same letter to my local town's evening and weekly papers. Inside three days I had two interviews.

'I bought a new shirt, tie and jacket and turned up to see Michael Taylor, the editor of the *Lancashire Evening Post* in Wigan. I felt I impressed this man who, half-way into my interview, took me round the deserted newsroom. It was 4.30pm and the evening final edition had gone "down to the works". As for the staff, they were heading home. They start prompt at 7.30am, he told me. I gulped. Students never see 7.30am, let alone the hour you'd have to get up to arrive there by public transport.

'Six years there taught me I loved papers, enjoyed reviewing, liked writing, didn't mind telephone interviewing and absolutely loathed knocking on doors asking people about their misfortunes.

'I next took a job as a news editor (number 3 in the chain of command) at a small-circulation, paid-for weekly paper in Leicestershire. The promise of training as a sub-editor was kept, but my fondness for "*Sun*-style" sensational reporting ruffled the owner's feathers too much. I was sacked and simply moved down the road to the nearest largest town, where I more or less performed the same role.

'Three years in small local newspapers gave me enough clout to be employed by *The Birmingham Post.* I had also worked for a few Fleet Street papers on a casual basis, so three years later I decamped to London.

'I became a writer/sub with Teletext, about to take over from Oracle as provider of teletext for ITV and C4 on 1 January 1993. They retrained me for the medium and I have stayed there ever since. At the same time, I go regularly into the national newspapers of an evening to "keep my hand in" with newspapers – which helps raise my standard of living.

'If I had been more ambitious, I would have been very much wealthier than I am. I probably earn what a deputy headmaster in a middle-sized school does – for an average 56-hour week at my desk. The "big-name" royal reporters and star feature writers can earn five times that.'

 Activity

Discuss which of the employment trends described above are reflected in Roger's career.

Methods of training in the media industries

Media work has a glamorous image, and there is a lot of competition for training and jobs. There are several ways to gain entry into the different industries and to become qualified so that your career can progress. Basically, your training may be **pre-entry** (college, school or university courses, work experience or voluntary work) or **in-company**, sometimes called on-the-job (where you receive training and can study for qualifications whilst working).

As a student, you should already be preparing a **portfolio of work** which you can take to interviews, whether for a job or for a higher education course. This should be well presented and contain a few examples of your best work, relating to the area of study or industry you are hoping to join.

Here are some examples of items Skillset considers would be useful evidence in a portfolio:

- audio-taped interviews
- recording of a show you have presented
- showreel of different techniques
- collection of your film/TV reviews
- portfolio of still photos
- short film or video
- scripts for commercials.

You should also include anything else you feel demonstrates a relevant practical skill.

Activity

Make a similar list of items which could be included in the portfolio of someone interested in a career in one of the print and graphics industries.

Pre-entry training

Figure 32.4 is a diagram showing the relative value of the different certificated courses, such as GNVQs, NVQs and GCSEs.

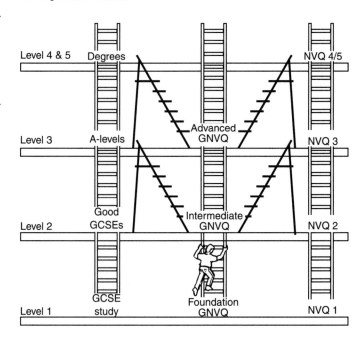

Figure 32.4 Comparing GNVQs and other qualifications

GNVQ – Intermediate and Advanced level

GNVQs are excellent qualifications, which give students an overview of the various media industries. Advisers from the industries have assisted in designing the courses. There is a strong vocational element as well as theoretical depth. Just as a history A-level does not mean you are going to be an archaeologist, or a French A-level mean that you will become an interpreter, neither does the Media GNVQ mean that you will become a camera operator or a journalist. This is a starting point and teaches many practical and organisational skills that are transferable to other vocational areas. Students with an Advanced GNVQ have been very successful in gaining offers of places at university, although most have been conditional on achieving the qualification at merit level.

Work experience

Whilst doing your GNVQ programme you will have had opportunities to work in certain areas. This provides invaluable experience. It will probably have made you realise all the hard work behind the glamorous image of the media.

If you have worked hard, shown initiative, produced quality work, and got on well with other people, you may even be lucky enough to be offered a permanent job with the company you have worked for. Many firms are keen to take on someone they know has fitted in well with their other staff and already knows the organisation.

At interviews, prospective employers are always interested in work experience, particularly if you have volunteered to do it in your spare time, at weekends or in the holidays. Work experience at **hospital radio** is a recognised route into the radio industry, whether you want to be a DJ or work on the technical side. These days there are also opportunities to work on community video projects or on **community cable channels**. Producing the **college magazine** is another form of work experience. **Local newspapers** are often pleased to accept articles written by the public, but don't expect to be paid for them!

Activity

Make a list of organisations or companies where you might be able to find work experience. Note down names and addresses, telephone numbers and contact names.

Other courses

Whilst studying for your main qualifications, you should also consider other courses, which may help show your dedication to a particular area or broaden your skills or knowledge. This could be a short course in animation or one leading to an instrumental qualification, shorthand lessons or tuition in a foreign language.

Degrees and HNDs

A minimum of two A-levels or a GNVQ is usually expected of students applying for an honours degree. Mature students or students with alternative qualifications or work experience may also be accepted. Media degrees and HNDs (Higher National Diplomas) are extremely popular and every year there are more offered by the universities. Some are geared towards technical skills, others towards the sociological side of the media. Most honours degree courses last for three years and HNDs, which tend to be more practical, for two. Of course, if you have completed a Media GNVQ there are other areas you might like to consider, such as graphic design or history, business studies or English. There is no real reason why you have to continue with another media qualification. In fact, this may be the opportunity for you to acquire a depth of knowledge in another area.

To find out what courses appeal to you, you will first need to consult the Universities and Colleges Admissions Service (UCAS) handbook. This gives details of all university and college courses. Your school or college careers adviser should have a copy for you to look at.

If you require more details about a course, you should refer to the university prospectus – your college or local careers adviser may well have copies. Alternatively, you could write to the individual university or pay it a visit. Applications to universities should be made in the autumn of the year before you wish to start. One thing you need to consider when applying for university is finance. Grants are very small these days and, rather than take out a loan, some students apply to university and then defer entry for a year so that they can work in order to save money.

After completing a degree you may still need further professional qualifications. These are listed below.

Journalism

About half the intake of trainees into the newspaper industry are recruited after attending a one-year full-time course at a college accredited by the **National Council for the Training of Journalists (NCTJ)**. The NCTJ is a charity running independent training schemes for print journalists.

All the courses cover not only writing skills, including shorthand, but aspects of law and public affairs necessary for journalists to know, so that they can work effectively, legally, ethically and safely. After completing a full-time journalism course, you will serve a three-month probationary period before entering into a training contract. You will still have to prove your competence before you are given a permanent contract. Competition for courses is keen and to be accepted you should have undertaken work experience with a newspaper.

You can find the list of NCTJ accredited colleges in The Media Guide published by *The Guardian,* or by writing to the NCTJ at Latton Bush Centre, Southern Way, Harlow, Essex CN18 7BL.

Activity

Read the list of desirable attributes (below) given by the Newspaper Society to would-be journalists. Could you demonstrate the following to an editor?

- an interest in current affairs at all levels
- a lively interest in people, places and events
- an ability to write in a style which is easy to understand
- good spelling, grammar and punctuation
- an appreciation of the part a local newspaper plays in the community
- a willingness to accept irregular hours and an ability to work under pressure to meet deadlines
- determination and persistence.

Photojournalism

There is a lot of competition in this area and applicants will be expected to have a strong portfolio showing examples of their photographic work. Courses are for one year.

Periodicals Training Council

This acts as a focus for magazine training. It accredits vocational courses in periodical journalism. A list of their accredited courses can be obtained from the Periodical Publishers Association, 15 Kingsway, London WC2B 6UN.

Printing

If you are interested in a career in printing then you should read the *Guide to Educational Courses in the Printing Industry* published by the **Institute of Printing**, 8 Lonsdale Gardens, Tunbridge Wells, Kent TN1 1NU.

Broadcasting

The best information on the broadcasting and film industries is available from **Skillset**. They identify the different jobs and describe the necessary educational background and skills needed. Anyone considering a job in this area should start here. For example, see Figure 32.5.

Skillset is a small professional organisation, launched in 1992, which is solely concerned with the promotion and development of training within the broadcast, film and video industry.

It is funded and managed by leading bodies, including the BBC, AVFPA, C4, the Federation of Entertainment Unions, ITVA, IVCA and PACT (see page 568 below). They conduct research to find out about employment trends, working practices and training needs. One of their particular concerns is to support training for freelances. A wealth of information about their work is contained in their

Transmission:	Announcers:
Technicians and engineers work to exhibit the production in a high-quality form which can involve projecting images or operating transmission equipment linking electronic signals from the studios to a transmitter.	Announcers work to detailed and carefully timed scripts, communicating information to the viewer from a soundproofed 'behind the scenes' office. They sometimes write or adapt their own material.
Essential skills: High level of technical ability. Self-motivated. Attention to detail. Quick thinking and problem solving.	**Essential skills:** Ability to work independently for long periods. Clear communication. Attention to detail. Calm and 'user friendly' manner.
Useful background: Relevant qualification with practical experience of telecommunications or computers.	**Useful background:** Any general working experience (especially drama or teaching), TV administration.

Figure 32.5 Information on work areas in broadcasting and film (source: Skillset)

careers handbook, which is freely available to schools and colleges.

The **British Kinematograph, Sound and Television Society** (**BKSTS**) validates eleven courses and runs its own training courses. This organisation was founded in 1931 and covers all technical aspects of film, television, sound and other associated industries. It has played a leading role in the development of technical standards. It holds many training courses to update people on the latest technology. A list of accredited courses can be obtained from M6–M14 Victoria House, Vernon Place, London WC1B 4DF.

CSV Media is the largest independent media training agency in the UK. Much of its training is offered to charities, voluntary and community groups or the unemployed. They offer practical courses which take place in radio or TV studios. They claim that 80 per cent of their students subsequently find work in the media.

The **Broadcast Journalism Training Council** (formerly the National Council for the Training of Broadcast Journalists) is a voluntary organisation, representing all sides of the TV and radio industries, which in particular is interested in maintaining high standards. It accredits eight postgraduate courses and seven more are seeking accreditation. A few places are available to non-graduates. A list of accredited courses can be obtained from 188 Lichfield Court, Sheen Road, Richmond, Surrey TW9 1BB.

Radio

The Skillset report for 1993/4 estimated that there were approximately 3800 people in paid employment in radio production and technical jobs. This does not include journalists or marketing and management teams.

The Association of Independent Radio Companies (**AIRC**) keep a large database of courses in radio training. They can be contacted at 46 Westbourne Grove, London W2 5SH.

The Community Radio Association is supported by the European Social Fund and local public agencies and it offers 500 training places annually. The courses are free and take place in community radio stations. Ethnic minority groups are encouraged to take part. Write to 15 Paternoster Row, Sheffield S1 2BX.

The Radio Training Unit, Leicester (**RTU**) gives training for people wishing to enter the industry as well as those who are already employed. It runs a

number of schemes, one of which is a type of apprenticeship which involves a work placement in an ILR or BBC station. Most course members are graduates who have been unemployed for six months or more. It also provides short courses on media techniques such as giving interviews, writing press releases, etc.

Film and video

The National Film and Television School is financed by the European Social Fund. It usually runs two short courses a year for people who have recently entered or are new to the industry. Its address is Station Road, Beaconsfield, Bucks HP9 1LG.

First Film Foundation is a charity set up to help young film-makers. It offers regular one-day courses as well as longer training in scriptwriting and editing, budgeting, scheduling, packaging, etc. Write to 222 Kensal Road, London W10 5BN.

The **National Association for Higher Education in Film and Video** promotes links between industry and educational establishments and can give information on many different courses. It can be contacted at 24 Shelton Street, London WC2H 9HP.

Specialist courses

Manufacturing and facilities companies, such as JVC, Kodak, Sony and Metromedia, all run courses aimed at people who are already technicians and engineers.

In-company training

The advantage of recruiting someone who is not yet trained to be an editor or producer, is that you are probably local, know the area and people, have fresh ideas and can be paid less than someone who is qualified. You can also be trained in the particular house style and working practices of the company. On the other hand it gives you the chance to see if you are going to like the job before you spend a couple of years gaining a professional qualification.

Broadcasting

In broadcasting most entry-level jobs occur in the following areas:

- air-time sales
- administrative and secretarial
- camera, sound or other technical assistant

- runners and gofers
- assistant floor manager.

You may never see these jobs advertised. You are best advised to write directly to companies or make contacts through work experience. If you hope to work in radio, it is not enough simply to send one demo tape and a CV, showing you have a media qualification and have worked in hospital radio, and hope that it will impress a producer sufficiently to offer you a job as DJ. You will have to visit the radio station and meet people. You may have to start off working at reception to get a foot in the door, or offer to work for free (and this may be for months without further progression). However, one day someone may be ill, your twentieth demo tape may show improvement and you may find yourself on air doing the late-night shift!

It is very important now, with the growing trend towards using small producers, that you can show that you have experience and love the job so much that initially you are prepared to work hard for very little financial reward.

National Vocational Qualifications (NVQ) and **Scottish Vocational Qualifications (SVQs)** have been on offer in the media industries since the early 1990s, in both journalism and in broadcasting, and the number will gradually increase. What this means is that people can be assessed at their place of work for the work that they are doing. They have to prove to an experienced assessor that they are competent in a particular area or skill. NVQs have been described as a 'guarantee of competence'.

Many employers in industry are convinced that this is the most appropriate way for people to gain qualifications, particularly in practical areas. Many colleges cannot afford to buy the sophisticated equipment used in the media industries, so it makes more sense for employees to be trained and assessed on the equipment used in their particular company.

The **BBC** has dramatically reduced the number of trainee vacancies over the past few years. These are advertises in the national press or on Ceefax. It publishes a free brochure called *The Way In: Job Opportunities*. This explains what each job entails and the personal qualities and qualifications needed, whether it is for a designer or for an engineering job.

Some **ITV** companies recruit and train people to become multi-skilled operatives, or specialist in certain technical or management areas. These few highly specialised trainee posts are advertised but often TV companies will recruit from colleges in their franchise area.

CAMERA OPERATORS

The camera is the eye of the viewer. Camera operators must know to within very fine limits the capabilities of their equipment. They work closely with producers, translating the images they have in their mind on to the screen. A good camera operator will have creative flair as well as technical skill. You learn by experience, by working with operators as a junior member of the camera team both in the studio and on location. We look for an interest in the visual arts, especially photography, and the ability to work as part of a team. A career progression can be into lighting, vision control and vision mixing.

TRAINING:

The way in: Most operational staff join as trainees and begin by attending a ten-week residential course at Wood Norton, our Training Centre in Worcestershire. There then follows a period of on-the-job training, most of which is practical, reinforced by further training at Wood Norton.

For operational jobs we look for people with a genuine interest in broadcasting and active involvement in areas such as audio recording, hospital radio, photography, film or video making, together with a good general education. However, many of the people who join us do have higher qualifications and openings also appeal to graduates and career changers.

Certain departments use a common system of training which gives trainees hands-on experience in related areas outside their own.

Figure 32.6 Details of a BBC camera operator's job and the training required

---

C4 does not make its own programmes but commissions them from independent organisations. However, it funds training via the *Skillset Freelance Training Fund.* C4 also funds a production scheme every two years called *FourFit,* which is aimed at people from an ethnic background. This two-year training scheme consists of both in-company and college-based instruction.

Other schemes within the independent production sector are:

- **ft2 – Film and Television Freelance Training**
  The 32 places on this scheme are financed by the European Social Fund. Trainees are attached to a variety of productions over two years and are paid a monthly grant. In their second year, they concentrate on a particular area such as camera or make-up.

- **CYFLE**
  This is financed by S4C, the European Social Fund, local TECs and TAC (which promotes the Welsh language in broadcasting) to train people specifically for Welsh Film and Television. Training is offered on a full-time one- or two-year course for six to eight people, who must speak Welsh. Most training is on location. The Scottish Television Companies run a similar scheme for

trainees who speak Gaelic through the **Gaelic Television Training Trust**.

- **Intermedia Film and Video**
  This is a media development agency offering a range of production courses, including NVQs. It works very closely with television and film companies.

- **British Animation Training Scheme**
  This is vocational training for those already working in the industry. Day release is given for training as Assistant Directors.

- **The Radio Training Unit, Leicester (TRU)**
  The RTU has close links with the commercial station, Leicester Sound, and operates a graduate-entry programme where 60 people will be working towards NVQs in Broadcast Journalism and Radio Sales.

Newspapers

You may be recruited into journalism direct from school or university. You are most likely to be accepted on to the editorial team first by a local or small regional newspaper near where you live. The first six months are likely to be a probationary period, while you and the editor decide whether you are suitable and fit in.

Then you should be registered with the NCTJ, which will provide you with a learning pack which forms a foundation course. With the help of your employer,

Audio Visual	Published monthly, covering multimedia communications.
Broadcast	Published weekly for the TV and radio industries, it will keep you informed about current news and views.
Campaign	A weekly trade magazine, in touch with the advertising industry. Essential for anyone thinking of working in commercials or corporate production.
Creative Review	A monthly journal, reflecting the television and commercial business.
Direct	A quarterly newsletter from the Directors Guild of Great Britain for directors in film, TV and theatre industries.
Eyepiece	A bi-monthly, published by the Guild of British Camera Technicians.
IVCA Magazine	A monthly magazine for the non-broadcast production and facilities industry.
Image Technology	A monthly magazine providing information about new technical developments in film and TV.
Media Week	Concerned with the sales and marketing aspects of film and TV and the advertising business.
Moving Pictures Television	Published six times a year on international television news, data and analysis.
The PACT Magazine	Monthly, covering industry news, business and information serving the independent television production sector.
Screen Finance	Published by a *Financial Times* subsidiary. News and analysis of the film industry in the UK and abroad.
Screen International	Weekly news and reviews of the 'top end' of the film and TV trade.
Sight and Sound	Quarterly publication which carries interviews with people involved in film making plus lots of reviews.
Stage, Screen & Radio	The journal for BECTU members, but also available to anyone else on subscription.
Stage & Television Today	A weekly update, particularly for actors but of general interest.
Television	The journal of the Royal Television Society, reports on current developments in TV.
TV Business International	Published monthly on the business of world television.
Televisual	Covers all aspects of production and post-production in all sectors – including commercials, corporate, pop promos and graphics.
TV Production	Written for programme makers in broadcast and non-broadcast television and international (TVP) video.
TV World	Monthly, offering information/analysis on international sales/distributions. Published by EMAP.
UK Press Gazette	Weekly publication covering the media and journalism.
Variety	Weekly news of showbusiness developments with a heavy US bias.
Viewfinder	Three issues a year are published by the British Universities Film and Video Council (BUFVC). Of particular interest to people in higher education and research.
Zerb	Twice-yearly journal from the Guild Television Cameramen.

Figure 32.7 Useful magazines and journals

you will complete the units, the final one of which is a test which will determine whether you can go on to a 12-week period of college-based education and training. After a further period of work experience, you will achieve an **NVQ** at **level 4** or equivalent.

Some newspaper groups have their own training centres where off-the-job training is done. A list of these can be obtained from the NCTJ.

Newspapers recruit a small number of trainee photographers every year and entrants can gain an NVQ or National Certificate in Press Photography after a successful period of work experience.

If you wish to work in the sales team on a newspaper, you may well be accepted straight from school and trained within the company. There is a high turnover of staff in sales and it is possible not only to gain experience in different departments very quickly, but to get promotion if you are keen.

Magazines

The Periodicals Training Council helped set up NVQs in magazine journalism. The Council publishes an annual *Directory of Magazine Training*.

Further information

If you are serious about a career in a media industry, it is important to read about the latest developments and trends in your chosen area. Figure 32.7 shows a list of magazines recommended by Skillset for those who wish to work in the broadcast, film and video industry.

The nature and role of industry organisations

There are three types of organisations associated with employment within the media:

- employers' organisations
- trade unions
- trade associations.

There are times when these organisations might hold different views, on wages, the right to strike or relationships with the government. The aims and emphasis of these organisations may differ, but most are concerned with the following:

- representing the particular interests of members

- the development of the industry, e.g. funding, technology, training
- the forging of links within the industry and outside
- supplying information from databases, statistics and so on about the industry
- marketing the industry, presenting a favourable image for the public or consumers/audience
- giving advice on production methods and rates (cost of products or services)
- discussing terms and conditions of employment, e.g. wages, pensions, hours of employment
- advice on contracts
- developing codes of practice – working and ethical
- providing a united front to lobby both the UK and European Parliaments
- providing an information service to members
- providing legal services for members
- being a forum for debate
- uniting members through social activities
- organising competitions and giving awards for achievements in the industries
- keeping members in contact through magazines or newsletters.

Employers' organisations

These include the following:

- **Producers Alliance for Cinema and Television (PACT)**
  Founded in 1991, this is the trade association and employers' body for feature film and independent TV producers. It represents the film and independent television production sector. It runs an industrial relations service and arranges finance for international co-productions.

- **Advertising Videotape and Film Producers Association (AVFPA)**
  This association represents the interests of producers of commercials.

- **Association of Independent Radio Companies (AIRC)**
  The AIRC promotes the interests of independent radio.

- **The Newspaper Society**
  This is the trade association for publishers of the local press, founded in 1836. It lobbies both UK and EU policy makers on media legislation. It takes an interest in local newspaper training and organises marketing and management courses. It promotes the 'Newspaper in Education' schemes, which link schools and colleges with newspaper

companies. Although it does not accredit courses or training, it produces detailed information published in a booklet called *Making the Decision*.

- **Scottish Daily Newspaper Society**
  Daily newspapers published in Scotland are represented by this society.

- **Scottish Newspaper Publishers Association**
  This represents 68 Scottish publishers.

- **Periodical Publishers Association**
  This is the trade association for magazine publishers, representing 200 companies.

- **British Printing Industries Federation**
  A trade association for employers, this federation represents 3000 companies.

- **National Federation of Retail Newsagents**
  This federation represents the interests of 28 500 retailers.

- **Paper Federation of Great Britain**
  This is the employers' federation for all sectors of the paper industry.

- **Guild of British Animation**
  This represents the interests of the major animation companies.

Trade unions

Trade unions are bodies set up to represent the interests of certain groups of employees. They will negotiate pay and working conditions for the workers they represent. Trade unions are financed by regular contributions paid by their members, based on a percentage of their earnings. This money is used to pay for administration, and the salaries of full-time officials.

Sometimes a worker is required to belong to a union in order to work in a particular company or situation. For example, in order to act in professional theatre or television in the UK, an Equity card issued by the union is needed.

- **Federation of Entertainment Unions**
  This is a collective body representing the interests of 150 000 members in broadcasting and entertainment. It includes all these unions described below: Equity, BECTU, Musicians Union, NUJ, Writers Guild, AEEU, and Film Artistes Association. Where these organisations have common concerns, such as rights of freelances, or minimum wages, it will liaise between the unions and co-ordinate lobbying, publicity, representation and so on.

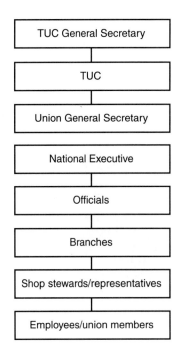

Figure 32.8 Union structure

- **Broadcasting, Entertainment, Cinematograph and Theatre Union**
  The largest trade union in broadcasting, with 55 000 members, BECTU represents non-performing staff and freelances in TV, radio, film, theatre and leisure. It gives employment, financial, legal and training advice. It has a monthly publication called *Stage, Screen and Radio*.

  Members pay 1 per cent of their salary. There is a student link-up scheme for people intending to make a career in any of these industries. Membership provides a range of opportunities to establish contacts within the industries, and gain up-to-date information to help with research projects. Student annual membership is £10.

- **Equity**
  This union is for actors, stage managers, opera singers, dancers, directors, designers, choreographers, variety artists, and performers in theatre, film, television, radio and variety venues. Its membership is approximately 45 000. An Equity card is needed to perform professionally in broadcasting and theatre.

- **Musicians Union**
  This union is responsible for pay and conditions for all musicians, whether classical or pop.

Figure 32.9 Publicity for BECTU

- **Directors Guild of Great Britain**
  The Directors Guild is the union for directors of all media – TV, film, radio and theatre.

- **Writers Guild of Great Britain**
  Representing the writers in film, TV, radio and theatre, this union has negotiated agreements with the BBC, ITV, and with PACT, for budget feature films, single TV movies, TV series and serials.

- **National Union of Journalists**
  The NUJ is the leading trade union representing both staff and freelance journalists and photographers. It also includes journalists who work in the broadcasting industry and has a Book Branch for those working in publishing. It has a membership of 29 000 including 12 800 student journalists. It is well known for its legal services and its campaigns for freedom of information. It publishes a journalists' code of conduct (see page 538) and holds conferences and training sessions.

- **Chartered Institute of Journalists**
  This is a smaller independent trade union, concerned with protecting standards, pay and conditions.

- **Society of Authors**
  The Society of Authors is an independent trade union founded in 1884 to promote the interests of authors and defend their rights. It has over 5500 members.

- **Amalgamated Engineering and Electrical Union**
  This has many members working in newspaper production and broadcasting.

- **Communication Workers Union**
  The CWU is the largest trade union in telecommunications.

- **Graphical, Paper and Media Union**
  This is the print and paper workers' trade union. It covers printing, papermaking, inkmaking, graphic arts, publishing, bookbinding and all allied trades.

Activity

Employment in the media is changing rapidly. Discuss in your group why trade unions could be important in protecting the rights of workers.

Professional and trade associations

These are many and varied. Many have a small, defined membership, others are larger. Some may offer a particular service, whereas others are more of a social club. They may be called associations, societies or guilds.

A few examples are given here:

- **The Royal Television Society**
  This society covers all areas of employment from production to mangement. It organises courses and seminars and is open to anyone interested in television, including students. It now offers student awards.

- **Women in Film and Television**
  This association is intended for professional women with at least three years' experience in the industry.

- **Cable Communications Association**
  At present one of the main aims of the CCA is to raise the profile of cable in the community. It has a free phone line for the public.

- **British Academy of Film and Television Arts**
  Formed in 1946, this association promotes high standards and encourages research and experiment. It organises the BAFTA TV awards.

- **Talking Newspaper Association**
  This is a national subscription service transposing over 900 newspapers and magazines to audio cassettes. It is a registered charity with over 500 local groups helping 150 000 visually impaired people.

- **Edinburgh International Film Festival**
  An international forum attracting prominent speakers, the film festival is held in August during the Edinburgh Festival and there are special opportunities arranged for students.

Activity

The British Film Institute (BFI) and Film Education are two organisations that can help you with your work. Find out where they are located and the type of work they do.

Employment legislation relevant to media industries

Employment legislation should help and protect both employers and employees, so that they can work effectively and safely.

Employment contracts

When you start work, whether full- or part-time, you will receive a written contract of employment. This may include the following information:

- title of the job to be done – e.g. VT editor, broadcast engineer, sales assistant
- date the job starts
- the hours of work
- the annual salary or the rate of pay, and method of payment
- holiday entitlement and special arrangements – there may be certain periods during which you will be expected to work, e.g. Christmas holidays
- period of notice that must be given – this ensures that the employer is not left in the lurch but has time to find a replacement
- details of any pension scheme – deductions can be made for the company pension scheme
- information on trade unions – employees are free to join the union of their choice
- rules of discipline – employees should be aware of the type of conduct that may lead to dismissal and the consequences of breaking rules; for example, operators of printing machinery will be sacked for drinking alcohol during working hours.

For details on health and safety legislation, see the appendix on health and safety. An employee can claim damages if an employer is negligent and fails to provide a safe working environment. At the same time, every employee is responsible for adhering to safe working practices.

If an employee breaks or cancels the contract of employment, then he or she can be dismissed. Behaviour such as dishonesty, violence, disclosing trade secrets, or refusing to obey reasonable orders can lead to dismissal.

Equal opportunities

Equal opportunities legislation such as the Sex Discrimination Act and the Race Relations Act states that jobs should be open to everyone regardless of gender, disabilities, ethnic background, etc. There should be no discrimination in recruitment, conditions of work, training, promotion or dismissal. This area also covers victimisation and sexual harassment at work.

If you think that discrimination has occurred, e.g. if you think someone was promoted from a production assistant to floor manager on the grounds of race or gender rather than their academic qualifications or work experience, then you can take your case to an industrial tribunal or a body such as the Race Relations Board.

As we have already noted, trade unions as well as individuals can negotiate rates of pay and working conditions with employers. If these different parties cannot reach agreement, industrial disputes can be taken before ACAS (the Advisory, Conciliation and Arbitration Service) which mediates between the employers and employees. It also handles cases of sex discrimination and unfair dismissal.

EU legislation

The UK is part of the European Union. The EU has its own legislation, and there are occasions when it overrides that of the UK Parliament.

All signatories to the European Union are bound by the European Social Chapter (1991) which covers basic human rights. Any individual citizen of a member country has a right to appeal to the European courts to adjudicate on matters where they feel that their country's legislation falls short of the European agreement.

The Social Chapter covers such things as:

- civil and political rights
- the right to work
- the right to just and favourable conditions of work
- trade union rights
- the right to social security
- rights relating to the protection of the family
- the right to an adequate standard of living
- the right to health
- the right to an education
- rights relating to culture and science
- the right to protection against discrimination on the grounds of race, colour, sex, language or religion.

However, the British government has elected to withdraw from the requirements of the EU Social Chapter, because it believes that the application of its employment rights would impose excessive costs upon British industry. The Conservative government has rejected the idea of a minimum wage, believing that this will lead to inflexibility and make the cost of manufactured products and services uncompetitive outside the European Union. The government claims that France and Germany have already found that the cost of their social welfare programmes is placing an excessive burden on resources and these countries are engaged in the process of cutting back on the privileges enjoyed by their populations. See also the section on the EU in the Legal and Ethical appendix.

Activity

Debate with members of your group whether it would benefit the media industries to have rules on minimum wages.

Applying for a job

If you are studying this unit towards the end of your two-year course, then you will have begun to think about your future career. Are you going to go on to higher education? Are you going to apply for a job? Whichever path you are considering, it is important that you prepare a good CV (curriculum vitae). This will help you to consider the extent and quality of your qualifications, and other factors which make

you suitable for further training or employment. You will also need practice in filling in application forms and letters of application.

Your CV should certainly be word processed. There are three good reasons for this:

- it will look well presented
- it can be updated regularly
- it can be adapted to suit different applications.

Some employers ask you to complete an application form. You will find these forms easier to complete if you have the information already compiled. Photocopy the form and fill in the copy as a practice run.

A video by Jumpcut (called *Talking Jobs*) shows how five candidates cope in an interview for a job with Yorkshire Television. Figure 32.10 shows a job specification for a communications operator, and an advertisement for the same job.

What should you put in a CV? Figure 32.11 gives you a checklist of headings and ideas of what you should include for each.

Job Specification

REGIONAL PROGRAMMES – COMMUNICATIONS OPERATOR

Reporting to:- Terry Mounsey   Production Manager Local Programmes

Purpose of the Job
The job holder is responsible for transporting goods and equipment, and for playing back recorded or live material from location to base.

Main Duties
1. Driving the transit van links vehicle, rigging and setting up radio links to transmit recorded material or live inserts into Local Programmes.
2. Playing-out tapes from regional offices to base.
3. The collection and delivery, by vehicle, of news video tapes.
4. To deliver spares and equipment to news crews in the field.
5. General driving duties involving the Volvo hatchback and transit van links vehicles.
6. Cleaning and routine maintenance of vehicles.

General Comments
Bearing in mind the nature of the Local Programmes news operation, the job holder needs to use initiative whilst maintaining a disciplined approach to the duties involved.

Job Advert

COMMUNICATIONS OPERATOR

YORKSHIRE TELEVISION – LOCAL PROGRAMMES

An interesting and varied opportunity has arisen, within our expanding Local Programmes News and Features area, for an experienced driver to work as a Communications Operator.

This programme area produces 400 hours of programme material for transmission in the Yorkshire region. The department is based in a purpose-built news centre adjacent to the Yorkshire Television Studio Centre.

The job involves driving cars and a transit van links vehicle throughout the region to deliver materials and set up microwave links to relay live and recorded news items back to the studios. Close liaison is maintained with the News Crews.

Deadlines form an important part of this role and as a result we are seeking a conscientious and bright person who is capable of taking decisions in potentially difficult circumstances.

The ability to use initiative is more important than academic qualifications.

A knowledge of the Yorkshire region would be an advantage. A clean driving licence and good colour vision are essential. Full training will be given in the use of all relevant technical equipment.

Figure 32.10 Job specification and advert

Curriculum Vitae

1	Name	Type your full name in capital letters.

2	Address	Type your full address, including the postal code.

3	Date of birth	Day, Month, Year – e.g. 18.10.78.

4 Education

You need enter only your last secondary school and further education: e.g.

John Cleveland College, Wolverton	92–94
North Warwickshire College, Stratford	94–96

5 Qualifications

Type all the qualifications gained, the grade and the year it was achieved: e.g.

GCSE	Mathematics	B	1994
	English	C	1994
	History	C	1994
BTEC GNVQ in Media		Distinction	1996

6 Work Experience

List all your work placements in date order. Give the employers' names, dates you worked, and brief description of work you were involved with: e.g.

1) *Wolverton Times* – 1 week 1994 work experience in the photographic department.
2) Castlemead Hospital Radio in summer holidays 1995, DJ.
3) *Stratford Mercury* – February 1996 – sales project.
4) Part-time employment – Haynes Newsagent June 1996 – shop assistant.

7 Residential Experience

List all the residentials attended and give BRIEF details of the purpose of each: e.g. visit to Prague 1995. Institutions visited – *Morning Post* newspaper, Praha Radio, Czech Television.

8 Interests and Hobbies

Employers are interested in your experience outside college. List any activities which will show what type of person you are: e.g. member of local theatre group, working backstage for 4 years.
Swimming
Watching films
Supporter of Wolverton Rugby Club
Remember that you will probably be questioned on these activities in an interview!

9 References

Always give the names and addresses of 2 referees. These should be people who have known you recently and should include someone who can comment on your achievements during your most recent course. The second referee may know you as a family friend or as an employee.
Type the names and addresses in 2 columns: e.g.

Ms S. Warr	Mr T. Haynes
BTEC Course Tutor	Haynes Newsagents
North Warwickshire College	High Street
	Wolverton

Figure 32.11 What to include in a CV

Activity

Compile your own CV. Discuss with your tutor what are your best qualities, for instance punctuality, meeting deadlines, creativity, completing tasks exactly as required, etc. Identify what it is about you that indicates you are suitable for the jobs which interest you.

You may decide to apply for a job after finishing this course. Some advertisers expect you to send in a letter of application (an example of which is given, opposite in Figure 32.12). Others may give only a telephone number, and ringing up to enquire about how to apply can involve you in the first stage of the selection procedure – this may well be an initial interview! So have the advertisement, a paper and pen and your CV near at hand.

Activity

Choose an advertisement from *The Guardian* and write a letter applying for the job.

Interviews

If you are luckily enough to get an interview, here are some points you should remember:

- confirm your acceptance of the interview appointment
- research the organisation and its products or services
- anticipate the type of questions you will be asked and prepare some answers – memorise key points (not whole speeches) about your background, hobbies, personal qualities and so on.
- find out exactly where the interview is, how to get there and how long it will take you
- dress appropriately for the occasion – neatly, tidily and with clean shoes!
- answer questions as fully as possible – don't just say yes or no
- appear committed to the job or organisation
- don't be embarrassed to point out good things about yourself, such as common sense, good communication skills, energy, attention to detail, curiosity, not afraid of getting your hands dirty, sensitivity, practicality, punctuality, etc.
- listen carefully to the questions and make sure you fully understand them before answering
- ask questions yourself – this shows that you have

```
                                    14 Beechwood Avenue
                                    Burbage
                                    BE10 1HQ
                                    2 November 1996

Mr B Brown
Bold Quality Printers
Burbage Industrial Estate
Burbage

Dear Mr Brown

Re vacancy for a trainee printer

I am replying to your advertisement in the
Burbage Times for a trainee printer.

I shall be leaving college in three weeks' time
after completing my Advanced GNVQ in Media:
Production and Communication. I should very
much like to work for your firm and receive
training in the printing business.

Whilst at college, I have worked on a major
project with the Charlton Mercury, designing
advertisements for a special supplement, and I
have helped produce the college magazine. I
have also enjoyed my work experience at Goldby
Printers in Nuneaton, where I assisted at
various stages of the print process.

During my vacations I have had a part-time job
working in the local newsagents.

I enjoy using computers and have used them to
design posters to publicise my friends' band. I
like meeting people and learning new practical
skills.

I am attracted to your company because it
produces a variety of quality publications. I
enjoy working hard and am sure that I could
benefit from your training and become an
effective and reliable member of your staff.

I look forward to hearing from you.

Yours sincerely

A.N. Buckley

A.N. Buckley
```

Figure 32.12 A letter of application

thought about the job and also gives you the opportunity to find out if you really want to work in the organisation
- act naturally – it is natural for you to be a little nervous! Take deep breaths to help yourself feel calm

575

- remember to be polite. Thank the person who shows you into the room. Say 'Good morning' (or 'Hello', if that is what they say to you) to the interviewer. Thank him or her at the end for seeing you.

Activity

Interview two people, one who works in publishing or in the printing industry and one who works in television, film or radio. Ask them to describe their position within the organisations, their responsibilities and what they enjoy about their jobs. Find out how they got their jobs.

Evidence assignment

In a group, design a series of wall posters showing the job titles of people employed in the media industries. The posters should describe their main functions and positions within the organisation.

Separate posters should identify and comment on how legislation, e.g. health and safety and equal opportunities legislation, has affected employment.

Using information from interviews and photographs taken on your work experience and industrial visits, write a case study for one media industry noting recent changes in employment patterns and the reasons for this. Describe training methods used for different jobs. Include a review of the nature and the role of relevant industry organisations

Investigating Media Industries: Unit Test

The following are the names of daily and Sunday newspapers. Use them to answer questions 1–3.

    a *The People*
    b *The Sun*
    c *The Financial Times*
    d *The Observer*

1 Identify which newspaper is owned by News International.

2 Which is owned by The Guardian Media Group?

3 Which is owned by the Mirror Group?

4 Which company owns the Daily Star?
    a Mirror Group
    b News International
    c United News and Media
    d Pearson

5 Another name for a broadsheet newspaper is:
    a quality
    b popular
    c mid-range
    d red banner

Below is a list of magazine titles. Use them to answer questions 6–8.

    a *Marie Claire*
    b *Smash Hits*
    c *Radio Times*
    d *Good Housekeeping*

6 Which magazine is owned by Emap?

7 Which magazine is owned by National Magazine Company?

8 Which magazine is owned by IPC?

9 Decide whether the following statements are true or false.
    i *New Musical Express* is produced by IPC
    ii IPC is part of Emap

    a i is true and   **ii** is true
    b i is true and   **ii** is false
    c i is false and   **ii** is true
    d i is false and   **ii** is false

10 The name of the publishing company that Picador is part of is:
    a Heinemann
    b Macmillan
    c Reed
    d Penguin

The following are the names of BBC national radio stations. Use them to answer questions 11–13.

    a Radio 2
    b Radio 3
    c Radio 4
    d Radio 5

11 Which station concentrates on sport and current affairs?

12 Which station is famous for drama?

13 Which station plays classical music?

14 Decide whether these statements are true or false.

    i Atlantic 252 broadcasts from Southern Ireland
    ii Atlantic does not need a British government licence to broadcast

    a i is true and   **ii** is true
    b i is true and   **ii** is false
    c i is false and   **ii** is true
    d i is false and   **ii** is false

The following is a selection of the names of independent local radio stations. Use them to answer questions 15–17.

   a Viking FM
   b Sunrise FM
   c Northants Supergold
   d Kiss 100FM

15 Which station is controlled by the Chiltern Radio network?

16 Which station belongs to Emap Radio?

17 Which station is part of the Metro Radio Group?

18 Which of these record companies is classed as 'Indie'?
   a EMI
   b CBS
   c XL
   d BMG

19 Which of these TV stations is a combination of public service and commercial broadcasting?
   a BBC2
   b C4
   c BSkyB
   d Cable

20 Decide whether these statements are true or false.

   i   MSO stands for Multiple Systems Operator
   ii TeleWest is an example of an MSO

   a i is true and   ii is true
   b i is true and   ii is false
   c i is false and   ii is true
   d i is false and   ii is false

21 Decide whether these statements are true or false.

   i   The American film industry is the largest in the world
   ii The UK makes fewer films than France, Germany or Italy

   a i is true and   ii is true
   b i is true and   ii is false
   c i is false and   ii is true
   d i is false and   ii is false

22 A film production company merges with the companies involved with the distribution and exhibition of the films it makes. What business term would most precisely describe this ownership pattern?
   a monopoly
   b take-over
   c horizontal integration
   d vertical integration

23 Which of these statements best describes the role of the BFI?

   a advises government on what films and TV programmes should be shown in public
   b produces information and educational publications on the film and TV industry and is also involved with film production
   c is an international commercial film production company
   d acts as a pressure group for the international film industry

24 Under which law could you be charged if you were accused of libel?
   a defamation
   b slander
   c contempt of court
   d the Public Order Acts

25 The owner of a musical composition is protected under:
   a the law of confidence
   b the Freedom of Information Act
   c copyright law
   d the Data Protection Act

26 Which technology is an essential component of multi-media publishing?
   a CD-ROM
   b RDS
   c e-mail
   d ISDN

27 Which of the following is the new broadcast-quality CD-ROM?
   a DAB
   b WEB
   c DVD
   d AVID

28 Which of the following is classed as a pre-entry vocational qualification?
  a NVQ
  b SVQ
  c GCSE
  d GNVQ

29 Who is responsible for health and safety in a studio production?
  a the producer
  b the floor manager
  c the director
  d the security officer

30 Which would be the most likely union for a camera operator to join?
  a BECTU
  b Equity
  c NUJ
  d CWU

Appendix: Media Organisations

Newspaper organisations

- **News International**
  This company, run by the Australian Rupert Murdoch, owns:

  The Sun (founded 1912)
  The Times (founded 1785)
  The News of the World (founded 1843)
  The Sunday Times (founded 1843)

- **Mirror Group**
  This company owns:

  The Daily Mirror (founded 1903)
  The Sunday Mirror (founded 1915)
  The Daily Record (founded 1847)
  The People (founded 1881)

  It also has a large number of shares in
  The Independent and *The Independent on Sunday*.

- **United News and Media/MAI**
  This company owns:

  The Daily Express (founded 1900)
  The Sunday Express (founded 1918)
  The Daily Star (founded 1978)

  It also owns 80 local newspapers.

- **Daily Mail and General Trust**
  This company owns:

  The Daily Mail (founded 1896)
  The Mail on Sunday (founded 1982)

  This trust also controls the Northcliffe Newspapers Group which owns many regional newspapers.

- **The Telegraph**
  This company, controlled by the Canadian Conrad Black, owns:

  The Daily Telegraph (founded 1855)
  The Sunday Telegraph (founded 1961)

- **Guardian Media Group**
  This company owns:

  The Guardian (founded 1821)
  The Observer (founded 1791)

- **Pearson**
  This company owns :

  The Financial Times (founded 1888)

Magazine publishers

- **Reed-Elsevier**
  This is one of the world's biggest publishing companies, formed in January 1993, when the British company Reed and the Dutch group Elsevier combined.

  The main British subsidiaries are:

1 **IPC Magazines**
  This is the UK's largest publisher of consumer and leisure magazines.

  Weekly titles include:

New Musical Express (NME)	*TV Times*
Woman	*Woman's Realm*
Horse and Hound	*Country Life*
New Scientist	*Woman's Own*
Amateur Photographer	*Melody Maker*

  Monthly titles include:

Family Circle	*Ideal Home*
Marie Claire	*Soccer Stars*
Classic Cars	*Options*

2 **Reed Business Publishing**
  This is the largest business publisher in Britain with such titles as:

Caterer & Hotel Keeper	*Computer Weekly*
Optician	*Media International*
Poultry World	*Television*

3 **Elsevier Science Publishers**
  This company publishes more than 400 academic, industrial and scientific journals. Titles include:

  Advances in Engineering Software
  Applied Acoustics
  Ceramics International
  Environmental Pollution
  Epilepsy Research
  Food Research International
  Ocean and Coastal Management

- **Emap**
  This company is the biggest rival to Reed-Elsevier
  There are two magazine divisions:

1 **Emap Business Communications**

   This publishes about 100 titles on architecture, communications, business, computing, fashion, transport, trade and retail, and finance.

2 **Emap Consumer Magazines**

   This division publishes about 90 titles, covering both specialist and general-interest magazines, which can be found on newsagents' shelves. Its magazines cover a wide variety of topics: bikes, cars, computer games, gardens, cameras, health, parenting, music, entertainment, retirement, sport, wildlife and women's interests. Some of its well-known magazines are:

Elle	*Angling Times*
Horse and Pony	*Mother and Baby*
Smash Hits	*More*
Garden News	*Q*
Just 17	*Motor Cycle News*
Practical Gardening	*Practical Photography*

- **United News and Media**
  This company owns about 120 magazines in Britain and 150 abroad. Its subsidiary companies are:

1 **Benn Business Publishing**
   This specialises in business, trade and professional magazines, with over 70 titles, including:

Music Business	*Timber Trades Journal*
DIY Week	*Leather*
Studio Sound	*Video Retailer*

2 **Miller Freeman**
   This has 100 business, technical, trade, construction and farming magazines including:

Building Design	*Farming News*
The Engineer	

- **BBC Worldwide Publishing**
  This owns BBC Magazines and includes many popular titles based around its television programmes. These include:

Gardeners' World	*Wildlife*
Clothes Show	*Good Food*
Homes and Antiques	*BBC Music Magazine*

  Its best-selling publication is the *Radio Times*.

- **National Magazine Company**
  Although American owned, this company publishes many titles popular in Britain including:

Country Living	*Good Housekeeping*
Cosmopolitan	*Esquire*
Harper's and Queen	*She*

- **Condé Nast Publications**
  This is another well-known American-owned publisher of lifestyle magazines. Its titles include:

Brides	*House and Garden*
Vanity Fair	*Tatler*
Vogue	

- **HMSO (Her Majesty's Stationery Office)**
  This publishes official magazines and reports including:

Economic Trends	*Hansard (Parliamentary reports)*
London Gazette	*Monthly Digest of Statistics*

- **Future Publishing**
  This company is now owned by Pearson. It was one of the first magazines in this country to give away free CDs and computer disks with its magazines. Titles include:

Sega Power	*Classic CD*

- **DC Thomson and Co.**
  This publishes some well-established titles dating back many decades such as:

My Weekly	*Bunty*
Beano	*Dandy*
People's Friend	

- **Argus Press**
  This is an example of a company which publishes both trade (approximately 90) and consumer publications (approximately 30), targeting groups or organisations with particular interests. For example:

Aeromodeller	*Fish Trader*
Model Railways	*Woodworker*

Below are three examples of publishers who concentrate on one particular field:

- **Cambridge University Press**
  This publishes over 120 academic journals.

- **Paul Raymond Publications**
  This is the biggest publisher of sex magazines in the UK. Titles include:

  Mayfair
  Razzle
  Men Only

- **Saga Publishing**
  This specialises in magazines for the retired.

The following two companies have very few publications but their titles are very well known:

- **Consumers Association**
  This company publishes five magazines, all concerned with consumer interests, including *Which?*

- **John Brown Publishing**
  This publisher produces:

  Classic FM – The Magazine
  Viz.

Book publishers

This list includes examples of some well-known and established companies. There are many more publishers!

- **Usborne Publishing**
  Founded in 1973, the managing director is Peter Usborne.

  Estimated annual turnover: approximately £14 million.

  They publish about 100 titles a year: non-fiction and fiction, puzzle books, educational books and music for children. A few titles are for parents.

- **Reader's Digest Association**
  Annual turnover: approximately £160 million.

  They publish about 10 titles a year. These include: *Family Medical Adviser, The Gardening Year, New DIY Manual, The Repair Manual.* They market their books strongly through mail-shots to selected houses.

- **HarperCollins Publishers Ltd**
  Owned by: News International Corporation.

  Annual turnover: approximately £200 million.

  They publish about 2200 titles. These are some of the names or **imprints** that authors are published under:

  - Crime Club, Eclipse, Flamingo (literary fiction)
  - HarperCollins Paperbacks, Harvill, Tolkien (science fiction and fantasy)
  - Thorsons, Aquarian Press, Pandora Press (health, popular psychology, feminism, yoga, mythology etc.)
  - Picture Lions, HarperCollins Audio, Jets, Young Lions, Lions, Armada, Tracks, Collins Non-fiction (children's)
  - Access Press, Birnbaum, HarperCollins Publishers, Collins, Collins English Library, CollinsGem (reference books, dictionaries, phrase books, travel, art, cookery etc.)
  - Collins Education (educational)
  - HarperCollins College (English editions of US academic imports)
  - HarperCollins, Fount, Marshall Pickering (religious books, bibles, prayer books, hymn books)
  - Bartholomew, Collins Longman, Nicholson, Times Atlases, Times Books, Invincible Press, HarperCollins Audiobooks (maps and guides)

Famous authors include: Jeffrey Archer, James Herbert, Fay Weldon and Len Deighton.

The company is intending to expand further into multimedia publishing; a newly formed division, Advanced Media, has electronic publishing rights. They have also established a broadcasting consultancy department to exploit TV and film rights across the company.

- **Macmillan Publishers Ltd**
  Founded in 1843.

  In 1986, they bought Sidgwick & Jackson.

  In 1987, they bought Pan Books.

  In 1995, they sold 65 per cent of their company to Holtzbrinck, one of Germany's biggest publishing groups.

  Estimated annual turnover for UK: approximately £100 million.

  This is the largest British privately owned publishing house.

  They publish about 1500 titles a year.

  There are five divisions:

  1 Macmillan Press Ltd – for medical and scientific journals, academic, professional textbooks, reference works.
  2 Macmillan Education – textbooks for schools and for the international education market.
  3 Macmillan General Books – non-fiction (Pan, Papermac, Macmillan, Sidgwick & Jackson) covering most subjects, such as biographies, history, hobbies, drama, travel, politics.
     - fiction (Macmillan, Pan) by authors such as Shirley Conran, Dick Francis, James Herriot, Lynda La Plante and Wilbur Smith.
  4 Picador – more serious literary works in fiction and non-fiction by international authors is such as Ian McEwan, Tom Wolfe, John Fowles, Umberto Eco and Edmund White.

5 Macmillan Children's Books – fiction and non-fiction, picture books and novelty books.

■ **Reed-Elsevier**
Principal subsidiaries include:

1 Reed Consumer Books

This includes the following imprints:

- William Heinemann (hardback): fiction and non-fiction. Authors include Robert James Waller, Clare Francis, Stephen Fry
- Secker & Warburg: literary fiction and non-fiction, hardback
- Minerva literary fiction and non-fiction, paperback
- Methuen: plays, drama, humour, fiction, music. Writers range from Brecht to Sue Townsend
- Mandarin: paperback fiction and non-fiction
- Sinclair-Stevenson: fiction and non-fiction. Authors include Susan Hill and Ralph Fiennes
- Hamlyn: well-illustrated popular non-fiction books on cookery, fashion e.g. *Larousse Gastronomique*
- Mitchell Beazley: illustrated encyclopaedias and quality books, e.g. *The New Joy of Sex, Miller's Antiques Price Guide*
- Osprey: military, aviation, car and natural history books
- George Philip: atlases, maps, astronomy books e.g. *Philips' Road Atlas of Great Britain*
- Conran Octopus: quality illustrated lifestyle books on gardening, cookery, etc.
- Pitkin Pictorials: souvenir guides e.g. *Cathedral Guides, The Queen and her Family*
- Heinemann Young Books: children's fiction e.g. *Thomas the Tank Engine, Animals of Farthing Wood*
- Mammoth Paperbacks : children's fiction e.g. *Winnie the Pooh*
- Methuen Children's Books: quality picture books and fiction for babies to early teens
- Brimax Books: mass-market picture books for children e.g. *Teddy Bear's Counting Book, Teddy Bear Tells the Time*
- Hamlyn Children's Books: illustrated non-fiction and reference books for children e.g. *The Animal Encyclopedia*.

2 Butterworth & Co. (Publishers) Ltd: books, some loose-leaf, on law, tax, accountancy, e.g. Halsbury's Laws of England, Butterworth's Business Tax Service.

3 Reed Educational & Professional Publishing

This includes:

- Butterworth-Heinemann: technical, medical and business books and journals
- Heinemann Educational: textbooks, literature and educational resources for schools and further education colleges
- Heinemann English Language Teaching: teaching books and materials
- Ginn: textbooks and other resources for primary schools.

4 Reed Business Information

Industrial and commercial reference books such as *Kelly's, Kompass.*

Financial books, such as *The Banker's Almanac.*

Media books, such as *Willings Press Guide, Kemp's Film, TV and Video Yearbook.*

Professional and careers books, such as *Directory of Directors, Who, Graduate Opportunities.*

Leisure books, such as *Historic Houses, Castles and Gardens.*

International reference books, such as *USA Industrial Directory.*

First Marketing Company – a newsletter publishing service.

Electronic publishing – including Reedbase On-line, Reedbase CD, Reed Business Journal Database – is an important part of Reed-Elsevier's business.

Independent Local Radio (ILR) organisations

This list includes the main owners of local radio stations:

■ **Capital Radio**
This owns:

BRMB-FM	Southern FM
Capital Gold	Capital FM
Invicta FM	Invicta Supergold
Ocean FM	Power FM

■ **Chiltern Radio Network**
This owns:

Chiltern	Chiltern Supergold
Galaxy	Horizon
Northants	Northants Supergold
Severn Sound	Severn Sound Supergold

- **Emap Radio** has a 51 per cent shareholding in Transworld Communications, so effectively owns:

Kiss 100FM	Key 103FM
Picadilly Gold	Radio Aire FM
Magic 828 AM	Red Dragon FM
Touch AM	Red Rose
City FM	

- **GWR Group**
  This owns:

Beacon	Brunel Classic Gold
CN FM	Gem AM
GWR FM	Hereward
Isle of Wight	KL FM
Leicester Sound	Mercia FM/Classic Gold
Ram FM	Trent FM
2CR FM/Classic Gold	210 FM/Classic Gold
Beacon/WABC	

- **Metro Radio Group**
  This owns:

Hallam FM	Great North
Great Yorkshire	Metro FM
The Pulse	TFM
Viking FM	

- **Scottish Radio Holdings**
  This owns:

Clyde 1 FM/2	Forth RFM
Max AM	Tay
Northsound Borders	

- **Sunrise Radio Group**
  This owns:

Sunrise	Sunrise East Midlands
Sunrise FM	

- **Transworld Communications**
  This organisation owns:

Aire FM	Magic 828
Touch FM	

ITV (Channel 3) regional companies

1 **Anglian Television Ltd**
   Covers East Anglia and the East Midlands.
   Owned by MAI.

   Network programmes include:

   The Chief
   Knightmare
   Survival.

2 **Border Television plc**
   Covers the Scottish Borders, the Lake District and the Isle of Man.

   Owned by Border Television, largest shareholder Cumbrian Newspapers group (18 per cent).

   Network programmes include:

   Innovators
   Union and the League.

3 **Carlton Broadcasting Ltd**
   Covers the London area during weekdays.

   Owned by Carlton Communications.

   Network programmes include:

   99–1
   Class Act
   Frank Stubbs
   The Good Sex Guide
   The Hypnotic World of Paul McKenna
   The Brit Awards
   Talking Telephone Numbers.

4 **Central Broadcasting Ltd**
   Covers the Midlands.

   Owned by Carlton Communications.

   Network programmes include:

   Outside Edge
   Peak Practice
   Sharpe
   Soldier, Soldier
   Cadfael
   Celebrity Squares
   The Cook Report
   Spitting Image.

5 **Channel Television Ltd**
   Covers the Channel Islands.

   Owned by Channel Islands Communications (TV), largest shareholders are Bois Trustees (8.9 per cent) and 3i Capital (8.5 per cent).

   Network programmes include:

   Channel Report
   Him .. and Other Animals
   Murder in the Family

6 **Grampian Television plc**
   Covers North and North-east Scotland.

   Owned by Grampian Television, largest shareholder Abtrust Scotland Investment Co. (7.8 per cent).

Network programmes include:

We the Jury
Country Matters
Crossfire
Top Club
The Way it Was.

7 **Granada Television Ltd**
Covers North-west England.

Owned by Granada Group, largest shareholder is SG Warburg Group (16.4 per cent).

Network programmes include:

Coronation Street
Cracker
Prime Suspect
World in Action
You've been Framed
Animal Crazy
The Memoirs of Sherlock Holmes
Stars in their Eyes
Surgical Spirit.

8 **HTV Group plc**
Covers Wales, Avon, Gloucestershire and Somerset.

Owned by HTV Group, largest shareholder Flextech (19.9 per cent).

Network programmes include:

Grass Roots
A Slice of Life
Wales and Westminster
Countrywatch
Garden Club
Wycliffe
You're the Boss.

9 **London Weekend Television (Holdings) plc**
LWT covers the London area at the weekends.

Owned by Granada Group.

Network programmes include:

London's Burning
The South Bank Show
You Bet!
Barrymore
Beadle's About
Blind Date
The Knock.

10 **Meridian Broadcasting Ltd**
Covers South and South-east England.

Owned by MAI (61 per cent), Carlton Communications (20 per cent) and SelecTV (15 per cent).

Network programmes include:

Doing it up
Loud and Clear
Serve you Right
Seven Days
Ruth Rendell series
ZZZAP!

11 **Scottish Television plc**
Covers Central Scotland and South-west Highlands.

Owned by Scottish Television, largest shareholder Mirror Group Newspapers (19.9 per cent).

Network programmes include:

Doctor Finlay
Taggart
Take the High Road
Wheel of Fortune
Kirsty
Scotland Today
Win, Lose or Draw.

12 **Tyne Tees Television Ltd**
Covers North-east England and North Yorkshire.

Owned by Yorkshire Tyne Tees Television Holdings.

Network programmes include:

The Cinder Path
The Dwelling Place
Cross Wits
Firm Friends
Gimme 5
The Dales Diary
Earth Movers.

13 **Ulster Television plc**
Covers Northern Ireland.

Owned by Ulster Television.

Network programmes include:

The Chieftains and Guests
High Days and Holidays
Kelly
Sailortown.

14 **Westcountry Television Ltd**
Covers Cornwall and Devon.

Owned by Westcountry Television, main shareholders are Associated Newspapers

(19.42 per cent), South West Water (22.56 per cent) and Brittany Ferries (16.92 per cent).

Network programmes include:

Brief Encounters
Commando
Roadrunner
Cobblestones, Cottages and Castles
My Story.

15 Yorkshire Television Ltd

Covers Yorkshire, Humberside, Derbyshire, Nottinghamshire and Lincolnshire.

Owned by Yorkshire-Tyne Tees Television, largest shareholders are Granada Group (14.2 per cent) and Pearson plc (14 per cent).

Network programmes include:

Bad Influence
Circle of Deceit
Emmerdale
Heartbeat
A Touch of Frost
Countdown
The Darling Buds of May
Jimmy's
Through the Keyhole
Whicker's World.

16 GMTV Ltd

Produces the ITV network breakfast-time service from 6.00 to 9.25 am every weekday.

Owned by Walt Disney (25 per cent), the Granada Group (20 per cent), Scottish TV (20 per cent), Carlton Communications (20 per cent) and the Guardian Media Group (15 per cent).

Appendix: Health and Safety

Introduction

Health and safety affects everyone. At work it is the responsibility of both the employer and the employee to maintain a healthy, safe and effective working environment. This also includes preventing the spread of illness, and so cleanliness and good personal hygiene are vital.

 Activity

When was the last time you:

- had an accident at work or college e.g. fell over, bumped into something or dropped something?
- lost work or property?

Why do you think it happened, and was there anything you could have done to prevent it?

Accidents are usually the result of someone being careless or making a mistake. The main reasons are:

- complacency – becoming over-confident
- distraction – day-dreaming, interruptions
- hurry – not allowing yourself enough time
- unfamiliarity – not knowing how to use equipment properly.

Did any of these play a part in what happened to you or your belongings?

Good organisations take health and safety (and risk assessment – see below) seriously. It is not only legally and morally correct, but also makes good economic sense. If a workplace is unsafe the company can be closed down, or the employer can be sued if someone is injured. Generally speaking, workers will be more productive, have less time off sick and have more respect for their organisation if they feel that the organisation has respect for them and shows concern for their well-being.

The purpose of health and safety policies is to minimise all accident and dangers to health. Policies must include the public as well as employers and employees.

Health and Safety at Work Act 1974

In order to protect the workforce, health and safety is enshrined in law. The main Act of Parliament is the Health and Safety at Work Act 1974. This means that your health, safety and welfare at work are protected by law. Your employer has a duty to protect you and to keep you informed about health and safety. But also you have a legal responsibility to look after yourself and others. If you find a problem, discuss it with your employer or your safety representative, if there is one.

Section 6 of the 1974 Act also places a duty on manufacturers, designers, suppliers and importers of articles for use at work to ensure, as far as is reasonably practicable, that the article is designed and constructed so as to be safe and without risks to health.

Employer's responsibilities

Under Section 2 of the Act the employer has certain responsibilities, such as:

- making the workplace safe and minimising risks to health
- keeping dust, fumes and noise under control
- ensuring plant and machinery are safe and that safe systems of work are established and followed by all employees
- ensuring articles and substances are moved, stored and used safely
- providing adequate welfare facilities
- giving employees the information, instruction, training and supervision necessary for health and safety.

The employer must also:

- draw up a health and safety policy statement if there are five or more employees, including the health and safety requirements and arrangements in force, and bring it to employees' attention
- provide free and protective clothing and equipment, as specifically required by health and safety law
- report certain injuries, diseases and dangerous occurrences to the enforcing authority

- provide adequate first-aid facilities
- consult a safety representative, if one is appointed by a recognised trade union, about matters affecting health and safety
- set up a safety committee if asked in writing to do so by two or more safety representatives
- take precautions against fire, and provide adequate means of escape and means for fighting fire.

In many workplaces employers may have specific duties such as to:

- maintain a workroom temperature of at least 16°C after the first hour of work where employees do most of their work sitting down
- keep the workplace clean
- provide, maintain and keep clean washing and toilet facilities, and accommodation for clothing, and supply drinking water
- see that workrooms are not overcrowded and that they are well ventilated and lit
- ensure that floors, steps, stairs, ladders, passages and gangways are well constructed and maintained and not obstructed
- take special precautions before allowing employees to enter and work in a confined space
- ensure that employees do not have to lift, carry or move any load so heavy that it is likely to injure them
- guard all dangerous parts of machines
- see that employees, especially young people, are properly trained or under supervision before using dangerous machines
- give employees suitable eye protection or protective equipment for certain jobs
- take proper precautions to prevent employees being exposed to substances which may damage their health
- take precautions against danger from electrical equipment and radiation.

The Management of Health and Safety at Work Regulations 1992 amended the 1974 Act. They include requirements for employers to:

- assess risks
- make arrangements for effective planning, organisation, control, monitoring and review of preventive and protective measures
- appoint competent people to assist the employer in complying with health and safety law
- co-operate and co-ordinate health and safety where the activities of different employers interact
- provide appropriate health surveillance, information and training.

Supplementary Regulations

Health and safety at work is also monitored by Regulations which are published as a supplement to the major legislation. We have mentioned above the Management of Health and Safety at Work Regulations (1992). Other examples include the following:

- Reporting of Injuries, Diseases and Dangerous Occurrences Regulations (1985) (RIDDOR)
- Control of Substances Hazardous to Health (1988) (COSHH)
- Electricity at Work Regulations (1989)
- Noise at Work Regulations (1989)
- Workplace (Health, Safety and Welfare) Regulations (1992)
- Health and Safety (Display Screen Equipment) Regulations (1992)
- Manual Handling Operations Regulations (1992)
- Provision and Use of Work Equipment Regulations (1992).

Insurance

Companies must be insured with an authorised insurer to cover Employers' Liability and Public Liability. A certificate of insurance must be clearly displayed within the premises. For some organisations, it is also a good idea to take out insurance to cover bad weather or cancellations, etc.

Responsibilities of employees

It is the responsibility of employees to report all accidents to the management (see below, page 593).

Employees must also co-operate with the employer to meet health and safety requirements. So workplaces generally state that employees are not allowed on the premises under the influence of alcohol or drugs. If they abuse alcohol or drugs, employees can be instantly dismissed. If you are asked to use machinery, you should inform your supervisor if you are using prescription or over-the-counter drugs.

Importance of health and safety

A good workplace will expend considerable time and effort to make sure the working environment is safe and secure. Training staff and raising awareness is not just something that should take place when people first start work, although this is of course important: it should be an on-going activity.

One of the biggest problems is the lack of importance given to potential dangers at work. A common cause of this is bravado, when people show off or try to show they're not frightened or worried. Another reason is a sense of complacency, when people become over-familiar with their jobs and their places of work. Training and raising awareness should therefore be a continuous process to stop people developing a careless attitude, and also because there are always changes taking place. Legislation is vast and complex, so employers need to keep up to date with it.

> *'The rate of change in health and safety legislation is phenomenal and no "policy" is fixed for more than a few months.'*
>
> (Steve Salmen, printing company director)

Activity

Check through the information given so far and then briefly list what you would consider to be your responsibility as an employee concerning health and safety issues. You should look at this question from a moral standpoint as well as from a legal point of view.

Risk assessment

In addition to health and safety, there is something called **risk assessment**. This is concerned with anticipating potential problems in a particular working area by carrying out a survey. The area could be, for example, a recording studio, an office, a cinema, print room or out on location. The idea is to assess the potential risks, both to people and equipment, and design ways to minimise or neutralise those risks.

Risk assessment covers more than just health and safety, because it deals with the potential for loss or damage of equipment and materials. For example, if you were going to take video or audio recording equipment out on location, you would have to assess the risk of the equipment being stolen or broken. After weighing up the situation you or your tutors may well decide that it is not worth the risk; or you may devise a policy of always having someone with you, solely to keep an eye on things.

Description of chemical: fixing solution used in plate making

Risks involved:

		Affecting:
1	Irritation to skin and eyes	Specifically employees working in the print room
2	Carrying bulk (1 × 10 litres)	Any employee
3	Decanting	Specifically employees working in the print room
4	Disposal of waste chemical	Specifically employees working in the print room
5	Disposal of waste containers	Any employee

Action taken to minimise risk:

1 Avoid contact with skin or eyes. Use barrier cream. Use the gloves or goggles provided for your personal use. Wash hands, gloves and goggles after use. If irritation occurs or eyes are affected, rinse copiously with water. If symptoms persist, contact your medical adviser.

2 Lift correctly using your leg muscles and a straight back to avoid straining the back.

3 There is always a risk of splashes to the skin and eyes when decanting. Wear the gloves and goggles provided for your personal use. Use the apron provided to avoid splashes to clothing. Pour directly from 10 litre bottle into dip tank. Avoid spills to the floor. Wipe up any spillage with P-Tork. Used P-Tork should be placed in the fire-retardant bins provided, which are emptied daily as part of our normal daily/weekly routines and will be disposed of to our normal landfill site via an authorised waste carrier.

4 As the dip tank is a continuous system, it is unlikely that any undiluted chemical would need to be disposed of. If it does, the directors will arrange for its correct disposal, which is by dilution with water to the sewerage system.

5 All empty containers should be bagged up as part of our normal daily/weekly routines and will be disposed of to our normal landfill site via an authorised waste carrier.

Remaining hazard

1 Chemical entering a cut or abrasion
2 Environmental effects of discharge to sewerage system

Action to minimise remaining hazard/action to be taken

1 Use the gloves and goggles provided for your personal use. Wash hands, gloves and goggles after use. If irritation occurs, rinse copiously with water. If symptoms persist, contact your medical adviser.

2 Contact Water Authority to discuss. Review 31.12.96.

Case study

Read the extract on the previous page from a professional printer's risk assessment.

Now carry out a risk assessment for an area of your workplace, such as a sound studio or even a classroom.

People should also carry out their own risk assessment to protect their work. You should, for example, break off the write-protect tabs on your tapes, clearly label recordings, and make back-up copies of your work, particularly computer files. In order to protect recordings, sound studios should have a sign – preferably red and green lights – to let people know when they can enter a recording area.

Health and safety inspectors

If a safety problem remains, or you need more help, health and safety inspectors can give advice on how to comply with the law. They also have the power to enforce it through the work of the Health and Safety Executive, which was set up as an enforcement agency under the HSWA.

Inspectors appointed under the Act, such as a factory inspector, environmental health officer, or safety inspector, have the powers to:

- enter premises at any reasonable time, or any time if they have reason to believe a dangerous situation exists
- make examinations/investigations if there may have been a breach of the law
- seize and destroy articles/substances that may cause serious personal injury
- inspect copies of relevant documents
- give information to safety representatives.

An inspector who is concerned about unsafe working practices may serve two types of notice:

- an **improvement notice** – where improvements must be done within a specified period of time
- a **prohibition notice** – to stop operations at once if the inspector considers that a work activity involves or will involve a risk of serious personal injury. This has immediate effect or may be deferred until the situation is remedied.

If the notices are not complied with, the person responsible can be prosecuted. However, there are a limited number of health and safety inspectors so it is difficult for them to get around to all places of work.

Health and safety and you

General safety

The following notices should be displayed in the rest-room or on the staff notice board:

- Certificate of Employers' Liability Insurance
- Health and safety at work – what you should know
- Details of first-aiders and location of the First Aid box
- Details of fire procedures.

Instruction, training and supervision

No employee should do any task without being trained for it. Before an employee works unsupervised there should be:

- A period with a trained employee who undertakes the task. This will familiarise the trainee with the organisation of the task. The task can be explained with an outline of the problem/risk area.
- A period of working totally supervised, where the supervisor explains the task whilst the trainee does it. The trainee should understand the task and the risks at this stage.
- A period of working partially supervised. The supervisor will be working close by but not watching every move. Trainees will not be left alone until they and their supervisors agree that they are capable of working unsupervised.

At any time trainees may ask for further instruction or retraining for a deeper understanding or clarification of the task.

If an engineer is correcting a fault or maintaining a machine the usual operator should accompany him or her.

Places of work

As an employee you should always work tidily and clean up after yourself. Don't leave blades (for example, scalpels) lying about, and clear up mess before it builds up and gets in the way. Do not leave objects such as your bag lying on the floor. An untidy area is a dangerous area, so working tidily will help you to work efficiently and safely.

Statutory breaks

Employers are required to provide breaks in the working day, according to the number of hours worked by an employee. These breaks are:

- 15 minutes between 10.00 am and 11.00 am
- 30 minutes between 12.00 noon and 2.00 pm
- 15 minutes between 2.00 pm and 4.00 pm.

Computers

All VDUs come under the Health and Safety (Display Screen Equipment) Regulations (1992). These are directed mainly at the protection of users, i.e. employees who habitually use display screen equipment as a significant part of their normal work.

According to the Regulations, employers must:

- assess and reduce risks
- make sure new work-stations meet minimum requirements covering equipment, furniture, task design and software.
- provide eye tests and glasses if necessary
- provide breaks or changes of activity
- give information and training.

The Workplace (Health, Safety and Welfare) Regulations (1992) also include requirements for lighting, workspace, work-station arrangements, seating and facilities for rest.

The two main problems associated with VDUs are visual fatigue and postural fatigue.

The screen must:

- have well-defined characters of adequate size and spacing
- be stable and free from flicker
- have easily adjustable brightness and contrast controls
- freely tilt and swivel to suit the user
- be free of reflection and glare.

Where there is little choice in the positioning of the screen, the use of screen filters may be beneficial.

The keyboard must:

- have 50 mm between it and the edge of the work surface to provide hand/arm support.

The chair must:

- be stable and allow freedom of movement
- be adjustable in height
- have a back rest adjustable in height and tilt
- have a footrest if user requests.

It is suggested that document holders should be used as much as possible to minimise head and body movements.

The work area must be:

- positioned so as to minimise noise
- maintained at a reasonable temperature and humidity (40 to 60 per cent)

The software must:

- be efficient and suitable for the task
- be adaptable for the ability of the user
- not measure the user's speed or accuracy without his or her knowledge
- allow information to be displayed in a format and at a pace suitable for the user.

Each user is entitled to undergo an appropriate eye test. The employer has to pay the basic cost of suitable lenses and frames where these are prescribed for VDU use. In order to prevent eye strain, VDUs should be of the low radiation variety and be fitted with anti-glare shields.

It is recommended that employees do not work for longer than one hour on a VDU without a break.

Electrical safety

All machinery should comply with the Electricity at Work Regulations 1989. The Health and Safety Executive (HSE) now states that there must be regular inspection of all wiring, flexes, etc. The electrical system should have live overload and neutral/earth leakage safety breakers on every circuit.

Employers should:

- allow use of the electrical system within safe working limits, allowing for surges, etc.
- maintain all conductors with suitable insulation
- provide and maintain earthing to all conductors
- provide means to isolate supply to the system
- take adequate precautions to prevent isolated equipment from becoming electrically charged.

Electrical safety is primarily concerned with protecting people from electric shock, which could have fatal results, and from fire and burns arising

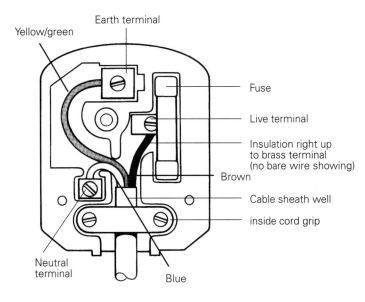

Yellow/green

Earth terminal

Fuse

Live terminal

Insulation right up to brass terminal (no bare wire showing)

Brown

Cable sheath well

inside cord grip

Neutral terminal

Blue

from contact with electricity. Measures against this are:

- protection from direct contact, i.e. proper insulation
- protection from indirect contact, e.g. effective earthing.

Earthing implies contact to the general mass of earth in such a manner as will ensure at all times an immediate discharge of electrical energy without danger.

Safety points

Do not overload electricity sockets by putting on additional plugs. Use **four-way adaptors**, with one plug per socket.

Fuses are basically strips of metal of such a size as would melt at a predetermined value of current flow. A fuse is placed in an electrical circuit and, on melting, cuts off the current to the circuit. The correct fuse to use should be of a type and rating appropriate to the circuit and the appliance it protects.

Circuit breakers 'trip' a switch from the 'on' to the 'off' position if an excess current flows in the circuit. A circuit breaker should be of the type and rating appropriate to the circuit and appliance it protects.

Earth leakage circuit breakers (residual current circuit breakers) are also necessary because fuses and circuit breakers do not always provide total

protection against electric shock. ELCBs provide protection against earth leakage faults.

Causes and effects of shock

An electric current flowing through the body has a direct effect on body organs and the central nervous system. This effect is fatal if the heart rhythm is disturbed for long enough to stop blood flowing to the brain. Emergency action to help victims is vital. Mouth-to-mouth resuscitation must be commenced quickly.

The extent of an electric shock is partly dependent upon the voltage of the current. However, the amperage is more important than the voltage and an alternating current is more dangerous than a direct one. A current through dry clothing is less dangerous than through wet clothing or directly on to bare skin. All currents are more dangerous when the body is earthed than when insulation is provided by rubber-soled shoes or a rubber mat.

Fire safety

The two principal areas where fires at work can spread are production areas and storage areas. The main causes of the spread of fires in buildings include:

- lack of fire-separating walls between specific areas
- poor housekeeping, resulting in combustible waste being stored in production and storage areas
- the presence of vertical and horizontal features, such as lift shafts and staircases
- presence of high levels of dust.

Fire extinguishers

There are three main techniques for extinguishing fires:

1 **Cooling** – water in spray form is more effective than water jets or buckets
2 **Smothering** – applying a blanket or foam
3 **Starvation** – taking away the fuel, which includes air. If you deprive a fire of oxygen it will go out.

Any work premises where explosive or highly flammable materials are stored, require a Fire Certificate. This requires employers to:

- ensure that all existing means of escape can be safely and efficiently used at all times and are not blocked up with rubbish, etc.

- train all employees in the procedures to be followed in case of fire
- maintain fire-fighting equipment in efficient working order
- not block access for emergency vehicles by allowing parking in the wrong places
- enforce no smoking rules.

Employees should know where all fire extinguishers are located and their uses (see table). Under EU legislation all fire extinguishers are to become red, with labels in the appropriate colour to show their use.

Colour	Type of extinguisher	Type of fire
Red	**Water**	Wood or paper only
Blue	**Dry chemical powder**	Electrical or flammable liquids (extremely effective for these)
Black	**Carbon dioxide gas** (produces a foam on meeting the fire)	Electrical or flammable liquids
Green	**Halon gas** (a vaporising liquid)	Particularly effective for electrical fires
Cream	**Foam**	Best used for liquid spillages or for small oil tanks

There are two types of water appliance: stored pressure and gas cartridge.

In the event of fire:

- clear the building: make sure that everyone leaves
- close all doors as you leave
- isolate electricity, if you can without staying in the building

- call the fire brigade
- tackle the fire only if you are in a position to do so without endangering yourself or others
- do not stay to pick up equipment, personal possessions, etc.
- do not use lifts.

If there is a fire at work, all employees should collect at the designated Fire Assembly Point. This is important so that fire officers can find out if anyone is left in the building.

Fire protection systems include:

- heat sensors
- smoke detectors
- flame detectors.

Reporting accidents

The Reporting of Injuries, Diseases and Dangerous Occurrences Regulations (1985) specify reporting for a wide range of accidents.

In all cases, whether an accident is serious or minor, a written note should be given to management within 24 hours, stating details of who was injured, when, what the injury was, how the injury occurred and any witnesses to the accident. In most cases this report will take the form of an entry in an Accident Book. Management should consider if the injury was preventable and what action should be taken to avoid a further occurrence. In certain circumstances the Health and Safety Executive should be informed.

Activity

Find out about the following health and safety procedures in your college or school:

- where are the fire extinguishers located and what types are they?
- where are the fire exits in your work/study area?
- where is your fire assembly point?
- where is the Accident Book kept?

General health and safety

Heat/temperature

It is uncomfortable and unhealthy to work in an environment where it is too hot or too cold. Normal temperatures should be between 16°C and 19°C. It is important to ensure good ventilation, as stale air causes headaches. Employees should be encouraged to drink water regularly, and supplies of fresh drinking water should be freely available. Drinks such as tea, coffee or canned drinks tend to have a dehydrating effect.

Safety and warning signs and labels should be displayed prominently in all work environments. Instructions on using equipment should also be readily available and employees should always follow manufacturers' advice regarding machinery and chemicals.

Mental health

All types of work can involve pressure, but this need not be a problem (it can even be quite good) providing you don't become over-stressed. Healthy eating habits (instead of a constant diet of burgers, chips, crisps and fizzy drinks), plenty of exercise and enough sleep can also all make a significant improvement to your outlook and attitude. These matters are part of your personal responsibility for your own health and safety.

Safety on location

Interviewing

It is vital to think carefully about your personal safety when arranging visits or interviews. Never go anywhere without telling someone where you are going and who you are meeting. Do not agree to carry out interviews alone at someone's house or other private place. Instead, meet in a public area or bring someone with you.

Clothing

Film crew, researchers, reporters and photographers should wear suitable shoes, and clothing that is appropriate for the location. For example, if they are in a war zone they should wear flak jackets. If visiting a building site, steel works, power station, etc. they should wear hard hats. In general, permission should always be sought before entering sites and factories.

Working abroad

Many of the risks connected with working abroad are general travelling hazards.

Food and **water** may be contaminated in a variety of ways, including water in lakes, swimming pools and the sea, so try not to swallow water when bathing, and only drink purified water.

Diarrhoea, as well as diseases such as cholera, typhoid and hepatitis, can be caught from contaminated food and water. There are vaccines available for immunisation. However, you can help to minimise the risks by simple precautions:

- always wash hands before handling food and eating
- boil or sterilise water or drink bottled water
- avoid ice in drinks and ice cream from street stalls, etc.
- eat freshly cooked food
- avoid food which has been re-heated or kept warm
- avoid food exposed to flies
- avoid (or boil) unpasteurised milk
- avoid fish and shellfish which can carry infections in some countries
- do not eat salads, and eat only fruit you can peel, unless you know they have been washed in purified water.

It is important to take care in the sun to avoid sunstroke or heatstroke: i.e. wear a hat and protective clothing, wear a suitable sun-screen and do not go out in the midday sun in countries where the sun is very strong. Drink plenty of non-alcoholic and non-fizzy drinks to prevent dehydration.

Diseases

Insect and animal bites can be dangerous in certain parts of the world. In tropical areas, malaria and yellow fever are spread by insects, particularly mosquitoes and ticks. Use insect repellent and wear appropriate clothing that covers arms and legs. Use a mosquito net around the bed at night.

Rabies occurs in animals in Europe and North America. You can contract the disease if bitten by an infected animal. A rabies antidote can work if available.

HIV is endemic in some parts of the world. Like hepatitis B, it can be passed on through unprotected sex, by transfusions of HIV-infected blood, tattooing or ear piercing without sterile equipment, and through the use of infected syringes, medical and dental instruments. To protect yourself, use condoms and do not inject drugs. (Some travellers carry their own first-aid kits with needles in case any injections might be required.)

Tetanus is a dangerous disease caught by the introduction of bacteria into a wound – even a slight scratch can become infected. Everyone should be protected by immunisation.

As soon as a journalist or photographer knows that he or she is travelling to foreign parts it is important to consult a doctor as vaccinations may take time to give full protection. It is also necessary to find out what treatment is available in specific countries and to take out adequate health insurance.

Activity

A good first-aid kit is essential equipment when working on location. Find out from your college (or work experience) what it should contain.

Safety equipment for location work

Safety equipment should be ordered after consultation with the production manager who is responsible for safety. You may need life jackets for filming at sea, safety helmets and harnesses for working on high buildings or construction sites, fluorescent jackets and armbands for traffic control or night filming, fire extinguishers where there may be a fire hazard, etc. All technical safety equipment, such as bollards, life belts, torches and so on must be booked in advance.

All firearms are subject to police regulations and it is forbidden for any unauthorised person to attempt to obtain weapons other than through the proper channels. BBC London has an armoury. If any ammunition – either real or blanks – is to be fired, then an armourer is usually in attendance. If a dummy weapon that looks realistic is used in a public place, for example in a scene where an actor holds up the post office, then local police supervision must be arranged.

The BBC's London Visual Effects Department can produce special effects involving pyrotechnics, such as ships on fire at sea, explosions, etc.

The assistant floor manager is responsible for collecting a first aid kit from the surgery and taking it to location. Sometimes something specific is needed, such as insect repellent for filming near stagnant water.

On location as well as in the studio the floor/studio manager is generally responsible for health and safety, so should have basic training in first aid. A general rule is not to hand out any medicine without first checking if the patient is allergic to it. If the complaint does not clear up, then a local doctor should be consulted.

When **stunts** are part of the script, personnel need to be properly trained and the stunt practised first under safe conditions.

When **animals** are used, a handler must also be booked. Normally professional walk-ons are used to appear in shot with an animal unless the handler is a member of Equity or the shot involves a degree of danger. Animals are always a hazard and should never be tied to anything that moves or is likely to be moved.

If a police vehicle is required the local police must be notified.

Safety in the studio

Normally alcoholic liquor is forbidden on sets. With the aid of blackcurrant and ginger cordials, or burnt sugar solution, the look of all shades of wines and spirits can be achieved. Beware of the dangers of all of these if the actor is diabetic. For beer, use alcohol-free shandy. (There is no convincing non-alcoholic substitute for Pernod!)

Be aware of the danger of trailing leads. Make sure that all cables and leads are taped down or covered with mats or safety (cable) ramps.

Other important safety points to remember include:

- check that all studio doors are closed before the start of recording
- if there is a live studio audience, inform them of fire emergency procedures and exits
- switch off individual pieces of equipment before switching off at the socket
- disconnect plugs after use
- lock down camera pedestals
- attach safety chains to lighting rigs
- check audio levels before putting on headphones, so as not to damage your ears
- store razor blades and scalpels safely by putting them in a protective sheath. Do not leave a blade mixed up with the edited lengths of audio tape.

595

Safety in the newspaper office

The 1974 HSW Act is extended to include all contractors, sub-contractors and **visitors**. The following rules should apply to all newspaper, magazine and publishing offices:

- Keep the work area tidy. Items not in use should be stored away.
- Waste should be stored in bins which are emptied regularly.
- Heavy items, such as ledgers, should not be placed on top of cabinets.
- Harmful items, such as light bulbs, should be separately stored and disposed of.
- Passages and doorways should be kept clear.
- Spillages should be cleared up immediately.
- Damaged floor coverings should be replaced.
- An established cleaning schedule should be maintained.

Ergonomics

This is the scientific study of the relationship between people and their workplace, particularly the human–machine interface. The elimination of operator error is one of the principal objectives of ergonomic design, through attention to:

- *vision* – the operator should be able to set and read with ease any controls, specific instruments, etc.
- *posture* – abnormal working posture increases the potential for fatigue, accidents and long-term injury
- *layout* – congested and over-populated areas cause fatigue and danger
- *comfort* – lighting levels, ventilation and humidity directly affect the operator
- *work rate* – this should always be set to suit the individual operator.

Safety at the printer's

There are many health and safety hazards at a printing works, ranging from dangerous machinery, high noise levels and toxic chemicals to excessive dust, which can lead to respiratory and skin problems, and even cause an explosion or fire.

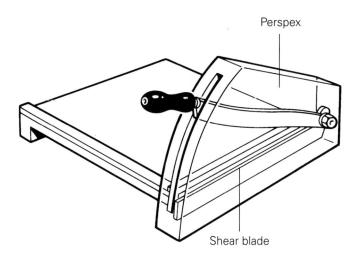

Perspex

Shear blade

Provision and maintenance of plant and systems of work

All machinery should be:

- easily isolated from the electrical supply as necessary
- stabilised where there is a danger of it falling over
- suitably and sufficiently lit
- constructed to allow ease of maintenance
- clearly marked with health and safety signs.

The operator of each item of plant should understand how it works and how it can go wrong. All plant machinery should receive regular attention and maintenance.

Employees should wear clean, close-fitting clothes which are not snagged or torn. They should not wear jewellery, including watches, which could become caught in machinery. Long hair must be tied back or secured with an appropriate band.

Before starting a job involving machinery, employees should ask themselves:

- Am I trained for this task?
- Do I require supervision?
- Is the plant safely guarded?

After work is completed they should ask:

- Were there any faults during the operation?
- Am I trained to correct these?
- Do I need to involve the supervisor?
- Do I need to book an engineer?

Dangerous machinery

Guards should be fitted to machines as appropriate, and electrical cut-out switches should be fitted to operate correctly when guards are not in place.

Guillotines and guillotine blades are specifically noted as dangerous. If a blade is to be changed or maintained, two people must be present. Power should be disconnected at an early stage. No one under the age of 18 years is allowed to handle or maintain a guillotine, guillotine blade or stitcher.

The workplace

The workplace should be tidy and clean. At a printer's the office, artwork room, rest-room and stairs are often covered in industrial-grade carpet, bonded to the floor and protected at the edges of steps with edging strips. Loading and plant areas should be covered with suitable non-slip flooring which is water repellent.

The temporary storage of waste should be in an area designated for rubbish in the outside yard. Screwed-up paper waste takes up more room and creates a potentially greater hazard.

Dust

There is a threefold hazard arising from excessive dust – respiratory problems, skin and eye damage, and risk of fire and explosion.

The sources of excessive dust are paper dust from cut paper, and powder spray, which can finely coat individual sheets of paper.

The solution to the problem of dust is to:

- run extractor fans continuously when printing in any room where powder spray is used
- clean up, using vacuum cleaners with a fine filter.

Regular vacuum cleaning reduces the amount of airborne dust and particles.

Printing companies also supply their staff with **face masks** with filters for removing either dust or fumes or vapours from the air supply. The use of solvents to clean machinery should be undertaken only where there is an adequate air supply. If a build-up of fumes occurs, clear the area and warn other employees of the danger.

A face mask is effective only if used and fitted correctly and in good condition.

Chemicals

A number of potentially dangerous chemicals are used at a printer's and great care must be taken at all times. In particular:

- use a funnel when decanting
- all empty containers should be bagged up and disposed of at a landfill site.

The solvents used by a small printer are alcohols (propanol and industrial methylated spirit) or aliphatic/aromatic hydrocarbons, which are flammable, toxic and can be narcotic and cause dermatitis. The following guidelines must be observed:

- always keep use to a minimum
- use disposable gloves
- avoid contact with the skin or eyes
- always use in well-ventilated conditions
- use a heavy-duty apron, face mask, gloves and goggles when decanting
- always return all containers to the metal cupboards as soon as is practically possible
- if swallowed, drink copious amounts of water and seek medical attention at once.

Barrier cream can protect the skin from irritation and/or **dermatitis**. It is effective for up to two or three hours and should be used in conjunction with regular handwashing/drying and gloves. Dermatitis is damage to the skin which is caused by the skin coming into contact with and reacting to some chemical or other agent.

As mentioned above, employees are recommended to use an apron in conjunction with heavy-duty gauntlets, goggles and face mask in the decanting of petroleum distillate or other liquid chemicals.

There are three types of hand protection available to employees in the form of gloves/gauntlets.

- Disposable latex gloves – to be used at any time to reduce the risk of dermatitis, especially during cleaning and maintenance operations where petroleum distillates are used. They are not strong so several pairs may be used during a normal day. They should be disposed of after one use.
- Heavy duty gloves – to be used for handling bagged waste. Because of their bulk they are unsuitable to be used whilst operating or maintaining machinery.
- Heavy duty gauntlets – to be used as for above but also for handling and decanting liquid chemicals in conjunction with apron, goggles and face mask.

Much of this advice is also relevant to the health and safety hazards of the photographic studio and darkroom (see page 599).

Noise

Under the Noise at Work Regulations (1989), employers are required to offer varying levels of hearing protection to all employees exposed to certain levels of noise over a designated period of time. Because of the high levels of **printing noise** it is imperative to wear ear defenders in the print room. The noise of the presses is above the safety limit and will damage the ear drums.

There are four ways of limiting or controlling noise:

■ reduction of noise at source
■ isolation of the source of the noise
■ provision of ear protection for workers at risk
■ reduction of time that workers are exposed to risk.

In both print and finishing rooms, employees are advised to use ear muffs which offer protection up to 120 decibels over an eight-hour day. It is important that personal stereos should not be worn underneath ear protectors because they negate the effectiveness of the ear protectors/muff.

Work-related upper limb disorders

Certain types of upper limb disorders are commonly found among those working in the printing industry. These are complaints of the arm, hand and shoulder, caused by undue loading of muscles, tendons and joints. They are called **repetitive strain injuries** (RSI). Pain may also be felt in the neck, upper back and chest, hands and arms.

What can cause these problems?

■ lifting or manipulating something that is too heavy or awkward
■ working too fast
■ long periods of repetitive work
■ awkward or rigid posture.

The **specific causes** of such injuries can include:

■ *Application of force,* i.e.
  – gripping, squeezing or pressing with the palm of the hand
  – applying force with the arm joints or a bent wrist in a semi-mechanised operation, such as fixing covers to books
  – keeping arms in a fixed position to hold an object or start a machine

  – using controls made stiff by inadequate maintenance, for instance, the operation of a hand wheel to insert or remove printing plates at small offset presses.

■ *High frequency or long duration of movement,* i.e.
  – where an operator repeats a single manipulation, often at speed
  – when the pace of work is set by the machine, for example in a newspaper's print room the operator has to change the 'web'
  – long periods without breaks
  – payment systems which discourage the taking of proper breaks
  – where the fingers, hand or wrist are positioned awkwardly
  – where the arm is raised or outstretched, for example the use of squeegees on large screen frames
  – where the upper arm is held away from the vertical, such as when someone is knocking up large sheets
  – when people need to stand on their toes or stretch uncomfortably in order to reach
  – where the employee has to lean sideways to work
  – when the working or seat height cannot be adjusted.

In addition to this, even apparently light work can involve prolonged tension of certain muscles. Deadlines or increased pace of work can put people under considerable stress, leading to increased muscle tension. Also, the body size and physique of individuals can vary greatly and there are differences in people's speed and dexterity.

Prevention of injuries

In order to prevent such disorders occurring, it is useful to apply **ergonomic** principles to machines, tools, work-stations, work methods and the environment, so that the job is made to fit the person and not vice versa.

In particular, it is possible to:

■ reduce high force levels, for example by maintaining equipment properly, by spreading the force over several fingers and by using tools with correctly designed handles
■ balance periods of frequent repetition with non-repetitive work, i.e. the employer can provide more varied tasks

- carry out tasks with either hand, for instance sharing mouse operations with either hand when using a keyboard
- use automation where appropriate, for example mechanised insertion work
- adjust machine pace and use self-pacing systems
- rotate jobs amongst the staff
- change posture
- modify the operation or product
- redesign work so that the wrist is kept straight
- change the operator's positioning in relation to the work.

It is also important for the employer to provide sufficient rest or recovery time, by means of breaks or changes of activity, and these should be introduced when they do not occur naturally. They should take place *before* the onset of fatigue. Remember that short, frequent breaks are better than longer occasional breaks.

Employers must pay attention to new employees, starting them at a slower work rate, with gradual upgrading to allow for the development of skills and strength.

It is important to remember that inadequate light levels and glare or reflections can cause hunching and other awkward postures, and introduce the risk of headaches. Also, excessively cold temperatures can reduce muscle efficiency and increase the risk of injury. Sufficient working space to do the job must also be provided.

Principles of correct handling

Incorrect methods of lifting or carrying large or heavy objects can cause many injuries, particularly to the back. It is therefore vital to observe these rules when lifting or handling objects:

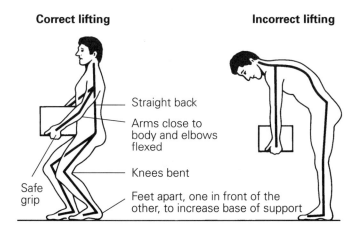

Correct lifting

Straight back

Arms close to body and elbows flexed

Knees bent

Safe grip

Feet apart, one in front of the other, to increase base of support

Incorrect lifting

- lift with a straight back, keeping the object close to the body
- use correct feet position, i.e. feet apart
- use body weight, keeping knees bent and arms close to body
- use correct grip, using as much of the palms of the hands as possible.

Safety in the photographic studio

There are a number of potential problems in the photographic studio. Health and safety hazards to be considered and controlled include photographic chemicals for developing film (see below). Proper ventilation is required and, in order to prevent irritation or burning of the skin, protective gloves should be worn when handling these substances. It is important that chemicals should always be kept in sealed containers. Aerosol sprays for mounting photographs must be handled with caution because of the risk of toxic poisoning. Scalpels and guillotines are also common equipment in photography, and need to be used and stored with care.

A darkroom floor should be covered with a non-slip water-repellent flooring. In addition, a darkroom should have linked intake/extract fans of fixed speeds, which provide a rapid turnover of air in a relatively small room. This is to dissipate heat and some of the fumes generated by the normal darkroom processes, involving chemicals and dangerous substances (see below). In addition, many of the precautions advised for preventing health and safety problems at the printer's also apply here (see page 597).

Dangerous substances

The Classification, Packaging and Labelling of Dangerous Substances Regulations (1984) include the following definitions in the classification of dangerous substances:

- *toxic* – a substance which if inhaled or ingested or if it penetrates the skin may involve serious, acute or chronic health risks and even death
- *corrosive* – a substance which on contact with living tissues destroys them
- *irritant* – a non-corrosive substance which through immediate, prolonged or repeated contact with skin or mucous membranes can cause dermatitis or inflammation

- *explosive* – a substance which may explode when in contact with a flame or is sensitive to shocks or friction
- *oxidising* – a substance which gives off a lot of heat when in contact with other substances
- *flammable* – a liquid having a flash point equal to or greater than 21°C and less than or equal to 55°C. Can form the contents of an aerosol dispenser
- *radioactive* – a substance which emits ionising radiations
- *carcinogenic* – a substance which can cause cancer.

According to the Control of Substances Hazardous to Health (COSHH) Regulations (1988) the employer must take account of the substances used at work and has the duty to:

- make health risk assessments
- control exposure
- carry out monitoring
- arrange for health surveillance.

First aid

Notices giving information on who first-aiders are, where they can be found, and the location of the First Aid box, should be prominently displayed on the staff notice board or in the rest-room.

The aims of first-aid treatment are to

- preserve life
- prevent deterioration in an existing condition
- promote recovery.

First aid is the approved method of treating a casualty until the person can be placed – if necessary – in the care of a doctor or taken to hospital.

Casualties should be seated or lying on their side in the recovery position (see below) while being treated. They should not be left on their backs as they may suffocate or choke on vomit. Cover them with a coat or blanket, even if it doesn't seem particularly cold. Casualties can get very cold if they go into shock.

1 RECOGNISE A LACK OF OXYGEN

Recovery position

2 ACT AT ONCE

Get a clear airway …
Remove any
obstruction … then

TILT HEAD
BACK

LIFT JAW

BREATHING MAY RESTART … IF NOT …

3 APPLY RESUE BREATHING

Start with four quick deep breaths

Seal nose and blow into mouth

Maintain head position

After blowing into mouth watch casualty's chest fall as you breathe in

Repeat every 5 secs

After first four breaths test for recovery signs
1. Pulse present?
2. Pupils less large?
3. Colour improved?

PULSE
POINTS

4 IF NONE, COMBINE RESCUE BREATHING & HEART COMPRESSION

Place casualty on a firm surface

Commence heart compression

Heel of hand only on lower half of breastbone, other hand on top. Fingers off chest

Keep arms straight and rock forward to depress chest 1.5 inches (4 cm)

Apply 15 compressions, one per second … then give two breaths

Re-check pulse … if still absent continue with 15 compressions to two breaths

If pulse returns cease compressions but continue rescue breathing

BREASTBONE

HEART

The first thing to check for is whether someone is breathing. If not – is there an obstruction which needs to be removed from the person's airway? If breathing still does not start, artificial ventilation (i.e. mouth-to-mouth) needs to be started at once.

Mouth-to-mouth ventilation

If the casualty is not breathing, place the person on his or her back, open the mouth and check it is clear. Tilt the head back. Maintain this position throughout. Kneel beside the casualty. While keeping the person's head tilted backwards, open the mouth and pinch the nose. Open your mouth and take a deep breath. Seal the casualty's mouth with yours and breathe out firmly into it.

The casualty's chest should rise. Remove your mouth and let the chest fall. If the chest does not fall, check that the head is tilted back sufficiently. Continue at a rate of 12 times a minute until the person is breathing on his or her own. Then place the casualty in the recovery position (see diagram on the previous page).

Other first-aid emergencies

In the case of **severe bleeding**, remove any visible foreign bodies from the wound and apply direct pressure on the bleeding point with fingers and thumb. Apply a sterile dressing and, if the wound is in a limb which is not broken, raise it to reduce the flow of blood. Seek medical help at once.

If you are dealing with **broken bones** you should not move the casualty unless there is a serious danger of further injury. This is particularly crucial where spinal injuries are concerned. Again, medical aid is required urgently.

If someone suffers a **chemical burn**, or a chemical splash to the eyes, wash continuously with clean, cool water for 15 minutes. Apply a loose dressing and take the casualty to hospital.

In the case of **electric shock**, switch off the supply before touching the victim. If the casualty has stopped breathing, it will be necessary to perform mouth-to-mouth ventilation (as above).

First-aid training

Some first-aid knowledge is helpful but is not a substitute for doing a first-aid course. First-aid training is always a useful qualification, whatever the size of organisation you end up working in (by law, companies of a certain size must have people trained in first aid on the premises). 'Trained' first-aiders have been on an approved training course, for example run by the Red Cross or St John Ambulance Association, and are awarded a certificate proving they are competent at administering first aid. In order to remain qualified, first-aiders must do a refresher course and be re-examined every three years.

First-aid training is a valuable life skill, it may be particularly useful if you often have to work away on location, or in small teams, or even on your own.

Appendix: Legal and Ethical Issues

Introduction

Legal responsibilities and ethical considerations will underpin much of your work in the media. You must meet your legal obligations – as required by the law of the land – or you will find yourself in court. You also have a moral obligation to act in an ethical manner – according to various established codes of practice – or you are likely to find yourself without a job.

The legal issues we will be looking at include: blasphemy, breach of confidence, contempt of court, defamation, EU legislation, obscenity, performing rights, and legislation concerned with race relations, equal opportunities, sex discrimination and national security.

The ethical matters covered here are: accuracy of sources, avoidance of exploitation and sensationalism, offensive material and issues of representation (also including confidentiality and privacy).

Note: The topics to be considered in this Appendix have been ordered alphabetically, within the two areas of law and ethics, to reflect the view that they cannot and should not be put in any order of importance.

Legal issues

Blasphemy

This law applies only to the Christian faith. Blasphemy is concerned with the use of material which Christians may find offensive. In 1977, *Gay News* was fined £1000 for publishing a make-believe letter in poetic form, supposedly from a Roman soldier, which discussed homosexual feelings relating to Christ. Although the content was apparently meant as a way of expressing love for God, this defence was not accepted. The law looks at alleged blasphemy to see whether it may cause a **breach of the peace**. It is the effect it has on people (for example, does it shock and outrage them?) rather than the *intention* that is important.

Breach of confidence

The law of confidentiality is used to prevent employees and former employees from giving away commercial secrets to rivals. It can also be used to 'protect' public secrets, and to keep local councillors and public service workers from disclosing certain matters.

Civil servants and former members of the security services may be liable to prosecution under this law, although they can also be charged under the Official Secrets Act. It appears that it has been easier to prosecute under confidentiality laws rather than the Official Secrets Act; for example, the government tried (unsuccessfully) to prosecute the author of *Spycatcher,* Peter Wright, under confidentiality laws, because of revelations in his book about the secret services.

Actions under confidentiality laws usually work by seeking an **injunction**, for example, against a newspaper, forbidding it to publish something which is considered to be 'not in the public interest'.

Cable regulations

Cable television has been regulated by the ITC. You should refer to Chapter 30 (page 532) for information about the regulatory framework.

Contempt of court

The relevant piece of legislation here is the Contempt of Court Act 1981. Someone can be in contempt of court if the judge decides that the person has harmed the legal process. A journalist can be indicted under the act for publishing material which may prejudice a fair trial. For example, it may be revealed in an article that an accused person had already been convicted of similar crimes. This may have an effect on a jury's judgement, although it is something they should not take into consideration.

Contempt also covers the revealing of sources and it can put journalists in a difficult position both legally and ethically. If a journalist is passed information and refuses to reveal the source when asked in court, then he or she can be in contempt of court. There are ethical issues at stake here. How many journalists, or their editors, find some information too hot to handle? Decisions may be taken not to print stories if it is thought that the journalists involved will be forced to reveal their sources. How many civil servants have decided against reporting a scandal because they know they may be exposed if the court threatens the journalist with prosecution for contempt?

A journalist, editor, producer or, indeed, any member of the public, can receive up to two years' imprisonment and an unlimited fine for being in contempt of court. There is always a risk that a comment, photograph or an interview could be held to be in contempt if their contents refer to a person or event that is relevant to a court case taking place at the time. Therefore, newspapers and broadcasters normally seek legal advice on any court case that is 'active'. (For this reason, the major newspapers and broadcasters have retained solicitors).

Copyright

Copyright is part of **intellectual property** law. If you use someone else's material without permission, for example reproducing a photograph or illustration in an article, or using a piece of recorded music as an introduction to something else, then you are breaking copyright law. All books have a copyright notice in the first few pages, and it is illegal to photocopy more than a few pages for academic use.

Under the Copyright, Designs and Patents Act 1988, copyright applies to songs and instrumental music, books, articles, poems, films, radio plays, stage productions, etc. Chapter 30 deals with copyright in more detail. See also **Performing rights** below.

Data protection

The 1984 Data Protection Act gives people a right to privacy concerning information that is held about them on computer. This is necessary because such information can be disseminated very widely and also very easily. It does not apply to handwritten records.

Essentially, individuals are entitled to see any information that is held in electronic storage. This information should be for lawful purposes and be no more or no less than is necessary to represent a person fairly. It should also be maintained properly

and kept up to date in order to ensure that it does not give a misleading picture of that person. In addition, it should not be kept longer than necessary and should be kept properly secure, with risk assessment carried out to ensure that validation procedures are put in force. Subscription lists in electronic form, for such products as mail-order books or music, should not be sold to other commercial parties without the consent of those whose names are on the list.

Defamation

The purpose of defamation law (Defamation Act 1952) is to protect a person's private and professional reputation from unjustified attack. **Libel** is part of this law, and a libel takes place when the unjustified attack is written, published or broadcast in some way. A verbal defamation is called **slander.**

Defamation can be a very problematic area for journalists and presenters. The problems, and media 'defences' (such as 'fair comment') are dealt with more fully in Chapter 30 (see page 533).

Deregulation

For full information on deregulation and its legal implications for broadcasting you should refer to Chapter 30.

Discrimination

It is illegal to discriminate against anyone on grounds of sex, age, disability or ethnic origin either when recruiting or in the workplace. The relevant pieces of legislation to know about are the **Sex Discrimination Act 1974** and the **Race Relations Act 1976,** also the Equal Opportunities Acts.

Discrimination can be *direct,* for example if a woman is paid less than a man for the same job. In 1996, the BBC finally agreed to pay the female stars of the hit comedy series *Men Behaving Badly* the same as the male stars. However, *indirect discrimination* can be more difficult to identify. An example is when an advertisement for a video editing job states that it is open to people with disabilities. In practice, lack of training can mean that disabled people are unlikely to apply. Skillset has observed that training schemes for the disabled have been cut. There are quotas by which large organisations must employ a certain proportion of people with disabilities. However, the contraction of the BBC and the rise of small independent companies means fewer opportunities for employment in television for the disabled. In the higher ranks, there is a noticeable lack of women and black people in both television and journalism. The *Media Guide 1996* quoted a survey in which it found that, in the 15 ITV companies, only four of the 106 executive directorships were held by women.

Under the **Public Order Act 1986** it is an offence to publish anything that can be construed as threatening, insulting or which *incites racial hatred*. A newspaper report of, for example, a racist speech does not have to agree with that speech in order to break the law. If the language used in the speech is unlawful and the newspaper uses that language in its report, then it too breaks the law. Therefore the newspaper would have to paraphrase the speech, using more moderate language.

Equal opportunities

We have mentioned equal opportunities in job applications when talking about this area of the law. Discrimination can, of course, also go on in the workplace, especially with regard to promotion. As mentioned above, women, for example, are usually poorly represented in senior management positions.

Activity

Some employers argue that women tend to leave their jobs to raise families and 'that's their *choice* but they can't have it both ways'. Others point out that there should be more support so that women (and men) can have time off to be with their families, and yet still have successful careers. They point out that other countries have more enlightened attitudes to paid time off for mothers and fathers. In addition, work hours can often be re-structured to suit school times, so that women can go back to work.

Where do you stand on this issue? What do you think of the choices available to parents? Find out as much as you can about how many women are employed as editors, deputy editors, managers and producers in a media industry of your choice. You can gain some information from the *Radio Times*, *TV Times*, *Guardian* 'Media Guide', *Willings Press Guide* and Benn's *Media Directory*. In addition, you should gather evidence from some examples of television programmes by looking at the credits at the end. You should also refer to the Media Organisations appendix.

European Union

The UK is part of the European Union (formerly known as the EC or 'Common Market') along with these other countries: France, Germany, Belgium, Netherlands, Luxembourg, Spain, Portugal, Italy, Greece, Sweden, Ireland, Denmark, Finland and Austria. (See map below.)

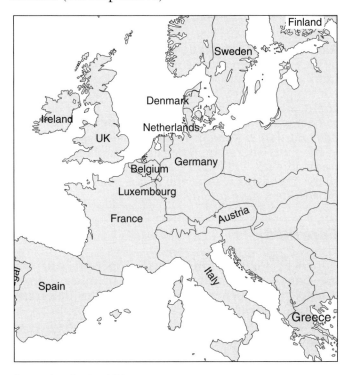

Countries in the EU

Many laws and regulations are the same for all countries within the union. However, Britain decided to 'opt out' of part of European employment legislation called the **Social Chapter**. The idea of this is to help to develop a sense of fair employment where a minimum wage level and conditions of employment are established in law.

Employers would therefore not be allowed to compete against each other simply on the grounds of low wages. At present, unscrupulous employers can offer a product at a cheaper price solely by paying low wages. When the economy is on a 'downturn' people can be offered low pay, with employers knowing that they can do this because people need the work. This, it is argued, has a negative 'knock-on' effect for society because it can lead to financial hardship and thus social tension. More families will need state support to survive, others will suffer domestic crises and some people may turn to crime.

However, in the UK and also in the USA, unemployment levels are generally lower than in the EU. Some politicians argue that this is because there is more flexibility in employment law, i.e. there is no minimum wage and Wages Councils were abolished in Britain in the early 1990s. Some people feel that such a 'free-market economy' leads to greater competitiveness amongst businesses and benefits the country as a whole. Those who call for a minimum wage for all dispute this.

Activity

Do you think there should be a minimum wage? List your reasons either for or against. Find out what you can about the Social Chapter and hold a group discussion to consider its advantages and disadvantages for participating countries.

Health and safety

The statutory legislation referring to health and safety is the Health and Safety at Work Act 1974 (HSWA), which has been updated now by the Workplace (Health, Safety and Welfare) Regulations 1992. The 1974 Act generally overshadows the Offices, Shops and Railway Premises Act of 1963, but the latter is still on the statute books and can be referred to in some situations.

The HSWA applies to all work premises and covers anyone who is on the premises – whether employee, employer or visitor. It requires all *employers* to:

- ensure the health, safety and welfare at work of their employees 'as far as is reasonably practicable'
- provide an on-going written statement on the health and safety policy of the company
- allow for the appointment of safety representatives selected by a recognised trade union.

The Act also requires all *employees* to:

- take reasonable care of their own health and safety and that of others who may be affected by their activities
- co-operate with the employer to meet health and safety requirements.

For more details of health and safety and risk assessment issues, please refer to the Health and Safety appendix.

Libel

See *Defamation* for details of the law referring to libel and slander.

Money

Because of restrictions by the Bank of England, facsimiles of banknotes cannot be used in drama productions – only blank paper cut to size and in the appropriate colour. If the money is to be shown in close-up (e.g. on TV) then the genuine article must be used.

Obscene Publications Act

The law states that a work is obscene if, when taken as a whole, it tends to deprave or corrupt. However, the defence can now argue that the work was '.... in the interests of science, literature, art or learning or of other objects of public concern'. Media producers should paraphrase any obscene examples in such a way as to avoid the dissemination of this kind of material under the spurious guise of serious investigation.

A famous case in the 1960s concerned the publication in paperback of D.H. Lawrence's novel *Lady Chatterley's Lover*. The publishers were brought to trial under this act but were acquitted as a result of using the defence mentioned above.

Performing rights

This is part of copyright law. It covers the performing right for music under the Performing Rights Society and mechanical copyright under the Mechanical-Copyright Protection Society.

The Performing Rights Society Limited (PRS) is an association of composers, authors and publishers of musical works. It grants licences to radio and TV stations (including satellite and cable) and concert halls, discos, clubs, etc. where music is broadcast or played live or recordings are played.

The copyright owner of a piece of music receives royalties via the PRS whenever his or her music is performed or broadcast.

The copyright owner (which could be the artist or publisher) is also protected by 'mechanical' rights. Generally permission will be given for a work to be recorded by record companies, radio, TV and video companies, etc., providing a royalty is paid. Recording rights involve not only music for sale in shops but also music incorporated into TV and radio programmes. (See *Copyright* above).

Product placement

See Chapter 27.

Sex discrimination

See *Discrimination* above.

Slander

See *Defamation* above for details of slander and libel.

Ethical issues and codes of practice

Accuracy of sources

It is good practice always to check your source material, whether it is for a fiction or a non-fiction product. Units 2 and 3 impress upon you the importance of checking the accuracy of names, addresses and other facts. Getting these wrong can cause not just annoyance and embarrassment, it can also cause litigation. For example, if a newspaper mixes up the name of an honest company with that of one they are exposing as being dishonest and fraudulent, there will be red faces all round. At the very least the paper will be asked to print an explanation or correction. In a busy daily news-room the potential for inaccuracy is enormous. The reporters and sub-editors must carry out stringent checks. It is too easy to get two people with the same name confused, or for the captions on photographs to become mixed up.

In addition, you should not be prepared to take one person's word without corroborating evidence, as this could lead to defamation and misrepresentation. You should always strive for 'balance' in a story.

Other chapters of this book have given examples of the need to maintain standards of accuracy. Chapter 6 points out the dangers of misquoting by paraphrasing.

Avoidance of exploitation

There have been numerous controversies about using images of people in distressed circumstances in order to provide sensational or dramatic images for the public. In the Ethiopian famine of the mid-1980s some photographers were accused of just waiting around for starving people to die so that they could capture the moment on film.

Although it is also a **stereotyping** issue, many people argue that women are exploited by the way they are portrayed in media products, such as sex magazines, or in TV game shows where their main role appears to be to stand around looking 'glamorous'. Some people argue that this helps to stereotype all women and even exploits men because of the false images of women that are conveyed.

Advertising generally is another controversial area for issues of exploitation. Some advertisements work on people's feelings of anxiety or insecurity. For example, parents are naturally concerned about their children's welfare and they are therefore susceptible to advertising that persuades them to take out extra insurance, or pay for extra educational activities. Adverts also make use of experts who sound authoritative and will tell you that a certain washing powder will wash 'brilliantly white and fresh', or that a particular shampoo will make your hair look as if you'd just stepped out of the hairdressers.

Other ads can exploit people's ambitions or sense of greed, whether this is a desire to be rich and successful or popular and glamorous.

 Activity

How do you feel about the examples of exploitation given above?

Avoidance of sensationalism

Large areas of the media tend to see themselves as providing entertainment rather than information. Even the news can become as much entertainment as information: so a story of a large arms sale to another country could be accompanied by archive footage of similar armaments being used in a war somewhere else in the world. This, it can be argued, would sensationalise the story, although others would defend it, saying it is useful because it 'brings the story to life'.

Sensationalising a news story to provide entertainment can result in unwelcome intrusions into people's lives, particularly if they are celebrities. Often, a photograph is obtained which, by itself, can be quite innocuous, perhaps of a rock star arriving at Heathrow Airport or entering a film première or a nightclub. The caption and the story that accompany this photo will, however, contain speculation about what the star is really up to, who he or she is supposedly with and so on. Tabloid newspapers and gossip magazines are full of this kind of conjecture, which may have little evidence to support it. Nevertheless it sensationalises what would otherwise be a dull story, or indeed no story at all!

Another example of what may be construed as sensationalism is the dramatisation of crime reconstructions. Programmes showing video footage of, for example, drivers behaving badly, police chases, etc. are often accused of sensationalising crime and bad behaviour whilst purporting to raise the public's awareness of it. Furthermore, some commercial radio stations now play a bed of music underneath the newsreader's voice to make the news sound more dramatic and pacey.

Activity

Do you think such techniques make the news sound trivial or gratuitously exciting?

Offensive material

In Unit 6 (Chapters 21 to 24) we looked at the interaction of audience and the media. There is a widespread belief that the media, and particularly television, do influence people profoundly. Children are seen as especially vulnerable, which is why there is the **nine o'clock watershed**. Programmes before this time should not contain bad language, excessive violence, or sexually explicit scenes. There are also restrictions on the portrayal of smoking and drinking and such scenes as hangings and suicides.

There are regulatory bodies to keep a check on media content. For all broadcasting (TV, radio, BBC and independent) there is the **Broadcasting Standards Council**, which deals with the portrayal of sex and violence and matters of taste and decency. Merged with this body is the **Broadcasting Complaints Commission**, which is concerned with unjust or unfair treatment or infringements of **privacy**.

The extent of the BSC's remit and its powers are stated on the cover of their monthly *Complaints Bulletin*, which records the complaints made by members of the public, the response of the particular broadcaster and the findings of the BSC. This states:

> *The BSC is a statutory organisation under the 1990 Broadcasting Act. Its role is to monitor the portrayal of violence, of sex and matters of taste and decency (such as bad language or the treatment of disasters) in all television, radio, cable and satellite services. The council works as an advisory body, monitoring the content of broadcasting, considering audience complaints and reporting on public opinion, which it tests by means of independent research.*

> *The council can only consider complaints about programmes or advertisements that have already been broadcast. It does not have the power to preview programmes or to censor broadcasting.*

There are no hard and fast rules about what is tasteful and decent, and ideas about public morality change in different cultures, in different contexts and in different time-periods. The BSC therefore tries to set standards as a 'benchmark' for broadcasters, and also tries to interpret the concerns and worries of the public.

Bad language (including derogatory terms for racial groups), sex and violence are the three areas of particular concern to the public. Extensive research is carried out to discover the public's attitude to these three areas in broadcasting.

The results of the research and findings are published by the BSC. Although interesting and useful these are very detailed and beyond the scope of this book. We recommend that you refer to the BSC publications themselves, such as their *Annual Reviews* dealing separately with: *Taste and Decency in Broadcasting, A Matter of Manners? (The Limits of Broadcasting Language), Violence in Factual Television* and *Sex and Sexuality in Broadcasting,* all by Andrea Millwood Hargrave, as well as *Violence in Television Fiction* by David Docherty, the BSC's *Code of Practice* and *Survivors and the Media* by Ann Shearer, as well as the monthly reports already mentioned. These give an excellent insight into the complexity of the issues and the diversity of opinions. There are plenty of concrete examples (including lots of qualitative research findings), which will fuel a worthwhile debate. These publications in turn carry their own lists of other titles available.

Generally speaking, the public's attitude to what is said or portrayed depends to a certain extent on the context. That is, if something enhances our understanding of the event being portrayed (for example, a nude scene in a play), then it is not as bad as the same thing used purely for its shock or titillation value. But people's opinions are, naturally enough, divided. There are differences in views between young and old, and male and female.

Here are some of the numerous examples of things people have objected to or commented on:

- TV ads for female 'personal hygiene' products
- a documentary on a mass murderer filmed in his prison, describing how he cut people up and disposed of their bodies
- the BBC TV children's series *Grange Hill* with its portrayal of drugs, bullying, etc.

Activity

Read the following quotes from two 18–19-year-old female respondents (from *Sex and Sexuality in Broadcasting*):

'Personally I don't want to see scenes of lesbianism, but I don't want to stop things being televised. You could show what you like after midnight.'

'Yes, I don't agree with censorship. You can just turn it off. I hate it when they cut bits out of films. It's up to you to turn it off. Rape scenes or child sex abuse I wouldn't want to watch myself but I don't object to showing it.'

Discuss these issues with your colleagues. What is your viewpoint?

There is often some heavy criticism, particularly of the press, for their insensitivity in dealing with people who have, for example, survived a tragedy or crime, or who are friends or relatives of victims. Coverage of the Hillsborough tragedy, where nearly 100 football supporters were crushed and suffocated to death in front of the press and TV cameras, caused particular outrage and grief in this respect to many members of the public and especially to the families of victims. *The Sun* newspaper was particularly castigated, and it suffered a mass boycott by the people of Liverpool for what they saw as the unsympathetic portrayal of the city's football fans.

Other matters connected with invasion of privacy and insensitivity to people's feelings have included the treatment of the royal family and other public figures.

Activity

In all the examples given above, the media organisation concerned will usually claim that its reporting is 'in the public interest' and that 'the public have a right to know'.

Critics of this defence claim that the press use coverage of tragedies or prominent people's problems in order to sell newspapers. Do you think this is true and – if so – are the papers justified?

Use press coverage of the following cases to support your arguments:

- the divorce of the Prince and Princess of Wales
- the Frederick and Rosemary West murder case
- the Zeebrugge ferry disaster.

Public interest vs. entertainment

Even crime reconstruction programmes and documentaries seem to have as much to do with entertainment as public support for the work of the police.

Areas of concern include the use of video footage of high-speed police chases, and the sale to the public of videos depicting real-life executions, or surgical training for doctors showing real operations.

Broadcast adverts and sponsorship

In addition to the BSC (and BCC) there is the **BBC Complaints Unit**, and the **ITC** (**Independent Television Commission**) which awards licences to independent (non-BBC) broadcasters, including cable

---

ITC responsibilities

Under its powers derived from the Broadcasting Act 1990 and the Broadcasting Act 1996, the ITC:

- **licenses** commercial television services in the UK (i.e. non licence-fee or non-government funded) whether delivered by analogue or digital means, terrestrially or by cable and satellite, public teletext and certain other text and data services;
- **regulates** these services through its licences and codes of practice on programme content, advertising, sponsorship and technical standards and has a range of penalties for failure to comply with them;
- has a duty to ensure that a **wide range of television services** is available throughout the UK and that, taken as a whole, the services are of a high quality and appeal to a variety of tastes and interests;
- has a duty to ensure **fair and effective competition** in the provision of these services.

ITC Sponsorship Code

The ITC issued the first *Code of programme sponsorship* in 1991. This was revised after consultation and in the light of the first two years' operating experience of sponsorship, and re-issued in January 1994 with some minor modifications. The ITC is in the process of reviewing this code again and aims to issue a revised version in early 1997.

<u>Definition</u>. The code defines programme sponsorship in the following terms:

'A programme is deemed to be sponsored if any part of its costs of production or transmission is met by an organisation or person other than a broadcaster or television producer, with a view to promoting its own or another's name, trademark, image, activities, products, or other direct or indirect commercial interests'.

The <u>aim</u> of the code is to protect editorial independence, to limit the intrusion of advertising messages into programmes and to make sponsorships clear and transparent to viewers without reducing creative and commercial flexibility.

The overriding principles which inform the ITC's sponsorship rules are the:

- maintenance of editorial integrity
- separation of programming from advertising.

<u>Prohibitions</u>. News and current affairs programmes cannot be sponsored; this includes business and financial reports which contain interpretation or comment. Manufacturers of tobacco products, prescription drugs and normally any other advertisers prohibited from advertising on television are not allowed to sponsor programmes.

<u>Content.</u> A sponsor is not permitted to influence the content or scheduling of a programme. No promotional reference to any advertiser or sponsor, or to any product or service, is permitted within any programme. The code contains several rules which apply to all television programmes, whether or not they are sponsored. The aim is to restrict the opportunity for commercial influence within programmes, again reinforcing the principle of editorial integrity.

<u>Sponsor credits</u>. The code contains detailed rules on sponsor credits. Sponsored programmes must have either a front or an end credit or both. The rules are designed to make the sponsor's association with the programme clear to the viewer while not blurring the distinction between programmes and the sponsorship attached to programmes.

<u>Product placement</u> is prohibited by the EC Directive and is therefore illegal in all EU member states. It is defined in the code as 'the inclusion of, or reference to, a product or service within the programme in return for payment or other valuable consideration to the programme maker or ITC licensee (or any representative of either)'.

<u>Undue prominence</u>. Rule 10.6 of the *ITC programme code* supports the principle of editorial integrity. This states that 'No undue prominence may be given in any programme to a commercial product or service. In particular, any reference to such a product or service must be limited to what can clearly be justified by the editorial requirements of the programme itself'.

<u>Advertiser-supplied programmes</u>. The code includes specific requirements in relation to programmes made for, or substantially funded by, an advertiser. These are permissible with stringent rules.

Advertising Code

The ITC code of advertising standards and practice gives guidance on the content of television advertising. The underlying principles are that advertising:

- should not be misleading
- should not encourage or condone harmful behaviour
- should not be offensive to the generality of views, taking account of when it is shown.

There is scope for controversy in all these areas but the ITC seeks to adopt standards reflecting as wide a consensus as possible while recognising that unanimity is impossible. There must be sound reasons for prohibiting the advertising on television of products or services which are legally available.

In addition to general rules the code refers to particular categories of advertising, including alcoholic drinks, financial services, medical products, advertising to children and advertising by religious and charitable groups.

ITC rules on advertising breaks sets out the rules which the ITC requires its licensees to observe on the amount, distribution, separation and scheduling of advertising. ITV, Channel 4 and the proposed Channel 5 are limited to an average of seven minutes of advertising per hour (seven and a half in peaktime); cable and satellite are permitted nine minutes average. In both cases this is calculated by averaging out the amount of advertising over the whole transmission day. The maximum of 12 minutes of spot advertising in any one hour applies to all services.

and satellite, and regulates their contents, including advertisements. The ITC's powers are derived from the Broadcasting Act 1990. Its code of practice also covers such matters as the portrayal of violence and sex, and issues of blasphemy, stereotyping and impartiality. It would be useful for you to obtain a copy of the code and study it carefully.

For radio there is the **Radio Authority** which awards the licences and regulates the content of independent radio, including advertising.

Both the RA and the ITC have to ensure that broadcasters observe certain standards in their advertising. In order to do this the broadcasters themselves set up an organisation called the *Broadcast Advertising Clearance Centre,* which works closely with the ITC and RA to give advice and clearance to advertisers. They will check production scripts and storyboards and must give clearance for an ad before it is broadcast.

There is a vast number of issues that the BACC (on behalf of the RA and ITC) have to consider before clearance is given. Here are some examples:

- ads should not exaggerate facts about a product or its performance
- there should be sensitivity in the way race, gender, disabilities (including relatively minor ones, such as being hard of hearing or short-sighted), the elderly, religion, suffering and distress are portrayed, in order to avoid hurtful, patronising or damaging stereotyping
- serious crime should not be portrayed
- ads should not connect drink with sexual attraction or with driving
- bad manners and loutish behaviour should not be shown
- the portrayal or promotion of smoking is generally unacceptable, including a shot of, for example, a motor race with a tobacco company logo visible
- ads should not encourage any unsafe or illegal behaviour
- children, particularly, should not be shown doing anything dangerous, such as climbing up to high shelves to reach the biscuit tin, or playing in a busy street. Young children should not appear to be unaccompanied.

Print advertising is monitored by the Advertising Standards Authority which, as we mentioned in Chapter 27, also covers cinema commercials, posters, direct mail and sales promotions. It operates a voluntary code of practice which states that advertising should be legal, decent, honest and truthful.

Adverts should be:	
LEGAL	An advert should not encourage or appear to condone illegal or criminal acts.
DECENT	An advert should not cause grave or widespread offence to the standards of decency of those likely to see it.
HONEST	An advert should not make claims which cannot be verified. Superlatives (e.g. best/finest) should only be used when they are likely to be understood as obvious exaggeration. An advert should not deliberately mislead the consumer.
TRUTHFUL	An advert should not misuse scientific or medical research or data to make exaggerated claims for the product.

Advertising Standards Authority

Representation

Chapter 2 concentrates on the concept of representation and the issues and controversies surrounding it. You will need to refer again to Chapter 2 in order to obtain a full picture of this important area of media studies. However, as a reminder, the important point to bear in mind is that the media do not, strictly speaking, *present* people, facts, opinions and events, they *re-present* them. The very act of using a newspaper, magazine, television or radio as a medium means that there is an interaction between these media and the subjects they are covering. They are not neutral 'mirrors' that reflect exactly and accurately what is going on in the world. Many strive honestly towards objectivity, but topics are still subject to **mediation**. That is, they are a selection and interpretation of events, and reflect the values and priorities (what to leave in, what to take out) of media institutions, owners, editors and other decision-makers. Representation is the result of this mediation process.

In this section we will look at the ways in which different groups and issues are represented. As a journalist or a researcher you have a duty to represent people or situations fairly and accurately. You therefore need to check your sources of information to find out whether they are entirely reliable in the way they depict a person or event.

Case study

A Public Health Officer was asked by a TV documentary producer to assist in the production of a programme concerning noise pollution.

One of the duties of a Public Health Officer is to investigate complaints from members of the public. The official was filmed and interviewed carrying out his duties for one day. There were no problems in the interaction between the official and the public and in fact it was a rather routine, even dull, day.

When the official saw the broadcast, however, he was appalled to see that the film speed had been increased, so he was depicted going about his duties in a comical manner reminiscent of a 'Charlie Chaplin' movie. This gave the impression that the Public Health Officer was a rather officious busybody, whose working day consisted of whizzing about, behaving in a bureaucratic manner and achieving very little.

This was a *misrepresentation*. The reality was that the official had a good working relationship with the public and was carrying out his public duties in a professional manner. Apparently, this was not exciting enough for the programme makers, who felt they had to entertain the public as well as inform them.

Politics

Newspapers do tend to have political leanings which, with few exceptions, are towards the right of the political spectrum. This can create an in-built bias towards certain **social groups** or **social issues**. Protesters and strikers are frequently portrayed as trouble-makers; people receiving benefits can be seen as scroungers, particularly (female) single parents. Other groups that are castigated periodically include social workers, teachers, politicians, homosexuals, the 'Loony Left' or 'Europe'.

Some tabloids print only simplified arguments, whereas the quality press can contain a large amount of analysis and comment. TV news reports do not have much time available, so tend to be driven more by interesting pictures than by detailed analysis. TV news can thus become as simplified as the reports in the tabloids, which can lead to the misrepresentation of people and events. This may not be a deliberate policy, but it can still happen.

Activity

Find examples of the ways in which certain controversial groups in society, such as new age travellers or anti-road protesters, are represented in the media.

When TV or press reports portray, for example, the suffering of refugees in Kurdistan or Bosnia, we see desperate and destitute people who have been living out in the open, exposed to the elements, having had to flee for their lives. They may be beside themselves with grief and worry over the loss of children and other loved ones. They could well have witnessed atrocities and suffered brutal treatment or rape. We look at these pictures but we don't understand why these events have happened, and we don't understand the people as they cry and exclaim in their own languages. We have very little in common with them. What we may not realise is that a few days before they may have been like us with families, jobs and houses.

Many reporters are courageous and dedicated in their efforts to bring home to us the tragedy afflicting people's lives in these terrible situations. The problem is that the news is very immediate. Only a small proportion of news coverage (such as Channel 4's 7pm news programme) devotes time to any real analysis. The nature of the popular media – the tabloid press and the short news bulletins – results in emphasis being placed on 'packaging' news into absorbable 'sound-bites' for the audience.

News reports, generally speaking, do not spend time going into the background of an event or in following through their coverage; this is the job of the documentary. Instead, we restlessly move from one crisis to the next and what was prominent in the news for one day or one week then disappears without trace. For example, the Gulf War displaced images of famine in Africa, but the coverage of the aftermath of the war (the plight of the Kurds, Shiites and other Iraqis) was in turn taken over by the unfolding conflicts in Yugoslavia.

Audiences have grown used to this kind of coverage, and perhaps they now want fresh news rather than to linger over unpleasant events that they feel powerless to do very much about. *Compassion fatigue* is the term used to describe the wearying effect of the depiction of suffering on mass media audiences. William Shawcross described it as a sickness of our time:

> *'The symptoms are first a rush of concern for a distant and obviously suffering group, followed by tedium and a feeling of withdrawal that sometimes descends into disdain. Compassion fatigue is nurtured by the speed and plethora of communications that bewilder and disorientate people everywhere.'*

> ('Living in Limbo' Guardian 21 April 1989).

611

Representation and mediation are at the heart of the study of the media. As we discussed in the opening chapters of this book, issues of representation and the mediating process are complicated by the pressures of time and money (in terms of production costs), a competitive environment with its concern over audience figures, and the values and perceptions of the media producers and the audience, all inter-connecting and interacting with one other. The challenge for those who study or work in the media is to look out for and recognise these influences on our everyday lives. We need to become active 'readers' of media representations rather than passive consumers of media messages. Developing skills at reading media texts will also enhance our understanding and enjoyment of them, as well as developing a much-needed questioning response to the most powerful network of mass communication that the world has ever seen.

Appendix: Bibliography

BBC. *Extending Choice: The BBC's Role in the New Broadcasting Age*, BBC, 1992

BFI. *Film and Television Handbook 1996*, British Film Institute, 1995

Bagnell, Nicholas. *Newspaper Language*, Focal Press, 1993

Barrat, David. *Media Sociology*, Routledge, 1986

Benn's Media 1995. M-G Information Services Ltd (published annually)

Chantler, Paul and Sim Harris. *Local Radio Journalism*, Focal Press, 1992

Chater, Kathy. *The Television Researcher's Guide 1992*, BBC Television Training

Cheney, Theodore A. Rees. *Getting the Words Right: how to re-write, edit and revise*, Writer's Digest Books, 1983

Cheshire, David. *The Complete Book of Video*, Dorling Kindersley Limited, 1990

Clayton, Joan. *Interviewing for Journalists*, Judy Piatkus Publishers Ltd, 1994

Cook, Pam. *The Cinema Book*, BFI, 1985

Crisell, Andrew. *Understanding Radio*, Methuen and Co., 1986

Darbyshire, Lydia (editor). *Practical Graphic Design Techniques*, Tiger Books, 1991

Davis, Anthony. *Magazine Journalism Today*, Butterworth-Heinemann, 1988

Dimbleby, Nick, Richard Dimbleby and Ken Whittington. *Practical Media*. Hodder and Stoughton, 1994

Donovan, Paul. *The Radio Companion*, Grafton, 1992

Dutton, Brian with John Mundy. *Media Studies – An Introduction*, Longman Group Ltd, 1995

Film Education. Many publications, free on request to schools and colleges

Goddard, Ken. *Informative Writing*, Cassell, 1995

Guardian Guide to the UK's Top Companies, Roger Cowe (editor). Fourth Estate Ltd, 1993.

Hall, Celia. *Editing for Everyone*, National Extension College, 1983

Halliwell's Film Guide, John Walker (editor). HarperCollins (eighth edition) 1991

Harris, Geoffrey and David Spark. *Practical Newspaper Reporting*, Focal Press, 1966

Hart, Christopher. *Everything you Ever Wanted to Know About Cartooning but Were Afraid to Draw*, Watson-Guptill Publications 1994

Hart, Christopher. *How to Draw Cartoon Animals*, Watson-Guptill Publications, 1995

Hennessy, Brendan. *Writing Feature Articles*, Focal Press, 1993

Horstmann, Rosemary. *Writing for Radio*, A & C Black, (second edition), 1991

Hutt, Allen and Bob James. *Newspaper Design Today: a Manual for Professionals*, Lund Humphries Publishers Ltd, 1989

ITC. *Factfile 1995*. Free on request

Kent, Raymond (ed). *Measuring Media Audiences*, Routledge, 1994

Langham, Josephine. *Lights Camera Action! Careers in Film, Television and Video*, BFI, 1993

Longmate, Norman. *Writing for the BBC*, BBC Books, 1988

Media Guide 1996, Steve Peak (editor). Guardian Books, 1995

Media and Marketing Pocket Book Series. NTC Publications Ltd, 1995. The series includes: *The Media Pocket Book, Marketing Pocket Book, UK Marketing Source Book, Regional Marketing Pocket Book, Lifestyle Pocket Book*

Meighan, Paul and Bernard McWilliams. *Photography Exposed – an Easy Guide*, Impact Books, 1984

Mellor, David. *Recording Techniques for Small Studios*, P. C. Publishing, 1993

Millerson, Gerald. *Video Production Handbook*, Focal Press, 1992

Millwood Hargrave, Andrea (editor). *A Matter of Manners? The Limits of Broadcast Language*

Millwood Hargrave, Andrea. *Taste and Decency in Broadcasting*, Broadcasting Standards Council, 1991

Nazzaro, Joe. *The Making of Red Dwarf*, Penguin Books, 1994

Paice, Eric. *The Way to Write for Television*, Elm Tree Books, 1987

Parker, Roger C. *Looking Good in Print*, Roger C. Parker, 1988

Phillips, Brian. *Stand by Studio*, BBC Television Training, 1987

The Print Book. National Extension College, 1985

Rumsey, F. and Tim McCormick. *Sound and Recording: An Introduction*, Focal Press 1992

Schihl, Robert J. *Studio Drama Processes and Procedures*, Focal Press, 1992

Schihl, Robert J. *Talk Show and Entertainment Program*, Focal Press, 1992

Shearer, Ann. *Survivors and the Media*, Broadcasting

Standards Council, 1991

Skillset. *Careers Handbook: A Career in Broadcast, Film and Video,* Skillset, 1996. Free on request

Social Trends 1995, Jenny Church (editor). HMSO, 1995

Stafford, Roy. *Hands On: A Teacher's Guide to Media Technology*

O'Sullivan, Tim, Brian Dutton and Philip Rayner. *Studying the Media: an Introduction,* Edward Arnold, 1994

Usborne Book of Graphic Design, Usborne Publishing, 1987

Watson, James and Anne Hill. *A Dictionary of Communication and Media Studies,* Edward Arnold, (third edition) 1993

Welsh, Tom and Walter Greenwood. *McNae's Essential Law for Journalists,* Butterworth, 1992

Willings Press Guide. British Media Publications (published annually)

Writers' and Artists' Yearbook 1996. A&C Black, London

The Writer's Handbook 1995, Barry Turner (editor). Macmillan Reference Books, 1994

Application of number (level 3)

There are many examples of data within the book which students and teachers can use to link mathematical exercises to the vocational area. There are also plenty of activities through which students can collect evidence for Application of Number. The grid on page 617 shows the elements where the majority of these can be found. The **production handbook** compiled for Unit 2 Element 1 (Chapter 5) is ideal for storing much of this work.

3.1 Collect and record data

The two reports and data collection sheets must cover a variety of tasks involving money, measurement of physical dimensions, scheduling, statistical trends, etc. Students will need to justify why they have chosen to collect certain data or use specific sample groups. They should be able to identify in each case the consequences of inaccurate data and poor record keeping. Evidence can be based on activities such as the following.

Concerning money

- budgeting for a product p165, p183, p255, p293
- calculating promotions, sales and distribution costs p238
- calculating advertising space and rates p469
- making calculations using rate cards p297, p460

Concerning physical measurements

- scaling illustrations p234
- working out page layout p235
- carrying out a recce p190, p305
- working out the volume of buildings p265
- designing floor plans p299
- making a lighting plot p300
- collecting data on poster sites p357

Concerning measurement of another property, e.g. time

- designing a programme schedule p249
- writing a treatment p193

- scheduling a running order p308
- measuring deviations from production schedules p236
- scheduling an advertising campaign p468, p471
- calculating tape speeds p257
- keeping a footage log p322, p324
- logging tapes p273
- editing p275, p328

Other possible data collection

- identifying research objectives and methodology p346, p367, p405
- designing a questionnaire p405
- collecting statistical data about a product/producer regarding circulation, revenue, expenditure, etc. p449, p452, p491, p494, p498, p504, p508, p519, p522
- collecting statistics on employment figures p510, p559
- designing a marketing plan p453, p455
- collecting feedback on a product p240, p280, p336

3.2 Tackle problems

Evidence of a range of techniques should be incorporated into reports or projects, showing that techniques have been used at least twice for calculations covering numbers, measurements of space and shapes, and data handling. The grid shows where teachers and students can find material and activities to use. All of the data found above for element 3.1 can be used again here, to solve specific problems or be used for a specific purpose, but some additional suggestions are given below.

Calculations covering numbers

- calculating camera shutter speeds, depth of field p141, p144
- calculating frequencies and decibels p160
- converting a budget from pounds to dollars p183
- calculating the cost of newsprint and ink p208
- working out the tonnage of newsprint needed p208

- calculating the time needed for print runs p208
- measuring the speed of a print run p208
- calculating the cost per minute of making the newspaper p208
- calculating distribution costs p238
- working out the amount of tape needed for different programme lengths using different recording speeds p258

Measurement of space and shapes

- preparing artwork and producing a paste-up p149
- working out point sizes p233
- calculating the volume of rockwool needed to soundproof a studio p258
- calculating the length of cables needed p318

Data handling

- comparing costs of different programmes p184
- using data relating to audience statistics pp380–90, 393–6
- using data relating to products/producers p491, p495, p500, p508, pp523–30
- calculating marketing data p436, pp438–42

3.3   Interpret and present data

Either numerical data collected in element 1 or calculations made in element 2 can be presented as evidence here. The grid shows the obvious places where this occurs. The following are examples of information being interpreted and presented in a diagrammatical or symbolic way, using industrial conventions:

- writing specification or proposals where ideas have been evaluated through assessing resources in terms of time, finance and materials Units 2, 3, 4 and 5
- producing the production handbook Unit 2
- producing budgets Units 2, 3, 4 and 5
- producing schedules Units 2, 3, 4 and 5
- producing floor plans Units 4 and 5
- producing a location recce Units 4 and 5
- producing a page layout Unit 3
- producing lighting plots Unit 5
- producing camera scripts Unit 5
- producing a script for a news programme Unit 4
- presenting research data Unit 6
- presenting marketing plans Unit 7
- producing reports on media companies Unit 8
- producing diagrams on employment trends Unit 8

EVIDENCE ASSIGNMENT TRACKING SHEET FOR APPLICATION OF NUMBER

Chapter		Unit 2				Unit 3				Unit 4				Unit 5				Unit 6				Unit 7				Unit 8			
		5	6	7	8	9	10	11	12	13	14	15	16	17	18	19	20	21	22	23	24	25	26	27	28	29	30	31	32
Application of Number Element 3.1	1			✔	✔	✔		✔	✔	✔		✔	✔	✔	✔	✔	✔	✔			✔	✔	✔			✔			✔
	2			✔	✔	✔		✔	✔	✔		✔	✔	✔	✔	✔	✔	✔			✔	✔	✔			✔			✔
	3			✔	✔	✔		✔	✔	✔		✔	✔	✔	✔	✔	✔	✔			✔	✔	✔			✔			✔
	4			✔	✔	✔		✔	✔	✔		✔	✔	✔	✔	✔	✔	✔			✔	✔	✔			✔			✔
	5			✔	✔	✔		✔	✔	✔		✔	✔	✔	✔	✔	✔	✔			✔	✔	✔			✔			✔
	6			✔	✔	✔		✔	✔	✔		✔	✔	✔	✔	✔	✔	✔			✔	✔	✔			✔			✔
	7			✔	✔	✔		✔	✔	✔		✔	✔	✔	✔	✔	✔	✔			✔	✔	✔			✔			✔
Application of Number Element 3.2	1	✔	✔	✔	✔	✔		✔	✔	✔		✔	✔	✔	✔	✔	✔			✔		✔	✔			✔	✔		
	2	✔	✔	✔	✔	✔		✔	✔	✔		✔	✔	✔	✔	✔	✔			✔		✔	✔			✔	✔		
	3	✔	✔	✔	✔	✔		✔	✔	✔		✔	✔	✔	✔	✔	✔			✔		✔	✔			✔	✔		
	4	✔	✔	✔	✔	✔		✔	✔	✔		✔	✔	✔	✔	✔	✔			✔		✔	✔			✔	✔		
	5	✔	✔	✔	✔	✔		✔	✔	✔		✔	✔	✔	✔	✔	✔			✔		✔	✔			✔	✔		
	6	✔	✔	✔	✔	✔		✔	✔	✔		✔	✔	✔	✔	✔	✔			✔		✔	✔			✔	✔		
	7	✔	✔	✔	✔	✔		✔	✔	✔		✔	✔	✔	✔	✔	✔			✔		✔	✔			✔	✔		
	8	✔	✔	✔	✔	✔		✔	✔	✔		✔	✔	✔	✔	✔	✔			✔		✔	✔			✔	✔		
	9	✔	✔	✔	✔	✔		✔	✔	✔		✔	✔	✔	✔	✔	✔			✔		✔	✔			✔	✔		
Application of Number Element 3.3	1	✔	✔	✔	✔	✔		✔	✔	✔		✔	✔	✔	✔	✔	✔			✔		✔		✔		✔	✔		✔
	2	✔	✔	✔	✔	✔		✔	✔	✔		✔	✔	✔	✔	✔	✔			✔		✔		✔		✔	✔		✔
	3	✔	✔	✔	✔	✔		✔	✔	✔		✔	✔	✔	✔	✔	✔			✔		✔		✔		✔	✔		✔
	4	✔	✔	✔	✔	✔		✔	✔	✔		✔	✔	✔	✔	✔	✔			✔		✔		✔		✔	✔		✔
	5	✔	✔	✔	✔	✔		✔	✔	✔		✔	✔	✔	✔	✔	✔			✔		✔		✔		✔	✔		✔

Communication (level 3)

The area of study covered by this course is all about communication, so the grid on page 619 only indicates major assignments which will provide evidence.

3.1 Take part in discussion
3.2 Produce written material
3.3 Use images

For the above elements, students have to prove that they can communicate on a one-to-one basis (e.g. when interviewing someone for a news story) as well as in a group (e.g. whilst working as part of a video crew) and to different audiences. Some suggestions are given below.

People familiar with the subject who know the student

■ presenting to the class
■ debating in the class
■ discussing media products in a group
■ evaluating ideas and progress with the production team
■ interviewing students and tutors at college
■ completing a booking form

People familiar with the subject who do not know the student

■ writing letters to media companies
■ talking to people when performing a location recce
■ interviewing the public about well-known topics
■ interviewing a specialist for a feature article
■ writing a memo to a member of staff in another department
■ conducting a radio phone-in
■ doing vox-pops
■ producing a camera script
■ producing a product proposal/specification/treatment for a client

People not familiar with the subject who know the student

■ asking family or friends to evaluate products made by the student
■ presenting ideas to teaching staff for a programme or print product based on a specialised subject or hobby known to the student
■ giving a marketing presentation for a particular product to a teacher
■ presenting an analysis of a media product of the student's choice to the rest of the class
■ presenting media research to a teacher of another subject

People not familiar with the subject who do not know the student

■ writing letters, e.g. to *Points of View*
■ writing letters or phone calls to potential advertisers in a student newspaper
■ designing cartoon strips
■ writing a hard news story or a feature article
■ producing a radio play or moving image product

3.4 Read and respond to written materials

Besides the evidence assignments indicated on the grid, there are many activities where evidence can be gained. Media students continually have to summarise written information, whether they are adapting a short story to make it suitable for a play, editing an interview for a newspaper or condensing research data for a presentation. After all, the media is about re-presenting the real world!

The following grid records evidence assignments (✓) across Units 1–8 (numbered tasks 1–32) for Communication Elements 3.1–3.4.

Unit	Task	3.1-1	3.1-2	3.1-3	3.1-4	3.1-5	3.2-1	3.2-2	3.2-3	3.2-4	3.2-5	3.3-1	3.3-2	3.3-3	3.4-1	3.4-2	3.4-3	3.4-4
Unit 1	1														✓	✓	✓	✓
	2											✓			✓	✓	✓	✓
	3												✓		✓	✓	✓	✓
	4													✓	✓	✓	✓	✓
Unit 2	5	✓	✓	✓	✓	✓												
	6	✓	✓	✓	✓	✓	✓	✓	✓	✓	✓	✓	✓					
	7	✓	✓	✓	✓	✓						✓	✓					
	8	✓	✓	✓	✓	✓	✓	✓	✓	✓	✓	✓	✓	✓				
Unit 3	9						✓	✓	✓	✓	✓							
	10	✓	✓	✓	✓	✓	✓	✓	✓	✓	✓	✓	✓					
	11						✓	✓	✓	✓	✓	✓	✓	✓				
	12	✓	✓	✓	✓	✓	✓	✓	✓	✓	✓				✓	✓	✓	✓
Unit 4	13	✓	✓	✓	✓	✓	✓	✓	✓	✓	✓							
	14	✓	✓	✓	✓	✓	✓	✓	✓	✓	✓							
	15						✓	✓	✓	✓	✓							
	16	✓	✓	✓	✓	✓	✓	✓	✓	✓	✓				✓	✓	✓	✓
Unit 5	17	✓	✓	✓	✓	✓	✓	✓	✓	✓	✓	✓	✓	✓				
	18						✓	✓	✓	✓	✓	✓	✓	✓				
	19											✓	✓	✓				
	20	✓	✓	✓	✓	✓	✓	✓	✓	✓	✓	✓	✓	✓	✓	✓	✓	✓
Unit 6	21						✓	✓	✓	✓	✓				✓	✓	✓	✓
	22	✓	✓	✓	✓	✓	✓	✓	✓	✓	✓				✓	✓	✓	✓
	23	✓	✓	✓	✓	✓	✓	✓	✓	✓	✓	✓	✓		✓	✓	✓	✓
	24	✓	✓	✓	✓	✓	✓	✓	✓	✓	✓	✓	✓		✓	✓	✓	✓
Unit 7	25						✓	✓	✓	✓	✓	✓	✓		✓	✓	✓	✓
	26	✓	✓	✓	✓	✓	✓	✓	✓	✓	✓	✓	✓					
	27						✓	✓	✓	✓	✓	✓	✓					
	28	✓	✓	✓	✓	✓	✓	✓	✓	✓	✓	✓	✓					
Unit 8	29											✓	✓	✓	✓	✓	✓	✓
	30	✓	✓	✓	✓	✓									✓	✓	✓	✓
	31						✓	✓	✓	✓	✓				✓	✓	✓	✓
	32						✓	✓	✓	✓	✓	✓	✓	✓	✓	✓	✓	✓

Information technology (level 3)

It would be impossible to pursue this course effectively without using information technology. The mass media rely heavily on IT both to produce and to communicate messages.

3.1 Prepare information
3.2 Process information
3.3 Present information

Students must prepare and enter information from existing sources, such as figures from a marketing report, but also develop information during input, e.g. write a script. They should be able to call up this information for processing and editing, and combine it with material from another source. Then the work should be presented in a suitable form. Evidence should show at least two examples each of the use of IT for text, graphics and numbers. Regular saving of work and print-outs are expected.

The grid on page 622 shows elements where it is easiest to assess this work. However, students will find that in a vocational area where high standards of presentation are the norm, there are numerous assessment opportunities. Below are some suggestions for suitable IT work.

Text

- word processing an agenda p112
- word processing a specification p116
- compiling a production handbook as a database p119
- presenting body copy p139
- designing an expense/budget sheet for an AV production p164, p294
- designing a playlist form for a radio station p164
- designing an equipment booking form p165, p257, p319
- word processing a proposal/brief for an AV production p171, p187, p286
- word processing a script/treatment for an AV production p173, p179, p193, pp195–8, p201, p266, p289, p310
- designing a budget sheet p183
- word processing a schedule p211, p221, p266, p309

- word processing letters p354, p472
- compiling a bibliography p376
- inputting information on current media debates p378
- writing a questionnaire p407
- preparing information for a marketing plan p449, p453, p455
- producing a schedule for an advertising campaign p471
- producing evaluation forms p243, p279, p338, p484
- designing an evaluation form p243, p279, p338

Text and graphics

- designing a film poster using a computer p153
- producing a hard news story, feature article, a short story for children, a horoscope, an advertisement, a photograph with captions p157, p229
- producing computer-generated animation p293
- preparing computer-generated titling for moving image products p327
- designing a recce form p190
- producing the layout for an advertisement p469, p473
- preparing OHTs p480
- designing a wall poster on employment using graphics p576
- designing a dummy page and organising text and graphics p212, p218
- editing print materials p227

Numbers

- analysing statistical data p380, p401
- analysing a questionnaire p413
- inputting and analysing data on revenue and expenditure of media products p530

Automated routines

- standard letters p354, p472
- bibliographies p376
- dummy pages p212
- equipment booking forms p165, p257, p319
- evaluation forms p243, p279, p338, p484

- mail merge – letters to contact names in production handbook p119
- analysing questionnaires p413

3.4 Evaluate the use of information technology

The student should write a short report describing, explaining and justifying the choice of three different systems to perform tasks suggested above. There should be an evaluation and comparison of these methods with alternative systems. As they perform the tasks, students should log any problems and describe their effects on the work. The Health and Safety appendix will help to explain the importance of working safely.

Below are some tasks where students can compare manual methods with those which use computers.

Unit 2

- compiling a production handbook manually

or

- compiling a production handbook on a computer database

- poster design using stencils and hand drawings

or

- poster design using a software package such as Coreldraw

Unit 3

- page layout consisting of a dummy page and a paste-up

or

- electronic page layout using a DTP package and a scanner

Unit 5

- hand-drawn cartoons

or

- computer animation

- manual titling for videos

or

- computer titling for videos

- assembly or insert video editing

or

- non-linear editing

Units 6, 7, 8

- collating and storing data manually, e.g. company information, marketing statistics, names and addresses

or

- collating and storing data on computer

- producing graphs, pie charts, etc. by hand

or

- producing these on computer

EVIDENCE ASSIGNMENT TRACKING SHEET FOR INFORMATION TECHNOLOGY

Chapter		Information Technology Element 3.1					Information Technology Element 3.2							Information Technology Element 3.3						Information Technology Element 3.4					
Unit	Ch	1	2	3	4	5	1	2	3	4	5	6	7	1	2	3	4	5	6	1	2	3	4	5	6
Unit 1	1																								
	2																								
	3																								
	4																								
Unit 2	5	✓	✓	✓	✓	✓	✓	✓		✓	✓			✓		✓						✓			
	6	✓	✓	✓	✓	✓	✓	✓		✓	✓	✓	✓	✓	✓	✓	✓	✓		✓	✓	✓	✓	✓	✓
	7	✓	✓	✓	✓	✓	✓	✓		✓	✓		✓	✓	✓	✓	✓					✓			
	8	✓	✓	✓	✓	✓	✓	✓		✓	✓		✓	✓	✓	✓	✓					✓			
Unit 3	9	✓	✓	✓	✓	✓	✓	✓		✓	✓	✓	✓	✓	✓	✓						✓			
	10	✓	✓	✓	✓	✓	✓	✓		✓	✓			✓	✓	✓						✓			
	11						✓	✓		✓	✓	✓		✓	✓	✓		✓	✓	✓	✓	✓	✓	✓	✓
	12						✓	✓		✓	✓			✓	✓	✓						✓			
Unit 4	13	✓	✓	✓	✓	✓	✓	✓		✓	✓		✓	✓		✓						✓			
	14																								
	15																								
	16						✓	✓		✓	✓			✓		✓						✓			
Unit 5	17	✓	✓	✓	✓	✓	✓	✓		✓	✓	✓		✓		✓						✓			
	18																								
	19						✓	✓		✓	✓	✓		✓	✓	✓				✓	✓	✓	✓	✓	✓
	20						✓	✓		✓	✓			✓		✓						✓			
Unit 6	21	✓	✓	✓	✓	✓	✓	✓	✓	✓	✓		✓	✓		✓						✓			
	22	✓	✓	✓	✓	✓	✓	✓		✓	✓			✓		✓						✓			
	23	✓	✓	✓	✓	✓	✓	✓		✓	✓			✓		✓						✓			
	24	✓	✓	✓	✓	✓	✓	✓		✓	✓	✓		✓	✓	✓				✓	✓	✓	✓	✓	✓
Unit 7	25	✓	✓	✓	✓	✓	✓	✓		✓	✓			✓		✓				✓	✓	✓	✓	✓	✓
	26	✓	✓	✓	✓	✓	✓	✓		✓	✓			✓		✓				✓	✓	✓	✓	✓	✓
	27	✓	✓	✓	✓	✓	✓	✓		✓	✓	✓		✓		✓						✓			
	28	✓	✓	✓	✓	✓	✓	✓	✓	✓	✓	✓		✓	✓	✓						✓			
Unit 8	29	✓	✓	✓	✓	✓	✓	✓	✓	✓	✓			✓		✓		✓	✓	✓	✓	✓	✓	✓	✓
	30																								
	31																								
	32	✓	✓	✓	✓	✓	✓	✓		✓	✓			✓		✓						✓			

Answers

Unit 1 Investigating the Content of Media Products

1	b	11	b	21	b
2	a	12	d	22	d
3	b	13	a	23	d
4	c	14	b	24	a
5	a	15	c	25	c
6	d	16	c	26	c
7	b	17	b	27	b
8	b	18	a	28	b
9	d	19	d	29	b
10	a	20	b	30	b

Unit 2 Planning and Research for Media Production

1	c	11	d	21	a
2	b	12	c	22	c
3	d	13	a	23	d
4	b	14	d	24	c
5	a	15	a	25	c
6	c	16	c	26	b
7	a	17	b	27	a
8	d	18	d	28	d
9	b	19	d	29	c
10	a	20	b	30	b

Unit 3 Producing Print Products

1	c	11	c	21	d
2	c	12	d	22	c
3	b	13	b	23	b
4	d	14	a	24	a
5	a	15	b	25	d
6	c	16	c	26	b
7	d	17	a	27	d
8	c	18	c	28	c
9	a	19	d	29	b
10	b	20	a	30	a

Unit 4 Producing Audio Products

1	c	11	d	21	b
2	d	12	c	22	d
3	d	13	a	23	d
4	b	14	b	24	a
5	b	15	a	25	c
6	d	16	b	26	a
7	a	17	d	27	c
8	a	18	c	28	d
9	b	19	b	29	b
10	c	20	a	30	a

Unit 5 Producing Moving Image Products

1	c	11	a	21	b
2	c	12	c	22	b
3	b	13	b	23	d
4	a	14	d	24	c
5	d	15	b	25	a
6	a	16	a	26	d
7	b	17	b	27	b
8	d	18	d	28	c
9	c	19	c	29	c
10	d	20	a	30	c

Unit 6 Investigating and Carrying Out Audience Research and Analysis

1	c	11	a	21	b
2	d	12	b	22	a
3	a	13	c	23	c
4	b	14	a	24	c
5	d	15	b	25	d
6	c	16	d	26	b
7	a	17	a	27	a
8	b	18	c	28	c
9	c	19	d	29	d
10	d	20	b	30	b

Unit 7 Investigating and Carrying Out Media Marketing

1	c	11	c	21	d
2	c	12	d	22	c
3	b	13	b	23	b
4	d	14	a	24	a
5	a	15	b	25	d
6	c	16	c	26	b
7	d	17	a	27	d
8	c	18	c	28	a
9	a	19	d	29	b
10	b	20	c	30	a

Unit 8 Investigating Media Industries

1	b	11	d	21	c
2	d	12	c	22	d
3	a	13	b	23	b
4	c	14	a	24	a
5	a	15	c	25	c
6	b	16	d	26	a
7	d	17	a	27	c
8	a	18	c	28	d
9	b	19	b	29	b
10	b	20	a	30	a

Index